Justifying Strict Liability

Justifying Strict Liability

A Comparative Analysis in Legal Reasoning

MARCO CAPPELLETTI

St John's College, University of Oxford

OXFORD
UNIVERSITY PRESS

Great Clarendon Street, Oxford, OX2 6DP,
United Kingdom

Oxford University Press is a department of the University of Oxford.
It furthers the University's objective of excellence in research, scholarship,
and education by publishing worldwide. Oxford is a registered trade mark of
Oxford University Press in the UK and in certain other countries

© Marco Cappelletti 2022

The moral rights of the author have been asserted

First Edition published in 2022

Impression: 1

All rights reserved. No part of this publication may be reproduced, stored in
a retrieval system, or transmitted, in any form or by any means, without the
prior permission in writing of Oxford University Press, or as expressly permitted
by law, by licence or under terms agreed with the appropriate reprographics
rights organization. Enquiries concerning reproduction outside the scope of the
above should be sent to the Rights Department, Oxford University Press, at the
address above

You must not circulate this work in any other form
and you must impose this same condition on any acquirer

Public sector information reproduced under Open Government Licence v3.0
(http://www.nationalarchives.gov.uk/doc/open-government-licence/open-government-licence.htm)

Published in the United States of America by Oxford University Press
198 Madison Avenue, New York, NY 10016, United States of America

British Library Cataloguing in Publication Data

Data available

Library of Congress Control Number: 2022933008

ISBN 978-0-19-285986-0

DOI: 10.1093/oso/9780192859860.001.0001

Printed and bound by
CPI Group (UK) Ltd, Croydon, CR0 4YY

Links to third party websites are provided by Oxford in good faith and
for information only. Oxford disclaims any responsibility for the materials
contained in any third party website referenced in this work.

Ai miei genitori,
a Fabiana

Preface

This book is a revised and substantially expanded version of a doctoral thesis completed at Oxford in 2020. The idea to write a monograph on the justifications for strict liability in tort came to me as I realized that these are the object of considerable controversy. As a comparative legal scholar, I could see that this is true for several legal systems, including those discussed in this book. I also noticed that most comparative contributions on strict liability focus on substantive law rather than on the justifications for it, and that the writings which explore at some length these justifications either single out specific torts for analysis or discuss only one legal system. In sum, there has been so far no systematic or in-depth *comparative* treatment of the main arguments put forward to justify strict liability in tort. This book seeks to fill this gap.

Given its comparative nature and its focus on individual justifications, the analysis I have undertaken here is, I think, the first of its kind. This has made the writing of this book particularly challenging and it is only thanks to the support and help of many people that I managed to bring it to completion. My gratitude is due first and foremost to Professor Simon Whittaker, who supervised my DPhil. He provided enlightening guidance in the countless meetings and discussions we had throughout my doctoral studies. After I successfully defended my thesis in September 2020, Professor Whittaker and I continued to discuss my work and this book has benefited immensely from our conversations. For all this and for his extraordinary mentorship, which continues to this day, I express my deepest gratitude to him.

My thanks are further due to Professor John Bell and Professor Birke Häcker for acting as my DPhil examiners and for providing invaluable comments on my work. I would also like to thank Professor Jean-Sébastien Borghetti, Professor Guido Calabresi, and Professor John CP Goldberg, with whom I have discussed my work at various stages, as well as OUP's anonymous reviewers, for all their very helpful comments and suggestions.

For the most part, I wrote this book at St John's College, Oxford, first as a DPhil candidate and then as a Junior Research Fellow. St John's has been my academic home for many years and I would like to thank the President and the Fellows of the college for giving me the opportunity to study and work in this wonderful place. I am also grateful to Sir Roy Goode and to the Oxford Law Faculty for the financial support I received during my doctoral studies.

Finally, I would like to thank my parents, Claudio and Marisa, and my wife, Fabiana. My parents have always supported me throughout my education and they

viii   PREFACE

have instilled in me a deep love for learning and studying. Fabiana, who became my wife in August 2021, has always encouraged me to pursue my desire for an academic career, well before I started my DPhil in 2016. She has endured countless conversations on this book and provided many criticisms and suggestions that have made this work much better than it would have otherwise been. Without their constant support and encouragement I could not have completed, or even started, this book and the thesis on which it is based. To them this book is dedicated with my love and gratitude.

St John's College, Oxford
November 2021
Marco Cappelletti

Contents

Table of Cases	xiii
Table of Legislation	xxiii
List of Abbreviations	xxvii

1.	General Introduction	1
	1.1 Justifying Strict Liability	1
	1.2 Scope of the Book	3
	1.3 Sources of Analysis and Use of Materials	8
	1.4 Methodology	10
	1.5 Structure of the Book	11

2.	Strict Liability in the Four Tort Systems: An Overview	13
	2.1 Introduction	13
	2.2 Strict Liability in English Law	13
	2.3 Strict Liability in the Law of the United States	26
	2.4 Strict Liability in French Law	37
	2.5 Strict Liability in Italian Law	49
	2.6 Concluding Remarks	61

3.	The Justifications for Strict Liability: A Comparative Analysis	65

3.1.	Introduction	67

3.2.	Risk	73
	3.2.1 The Risk-based Justifications of Strict Liability	73
	3.2.2 The Pervasive Nature of Risk in French Strict Liability	74
	3.2.3 Risk in Italian Law: The Varied Importance of its Permutations	84
	3.2.4 Risk in the United States: All Five Permutations at Play	93
	3.2.5 Risk in English Law: Controversy and Context-Dependence	103
	3.2.6 Concluding Remarks	114

3.3.	Accident Avoidance	119
	3.3.1 Accident Avoidance as a Justification for Strict Liability	119
	3.3.2 The Pervasive Nature of Accident Avoidance in the United States	120
	3.3.3 Accident Avoidance in Italy: A Leading Justification	129
	3.3.4 Accident Avoidance in English Law: Not (Yet?) a Leading Justification	137
	3.3.5 Avoiding Accidents: (Not) a Concern of French Strict Liability?	145
	3.3.6 Concluding Remarks	151

X CONTENTS

3.4. Deep Pockets 155
   3.4.1 The Deep-Pockets Justification of Strict Liability 155
   3.4.2 Deep Pockets in France: On the Way Towards the Socialization of Losses 156
   3.4.3 Deep Pockets in Italy: A Justification Belonging to the Past? 158
   3.4.4 The Minor Significance of the Deep-Pockets Argument in the United States 162
   3.4.5 Deep Pockets in England: A Justification of Modest Significance, with an Exception 166
   3.4.6 Concluding Remarks 170

3.5. Loss Spreading 173
   3.5.1 The Loss-Spreading Justification of Strict Liability 173
   3.5.2 Loss Spreading in France: A Panacea? 175
   3.5.3 Loss Spreading in the United States: A Leading and Flexible Justification 185
   3.5.4 Loss Spreading in Italy: A Neglected Argument? 195
   3.5.5 Loss Spreading in England: The Most Controversial Argument of All? 205
   3.5.6 Concluding Remarks 216

3.6. Victim Protection 221
   3.6.1 Victim Protection as a Justification for Strict Liability 221
   3.6.2 The Ultimate Reason for Strict Liability in France? 222
   3.6.3 An Essential Justification, but Not All that Matters in Italian Reasoning 226
   3.6.4 The Protection of Victims in the United States: A Falling Star? 230
   3.6.5 Victim Protection in English Law: An Argument to Be Handled with Care 234
   3.6.6 Concluding Remarks 239

3.7. Reduction in Administrative Costs 241
   3.7.1 Reduction in Administrative Costs as a Justification for Strict Liability 241
   3.7.2 The Ambiguous Significance of Reducing Administrative Costs in the United States 242
   3.7.3 Reducing Administrative Costs in Italy: A Concern for the Legal Economists Only? 246
   3.7.4 The Modest Significance of Administrative Cost Reduction in England 250
   3.7.5 Reducing Administrative Costs in France: An Insignificant Argument 253
   3.7.6 Concluding Remarks 256

3.8.	Individual Responsibility	259
	3.8.1 Individual Responsibility as a Justification for Strict Liability	259
	3.8.2 Individual Responsibility in the United States: An Argument of Moderate Significance	260
	3.8.3 The Limited Significance of Individual Responsibility in English Law	271
	3.8.4 Individual Responsibility in Italian Law: An Insignificant Argument	281
	3.8.5 Individual Responsibility, an Argument at Odds with French Strict Liability	286
	3.8.6 Concluding Remarks	290
4.	Concluding Reflections	293
	4.1 Justifications and Contexts of Liability	293
	4.2 Some Reflections on the Patterns of Reasoning in Strict Liability	295
	4.3 Justifying Strict Liability: Arguments, Values, and Goals	301
	4.4 Further Critical and Comparative Thoughts	313

Bibliography	317
Index	339

Table of Cases

ENGLAND

A v National Blood Authority, [2001] 3 All ER 289 . . . . 21–24, 236, 237–38
Allen v Gulf Oil Refining Ltd, [1980] QB 156, [1981] AC 1001 . . . . 17, 24–26, 111–12
Armagas Ltd v Mundogas Ltd, The Ocean Frost, [1986] AC 717 19–20
Armes v Nottinghamshire County Council, [2017] UKSC 60,
    [2018] AC 355. . . . . 19–20, 103–4, 112–13, 141–42,
                          167–68, 210–13, 214–16, 234–36, 238–39
Baker v Snell, [1908] 2 KB 825. 107–8
Bamford v Turnley, (1862) 3 B & S 66. 143–44
Barclays Bank Plc v Various Claimants, [2020] UKSC 13,
    [2020] 2 WLR 960. . . . . 18, 167–68, 207–9
Batchellor v Turnbridge Wells Gas Co, (1901) 84 LT 765 14–15
Behrens v Bertram Mills Circus Ltd, [1957] 2 QB 1 . . . . 17–18, 107–8, 109, 138–40
Biffa Waste Services v Maschinenfabrik Ernst Hese GmbH,
    [2008] EWCA Civ 1257 109–11
Bogle v McDonald's Restaurants Ltd, [2002] EWHC 490 21–24
Box v Jubb, (1879) 4 Ex D 76 15–16
Cambridge Water v Eastern Counties Leather, [1994] 2 AC 264 . . . . 14–16, 109–11
Cassidy v Ministry of Health, [1951] 2KB 343 20–21
Charing Cross Electricity Co v Hydraulic Power Co, [1914] 3 KB 772 . . . . 15–16, 24–26
Chester v Afshar, [2004] UKHL 41, [2005] 1 AC 134. 280
Collins v Hertfordshire CC, [1947] KB 598. 18
Coltman v Bibby Tankers, [1988] AC 276 237
Cooper v Wandsworth Board of Works, (1863) CBNS 180. .24–26
Coventry v Lawrence, [2014] UKSC 13, [2014] AC 822 17
Cox v Ministry of Justice, [2016] UKSC 10, [2016] AC 660 . . . . 19–20, 103–4, 112–14,
                              141–42, 168–69, 214–16, 219–20
Craner v Dorset CC, [2008] EWCA Civ 1323, [2009] ICR 56. .237
Dennis v Ministry of Defence, [2003] EWHC 793 (QB) 210–12
Donoghue v Stevenson, [1932] AC 562 21–24
Dorset v Home Office, [1970] AC 1004 210–12
Dubai Aluminium Co Ltd v Salaam and Others, [2003] 2 AC 366. . . . . 103–4, 207–9
Dugmore v Swansea NHS Trust, [2002] EWCA Civ 1689; [2003] ICR 574. 138–40
Dunne v North Western Gas Board, [1964] 2 QB 806 24–26
E v English Province of Our Lady of Charity, [2013] QB 722 18
Entick v Carrington, (1765) 19 St Tr 1030 24–26
Filburn v People's Palace and Aquarium Co Ltd, (1890) 25 QBD 258 . . . . 17–18, 29–30,
                                    107–8, 109, 138–40
Gee v DePuy International Ltd, [2018] EWHC 1208 . . . . 21–24, 138–40, 236
Gill v Edouin, (1894) 71 LT 762 15–16
Gore v Stannard, [2014] QB 1 . . . . 103–4, 107–8, 111–12, 206–7, 298–99
Gray v Pullen, (1864) 5 B & S 970 20–21
Green v Chelsea Waterworks Co, (1894) 70 LT 547 15–16
Greenock Corp v Caledonian R, [1917] AC 556. 15–16

xiv TABLE OF CASES

Groves v Wimborne (Lord), [1898] 2 QB 402 237
Gunter v James, (1907-1908) 24 Times L Rep 868 . . . . 107–8, 111–12
Hale v Jennings Bros, [1938] 1 All ER 579 . . . . 14–15, 107–8, 111–12
Hammersmith and City Railway Co v Brand, (1866-67) LR 2 QB 223 . . . . . 143–44, 209–10
Hill v Chief Constable of West Yorkshire, [1989] AC 53 24–26
Hoare & Co v McAlpine, [1923] 1 Ch 167 . . . . 14–15, 235–36
Honeywill & Stein Ltd v Larkin Bros (London's Commercial
    Photographers) Ltd, [1934] 1 KB 191 . . . . .20–21, 107–8, 109–11, 116–17
Hunter v Canary Wharf Ltd, [1997] AC 655 13–15
Hunter v Severs, [1994] 2 AC 350 213–14
Iman Abouzaid v Mothercare (UK) Ltd, [2000] 12 WLUK 627 21–24
JGE v English Province of Our Lady of Charity, [2013] QB 722 . . . . .18, 280
Jones v Festiniog Ry, (1867-68) LR 3 QB 733 . . . . 14–15, 107–8
Kiddle v City Business Properties Ltd, [1942] 1 KB 269 17
Knowles v Liverpool City Council, [1993] 1 WLR 1428 237
Lamb v Camden LBC, [1981] 1 QB 625 205
Leach v Money, (1765) 19 St Tr 2002 24–26
Limpus v London General Omnibus Co, (1862) 1 H & C 526 .112–13
Lister v Hesley Hall Ltd, [2002] 1 AC 215 . . . . .19–20, 103–5, 112–13, 207–9
LPTB v Upson, [1949] AC 155 27
Majrowski v Guy's and St Thomas's NHS Trust, [2006] UKHL 34 . . . . 103–4, 138–40,
                                                                                   167–68, 207–9, 235–36
Marcic v Thames Water Utilities Ltd, [2003] UKHL 66, [2004] 2 AC 42 210–12
Mckenna v British Aluminium Limited, [2002] Env LR 30 15–16
Michael v Chief Constable of South Wales, [2015] UKSC 2, [2015] AC 1732 24–26
Midwood v Manchester Corporation, [1905] 2KB 597 . . . . 24–26, 108–9, 111–12
Miles v Forest Rock Co Ltd, (1918) 34 TLR 500 . . . . 14–15, 107–8
Mirvahedy v Henley, [2003] 2 AC 491 . . . . 107–8, 138–40, 206–7
Mohamud v WM Morrison Supermarkets Plc, [2016] UKSC 11, [2016] AC 677 19–20
Morgans v Launchbury, [1973] AC 127 . . . . 19–20, 205, 234–35
Morris v Ford Motor Co Ltd, [1973] QB 792 . . . . 112–13, 205
National Telephone Co v Baker, [1893] 2 Ch 186 14–15
Nettleship v Weston, [1971] 2 QB 691 . . . . .13–14, 205
Nichols v Marsland, (1876) 2 Ex D 1 15–16
Noble v Harrison, [1926] 2 KB 332 107–8
Northwestern Utilities Ltd v London Guarantee and Accident Ltd,
    [1936] AC 108 . . . . 15–16, 107–8
O'Rourke v Camden LBC, [1998] AC 188 24–26
Ormrod v Crosville Motor Services Ltd, [1953] 1 WLR 1120 19–20
Pearson v Coleman Bros, [1948] 2 KB 359 17–18
Perry v Kendricks Transport Ltd, [1956] 1 WLR 85 . . . . 15–16, 138–40
Peters v Prince of Wales Theatre, [1943] 1 KB 73 15–16
Phelps v Hillingdon LBC, [2001] 2 AC 619 24–26
Powell v Fall, (1880) 5 QBD 597 . . . . 107–8, 111–12, 143–44
Pride of Derby and Derbyshire Angling Association Ltd v British
    Celanese Ltd, [1953] Ch 149 24–26
Racz v Home Office, [1994] 2 AC 45 24–26
Rainham Chemical Works v Belvedere Fish Guano, [1921] 2 AC 465 14–15
Rapier v London Tramways Company, [1893] 2 Ch 588 138–40
Read v J Lyons, [1947] AC 156 . . . . 14–15, 107–8, 109–11, 138–40, 277–79
Rickards v Lothian, [1913] AC 263 . . . . 15–16, 107–8
Robinson v PE Jones (Contractors) Ltd, [2011] EWCA Civ 9 7–8

TABLE OF CASES   xv

Romford Ice and Cold Storage v Lister, [1957] AC 555 . . . . 112–13, 213–14
Rowling v Takaro Properties Ltd, [1988] AC 473 24–26
Rylands v Fletcher, (1868) LR 3 HL 330 . . . . 13–16, 24–26, 27–29, 37, 44–45,
61–63, 94–96, 103–4, 107–8, 109–12, 116–17,
138–40, 141–42, 143–44, 152–53, 162–63,
166–67, 206–7, 210–12, 214–16, 235–36,
264–65, 266–67, 269–70, 277–80, 298–99
Sedleigh-Denfield v O'Callaghan, [1940] AC 880. 17
Shiffman v Order of St John, [1936] 1 All ER 557 14–15
Smeaton v Ilford Co, [1954] Ch 450 24–26
Smith v Northamptonshire CC, [2009] UKHL 27, [2009] ICR 734 . . . . 111–12, 138–40
Stovin v Wise, [1996] AC 923 24–26
Three Rivers DC v Bank of England (No.3), [2001] UKHL 16, [2003] 2 AC 1 24–26
Transco plc v Stockport MBC, [2003] UKHL 61, [2004] 2 AC 1 . . . . 14–17, 107–8,
109–11, 138–40, 144, 210–12, 214–16
Trevett v Lee, [1955] 1 WLR 113 17
Various Claimants v Catholic Child Welfare Society, [2012] UKSC 56,
[2013] 2 AC 1 . . . . 18, 103–5, 112–13, 141–42, 167–69,
207–9, 212–13, 214–16, 234–36
Viasystems (Tyneside) Ltd v Thermal Transfer (Northern) Ltd, [2006] QB 510 112–13,
138–40, 167–68, 207–9
Weddall v Barchester Healthcare Ltd, [2012] EWCA Civ 25 112–13
Welsh v Stokes, [2007] EWCA Civ 796 . . . . 138–40, 206–7
West v Bristol Tramways Co, [1908] 2 KB 14 14–16
Wilkes v Depuy International Ltd, [2016] EWHC 3096 . . . . .21–24, 236
Wilson and Clyde Coal Co v English, [1938] AC 57 20–21
WM Morrison Supermarkets plc v Various Claimants, [2020]
UKSC 12, [2020] 2 WLR 941 . . . . 19–20, 207–9, 214–16
Woodland v Swimming Teachers Association, [2013] UKSC 66,
[2014] AC 537 . . . . 20–21, 109–11
Wyatt v Rosherville Gardens Co, (1886) 2 TLR 282 17–18
X (Minors) v Bedfordshire CC, [1995] 2 AC 633 24–26

FRANCE

Civ 27.11.1844 45
TC 8.2.1873 (*Blanco*) 4–6, 46–47
TC 30.7.1873 (*Pelletier*) 46–47
CE 21.6.1895 (*Cames*) 74–76
Civ 16.6.1896 (*Teffaine*) 39–40, 77
CE 3.2.1911 (*Anguet*) 46–47
CE 26.7.1918 (*Lemonnier*) 46–47
CE 28.3.1919 (*Regnault- Desroziers*) 47–49, 79–81
CE 30.11.1923 (*Couitéas*) 47–49, 181–82
Civ 21.2.1927 (*Jand'heur*) 79–81
Ch réun 13.2.1930 (*Jand'heur*) 39–40, 77, 79–81
CE 24.7.1931 (*Comm de Vic- Fezensac*) 47–49
CA Paris 20.10.1934 224–25
CE Ass 14.1.1938 (*La Fleurette*) 47–49, 181–83
Ch réun 2.12.1941 (*Franck*) 39–40, 77, 149–50
CE 5.3.1943 (*Chavat*) 47–49
Cass civ 23.1.1945 39–40

xvi TABLE OF CASES

CE Ass 22.11.1946 (*Commune Saint-Priest-la-Plaine*)............................47–49
Trib Seine 2.4.1949..77
CE Ass 24.6.1949 (*Lecomte et Daramy*) 47–49, 79–81, 183–84
CE Ass 28.7.1951 (*Laruelle et Delville*)...................................46–47
CE 7.11.1952 (*Grau*)...47–49
CE 17.4.1953 (*Pinguet*)..47–49
Civ (2) 12.10.1955...41
Civ (2) 5.1.1956..145–46
CE 3.2.1956 (*Thouzellier*)..47–49, 79–81
CE 4.10.1957 (*Beaufils*) 47–49
CE 28.6.1961 (*André-des-Alpes*) 46–47
Civ (1) 3.3.1964..40
CE Ass 30.3.1966 (*Compagnie Générale d'Energie Radio-Electrique*)..............47–49
CE 20.11.1968 (*Compagnie d'Assurances 'La Fortune'*).......................46–47
CE 25.9.1970 (*Tesson*) 47–49
Civ (3) 4.2.1971..45
CE 26.1.1973 (*Driancourt*) 46–47
CE 14.11.1973 (*Leynaert*)...47–49
CE Ass 20.3.1974 (*Navarra*) 47–49
CE 29.5.1974 (*Reyboz*)...47–49
Cass crim 20.5.1976..42
CE 20.10.1976 (*Alfortville*) 46–47
CE 29.10.1976 (*Burgat*) 47–49
CE 27.5.1977 (*SA Victor-Delforge*)......................................47–49
Civ (2) 19.3.1980...79–81
CE 20.11.1981 (*Rodal*) 47–49
Civ (2) 21.7.1982 (*Desmares*)..........................44–45, 178–79, 253–54
Civ (2) 22.2.1984...149–50
Ass plén 9.5.1984 (*Fullenwarth*) 41
CE 22.6.1984 (*Sealink*)...47–49
CE 8.10.1986 (*Langlet et Centre hospitalier général de Château-Thierry*)............46–47
Civ (2) 6.4.1987..39–40, 44–45
CE 27.1.1988 (*Giraud*) 46–47
Ass plén 19.5.1988..42
CA Limoges 23.3.1989 (*Blieck*)..178
CE 9.5.1989 (*Centre Hospitalier de Castelnaudry*) 46–47
Conseil Constitutionnel 4.7.1989 no 89-254.................................47–49
Ass plén 29.3.1991 (*Blieck*) 40–41
Civ (3) 12.2.1992..45
Civ (2) 19.2.1992..40
Civ (1) 9.6.1993...145–46, 149–50
Civ (2) 22.5.1995..40–41
CE Ass 26.5.1995 (*N'Guyen*) 47–49
Civ (2) 28.6.1995..45
Civ (1) 5.11.1996..6–7
Civ (2) 19.2.1997 (*Bertrand*) 41, 145–46, 176–78, 253–54
Civ (2) 2.12.1998..41
Civ (2) 10.5.2001 (*Levert*) 41, 145–46, 176–78, 253–54
Ass plén 14.12.2001..176–78
Civ (2) 12.12.2002...40–41
Ass plén 13.12.2002 ....41, 253–54
Cass com 1.7.2003 n.01-13.052..6–7

Civ (2) 5.2.2004 45
Civ (2) 29.4.2004 41
Ass plén 14.4.2006 39–40
Civ (1) 12.7.2007 176–78
Cass com 27.5.2008 n.07-14.422 6–7
Civ (3) 9.9.2009 6–7
Civ (1) 3.6.2010 6–7
Cass com 28.9.2010 n.09-69.272 6–7
Cass soc 17.5.2011 6–7
Cass crim 29.6.2011 . . . . 156–57, 224–25
Civ (3) 10.12.2014 45
Civ (3) 18.1.2018 n.16-20.563 6–7

ITALY

Civ sez un 26.10.1957 n.4156 55
App Brescia 4.5.1958 248–50
Civ (III) 23.1.1962 n.95 90–93
Civ (III) 30.11.1977 n.5222 51–52
Civ (III) 29.1.1981 n.693 . . . . .90–91, 135
Civ (III) 27.3.1987 n.2994 86–87
Civ (III) 1.7.1987 n.5764 51–52
Civ (III) 24.5.1988 n.3616 51–52
Civ (III) 29.5.1989 n.2584 . . . . 86–87, 199–200
Civ (III) 27.7.1990 n.7571 51–52
Civ sez un 14.3.1991 n.2726 51–52
Civ sez un 11.11.1991 n.12019 135
Civ (II) 25.3.1995 n.3553 52–53
Civ (III) 30.8.1995 n.9205 51–52
Civ (I) 1.9.1995 n.9211 51–52
Trib Massa Carrara 27.2.1996 51–52
Civ (III) 19.6.1997 n.5485 50
Civ (III) 26.10.1998 n.10629 226–27
Civ (III) 4.12.1998 n.12307 54
Civ sez un 22.7.1999 n.500 58–60
Civ (III) 22.5.2001 n.6970 91–93
Civ (III) 20.6.2001 n.8381 . . . . 86–87, 134–35, 199–200
Cons St 6.8.2001 n.4239 58–60
Trib Monza 22.10.2001 134–35
Civ (III) 20.7.2002 n.10641 52–53
Civ (III) 10.2.2003 n.1954 51–52
Civ (III) 4.5.2004 n.8457 51–52
Civ (III) 22.10.2004 n.20588 199–200
Civ (III) 16.6.2005 n.12965 50
Trib Brescia 10.8.2005 134–35
Civ (III) 20.2.2006 n.3651 54–55
Civ (II) 9.3.2006 n.5080 51–52
Civ (III) 6.7.2006 n.15383 . . . . 52–53, 134–35, 160
Civ (III) 12.7.2006 n.15779 135
Civ (III) 13.3.2007 n.5839 51–52
Civ (III) 7.5.2007 n.10300 51–52
Civ (III) 15.5.2007 n.11193 51–52

xviii   TABLE OF CASES

Civ (III) 22.6.2007 n.14578 54–55
Civ (III) 19.2.2008 n.4279 . . . . 134–35, 160
Civ (III) 25.2.2008 n.4718 135
Civ (III) 6.3.2008 n.6033 . . . . 86–87, 134–35
Civ (III) 25.7.2008 n.20427 135
Trib Roma 28.1.2009 n.1828 134–35
Cons St 13.2.2009 n.775 58–60
Trib Mantova 5.8.2009 n.789 51–52
Trib Milano 3.10.2009 n.11786 54–55
Civ (III) 17.12.2009 n.26516 . . . . 51–52, 134–35, 160
Civ (sezione lavoro) 11.1.2010 n.215 . . . . 86–87, 134–35, 199–200
Civ (III) 21.1.2010 n.1002 54
Cons St 12.3.2010 n.1467 58–60
Civ (III) 16.3.2010 n.6325 54–55
Cons St Ad Plen 23.3.2011 n.3 58–60
Civ (III) 19.5.2011 n.11016 90–93
Civ (III) 18.7.2011 n.15733 51–52
Civ (III) 6.12.2011 n.26200 50
Civ (III) 8.2.2012 n.1769 . . . . .52–53, 135
Civ (III) 20.3.2012 n.4395 135
Civ (III) 9.5.2012 n.7048 6–7
Civ (III) 19.7.2012 n.12448 . . . . 86–87, 134–35, 199–200
Civ (III) 26.7.2012 n.13214 51–52
Civ (III) 11.12.2012 n.22632 . . . . .54, 90–91, 135
Civ (III) 29.5.2013 n.13458 56
Civ (VI) 4.10.2013 n.22684 . . . . .52–53, 135
Trib Bari 12.12.2013 90–93
Civ (III) 19.2.2014 n.3964 135
Civ (III) 21.5.2014 n.11270 226–27
Trib Milano 11.7.2014 n.9235 . . . . 51–52, 134–35
Civ (III) 10.10.2014 n.21426 . . . . 86–87, 134–35, 199–200
Civ (III) 18.11.2014 n.24475 50
Civ (III) 13.1.2015 n.295 135
Civ (III) 9.4.2015 n.7093 . . . . 51–52, 90–91
Civ sez un 29.4.2015 n.8620 . . . . .52, 88, 90–93
Civ (III) 29.7.2015 n.16052 51–52
Civ (III) 31.7.2015 n.16276 58–60
Civ (III) 18.9.2015 n.18317 52–53
Civ (III) 22.12.2015 n.25738 54
Civ (III) 26.1.2016 n.1321 50
Civ (III) 19.2.2016 n.3258 56
Civ (I) 9.5.2016 n.9337 135
Civ (III) 25.5.2016 n.10757 54–55
Civ (III) 27.6.2016 n.13208 6–7
Civ (II) 2.8.2016 n.16074 6–7
Cons St 13.2.2017 n.602 58–60
Civ (II) 17.2.2017 n.4252 6–7
Cons St 17.2.2017 n.730 58–60
Civ (III) 9.3.2017 n.6033 90–91
Cons St 27.3.2017 n.1364 58–60
Civ (III) 12.5.2017 n.11785 . . . . 57–58, 90–91

TABLE OF CASES   xix

Civ (III) 29.9.2017 n.22839 135
Civ (III) 1.2.2018 n.2480 52–53
Civ (III) 14.3.2018 n.6141 135
Civ sez un 16.5.2019 n.13246 57–58
Cons St Ad Plen 23.4.2021 n.7..58–60

UNITED STATES

Ambort v Nowlin, 709 S.W.2d 407 (Ark.1986) 29–30
American Tobacco Co, Inc v Grinnell, 951 S.W.2d 420 (Tex.1997) 27–29
Anderson v Marathon Petroleum Company, 801 F.2d 936 (7th Cir.1986).......31, 123–26
Anderson v Owens-Corning Fiberglas Corp, 810 P.2d 549 (Cal.1991) 33–34
Appelhans v McFall, 757 N.E.2d 987 (Ill.2001)................................31–32
Ayers v Johnson & Johnson Baby Prods Co, 818 P.2d 1337 (Wash.1991) 33–34
Barker v Lull, 573 P.2d 443 (Cal.1978) 33–34
Becker v Interstate Properties, 569 F.2d 1203 (3rd Cir.1977) 100–2, 123–26
Bell v Jet Wheel Blast, 462 So.2d 166 (La.1985)..............................191–92
Berkovitz v United States, 486 US 531 (1988) 34–37
Beshada v Johns-Manville Products Corp, 447 A.2d 539 (N.J.1982) 33–34, 100–2,
                  187, 193–94, 231–33, 242–43, 245–46
Bianchini v Humble Pipe Line Co, 480 F.2d 251 (5th Cir.1973) 27–29
Bierman v City of New York, 60 Misc.2d 497 (N.Y.1969) 93–94, 123–26
Bivens v Six Unknown Named Agents of Federal Bureau of Narcotics,
    403 US 388 (1971) 34–37, 123–26, 231–33
Blankenship v Gen Motors Corp, 406 S.E.2d 781 (W.Va.1991)......................186
Bowling v Heil Co, 511 N.E.2d 373 (Ohio 1987)...................... 164–65, 191–92
Brooks v Beech Aircraft Corp, 902 P.2d 54 (N.M.1995)............. 33–34, 100–3, 191–92
Brown v Collins, 53 NH 442 (N.H.1873)..27–29
Brown v Kendall, 60 Mass 292 (Mass.1850) 27
Carey v Piphus, 435 US 247 (1978)...34–37
Chavez v Southern Pacific Transportation, 413 F.Supp. 1203
    (Cal.1976) 98–100, 186, 187, 192–93, 231–33
Chicago, Indianapolis & Louisville Railway v Stierwalt, 153 N.E. 807 (Ind.1926) 31–32
Cities Service Co v State, 312 So.2d 799 (Fla.1975) 98–100, 231–33
Codling v Paglia, 298 N.E.2d 622 (N.Y.1963) 186, 191–92
Curry v Superior Court, 20 Cal.App.4th 180 (Cal.1993) 123–26
Dalehite v United States, 346 US 15 (1953) 34–37
Daly v General Motors Corp, 575 P.2d 1162 (Cal.1978).........................33–34
Dart v Pure Oil Co, 27 N.W.2d 555 (Minn.1947) 27–29
Dippel v Sciano, 155 N.W.2d 55 (Wis.1967) 93–94
Dyer v Maine Drilling & Blasting, Inc, 984 A.2d 210 (Me.2009) 27–29, 98–102,
                  123–26, 191–92
Elias v Unisys Corp, 573 N.E.2d 946 (Mass.1991) 231–33
Escola v Coca Cola Bottling Co, 150 P.2d 436 (Cal.1944) 123–26, 186–87,
                  231–33, 242–43
Essig v United States, 675 F.Supp. 84 (N.Y.1987)..............................269–70
Exner v Sherman Power Construction, 54 F.2d 510 (2nd Cir.1931).................27–29
Farmers Ins Exchange v State of California, 175 Cal.App.3d 494 (Cal.1985) 34–37
Farmers Ins Group v County of Santa Clara, 906 P.2d 440 (Cal.1995)..............231–33
Feldman v Lederle Laboratories, 479 A.2d 374 (N.J.1984) 33–34
Fifer v Dix, 608 N.W.2d 740 (Wis.2000).......................................29–30

XX TABLE OF CASES

Findlay v Copeland Lumber Co, 509 P.2d 28 (Ore.1973)...........................33–34
France v Southern Equip Co, 689 S.E.2d 1 (W.Va.2010) 31
Francioni v Gibsonia Truck Corp, 372 A.2d 736 (Pa.1977)........123–26, 191–92, 231–33
Fruit v Schreiner, 502 P.2d 133 (Alaska 1972)............................. 186, 191–92
Gantes v Kason Corp, 679 A.2d 106 (N.J.1996).................................123–27
GJ Leasing Co, Inc v Union Elec Co, 54 F.3d 379 (7th Cir.1995).....................122
Godoy ex rel. Gramling v E.I. du Pont de Nemours & Co, 768 N.W.2d 674
   (Wis.2009)..33–34
Golden v Amory, 109 N.E.2d 131 (Mass.1952)................................27–29
Gossett v Simonson, 411 P.2d 277 (Or.1966)........................... 102–3, 123–26
Green v Smith & Nephew AHP, Inc, 629 N.W.2d 727 (Wis.2001) 33–34, 93–94,
   100–3, 127–28, 191–92, 296–98
Greenman v Yuba Power Products, Inc, 377 P.2d 897 (Cal.1963)..................33–34
Halphen v Johns-Manville Sales Corp, 484 So.2d 110 (La.1986) 242–43
Harris v Trojan Fireworks Co, 120 Cal.App.3d 157 (Cal.1981)....................269–70
Heath v Sears, Roebuck & Co, 464 A.2d 288, 293 (N.H.1983) 100–3, 123–26
Hinman v Westinghouse Electric Company, 471 P.2d 988 (Cal.1970).......100–3, 164–65,
   186, 191–92
Holland v Buckley, 305 So.2d 113 (La.1971) 94–96, 100–2
Hoven v Kelble, 256 N.W.2d 379 (Wis.1977)....................................100
Hutchinson v Capeletti Brothers, Inc. 297 So.2d 952 (Fla.1981)............. 186, 191–92
In re Bomb Disaster at Roseville, 438 F.Supp. 769 (Cal.1977)....................34–37
In State Department of Environmental Protection v Ventron Corp,
   468 A.2d 150 (N.J.1983)...231–33
Indian Towing Company v United States, 350 US 61 (1955).....................34–37
Ira S Bushey & Sons, Inc v United States, 398 F.2d 167 (2d Cir.1968).......... 269–70, 280
Isaacs v Powell, 267 So.2d 864 (Fla.1972)........................29–30, 100–2, 298–99
Johnson v Raybestos-Manhattan, Inc., 740 P.2d 548 (Haw.1987)..................33–34
Johnson v State of California, 447 P.2d 352 (Cal.1968) 34–37, 188–90
Johnston v Long, 181 P.2d 645 (Cal.1947).............................. 186, 191–92
Jost v Dairyland Power Cooperative, 172 N.W.2d 647 (Wis.1970)..................32–33
Kansallis Finance Ltd v Fern & Others, 659 N.E.2d 731 (Mass.1996) 31–32
Kennedy v City and County of Denver, 506 P.2d 764 (Colo.1972) 29–30
Kenney v Liston, 760 S.E.2d 434 (W.Va.2014)................................269–70
Keyser v Phillips Petroleum Co, 287 So.2d 364 (Fla.1973) 29–30
King v Blue Mountain Forest Association, 123 A.2d 151 (N.H.1956) 29–30
Klein v Pyrodyne Corp, 810 P.2d 917 (Wash.1991) 27–29
Laird v Nelms, 406 US 797 (1972)............................34–37, 96–100, 188–90
Langan v Valicopters, 567 P.2d 218 (Wash.1977) 27–29, 100–2
Leichtamer v Am Motors Corp, 424 N.E.2d 568 (Ohio 1981)....................123–27
Li v Yellow Cab Company of California, 532 P.2d 1226 (Cal.1975) 31
Lisa M v Henry Mayo Newhall Mem Hosp, 907 P.2d 358 (Cal.1995)........... 31, 123–26,
   127–28, 191–92, 231–33
Lively v United States, 870 F.2d 296 (5th Cir.1989)............................34–37
Losee v Buchanan, 51 N.Y. 476 (N.Y.1873) 27–29
Lubin v Iowa City 131 N.W.2d 765 (Iowa 1964) 188–90
Luth v Rogers & Babler Constr Co, 507 P.2d 761 (Alaska 1973)....................102–3
Mahowald v Minnesota Gas Co, 344 N.W.2d 856 (Minn.1984) 187, 231–33
Malchose v Kalfell, 664 N.W.2d 508 (N.D.2003)...............................31–32
Mary M v City of Los Angeles, 814 P.2d 1341 (Cal.1991).......... 123–26, 127–28, 231–33
Maselli v Ginner, 809 P.2d 1181 (Idaho 1991)................................31–32

TABLE OF CASES xxi

McLane v Northwest Natural Gas, 467 P.2d 635, 638 (Or.1970) 93–94, 96–98, 296–97
McPhee v Tufty, 623 N.W.2d 390 (N.D.2001) 31–32
Michaelsohn v Smith, 113 N.W.2d 571 (ND.1962). 231–33
Miller v United States, 463 F.3d 1122 (10th Cir.2006) 34–37
Mills v Smith, 673 P.2d 117 (Kans.1983) 29–30
Monell v Department of Social Services of the City of New York,
    436 US 658 (1978) 34–37, 188–90, 231–33
Montague v AMN Healthcare, Inc, 223 Cal.App.4th 1515 (Cal.2014). 188–90, 231–33
National Steel Service Center v Gibbons, 319 N.W.2d 269 (Iowa 1982). 27–29,
    123–26, 185–86
Old Island Fumigation v Barbee, 604 So.2d 1246 (Fla.1992). .27–29
Owen v City of Independence, 445 US 622 (1980) 34–37, 123–26, 188–90, 231–33
Patterson v Blair, 172 S.W.3d 361 (Ky.2005) 31
Peterson v Lou Bachrodt Chevrolet Co, 329 N.E.2d 785 (Ill.1975) 94–96
Price v Shell Oil Co, 466 P.2d 722 (Cal.1970). 187
Promaulayko v Johns Manville Sales Corp, 562 A.2d 202 (N.J.1989). 191–92
Pusey v Bator, 762 N.E.2d 968 (Ohio 2002). 31
Queen City Terminals, Inc v Gen Am Transp Corp, 653 N.E.2d 661
    (Ohio 1995). 123–26, 127–28, 191–92, 297–98
Rayonier, Inc v United States, 352 US 315 (1957). 190–91, 230
Richman v Charter Arms Corp, 571 F.Supp 192 (La.1983) 188–90
Riss v City of New York, 240 N.E.2d 860 (N.Y.1968) 123–26
Riviello v Waldron, 391 N.E.2d 1278 (N.Y.1979) 162–63
Rodebush v Oklahoma Nursing Homes, Ltd, 867 P.2d 1241 (Okla.1993). 31
Rodgers v Kemper Constr Co, 50 Cal.App.3d 608 (Cal.1975). 269–70
Roditis v United States, 122 F.3d 108 (2nd Cir.1997) 34–37
SaBell's, Inc v Flens, 627 P.2d 750 (Colo.1981) 29–30
Safford Animal Hosp v Blain, 580 P.2d 757 (Ariz.1978). 29–30
Schump v Firestone Tire and Rubber Co, 541 N.E.2d 1040 (Ohio 1989). 188–90
Seely v White Motor Co, 403 P.2d 145 (Cal.1965). 187, 231
Siegler v Kuhlman, 502 P.2d 1181 (Wash.1972) 27–29, 188–90
Smith v Lockheed Propulsion Co, 247 Cal.App.2d 774 (Cal.1967) 100–2
Spalding v Waxler, 205 N.E.2d 890 (Ohio 1995). 31–32
Sternhagen v Dow Co, 935 P.2d 1139 (Mont.1997) 33–34
Suvada v White Motor Co, 210 N.E.2d 182 (Ill.1965) 100–2
T & E Industries, Inc v Safety Light Corp, 587 A.2d 1249 (N.J.1991) 27–29, 191–92
Toms v Calvary Assembly of God, Inc, 132 A.3d 866 (Md.2016) 27–29
Townsend v Sears, Roebuck & Co, 879 N.E.2d 893 (Ill.2007) .33–34
Toyota Motor Sales U.S.A., Inc v Superior Court, 220 Cal.App.3d 864 (Cal.1990). . . .269–70
Trotter v Callens, 546 P.2d 867 (N.M.1976). 27–29
United States v Gaubert, 499 US 315 (1991) 34–37
US Airways v Elliott Equipment Co, No. CIV.A. 06-1481, 2008 WL
    4461849 (Pa.2008) 191–92
Vandermark v Ford Motor Co, 391 P.2d 168 (Cal.1964) 231–33
Vassallo v Baxter Healthcare Corp, 696 N.E.2d 909 (Mass.1998). 33–34
Vincent v Lake Erie, 124 N.W. 221 (Minn.1910). 264–65
Weber v Stokely-Van Camp, Inc, 144 N.W.2d 540 (Minn.1966). .163
Williams v Tysinger, 399 S.E.2d 108 (N.C.1991). 29–30
Young v Beck, 251 P.3d 380 (Ariz.2011). 31–32, 231–33
Yukon Equipment v Fireman's Fund Insurance, 585 P.2d 1206
    (Alaska 1978) 27–29, 98–102

AUSTRALIA

Chappel v Hart, [1999] 2 LRC 341, (1998) 72 ALJR 1344 280

CANADA

KLB v British Columbia, 2003 SCC 51, [2003] 2 SCR 403........................141–42

EUROPEAN UNION

Commission v France, Case C-52/00...43–44
Commission v Portugal, Case C-275/03 58–60
Commission v Portugal, Case C-70/06 58–60
Commission v United Kingdom, Case C-300/95...............................21–24
Stadt Graz v Strabag AG and Others, Case C-314/09...........................58–60

SCOTLAND

Cairns v Northern Lighthouse Board, [2013] CSOH 22, 2013 SLT 645...... 138–40, 206–7

Table of Legislation

ENGLAND

Animals Act 1971 . . . 15–16, 17–18, 138–40
 s 2(1) 15–16, 17–18
 s 2(2) 17–18
 ss 3–4 17–18
 s 5(1)–(6) 17–18
 s 6(2) 17–18
 s 10 17–18
Automated and Electric Vehicles
 Act 2018. 20–21
Consumer Protection Act 1987. 21–24,
 26, 106–7
 s 4(1). 21–24, 26
Control of Substances Hazardous to Health
 Regulations 1988 and 1994
 s 7(1). 138–40
Crown Proceedings Act 1947 24–26
 s 2(1) 24–26
 s 2(2) 24–26
 s 2(3) 24–26
Employer's Liability (Defective Equipment)
 Act 1969. . . . . .20–21, 237
 s 1(1). 20–21
Employers' Liability (Compulsory
 Insurance) Act 1969. 206–7
Enterprise and Regulatory Reform
 Act 2013. . . . . . . 20–21, 61–62, 209, 237
 s 47 20–21
 s 69 20–21
Environmental Protection Act 1990
 s 73(6). 15–16, 107–8
Factory and Workshop Act 1878. 237
Gas Act 1965
 s 14 . . . . 15–16, 107–8
Health and Safety at Work etc. Act 1974
 s 15 20–21
 s 47 20–21
Human Rights Act 1998. 210–12
 s 7 24–26
 s 8 24–26
Land Compensation Act 1973. 210–12
Nuclear Installations Act 1965
 s 7 107–8
 s 12 . . . . 15–16, 107–8

Police Act 1996
 s 88 19–20
Provision and Use of Work Equipment
 Regulations 1998 . . . . .138–40, 237
 s 4(1). 20–21
 s 5(1). 20–21
Vaccine Damage Payment
 Act 1979. 210–12
Water Industry Act 1991
 s 209 . . . . 15–16, 107–8
Workplace (Health, Safety and Welfare)
 Regulations 1992 237

FRANCE

Code civil. 4–6, 37–40,
 41, 44–45, 46–47, 49–50, 52–53,
 54, 74–76, 88, 109–11, 287
 art 1218 .39–40
 art 1240 6–7
 art 1242 . . . . 39–41, 42, 176–78
 art 1242(1) 11, 39–41, 81–82,
 222–23
 art 1242(2) 39–40
 art 1242(4) 40–41
 art 1242(5) 40–41, 42–43
 art 1242(6) 38–39, 40–41, 42–43
 art 1242(7) 40–41, 42–43
 art 1242(8) 38–39, 40–41, 42–43
 art 1243 .39–40
 art 1244 .39–40
 arts 1240–1241 37–38
 arts 1240–1244 11
 arts 1242–1244 38–39
 arts 1245–1245-17 43–44
 art 1245-10. 43–44
 (former) art 1382 74–76
 (former) art 1384(1) 11, 39–40,
 74–76, 77, 79–82, 222–23
 (former) art 1385 40
 (former) art 1386 40
 (former) arts 1382–1383 37–38
 (former) arts 1384–1386 38–39
Code de l'aviation civile
 art L 141-2 44–45

xxiv TABLE OF LEGISLATION

Code de la santé publique 45
   art L 1142-1 45
Code pénal
   art 111-1. 4–6
Déclaration des droits de l'homme et du
   citoyen
   art 13. 181–82
Loi du pluviôse an VIII
   art 4. 47–49
Loi 20.7.1899. 42–43
Loi 5.4.1937. .42–43
Loi no 85-677 of 5.7.1985
   (loi Badinter) 39–40, 44–45,
         61, 77–78, 79–81, 145–46,
         178–79, 181, 253–54
   art 1. 44–45
   art 2. 44–45
   art 3. 44–45
   art 5. 44–45
Loi no 98-389 of 19.5.1998. 43–44
Loi no 2002-303 of 4.3.2002 44–45
Loi no 2018-287 of 20.4.2018 37–38
Ordonnance no 2016-131 of
   10.2.2016. .37–38

ITALY

Codice civile 4–6, 9, 49–50, 51–53,
       55–56, 57–58, 60, 62, 84, 88,
       196–97, 198, 200, 284–85
   art 844. 55
   art 1218 56–57
   art 1227 . . . . 51–52, 134–35
   art 1228 56–57
   art 2043 . . . . 6–7, 11, 37–38,
       49–50, 52–53, 54–55,
       56–60, 284–85
   art 2047 49–50
   art 2048 50
   art 2049 . . . . .54–55, 56–58,
       90–93, 199–200, 226–27
   art 2050 . . . . .11, 51–52, 62, 88–89,
       91–93, 132–35, 200,
       229, 247–48, 304–5
   art 2051 . . . . .52–53, 57–58, 88,
       91–93, 135, 200, 226–27
   art 2052 . . . . .53–54, 57–58, 88,
       90–93, 226–27
   art 2053 . . . . .54, 88, 226–27
   art 2054 . . . . 52, 88–89,
       134–35, 226–27
   art 2054(1). 52

art 2054(2) 52
art 2054(3) 52, 90–93, 226–29
art 2054(4) 52, 86–87, 88,
       90–93, 226–29
arts 2047–2054 . . . . . . 11, 49–50, 284–85
arts 2049–2054 85–86
arts 2050–2054 88–89
arts 2051–2053 91–93
Codice del consumo
   arts 114–127 56
Codice del processo amministrativo
   art 7. 57–58
Codice della navigazione
   art 965. . . . . 56, 88
Codice penale
   art 39. 4–6
Costituzione della Repubblica
   Italiana (Italian
   Constitution) 199–200, 304
   art 2. 198
   art 28. 57–58
D Lgs 6.9.2005 n.206 56
D.M. 20.3.1979 . . . . 56, 88
D.P.R. 10.1.1957 n.3
   arts 22–23. 57–58
D.P.R. 24.5.1988 n.224 56
D.P.R. 10.5.1975 n.519 . . . . 56, 88
legge 31.12.1962 n.1860. . . . . 56, 88
legge 8.3.2017 n.24
   art 7(1) 56–57
   art 7(3) 56–57
r.d. 29.7.1927 n.1443
   art 31. . . . . 56, 88

UNITED STATES

42 USC § 1983. . . . . .34–37, 94–96,
       126–27, 188–91, 231–33
Ann Cal Civ Code (Annotated California
   Civil Code)
   § 1714.1 31–32
Ann Cal Gov Code (Annotated California
   Government Code)
   §§ 814–895.8 34–37
   § 815.2 34–37
   § 862(b) 34–37
CRSA (Colorado Revised Statutes
   Annotated)
   § 24-10-106(4). 34–37
   § 24-10-106.1(4) 34–37
FTCA (Federal Tort Claims Act) . . . 34–37,
       188–90

TABLE OF LEGISLATION xxv

28 USC § 2674 34–37
28 USC § 2679(b) 34–37
28 USC § 2680(h) 34–37
FLA (Florida Statutes Annotated)
§§ 767.01, 767.04. 29–30
HRS (Hawaii Revised Statutes Annotated)
HRS D 4, T 36, Ch 662 34–37
IC (Idaho Code Annotated)
IC T 6, Ch 9 34–37
ICA (Iowa Code Annotated)
ICA T XV, Subt 5, Chs 669–670. . . .34–37
Ill Comp Stat Ann (Illinois Compiled
Statutes Annotated)
510 ILCS 5/16 29–30
MGLA (Massachusetts General Laws
Annotated)
Ch 231, § 85G 31–32
Ch 258, §§ 2, 10 34–37
MSA (Minnesota Statutes Annotated)
§ 3.736 34–37
§ 466.02 34–37
New York General Obligations Law
§ 3-112 31–32
New York Vehicle and Traffic Law
§ 388 31–32
NJSA (New Jersey Statutes Annotated)
§ 59:2-2. 34–37

§§ 59:2-3–59:2-10 34–37
§ 59:9-2. 34–37
NMSA (New Mexico Statutes Annotated)
§ 41-4-2 34–37
NRS (Nevada Revised Statutes Annotated)
§ 41.031 34–37
ORCA (Ohio Revised Code Annotated)
§ 4513.20 31–32
PaCSA (Pennsylvania Statutes and
Consolidated Statutes)
42 PaCSA PA ST Pt VII, Ch 85 34–37
RCWA (Revised Code of Washington
Annotated)
§ 4.92.090. .34–37
§ 4.96.010. .34–37
VSA (Vermont Statutes Annotated)
12 VSA § 5601 34–37

EUROPEAN UNION

EU Directive 374/85 (Product Liability
Directive). 21–24, 26,
37–38, 39–40, 43–44, 56,
138–40, 141–42, 178–79,
200–2, 214–16, 236–38
art 7. 21–24
art 7(e) 21–24

List of Abbreviations

Agency Restatement	Restatement (Third) of Agency (2006)
Akron L Rev	Akron Law Review
AJCL	American Journal of Comparative Law
AJDA	Actualité juridique: droit administratif
Arch dir pubbl	Archivio di diritto pubblico
Arch phil dr	Archives de philosophie du droit
Ariz St LJ	Arizona State Law Journal
Ass plén	Assemblée pléniere de la Cour de cassation
B & S	Best and Smith's Reports, Queen's Bench (ER vols 121-122)
Baylor L Rev	Baylor Law Review
BGB	Bürgerliches Gesetzbuch (Germany, 1900)
Bull AP	Bulletin des arrêts Cour de Cassation Assemblée plénière
Bull civ	Bulletin des arrêts de la Cour de cassation, Chambres civiles
CA	Cour d'appel; Court of Appeal
Cal L Rev	California Law Review
Can JL Juris	Canadian Journal of Law and Jurisprudence
Cardozo L Rev	Cardozo Law Review
Cass civ	Chambre civile de la Cour de cassation française
Cass com	Chambre commerciale de la Cour de cassation
Cass crim	Chambre criminelle de la Cour de cassation
Cass soc	Chambre sociale de la Cour de cassation
Cc	Code civil français
CE	Conseil d'État
CE Ass	Assemblée du Conseil d'État
Cf/cf	Compare
CG	Corriere giuridico
Ch	Law Reports, Chancery Division (1890-)
Ch/ch	Chapter
Ch réun	Chambres réunies de la Cour de Cassation
Ch J Comp L	Chinese Journal of Comparative Law
Civ sez un	Sezioni unite della Corte di cassazione italiana
Civ (1), (2) and (3)	Première, deuxième and troisième chambre civile de la Cour de cassation française
Civ (I), (II), (III), and (VI)	Prima, seconda, terza, e sesta sezione civile della Corte di cassazione italiana
Civ (sezione lavoro)	Sezione lavoro della Corte di Cassazione italiana
CJEU	Court of Justice of the European Union
CLJ	Cambridge Law Journal
CLP	Current Legal Problems

xxviii LIST OF ABBREVIATIONS

CLWR	Common Law World Review
Cmnd	command (identifier for published parliamentary papers)
Cod civ	Codice civile
Colum L Rev	Columbia Law Review
comm	commentaire
concl	conclusions
Cons St	Consiglio di Stato
Cons St Ad Plen	Adunanza Plenaria del Consiglio di Stato in sede giurisdizionale
CPA 1987	Consumer Protection Act 1987
CUP	Cambridge University Press
D	Recueil Dalloz
D aff	Recueil Dalloz, Cahier droit des affaires
D chron	Dalloz chronique
D Lgs	Decreto Legislativo
DH	Dalloz, Recueil hebdomadaire de jurisprudence (1924–1940)
Dig disc priv	Digesto delle discipline privatistiche
Dir giur	Diritto e giurisprudenza
DR	Danno e Responsabilità
Dr & patrim	Droit & patrimoine
ed(s)	editor(s)
EDCE	Etudes et documents du Conseil d'État
edn	edition
Eg/eg	for example
Enc Dir	Enciclopedia del diritto
Enc Giur	Enciclopedia giuridica Treccani
esp	especially
et al	and others, *et alii*
EU	European Union
EWCA Civ	Decision of the Court of Appeal (Civil Division)
EWHC	Decision of the High Court
Fasc	fascicule
Fam Dir	Famiglia e Diritto
Fla St U L Rev	Florida State University Law Review
Fordham L Rev	Fordham Law Review
Fordham L Rev Res Gestae	Fordham Law Review Res Gestae
Foro It	Il Foro Italiano
Foro Pad	Il Foro Padano
FTCA	Federal Tort Claims Act
Ga L Rev	Georgia Law Review
Gaz Pal	Gazette du Palais
GC	Giustizia civile
Geo LJ	Georgetown Law Journal
Geo Wash L Rev	George Washington Law Review
GI	Giurisprudenza italiana

GM	Giurisprudenza di merito
Harv L Rev	Harvard Law Review
HL	House of Lords
HUP	Harvard University Press
ILJ	Industrial Law Journal
Indiana LJ	Indiana Law Journal
Inst	Institutiones (Institutes of Justinian)
Int Rev Law Econ	International Review of Law and Economics
Iowa L Rev	Iowa Law Review
J	Mr Justice
JCl	Juris-Classeur
JCl Admin	Juris-Classeur Administratif
JCl E	Juris-Classeur Europe
JCLI	Journal of Contemporary Legal Issues
JETL	Journal of European Tort Law
JTL	Journal of Tort Law
JCP	Juris-classeur périodique, La semaine juridique
JCP E	Juris-classeur périodique, La semaine juridique, entreprises et affaires
JCP G	Juris-classeur périodique, La semaine juridique, édition générale
JEL	Journal of Environmental Law
JPIL	Journal of Personal Injury Law
J Legal Stud	Journal of Legal Studies
KB	Law Reports, King's Bench Division (1901-1952)
Law Com	Law Commission
Law and Phil	Law and Philosophy
LGDJ	Librairie générale de droit et jurisprudence
LJ	Lord Justice of Appeal
Loy LA L Rev	Loyola of Los Angeles Law Review
LPA	Les petites affiches
LQR	Law Quarterly Review
LRC	La Responsabilità Civile
LR Ex	Law Reports, Exchequer Cases (1865-1875)
LR HL	Law Reports, English & Irish Appeals (1866-1875)
LR QB	Law Reports, Queen's Bench (First Series) (1865-1875)
LS	Legal Studies
LT	Law Times Reports
Ltd	Limited
Md L Rev	Maryland Law Review
Mich L Rev	Michigan Law Review
Minn L Rev	Minnesota Law Review
MLR	Modern Law Review
n/nn	footnote/footnotes
NCL Rev	North Carolina Law Review
NJCL	National Journal of Constitutional Law
Noviss Dig It	Novissimo Digesto Italiano

LIST OF ABBREVIATIONS

NGCC	Nuova giurisprudenza civile commentata
Nottingham LJ	Nottingham Law Journal
obs	observation
OJLS	Oxford Journal of Legal Studies
Okla City U L Rev	Oklahoma City University Law Review
OUCLJ	Oxford University Commonwealth Law Journal
OUP	Oxford University Press
para(s)	paragraph(s)
Pol dir	Politica del diritto
PN	Professional Negligence
Product Liability Directive	EU Directive 374/85
Products Liability Restatement	Restatement (Third) of Torts: Products Liability (1998)
Projet de réforme	Ministère de la Justice, *Projet de réforme de la responsabilité civile*, March 2017, available at <http://www.justice.gouv.fr/publication/Projet_de_reforme_de_la_responsabilite_civile_13032017_pdf>
Pt	Part
PUAM	Presses Universitaires d'Aix-Marseille
PUF	Presses Universitaires de France
QB	Court of Queen's Bench Law Reports, Queen's Bench Division (1891-1901, 1952-)
QBD	Queen's Bench Division of the High Court of Justice; Law Reports, Queen's Bench Division (1875-1890)
RabelsZ	Rabels Zeitschrift für ausländisches und internationales Privatrecht
Rapport Bigot-Reichardt	Rapport d'information no 663 fait au nom de la commission des lois constitutionnelles, de législation, du suffrage universel, du Règlement et d'administration générale sur la responsabilité civile, par MM. Jacques BIGOT et André REICHARDT, Sénateurs, 22 juillet 2020
RCA	Responsabilité civile et assurances
RCDP	Rivista critica del diritto privato
RCLJ	Revue critique de législation et jurisprudence
RCP	Responsabilità civile e previdenza
RDP	Revue du droit public
Rec	Recueil des Décisions du Conseil d'État
Rep Foro It	Repertorio del Foro Italiano
Req	Chambre des requêtes de la Cour de cassation
RIDC	Revue internationale de droit comparé
Riv Dir Civ	Rivista di diritto civile
Riv Dir Comm	Rivista del diritto commerciale e del diritto generale delle obbligazioni
Riv Dir Priv	Rivista di diritto privato
Riv It Sc Giur	Rivista italiana delle scienze giuridche
RTDPC	Rivista trimestrale di diritto e procedura civile

RRJ	Revue de la recherche juridique, Droit prospectif
RTD civ	Revue trimestrielle de droit civil
S	Recueil Sirey
SCR	Supreme Court Reports (Canada)
Second Restatement	Restatement (Second) of Torts
s(s)	section(s)
Suff U L Rev	Suffolk University Law Review
S Cal L Rev	Southern California Law Review
TC	Tribunal des conflits
Tex L Rev	Texas Law Review
Third Restatement LPEH	Restatement (Third) of Torts: Liability for Physical and Emotional Harm (2010)
TLR	Times Law Reports
TR	Term Reports, King's Bench (ER vols 99-101)
Trib	Tribunale
Tul Civ LF	Tulane Civil Law Forum
Tul L Rev	Tulane Law Review
U Chi L Rev	University of Chicago Law Review
U Mem L Rev	University of Memphis Law Review
U Pa L Rev	University of Pennsylvania Law Review
UCLA L Rev	UCLA Law Review
UKHL	Decision of the House of Lords
UKSC	Decision of the UK Supreme Court
USC	United States Code
Va L Rev	Virginia Law Review
Vand L Rev	Vanderbilt Law Review
vol(s)	volume(s)
Yale LJ	Yale Law Journal
YEL	Yearbook of European Law
YUP	Yale University Press
W Ontario L Rev	Western Ontario Law Review
WLR	Weekly Law Reports

1

General Introduction

1.1 Justifying Strict Liability

Liability for fault has traditionally attracted widespread recognition in many jurisdictions around the world and is often seen as the main form of liability in tort. Since the late nineteenth century, though, the idea that a party may be liable even though they were not at fault has gained the attention of legislators, courts, and legal scholars. In different ways and to varying degrees across legal systems, this 'strict' liability has been relied upon in a variety of areas of human activity. Yet, strict liability remains controversial and lively discussions have taken place over the years about its theoretical foundations. Should we make room for strict liability in tort law and, if so, when should it apply, and in what form? In responding to these questions, legal actors within and across jurisdictions have put a lot of effort into seeking to provide proper justifications for strict liability, whether in general or in relation to specific contexts, but they have by no means agreed on what they should be. For example, why do or should we impose strict liability on employers for the torts committed by their employees, or on a person for the harm caused by their children, animals, activities, or things? These sorts of questions can receive very different answers, with a wide variety of justifications and lines of argumentation being put forward. As a result, the justificatory basis of strict liability remains the object of vigorous debate.

This study explores the justifications for strict liability found in four legal systems, namely England, the United States, France, and Italy. These jurisdictions belong to different legal traditions—civil law and common law—and each of them has its own distinctive ways of thinking and theorizing about tort law and tort liability in general and strict liability in particular. They therefore offer an excellent perspective on the variety of reasoning on strict liability in tort law and how it compares across different laws.

This book has four principal aims. A first aim is to identify clearly the main arguments put forward to justify strict liability, to explain their significance, and to explore their interrelationship within the four legal systems. By comparing the treatment that each argument receives in the four laws, a complex picture will emerge reflecting the different ways in which individual justifications can be used as well as the differing weight that is attributed to them. A second aim of this study is to shed light on the patterns of reasoning in strict liability, that

Justifying Strict Liability. Marco Cappelletti, Oxford University Press. © Marco Cappelletti 2022.
DOI: 10.1093/oso/9780192859860.003.0001

is on the ways in which the arguments are used to justify strict liability. As will be seen, these patterns differ in several important respects and they provide significant indications about the attitude of legal actors to the justificatory basis of strict liability across the four systems. Thirdly, the book seeks to advance our understanding of the contrasting '*cultures* of tort' in the four systems, notably by highlighting the intimate relationship between the arguments for strict liability and the commitments to wider values and goals within the four systems. Indeed, apparently identical arguments can have specific connotations and embody different understandings of strict liability, depending on the values or goals their proponents are committed to. Since distinct commitments can coexist within the same legal system, it will be possible to see interactions and clashes of views that both characterize the legal reasoning on strict liability and shape the wider tort cultures in the four systems. Finally, the comparative analysis of legal reasoning set out in this book will allow us to appreciate the shifting justificatory basis of 'strict liability' which varies according to the patterns of reasoning chosen, to the arguments used, and to the broader values and goals which inspire the reasoning on strict liability.

While this book focuses on the arguments put forward to justify strict liability and on the criticisms that these arguments attract, it does not explore arguments that justify fault-based liability, nor does it consider the reasons for adopting rules of no liability (ie rules which let the loss lie where it falls). It is certainly true that, at least sometimes, the reasons in favour of fault-based liability or no liability are used to criticize arguments justifying strict liability, and that sometimes an argument which is used to justify strict liability may be used in a different way to justify fault-based liability or no liability. Notwithstanding these overlaps, the focus of my investigation remains on strict liability and on the arguments put forward to justify it. Indeed, unlike fault liability or no liability, strict liability is often seen as requiring some special justification and, as already mentioned, these justifications are very much open to debate and the object of considerable disagreement across and within different legal systems.

Secondly, in discussing the arguments for strict liability it is tempting to assess their validity. For example, is the spreading of losses an attractive justification for strict liability? Should we decide between strict, fault-based, or no-liability regimes on the basis of considerations such as avoiding accidents or compensating victims? Is there any particular understanding of individual responsibility which convincingly supports the imposition of strict liability? These are clearly important questions, but I will not try to answer them here, nor will I suggest a novel approach as to when and why strict liability should be imposed. Instead, I will seek to produce a picture of the legal reasoning used in strict liability, so that our understanding of this type of liability and of the reasoning surrounding it may be enhanced.

1.2 Scope of the Book

Given the subject matter and the comparative nature of this book, it is necessary to clarify what I mean by 'strict liability' and 'tort law'.

As regards strict liability, the meaning of this notion will be clarified by explaining how each of the four legal systems understands it. While it is more convenient to postpone this task to Part 2 of the book, where I provide an overview of the four laws, it is necessary at this point to explain why I adopt this strategy. First of all, given that my investigation is about the reasoning justifying strict liability in a plurality of legal systems, it is indispensable to know what *these systems* mean by strict liability before we can understand the relevant reasoning put forward in each of them. Moreover, the very term 'strict liability' is clearly not system-neutral, as it refers to a distinct form of liability recognized as such in common law systems such as those in England and in the Unites States. As will be seen, in these two legal systems strict liability is often portrayed as 'liability without fault'.[1] The same term 'liability without fault' can be also found in the two civil law systems (*responsabilité sans faute* in France, and *responsabilità senza colpa* in Italy).[2] However, and very importantly, these three terms (liability without fault, *responsabilité sans faute*, and *responsabilità senza colpa*) do not necessarily refer to the same phenomenon in the four laws, for 'fault' (*faute*, *colpa*) can take on different meanings across (and sometimes even within) them, therefore proving to be a highly ambiguous notion.[3] In light of this, I do not attempt to provide an abstract, system-neutral definition of strict liability but instead explain how 'strict liability' is understood in the four legal systems, including its relationship with fault. As will be seen, legal actors in all four systems are aware that it is difficult to distinguish sharply between 'fault' and 'strict liability' but, notwithstanding this difficulty, 'strict liability' is often depicted as clearly distinct from, if not opposed to, fault-based liability and it is widely used to refer to groups of situations where, at least in principle, the defendant's 'fault' (generally understood as lack of reasonable care or ordinary diligence) is seen as irrelevant to the determination of liability.[4]

---

[1] See sections 2.2 and 2.3.

[2] See sections 2.4 and 2.5.

[3] For a brief discussion concerning several common law systems, see Allan Beever, *A Theory of Tort Liability* (Hart Publishing 2016) 28–33. For a discussion of the extraordinary breadth of fault (*faute*) in French law, see Simon Whittaker, 'The Law of Obligations' in John Bell and others (eds), *Principles of French Law* (2nd edn, OUP 2008) 294, 364–81. For a discussion of the various meanings of 'fault' (*colpa*) in Italy, see Massimo Franzoni, *L'illecito. Trattato della responsabilità civile* (2nd edn, Giuffrè 2010) 175ff.

[4] Therefore, the expression 'liability without fault' should not be taken to mean liability conditional upon the absence of fault but rather liability regardless of fault: see Peter Cane, 'Responsibility and Fault: A Relational and Functional Approach to Responsibility' in Peter Cane and John Gardner (eds), *Relating to Responsibility: Essays in Honour of Tony Honoré on his 80th Birthday* (Hart Publishing 2001) 81, 99–100.

4   JUSTIFYING STRICT LIABILITY

Secondly, I need to explain the meaning of 'tort law'. The term is not system-neutral, as it refers to a particular body of law in England and in the United States,[5] which primarily governs situations where a party, independently of the existence of a contract or other, equitable duty,[6] has caused some harm to another party.[7] The bodies of law generally concerned with these types of situations in France and Italy are the laws of extra-contractual liability (*responsabilité extracontractuelle, responsabilità extracontrattuale*).[8] While overlapping to a large extent, the laws

---

[5] The birth of tort law as a 'separate' legal domain can be traced back to the mid-nineteenth-century abolition of the forms of action and the consequent need to work out the substance of the law beneath the old writs: see Michael Lobban, 'Tort' in William Cornish and others (eds), *The Oxford History of the Laws of England, Volume XII—1820-1914: Private Law* (OUP 2010) 877, 887ff; G Edward White, *Tort Law in America: an Intellectual History* (OUP 2003) 3ff. Since then, both in England and in the United States, scholars have tried to rationalize tort law and to present it as a coherent whole: early attempts are owed, in England, to Charles G Addison, *Wrongs and Their Remedies: Being a Treatise on the Law of Torts* (Stevens and Sons 1860) and, in the United States, to Francis Hilliard, *The Law of Torts or Private Wrongs* (Little, Brown and Company 1859). Whether tort law can be rationalized under a unifying principle or whether it is just a gallery of disparate 'wrongs' has always been much controversial and the issue is nowhere close to a resolution. The first manifestation of disagreement dates back to the rivalry between Frederick Pollock's view that the whole law of torts could be explained by reference to an overarching theory (Frederick Pollock, *The Law of Torts: a Treatise on the Principles of Obligations Arising from Civil Wrongs in the Common Law* (1st edn, Stevens 1887) vi–viii) and John Salmond's position that tort law consisted of 'a number of specific rules prohibiting certain kinds of harmful activity' (John Salmond, *The Law of Torts: a Treatise on the English Law of Liability for Civil Injuries* (2nd edn, Stevens and Haynes 1910) 9).

[6] As to the relationship between torts and equitable wrongs, see eg Nicholas J McBride and Roderick Bagshaw, *Tort Law* (6th edn, Pearson Education 2018) 21–23; John Gardner, 'Torts and Other Wrongs' (2012) 39 Fla St U L Rev 43, 51; cf James Edelman, 'Equitable Torts' (2002) 10 Torts Law Journal 64.

[7] Some terminological clarification is in order here. I will use the terms 'harm', 'loss', or 'damage' to refer to the detrimental effects that an individual might suffer as a result of tortious conduct. These will typically include death, personal injury, pain and suffering, emotional distress, or damage to property. By contrast, I will use the term 'damages' to refer to the monetary award that the defendant is ordered to pay to the claimant in respect of those losses.

[8] In Italian and French law there is a variety of terms which have been and are used to refer to the same area of law, most notably 'delictual liability', 'civil liability', and 'extra-contractual liability'. The term 'delictual liability' can be traced back to the Roman *delictum* (from *delinquere*, which hardly needs translation). In Justinian's *Institutes*, 'delicts' are presented as one of the four prongs in the taxonomy of the private law of obligations: those arising from contracts, as though from contracts, from delicts, as though from delicts (Inst.3.13.2). The modern equivalent of the law of delicts is the law of torts, but in Roman times there was no clear-cut distinction between the law of delicts and the criminal law. Indeed, the former presented a strong penal element, with several remedies being calibrated to both compensate and punish: see eg Barry Nicholas, *An Introduction to Roman Law* (rev edn, OUP 2008) 207–11. It seems no accident, then, that in modern civil law systems such as Italian and French law the term 'delict' features prominently in the criminal law: article 39 of the Italian Criminal Code (*Codice penale*) distinguishes between delicts and contraventions according to the seriousness of the punishment, while article 111-1 of the French Criminal Code (*Code pénal*) distinguishes among crimes, delicts, and contraventions according to the seriousness of the offence. In private law, the term 'delictual liability' has gradually lost much of its past currency, to the benefit of terms such as 'extra-contractual' and 'civil liability'. At the time of its enactment, in 1804, the French Civil code (*Code civil*) spoke of 'delicts' and 'quasi-delicts' (*Des délits et des quasi-délits*, this being the heading of Chapter II, Title IV, Book III of the *Code*); the same terminology was adopted in the 1865 Italian Civil code (*Codice civile*), where Section III in Chapter I, Title IV, Book III, was titled '*Dei delitti e dei quasi-delitti*'. 'Delictual liability' (*responsabilité délictuelle*) has been widely used in France in the twentieth century, with the title of canonical works on the subject reflecting this tendency: eg Henri and Leon Mazeaud, *Traité théorique et pratique de la responsabilité civile et délictuelle* (6th edn, Montchrestien 1965). More recently, the term 'extra-contractual liability' has gained increasing popularity although the term 'delictual liability' is still commonly used as a shorthand for referring to the same area of law (see eg Muriel Fabre-Magnan, *Droit*

of torts and the laws of extra-contractual liability are by no means coextensive legal domains. A particularly important example relates to situations where a private party brings an action not against another private party but against the state or some public authority. In English and US law this type of dispute is generally governed by ordinary tort doctrines, though sometimes qualified or specially adapted.[9] Similarly, in Italian law, the law of extra-contractual liability is widely seen as the general basis of public liability for the infringement of private rights or other legally protected interests (*responsabilità della pubblica amministrazione*),[10] even though the applicable law is modified in significant ways so as to take into account the public nature of defendants.[11] In these three legal systems, then, the liability of public authorities is seen as part of the general law of torts or of the law of extra-contractual liability and, therefore, it is necessarily included in my analysis. By contrast, in France in principle the application of the general law of extra-contractual liability to public authorities is excluded and their liability is instead typically governed by a distinct and special body of principles and rules known as 'administrative liability' (*responsabilité administrative* or *responsabilité de la*

---

des obligations. 2—Responsabilité civile et quasi-contrats (4th edn, PUF 2019) [3], [18]; cf Jean-Sébastien Borghetti, 'L'avant-projet de réforme de la responsabilité civile. Vue d'ensemble de l'avant-projet' D 2016.1386, fn 9, criticizing the use of the term 'extra-contractual liability' at least insofar as the term is used to cover liability for bodily injuries arising in a contractual setting). This shift in language has been formally upheld in the 2016 reform of the French *Code civil*, which dropped the terms 'delict' and 'quasi-delict' and replaced them with 'extra-contractual liability' (Sub-Title II, Title III, Book III of the *Code*). Moreover, in the 2017 *Projet de réforme* of the *Code civil*, Sub-Title II is renamed 'Civil Liability' (*Responsabilité Civile*), a term which is understood as including both contractual and extra-contractual liability. Within Sub-Title II, Chapter II sets out the conditions for the imposition of civil liability: the first Section presents rules common to contractual and extra-contractual liability; the second deals with the conditions for the imposition of extra-contractual liability; the third with provisions specific to contractual liability. The design of this part of the *Code* reflects the prevailing view in the French academy which sees civil liability as an umbrella term including both contractual and extra-contractual liability: see eg Geneviève Viney, *Introduction à la responsabilité. Traité de droit civil* (4th edn, LGDJ 2019) [1]. In Italian law, the evolution in language has been quite different. Delictual liability (*responsabilità delittuale*) fell into disfavour already towards the end of the nineteenth century, proof of this being the disappearance of the terms *delitti* and *quasi-delitti* from the new Italian *Codice Civile*, enacted in 1942 (see Michele Graziadei, 'Liability for Fault in Italian Law: The Development of Legal Doctrine from 1865 to the End of the Twentieth Century' in Nils Jansen (ed), *The Development and Making of Legal Doctrine* (CUP 2010) 126, especially fn 1). This does not mean that the term 'delictual liability' has disappeared altogether from Italian writings, but today academics and courts most commonly employ the term *responsabilità extracontrattuale*, although this expression has not found formal recognition in the *Codice Civile* (Title IX, Book IV, speaks of *fatti illeciti*, literally 'unlawful facts'). Furthermore, frequent use is made of 'civil liability' (*responsabilità civile*): although the term technically encompasses both contractual and extra-contractual liability (see Franzoni (n 3) 5–9), it is very often used as a shorthand for extra-contractual liability (see eg Pier Giuseppe Monateri, 'Responsabilità civile' Dig Disc Priv (UTET 1998) XVII, 1).

[9] For English law, see Paul Craig, *Administrative Law* (9th edn, Sweet & Maxwell 2021)chs 29–30. For US law, see Dan B Dobbs, Paul T Hayden, and Ellen M Bublick, *Hornbook on Torts* (2nd edn, West Academic Publishing 2016)ch 22.

[10] See eg Francesco Caringella, *Manuale di diritto amministrativo. I. La responsabilità della pubblica amministrazione* (Dike 2012) 10–12, 49–55.

[11] Luisa Torchia, 'La responsabilità' in Sabino Cassese (ed), *Trattato di Diritto Amministrativo. Diritto amministrativo generale*, vol II (2nd edn, Giuffrè 2003) 1649, 1654–55.

6 JUSTIFYING STRICT LIABILITY

puissance publique).[12] In light of this, as a matter of proper comparative law methodology the book includes references to French administrative liability as well and discusses the reasoning put forward to justify its strict forms. An additional benefit of including public liability in my analysis is that it shows how the justifications which feature in the reasoning concerning the strict liability of private parties resonate with or, on the other hand, differ from, the arguments put forward to justify the strict liability of public bodies.

Another difference between the laws of torts and the laws of extra-contractual liability may be identified at the level of the conditions of liability. While in all the four systems the courts must verify that the relevant causation and conduct elements are met, only the French and Italian laws generally require that the claimant has suffered some sort of harm.[13] In these two civil law systems, the infringement of a legally protected interest is not enough to obtain a favourable judgment in tort; instead, the infliction of harm is necessary.[14] By contrast, the English and US laws include a number of torts which do not depend upon the occurrence of some harm to the claimant's detriment; in these cases, the defendant's infringing conduct constitutes and completes the tort by itself and no (proof of) harm is required for a finding of liability; torts of this kind are usually labelled as actionable *per se*.[15] It is true that this difference between the laws of torts and the laws of extra-contractual liability may have become one of degree rather than one of kind as situations have emerged in the Italian and (especially) French laws where the existence of liability *per se* may be occasionally admitted.[16] Even so, liability *per se* remains exceptional

---

[12] TC 8.2.1873 (*Blanco*), D 1873.3.17. See generally René Chapus, *Droit administratif général*, vol 1 (15th edn, Montchrestien 2001) [1399]ff.

[13] For a general comparative discussion on this, see Helmut Koziol, 'Comparative Conclusions' in Helmut Koziol (ed), *Basic Questions of Tort Law from a Comparative Perspective* (Jan Sramek Verlag KG 2015) 683, 748–50; Helmut Koziol, 'Schadenersatzrecht and the Law of Torts: Different terms and different ways of thinking' (2014) 5(3) JETL 257, 263–67. This difference between common law and civil law systems is connected to further divergences, such as the types of the remedies available for liability in tort, which however need not detain our attention here.

[14] See eg article 2043 of the Italian *Codice civile* and article 1240 of the French *Code civil*.

[15] See eg Peter Cane, 'Fault and Strict Liability for Harm in Tort Law' in William Swadling and Gareth Jones (eds), *The Search for Principle: Essays in Honour of Lord Goff of Chieveley* (OUP 1999) 171, 172–73 (on trespass to land, conversion, and battery); Robert E Keeton, Lewis D Sargentich, and Gregory C Keating, *Tort and Accident Law—Cases and Materials* (4th edn, Thomson West 2004) 155ff (on defamation); Gregory C Keating, 'Strict Liability Wrongs' in John Oberdiek (ed), *Philosophical Foundations of the Law of Torts* (OUP 2014) 292, 297–300 (on trespass to land, conversion, and battery); James Goudkamp and Donal Nolan, *Winfield & Jolowicz on Tort* (20th edn, Sweet and Maxwell 2020) [4-004] (on trespass to the person), [4-007] (on battery), [13-031]–[13-032] (on libel and some types of slander), [14-003] (on trespass to land).

[16] In French law, 'acts of unfair competition give necessarily rise to ... some harm, even if just of a moral nature' (Cass com 1.7.2003 n.01-13.052; Cass com 27.5.2008 n.07-14.422; Cass com 28.9.2010 n.09-69.272); the failure to provide patients with information relating to subsequent medical treatment creates in itself 'a damage [*préjudice*] that the judge cannot leave without reparation' (Civ (1) 3.6.2010, RTD civ 2010.571 note Jourdain); certain courses of action by the employer 'necessarily cause a prejudice' to the employee who is therefore entitled to get damages (eg Cass soc 17.5.2011, JCP S 2011); 'according to article 9 of the Civil code, reparation is owed as soon as an invasion of private life has been established' (Civ (1) 5.11.1996, D 1997.289 note Jourdain; Jean-Sébastien Borghetti, 'Liability for False Information in French Law: The Limits of Civil Law' in Helmut Koziol (ed), *Tatsachenmitteilungen und*

GENERAL INTRODUCTION 7

in the two civil law systems and it is still unclear whether this type of liability will attract enough support to become an established or even expanding pattern of liability. For present purposes, it suffices to say that liability *per se* is not explored here, as my focus is on situations where the claimant has suffered some sort of harm. This is in part because it is here that the justifications for the imposition of strict liability are most interesting, and in part for reasons of space.

A final point is in order in delineating the scope of the book. It is clear that strict liability does not belong only to the province of tort law as it features in other legal domains such as, most notably, the law of contract. Given that the distinction between tort and contract is much discussed and that there is considerable disagreement as to where and how the line between the two should be drawn,[17] it is important to clarify for present purposes the relationship between them. According to a traditional view, contractual obligations stem from the voluntary agreement of the contracting parties, whereas tort duties are established by the law itself.[18] This approach, perhaps still useful as a starting point,[19] does not however consider important developments in modern legal systems which suggest that

---

Werturteile: Freiheit und Verantwortung (Jan Sramek Verlag 2018) 133, 141ff); finally, 'reparation is owed as soon as an infringement of property rights has been established' (Civ (3) 9.9.2009, D 2010.49 note P Brun and O Gout, but cf Civ (3) 18.1.2018 n.16-20.563). Whether or not these two last situations constitute instances of liability *per se* is controversial: see Laurène Gratton, 'Le dommage déduit de la faute' RTD civ 2013.275. Italian law as well is committed to the principle that there cannot be any liability in tort without detrimental consequences (*danno-conseguenza*) resulting from the defendant's infringement of the claimant's legally protected interest (see C Massimo Bianca, *Diritto civile. V—La responsabilità* (3rd edn, Giuffrè 2021) 119). Nevertheless, some uncertainty is shown in relation to liability for private nuisance: some decisions suggest that the infringing conduct may be enough to trigger damages (eg Civ (III) 9.5.2012 n.7048, (2012) 12 DR 1179); other decisions (eg Civ (II) 2.8.2016 n.16074) limit this position to one particular type of harm ('*danno esistenziale*', consisting in some deterioration of the relational dimension of one's own life and the accompanying change in one's own living habits); still other decisions exclude altogether liability *per se* in the context of private nuisance (eg Civ (III) 27.6.2016 n.13208). Moreover, in relation to the 'illegitimate occupation of another's immovable', some courts have stated that the harm is automatic and derives from the impossibility to enjoy the thing and its 'civil fruits' (eg Civ (II) 17.2.2017 n.4252). See also Matteo Ambrosoli, 'I diritto reali e la responsabilità extracontrattuale' in Antonio Gambaro and Umberto Morello (eds), *Trattato dei diritto reali. Volume I—Proprietà e possesso* (Giuffrè 2008) 1033, 1072–74.

[17] See eg Patrick S Atiyah, *Essays on Contract* (Clarendon Press 1986) 40–42; Peter Birks, 'The Concept of a Civil Wrong' in David G Owen (ed), *Philosophical Foundations of Tort Law* (OUP 1995) 31, esp 47ff; Peter Cane, *The Anatomy of Tort Law* (Hart Publishing 1997) 183–86; Andrew Burrows, *Understanding the Law of Obligations: Essays on Contract, Tort and Restitution* (Hart Publishing 1998) 8–14; Gardner (n 6) 58–61; Curtis Bridgeman and John CP Goldberg, 'Do Promises Distinguish Contract from Tort?' (2012) 45 Suff U L Rev 873; Viney (n 8) [225]ff; Franzoni (n 3) 14–16.

[18] eg Sir Percy Henry Winfield, *Province of the Law of Tort* (The University Press 1931) 40 ('tort and contract are distinguishable from one another in that the duties in the former are primarily fixed by the law, while in the latter they are fixed by the parties themselves'; and 'in tort the duty is towards persons generally, in contract it is towards a specific person or specific persons'); Charles Sainctelette, *De la responsabilité et de la garantie: accidents de transport et de travail* (Bruylant-Christophe 1884) 6–15; Adriano De Cupis, *Il danno: teoria generale della responsabilità civile*, vol I (3rd edn, Giuffrè 1979) 113.

[19] eg *Robinson v PE Jones (Contractors) Ltd*, [2011] EWCA Civ 9, [79] (Jackson LJ); Simon Whittaker, 'Contract Law and other Legal Categories' in Hugh Beale (ed), *Chitty on Contracts*, vol 1 (34th edn, Sweet & Maxwell 2021) ch 3, [3-003].

reliance on voluntary agreement cannot distinguish neatly between tort and contract. First, the incidents of a contractual relationship as well as the consequences of a breach of contract are very often determined, in whole or in part, by the law itself. Secondly, and conversely, the parties' agreement on occasion may give rise to tortious obligations or, at other times, may limit the scope of, or even exclude altogether, particular obligations already imposed by the law of torts.[20] In view of this, it seems more accurate to say that contractual obligations are *typically* triggered by the parties' agreement,[21] and that tort duties are *typically* triggered by the law itself. It is on this basis that I distinguish tort from contract and that I focus my discussion on liability in tort rather than on liability in contract.

1.3 Sources of Analysis and Use of Materials

The justifications for the imposition of strict liability can be found in a wide range of sources across the four legal systems studied. The most useful ones to understand how strict liability is justified are judicial decisions and academic writings. As regards the former, judgments present remarkable differences in style across the four legal systems. The opinions of judges in common law systems are usually overt and elaborate, therefore constituting an ideal source of understanding why the law is in a certain state (in our case, why strict liability is adopted in certain situations). Sometimes, as I will show, judicial opinions can contain a multitude of justifications that disclose strikingly complex and rich patterns of argumentation. By contrast, in the two civil law systems, judgments do not contain the opinions of the individual judges, but only the unitary decision of the court. This typically means that there is a less elaborate judicial reasoning, although there is a considerable difference between Italy and France. Indeed, the judgments of Italian courts still contain a good deal of reasoning, while French judgments are famous for their brevity and syllogistic nature. As a result, the work of French legal scholars becomes key to identifying the justifications for strict liability, to understand their role in the relevant legal system, and more generally to appreciate the intellectual climate in which the courts operate.[22] What is more, the overt nature of French academic reasoning allows us to appreciate a certain self-awareness in the French legal culture

---

[20] eg Whittaker (n 19) [3-003]; Goudkamp and Nolan (n 15) [1-004]–[1-007]; John CP Goldberg and others, *Tort Law: Responsibilities and Redress* (5th edn, Wolters Kluwer 2021) 36–37; Viney (n 8) [271], [301]; Massimo Franzoni, *Il danno risarcibile. Trattato della responsabilità civile* (2nd edn, Giuffrè 2010) 773ff.

[21] See Simon Whittaker, 'Privity of Contract and the Tort of Negligence: Future Directions' (1996) 16 OJLS 191.

[22] On the key role that French academics play in explaining and clarifying the meaning and scope of French judicial decisions, as well as on their role in French law more generally, see Jean-Sébastien Borghetti, 'Legal Methodology and the Role of Professors in France—*Professorenrecht* is not a French Word!' in Jürgen Basedow, Holger Fleischer, and Reinhard Zimmermann (eds), *Legislators, Judges, and Professors* (Mohr Siebeck 2016) 209.

about the key role of strict liability in their law. This does not mean, of course, that in the other three legal systems the role of legal scholars is less important. On the contrary, for the purpose of understanding the functioning of a legal system, which includes the reasoning taking place in it, academic reasoning is as essential as judicial reasoning and it is therefore given the utmost importance in this work.[23]

Besides academic writings and judicial decisions, I have also used Reports of the Law Commission for England and Wales, the Report of the Pearson Commission, and the Restatements on the law of torts in the United States, because these all include extended discussions about the justifications for strict liability. Equivalent sources do not exist in France and Italy, although I do refer in a few instances to the Report of the Italian Ministry of Justice to the *Codice civile*,[24] and to a few proposals to reform French tort law which have been put forward in recent times.[25] Finally, while Parliamentary debates or documentation could have been useful sources, they are not considered in this work; on the one hand, it is unlikely that they would have added to the range of arguments already identified and, on the other hand, a thorough study of Parliamentary materials across the four legal systems (one of which comprises fifty-one jurisdictions) would have extended the boundaries of this research beyond a manageable limit.

As a final point, my discussion generally adopts the present tense to illustrate the reasoning of legal actors, even if they wrote in the nineteenth or twentieth century. The reason for this is that in all the four systems contemporary legal actors still refer to these 'old' instances of reasoning as providing authoritative statements about the justifications for the imposition of strict liability. In a meaningful way, then, legal actors (especially scholars) who wrote several decades ago still participate actively in the conversation regarding the justifications for strict liability.

---

[23] The book occasionally considers the work of legal scholars who, while contributing to a particular national discourse, are also associated with another jurisdiction. For example, Ernest Weinrib is a Canadian scholar based in Toronto, but I will mention his writings while discussing the reasoning on strict liability in the United States, as he actively participates in the tort debate taking place there and his work is particularly influential among US legal scholars. Similarly, John Fleming was born in Germany, received his legal education in England, and taught in Australia and in the United States; his scholarly contributions were and remain highly regarded throughout the common law world, even though they seem to have more echo in England (and Australia), and there are indications that he saw himself more as an English than as a US lawyer (see Paul Mitchell, 'Professor John G Fleming (1919–1997): "A Sense of Fluidity"' in James Goudkamp and Donal Nolan (eds), *Scholars of Tort Law* (Hart Publishing 2019) 289, 301). As a result, for the purposes of this book, Fleming's view on strict liability will be treated as part of the English discourse.

[24] 'Relazione del Ministro Guardasigilli Grandi al Codice Civile del 1942': available at <https://www.consiglionazionaleforense.it/web/cnf/collana-studi-storici-e-giuridici?largefont> (accessed 26 August 2021).

[25] Pierre Catala (ed), *Avant-projet de réforme du droit des obligations et du droit de la prescription: Rapport à Monsieur Pascal Clément Garde des Sceaux, Ministre de la Justice, 22 Septembre 2005* [Avant-projet Catala]; François Terré (ed), *Pour une réforme du droit des contrats* (Dalloz 2009); François Terré (ed), *Pour une réforme du droit de la responsabilité* (Dalloz 2011); François Terré (ed), *Pour une réforme du régime général des obligations* (Dalloz 2013)[Avant-projet Terré].

1.4 Methodology

Given its nature and aims, the book does not rely on the traditional methodology of comparative functionalism.[26] Indeed, by seeking to 'find rules or institutions ... serving a certain social function',[27] functionalism is interested in how such rules and institutions operate and in the effects they produce across legal systems, and therefore it cannot provide the methodological support needed by a work that concentrates on legal reasoning rather than on the substantive laws themselves. Instead, given its focus on legal reasoning, the book combines two other methods of comparative law, namely the 'jurisprudential' and the 'structural' approach.[28] The former approach aims for 'an understanding of conscious ideas at work' in legal systems, 'that is the principles, concepts, beliefs, and reasoning that underlie ... legal rules and institutions'.[29] This approach is connected to one of the aims of the book which, by exploring the substantive justifications for strict liability, seeks to advance our understanding of the ideas that lie behind strict liability and therefore inspire its imposition across the four legal systems studied. Secondly, my emphasis on legal arguments finds support in Sacco's structural approach to comparative law. According to this approach, the reasons through which legal actors reach a certain solution constitute one of the 'legal formants' which shape the legal system and which 'have a life of their own';[30] this is so true that '[l]egal systems where the conclusion is supported by different justifications cannot be regarded as identical'.[31] Legal structuralism promises to improve our understanding of a system or framework and of its constituent elements by observing the relationship among the elements themselves.[32] If we think of the arguments for strict liability as an independent legal formant of the tort system, identifying and comparing them will improve our understanding of strict liability and of the tort system more generally as well as illuminating their own significance. Moreover,

---

[26] On functionalism, see generally Konrad Zweigert and Hein Kötz, *An Introduction to Comparative Law* (Tony Weir (tr), 3rd edn, OUP 1998) 32–47; Michele Graziadei, 'The Functionalist Heritage' in Pierre Legrand and Roderick Munday (eds), *Comparative Legal Studies: Traditions and Transitions* (CUP 2003) 100; Ralf Michaels, 'The Functional Method of Comparative Law' in Mathias Reimann and Reinhard Zimmermann (eds), *The Oxford Handbook of Comparative Law* (2nd edn, OUP 2019) 345.

[27] Jaakko Husa, 'Farewell to Functionalism or Methodological Tolerance?' (2003) 67 RabelsZ 419, 423.

[28] For a brief overview of these two methods of comparative law, see Mathias Siems, *Comparative Law* (CUP 2018) 123–27 (arguing that the two overlap).

[29] William Ewald, 'The Jurisprudential Approach to Comparative Law: A Field Guide to Rats' (1998) 46 AJCL 701, 705. See also Catherine Valcke, 'Comparative Law as Comparative Jurisprudence—The Comparability of Legal Systems' (2004) 52 AJCL 713.

[30] Rodolfo Sacco, 'Legal Formants: A Dynamic Approach to Comparative Law' (1991) 39 AJCL 1, 30. See also Ugo Mattei, 'The Comparative Jurisprudence of Schlesinger and Sacco: A Study in Legal Influence' in Annelise Riles (ed), *Rethinking the Masters of Comparative Law* (Hart Publishing 2001) 238, 251ff.

[31] Sacco (n 30) 30.

[32] Mattei (n 30) 251. See also Geoffrey Samuel, 'Can Legal Reasoning Be Demystified?' (2009) 29(2) LS 181, 194.

a legal system's reliance on one or more justifications for strict liability is likely to show its commitment to certain goals or values in relation to accidents. These goals and values may be seen as a reflection of the mindset of the legal actors operating within that system or, in other words, as a reflection of an aspect of the legal culture characterizing that system.[33] Therefore, by focusing on the reasoning which surrounds strict liability, our comprehension of the various legal cultures featuring in the four systems under consideration may be enhanced as well. Finally, as a further result of this study, national lawyers may be encouraged to reflect on elements and features of their own legal system that at present may be either neglected or misapprehended.

1.5 Structure of the Book

This book is structured in a way that reflects its aims and methodology. Following this General Introduction, Part 2 sets the scene for the comparative discussion of arguments taking place in Part 3 of the book, by outlining the main traits of the four substantive laws as relevant for present purposes. In particular, it first clarifies how the four systems understand 'strict liability' and then it identifies and discusses the contexts where strict liability is imposed in each of them. By the expression 'context(s) of liability' I refer throughout the book to a group of situations in which liability is imposed: these will normally coincide with what English and US lawyers call 'torts' and with what French and Italian lawyers consider the 'heads of liability'.[34] While expressions such as *régimes/cas de responsabilité*, or *regimi/ regole di responsabilità* may sometimes be used in France and Italy, respectively, there is no agreed term in French and Italian law to indicate the various heads of liability: these are more often referred to by simply mentioning the relevant provision included in the civil codes or in the statutes,[35] or by mentioning the action or activity on which the context of liability rests.[36]

---

[33] See generally Roger Cotterrell, 'Comparative Law and Legal Culture' in Mathias Reimann and Reinhard Zimmermann (eds), *The Oxford Handbook of Comparative Law* (2nd edn, OUP 2019) 710, 711 (arguing that the notion of legal culture 'might include underlying values or principles of a legal system, as well as traditions, shared beliefs, common ways of thinking, constellations of interests or patterns of allegiances of lawyers, lawmakers, and citizens').

[34] On whether the French law of civil liability (contractual and extra-contractual) may be seen as structured around separate heads of liability rather than around overarching principles of liability, see Jean-Sébastien Borghetti and Simon Whittaker, 'Principles of Liability or a Law of Torts?' in Jean-Sébastien Borghetti and Simon Whittaker (eds), *French Civil Liability in Comparative Perspective* (Hart Publishing 2019) 455.

[35] eg articles 1240–1244 of the French *Code civil* (Cc), or articles 2043, 2047–2054 of the Italian *Codice civile* (Cod civ).

[36] eg 'liability for the deeds of things' (*responsabilité du fait des choses*) under article 1242(1) (former article 1384(1)) Cc, or 'liability for dangerous activities' (*responsabilità per l'esercizio di attività pericolose*) under article 2050 Cod civ.

The aim of Part 2 is to provide some general substantive background to the subsequent discussion of arguments. Exploring the contexts of strict liability is key to understanding how and to what extent different legal systems rely on strict liability. Moreover, the various justifications for strict liability show a degree of context-dependence in each legal system, meaning that some of them may be seen as convincing in certain contexts of liability, but left aside in others. As a result, it is necessary to have a clear picture of where and how strict liability applies before being able to understand the reasoning for its imposition. Having said that, some readers may already know the substantive law of one or more of the tort systems studied, in which case they may not need to read the relevant sections in Part 2 and, for those systems, proceed directly to Part 3.

Part 3, which is the core of the book, sets out the comparative analysis of the arguments used to justify strict liability in the four legal systems. Given that this analysis seeks to explore the usages and significance of each argument *within* and *across* the four laws studied, the most fruitful way of organizing the discussion appeared to be by arguments. To help navigate the complexities of legal argumentation, Part 3 begins by providing the framework of analysis which I have elaborated to explore the various patterns of reasoning and the significance of the arguments in and across the four laws. The seven main sections of Part 3 analyse the arguments in turn: each section explores the core idea behind the argument, its internal variations, and then discusses its usages and significance in the four laws, comparing and contrasting the treatment the argument receives across them. Each section provides some concluding remarks in relation to the argument examined. Finally, Part 4 of the book offers further, more general insights on the patterns of use and on the significance of the arguments discussed in Part 3, it provides critical reflections on the nature of the reasoning in strict liability across the four laws, and it reflects on the broader values and goals which influence such reasoning.

2

Strict Liability in the Four Tort Systems

An Overview

2.1 Introduction

How do the four legal systems understand 'strict liability'? To answer this, it is necessary to look at the four substantive laws and to set out the contexts of strict liability which can be identified in each of them. To do so, this Part of the book presents the four laws separately, so as to convey a clear sense of their own specificities vis-à-vis the role of strict liability, while also pointing out similarities and differences among them. This will provide the necessary background for the comparative discussion of legal reasoning in Part 3, where the various arguments are not discussed in a vacuum, but rather in relation to the specific contexts of liability for which they typically are invoked.

2.2 Strict Liability in English Law

English tort law comprises a wide range of distinct torts (or 'contexts of liability'). On the list we find well-known 'entries' such as the torts of negligence, trespass (to land or the person), nuisance, the rule in *Rylands v Fletcher*, and many others.[1] As each tort has its own rules, authorities, and focus,[2] important variations exist from one tort to another, whether in relation to the nature of the claimant's protected interests,[3] or to the standard of conduct expected of the defendant. In this second respect, English lawyers often distinguish between torts based on fault and torts involving strict (or stricter) liabilities. The former type of tort refers to situations where the defendant should have acted differently, either because they acted intentionally or because they failed to take reasonable care, the most important example being the tort of negligence.[4] By contrast, the latter type of torts—those

---

[1] According to Bernard Rudden, 'Torticles' (1991–1992) 6 Tul Civ LF 105, there are around seventy torts across common law jurisdictions.

[2] See Tony Weir, *An Introduction to Tort Law* (2nd edn, OUP 2006) 11; Simon Whittaker, 'The Law of Obligations' in John Bell and others, *Principles of French Law* (2nd edn, OUP 2008) 294, 360; Simon Deakin and Zoe Adams, *Markesinis and Deakin's Tort Law* (8th edn, OUP 2019) 23–25.

[3] For example, while the main concern of the tort of negligence is to safeguard property interests and bodily integrity, the tort of private nuisance and the rule in *Rylands v Fletcher* are confined to the protection of the former only: see *Hunter v Canary Wharf Ltd*, [1997] AC 655.

[4] See eg *Nettleship v Weston*, [1971] 2 QB 691.

Justifying Strict Liability. Marco Cappelletti, Oxford University Press. © Marco Cappelletti 2022.
DOI: 10.1093/oso/9780192859860.003.0002

14 JUSTIFYING STRICT LIABILITY

of strict liability—are typically described as imposing 'liability without fault', that is regardless of whether the defendant complied with the standard of the reasonable person.[5] At a conceptual level, therefore, it appears that fault and strict liability *can* be seen as clearly distinct, if not opposed; at the same time, English lawyers also acknowledge that, in practice, a sharp distinction between strict liability and fault-based liability may be difficult to draw and suggest that the degree of strictness across liability rules varies depending on the way in which the constituent elements of the various torts are set up, interpreted, and applied as well as on the available defences.[6] As a result, it may be useful to imagine the different torts along a continuum which classifies them according to their degree of strictness.[7] Yet, on the basis of the conceptual distinction seen above, the term 'strict liability' is still commonly used to refer to those situations where compliance with the standard of reasonable care does not exempt the defendant from a finding of liability. And while the tort of negligence certainly constitutes the main avenue of civil redress in English tort law, there are several torts which are widely seen as torts of strict liability and which appear to play an important role as well in English law. To these torts, or contexts of liability, I now turn.

A first context of strict liability concerns the famous rule established in *Rylands v Fletcher*.[8] In that case, the Exchequer Chamber held that a

> person who for his own purpose brings on his lands and collects and keeps there anything likely to do mischief if it escapes, must keep it in at his peril, and, if he does not do so, is prima facie answerable for all the damage which is the natural consequence of its escape.[9]

In other words, in its early days the rule in *Rylands v Fletcher* imposed strict liability for the harm caused by the escape of a dangerous thing,[10] it covered both

---

[5] Peter Cane, 'Fault and Strict Liability for Harm in Tort Law' in William Swadling and Gareth Jones (eds), *The Search for Principle: Essays in Honour of Lord Goff of Chieveley* (OUP 1999) 171, 191; John Gardner, 'Some Rule-of-Law Anxieties about Strict Liability in Private Law' in Lisa M Austin and Dennis Klimchuk (eds), *Private Law and the Rule of Law* (OUP 2014) 207.

[6] See eg James Goudkamp and Donal Nolan, *Winfield & Jolowicz on Tort* (20th edn, Sweet and Maxwell 2020) [1-044]; Jenny Steele, *Tort Law, Text, Cases, and Materials* (4th edn, OUP 2017) 847; Christian Witting, *Street on Torts* (16th edn, OUP 2021) 401.

[7] See WV Horton Rogers, 'England' in Bernard A Koch and Helmut Koziol (eds) *Unification of Tort Law: Strict Liability* (Kluwer Law International 2002) 101; Keith M Stanton, 'The Legacy of Rylands v Fletcher' in Nicholas J Mullany and Allen M Linden (eds), *Tort Tomorrow, a Tribute to John Fleming* (LBC Information Services 1998) 84, 99; Goudkamp and Nolan (n 6) [1-044]; Steele (n 6) 847. cf Cane (n 5) 172 (criticizing the continuum idea and arguing that the standards of liability in tort should instead be seen 'as consisting of a number of distinct elements which can be put together in different combinations to produce complex amalgams of the two types of responsibility recognized in tort law', ie strict liability and liability for fault).

[8] (1865) 3 H & C 774 (Court of Exchequer); (1866) LR 1 Ex 265 (Court of Exchequer Chamber); (1868) LR 3 HL 330.

[9] (1866) LR 1 Ex 265, 279.

[10] The rule was held to apply to a number of types of things: eg gas (*Batchellor v Turnbridge Wells Gas Co*, (1901) 84 LT 765); electricity (*National Telephone Co v Baker*, [1893] 2 Ch 186); fumes (*West*

STRICT LIABILITY IN THE FOUR TORT SYSTEMS: AN OVERVIEW   15

damage to property and personal injuries,[11] and it applied regardless of whether the claimant had any interest in the land affected by the escape of the thing.[12] With the passing of time, however, the scope of application of the rule and, more generally, its role in English tort law have been dramatically reduced. This has occurred through judicial and academic statements suggesting that the rule in *Rylands* would be part of the tort of private nuisance.[13] In *Read v J Lyons*, Lord Macmillan observed, even if *obiter*, that the rule in *Rylands* 'derives from a conception of mutual duties of adjoining or neighbouring landowners and its congeners are trespass and nuisance', and that this rule 'is truly a case on the mutual obligations of the owners or occupiers of neighbouring closes'.[14] It followed from this, first, that *Rylands* could not apply unless the dangerous substance escaped from the defendant's land to a place outside such land, so that if the claimant suffered some harm within the defendant's property, they could not recover under *Rylands v Fletcher*.[15] Secondly, it was no longer possible to recover damages for personal injuries, but only for damage to the claimant's property.[16] In 1993 in *Cambridge Water v Eastern Counties Leather*,[17] Lord Goff stated that *Rylands* may be seen as an 'extension of the law of nuisance to cases of isolated escape'.[18] A decade later, the Law Lords reiterated this view in *Transco plc v Stockport MBC* by arguing that the rule in *Rylands* is a sub-species of private nuisance and that, since private nuisance is a tort against land,[19] *Rylands* itself is also best regarded as a tort against land.[20]

As a result, the rule in *Rylands* applies today only where the following requirements are met: the defendant must have brought or kept on land an exceptionally dangerous or mischievous thing;[21] the harm must have been a reasonably

---

v Bristol Tramways Co, [1908] 2 KB 14); blasting and munitions (*Miles v Forest Rock Co Ltd*, (1918) 34 TLR 500; *Rainham Chemical Works v Belvedere Fish Guano*, [1921] 2 AC 465); fire (*Jones v Festiniog Ry*, (1867–68) LR 3 QB 733); a flag pole (*Shiffman v Order of St John*, [1936] 1 All ER 557); a chair-o-plane in a fairground (*Hale v Jennings Bros*, [1938] 1 All ER 579); vibrations (*Hoare & Co v McAlpine*, [1923] 1 Ch 167).

[11] *Rylands v Fletcher* itself provides an example of the operation of the rule relating to damage to property: the claimant's mines were flooded by water which escaped from the defendant's reservoir and reached his property through some old shafts. In relation to the rule in *Rylands* covering personal injuries, see eg *Jennings Bros* (n 10) 585; *McAlpine* (n 10) 174; *Shiffman* (n 10) 561–62.

[12] See eg *Shiffman* (n 10); *Forest Rock Co Ltd* (n 10).

[13] For a critique of the assimilation of *Rylands* into private nuisance, see Roderick Bagshaw, 'Rylands Confined' (2004) 120 LQR 388; John Murphy, 'The Merits of Rylands v Fletcher' (2004) 24 OJLS 643; Donal Nolan, 'The Distinctiveness of *Rylands v Fletcher*' (2005) 121 LQR 421.

[14] [1947] AC 156, 173–74.

[15] ibid 168.

[16] ibid 173.

[17] [1994] 2 AC 264.

[18] *Cambridge Water* (n 17) 304. To achieve this result, the House of Lords relied on Lord Macmillan's *dicta* in *J Lyons* and on a 1949 journal article by FH Newark, 'The Boundaries of Nuisance' (1949) 65 LQR 480.

[19] See *Canary Wharf* (n 3) 702–07.

[20] *Transco plc v Stockport MBC*, [2003] UKHL 61, [2004] 2 AC 1, [9], [34]–[35].

[21] For an overview of the things that have been found to be dangerous, see the case law mentioned in n 10.

foreseeable consequence of the escape, regardless of whether the escape itself was foreseeable or not;[22] the defendant's use of the land from which the thing escaped must have been extraordinary and unusual;[23] the thing must have escaped into or onto the claimant's land;[24] and the escape must have damaged the claimant's land.[25] Finally, even if all these requirements are met, the defendant can still avoid liability on the basis of an act of God,[26] act of a stranger,[27] default or consent of the claimant,[28] and statutory authority.[29] This emasculation of the rule in *Rylands* means that, unlike the US and Italian tort systems,[30] English law does not contain any general and strict liability for dangerous activities. These are instead governed either by the tort of negligence or through specific pieces of legislation, with statutory strict liability being imposed in a variety of circumstances, including where harm is caused by nuclear installations,[31] the underground storage of gas,[32] waste disposal,[33] burst water mains,[34] or the keeping of dangerous animals.[35] Therefore, insofar as dangerous activities and things are concerned, strict liability rules apply only occasionally (whether under *Rylands* itself or particular statutes), with the tort of negligence being the default rule.

---

[22] See *Cambridge Water* (n 17) 301–06. cf *Bristol Tramways Co* (n 10), where *Rylands* was applied to a risk of harm which was unforeseeable.

[23] Originally, this requirement was labelled as 'non-natural use' test in *Rylands v Fletcher*, (1868) LR 3 HL 330, 338–40. For a brief overview of its development and current significance, see Goudkamp and Nolan (n 6) [16-012]–[16-020].

[24] See n 15 in this section.

[25] This requirement means not only that personal injuries are excluded from the scope of application of *Rylands*, but also that, to have *locus standi*, the claimant must have an interest in the land affected by the escape of the dangerous substance: see *Mckenna v British Aluminium Limited*, [2002] Env LR 30, [21].

[26] See *Nichols v Marsland*, (1876) 2 Ex D 1; *Greenock Corp v Caledonian R*, [1917] AC 556. The expression 'act of God' refers to 'those events which involved no human agency and which it was not realistically possible for a human to guard against' (*Transco* (n 20) [59]).

[27] If the escape is caused by the unforeseeable act of a third party, the defendant is not liable: see *Box v Jubb*, (1879) 4 Ex D 76; *Rickards v Lothian*, [1913] AC 263; *Perry v Kendricks Transport Ltd*, [1956] 1 WLR 85. See also *Northwestern Utilities Ltd v London Guarantee and Accident Ltd*, [1936] AC 108.

[28] In *Rylands v Fletcher*, Blackburn J included the claimant's default among the available defences ((1866) LR 1 Ex 265, 280), which applies only if the harm is due wholly to the claimant's act or default. As regards the defence of consent of claimant, this refers to situations where the claimant consented to the presence of the dangerous thing on the defendant's premises and the escape was not owed to the defendant's negligence: see *Gill v Edouin*, (1894) 71 LT 762; *Peters v Prince of Wales Theatre*, [1943] 1 KB 73.

[29] The defendant may try to escape liability if they were statutorily authorized to perform the activity that eventually caused harm, but if liability can be excluded depends on the construction of the statute: see eg *Green v Chelsea Waterworks Co*, (1894) 70 LT 547; *Charing Cross Electricity Co v Hydraulic Power Co*, [1914] 3 KB 772.

[30] See text to nn 117–131 in section 2.3 and nn 291–301 in section 2.5.

[31] Nuclear Installations Act 1965, s 12.

[32] Gas Act 1965, s 14.

[33] Environmental Protection Act 1990, s 73(6).

[34] Water Industry Act 1991, s 209.

[35] Animals Act 1971, s 2(1). For a list of further statutes imposing liability stricter than fault liability, see Rogers (n 7) 106–07.

Another context of strict liability is the tort of private nuisance. The creator of a nuisance may take all reasonable precautions in operating their activity so as to avoid interfering with the claimant's interest in the use and enjoyment of their land, and yet they may not be able to do so and be found liable. For example, despite adopting latest pollution filters, a factory may nevertheless emit noxious substances and affect detrimentally a neighbour's enjoyment of their residential house. If the interference is so substantial that it would be unreasonable to expect the claimant neighbour to put up with it, the defendant factory will be liable and proof of reasonable care on their part will be immaterial.[36] It is therefore clear that, at least in this sort of case, private nuisance is a tort of strict liability, and the defendant can escape liability only if they acquired by grant or prescription the right to commit a nuisance,[37] if the nuisance was authorized by statute[38] or caused by an act of God,[39] or if the claimant consented to it,[40] or they were contributorily negligent.[41]

A further area where English law imposes strict liability relates to the harm caused by animals. First, a person may be strictly liable in nuisance or under the rule in *Rylands* for the harm caused by their own animals, provided that the requirements of the two torts are met.[42] Moreover, strict liability for animals is statutorily imposed through the Animals Act 1971 in four distinct categories of cases. First, under section 2(1) of the Act strict liability applies to the keepers of animals belonging to a 'dangerous species', meaning that these animals 'have such characteristics that they are likely, unless restrained, to cause severe damage or that any damage they may cause is likely to be severe'.[43] Typical examples include lions, tigers, elephants, and bears.[44] The second category of cases is governed by section 2(2) of the Act, which imposes strict liability on the keeper of a non-dangerous animal if a number of conditions are met. First, it is necessary that the damage caused by the animal is either likely to be caused or likely to be severe. Secondly, it is required that such likelihood of harm or of severity of harm is due to characteristics which the animal possesses but which are not normally found in animals of the same species. Thirdly, the keeper must have known that the animal possessed such characteristics.[45] Unlike under the rule in *Rylands v Fletcher* and under the tort

---

[36] For a statement on the strict nature of the tort of private nuisance, see *Transco* (n 20) [26] (Lord Hoffmann).

[37] See *Coventry v Lawrence*, [2014] UKSC 13, [2014] AC 822, [28]–[46].

[38] See eg *Allen v Gulf Oil Refining Ltd*, [1981] AC 1001.

[39] See *Sedleigh-Denfield v O'Callaghan*, [1940] AC 880, 886.

[40] *Kiddle v City Business Properties Ltd*, [1942] 1 KB 269.

[41] See *Trevett v Lee*, [1955] 1 WLR 113, 122. In this scenario, the defendant may obtain a reduction in damages depending on the extent of the claimant's negligence.

[42] See Peter North, *Civil Liability for Animals* (OUP 2012) [6.07]–[6.11].

[43] Animals Act 1971, s 6(2).

[44] *Wyatt v Rosherville Gardens Co*, (1886) 2 TLR 282, 283 (bears); *Filburn v People's Palace and Aquarium Co Ltd*, (1890) 25 QBD 258 (elephants); *Pearson v Coleman Bros*, [1948] 2 KB 359 (lions); *Behrens v Bertram Mills Circus Ltd*, [1957] 2 QB 1, 17–18 (tigers).

[45] Animals Act 1971, s 2(2).

18   JUSTIFYING STRICT LIABILITY

of private nuisance, liabilities under section 2 of the Animals Act 1971 also cover personal injuries. In terms of defences, section 5(1)–(3) of the Act provides that strict liability does not apply if the harm is due wholly to the claimant's fault, if the claimant voluntarily exposed themselves to the risk of such harm, or if the animal injured a trespasser. Furthermore, the defence of contributory negligence should apply as well.[46] By contrast, neither act of God nor act of a third party are applicable defences in relation to liability under section 2 of the Animals Act 1971,[47] therefore subjecting the keepers of dangerous (and sometimes non-dangerous) animals to a very rigorous regime. Finally, the third and fourth categories of strict liability under the Animals Act 1971 concern dogs injuring another's livestock and straying livestock causing damage to another's property, respectively.[48] In both cases, proof of fault in the owner or keeper of the damaging or injuring animal is not required, and the defendant can have their liability reduced if the claimant was contributorily negligent,[49] or escape it altogether if the harm was due wholly to the claimant's fault.[50]

Another context in which strict liability is prominent is liability for the action of another. Today, in order to decide whether a party is vicariously liable, English courts run a two-stage test. First, they explore the nature of the relationship between the defendant and the physical author of harm and verify whether this relationship is 'one that is capable of giving rise to vicarious liability'.[51] The classic relationship is that between employer and employee, whose existence may be assessed either on the basis of the 'control test' or, more prominently in recent times, on the basis of the 'entrepreneur test'.[52] However, modern case law has extended the scope of vicarious liability beyond the boundaries of the traditional employment relationship, and today it applies to any relationship 'akin to that between an employer and an employee'.[53] When assessing whether a relationship is akin to employment, courts may consider whether:

(i) the employer is more likely to have the means to compensate the victim than the employee and can be expected to have insured against that liability; (ii) the

---

[46] North (n 42) [2.160].

[47] See North (n 42) [2.165]; Law Commission, *Civil Liability for Animals* (Law Com No 13, 1967) [24].

[48] See Animals Act 1971, ss 3 and 4.

[49] Animals Act 1971, s 10.

[50] ibid s 5(1). For defences specific to the third and fourth categories of liability, see ibid s 5(4) and s 5(5)–(6), respectively.

[51] *Various Claimants v Catholic Child Welfare Society*, [2013] 2 AC 1, [21] [*CCWS*].

[52] The 'control test' is satisfied when the employer 'can not only order or require what is to be done, but how it shall be done': see *Collins v Hertfordshire CC*, [1947] KB 598, 615. By contrast, the 'entrepreneur test' seeks to distinguish between employee and independent contractor by suggesting that 'an employee works for his employer', whereas an 'independent contractor is in business on his own account': see *JGE v English Province of Our Lady of Charity*, [2013] QB 722, [64] (Ward LJ); and also *Barclays Bank Plc v Various Claimants*, [2020] UKSC 13, [2020] 2 WLR 960. For a brief discussion of both tests, see Goudkamp and Nolan (n 6) [21-010]–[21-011].

[53] *CCWS* (n 51) [47] (quoting *E v English Province of Our Lady of Charity*, [2013] QB 722).

tort will have been committed as a result of activity being taken by the employee on behalf of the employer; (iii) the employee's activity is likely to be part of the business activity of the employer; (iv) the employer, by employing the employee to carry on the activity will have created the risk of the tort committed by the employee; (v) the employee will, to a greater or lesser degree, have been under the control of the employer.[54]

Once a court is satisfied that, on the basis of these factors, the relationship between the defendant and the physical author of harm is capable of giving rise to vicarious liability, it will run the second stage of the test and will assess whether there is a sufficiently close connection between this relationship and the tortious conduct. In the traditional employment scenario, this test amounts to seeing whether the employee committed the tort in the ordinary course of their employment. Traditionally, this requirement was thought to be satisfied where the tortious act was expressly or impliedly authorized by the employer or if it could be considered as an unauthorized mode of doing the job that the employee was employed to do.[55] But given that some types of conduct cannot be described as modes of performing one's own job, for example where the tortfeasors sexually abuse the children that they are supposed to care for, courts have recently moved to a more flexible approach which assesses whether the tortious action has a sufficiently close connection with the relationship between the defendant and the physical author of harm.[56] This enquiry is highly fact-sensitive and it takes into account a variety of distinct considerations depending on the facts of the case being litigated.[57] In general terms, then, if a court is satisfied that the relationship between the defendant and the physical author of harm is capable of giving rise to vicarious liability and if the tortious conduct is sufficiently connected with this relationship, a court will hold the defendant vicariously liable.[58] By contrast, the defendant will not be liable if either of these requirements is not met, or if the physical author of harm were not themselves liable in tort (because, eg, they had a valid defence against the claimant); alternatively, the defendant may obtain a reduction in damages by

---

[54] ibid [35].

[55] See John W Salmond, *The Law of Torts: A Treatise on the English Law of Liability for Civil Injuries* (1st edn, Stevens and Haynes 1907) 83.

[56] See *Lister v Hesley Hall Ltd*, [2002] 1 AC 215. Depending on the facts of the case, the close connection test may be specially adapted, as it happens with cases concerning the abuse of children: see eg *WM Morrison Supermarkets plc v Various Claimants*, [2020] UKSC 12, [2020] 2 WLR 941, [36] and [23].

[57] See Goudkamp and Nolan (n 6) [21-021]–[21-037].

[58] The breadth of this two-stage test has allowed the UK Supreme Court to hold liable: the Ministry of Justice for the injury that a prisoner working in the prison kitchen caused to the claimant catering manager (*Cox v Ministry of Justice*, [2016] UKSC 10, [2016] AC 660); a private employer for the harm that one of his employees caused to a customer by way of verbal and physical assault (*Mohamud v WM Morrison Supermarkets Plc*, [2016] UKSC 11, [2016] AC 677); a local authority for the sexual abuse that a child suffered as a result of the acts of her foster parents, in whose care the child had been placed by the local authority (*Armes v Nottinghamshire County Council*, [2017] UKSC 60, [2018] AC 355).

proving that the claimant was contributorily negligent. Finally, there are special rules of liability for the actions of others that it may be difficult to see as arising out of an employment relationship or of a relationship akin to employment.[59] For example, traffic accidents are generally governed by the tort of negligence,[60] but strict liability is imposed on a vehicle owner where someone else drives the car for the owner's purposes and under delegation of a task or duty.[61] Similarly, chief police officers are liable for the torts committed by policer officers in the performance of their functions.[62] Again, principals are liable for the torts of their agents whenever the latter act within the actual or ostensible scope of their authority as agents.[63] What all these liabilities for the actions of others have in common is that they are strict, because proof of the defendant's diligent conduct is no answer to a claim for damages.

Other rules of strict liability featuring in English law relate to the so-called liability for breach of a non-delegable duty, which may be created either by courts or by statute and which applies across a variety of different situations. For example, in relation to the operation of dangerous activities, employers are under a non-delegable duty to ensure that their activity will not result in any damage and, therefore, they are strictly liable for the harm negligently caused by the independent contractor to whom they entrusted such activity.[64] Similarly, hospitals and schools have a non-delegable duty to ensure the physical safety of the patients and pupils put in their care, with the result that they are strictly liable for the harm caused to them by independent contractors while performing teaching or medical functions.[65] Again, those who undertake operations on the highway have been held strictly liable for the harm caused by their independent contractors while carrying

---

[59] Nicholas J McBride and Roderick Bagshaw, *Tort Law* (6th edn, Pearson Education 2018) 832–33; Goudkamp and Nolan (n 6) [21-016]–[21-017].

[60] Roderick Bagshaw, 'The Development of Traffic Liability in England and Wales' in Wolfgang Ernst (ed), *The Development of Traffic Liability* (CUP 2010) 12, 49; Peter Cane and James Goudkamp, *Atiyah's Accidents, Compensation and the Law* (9th edn, CUP 2018) 188. Note that under s 2(1) of the Automated and Electric Vehicles Act 2018, insurers are strictly liable for the damage 'caused by an automated vehicle when driving itself on a road or other public place', provided that the vehicle in question is insured at the time of the accident. Given the low number of automated vehicles today on the road, this strict liability is still of limited practical significance.

[61] *Ormrod v Crosville Motor Services Ltd*, [1953] 1 WLR 1120; *Morgans v Launchbury*, [1973] AC 127, reversing the decision of the Court of Appeal, where Lord Denning MR extended the vicarious liability of vehicle owners 'to a case when the car is being driven by the driver for his own purposes on an occasion in which the owner has no interest and for which he has not given permission': see *Launchbury v Morgans*, [1971] 2 QB 245, 254–55. cf the position in the United States, on which see text to nn 156–159 in section 2.3.

[62] Police Act 1996, s 88. Note, though, that the chief police officer is not personally liable and that the money to pay any award of damages comes from the police fund.

[63] See *Armagas Ltd v Mundogas Ltd, The Ocean Frost*, [1986] AC 717.

[64] *Honeywill & Stein Ltd v Larkin Bros (London's Commercial Photographers) Ltd*, [1934] 1 KB 191. In *Woodland v Swimming Teachers Association*, [2013] UKSC 66, [2014] AC 537, [6], Lord Sumption cast doubt on the basis of this type of non-delegable duty and added that in future cases the *Honeywill* decision and its progeny may be re-examined.

[65] See *Cassidy v Ministry of Health*, [1951] 2 KB 343 (hospitals); *Woodland* (n 64) (schools).

STRICT LIABILITY IN THE FOUR TORT SYSTEMS: AN OVERVIEW   21

out the relevant works.[66] Also, employers are under a non-delegable duty to see that reasonable care is taken in providing their employees with competent staff, adequate material, a proper system of working, effective supervision, and a safe place of work,[67] although it is controversial whether this liability is strict or based on fault.[68] It is instead clear that employers are strictly liable for breach of statutory duty for harm caused to their employees by a defect in the equipment provided to them, even if such defect is due wholly or partly to the fault of a third party (typically the manufacturer of the equipment).[69] Moreover, at least as far as pre-2013 work accidents are concerned, employers may be held strictly liable to their employees in a wide variety of circumstances for breach of health and safety regulations, as where, for example, employers do not ensure that 'work equipment is so constructed or adapted as to be suitable for the purpose for which it is used or provided', or that 'work equipment is maintained in an efficient state, an efficient working order and in good repair'.[70] By contrast, for accidents occurring on or after 1 October 2013 as a result of a breach of health and safety regulations, employers will be generally liable to their employees only upon proof of negligence, following changes made by the Enterprise and Regulatory Reform Act 2013.[71]

A further context of strict liability can be identified in the English law of liability for defective products. Since *Donoghue v Stevenson*, the main avenue of civil redress for victims of accidents involving products has been the tort of negligence,[72] where the manufacturer is liable only if they negligently expose others to an unreasonable risk of harm which then materializes in the form of personal injury or damage to

---

[66] See eg *Gray v Pullen*, (1864) 5 B & S 970; *Woodland* (n 64) [23] (Lord Sumption referring to the 'highway cases').

[67] See *Wilson and Clyde Coal Co v English*, [1938] AC 57, 78.

[68] Compare Goudkamp and Nolan (n 6) [9-017], [9-024] (suggesting that the non-delegable duty in question is modelled on the duty of care in the tort of negligence) with Witting (n 6) 626, 630 (arguing that liability for breach of a non-delegable duty, including that of employers, is strict).

[69] Employer's Liability (Defective Equipment) Act 1969, s 1(1).

[70] See the Provision and Use of Work Equipment Regulations 1998, s 4(1) and s 5(1), respectively.

[71] Before 2013, the Health and Safety at Work etc. Act 1974, s 47 established that breach of health and safety regulations which caused harm was actionable unless provided otherwise by the relevant legislation. The Enterprise and Regulatory Reform Act 2013, s 69 reverses this presumption of actionability, and s 47 now establishes that '[b]reach of a duty imposed by ... health and safety regulations shall not be actionable except to the extent that regulations under this section so provide'. The Explanatory Notes to this reform make clear that 'it will only be possible to claim for compensation in relation to breaches of affected health and safety legislation where it can be proved that the duty holder (usually the employer) has been negligent. This means that in future, for all relevant claims, duty-holders will only have to defend themselves against negligence': see [465]. This move towards fault seems driven by a desire to protect firms from the burden of excessive liability: see Cane and Goudkamp (n 60) 86, and cf Michael A Jones (ed), *Clerk & Lindsell on Torts* (23rd edn, Sweet & Maxwell 2020) [12-02]. Only health and safety regulations which are neither made under the Health and Safety at Work etc. Act 1974, s 15, nor listed in its Schedule 1 are unaffected by the 2013 reform, as for example the Employer's Liability (Defective Equipment) Act 1969.

[72] For an overview of the different phases of product liability in English law, see Simon Whittaker, 'The Development of Product Liability in England' in Simon Whittaker (ed), *The Development of Product Liability* (CUP 2010) 51.

property other than the product itself.[73] By implementing the European Directive on liability for defective products,[74] however, the Consumer Protection Act 1987 (CPA 1987) provides claimants with an additional route to compensation for harm caused by products, although it is not entirely clear whether this liability is strict or based on fault. Under the Act, the liability of manufacturers is formally divorced from any notion of fault, but it is required that the product in question be defective. This requirement has sparked a lively debate as to the nature of liability, with some legal scholars suggesting that the standard of conduct imposed on manufacturers is not substantially different to that in the tort of negligence,[75] and with others arguing instead that liability is strict because independent of any regard for the avoidability of the defect and the taking of reasonable precautions.[76] Some of the leading cases in the field suggest that, at least insofar as manufacturing defects are concerned, English courts do not give any consideration to the defendant's conduct and see product liability as strict.[77] Where, instead, the product is defective in design, courts engage in a more inclusive balancing exercise and take into account whether the defect was avoidable and at what cost, in the context of a broader risk–utility test.[78] It is not entirely clear whether this way of assessing design defects may amount to imposing strict liability or liability based on fault, but the courts' focus on the product rather than on the producer's conduct suggests that liability for design defects is markedly more rigorous than fault liability.[79] Similarly, some leading scholars argue that performing a risk–utility calculus in cases of defective design 'would not be reintroducing negligence by the back door',[80] and that liability would be strict on the grounds that the assessment of the avoidability of defect would be made in hindsight (at the time of the trial) and that its focus would not

---

[73] *Donoghue v Stevenson*, [1932] AC 562, which marked the emergence of the tort of negligence as an autonomous tort, concerned itself a case of liability for defective products.

[74] EU Directive 374/85 (Product Liability Directive). On the implementation process, see Simon Whittaker, *Liability for Products* (OUP 2005) 465–75.

[75] See Simon Whittaker, 'The EEC Directive on Product Liability' (1985) 5 YEL 233, 242–46; Jane Stapleton, 'Products Liability Reform—Real or Illusory?' (1986) 6 OJLS 392.

[76] See eg Elspeth Deards and Christian Twigg-Flesner, 'The Consumer Protection Act: Proof at Last that it is Protecting Consumers?' (2001) 10 Nottingham LJ 1.

[77] *A v National Blood Authority*, [2001] 3 All ER 289 [*NBA*] (putting forward a distinction between standard and non-standard products, which mirrors the US distinction between products with design defects and products with manufacturing defects: see eg Deakin and Adams (n 2) 604, fn 195). See also Donal Nolan, 'Strict Product Liability for Design Defects' (2018) 134 LQR 176, 177 (suggesting that the distinction between design and manufacturing defects 'is rightly viewed as fundamental to the analysis of the defectiveness issue in strict product liability regimes in other jurisdictions, since a coherent approach to that question seems to be impossible without it').

[78] *Wilkes v Depuy International Ltd*, [2016] EWHC 3096, [85]. See also *Bogle v McDonald's Restaurants Ltd*, [2002] EWHC 490, [80]; *Gee v DePuy International Ltd*, [2018] EWHC 1208, [141]–[143] (suggesting that 'the avoidability or impossibility of taking precautionary measures; the impracticality, difficulty or cost of taking such measures; and the benefit to society or utility of the product' may be relevant even in cases involving non-standard products).

[79] *Wilkes* (n 78) [63]; Goudkamp and Nolan (n 6) [11-034].

[80] Deakin and Adams (n 2) 607.

shift back from the product to the manufacturer's conduct.[81] As far as defences are concerned, the CPA 1987 follows the Product Liability Directive.[82] Among these, particularly significant is the so-called development risk defence which, broadly speaking, shields manufacturers from liability if the relevant risk of harm was unforeseeable according to the scientific and technical knowledge available at the time when the product was put into circulation. While article 7(e) of the Product Liability Directive takes a rigorous approach whereby the defendant is exempted from liability if that knowledge 'was not such as to enable the existence of the defect to be discovered', the CPA 1987 adopts an apparently more subjective test and shields a manufacturer from liability if 'the state of scientific and technical knowledge at the relevant time was not such that a producer of products of the same description as the product in question might be expected to have discovered the defect if it had existed in his products while they were under his control'.[83] Notwithstanding the different wording, it is unclear whether the English provision will lead to different results from those that would be achieved under article 7(e) of the Directive. Indeed, in the leading case, *NBA*,[84] the court referred directly to the Product Liability Directive rather than to the CPA 1987 and therefore adopted a rigorous approach to the defence,[85] making it very difficult for defendants to rely successfully on it. While it remains to be seen whether this stance will be confirmed in future cases or if instead English courts will prefer adopting a more lenient approach towards manufacturers, it seems clear that the development risk defence reduces to some extent the rigour of liability for defective products. In sum, as seen above,[86] while there is no settled view as to the nature of product liability under the CPA 1987, several legal scholars and some leading judgments suggest that liability

---

[81] Nolan (n 77) 178–79. See also *Wilkes* (n 78) [89]; *Iman Abouzaid v Mothercare (UK) Ltd*, [2000] 12 WLUK 627; *Gee* (n 78) [84].

[82] CPA 1987, s 4(1); Product Liability Directive, art 7.

[83] CPA 1987, s 4(1)(e). As a result of this difference, the European Commission instituted proceedings against the United Kingdom for failure to transpose correctly the Directive, but the CJEU rejected the Commission's view on the ground that it failed to identify UK case law interpreting the development risk defence in a way that was inconsistent with the Directive: see *Commission v United Kingdom*, Case C-300/95, [1997] All ER (EC) 481. In following Advocate General Tesauro, the CJEU also clarified that the defence must be assessed objectively, ie regardless of the circumstances or abilities of the particular manufacturer (para [27] of the judgment), that the relevant state of scientific and technical knowledge refers not to the knowledge available in the sector in which the manufacturer operates, 'but, unreservedly, at the state of scientific and technical knowledge, including the most advanced level of such knowledge' (ibid [26]). On the other hand, the manufacturer can escape liability if such knowledge is available only in some inaccessible form, as would be the case if the relevant piece of information were only contained in 'research carried out by an academic in Manchuria published in a local scientific journal in Chinese, which does not go outside the boundaries of the region' (at para [23] of the Advocate General's opinion).

[84] *NBA* (n 77).

[85] Burton J held that the defence does not apply to known but unavoidable risks (ibid [74]), and regarded as 'non-Manchurianly accessible' knowledge only 'unpublished document or unpublished research not available to the general public, retained within the laboratory or research department of a particular company' (ibid [49]).

[86] See text to nn 75–81 in this section.

is strict as far as manufacturing defects are concerned and that it may be strict even in relation to design defects.

Finally, I should note the position of public entities in English law in relation to strict liability. Here it is necessary to distinguish between the Crown and other public bodies. Unlike any other public body, the Crown has enjoyed for a long time an immunity from tort liability based on the idea that 'the King can do no wrong'. The Crown Proceedings Act 1947 removed this privilege, though, and today the Crown is liable in tort as 'if it were a person of full age and capacity'.[87] On this basis, the Crown is made liable for the torts of its servants and agents, for breach of the duties it owes to them as their employer, and for breach of the duties attaching at common law to the ownership, occupation, possession, or control of property.[88] In addition to this, the Crown is liable for breach of statutory duty where it is bound by a duty which is binding also upon other persons,[89] and it is also liable for the torts committed by its officers while performing functions directly imposed on them either by statute or by common law rules, as if those functions were imposed on them by virtue of instructions from the Crown.[90] In sum, the Crown Proceedings Act 1947 has subjected the Crown to rules which are, with some adaptation, the same as those governing ordinary tort actions,[91] and therefore it has put it on a similar footing with other public authorities, as these have always been liable in tort like any other subject of the Crown.[92] Today, then, English public bodies can be held liable for torts such as negligence, breach of statutory duty, nuisance, or the rule in *Rylands v Fletcher*, and they can also be held vicariously liable for the torts of their employees.[93] Importantly, however, English courts are more cautious in imposing liability on public bodies than they are in relation to

---

[87] Crown Proceedings Act 1947, s 2(1).

[88] ibid.

[89] Crown Proceedings Act 1947, s 2(2).

[90] Crown Proceedings Act 1947, s 2(3).

[91] Paul Craig, *Administrative Law* (9th edn, Sweet & Maxwell 2021) [29–001].

[92] eg *Entick v Carrington*, (1765) 19 St Tr 1030; *Leach v Money*, (1765) 19 St Tr 2002; *Cooper v Wandsworth Board of Works*, (1863) CBNS 180; *Pride of Derby and Derbyshire Angling Association Ltd v British Celanese Ltd*, [1953] Ch 149. On this approach to public liability, see Albert V Dicey, *Lectures Introductory to the Study of the Law of the Constitution* (Macmillan 1885) Lecture V, esp 177–208.

[93] See Sue Arrowsmith, *Civil Liability and Public Authorities* (Earlsgate Press 1992) chs 5–8; Henry WR Wade and Christopher F Forsyth, *Administrative Law* (11th edn, OUP 2014) chs 20–21; Craig (n 91) chs 29–30. Among the torts for which a public body can be held vicariously liable there is the specific public law tort of misfeasance in public office, which is committed where a public officer causes a loss to another by dishonestly abusing their governmental power: see *Racz v Home Office*, [1994] 2 AC 45; *Three Rivers DC v Bank of England (No.3)*, [2001] UKHL 16, [2003] 2 AC 1. Moreover, a public body can be held liable if it acts in violation of the Human Rights Act 1998: under s 7, the victim of such violation may sue the relevant public authority and, according to s 8, the court 'may grant such relief or remedy, or make such order, within its powers as it considers just and appropriate', this including a damages award. Finally, note that public employees may be sued personally for their torts and that, if their employer is also sued and ordered to pay damages to the claimant, the employees are subject to the employer's recourse action, even though this occurrence is very rare: see Ken Oliphant, 'The Liability of Public Authorities in England and Wales' in Ken Oliphant (ed), *The Liability of Public Authorities in Comparative Perspective* (Intersentia 2016) 127, [33].

private parties. For example, in claims against public authorities in the tort of negligence, English judges assess whether or not the matter of the case is justiciable, in other words whether it is suitable for judicial resolution. Courts are very likely to consider as non-justiciable cases which would require them to scrutinize a public body's policy determination such as 'discretionary decisions on the allocation of scarce resources or the distribution of risks'.[94] Also, courts sometimes invoke policy considerations so as to rule out the existence of a duty of care,[95] and this type of consideration is given greater weight in claims against public entities than in claims against private parties.[96] In the tort of breach of statutory duty, a claimant must show that the relevant duty was imposed to protect a limited class of individuals and that the statute intended to confer private rights of action, this depending on statutory construction.[97] A number of 'indicators' are used to decide the latter issue, including whether the statute already provides for remedies other than a private right of action,[98] whether the statute is intended to benefit society in general,[99] and whether a 'good deal of judgment' on the part of the relevant public authority is involved.[100] In general, English courts have been reluctant to find public bodies liable for breach of statutory duty,[101] sometimes because they felt that it would be too much to impose strict liability on them.[102] Again, claimants do not easily succeed against public bodies in claims based on private nuisance or on the rule in *Rylands v Fletcher*. As to nuisance, the defence of statutory authority is applied in such a way as to constitute 'the principle hurdle for claimants suing public authorities',[103] for no action will lie whenever the harm caused is the inevitable consequence of the exercise of statutory authority.[104] As to the rule in *Rylands*, courts have on occasion denied liability in public bodies by holding that, while the rule requires that the defendant acted 'for its own purposes', public bodies act for the public benefit, with the result that the rule cannot apply to them.[105] Moreover, if a public body is acting under a statutory power it may be held liable under the rule in *Rylands* only if there is a 'nuisance clause', that is a clause or section in the statute which preserves

---

[94] *Rowling v Takaro Properties Ltd*, [1988] AC 473, 501 (Lord Keith).

[95] See *Stovin v Wise*, [1996] AC 923, 952 (Lord Hoffmann); *Rowling* (n 94) 502; *Hill v Chief Constable of West Yorkshire*, [1989] AC 53, 63 (Lord Keith).

[96] Oliphant (n 93) [10], [16].

[97] See *X (Minors) v Bedfordshire CC*, [1995] 2 AC 633, 731–32 (Lord Browne-Wilkinson).

[98] ibid.

[99] ibid. See also *O'Rourke v Camden LBC*, [1998] AC 188, 192–93.

[100] *O'Rourke* (n 99) 194.

[101] ibid; *Phelps v Hillingdon LBC*, [2001] 2 AC 619, 652; *Michael v Chief Constable of South Wales*, [2015] UKSC 2, [2015] AC 1732, [113]–[114]. For further examples, see Craig (n 91) [30–034]–[30–035], including the case law referenced in fn 155.

[102] See Craig (n 91) [30–035].

[103] ibid [30–054].

[104] *Gulf Oil Refining* (n 38).

[105] *Dunne v North Western Gas Board*, [1964] 2 QB 806, 832–833; Wade and Forsyth (n 93) 659–60 (discussing and criticizing this approach). cf *Smeaton v Ilford Co*, [1954] Ch 450, 468–71 (Upjohn J) (observing that it would be improper to exclude the application of *Rylands v Fletcher* on the ground that the public authority acted for the general benefit of the community).

26 JUSTIFYING STRICT LIABILITY

liability in nuisance.[106] If, instead, a public authority is under a statutory duty, there is no liability (whether or not there was a nuisance clause) 'if what had been done was ... expressly required by statute ... or was reasonably incidental to that requirement and was done without negligence'.[107] In sum, a variety of limitations inherent in the torts themselves may thwart the hopes of claimants to obtain tort compensation from public defendants, including in strict liability claims. Overall, then, it seems fair to say that English law handles with care the liability of public bodies and that its approach to strict liability is rather restrictive, especially if compared to other legal systems such as French law, which, as will be seen in section 2.4, imposes a wide range of strict liabilities on public authorities.[108]

To conclude, in a setting where negligence dominates the scene, strict liability plays nevertheless a role. On the one hand, over the twentieth century, English legal actors have been reluctant to admit or expand strict liability in tort. This can be seen in the fall of the rule in *Rylands v Fletcher*, the introduction of strict product liability only as a result of a European directive, the possible watering down of the rigour of the development risk defence under section 4(1)(e) of CPA 1987, the demise of employers' strict liability for breach of statutory duty, as well as the fact that an important area such as traffic accidents is based, by and large, on negligence. On the other hand, both the courts and the legislature are willing to support, in a variety of settings, the imposition of strict liability, as shown in contexts such as liability for animals, liability for private nuisance, liability for products, liability for breach of certain non-delegable duties, and, most importantly given its recent expansion, vicarious liability for the torts of others. In sum, although the tort of negligence (and its focus on fault) constitutes the centre of gravity of the English tort system, some types of accidents escape its gravitational pull and are governed by rules of strict liability.

2.3 Strict Liability in the Law of the United States

While there are fifty-one tort regimes in the United States, one for each of the jurisdictions forming part of the Union, there is a degree of uniformity among them which makes it possible to approach tort law in the United States as if there were one body of law.[109] In this respect, the Restatements of the American Law Institute are of great assistance, as they 'restate' systematically the common law of torts on the basis of the rules adopted in the majority of states and therefore they make it

---

[106] See *Midwood v Manchester Corporation*, [1905] 2KB 597; *Charing Cross Electricity Co* (n 29). See also Craig (n 91) [30–059].

[107] See *Dunne* (n 105) 834–35. See also *Smeaton* (n 105) 476–77.

[108] See section 2.4.

[109] Kenneth S Abraham, *The Forms and Functions of Tort Law* (5th edn, Foundation Press 2017) 1.

relatively easy to identify the tort rules which have broad acceptance across the United States.[110]

In keeping with the English approach, US tort law is organized around a collection of torts. From the perspective of the standard of conduct, they are often distinguished on the basis of whether or not they rest on the defendant's fault. Torts based on fault involve either intentional wrongdoings or carelessly inflicted harm, with the tort of negligence clearly dominating the scene.[111] In contrast, liability rules which do not require any failure to act as a reasonable person should have done in the circumstances constitute instances of strict liability.[112] Therefore, in keeping with the English approach, a conceptual distinction between fault-based liability and strict liability appears to be viable.[113] At the same time, though, some legal scholars show that sharp boundaries between fault and strict liability may be difficult to draw,[114] and that different liability rules may be located along a continuum on the basis of their degree of strictness.[115] Nevertheless, the term 'strict liability' is commonly seen in opposition to fault, and it is therefore used to refer to a variety of torts which do not make liability depend upon the violation of the standard of the reasonable person. As a result, and despite the prominence of the tort of negligence, strict liability takes on an important role in the United States.

To begin with, after an initially cold reception by a majority of courts,[116] the English rule in *Rylands v Fletcher* has been accepted in most states and, in sharp contrast with the English approach, it has developed into a common law rule of

---

[110] In some cases, particularly if the state courts are split on a particular issue and it is not possible to identify a majority view, the Restatement may reflect the drafters' own preferences (this being usually made clear in the comments to the relevant section in the Restatement).

[111] As in English law, the tort of negligence is based on a failure to take reasonable care: see *Brown v Kendall*, 60 Mass 292 (Mass.1850). Note that, under the US doctrine of negligence *per se*, the mere violation of a statutory rule constitutes by itself—*per se*—negligence, whether or not the defendant's non-compliant conduct was reasonable, and that this doctrine is seen as part of negligence law: see eg John CP Goldberg and others, *Tort Law: Responsibilities and Redress* (5th edn, Wolters Kluwer 2021) 424–39. In English law, by contrast, the action for breach of statutory duty is today entirely separate from the tort of negligence: see Goudkamp and Nolan (n 6) [8-003]. This is not to say that English law never contemplated 'statutory negligence': see Glanville Williams, 'The Effect of Penal Legislation in the Law of Tort' (1960) 23 MLR 233, 236; Keith M Stanton, *Breach of Statutory Duty in Tort* (Sweet & Maxwell 1986) 25ff. This approach was eventually rejected in England with *LPTB v Upson*, [1949] AC 155, 168–69 (Lord Wright).

[112] See eg Robert E Keeton, Lewis D Sargentich, and Gregory C Keating, *Tort and Accident Law—Cases and Materials* (4th edn, Thomson West 2004) 805.

[113] See Steven Shavell, 'Strict Liability versus Negligence' (1980) 9 J Legal Stud 1; Robert Cooter and Thomas Ulen, *Law & Economics* (6th edn, Pearson 2012) 196–98. See also, though from an entirely different perspective, Gregory C Keating, 'Is There Really No Liability Without Fault?: A Critique of Goldberg & Zipursky' (2017) 85 Fordham L Rev Res Gestae 24, 29.

[114] See eg John CP Goldberg and Benjamin C Zipursky, 'The Strict Liability in Fault and the Fault in Strict Liability' (2016) 85 Fordham L Rev 743.

[115] See eg the classification of liability rules put forward by Guido Calabresi and Alvin K Klevorick, 'Four Tests for Liability in Torts' (1985) 14 J Legal Stud 585.

[116] Famous examples are *Brown v Collins*, 53 N.H. 442 (NH 1873); and *Losee v Buchanan*, 51 N.Y. 476 (NY 1873). See also Morton J Horwitz, *The Transformation of American Law 1870–1960: The Crisis of Legal Orthodoxy* (OUP 1992) 13, 124; Lawrence M Friedman, *A History of American Law* (4th edn, OUP 2019) 461–62.

28   JUSTIFYING STRICT LIABILITY

strict liability for harm caused by abnormally dangerous activities.[117] In determining whether an activity is abnormally dangerous, courts rely on several factors. In particular, they primarily consider the likelihood and severity of harm, whether the risk of harm can be avoided by the exercise of reasonable care, and whether the activity generating such risk is in common usage.[118] The relevance of other factors such as the locational appropriateness and the social value of the defendant's activity has varied over time,[119] but they appear to be of limited importance today.[120] Examples of abnormally dangerous activities include blasting,[121] storage of explosives,[122] processing of hazardous materials,[123] transportation of flammable or explosive materials,[124] crop dusting,[125] and fireworks displays.[126] Liability for harm caused by abnormally dangerous activities is clearly strict because the defendant is liable even if they exercised due care to avoid the harm.[127] In terms of the defences available to defendants, a variety of approaches can be identified. For example, the Second Restatement adopts an extremely rigorous approach to intervening actions and events: § 522 provides that strict liability applies even if harm is 'caused by the unexpectable (a) innocent, negligent or reckless conduct of a third person, or (b) action of an animal, or (c) operation of a force of nature'. The position in the case law is more mixed. While some jurisdictions adopt the Second Restatement's approach,[128] others do not and hold that external causes of harm can exempt a defendant from liability, especially if they are unforeseeable.[129] Turning to the victim's

---

[117] cf the position of courts in Texas: see *American Tobacco Co, Inc v Grinnell*, 951 S.W.2d 420 (Tex.1997) [35]. There are also statutes that, in some states, protect minors from exposure to dangers by, for example, prohibiting the sale of dangerous products to them or by prohibiting their employment in dangerous occupations: see eg *Dart v Pure Oil*, 27 N.W.2d 555, 560–61 (Minn.1947); *Restatement (Second) of Torts* ('Second Restatement'), § 288 A, comment *c*.

[118] See factors (a)–(d) of § 520 of the Second Restatement, as well as § 20(b) of the 2010 *Restatement (Third) of Torts: Liability for Physical and Emotional Harm* ('Third Restatement LPEH').

[119] Compare comment *f* to § 520 of the Second Restatement with the Reporters' Note on comment *k* to § 20 of the Third Restatement LPEH.

[120] See Reporters' Note on comment *k* to § 20 of the Third Restatement LPEH. cf *Toms v Calvary Assembly of God, Inc*, 132 A.3d 866, 872 (Md.2016) (on the considerable importance of locational appropriateness in Maryland).

[121] *Dyer v Maine Drilling & Blasting, Inc*, 984 A.2d 210 (Me.2009).

[122] *Exner v Sherman Power Construction*, 54 F.2d 510 (2nd Cir.1931); *Yukon Equipment v Fireman's Fund Insurance*, 585 P.2d 1206 (Alaska 1978).

[123] *T & E Industries, Inc v Safety Light Corp*, 587 A.2d 1249 (N.J.1991).

[124] *Siegler v Kuhlman*, 502 P.2d 1181 (Wash.1972); *National Steel Service Center v Gibbons*, 319 N.W.2d 269 (Iowa 1982).

[125] *Langan v Valicopters*, 567 P.2d 218 (Wash.1977).

[126] *Klein v Pyrodyne Corp*, 810 P.2d 917 (Wash.1991). For further examples, see Victor E Schwartz, Kathryn Kelly, and David F Partlett, *Prosser, Wade, and Schwartz's Torts—Cases and Materials* (13th edn, Foundation Press 2015) 755–56.

[127] § 519 of the Second Restatement; § 20(b)(1) of the Third Restatement LPEH.

[128] eg *Yukon* (n 122) 1211–12 (intentional conduct by a third party not a good defence); *Old Island Fumigation v Barbee*, 604 So.2d 1246, 1248 (Fla.1992) (negligence by a third party not a good defence).

[129] eg *Golden v Amory*, 109 N.E.2d 131, 133 (Mass.1952) (considering act of God as a good defence because 'plainly beyond the capacity of anyone to anticipate'); *Klein* (n 126) 925 (considering as good defences events which a defendant could not be reasonably expected to anticipate); *Bianchini v Humble Pipe Line Co*, 480 F.2d 251, 254–55 (5th Cir.1973) (seeing the action of a third party as a good defence); *Trotter v Callens*, 546 P.2d 867, 869 (N.M.1976) (considering act of God as a good defence if the act is

own conduct, there is again a variety of approaches. For example, §§ 523–524(2) of the Second Restatement suggest that the defendant should be able to escape liability if the victim voluntarily assumes the risk of harm generated by the abnormally dangerous activity, but not if the victim was contributorily negligent.[130] By contrast, a radically different approach is adopted by the Third Restatement LPEH. In seeking to reflect the evolution of the case law intervening after the drafting of the Second Restatement, § 25 abolishes contributory negligence as a complete bar to recovery and suggests a regime of comparative responsibility, where liability is apportioned depending on the defendant's and claimant's respective conduct.[131]

Another context of strict liability in the United States regards the harm caused by animals. In this respect, in resemblance with the English approach, a distinction is drawn between trespassing (or intruding) animals, animals wild by nature, and domesticated animals.[132] As regards trespassing animals, the position of most US courts is essentially that a possessor of livestock is liable for any harm done while upon the land of another although they exercised the utmost care to prevent them from intruding.[133] In the approach of the Third Restatement LPEH, this rule is now extended to all animals other than dogs and cats.[134] Furthermore, in some states the owner or possessor of trespassing animals can escape strict liability if the claimant landowner failed to protect their own land by fencing out,[135] while in other jurisdictions this defence is not available.[136] Moving to wild animals, most states impose strict liability on their owners and possessors for any harm caused to third parties,[137] with the exception of public zoos, which are liable only

---

'so extraordinary' that it 'cannot be prevented by human care, skill or foresight'). Note that, according to the Reporters' Note on comment *d* to § 34 of the Third Restatement LPEH, '[t]he American case law on intervening cause [in contexts of strict liability] is thin, and the case law is inconsistent in how much emphasis it places on the foreseeability of the intervening act'.

[130] Here contributory negligence refers to situations where the victim 'merely fails to exercise reasonable care to discover the existence or presence of the activity or to take precautions against the harm that may result from it': see comment *a* to § 524. See also the Reporter's Note on § 524 for reference to the relevant case law.

[131] A regime of comparative responsibility is today adopted in an increasing number of jurisdictions across the United States: see comment *c* to § 25 of the Third Restatement LPEH. See also Goldberg and others (n 111) 974.

[132] Charles E Cantu, 'Distinguishing the Concept of Strict Liability in Tort from Strict Products Liability: Medusa Unveiled' (2003) 33 U Mem L Rev 823, 827, 828ff.

[133] § 504(1) of the Second Restatement. While the Second Restatement speaks only of possessors, it seems clear that, at least in modern times, the rule of strict liability applies to owners as well: see the Reporters' Note on comment *f* to § 21 of the Third Restatement LPEH, and the case law mentioned therein.

[134] See § 21.

[135] See eg *SaBell's, Inc v Flens*, 627 P.2d 750 (Colo.1981).

[136] See comment *c* to § 21 of the Third Restatement LPEH.

[137] See § 22 of the Third Restatement LPEH (see the Reporters' Note on comment *b* for a rich sample of decisions regarding wild animals). The rule of strict liability for wild animals was already recognized in § 507(1) of the Second Restatement, which traced it back to the English case *Filburn v People's Palace & Aquarium Co*, 25 QBD 258 (1890). cf *King v Blue Mountain Forest Association*, 123 A.2d 151 (N.H.1956) rejecting this rule for New Hampshire.

30 JUSTIFYING STRICT LIABILITY

if negligent.[138] More complicated is the position regarding domesticated animals. An owner or possessor of this type of animal, whose classic example would be a dog or cat, is strictly liable only if they know or have reason to know that the animal has 'dangerous tendencies abnormal for the animal's category'.[139] However, many states have enacted statutes which hold owners or possessors of dogs strictly liable regardless of any scienter requirement, therefore creating an important statutory exception—confined to dogs—to the common law position.[140] If instead a domesticated animal does not have any abnormally dangerous tendency, the negligence standard applies.[141] In terms of defences, the position is complex. As regards intervening actions by third parties or natural events, the Second Restatement suggests that, for trespassing animals, strict liability does not apply if harm is 'brought about by the unexpectable operation of a force of nature, action of another animal or intentional, reckless or negligent conduct of a third person';[142] by contrast, in relation to wild animals as well as to domestic but vicious animals, strict liability applies even if the harm occurred because of the 'unexpectable ... innocent, negligent or reckless conduct of a third person, or ... action of another animal, or ... operation of a force of nature'.[143] Adopting a different approach, the Third Restatement LPEH 'employs a unitary standard' which takes into account the foreseeability of intervening actions or events and which arguably excludes strict liability if such actions or events are not reasonably foreseeable by the defendant.[144] As to the victim's conduct, the approach of the Second Restatement and of some courts is similar to that adopted for abnormally dangerous activities, for the defendant can escape liability in cases of victim's assumption of risk, but not of contributory negligence.[145] By contrast, the Third Restatement LPEH and the case law of many state courts adopt a regime of comparative responsibility.[146]

---

[138] See *Kennedy v City and County of Denver*, 506 P.2d 764 (Colo.1972). See also *Isaacs v Powell*, 267 So.2d 864 (Fla.1972) (imposing strict liability on a *privately* owned zoo).

[139] § 23 of the Third Restatement LPEH. On the varying interpretation given across US courts to the scienter requirement, see the Reporters' Note on comment *c* to § 23.

[140] eg FLA §§ 767.01, 767.04 (Florida Statutes Annotated); 510 Ill Comp Stat Ann 5/16 (Illinois Compiled Statutes Annotated). The complete list can be found in the Reporters' Note on comment *d* to § 23 of the Third Restatement LPEH.

[141] eg *Safford Animal Hosp v Blain*, 580 P.2d 757 (Ariz.1978) (cows); *Williams v Tysinger*, 399 S.E.2d 108 (N.C.1991) (horses). See also the Reporters' Note on comment *i* to § 23 of the Third Restatement LPEH.

[142] § 504(3)(c). See also comment *i* to this section and the Reporter's Note on this comment for reference to the relevant case law.

[143] § 510. Note, though, that '[a]uthority relevant to this Section is sparse and indecisive': see the Reporter's Note on § 510.

[144] See the Reporters' Note on comments *d* and *e* to § 34.

[145] § 515 of the Second Restatement. See eg *Keyser v Phillips Petroleum Co*, 287 So.2d 364 (Fla.1973). For reference to further case law, see the Reporter's Note to this section.

[146] See § 25 of the Third Restatement LPEH. For some examples, see eg *Ambort v Nowlin*, 709 S.W.2d 407 (Ark.1986) (dog bite); *Mills v Smith*, 673 P.2d 117 (Kans.1983) (wild animal); *Fifer v Dix*, 608 N.W.2d 740 (Wis.2000) (dog injury statute). In addition to this, § 24 of the Third Restatement LPEH mentions another defence (available also in the context of abnormally dangerous activities): 'strict liability ... does not apply (a) if the person suffers physical or emotional harm as a result of making contact with or coming into proximity to the defendant's animal or abnormally dangerous activity for the

STRICT LIABILITY IN THE FOUR TORT SYSTEMS: AN OVERVIEW   31

Another context in which strict liability is prominent is liability for the action of another. In this area, the most significant doctrine is the vicarious liability of employers for the torts committed by their employees, generally known as *respondeat superior*. It is widely acknowledged that an employer/employee relationship exists if the employer 'controls or has the right to control the manner and means of the [employee's] performance of work'.[147] Furthermore, the employer is liable only if the tort is committed by their employee 'acting within the scope of employment',[148] meaning that the employee is 'performing work assigned by the employer or engaging in a course of conduct subject to the employer's control'.[149] The 'scope of employment' requirement can be interpreted in a broad way, with the result that liability may apply if, for example, the employee disregards the employer's instructions or even if the employee's action is intentionally wrongful.[150] The defendant will not be liable if there was no employer/employee relationship between them and the material author of harm, or if the 'scope of employment' requirement was not met, or if the employee was not himself liable in tort; alternatively, the defendant can obtain a reduction in damages by proving that the claimant's negligent conduct contributed to the causation of harm.[151] While it is therefore clear that, as a general rule, an employer is not vicariously liable for the tort of an independent contractor,[152] there are important exceptions to this. Most notably, someone who hires an independent contractor to carry out an abnormally dangerous activity or an activity that poses a 'peculiar risk' of harm to third parties is strictly liable for the harm caused by the latter,[153] as proof of the hirer's reasonable conduct is no answer to a claim for damages.

Another form of vicarious liability relates to parental liability. While at common law the general position resembles the English approach and therefore parents are

---

purpose of securing some benefit from that contact or that proximity; or (b) if the defendant maintains ownership or possession of the animal or carries on the abnormally dangerous activity in pursuance of an obligation imposed by law'.

[147] § 7.07(3)(a) of the *Restatement (Third) of Agency* ('Agency Restatement'). See *France v Southern Equip Co*, 689 S.E.2d 1 (W.Va.2010); Dan B Dobbs, Paul T Hayden, and Ellen M Bublick, *Torts and Compensation—Personal Accountability and Social Responsibility for Injury* (8th edn, West Academic Publishing 2017) 707–08.

[148] § 7.07(1) of the Agency Restatement.

[149] § 7.07(2) of the Agency Restatement.

[150] *Patterson v Blair*, 172 S.W.3d 361 (Ky.2005) (car dealership held vicariously liable for an employee's act of firing a pistol at a vehicle's tires in effort to repossess it while the claimant, a customer, was operating it); *Rodebush v Oklahoma Nursing Homes, Ltd*, 867 P.2d 1241 (Okla.1993) (nursing home held liable for an employee's act of slapping an elderly Alzheimer's patient). cf *Lisa M v Henry Mayo Newhall Memorial Hosp*, 907 P.2d 358 (Cal.1995) (hospital held not vicariously liable for sexual battery committed by an ultrasound technician on a pregnant patient after ultrasound examination).

[151] See *Li v Yellow Cab Company of California*, 532 P.2d 1226 (Cal.1975).

[152] See § 57 of the Third Restatement LPEH.

[153] See § 58 ('Work Involving Abnormally Dangerous Activities') and § 59 ('Activity Posing a Peculiar Risk') of the Third Restatement LPEH and, respectively *Anderson v Marathon Petroleum Company*, 801 F.2d 936, 939–41 (7th Cir.1986), *Pusey v Bator*, 762 N.E.2d 968 (Ohio 2002). See also § 60 (work on instrumentalities used in highly dangerous activities).

32 JUSTIFYING STRICT LIABILITY

held liable for the harm caused by their children only if they have been themselves negligent in supervising or controlling their offspring,[154] most states have enacted statutes which, with variations, provide for strict parental liability in cases of intentional misconduct by the minor.[155] Furthermore, many courts adopt the so-called family purpose doctrine, which is instead expressly rejected in England.[156] This doctrine, which establishes a form of vicarious liability in the context of traffic accidents, provides that the family member (typically a parent) who is owner of a vehicle is strictly liable for the harm carelessly caused by another family member (typically a child) while driving, so long as the driving occurs with the owner's permission, whether express or implied.[157] Finally, in some states, statutes have extended the scope of this form of vicarious liability so as to cover traffic accidents carelessly caused by any person, family member or not, who was driving the vehicle with the owner's permission.[158] In these cases, the defendant can benefit from any defence available to the driver.[159]

Leaving the realm of liability for the action of another, another context of strict liability is private nuisance. Here liability is at least sometimes strict because, as also discussed in relation to English law, the defendant may be found liable even though they took all reasonable precautions. The classic example is that of a factory which, despite adopting reasonably expensive measures and advanced technology, cannot bring the level of pollution below a certain threshold and cannot therefore avoid a substantial harm to the neighbour's interest in the use and enjoyment of

---

[154] See *Appelhans v McFall*, 757 N.E.2d 987, 993 (Ill.2001).

[155] See eg MGLA Ch 231, § 85G (Massachusetts General Laws Annotated); § 3-112 of the New York General Obligations Law; Ann Cal Civ Code § 1714.1 (Annotated California Civil Code). See also Gilbert Geis and Arnold Binder, 'Sins of Their Children: Parental Responsibility for Juvenile Delinquency' (1991) 5 Notre Dame JL Ethics & Pub Pol'y 303, 309–12; Pamela K Graham, 'Parental Responsibility Laws: Let the Punishment Fit the Crime' (2000) 33 Loy LA L Rev 1719, 1725–29; Lisa Gentile, 'Parental Civil Liability for the Torts of Minors' (2007) 16 JCLI 125.

[156] See n 61 and accompanying text.

[157] *McPhee v Tufty*, 623 N.W.2d 390 (N.D.2001); *Malchose v Kalfell*, 664 N.W.2d 508 (N.D.2003); *Young v Beck*, 251 P.3d 380 (Ariz.2011).

[158] See Goldberg and others (n 111) 630–31. An example is New York Vehicle and Traffic Law § 388. Moreover, statutes which prescribe rules of conduct in the interest of road safety may be interpreted and applied so as to impose strict liability for traffic accidents: see eg ORCA § 4513.20 (Ohio Revised Code Annotated), which imposes on operators of motor vehicles an obligation to ensure that these are equipped with well-functioning brakes; on this basis, in *Spalding v Waxler*, 205 N.E.2d 890 (Ohio 1995), the defendant was found liable for an accident caused by a failure in his foot brake, even though he showed that the vehicle was regularly serviced, that the brakes had been inspected and adjusted less than six months prior to the accident, and that he had no warning that his foot brake would fail. See also *Chicago, Indianapolis & Louisville Railway v Stierwalt*, 153 N.E. 807 (Ind.1926) (concerning the equipment of motor vehicles for interstate commerce). cf Third Restatement LPEH §15, comment *c* (suggesting that the exercise of reasonable care should be a defence against tort claims in damages for the failure to comply with statutory strict duties). Note that, apart from instances where strict liability may be imposed by statute, at common law it is the tort of negligence that governs traffic accidents.

[159] Further examples of liability for the action of another include the liability of partners of a partnership for the torts committed by other partners (see *Kansallis Finance Ltd v Fern & Others*, 659 N.E.2d 731 (Mass.1996)), as well as the liability of participants in a joint enterprise for the torts committed by one or more of the participants (*Maselli v Ginner*, 809 P.2d 1181, 1184 (Idaho 1991)).

land.[160] If a balancing of all the stakes involved suggests that the interference with this interest is unreasonable,[161] the defendant will be found liable even though they adopted all reasonable precautions to avoid harm.

More complicated is the US law of defective products. So much has been written on it that '[t]he topic of products liability has sufficient material to support a separate law school course'.[162] For present purposes, however, it is sufficient to emphasize only a few key points. Strict product liability emerged in the United States in 1963 with *Greenman v Yuba Power Products, Inc*,[163] a decision that deeply influenced the drafting of § 402A of the Second Restatement which, published in 1965, has represented the reference point of product liability law over the subsequent three decades. Since the 1970s US courts, with the help of legal scholars, identified three types of defect, namely manufacturing defects, design defects, and warning defects.[164] The required standard of liability has generally varied according to the type of defect affecting the product. While it is uncontroversial that manufacturing defects were and are governed by strict liability, warning and design defects have generated both a long-lasting debate on the most appropriate standard of liability and a case law oscillating between strict liability and liability based on negligence. In this respect, it hardly makes sense to characterize the US position as embracing a unitary view, given the variety of approaches adopted across the fifty-one jurisdictions. It can be nevertheless observed that the 1998 Products Liability Restatement recommends what is, in essence, a negligence-based regime for both design and warning defects, therefore departing from § 402A of the Second Restatement.[165] While many jurisdictions now follow this approach, others do not,[166] and there are examples from the case law of decisions which apply strict liability to design or warning defects.[167] It remains to be seen whether the approach of the Products Liability Restatement will eventually prevail or whether the courts will instead

[160] eg *Jost v Dairyland Power Cooperative*, 172 N.W.2d 647 (Wis.1970). See also Gregory C Keating, 'Nuisance as a Strict Liability Wrong' (2012) 4(3) JTL, article 2. On private nuisance more generally, see §§ 822–831 of the Second Restatement.

[161] For guidance on this, see §§ 826–828 of the Second Restatement.

[162] Schwartz, Kelly, and Partlett (n 126) 768.

[163] 377 P.2d 897 (Cal.1963).

[164] This trifurcation of defectiveness is formally adopted by the *Restatement (Third) of Torts: Products Liability*, published in 1998 ('Products Liability Restatement'). A definition of each type of defect can be found in § 2 of this Restatement. For a detailed account of defectiveness, see David G Owen, *Products Liability Law* (3rd edn, West Academic Publishing 2015) 336–432 (on defectiveness in general), 433–76 (on manufacturing defects), 477–549 (on design defects), and 550–96 (on warning defects). The now frequent practice in European legal systems to distinguish between manufacturing, design, and warning defects is, by and large, a result of the influence exerted by the US law of product liability.

[165] For a very recent and critical appraisal of the approach of the Products Liability Restatement, see Gregory C Keating, 'Products Liability as Enterprise Liability' (2017) 10(1) JTL 41, 75–77.

[166] For a complete list in relation to design defects, see John Fabian Witt, *Torts: Cases, Principles, and Institutions* (2nd edn, CALI eLangdell Press 2016) 595–96.

[167] eg *Barker v Lull*, 573 P.2d 443, 454, 457 (Cal.1978); *Beshada v Johns-Manville Prods Corp*, 447 A.2d 539, 545–49 (N.J.1982); *Ayers v Johnson & Johnson Baby Prods Co*, 818 P.2d 1337 (Wash.1991); *Sternhagen v Dow Co*, 935 P.2d 1139 (Mont.1997); *Green v Smith & Nephew AHP, Inc*, 629 N.W.2d 727 (Wis.2001). See also the analysis of Keating (n 165) 80–92.

34 JUSTIFYING STRICT LIABILITY

prefer imposing strict liability even for these defects,[168] although the approach of the Restatement seems to have gained the ascendancy in recent times. In terms of defences, some courts align with § 402A of the Second Restatement and therefore reject contributory negligence as a defence to a strict liability claim, while recognizing assumption of risk[169] and misuse of product as defences barring recovery.[170] A majority of courts, however, adopt a regime of comparative responsibility and typically reduce damages if the victim was at fault.[171] Finally, the vast majority of jurisdictions recognize the 'state-of-the-art' defence (which is similar in function to the 'development risk' defence in European systems),[172] while a few of them reject it and therefore adopt a very rigorous strict liability.[173] In sum, strict liability plays an important role in the US law of defective products: it certainly applies to manufacturing defects and, in some situations and various forms, it may also apply to design and warning defects.

Finally, in keeping with the English approach to the liability of the Crown,[174] both the federal government of the United States and state governments have for a long time been immune from tort claims under the doctrine of sovereign immunity.[175] In addition, the states granted some degree of immunity from tort actions to local governments, municipalities, and other political subdivisions within them.[176] At both the federal and state level as well as at the level of state political subdivisions, these immunities have been waived at least to some extent, and today US public bodies are subjected to ordinary tort law doctrines, though with important limitations and qualifications which affect, among other things, the imposition of strict liability. At the federal level, the Federal Tort Claims Act (FTCA) provides that the United States is liable 'in the same manner and to the same extent

---

[168] *Godoy ex rel. Gramling v E.I. du Pont de Nemours & Co*, 768 N.W.2d 674, 690 (Wis.2009).

[169] Comment *n* to § 402A: 'If the user or consumer discovers the defect and is aware of the danger, and nevertheless proceeds unreasonably to make use of the product and is injured by it, he is barred from recovery.' See *Findlay v Copeland Lumber Co*, 509 P.2d 28, 31 (Ore.1973).

[170] Comment *h* to § 402A: '[a] product is not in a defective condition when it is safe for normal handling and consumption. If the injury results from abnormal handling, as where a bottled beverage is knocked against a radiator to remove the cap, or from abnormal preparation for use, as where too much salt is added to food, or from abnormal consumption, as where a child eats too much candy and is made ill, the seller is not liable.'

[171] eg *Daly v General Motors Corp*, 575 P.2d 1162 (Cal.1978). For a rich list of authorities, see the Reporters' Note on comment *a* and comment *d* to § 17 of the Products Liability Restatement.

[172] See eg *Vassallo v Baxter Healthcare Corp*, 696 N.E.2d 909 (Mass.1998); *Feldman v Lederle Laboratories*, 479 A.2d 374 (N.J.1984) (restricting *Beshada* (n 167) to its own circumstances); *Anderson v Owens-Corning Fiberglas Corp*, 810 P.2d 549 (Cal.1991).

[173] *Johnson v Raybestos-Manhattan, Inc.*, 740 P.2d 548 (Haw.1987); *Sternhagen* (n 167) 1144–47; *Brooks v Beech Aircraft Corp*, 902 P.2d 54, 63 (N.M.1995); *Townsend v Sears, Roebuck & Co*, 879 N.E.2d 893, 898–99 (Ill.2007). For a systematic discussion of the state-of-the-art defence in the US law of product liability and a detailed assessment of its status across the United States, see Owen (n 164) 656–87.

[174] See text to nn 87–92.

[175] Dan B Dobbs, Paul T Hayden, and Ellen M Bublick, *Hornbook on Torts* (2nd edn, West Academic Publishing 2016) 549–51.

[176] ibid 565–657.

as a private individual under like circumstances',[177] 'for injury or loss of property, or personal injury or death arising or resulting from the negligent or wrongful act or omission' of its employees while acting within the scope of their employment.[178] Therefore, the federal government is subject to the doctrine of *respondeat superior*. However, the FTCA adopts a less rigorous version of this doctrine than that at common law as it excludes the government's vicarious liability for certain intentional torts which, by contrast, would determine the imposition of vicarious liability on private defendants.[179] Moreover, the federal government cannot be held liable for damage caused in the performance of 'discretionary acts', where some element of judgment or choice is involved in the pursuit of governmental policies, while no immunity is preserved in relation to 'ministerial acts', where the acting person is merely following a prescribed course of action.[180] In addition to this, as interpreted by the US Supreme Court, the FTCA excludes the imposition of strict liabilities other than *respondeat superior*,[181] therefore improving considerably the position of federal bodies as compared to that of private actors.[182]

---

[177] 28 USC § 2674.

[178] 28 USC § 2679(b)(1).

[179] 28 USC § 2680(h). Note that, unlike private employees, federal employees usually enjoy statutory immunity from personal liability for the torts they commit within the scope of their employment (see 28 USC § 2679(b)), and a similar approach has been adopted in many states (see also Goldberg and others (n 111) 553, 626). However, there are pockets of employees' personal liability: at the federal level the so-called *Bivens* doctrine subjects federal officers to liability for violation of constitutional rights (see *Bivens v Six Unknown Named Agents of Federal Bureau of Narcotics*, 403 US 388 (1971)) and, at the state or municipal level, public officials may be liable for deprivation of federal 'rights, privileges, or immunities secured by the Constitution and laws' under colour of state law (see 42 USC § 1983). Note also that, at least in some cases, the violation of a constitutional or federal right may be classified as actionable per se, as it is independent of any actual injury to the claimant: see *Carey v Piphus*, 435 US 247, 266 (1978) (holding that 'the right to procedural due process is "absolute" in the sense that it does not depend upon the merits of a claimant's substantive assertions, and because of the importance to organized society that procedural due process be observed, ... we believe that the denial of procedural due process should be actionable for nominal damages without proof of actual injury'). On the other hand, many claims concerning the violation of such rights do involve the infliction of physical harm: see Dobbs, Hayden, and Bublick (n 175) 582 (specifically on claims under § 1983).

[180] See *Berkovitz v United States*, 486 US 531 (1988); *United States v Gaubert*, 499 US 315 (1991). While not appearing in these very decisions, the term 'ministerial' is commonly used in the United States to refer to situations where the public employee/official does not have any choice but to adhere to the relevant statute, regulation, or policy. The distinction between discretionary and ministerial functions is not without challenges and sometimes it may be difficult to draw it: see the remarks made in *Johnson v State of California*, 447 P.2d 352, 360–62 (Cal. 1968). On the tendency of courts to interpret broadly the discretion-based immunity and therefore to favour public bodies, see Dobbs, Hayden, and Bublick (n 175) 553–58.

[181] See *Dalehite v United States*, 346 US 15 (1953); and *Laird v Nelms*, 406 US 797 (1972). In the latter case, the Supreme Court held that the property damage suffered as a result of the sonic boom generated by air force aircraft was not actionable under the FTCA on the ground that it was not shown that the damage had been caused by negligence, and that the FTCA does not authorize the imposition of strict liability of any sort on the government.

[182] Other courts followed this approach: eg *Lively v United States*, 870 F.2d 296, 300 (5th Cir.1989) (holding that 'strict liability ... claims are not cognizable under the FTCA'); *Miller v United States*, 463 F.3d 1122, 1125 (10th Cir.2006) (holding that strict liability under dram shop acts is 'not within the scope of the FTCA's immunity waiver'); *In re Bomb Disaster at Roseville*, 438 F.Supp. 769 (Cal.1977) (holding that the FTCA did not waive government's immunity from claims based on the theory of strict product liability); *Roditis v United States*, 122 F.3d 108, 111–12 (2nd Cir.1997) (holding that the FTCA

36 JUSTIFYING STRICT LIABILITY

In keeping with the federal approach, many states distinguish between discretionary and ministerial functions, with immunity from liability being preserved for the former but not for the latter.[183] While it is true that most states have waived their own immunity and the immunity of local entities within them from liability in tort, whether by statute or by judge-made law, there are variations across the fifty-one jurisdictions in terms of scope and conditions of liability, including whether and to what extent strict liability may or may not apply. A systematic overview of state laws is beyond the scope of this work but, in broad terms, it is possible to say that, in most states, public bodies are generally liable on a vicarious basis for the torts committed by their employees,[184] and that, with differences from state to state, other strict liabilities may also be imposed.[185] In sum, although any broad

precludes the federal government's liability for harm caused by an independent contractor, even if state law would impose liability in such circumstances).

[183] As noted by Michael D Green and Jonathan Cardi, 'The Liability of Public Authorities in the United States' in Oliphant (ed) (n 93) 537, [12], some states such as North Carolina, Texas, or Ohio do not rely on the discretionary/ministerial distinction, and still use the governmental/proprietary one, which has been criticized and rejected at the federal level in *Indian Towing Company v United States*, 350 US 61, 65 (1955).

[184] Note that, under 42 USC § 1983 (authorizing tort claims for deprivation of federal rights), *respondeat superior* does not apply to local entities. These, according to the United States Supreme Court, can be held liable only if the deprivation arises from the local government's own policy or custom (the so-called official policy requirement): see *Monell v Department of Social Services of the City of New York*, 436 US 658, 694 (1978); *Owen v City of Independence*, 445 US 622 (1980) fn 39.

[185] For example, Ann Cal Gov Code §§ 814–895.8 (Annotated California Government Code) regulate the liability of public bodies and employees in California, the 'practical effect' of § 815 being 'to eliminate any common law governmental liability for damages arising out of torts' (Legislative Committee Comments–Senate to § 815). Against this backdrop, California imposes vicarious (and therefore strict) liability on public bodies for the harm tortiously caused by their employees (see § 815.2). Moreover, the California Government Code arguably imposes strict liability on public entities for the harm caused by the use of pesticides (§ 862(b)), although the strict nature of this liability remains uncertain given the absence of a judicial determination on the matter (as acknowledged in the Law Revision Commission comments; and see also *Farmers Ins Exchange v State of California*, 175 Cal.App.3d 494, 504 (Cal.1985)). In Pennsylvania, the relevant statutory provisions exclude, in principle, any governmental liability and then provide for specific exceptions to this, giving rise to instances of vicarious liability which generally require negligence in the conduct of the public servant: see 42 PaCSA PA ST Pt VII, Ch 85 (Pennsylvania Statutes and Consolidated Statutes). In Colorado, the relevant statutory provisions provide for a general immunity of the state and other local entities (see CRSA § 24-10-106(1) (Colorado Revised Statutes Annotated)); however, a list of activities which exceptionally trigger liability is provided and, for *some* of them, it is added that '[n]o rule of law imposing absolute or strict liability' can apply to public entities or employees: see CRSA § 24-10-106(4), CRSA § 24-10-106.1(4). As a result, strict liability may apply to activities other than these (eg the operation and maintenance of gas, electrical, power, or swimming facilities). By contrast, other states adopt a different starting-point, establishing that public bodies are generally liable in tort and then providing their own list of exceptions in which immunity from liability is retained: see eg HRS D 4, T 36, Ch 662 (Hawaii Revised Statutes Annotated) (regulating tort liability of the state); IC T 6, Ch 9 (Idaho Code Annotated) (regulating tort liability of the state and of local entities); ICA T XV, Subt 5, Chs 669–670 (Iowa Code Annotated) (regulating tort liability of the state and of local entities); MGLA Ch 258, §§ 2, 10 (Massachusetts General Laws Annotated) (regulating tort liability of the state and of local entities); MSA § 3.736 and § 466.02 (Minnesota Statutes Annotated) (regulating tort liability of the state and of local entities, respectively); NRS § 41.031 (Nevada Revised Statutes Annotated) (regulating tort liability of the state and of local entities); 12 VSA § 5601 (Vermont Statutes Annotated) (regulating tort liability of the state). In these states, strict liability may be imposed on public bodies as if they were private actors, unless expressly excluded. Still different is the approach adopted in states such as New Jersey, where the relevant legislation first establishes a general principle

STRICT LIABILITY IN THE FOUR TORT SYSTEMS: AN OVERVIEW   37

proposition runs the risk of oversimplification, it appears that, in keeping with the English approach, the laws of the United States have remained cautious in imposing tort liability on public bodies and that, although the doctrine of *respondeat superior* is certainly a significant aspect of public liability, the idea of subjecting public bodies to rules of strict liability is handled with care.

To conclude, over the course of the twentieth century, many legal scholars and judges have devoted increasing attention to strict liability and have managed to carve out considerable space for it in US tort law. Occasional interventions of state legislatures have also supported an expansion of strict liability, especially in the context of liability for the action of another. Compared to the English approach, US law places comparatively more reliance on strict liability, as shown by the development of the rule in *Rylands v Fletcher* into a general liability for abnormally dangerous activities, by the adoption of the 'family purpose' doctrine, and by the enactment of statutes imposing strict liability on parents and of statutes providing for the strict liability of dog owners. Special mention deserves to be made to liability for defective products, for this has been the major catalyst of strict liability theorists and progressive judges over the past fifty years, and it is therefore unsurprising that some state courts understand and apply the relevant law in a particularly rigorous way. In sum, despite the predominance of the tort of negligence and the attractiveness of the fault paradigm to many US legal actors, strict liability constitutes an important part of tort law in the United States.

2.4 Strict Liability in French Law

The general law of what is now called French extra-contractual liability is set out in Book III ('The Different Ways of Acquiring Ownership'), Title III ('The Sources of Obligations'), Sub-title II ('Extra-Contractual Liability') of the *Code civil* (Cc).[186]

---

of vicarious liability for all public entities (NJSA §59:2-2), with exceptions (NJSA §§ 59:2-3 to 59:2-10), and then provides that '[n]o judgment shall be granted against a public entity or public employee on the basis of strict liability, implied warranty or products liability' (NJSA § 59:9-2) (New Jersey Statutes Annotated) (regulating tort liability of the state and of local entities). Similarly, in New Mexico the liability of public entities is based on 'the traditional tort concepts of duty and the reasonably prudent person's standard of care in the performance of that duty', and the state Tort Claims Act 'in no way imposes a strict liability for injuries upon governmental entities or public employees' (see NMSA § 41-4-2 (New Mexico Statutes Annotated). Finally, in some states the waiver of immunity is particularly broad, with the state or other local entity being liable in tort 'to the same extent as if [they] were a private person or corporation', this arguably including their exposure to any rule of strict liability which is recognized at common law: see eg RCWA § 4.92.090 and § 4.96.010 (Revised Code of Washington Annotated) (regulating tort liability of the state and of local entities, respectively). Note that neither legislators nor judges are generally liable in the United States for the harm they cause in the exercise of their legislative or judicial functions: see Dobbs, Hayden, and Bublick (n 175) 568, 577–78, 581; Green and Cardi (n 183) [36]–[37].

[186] The current structure of Book III is the result of the reform enacted by the 'Ordonnance of 2016' (*Ordonnance* no 2016-131 of 10.2.2016 *portant réforme du droit des contrats, du régime général et de la*

38 JUSTIFYING STRICT LIABILITY

Since its enactment in 1804, the *Code* has sought to regulate all cases of extra-contractual liability by a handful of very general rules.[187] From the perspective of the required standard of conduct, these rules are sometimes presented in a binary way, with 'liability for fault' (*responsabilité pour faute*) on one side and 'liability without fault' or 'strict liability' (*responsabilité sans faute, responsabilité de plein droit*) on the other.[188] Belonging to the first group are the first two provisions in Sub-title II, articles 1240–1241 (former articles 1382–1383) Cc, which establish respectively that '[a]ny human action whatsoever which causes harm to another creates an obligation in the person by whose fault it was caused to make reparation for it', and that '[e]veryone is liable for the harm which he has caused not only by his action, but also by his failure to act or his lack of care'. Under these provisions, a defendant is liable if they failed to act as a *bon père de famille* or as a *personne raisonnable* (the French equivalent of the 'reasonable person'), meaning that they failed to comply with 'a general norm of social conduct which requires of individuals to act with prudence and diligence'.[189]

By contrast, the second group of provisions, which is often portrayed in the literature as going under the banner of *responsabilité sans faute*, comprises articles 1242–1244 (former articles 1384–1386) Cc as well as other rules located outside the *Code civil*,[190] almost all of which now impose liability regardless of whether the

---

preuve des obligations as amended by *loi* no 2018-287 of 20.4.2018 *ratifiant l'ordonnance* no 2016-131 of 10.2.2016 *portant réforme du droit des contrats, du régime général et de la preuve des obligations*). For an overview of the changes introduced by the *Ordonnance* of 2016, see Pietro Sirena, 'The New Design of the French Law of Contract and Obligations: An Italian View' in John Cartwright and Simon Whittaker (eds), *The Code Napoléon Rewritten* (Hart Publishing 2017) 339.

[187] In 1998, however, many new provisions were added to the *Code* to implement the Product Liability Directive: see text to n 230. Moreover, in 2017 the French Ministry of Justice published a draft parliamentary bill (the *Projet de réforme*) which, if enacted, would introduce important substantive changes to this area of French law (the *Projet* is available at <http://www.justice.gouv.fr/publication/>). For a comparative discussion of many of these changes, see Jean-Sébastien Borghetti and Simon Whittaker (eds), *French Civil Liability in Comparative Perspective* (Hart Publishing 2019).

[188] See Jonas Knetsch, 'The Role of Liability without Fault' in Borghetti and Whittaker (n 187) 123, 125 (referring to François Terré and others, *Droits civil, Les obligations* (12th edn, Dalloz 2018) [905]ff). For a similar example, see Philippe Malaurie, Laurent Aynès, and Philippe Stoffel-Munck, *Droit des obligations* (11th edn, LGDJ 2020) 43. It should be noted that in French law the notion of *faute* goes beyond a defective conduct in the defendant. In keeping with the US approach, *faute* extends to the violation of statutory rules or administrative regulations, regardless of whether the defendant acted negligently: see Patrice Jourdain in Geneviève Viney, Patrice Jourdain, and Suzanne Carval (eds), *Les conditions de la responsabilité. Traité de droit civil* (4th edn, LGDJ 2013) [448]. But French law goes even farther than this: every criminal offence is in itself a 'fault' for the purposes of civil liability (see Whittaker (n 2) 368–73); furthermore, *faute* plays the role which in common law systems is performed by the defining characteristics of individual torts, such as the duty of care in the tort of negligence, and by the general clause of 'unlawfulness of harm' (*ingiustizia del danno*) in article 2043 of the Italian *Codice civile*, all setting the scope of liability by selecting the rights or interests deemed to deserve tort protection (for a comparative overview on this, see Pier Giuseppe Monateri, *La Responsabilità Civile. Trattato di Diritto Civile* (UTET 1998) 54–64).

[189] Jourdain (n 188) [450].

[190] See text to nn 240–253 in this section.

defendant acted as a *personne raisonnable*.[191] The French habit of presenting 'fault' (*responsabilité pour faute*) and 'strict liability' (*responsabilité sans faute*) as clearly distinct, if not opposed, reflects the idea that it is appealing to distinguish between the two, even if only for reasons of a clearer and neater exposition of the law.[192] At the same time, though, the positive law suggests that liability rules can vary in their degree of strictness,[193] at times even substantially, therefore suggesting that, in keeping with the English and the US position, these rules may be placed along a continuum. As will be seen below, French law contains many rules of strict liability, their number and (sometimes extreme) rigour showing very well the French strong attachment to strict liability as compared to the other three legal systems studied.

As a starting point, article 1242(1) (former article 1384(1)) Cc provides that 'one is liable not only for the harm which one causes by one's own action but also for that which is caused by the action of persons for whom one is responsible, or of things which one has in one's keeping'. While at the time of enactment of the *Code* this article was arguably meant to be merely an introduction to subsequent provisions,[194] in the late nineteenth century it was reinterpreted as an independent ground of liability for the harm caused by the deeds of things in one's 'keeping' (*garde*).[195] This rule applies in principle to all physical things, with no distinction being made on the basis of the thing's dangerousness or defectiveness.[196] The person liable is the 'keeper' (*gardien*), with la *garde* being defined as the 'the use, direction, and control' of the thing.[197] To escape liability, the *gardien* must show the existence of a fortuitous event—either a force of nature, an action of a third party, or an action, innocent or careless, of the victim—which is causally linked to the victim's harm and which bears the characteristics of *force majeure*: it must be 'unforeseeable' and 'irresistible'[198] as well as 'exterior to the thing'.[199][200] If the victim's conduct does not

---

[191] cf article 1242(6),(8) Cc, establishing that teachers are liable for the harm caused by their pupils if the claimant can prove the teacher's 'fault, lack of care or failure to act'.

[192] Knetsch (n 188) 125.

[193] ibid 126–27; Whittaker (n 2) 389–408.

[194] Malaurie, Aynès, and Stoffel-Munck (n 188) [115].

[195] Civ 16.6.1896 (*Teffaine*), D 1897.1.433 note Saleilles.

[196] Ch réun 13.2.1930 (*Jand'heur*), D 1930.1.57 note Ripert. However, article 1242 Cc does not apply to motor vehicle accidents falling within the scope of the *loi Badinter*, nor to accidents caused by defective products falling within the scope of the Product Liability Directive as implemented in France in 1998 below: Jean-Sébastien Borghetti and Simon Whittaker, 'Principles of Liability or a Law of Torts?' in Jean-Sébastien Borghetti and Simon Whittaker (eds), *French Civil Liability in Comparative Perspective* (Hart Publishing 2019) 455, 464. Furthermore, article 1242 Cc does not apply to liability for animals and to liability for ruinous buildings either, regulated respectively by articles 1243 and 1244. Finally, under article 1242(2), the person who holds property in which a fire has arisen will be liable to third parties for harm caused by that fire only upon proof of their fault or of the fault of persons for whom they are responsible.

[197] Ch réun 2.12.1941 (*Franck*), S 1941.1.217 note H Mazeaud.

[198] Ass plén 14.4.2006, Bull AP no 6, 2006.

[199] Cass civ 23.1.1945, S 1946-47.1.57. See also Malaurie, Aynès, and Stoffel-Munck (n 188) [123] (noting that 'exteriority to the thing' is no longer mentioned by the courts but that nevertheless it is an underlying ingredient of *force majeure* in the context of liability for the deeds of things).

[200] Jourdain (n 188) [667]. The defence of *force majeure* was already recognized in 1896 in *Teffaine* (n 195) and, since then, it has been defined judicially for extra-contractual matters. By contrast, in

constitute *force majeure*, but they were at fault and contributed to the realization of harm, the defendant's liability will be reduced accordingly (defence of *faute de la victime*).[201] Therefore, as absence of failures in the defendant's conduct is not a good defence, French liability for the deeds of things can be seen as strict, even if the intense process of elaboration, interpretation, and reinterpretation of the various elements of this liability has at times called into question its strict nature.[202]

Other strict liabilities are those for the action of animals and for ruinous buildings. Article 1243 (former article 1385) Cc imposes liability on the owner or user of an animal, and this includes any type of animal, except wildlife.[203] The fundamental condition for imposing liability is use of the animal, with liability being normally imposed on its owner, who is typically also its user.[204] The following provision, article 1244 (former article 1386) Cc, imposes liability for damage caused by a ruinous building, with the claimant having to prove that the damage was caused by a defect in the maintenance or construction of the building. As with liability for the deeds of things, under both articles 1243 and 1244 Cc liability can be avoided in cases of *force majeure* or its extent reduced in case of *faute de la victime*.[205] Again, as proof of diligence does not excuse the defendant, liability under both provisions is strict.

Other strict liabilities featuring in French law are those imposed for harm caused by another person's action, found in article 1242 Cc. Article 1242(1) provides that a person 'is liable for the harm caused by the action of persons for whom he is responsible'.[206] This general statement was originally meant to provide only an introduction to the specific liabilities envisaged in the subsequent *alinéas* of the same article: liability of parents for the harm caused by their children who live with them (article 1242(4), (7)), liability of masters and employers for the harm caused by their servants and employees (article 1242(5)), liability of teachers for the harm caused by their pupils (article 1242(6), (8)), and liability of craftsmen for the harm caused by their apprentices (article 1242(6)–(7)). More recently, however, the Cour de cassation has held that there may be additional instances of liability for another's action on the basis of article 1242(1) Cc in situations other than

contractual matters it is defined by article 1218 Cc. This 'asymmetry' between contract and tort would be removed by the *Projet de réforme*, as proposed article 1253 would provide a definition of *force majeure* that is specific to extra-contractual matters.

[201] Malaurie, Aynès, and Stoffel-Munck (n 188) [122]; Civ (2) 6.4.1987.

[202] Whittaker (n 74) 52–59, 633–34 (on the notion of *garde*, causation, and defences); Jourdain (n 188) [660], [675]–[675-1] (on *la garde*); Mireille Bacache-Gibeili, *Les obligations, La responsabilité civile extracontractuelle* (3rd edn, Economica 2016) [255]ff (on *la garde*).

[203] Malaurie, Aynès, and Stoffel-Munck (n 188) [113].

[204] However, if at the time of the accident the animal is with someone else who has its 'use, direction, and control', liability will be attributed to this person: ibid [114].

[205] Civ (1) 3.3.1964; Jourdain (n 188) [729] (ruinous buildings); Civ (2) 19.2.1992; Jourdain (n 188) [702] (animals).

[206] For an analysis which compares the French liability for the action of another (both in its current form and as envisaged in the *Projet de réforme*) with the relevant English and German law, see Birke Häcker, 'Fait d'autrui in Comparative Perspective' in Borghetti and Whittaker (n 187) 143.

STRICT LIABILITY IN THE FOUR TORT SYSTEMS: AN OVERVIEW   41

those encompassed by *alinéas* 4–7, although the scope and impact of this decision is not yet entirely clear.[207] The relevant case law has shaped two main categories of cases: the first regards situations where the defendant has the power to organize and control the way of life of another person, for example a delinquent minor or an adult with physical or mental impairments;[208] the second concerns situations where the defendant supervises or organizes the activity of another, without any need for the physical author of harm to be physically or mentally impaired.[209] Defendants in both categories of cases are subjected to strict liability,[210] as proof of diligence is no answer to a claim for damages and the defendant can escape liability by proving *force majeure* or obtain its reduction by proving *faute de la victime*.[211] Noteworthy is the fact that the regime applied to defendants in the second class of cases may change in the future and be based on a presumption of fault, should the *Projet de réforme* become law.[212]

Moving to the liability of parents (article 1242(4), (7) Cc), the *Code civil* states that parents can escape liability by proving that 'they could not avoid the harm' caused by their children. French courts long interpreted this defence as based on fault, meaning that parents could avoid liability by proving that they fulfilled their duties of upbringing and surveillance.[213] After a period of uncertainty and oscillating case law,[214] the Cour de cassation eventually held that parents are strictly liable for the harmful action of their children,[215] with the only available defences being *force majeure* and *faute de la victime*.[216] Moreover, it was later established that it is enough for the action of the minor to be the 'direct cause of harm',[217] without any need for the latter's conduct to be at fault in any way.[218] These judicial developments have rendered parental liability extremely strict.

---

[207] Ass plén 29.3.1991 (*Blieck*), JCP 1991.II.169, n.21673 note Ghestin. For a detailed analysis of the significance of *Blieck*, see Geneviève Viney in Viney, Jourdain, and Carval (eds), *Les conditions de la responsabilité. Traité de droit civil* (n 188) [789-8]–[789-27].

[208] See Viney (n 207) [789-15].

[209] Malaurie, Aynès, and Stoffel-Munck (n 188) [88]. This type of liability has been applied so far almost exclusively in the context of sporting events: see Civ (2) 22.5.1995, RTD civ 1995.899 note Jourdain (liability of a rugby club for the death and injuries that its own players caused to the players of the rival team); Civ (2) 12.12.2002, RTD civ 2003.305 note Jourdain (liability of a club of *majorettes* for the injuries one of the *majorettes* caused to another member by mishandling her baton).

[210] Viney (n 207) [789-21] (regarding the first type of cases) and [789-24] (regarding the second type of cases). The same solution is adopted in articles 1246–1247 *Projet de réforme*.

[211] ibid [789-23] and [789-27]; Malaurie, Aynès, and Stoffel-Munck (n 188) [88].

[212] Article 1248 *Projet de réforme*. See also *Rapport Bigot-Reichardt*, 32–33.

[213] Civ (2) 12.10.1955, D 1956.301 note Rodière.

[214] Viney (n 207) [870].

[215] Civ (2) 19.2.1997 (*Bertrand*), D 1997.265 note Jourdain; Ass plén 13.12.2002, D 2003.4.231 note Jourdain, 'La responsabilité des père et mère: une responsabilité principale et directe, indépendante de celle du mineur'.

[216] eg *Bertrand* (n 215); Civ (2) 2.12.1998, Bull civ II no 292, 1998; Civ (2) 29.4.2004, Bull civ II no 202, 2004.

[217] Ass plén 9.5.1984 (*Fullenwarth*), D 1984.525 note Chabas.

[218] Civ (2) 10.5.2001 (*Levert*), D 2001.2851 note Tournafond. This position was later confirmed in Ass plén 13.12.2002 (n 215). The current reform project, judging this development as too extreme, would remove it by requiring that the action of the physical author of harm be of a nature to engage their own

42 JUSTIFYING STRICT LIABILITY

Another remarkably strict liability is that of employers for the harm caused by their employees (article 1242(5) Cc).[219] There are three requirements for the imposition of this liability. First, there must be a 'relationship of subordination' (*lien de préposition*) between employer and employee, consisting in the employer's power to give orders or instructions to the employee in relation to the performance of the latter's functions. This relationship is not confined to cases of employment proper and is interpreted in a very expansive way, as shown by the case law.[220] Secondly, the harmful action must be of a nature to engage liability in the physical author of harm, the employee.[221] Thirdly, the harm must have been caused in the course of employment, the Cour de cassation finally holding that the employer is liable for the action of the employee unless the former proves that 'the employee acted outside the functions for which he was employed, without authorisation, and for purposes alien to his attributions'.[222] Employers' vicarious liability is clearly strict because once the claimant has shown that the three requirements above are met, the employer cannot escape liability by proving that they acted diligently or even that, from their point of view, the employee's action bore the features of *force majeure*.[223] If, though, the claimant's negligent conduct contributed to the causation of harm, the defendant will be able to obtain a reduction in damages.[224]

As to the liability of teachers for their pupils' actions, a series of legislative measures have been enacted, imposing strict liability on the state if the teacher whose fault allowed a pupil's harmful conduct works in public schools or in schools having a contract (*contrat d'association*) with the state.[225] If instead the teacher works in a private school, the teacher is personally liable only if their fault is proven under article 1242(6), (8) Cc,[226] while the school will be strictly liable as an employer pursuant to article 1242(5).[227] Finally, as to craftsmen, while article 1242(7)

---

liability in tort (see article 1245(1) *Projet de réforme*, and *Rapport Bigot-Reichardt*, 28). This approach is part of a view which sees liability for the action of another as combined with other heads of liability, such as liability for fault or liability for the deeds of things: the latter type of liability (for fault, for things) must be established in the physical author of harm before the defendant can be held vicariously liable for the damage caused: see generally on this Jean-Sébastien Borghetti and Denis Mazeaud, 'Imputation du dommage causé à autrui' in François Terré (ed), *Pour une réforme du droit de la responsabilité civile* (Dalloz 2011) 149, 154–55.

[219] While article 1242(5) Cc refers to the notions of *commettants* and *maîtres* as liable parties and to *domestiques* and *préposés* as the physical authors of harm, for reasons of convenience I simply refer to employers and employees.

[220] Cass crim 20.5.1976, RTD civ 1976.786 obs Durry (an election candidate was found liable for the harm that his supporters caused to those of another candidate, on the ground that he had the power to give them orders). For other examples, see Viney (n 207) [792].

[221] Malaurie, Aynès, and Stoffel-Munck (n 188) [100].

[222] Ass plén 19.5.1988. This solution is also adopted in article 1249 *Projet de réforme*.

[223] Viney (n 207) [809].

[224] ibid.

[225] *Loi* 20.7.1899 and *loi* 5.4.1937. See Muriel Fabre-Magnan, *Droit des obligations. 2—Responsabilité civile et quasi-contrats* (4th edn, PUF 2019) [425].

[226] See Malaurie, Aynès, and Stoffel-Munck (n 188) [93]; Fabre-Magnan (n 225) [424]–[425].

[227] Viney (n 207) [917].

STRICT LIABILITY IN THE FOUR TORT SYSTEMS: AN OVERVIEW   43

Cc subjects them to the same burden of proof envisaged for parents (no liability upon proof that 'they could not avoid the harm'), it is still unclear whether this imposes strict liability[228] or liability based on a presumption of fault.[229]

Another significant area of liability is that of defective products, currently governed by articles 1245–1245-17 Cc, implementing the Product Liability Directive.[230] Despite the fact that article 1245-10 Cc formally characterizes the producer's liability as strict and does not include proof of diligent conduct among the available defences, the nature of liability for products is controversial. Indeed, it has been suggested that the judicial assessment of the notion of defect actually involves an evaluation of the producer's conduct,[231] and that liability would be based on fault in cases of design defect or failures in the duty to warn, with strict liability operating in cases of manufacturing defect only.[232] However, and despite these controversies, the narrative of product liability as essentially strict is widespread among French legal scholars,[233] and it is reinforced by the debate which has preceded and accompanied the implementation of the Product Liability Directive.[234] In particular, the implementing process has been long and difficult because French law had already adopted a combination of contractual and extra-contractual rules resulting in a strict liability of sellers and manufacturers.[235] For this reason, French legal actors were hostile to some of the rules in the Directive, most notably that allowing the development risk defence,[236] which seemed to water down the protection already guaranteed to victims of defective products.[237] As a result, while

---

[228] ibid [893] (arguing that the liability of craftsmen is, in essence, assimilated to that of parents and would therefore be strict).

[229] Malaurie, Aynès, and Stoffel-Munck (n 188) [92]. Under article 1248 *Projet de réforme*, the liability of craftsmen for the action of their apprentices would be based on a presumption of fault.

[230] This was originally transposed in France by *loi* no 98-389 of 19.5.1998.

[231] See Whittaker (n 74) 483–84 (citing François Xavier Testu and Jean-Hubert Moitry, 'La responsabilité du fait des produits défectueux, Commentaire de la loi 98-389 du 19 mai 1998' Dalloz affaires (16 July 1998) Suppl to No 125, 5, 7).

[232] Jean-Sébastien Borghetti, *La Responsabilité du Fait des Produits: Etude de Droit Comparé* (LGDJ 2004) [667]–[669]. For more general remarks on the allegedly fault-based nature of product liability, see Pascal Oudot, 'L'application et le fondement de la loi du 19 mai 2008 instituant la responsabilité du fait des produits défectueux: les leçons du temps', Gaz Pal 15.11.2008, 6.

[233] Geneviève Viney in Geneviève Viney, Patrice Jourdain, and Suzanne Carval (eds), *Les régimes spéciaux et l'assurance de responsabilité. Traité de droit civil* (4th edn, LGDJ 2017) [14], [22]; Jérôme Huet, 'Responsabilité du fait des produits défectueux. Objectifs, portée et mise en œuvre de la directive 85/374' JCl E, fasc 2020 (updated 15.2.2017) [19], [60]; Jacques Flour, Jean-Luc Aubert, and Eric Savaux, *Droit civil. Les obligations. 2. Le fait juridique* (14th edn, Dalloz 2011) [300].

[234] See generally Jean-Sébastien Borghetti, 'The Development of Product Liability in France' in Simon Whittaker (ed), *The Development of Product Liability* (CUP 2010) 87.

[235] See Whittaker (n 2) 403–08.

[236] Viney (n 233) [54]–[57]. Other controversial issues regarded the liability of suppliers on the same basis as that of producers and the *obligation de suivi des produits* (an obligation of producers and suppliers to monitor the safety of their products once put on the market, its fulfilment working as a condition of the development risk defence), which were included in the French implementing law but later declared incompatible with the Directive by the CJEU (*Commission v France*, Case C-52/00, [36]–[48]): see Whittaker (n 74) 458–60; Pascal Oudot, 'La piège communautaire de la responsabilité du fait des produits défectueux' Dr & patrim, January 2003, no 111, 40, 42.

[237] Patrice Jourdain, 'Commentaire de la loi no 98-389 du 19 mai 1998 sur la responsabilité du fait des produits défectueux' JCP E 1998.1204, [77] ; Jean Calais-Auloy, 'Le risque de développement: une

44 JUSTIFYING STRICT LIABILITY

French law has in principle adopted this defence, it has departed from it where the harm is caused 'by an element of the human body or by its products'.[238] And the scope of application of this defence may be further reduced if the *Projet de réforme* of French tort law were enacted because the defence would no longer apply wherever the harm is caused 'by any health product for human use', which is the type of situation where the defence is most often invoked these days.[239] Here again, then, all the French propensity for strict and broad liability rules is displayed.

Further areas of strict liability can be found outside the *Code*, most notably traffic accidents, nuisance (*troubles du voisinage*), and medical accidents, all regulated by special legislation.[240] Traffic accidents were long governed by liability for the deeds of things but, due to the intensification of motoring and the increase in the number of deaths and injuries caused by traffic accidents, special legislation became necessary.[241] The French legislator, under the pressure of legal scholars and the Cour de cassation, eventually enacted the *loi* no 85-677 of 5 July 1985 (*loi* Badinter).[242] The regime set up by the *loi* is extremely strict: the driver or keeper of the vehicle is liable on the basis of the mere 'involvement' (*implication*) of the vehicle in the accident;[243] furthermore, liability cannot be avoided even if the harm was caused by

exonération contestable' in *Mélanges Michel Cabrillac* (Dalloz/Litec 1999) 81. cf François Ewald, 'La véritable nature du risque de développement et sa garantie' Risques, 1993, no 14, 9; Christian Gollier, 'Le risque de développement est-il assurable?' Risques, 1993, no 14, 49.

[238] Article 1245-11 Cc. This exception was admitted as a reaction to a major scandal involving the safety of blood products contaminated with HIV, on which see Whittaker (n 74) 149–51, 315–19, 324, 394–401.

[239] Article 1298-1 *Projet de réforme*. See Viney (n 233) [57].

[240] The *Projet de réforme* would incorporate the statutes governing traffic accidents and *troubles du voisinage* in the *Code civil* as articles 1285–1288 and 1244, respectively. By contrast, liability for medical accidents would continue to be regulated by *loi* no 2002-303 of 4.3.2002. Other examples of strict liability outside the *Code* include liability for nuclear installations (regulated by a plethora of international conventions and domestic laws) and liability for accidents caused by airplanes (article L 141-2 of the *Code de l'aviation civile*). For a general overview of these and other special contexts of liability, see Geneviève Viney, *Introduction à la responsabilité. Traité de droit civil* (4th edn, LGDJ 2019) [24].

[241] Geneviève Viney and Anne Guégan-Lécuyer, 'The Development of Traffic Liability in France' in Wolfgang Ernst (ed), *The Development of Traffic Liability* (CUP 2010) 50, 60–69.

[242] André Tunc, *La sécurité routière: esquisse d'une loi sur les accidents de la circulation* (Dalloz 1966); André Tunc, 'Les causes d'exonération de la responsabilité de plein droit de l'art. 1384, al. 1er du Code civil' D chron 1975.83. See also Civ (2) 21.7.1982 (*Desmares*), D 1982.449 note Larroumet, where the Cour held that the victim's fault could exclude liability only where it constituted *force majeure*. This decision pushed the legislator to take action and enact the *loi* Badinter. This statute in turn triggered a *revirement* of the Cour de cassation, which held that the victim's fault could impact on the defendant's liability even if it did not constitute *force majeure*: Civ (2) 6.4.1987.

[243] Article 1 of the *loi* Badinter. On the notion of *implication*, see Sabine Abravanel-Jolly, 'Art. 1382 à 1386—Fasc. 280-10: RÉGIMES DIVERS. —Circulation routière. —Indemnisation des victimes d'accidents de la circulation. —Droit à indemnisation' JCl Civil Code (updated 28.11.2018) [37]–[54]. For a striking application of this rule, see Civ (2) 23.5.2002, RCA 2002, comm n.258: a passenger got out of a motor vehicle which had stopped and was then killed by a rotten tree which fell on them and on the vehicle; the Cour de cassation held that, in holding the driver of the car not liable on the basis that the victim died because of the tree fall and 'independently of the presence of the vehicle close to where it fell', the lower court violated article 1 of the *loi* Badinter. Arguably, *implication* does not play in the *loi* Badinter the same role that causation plays in other heads of liability, as it does not link a *fait générateur* (eg 'fault', the 'deeds of things', or the 'action of another') to a harm but rather it works as a criterion of

force majeure,[244] and the victim's fault can be used as a defence only if it was at once inexcusable and the exclusive cause of injury.[245] The striking rigour with which the position of drivers and keepers of motor vehicles is treated constitutes a perfect example of the attractiveness of strict liability among French lawyers.

Turning to *troubles du voisinage*, French courts have developed this liability rule since the mid-nineteenth century,[246] and for a long time based it, at least formally, on fault.[247] Today, however, it seems enough that the defendant violates the principle that 'nothing must cause an excessive inconvenience as between neighbours' (*nul ne doit causer à autrui un trouble anormal du voisinage*),[248] whether or not they were at fault.[249] Liability is, again, strict, as it can be avoided only by proof of *force majeure*.[250]

In relation to medical accidents, legislation was enacted in 2002 to bring order in a rather chaotic area of French civil liability.[251] This legislation provides that, except where harm is caused by a defective product (where the law on liability for products applies), professionals such as doctors, midwives, or dental surgeons as well as 'any establishment, service or bodies in which individual acts of prevention, diagnosis or care take place are liable for the harmful consequences of acts of prevention, diagnosis or care only in the case of fault'.[252] Therefore, where individual 'acts of prevention, diagnosis or care' cause harm to a patient in a hospital or clinic, this will be strictly liable to them for the careless conduct of the person performing the harmful act. Furthermore, healthcare establishments are also strictly liable 'for harm resulting from hospital-acquired infections, unless they establish the existence of a *cause étrangère*' (ie *force majeure*).[253]

---

attribution of liability (*critère d'imputation*), in the sense that it identifies the party liable for the accident: see Jean-Sébastien Borghetti, 'L'accident fait générateur de responsabilité' RCA 7–8 July 2015, dossier 3, 12, [18]–[22].

[244] Article 2 of the *loi* Badinter, which applies to both bodily injury and damage to property.

[245] Article 3 of the *loi* Badinter. Moreover, this defence cannot apply (i) against victims aged less than sixteen or older than seventy; or regardless of their age, (ii) against victims whose disability is greater than 80 per cent at the time of the accident. For these classes of victims, the defendant can only escape liability if the victim exposed themselves intentionally to the harm (ibid). It must be noted, though, that in cases of damage to property, the victim's fault can reduce or exclude liability (article 5).

[246] Civ 27.11.1844, S 1844.1.211.

[247] See Patrice Jourdain in Viney, Jourdain, and Carval (eds), *Les régimes spéciaux et l'assurance de responsabilité* (n 233) [180].

[248] Civ (2) 28.6.1995, Bull civ II no 222, p 128, 1995.

[249] Civ (3) 4.2.1971, Bull civ III no 80, p 58, 1971; Civ (3) 12.2.1992, Bull civ III no 44, p 27, 1992; Civ (3) 10.12.2014, Bull civ III no 164, 2014.

[250] See Jourdain (n 247) [184]; Guy Courtieu, 'Art. 1382 à 1386—Fasc. 265-10: RÉGIMES DIVERS. — Troubles de voisinage' JCl Civil Code, 27.11.2017, [81], [85]. See Civ (2) 5.2.2004, Bull civ II no 49, p 40, 2004; Civ (3) 10.12.2014, Bull civ III no 164, 2014.

[251] *Loi* no 2002-303 of 4.3.2002, whose article 98 created Title IV of Book 1 of the legislative part of the *Code de la santé publique*. This statute does not make clear whether liability for medical accidents is contractual or extra-contractual.

[252] Article L 1142-1 of the *Code de la santé publique*.

[253] ibid.

46 JUSTIFYING STRICT LIABILITY

Finally, strict liability features conspicuously in French law in relation to the liability of public entities. Unlike in England and in the United States, where in principle the same body of law governs both disputes between private parties and disputes involving the state or some other public authority, French law possesses a special body of law governing the liability of public authorities (*responsabilité administrative* or *responsabilité de la puissance publique*) and also a separate administrative law jurisdiction, at the apex of which is the Conseil d'État.[254] In recognizing for the first time in 1873 in *Blanco* that the state could be liable to persons injured by the actions of its officials, the Tribunal des conflits rejected the applicability of the general provisions on delictual liability in the *Code civil* to public bodies on the ground that French public liability has its 'own special rules which vary according to the needs of the service and the necessity to reconcile the rights of the state with private rights'.[255] While the special character of French administrative law has sometimes protected French public bodies from liability, it has also imposed upon them special and strict liabilities. In contrast with the English or US approach, French law provides for an extensive regime of liabilities in public bodies, based on the distinction between 'administrative liability for fault' (*la responsabilité administrative pour faute*) and 'administrative liability without fault' (*la responsabilité administrative sans faute*).[256] In the realm of liability for fault, the key concept is that of *faute de service*, which refers to any malfunctioning in the administrative machinery or in the execution of a public service and which entitles the victims of such failures to claim damages for the losses suffered.[257] *Faute de service* covers both the fault of public employees, for whose harmful action the administration is liable,[258] and the fault of the administrative system taken as a whole,[259] examples of the latter being the inadequate education provided in school or the death of a

[254] See L Neville Brown and John S Bell, *French Administrative Law* (5th edn, OUP 1998)chs 3–6.

[255] TC 8.2.1873, D 1873.3.17 (*Blanco*) (trans L Neville Brown and John S Bell, *French Administrative Law* (5th edn, OUP 1998) 183). Note, however, that in situations where a public service is in concession to a private company instead of being run directly by the competent public body, liability of the company for the harm caused to third parties will be governed by the law of extra-contractual liability: see John Bell, 'The Reform of Delict in the Civil Code and Liability in Administrative Law' in Borghetti and Whittaker (n 187) 425, 426.

[256] Yves Gaudemet, *Droit Administratif* (23rd edn, LGDJ 2020) [367].

[257] See René Chapus, *Droit administratif général*, vol 1 (15th edn, Montchrestien 2001) [1450]–[1454]; John Bell, 'Administrative Law' in John Bell and others, *Principles of French Law* (2nd edn, OUP 2008) 168, 90; Duncan Fairgrieve and François Lichere, 'The Liability of Public Authorities in France' in Oliphant (ed) (n 93) 155, [30]–[32]. On the notion of *faute de service*, see generally Michel Paillet and Emmanuel Breen, 'FAUTE DE SERVICE. —Notion' JCl Admin, Fasc 818, 2008(updated in 2011).

[258] There are, however, limits to this administrative liability. If the employee's fault amounts to a 'personal fault' (*faute personnelle*), meaning that their harmful action was sufficiently detached from the public service, then the employee may be held personally liable (even though it is often open to the victim to sue both the employee and the administration): see TC 30.7.1873 (*Pelletier*), D 1874.3.5; CE 3.2.1911 (*Anguet*), S 1911.3.137; CE 26.7.1918 (*Lemonnier*), D 1918.3.9; CE Ass 28.7.1951 (*Laruelle et Delville*), D 1951.620 note Nguyen Do; Chapus (n 257) [1523]–[1535]; Bell (n 257) 191; Fairgrieve and Lichere (n 257) [37]–[42].

[259] Duncan Fairgrieve, *State Liability in Tort: A Comparative Law Study* (OUP 2003) 102–03; Bell (n 257) 190–92; Gaudemet (n 256) [368].

patient in a hospital due to staff shortages.[260] Moreover, French administrative law recognizes different degrees of *faute*, depending on the type of action or activity undertaken by the relevant public body. In many situations, an 'ordinary fault' (*faute simple*) will be necessary and sufficient, although sometimes a 'very serious fault' (*faute lourde*) is required though in fewer and fewer situations;[261] moreover, on occasion French courts have understood *faute de service* in a particularly rigorous way by focusing merely on the negative results of the administrative action rather than on the reasonableness of the public employee's conduct.[262] In addition to all this, the notion of *faute de service* extends to cover the mere illegality (or unlawfulness in a 'public law' sense) of an administrative act,[263] even in situations where an ordinarily diligent conduct was adopted, and it therefore gives rise to liabilities which would exceed the boundaries of liability for fault as understood in England and in the United States.[264] In sum, in French administrative law the notion of *responsabilité pour faute* is wide-ranging and, despite requiring *faute*, it can cover liabilities which would be typically seen as instances of strict liability in common law systems.

But there is more, for besides liability based on *faute* French administrative law features a wide and heterogeneous range of liabilities *sans faute*.[265] The main examples include, first, the operation of dangerous things or activities,[266] as where grenades which had been stored by military authorities in some bunkers exploded and caused substantial damage to a residential area.[267] Moreover, any person who, without being a public servant, assisted in a public service and as a result sustained some harm, is entitled to receive compensation from the public purse, classic examples being assistance in firefighting or the rescue of people in danger.[268] Again, if

---

[260] See, respectively, CE 27.1.1988 (*Giraud*), [1988] Rec 39; and CE 8.10.1986 (*Langlet et Centre hospitalier général de Château-Thierry*), AJDA 1986.723.

[261] See Gaudemet (n 256) [370]–[377]. On the reasons for the adoption of this heightened standard of conduct, see Chapus (n 257) [1463].

[262] See Fairgrieve (n 259) 104–05 (mentioning as relevant examples CE 28.6.1961 (*André-des-Alpes*), [1961] Rec 440; CE 20.11.1968 (*Compagnie d'Assurances 'La Fortune'*), [1968] Rec 579; CE 20.10.1976 (*Alfortville*), [1976] Rec 1116; CE 9.5.1989 (*Centre Hospitalier de Castelnaudry*), [1989] Rec 909).

[263] CE 26.1.1973 (*Driancourt*), [1973] Rec 78, AJDA 1973.245. See also Gaudemet (n 256) [369].

[264] Fairgrieve (n 259) 136. Note that, in situations where a serious fault is required, mere illegality may well not be enough for a finding of liability, for illegality does not constitute in itself a *faute lourde*: see ibid 35, 114.

[265] See generally Stéphanie Hennette-Vauchez, 'Responsabilité sans faute' in Répertoire de la responsabilité de la puissance publique (2017).

[266] François Vincent, 'Responsabilité sans faute' JCl Admin, Fasc 824, 2015 [4]–[49]; Fairgrieve (n 259) 138–42.

[267] CE 28.3.1919 (*Regnault-Desroziers*), S 1918–1919.3.25 note Hauriou. See also CE Ass 24.6.1949 (*Lecomte et Daramy*), D 1950.27 (on firearms and similar devices); CE 3.2.1956 (*Thouzellier*), RDP 1956.854 (on escapes from open borstals); CE Ass 26.5.1995 (*N'Guyen*), JCP 1995.II.22468 note Moreau (on contaminated blood products which were provided by a hospital). For further examples, see Chapus (n 257) [1488]–[1493].

[268] See eg CE 5.3.1943 (*Chavat*), [1943] Rec 62; CE 25.9.1970 (*Tesson*), D 1971.55. See also CE Ass 22.11.1946 (*Commune Saint-Priest-la-Plaine*), D 1947.375 note Blaevoet (concerning citizens who were injured while helping in the organization of communal events (display of fireworks, in this case); CE

48   JUSTIFYING STRICT LIABILITY

a person is harmed accidentally by the carrying out of 'public works' (*travaux publics*), compensation may be sought provided that the claimant had no prior connection with the public work;[269] if, however, the harm is not accidental but is instead the normal consequence of the public work, then liability will arise only if the harm is *anormal* and *spécial*, that is if it reaches a certain threshold of seriousness and it is specific to the claimant or to a limited class of persons.[270] Also, the regime governing medical accidents which I mentioned earlier applies to all practitioners and healthcare establishments (whether public or private), therefore imposing strict liability on public establishments for nosocomial infections as well as for the negligent conduct of their employees.[271] Finally, liability *sans faute* may also stem from harm caused by legislation,[272] including the ratification of an international treaty,[273] or by a lawful administrative act;[274] as in the case of non-accidental damage caused by public works, these liabilities are subject to the requirements of *anormalité* and *spécialité*.[275] While liability arising from legislation or international treaties is rare,[276] lawful administrative decisions can give rise to the liability of a public authority in a range of situations, as where the relevant authority refuses to enforce court orders,[277] chooses not to have recourse to force,[278] or decides not to enforce planning regulations.[279] As will be seen below,[280] a number of these strict liabilities have their own, special public law justification, which is the principle of 'equality before public burdens' (*égalité devant les charges publiques*), according to which a citizen harmed by action taken in the public interest should be compensated rather than having to bear a disproportionately large burden (*le charge*) of the public action.[281] While an idea of this nature is not unknown in the other legal

---

17.4.1953 (*Pinguet*), D 1954.7 note Morange (regarding a person who was injured while helping the police in putting a criminal under arrest).

[269] This liability is very ancient (dating back to 1799) and was introduced by statute (*loi du pluviôse an VIII*, article 4). See also CE 7.11.1952 (*Grau*); CE 4.10.1957 (*Beaufils*); CE 14.11.1973 (*Leynaert*). See Chapus (n 257) [1498]–[1500].

[270] See eg CE 24.7.1931 (*Comm de Vic-Fezensac*), D 1931.3.51 note P-L J; CE 29.5.1974 (*Reyboz*), [1974] Rec 326; CE 20.11.1981 (*Rodal*), RDP 1982.1445. See Chapus (n 257) [1509].

[271] See text to nn 251–253 in this section.

[272] CE Ass 14.1.1938 (*La Fleurette*), D 1938.3.41.

[273] CE 29.10.1976 (*Burgat*), RDP 1977.213. cf CE Ass 30.3.1966 (*Compagnie Générale d'Energie Radio-Electrique*), D 1966.582 note Lachaume.

[274] CE 30.11.1923 (*Couitéas*), D 1923.3.59 concl Rivet.

[275] See generally Chapus (n 257) [1507].

[276] See, respectively, Olivier Gohin, 'La Responsabilite de l'État en tant que Legislateur' (1998) 50(2) RIDC 595; Fairgrieve (n 259) 145–46, 148–50; and Roger Errera, 'The Scope and Meaning of No-Fault Liability in French Administrative Law' (1986) 39 CLP 157, 162.

[277] eg *Couitéas* (n 274).

[278] eg CE 27.5.1977 (*SA Victor-Delforge*), Revue administrative 1977.488; CE 22.6.1984 (*Sealink*), AJDA 1984.770.

[279] eg CE Ass 20.3.1974 (*Navarra*), D 1974.480 note Gilli. For many other examples of liability arising from lawful administrative decisions, see Vincent (n 266) [89]–[105].

[280] See subsection 3.5.2.

[281] I consider this argument as the French version, in the public law context, of loss spreading as burden–benefit proportionality, and I will therefore discuss it mainly in subsection 3.5.2. As to the meaning of burden–benefit proportionality, see subsection 3.5.1.

systems studied,[282] in the French context it has constitutional status, and therefore special importance.[283] Overall, then, strict liability is a key component of French public liability and, particularly in light of the existence of several pockets of *responsabilité sans faute*, it provides a striking contrast with the more cautious approach adopted in England and in the United States.

To conclude, it is clear that, compared to their English and US counterparts, French legal actors have a distinct taste for the idea of imposing liability regardless of any failure in conduct. Since the late nineteenth-century courts and legal scholars have relentlessly contributed to the development of strict liabilities, from the creation of liability for the deeds of things and the general liability for the action of another to a stricter interpretation of rules such as those on parental liability. The legislator too has fuelled this transformation through a series of interventions such as, most notably, that relating to traffic accidents which imposes a particularly strict liability in an area where deaths and personal injuries are an everyday occurrence. It is therefore clear that French law has undergone a process of transformation in which the general trend has been from fault to strict liability and that today it relies heavily on (sometimes very) strict liability regimes in a wide range of situations.

2.5 Strict Liability in Italian Law

The general law of Italian extra-contractual liability is set out in Book IV ('Of Obligations'), Title IX ('Of Unlawful Facts') of the *Codice civile* (Cod civ), enacted in 1942.[284] The opening provision of Title IX is article 2043, which sets out a general rule of 'liability for fault' (*responsabilità per colpa*) and provides that '[a]ny action which deliberately or negligently causes an unlawful harm to another person obliges the person who committed that action to compensate the harm'. In so providing, article 2043 imposes liability on defendants who failed to comply with the standard of diligence and prudence required of a reasonable person in like circumstances (the so-called *buon padre di famiglia*).[285] Article 2043 is followed by a panoply of provisions (article 2047 to article 2054) which govern specific contexts of liability and which are widely seen as embodying distinct criteria of imposition of

---

[282] See subsection 3.5.3 (United States), subsection 3.5.4 (Italy), and subsection 3.5.5 (England).

[283] See eg Conseil Constitutionnel 4.7.1989 no 89-254 DC, Journal officiel 5.7.1989, p 8382, at para [24]; Errera (n 276) 171–72.

[284] This codification is often portrayed as a 'hybrid' of the French *Code civil* and the German BGB, with its own originality in many respects: see Sirena (n 186) 341. See also Nadia Coggiola, 'The Influence of Foreign Legal Models on the Development of Italian Civil Liability Rules from the 1865 Civil Code to the Present Day' (2019) 5 The Italian Law Journal 441.

[285] Monateri (n 188) 74. Besides article 2043, a multitude of statutes and administrative regulations establish fault-based norms of conduct for a wide range of activities. The violation of these norms constitutes *colpa* and, if causative of an unlawful harm, it triggers liability: see Giovanna Visintini, *Fatti Illeciti* (Pacini Giuridica 2019) 106–07.

50   JUSTIFYING STRICT LIABILITY

liability.[286] Are these provisions instances of *responsabilità per colpa*, or do they depart from the standard of the reasonable person and therefore constitute examples of 'liability without fault' or 'strict liability' (*responsabilità senza colpa* or, more commonly today, *responsabilità oggettiva*)? Since the enactment of the *Codice civile*, the nature of most of these provisions has been disputed because they allow for defences which may be interpreted (and have in fact been interpreted) in a variety of ways. In this respect, then, the key question is to establish whether a lack of *colpa*, in other words whether the defendant acted as an ordinarily diligent person should have done in like circumstances, exempts them from liability. Here, therefore, we see again that, in keeping with the other three legal systems considered, the idea is that there is an 'exonerating level of diligence' which, at least in principle, allows to draw a distinction between *responsabilità per colpa* and *responsabilità oggettiva*.[287] At the same time, both the positive law and the work of some Italian scholars show that the picture may be more complicated than this, and that, from the standpoint of the standard of conduct, it is possible to think of liability rules as located along a continuum of strictness.[288] Nevertheless, the term *responsabilità oggettiva* is used to refer to contexts of liability where *colpa* is seen as irrelevant and which, therefore, constitute instances of strict liability in Italian law.

A good starting point is represented by articles 2047 and 2048 Cod civ, which govern liability of guardians for the harm caused by individuals lacking mental capacity (article 2047), and liability of parents, teachers, or craftsmen for the harm caused by, respectively, children, pupils, or apprentices (article 2048). Both these provisions provide that the defendants are liable 'unless they prove that they could not have prevented the harmful action'. This wording has proven to be highly ambiguous, with interpretations oscillating between fault and strict liability. While courts have often argued that defendants could avoid liability if their obligations of monitoring or upbringing were fulfilled,[289] the rigour with which courts assess the facts and the defendant's behaviour has led numerous authors to think that these liability rules are in reality strict, and proof of a diligent conduct is no answer to a claim for damages.[290]

---

[286] See Stefano Rodotà, *Il Problema della Responsabilità Civile* (Giuffrè 1964) 127ff.

[287] Monateri (n 188) 76–77.

[288] Pier Giuseppe Monateri, Gino MD Arnone, and Nicolò Calcagno, *Il dolo, la colpa e i risarcimenti aggravati dalla condotta* (Giappichelli 2014) 154–60.

[289] In relation to article 2047, see eg Civ (III) 19.6.1997 n.5485, (1998) Diritto ed economia delle assicurazioni 287; Civ (III) 16.6.2005 n.12965; Civ (III) 26.1.2016 n.1321, (2016) 11 CG 1357. In relation to article 2048, see Civ (III) 6.12.2011 n.26200, (2012) 3 DR 257; Civ (III) 18.11.2014 n.24475.

[290] In relation to article 2047, see Marco Comporti, *Esposizione al pericolo e responsabilità civile* (Morano editore 1965) 238; Monateri (n 188) 931–32 in combination with his remarks at 85–86 (although his observations at 939–41 suggest that he may see liability for the action of the 'incapable' as located somewhere between strict liability and fault); Massimo Franzoni, *L'illecito. Trattato della responsabilità civile* (2nd edn, Giuffrè 2010) 695–96. In relation to article 2048, see Liliana Rossi Carleo, 'La responsabilità dei genitori ex art. 2048 c.c.' (1979) II Riv Dir Civ 126; Luigi Corsaro, 'Funzione e ragioni della responsabilità del genitore per il fatto illecito del figlio minore' (1988) IV GI 225, 226–28; Monateri (n 188) 945; Giovanni Facci, 'La responsabilità dei genitori in caso di incidente stradale del figlio minore: per colpa o oggettiva?' (2006) 2 Famiglia e diritto 138, 140.

Difficulties of interpretation have also characterized article 2050 Cod civ, which regulates liability for dangerous activities.[291] This provision of the code does not define what amounts to a dangerous activity, with the consequence that, apart from where special legislation has been enacted, it will be for the courts to decide from case to case whether a certain activity qualifies as dangerous for the purposes of article 2050. In this respect, and contrary to the more restrictive approach of US courts vis-à-vis liability for abnormally dangerous activities,[292] Italian courts have interpreted the notion of 'dangerous activity' in a particularly generous way, thus giving article 2050 a strikingly broad scope of application. Examples of dangerous activity include the loading and unloading of things by operation of cranes or similar equipment,[293] the manufacture and distribution of gas cylinders,[294] and the storage of fuel at petrol stations.[295] The general idea behind this case law seems to be that an activity is dangerous if, by its nature and thus regardless of any culpability on the part of its operator, it possesses a 'high harmful potential', that is it gives rise to a serious risk of harm.[296] Furthermore, article 2050 imposes liability on the party who engages in a dangerous activity 'unless they prove that they took all suitable measures to avoid the harm'. While what constitutes 'all suitable measures' is determined from case to case, Italian courts have eventually clarified that article 2050 imposes strict liability,[297] because proof of ordinary diligence does not exonerate the defendant.[298] To escape liability, the defendant must either satisfy the court that they adopted 'all suitable measures to avoid the harm' or, if they did not, that a fortuitous event (*caso fortuito*), typically a natural force, an action of a third party or of the victim, was the exclusive cause of harm.[299] Apart from this last condition, the event must also be exceptional and objectively unforeseeable,[300]

---

[291] Article 2050 reads as follows: '[w]hoever causes harm to another in the performance of an activity dangerous by its nature or by reason of the means employed, is liable in damages, unless they prove that they took all suitable measures to avoid the harm'.

[292] See text to nn 121–126 in section 2.3.

[293] Civ (III) 1.7.1987 n.5764.

[294] Civ (III) 26.7.2012 n.13214, (2013) 6 DR 601.

[295] Civ (III) 29.7.2015 n.16052, (2016) 2 DR 155. Other examples are the production, transportation, and distribution of electric energy (Civ (II) 9.3.2006 n.5080; Civ (III) 15.5.2007 n.11193, (2007) 11 RCP 2303); the activities typical of the construction industry (Civ (III) 10.2.2003 n.1954, (2003) Archivio civile 933); activities involving the shooting of bullets, including hunting (Civ (III) 30.11.1977 n.5222, (1978) Archivio civile 500); the manufacturing and letting off of fireworks (Civ sez un 14.3.1991 n.2726, (1993) 1 GI 1118); the management of entertainment attractions in amusement parks such as bobsleigh (Civ (III) 27.7.1990 n.7571) and fairground bull ride (Trib Massa Carrara 27.2.1996, (1996) Archivio civile 1018); sporting activities such as operating a horse-riding school (Civ (III) 24.5.1988 n.3616); pool slides (Civ (III) 13.3.2007 n.5839); toxic waste disposal (Civ (I) 1.9.1995 n.9211, (1995) CG 1146).

[296] Civ (III) 27.7.1990 n.7571; Civ (III) 30.8.1995 n.9205, (1996) 1 GI 466; Civ (III) 7.5.2007 n.10300, (2007) 1 Foro It 1685. See Franzoni (n 290) 412–16; Monateri (n 188) 1019.

[297] Civ (III) 4.5.2004 n.8457, [2.1], (2004) 1 Foro It 2378; Trib Mantova 5.8.2009 n.789, (2009) 12 DR 1227; Civ (III) 17.12.2009 n.26516, [3.9], (2010) 6 DR 569; Trib Milano 11.7.2014 n.9235, (2015) 2 LRC 579.

[298] Civ (III) 9.4.2015 n.7093, [1.8], (2015) 5 GI 1062.

[299] Civ (III) 18.7.2011 n.15733, (2012) 1 Foro It 1560.

[300] ibid; Civ (III) 4.5.2004 n.8457 (n 297) [3.2].

52 JUSTIFYING STRICT LIABILITY

otherwise its causal impact will be deemed irrelevant and the defendant will be held liable. If, however, the fortuitous event consisted in a careless action of the victim and it contributed to the causation of harm, the defendant can obtain a reduction in damages pursuant to article 1227 Cod civ.[301] Clearly, then, those engaged in dangerous operations are subjected to a strict regime of liability.

A particular example of liability for dangerous activities is article 2054 Cod civ, which regulates liability arising from traffic accidents.[302] The nature of each of the four liability rules contained in article 2054 has been clarified by the Corte di cassazione in a very recent decision. Paragraph 1 establishes the driver's liability for damage to property or harm to the bodily integrity of another, unless they prove that they did everything possible to avoid it; paragraph 2 provides that in cases of collision between vehicles, drivers are presumed to have caused the harm in equal shares; paragraph 3 holds the owner of the vehicle (or the usufructuary or purchaser with reservation of ownership) jointly and severally liable with the driver for accidents under paragraphs 1 and 2, unless they prove that the vehicle was being operated against their will; paragraph 4 provides that '[i]n any case, the persons indicated in the preceding paragraphs are liable for damage arising from defects in the manufacture or maintenance of the vehicle'. In a climate of controversy and uncertainty on the nature of these rules, the *Sezioni Unite* have held that the first three paragraphs of article 2054 impose liability on the basis of lack of ordinary diligence.[303] By contrast, in agreement with most legal scholars,[304] the same court views paragraph 4 as providing for a truly strict liability rule,[305] for defendants can escape liability only on the basis of a fortuitous event which breaks the causal link between the accident and the defect in the manufacture or maintenance of the vehicle.[306]

In common with the French *Code* of 1804, the *Codice civile* contains a provision dealing with liability for 'damage caused by things in one's keeping' (*danno cagionato da cosa in custodia*). Article 2051 Cod civ provides that '[e]veryone is

---

[301] Civ (III) 18.7.2011 n.15733 (n 299).

[302] Civ sez un 29.4.2015 n.8620, [3.2], (2016) 1 RCP 205.

[303] ibid [3.1]–[3.3]. cf Carlo Castronovo, *Responsabilità civile* (Giuffrè 2018) 754–755 (arguing that, as constantly interpreted and applied by the courts, the first three paragraphs of article 2054 are instances of strict liability); Antonino Procida Mirabelli di Lauro, *La responsabilità civile: strutture e funzioni* (Giappichelli 2004) 114–18 (on the no-fault nature of all the four paragraphs of article 2054 Cod civ); Franzoni (n 290) 605–08, 613–16, 855–56 (arguing that paragraph 1, as interpreted by the courts, would be an instance of strict liability, and that paragraph 3 would instead be based on fault); Riccardo Mazzon, 'Il fenomeno della responsabilità oggettiva nella disciplina prevista dall'art. 2054 c.c. e concernenti la circolazione dei veicoli' in Paolo Cendon (ed), *Responsabilità civile*, vol III (2nd edn, UTET 2020) 4006, 4007 (seeing paragraph 3 as strict); Monateri (n 188) 1095–96 (arguing that paragraph 1 would be based on fault); Cesare Salvi, *La responsabilità civile* (3rd edn, Giuffrè 2019) 217 (arguing that, to escape liability, the driver must prove not that they were driving diligently, but that the accident was caused by an external event).

[304] eg Enzo Roppo, 'Sul danno causato da automobile difettose. Tutela dei danneggiati, regime di responsabilità e incidenza dell'assicurazione obbligatoria' (1978) 12(IV) GI 130, 132.

[305] Civ sez un 29.4.2015 n.8620 (n 302) [3.3].

[306] ibid.

liable for the damage caused by things in his keeping, unless he proves that the damage was the result of a fortuitous event'. The scope of article 2051 is very broad, as a result of the generous interpretation given to the concepts of thing and 'keeper' (*custode*). In particular, any physical thing, movable or immovable, in solid, liquid, or gaseous state falls within the scope of article 2051.[307] Any distinction between 'dangerous' or 'innocuous' things is irrelevant, as that between defective or non-defective things: liability will be triggered in any case.[308] However, in this respect differing from the French position,[309] the thing must not have been a 'mere instrument in the hands' of the defendant, as otherwise the thing will be seen as merely occasioning the accident, not as causing it, and article 2043 (ie fault-based liability) rather than article 2051 will apply.[310] As to the notion of *custode*, the defendant is identified as such if they were in a factual relation with the thing consisting in having physical control and power over it,[311] that is if the *custode* is in the position to 'control the thing, remove situations of danger that may have materialized, and exclude others from coming into contact with the thing'.[312] To escape liability, the defendant must prove the occurrence of a *caso fortuito* which had 'exclusive causal efficiency in producing the harm', meaning that it was 'autonomous, exceptional, unforeseeable, and inevitable'.[313] Otherwise, if the fortuitous event consisted in a faulty action of the victim and it contributed to the causation of harm, the defendant can obtain a reduction in damages.[314] In sum, since proof of the *custode*'s diligence is no answer to a claim in damages, liability for the harm caused by things in one's keeping appears strict.[315]

The same can be safely said of liability for damage caused by animals. Article 2052 establishes that

> [t]he owner of an animal, or one who makes use of it for the period of such use, is liable for damage caused by the animal, regardless of whether the animal was [at the time of the accident] in their keeping or strayed or escaped, unless they prove that the damage was the result of a fortuitous event.

---

[307] Alessandro Farolfi, 'Il danno cagionato da cose in custodia' in Cendon (n 303) 3849, 3855.

[308] Civ (III) 20.7.2002 n.10641, [5.1], (2002) 12 DR 1201.

[309] Jourdain (n 188) [659] (including fn 196).

[310] Civ (II) 25.3.1995 n.3553, (1995) Rep Foro It, voce *Responsabilità civile*, n.165; Monateri (n 188) 1039–40, 1053.

[311] Civ (III) 8.2.2012 n.1769, (2012) 9 GC 2047B.

[312] Civ (VI) 4.10.2013 n.22684, (2014) 6 DR 616.

[313] Civ (III) 18.9.2015 n.18317, [1.2], (2015) Rep Foro It, voce *Responsabilità civile*, n.257. See also Civ (III) 1.2.2018 n.2480, (2018) 1 Foro It 1243.

[314] Civ (III) 6.7.2006 n.15383, [7.1]–[7.6], (2006) 11 DR 1145.

[315] cf C Massimo Bianca, *Diritto civile. V—La responsabilità* (3rd edn, Giuffrè 2021) 692–95 (seeing the liability for the damage caused by things in one's keeping as based on a presumption of fault, mainly on the ground that the defence of *caso fortuito* would involve an assessment of the diligence of the defendant's conduct).

54 JUSTIFYING STRICT LIABILITY

As in French law, the notion of animal includes any type of animal, be it tame, tamed, or ferocious,[316] and the notion of use is understood broadly so that 'using' an animal for pure leisure is enough.[317] Furthermore, while the owner is often the person who uses the animal, at the time of the accident the animal may have been used by another person who, in this case, will be liable rather than the owner.[318] Finally, liability under article 2052 is seen as clearly strict, given that the defendant's conduct is irrelevant and the only available defence is, as usual and with the same rules seen above, proof of *caso fortuito*.[319]

Another significant provision is article 2053 Cod civ, which imposes liability on the owner of a building or other structure for the harm caused by its ruinous state. Contrary to the equivalent provision in the French *Code civil*, however, the claimant must only prove damage and causation, the onus being on the defendant to prove that the damage was not caused by a defect in its maintenance or construction. Furthermore, and again, the defendant can escape liability by proving a fortuitous event as the exclusive cause of damage or obtain a reduction in damages if the careless action of the victim contributed to the causation of harm.[320] Therefore, as the conduct of the building's owner is irrelevant to the determination of liability, this provision of the code constitutes a clear instance of strict liability.

Another context in which strict liability is prominent is the vicarious liability of employers, regulated in article 2049.[321] The essential requirements of liability are three. First, there must be a special relationship between the defendant and the physical author of harm, such that the former has the power to direct and monitor the activity of the latter (*rapporto di preposizione*). The typical example is that of the relationship between employer and employee, but many other types of relationship would also qualify, such as those arising in the contracts of mandate, agency, or mere collaboration.[322] The second requirement is that the employee has committed an unlawful action or omission (*fatto illecito*). On the meaning of *fatto illecito*, however, there is disagreement, as some believe that the action of the physical author of harm should be of a nature to engage their personal liability under article 2043, while others believe that an innocent action is enough to trigger the liability of employers.[323] The third and final requirement is that the tasks entrusted to the employee are of such a nature that they determine, make it easier or possible the occurrence of the harmful event (*nesso di occasionalità necessaria*); if this

---

[316] Franzoni (n 290) 532.

[317] Monateri (n 188) 1062–63.

[318] Civ (III) 22.12.2015 n.25738, [4.2]; Civ (III) 11.12.2012 n.22632, [6.3].

[319] Civ (III) 4.12.1998 n.12307, [6.1], (1999) 1 Foro It 1938.

[320] Civ (III) 21.1.2010 n.1002, [2.2], [3.2]–[3.5].

[321] While for convenience I refer to employers and employees, article 2049 Cod civ refers to employers and masters on the one hand, and to employees and servants on the other.

[322] See respectively Trib Milano 3.10.2009 n.11786; Civ (III) 22.6.2007 n.14578, (2007) Rep Foro It, voce *Responsabilità civile*, n.289; and Civ (III) 16.3.2010 n.6325, (2010) 11 DR 1033.

[323] For a brief overview of the various positions, see Franzoni (n 290) 769ff.

STRICT LIABILITY IN THE FOUR TORT SYSTEMS: AN OVERVIEW   55

requirement is met, the employer may be held liable even in situations where the employee abused their position, went beyond the limits of the assigned tasks, acted for strictly personal purposes, or harmed the claimant intentionally.[324] Article 2049 clearly imposes a strict liability, for the employer's diligent conduct is irrelevant and, once the requirements seen above are met, the employer can only obtain a reduction in damages if the claimant's negligent conduct contributed to the causation of harm.[325]

Beyond Title IX, Book IV of the *Codice civile* there is another provision in the code that deserves attention, namely article 844 on liability for nuisance (*Immissioni*). This article, which is located in Book III, Title II ('Of Ownership'), provides that a landowner has remedies against nuisances only if these exceed the threshold of 'normal tolerability', with the judge that may either order the adoption of further emission-reducing precautions, or inhibit the continuation of the emitting activity if there is no way to stop the intolerable nuisance. Importantly, article 844(2) regulates situations where the emissions come from a productive activity and establishes that where such emissions cannot be brought below an acceptable level through the adoption of reasonable precautions, the judge must decide the dispute by balancing the needs of production with the protection of property rights. In this scenario, emissions may be judged as 'lawful' (*lecite*) and therefore be allowed to continue, and in this case the claimant will be entitled to an indemnity from the other party for the interference with the use and enjoyment of their land.[326] In this type of situation, liability to pay the indemnity can be characterized as strict, for the fact that the defendant adopted all reasonable precautions to remove or minimize the emissions is irrelevant to the determination of their liability.[327]

---

[324] eg Civ (III) 25.5.2016 n.10757, [5].

[325] Marco Comporti, *Fatti Illeciti: le responsabilità oggettive—Artt. 2049-2053. Il Codice Civile—Commentario* (Giuffrè 2009) 123–24, fn 100. It is instead controversial whether the defendant can escape liability by proving *caso fortuito*: ibid 92, fn 33 (arguing that the defence should, in principle, be available); Civ (III) 20.2.2006 n.3651, (2006) 1 Foro It 2801, 2814 (excluding the application of *caso fortuito* to article 2049 Cod civ).

[326] See eg Monateri (n 188) 556. Note that the indemnity is not mentioned at all in article 844, and that it is instead a remedy created by the courts: see Civ sez un 26.10.1957 n.4156, (1958) 1 Foro It 1497. The nature of the indemnity has always been very controversial, with some scholars seeing it as pertaining to tort law, others as belonging to property law, and still others as a constituting a remedy to nuisance as a 'harmful lawful act' (*atto lecito dannoso*): for a critical overview of all these approaches, see generally Cesare Salvi, *Le immissioni industriali. Rapporti di vicinato e tutela dell'ambiente* (Giuffrè 1979) 249ff. Relatedly, Italian legal actors have long disagreed as to which provision in the civil code should ground claims seeking an indemnity award, the main candidates being article 844 and article 2043 Cod civ: see Monateri (n 188) 566–67. As to the quantification of the indemnity, there are two main views in the case law: some courts see it as the reduction in the profits earnable from the current use of the claimant's land; others think that it should correspond to the diminution in the market value of the land. For an overview of this issue, see Marcello Adriano Mazzola, *Responsabilità civile da atti leciti dannosi* (Giuffrè 2007) 281–95.

[327] See Pietro Trimarchi, *Rischio e responsabilità oggettiva* (Giuffrè 1961) 348; Giovanna Visintini, 'Immissioni e tutela dell'ambiente' [1976] RTDPC 689, 690; Antonio Gerardo Diana, *Le immissioni. Tipologie, azioni e tutele* (Giuffrè 2013) 366 (quoting Francesco Caringella and Giuseppe De Marzo, *Manuale di diritto civile* (Giuffrè 2007) 560). cf Salvi (n 326) 251; Monateri (n 188) 566–67.

56 JUSTIFYING STRICT LIABILITY

Outside the *Codice civile*, there are other areas of strict liability governed by special legislation.[328] Among these, the most significant is liability for defective products, currently governed by articles 114–127 of the 'Consumers code' (*Codice del consumo*),[329] which implement the Product Liability Directive.[330] By and large the Italian legislator has reproduced in a faithful way the key elements of the Directive, such as the notions of producer, defect, or compensable damage.[331] Moreover, Italian law has adopted all the grounds of exoneration envisaged in the Directive, none of which allows the producer to escape liability on the basis of their diligent conduct.[332] This circumstance, coupled with the fact that liability is typically seen as based on the causal connection between defect and harm, without any relevance accorded to the producer's conduct,[333] leads to liability for defective products being seen as generally strict. But this conclusion is unanimously accepted only in relation to manufacturing defects for, in keeping with the other three legal systems, it is controversial whether liability arising out of design defects or failures in the duty to warn is strict or based on the producer's fault.[334] Furthermore, it is doubted whether Italian courts, especially in recent times, always interpret liability for products as strict or if instead at times they 'succumb to the charm of fault'.[335]

Finally, a few words must be said in relation to medical accidents, an area recently reformed by legge no 24 of 8 March 2017. Here the Italian legislator has opted for a binary regime: the relationship between healthcare establishments and patients is contractual in nature, with the consequence that the former are liable in contract to the latter pursuant to articles 1218 and 1228 Cod civ for, respectively, any harm caused either by their own organizational failures or by the negligent or intentional conduct of their staff (whether or not there exists a formal contract of employment between the establishment and the professional who injured the patient).[336] While

---

[328] Examples include liability for nuclear installations (legge 31.12.1962 n.1860, D.P.R. 10.5.1975 n.519, and D.M. 20.3.1979), liability for accidents caused by airplanes (article 965 of *Codice della navigazione*), or liability for the exploitation of mines (article 31, r.d. 29.7.1927 n.1443). For a general overview of these and other special liabilities, see Franzoni (n 290) 649–76.

[329] Enacted with D Lgs 6.9.2005 n.206.

[330] The Directive was first implemented in Italy by D.P.R. 24.5.1988 n.224.

[331] Articles 115, 117, and 123 of the *Codice del consumo*. A thorough review of the implementing law and its points of departure from the Directive can be found in Roberto Pardolesi and Giulio Ponzanelli (eds), 'La responsabilità per danno da prodotti difettosi' (1989) (3) Le nuove leggi civili commentate 497.

[332] Article 118 of the *Codice del consumo*.

[333] Civ (III) 29.5.2013 n.13458, (2014) 5 DR 489; Civ (III) 19.2.2016 n.3258, [5.1].

[334] Giulio Ponzanelli, 'Dal biscotto alla "mountain bike": la responsabilità da prodotto difettoso in Italia' (1994) 1 Foro It 252, [3]; Pier Giuseppe Monateri, *Illecito e responsabilità civile—Tomo II. Trattato di diritto privato* (UTET 2002) 225ff; Bianca (n 315) 720–21. cf Giulio Ponzanelli, 'Il produttore è responsabile del danno cagionato da difetti del suo prodotto' in Pardolesi and Ponzanelli (n 331) 506, 508–09.

[335] Alessandro Palmieri, 'Difetto e condizioni di impiego del prodotto: ritorno alla responsabilità per colpa?' (2007) 1 Foro It 2415, 2418.

[336] Article 7, para 1 of legge 8.3.2017 n.24. For an overview of liability for medical accidents, see Rosanna Breda, 'La responsabilità—riformata?—della struttura sanitaria' in Nicola Todeschini (ed), *La responsabilità medica* (UTET 2019) 929.

the nature of the liability of health care establishments for their own failures under article 1218 is not yet entirely clear, with interpretations oscillating between fault and strict liability,[337] their liability under article 1228 is clearly strict, for this provision is, in contractual matters, the equivalent of article 2049 Cod civ. By contrast, the relationship between doctors (or other health care professionals) and patients is extra-contractual and the former are personally liable to the latter on the basis of fault pursuant to article 2043 Cod civ.[338]

The heads of strict liability discussed so far apply, in principle, to public authorities as well as to private persons or bodies. Indeed, article 28 of the Italian Constitution establishes that 'civil servants and employees of the State and public bodies are directly responsible, under criminal, civil and administrative law, for acts committed in violation of rights. In such cases, civil liability extends to the State and to public bodies'.[339] From the perspective of civil liability, this means that whenever the state or other public body violates, often by way of a 'physical activity' (*attività materiale*), another's 'legal right' (*diritto soggettivo*), that is a right directly protected by the law and therefore not subordinated to the exercise of any administrative power, liability will arise under articles 2043ff of the *Codice civile* (*responsabilità da comportamento*, or *responsabilità per attività materiale*).[340] In this way, the Italian administration is liable in the same manner and to the same extent as a private individual in like circumstances, though with some qualifications or adaptations to the ordinary tort rules.[341] For instance, it has long been controversial whether article 2049 could apply to public bodies, given the uncertain nature of their liability, which is sometimes seen as 'direct' and at other times as vicarious. While the majority view in Italy has for a long time been that the liability of public bodies is direct and that therefore article 2049 Cod civ should not apply,[342] the *Sezioni Unite* of the Corte di Cassazione have recently adopted a

---

[337] Breda (n 336) 946–47.

[338] Article 7, para 3 of legge 8.3.2017 n.24. If, however, the individual healthcare provider has undertaken themselves a contractual obligation vis-à-vis the patient, they will be liable in contract, not in tort.

[339] The wording of this provision has sparked a lasting debate on the nature of the liability of the Italian administration: for a brief overview, see Michele Corradino, *La responsabilità della Pubblica Amministrazione* (Giappichelli 2011) 8–11.

[340] Gian Domenico Comporti, 'Responsabilità della pubblica amministrazione' in *Dizionario di diritto pubblico*, vol V (Giuffrè 2006) 5125, 5133–34. Typical examples of *diritto soggettivo* include the right to one's own bodily integrity and the preservation of one's own property. Therefore, personal injuries and damage to property are the typical types of harm that substantiate the violation of a *diritto soggettivo*. Competent to hear claims regarding the violation of *diritti soggettivi* are ordinary courts, at the apex of which is the Corte di Cassazione. By contrast, administrative courts, at whose apex is the Consiglio di Stato, hear cases regarding the violation of *interessi legittimi* (on which see text to nn 347–348 in this section), as well as cases regarding the violation of *diritti soggettivi* though only in specific matters identified by statute: see article 7 of the 'Code of Administrative Process' (*Codice del processo amministrativo*).

[341] Public employees, by contrast, can be held personally liable only in cases of gross negligence or malice, as established by articles 22–23 of D.P.R. 10.1.1957 n.3. If the administration is found liable for the grossly negligent or malicious action of its employees, it will have a recourse action against them.

[342] See Angelo Piazza, *Responsabilità civile ed efficienza amministrativa* (Giuffrè 2001) 19–25, 122–56 (providing a detailed discussion and criticism of the majority view).

58   JUSTIFYING STRICT LIABILITY

different stance and held that, when a 'physical activity' is being performed, the relevant public authority will be vicariously liable under article 2049 for the action of its employees.[343] Moreover, article 2051 Cod civ on liability for the things in one's keeping is today specially adapted to the (sometimes considerable) size of things owned by the state or other public entities, as for example highways. While the traditional position was that the large size of the thing was a sufficient reason to deny compensation, this is no longer the case and today Italian courts assess all the facts of the case at hand before deciding the issue of liability.[344] Furthermore, in relation to animals, it is controversial whether public entities may be held strictly liable under article 2052 Cod Civ for harm caused by wildlife,[345] with the majority view apparently favouring fault liability under article 2043.[346] Despite these controversies, qualifications, and adaptations, the common understanding in Italian law is that public bodies are subject to the same law as private persons, and this means therefore that strict liability is seen as playing an important role in Italian administrative law.

However, the position is more complex in relation to 'liability for administrative acts' (*responsabilità per attività provvedimentale*). For a long time, private parties could not be compensated where the public administration infringed their 'legitimate interests' (*interessi legittimi*) by way of an unlawful act, but could only obtain the act's annulment.[347] *Interesse legittimo* may be described as the interest that an individual has in obtaining a favourable decision of the public administration,[348] and its violation attracted compensation only in 1999 with the ground-breaking decision no 500 of the Corte di cassazione.[349] Since that decision, if an *interesse legittimo* is infringed by an unlawful administrative act, a private person affected can obtain compensation for their harm. In this way, the range of legally protected

---

[343]   Civ sez un 16.5.2019 n.13246, (2019) 4 DR 493. See also Maria Pia Giracca, 'Responsabilità civile e pubblica amministrazione: quale spazio per l'art. 2049 c.c.?' (2001) 1 Foro It 3293.

[344]   See eg Civ (III) 12.5.2017 n.11785, [4], (2018) 1 DR 49.

[345]   See Annalisa Bitetto, 'Danni provocati da animali selvatici: chi ne risponde e perché?' (2003) 3 DR 275; Giovanni Comandé and Luca Nocco, 'The Liability of Public Authorities in Italy' in Oliphant (ed) (n 93) 251, [134]–[140].

[346]   See Katia Mascia, 'Responsabilità per i danni cagionati dagli animali' (2020) 4 DR 538, 543–46.

[347]   Comandé and Nocco (n 345) [19].

[348]   See Cons St Ad Plen 23.3.2011 n.3, [3.1], (2012) 3 Foro It 31. For a detailed discussion of *interesse legittimo*, see Francesco Caringella, *Manuale di diritto amministrativo. I. La responsabilità della pubblica amministrazione* (Dike 2012) 139–212. See also Fulvio Cortese, 'The Liability of Public Administration—A Special Regime between Formal Requirements and Substantial Goals' in Giacinto della Cananea and Roberto Caranta (eds), *Tort Liability of Public Authorities in European Laws* (OUP 2020) 61. Typical examples of *interesse legittimo* involve the grant or denial of authorizations, concessions, or licences which a private party believes should be granted (to them) or denied (to a third party).

[349]   Civ sez un 22.7.1999 n.500. For comments on this decision, see eg Filippo Satta, 'La sentenza n. 500 del 1999: dagli interessi legittimi ai diritti fondamentali' (1999) 5 Giurisprudenza Costituzionale 3233; Guido Alpa, 'Il révirement della Corte di cassazione sulla responsabilità per la lesione di interessi legittimi' (1999) 4–5 RCP 907; Roberto Caranta, 'La pubblica amministrazione nell'età della responsabilità' (1999) 1 Foro It 3201; Pier Giuseppe Monateri, 'Il Tort da illegittimo esercizio della funzione pubblica' (1999) 10 DR 978; Alessandro Palmieri and Roberto Pardolesi, 'La Cassazione riconosce la risarcibilità degli interessi legittimi. Il commento' (1999) 10 DR 980.

interests vis-à-vis the public administration is broadened, as the infringement of both *diritti soggettivi* and *interessi legittimi* may attract compensation. At the same time, though, it is more difficult for private individuals to obtain compensation for the infringement of an *interesse legittimo*, because liability is grounded on fault under article 2043 Cod civ[350] and the relevant standard of conduct has changed from *colpa in re ipsa*, where any unlawfulness in the administrative action amounted to a fault, to *colpa di apparato*, which exists where the adoption of an administrative act violates 'the rules of impartiality, fairness and good administration.'[351] Following criticism of this understanding of *colpa di apparato*,[352] later case law has tried to draw the features of this notion with greater precision,[353] clarifying that the unlawfulness of an administrative act is a very significant, but not conclusive, factor, and that certain excusable mistakes may exempt the administration from liability.[354] Importantly, it remains true that some sort of failure in the administrative machinery is seen as necessary for a finding of liability and that, as a result, liability of the Italian administration is generally portrayed as based on *colpa*. Occasionally, however, Italian public bodies may be subject to liability regardless of any *colpa* in their administrative action. For example, following a series of decisions by the Court of Justice of the European Union (CJEU) on the breach of public procurement laws,[355] Italian courts have concluded that Italian public

---

[350] Note that some Italian courts and legal scholars have argued that this type of liability would have a contractual or pre-contractual nature: see eg Massimo Severo Giannini, Intervento in *Atti del convegno nazionale sull'ammissibilità del danno patrimoniale derivante da lesione di interessi legittimi* (Giuffrè 1965) 511, 518–20; Carlo Castronovo, 'Responsabilità civile per la pubblica amministrazione' (1998) 3 Ius 647; Cons St 6.8.2001 n.4239, [31]–[36], (2002) 3 Foro It 1; Cons St 12.3.2010 n.1467, [5]–[6], (2010) RCP 1542. For a detailed discussion of the position of civil and administrative courts on this issue, see Corradino (n 339) 27–51. Eventually, Cons St Ad Plen 23.4.2021 n.7, (2021) 3 Foro It 394, has settled the matter and held that the liability of the administration for the infringement of an *interesse legittimo* has extra-contractual nature and is therefore based on article 2043 Cod civ.

[351] See Civ sez un 22.7.1999 n.500. See also Filippo Satta, 'Responsabilità della pubblica amministrazione' Enc Dir XXXIX (Giuffrè 1998) 1369, 1378–79.

[352] See eg Fabio Elefante, *La responsabilità della pubblica amministrazione da attività provvedimentale* (CEDAM 2002) 192–95; Alberto Zito, *Il danno da illegittimo esercizio della funzione amministrativa. Riflessioni sulla tutela dell'interesse legittimo* (Editoriale Scientifica 2003) 153–62; Orazio Ciliberti, 'L'elemento soggettivo nella responsabilità civile della pubblica amministrazione conseguente a provvedimenti illegittimi' in Enrico Follieri (ed), *La responsabilità civile della pubblica amministrazione* (Giuffrè 2004) 253, 269–72. See also Fabrizio Fracchia, 'L'elemento soggettivo nella responsabilità dell'amministrazione' in *Responsabilità della pubblica amministrazione per lesioni di interessi legittimi. Atti del 54° Convegno di Studi di Scienza dell'Amministrazione, Varenna—Villa Monastero, 18–20 settembre 2008* (Giuffrè 2009) 211, 241–59.

[353] For an overview of these developments, see Alberto Zito, 'Il problema della colpa nella tutela risarcitoria degli interessi legittimi: spunti ricostruttivi' in *Studi in memoria di Franco Ledda* (Giappichelli 2004) 1381; Corradino (n 339) 69–92; Franco Gaetano Scoca (ed), *Diritto amministrativo* (6th edn, Giappichelli 2019) 481–83.

[354] See Cons St 17.2.2017 n.730; Cons St 13.2.2009 n.775, [2.1]; Cons St 13.2.2017 n.602, [25.3]–[25.4]. See also Caringella (n 348) 259–64. As to the position of public employees, these may be held personally liable for the violation of an *interesse legittimo*, if they acted with malice or gross negligence: see Civ (III) 31.7.2015 n.16276, [2.1]–[2.6].

[355] See *Commission v Portugal*, Case C-275/03; *Commission v Portugal*, Case C-70/06; and especially *Stadt Graz v Strabag AG and Others*, Case C-314/09.

60 JUSTIFYING STRICT LIABILITY

authorities are strictly liable for this type of breach,[356] and a lively debate has arisen among legal scholars as to the appropriateness of strict liability in the administration both within and beyond that context.[357] Overall, it is clear that strict liability is a conspicuous feature of administrative liability for 'physical activity' (*attività materiale*), while it is less significant where public bodies are involved in the performance of 'administrative acts' (*attività provvedimentale*).

To conclude, strict liability plays an important role in Italian law. Besides employers' vicarious liability, which has always been generally treated as strict, several liability rules included in the *Codice civile* have become strict due to the gradual interpretive work of courts and legal scholars (for example liability for dangerous activities, for things in one's keeping, for the actions of animals, for ruinous buildings, and for traffic accidents at least insofar as the owner of the vehicle and the producer of a defective vehicle are concerned). But while occupying a considerable space in Italian law, strict liability is not as pervasive as it is in French law. Indeed, the nature of a number of liability rules remains controversial due to the ambiguous wording in the provisions of the code and is subjected to a variety of interpretations, oscillating between strict and fault-based liability (most notably, liability of parents for the actions of their children and that of guardians for the actions of individuals lacking mental capacity). Furthermore, in some areas where death and personal injuries are frequent occurrences, Italian law contrasts with French law in that the fault paradigm is still attractive, the paramount example here being the role it plays in the liability of drivers for traffic accidents. In addition to this, it is difficult to find in Italian law liability rules that are as strict as those that French law has envisaged, for example, in relation to liability for traffic accidents, parental liability, or liability for defective products vis-à-vis the limitations imposed on the development risk defence. All in all, then, it is true that Italian legal actors have progressively increased their reliance on strict liability and that this type of liability is today a central and widespread feature of Italian law. However, if compared to the French position, it is clear that greater caution has been adopted in Italy towards the introduction of strict liability and that the solutions envisaged by the Italian courts and legislator have generally been less radical and more prone to the influence of the fault paradigm.

---

[356] Cons St 27.3.2017 n.1364, [6]. See also Corradino (n 339) 92–107; Caringella (n 348) 264–71.

[357] See eg Alessandra Dominici, 'La responsabilità oggettiva in materia di appalti: il Consiglio di Stato si allinea alle pronunce del giudice comunitario' (2013) 1 Rivista amministrativa degli appalti 41; Ester Santoro, 'Il risarcimento del danno da aggiudicazione illegittima prescinde dall'accertamento della colpa? Riflessioni alla luce della giurisprudenza europea e del codice del processo amministrativo' (2011) 2 Foro amministrativo T.A.R. 679. For further examples of situations in which Italian public authorities may be liable regardless of *colpa*, see Comandè and Nocco (n 345) [181]–[195].

2.6 Concluding Remarks

In the four legal systems studied, strict liability is understood in loosely similar ways. On the one hand, strict liability is often presented as opposed to liability for failure to act as a reasonable and diligent person. In this way, strict liability and fault-based liability are seen as clearly distinct. On the other hand, it is recognized that it may be difficult to draw a clear-cut distinction between fault and strict liability, that certain contexts of liability may present a mixture of fault-based and strict elements, and that therefore the idea of a continuum may better represent variations among liability rules in terms of their strictness. Nevertheless, in all four systems strict liability is still a well-recognizable legal category and it is widely used to refer to several contexts of liability where, at least in principle, the defendant's 'fault' (understood as lack of reasonable care or ordinary diligence) is seen as irrelevant to the determination of liability. This remains true even though the understandings of 'fault' may themselves differ in the four laws.

So understood, strict liability features in all the four legal systems studied, but it does so in different ways and to conspicuously differing extents across the four laws. Trying to locate the four jurisdictions along a spectrum on the basis of their relative reliance on strict liability, French law would be at one extreme point. The relentless work of French jurists and courts since the late nineteenth century as well as the occasional interventions of the legislator have all contributed to the adoption of strict liability in a wide range of situations, from liability for the deeds of things or the actions of animals to vicarious liability for the action of another and liability for traffic accidents. Moreover, the degree of strictness of certain rules is striking, as shown by the *loi* Badinter on traffic accidents as well as by the limitations to the development risk defence in product liability. The absence of a distinct context of liability for dangerous activities should not be taken to mean that harm caused through the operation of these activities remains without redress. Either statutes regulating the specific activity in question or the general liability for the deeds of things will make up for this absence and therefore cover accidents that Italian law and US law subject to a dedicated strict liability for (abnormally) dangerous activities. Finally, strict liability is also particularly prominent in French administrative law, as there is a wide variety of situations where public entities may be liable regardless of fault. All this testifies to the heavy reliance of French law on strict liability, and it gives a clear sense of the French taste for it.

English law would instead be placed at the other extreme point of the spectrum. Here, strict liability is indeed imposed in a variety of contexts (eg animals, private nuisance, defective products, breach of certain non-delegable duties), and the recent expansionistic developments in the law of vicarious liability confirm that it has a role to play in English tort law. This occurs, though, in a setting where the tort of negligence is dominant and where, therefore, legal actors are generally very cautious before adopting or expanding rules of strict liability. A striking example

62 JUSTIFYING STRICT LIABILITY

of this attitude is the demise of the rule in *Rylands v Fletcher*, which went from potentially being a general rule of strict liability for dangerous activities to actually being, in the view of some scholars but especially of the highest courts, a 'subspecies' of the tort of private nuisance. Equally significant is the radical change that the Enterprise and Regulatory Reform Act 2013 has brought about in the law governing employers' liability for breach of statutory duty, with strict liability being generally replaced by a negligence standard. Moreover, in sharp contrast with French law, a key area such as that of traffic accidents remains governed by the tort of negligence. Additionally, where English law applies strict liability, the relevant rule is sometimes less broad in its scope of application than equivalent rules in the other three legal systems, a clear example being liability for the actions of animals. Finally, when it comes to imposing strict liability on public bodies, English courts adopt an even more cautious approach than is the case in disputes between private parties. In sum, if compared to the other three legal systems studied, English law shows greater attachment to fault and, therefore, fewer and less rigorous rules of strict liability.

Italy and the United States would be located somewhere in the middle of the spectrum. In Italian law, strict liability plays a very important role, in relation to both private parties and public entities. Even if the *Codice civile* sets out liability rules whose standard of conduct is not entirely clear, the interpretive work of courts and jurists has turned many of these rules into strict liabilities. Particularly striking here is the breadth of liability for dangerous activities under article 2050 Cod civ, with the courts interpreting the requirement of dangerousness in a very generous way. On the other hand, despite the widespread reliance of Italian law on strict liability, the notion of fault keeps exerting considerable attraction on national legal actors, with the result that interpretive uncertainty still characterizes contexts such as parental liability, and that key contexts such as the liability of drivers for traffic accidents remain the province of fault. In addition to this, it is difficult to identify in Italy liability rules that possess the same extreme rigour displayed occasionally by French law, in relation to both civil and administrative liability. In sum, while heavily relied on and certainly featuring more prominently than in English law, strict liability in Italy does not reach the peaks of frequency, breadth, and rigour that it instead experiences in France.

Similar conclusions can be drawn in relation to the United States. Here, unlike English law, the rule in *Rylands v Fletcher* was not restricted but rather developed into a general strict liability for abnormally dangerous activities. Moreover, again departing from the English approach, pockets of strict liability can be identified in relation to the harm caused by dogs, to the intentional misconduct of children, and to traffic accidents in situations where the 'family purpose' doctrine (or expanded statutory versions of it) apply. In addition to this, in the context of product liability some state courts apply strict liability even to design and warning defects, and do not afford manufacturers the protection of the development risk defence;

this position testifies to an extremely rigorous approach which, albeit currently in retreat, is still clearly present in the United States within this specific context of liability. On the other hand, US strict liabilities are sometimes less broad than those identifiable in France and Italy. For example, the US liability for abnormally dangerous activities does not include a high number of activities which are instead covered by its Italian equivalent, its rule of liability for the actions of animals does not apply to all animals, unlike the French and Italian ones, and its liability for the action of another person does not cover the wide range of situations falling within the scope of the French law on *le fait d'autrui*. Finally, the US approach to the strict liability of public bodies is more similar to the English one than to that of Italy or France. Overall, strict liabilities constitute an important part of US tort law, featuring more conspicuously here than in English law while not being as widespread, rigorous, or broad as in France or Italy.

In sum, all the four legal systems studied rely on strict liability. Certainly, there are important commonalities across the four laws, as each of them includes rules of strict liability for harms caused by animals, by the actions of other persons, by defective products, and by certain types of unreasonable nuisances. At the same time, though, the four systems differ markedly in the way in which they rely on strict liability and in the extent to which they do so. This diversity of significance reflects contrasting views as to the desirability of strict liability and its proper place in the tort system. Part 3 of the work seeks to advance our understanding of strict liability by exploring the substantive justifications put forward in the four jurisdictions to justify the imposition of this type of liability. Arguments will be discussed in relation to each legal system and comparatively by paying attention to the various contexts in which strict liability has been identified. In this way, it will be possible both to shed light on the role and purposes attributed to strict liability in each of the four legal systems studied and to bring to light the wide variety of values, ideals, and goals which are brought to bear on the imposition of such liability.

3

THE JUSTIFICATIONS FOR STRICT LIABILITY

A Comparative Analysis

3.1

Introduction

The imposition of strict liability across the four legal systems studied has been justified in the twentieth century by a wide variety of arguments. While some of these arguments have lost much of their force due to social changes and developments in legal thinking, others have continued to be relied upon by scholars and courts and to inform contemporary legal reasoning.

This Part of the book explores the main arguments put forward across the four legal systems to justify strict liability. Some of these arguments are based on the notion of risk and will be grouped under the label of 'risk-based arguments' (which include 'risk creation', 'abnormality of risk', 'nonreciprocity of risk', 'risk–benefit', and 'risk–profit'). Other arguments are premised on the desire to pursue goals such as the avoidance of accidents (here labelled as 'accident avoidance'), the financial protection of victims ('victim protection'), the reduction in the cost of administering tort liability rules ('administrative cost reduction'), the promotion of norms of individual responsibility ('individual responsibility'), and the redistribution of losses. This latter goal encompasses the 'loss-spreading' argument (which includes 'insurance spreading', 'enterprise spreading', 'proportionality of burdens and benefits', and 'taxation spreading') and the 'deep-pockets' justification. All the arguments discussed in this Part of the book feature a core idea, and some of them also present internal variations which reflect different ways of handling that core idea. Identifying core ideas and distinguishing between their internal variations provide a first step in exploring the complexities of legal reasoning in strict liability, for it allows us to unravel the *patterns* of reasoning with greater precision and to uncover the justificatory weight of the various arguments and of their internal variations within and across the four laws.

As I said in Part I, my aim is not to evaluate the persuasiveness or desirability of strict liability or of any of the arguments considered in the book, nor to put forward any novel approach to strict liability.[1] On the other hand, I have selected arguments on the basis of whether they can be treated as distinct justifications for strict liability. For this reason, I do not consider 'cost internalization' (*internalisation des coûts, internalizzazione dei costi*) and 'enterprise liability' (*responsabilité de l'entreprise, responsabilità d'impresa*) as themselves arguments for strict liability, but rather as 'empty boxes' that can be filled with, or surrounded by, a variety of

---

[1] See section 1.1.

Justifying Strict Liability. Marco Cappelletti, Oxford University Press. © Marco Cappelletti 2022.
DOI: 10.1093/oso/9780192859860.003.0003

68 JUSTIFYING STRICT LIABILITY

different justifications. In particular, in discussions on strict liability, 'cost internalization' amounts to no more than saying that a party should be strictly liable, ie that they should internalize the costs of accidents they caused, whether or not they were at fault: this says nothing about the *reasons* for holding that party strictly liable. Where it is used, the term 'cost internalization' is typically surrounded by ideas such as risk–profit, accident avoidance, or loss spreading, which constitute the reasons for forcing the defendant to internalize the costs of accidents they caused. Similarly, the term 'enterprise liability' merely means that a firm should be strictly liable but does not clarify at all the reasons why this should be so.[2] 'Enterprise liability' too is, therefore, an empty box that can be filled with all sorts of justifications. The focus of my discussion is not on these empty boxes, which do not constitute distinct reasons for imposing strict liability but rather on the justifications which give content to them. Similarly, I do not treat 'fairness' as a distinct justification for strict liability, as its content varies as much as its proponents and can be filled with all sorts of different arguments. Nor do I consider the mere causation of harm to be a meaningful justification either. Attributing liability on the basis of a causal link between the defendant's conduct and the claimant's harm does not indicate the reasons why a legal system does or should impose liability on such a purely causal ground: causal theories are rather rooted in a variety of justifications and these justifications, rather than 'pure' causation, are the focus of my analysis.[3] Finally, arguments based on the 'minimization of the costs of accidents' (sometimes expressed as the promotion of 'social welfare') could have been the object of a dedicated section. Developed in the field of 'law and economics', this idea suggests that the purpose of tort law is to minimize the sum of the costs of accidents and therefore to increase social welfare. In this respect, different types of costs can become relevant, including the costs represented by the losses themselves, the costs of avoiding such losses, the costs of failing to compensate for such losses, and the costs of administering the tort system. As will be seen, different approaches may prioritize the reduction of some of these costs while disregarding that of others, with consequent disagreements as to which legal arrangements ought to be made, including the choice between strict liability and fault.[4] Very importantly, this type

---

[2] This term was independently coined by Albert A Ehrenzweig, *Negligence Without Fault: Trends Toward An Enterprise Liability for Insurable Loss* (University of California Press 1951) (reprinted in (1966) 54 Cal L Rev 1422), and by Charles O Gregory, 'Trespass to Negligence to Absolute Liability' (1951) 37 Va L Rev 359.

[3] See eg Richard A Epstein, 'A Theory of Strict Liability' (1973) 2 J Legal Stud 151; Giacomo Venezian, 'Danno e risarcimento fuori dei contratti' in *Opere giuridiche, vol. 1—Studi sulle obbligazioni* (Athenaeum 1919) 1ff (this work was written in 1886 but published only thirty-three years later). Note that theories of pure causation have little purchase today: for criticisms of these theories see eg Pietro Trimarchi, *Rischio e responsabilità oggettiva* (Giuffrè 1961) 15–18; Stephen R Perry, 'The Impossibility of General Strict Liability' (1988) 1 Can JL Juris 147, 151, 159–66.

[4] Compare eg Guido Calabresi, *The Costs of Accidents: A Legal and Economic Analysis* (YUP 1970); William L Landes and Richard A Posner, *The Economic Structure of Tort Law* (HUP 1987); Louis Kaplow and Steven Shavell, *Fairness v Welfare* (HUP 2002) 85–154.

INTRODUCTION 69

of reasoning can be partitioned into arguments such as accident avoidance, administrative cost reduction, and the loss-spreading and deep-pockets justifications. It is for this reason that I have decided not to discuss cost minimization as a separate argument. Nevertheless, I will refer to it (or, interchangeably, to the promotion of social welfare) to highlight the specific connotation of certain arguments and the commitments which inspire certain legal actors when it comes to justifying strict liability (or, for that matter, tort liability more generally).

My comparative analysis of the justifications for strict liability unearths a variety of patterns, reflecting different ways in which the justifications are used in the four legal systems studied. Sometimes strict liability may be justified by reference to a single argument, labelled here a *stand-alone* argument, while sometimes multiple arguments may be used at once. Where the latter is the case, they may either be *combined* or simply *juxtaposed* within a broader reasoning. Where arguments are combined, they constitute building blocks of the relevant reasoning and present some level of interconnectedness or integration. Often, the reasoning of which they form part would not stand up if any of them were missing, for each argument constitutes a necessary element in the reasoning; often the justificatory value of each argument depends on its relationship with the other arguments featuring in the same reasoning. For example, reasoning justifying strict liability may include two arguments, with one embodying the fundamental goal that strict liability pursues and the other constituting the means of achieving it. In this case, the two arguments are interconnected and form a combination of arguments.

By contrast, where arguments are only juxtaposed, they look like a list of separate reasons which all point to strict liability but from different, independent directions. The significance of a juxtaposed argument does not depend on the other arguments in the reasoning; therefore, to understand its justificatory weight it is often helpful to take into account a variety of factors, as for example the existence of an explicit ranking of arguments provided by the relevant legal actor, the use of emphatic expressions, or the number of times an argument is repeated in the same reasoning. Finally, sometimes it may be particularly difficult to estimate whether the arguments put forward are being combined or juxtaposed and, where this is case, I will merely note that they are discussed or grouped together.

Another important pattern of reasoning which can be identified in the four legal systems concerns the context-dependent use of some arguments. An argument may be used to justify a specific context of strict liability but be ignored in relation to others, or its frequency of use may vary depending on the particular context or contexts of liability for which it is invoked. My analysis will pay attention to this pattern so as to appreciate correctly the overall significance of arguments in each of the four legal systems examined.

A further pattern of reasoning, which cuts across the previous ones, relates to the distinction between means and goals. At times, an argument may feature in the reasoning justifying strict liability as the goal that strict liability should pursue.

70 JUSTIFYING STRICT LIABILITY

Where this is the case, other arguments also considered in this work may act as means to achieve that goal. For example, strict liability may be justified on the ground that it is desirable to ensure that victims of accidents receive compensation for their losses, and the *same* reasoning may suggest that the best way to do so is to impose liability on the defendant because of their spreading abilities; in this case, loss spreading acts as a means to achieve the goal of victim protection. Moreover, arguments that sometimes act as means may, at other times, be themselves the goals which strict liability should accomplish. For example, accident avoidance and loss spreading may be seen as serving (and therefore as means to) the minimization of the overall costs of accidents, but they may also be seen as goals worth pursuing in themselves. Relatedly, the same argument may be used by legal scholars and judges as a means to achieve different goals. For example, the deep-pockets argument may be seen as serving the minimization of the costs of accidents or, quite differently, the protection of victims. Similarly, the risk–profit argument may be seen as promoting norms of individual responsibility or, quite the opposite, as part of a strategy of increased victim protection. All these variations characterize the relevant argument and confer on it a varying role and significance within and across legal systems.

Keeping track of all these patterns of reasoning and, therefore, of the different ways in which the various arguments are used will be key to understanding how legal actors in the four jurisdictions organize their thinking about strict liability.

As well as identifying these patterns, it is also important to assess and to characterize the justificatory weight of the arguments used across the four legal systems. In this respect, I characterize arguments depending on the weight or significance which they possess in individual instances of reasoning, though where the significance of arguments is not made explicit in the materials, I will assess them myself according to whether they are 'key', 'secondary', or 'make-weight' arguments. First, an argument may act as a 'key' reason for adopting strict liability, meaning that it is seen as a justification of great importance; this is invariably the case where the argument stands alone but it can also be the case where the argument is juxtaposed or combined with other justifications. In the latter two cases, the same reasoning may include one or more key arguments, each being of equal importance. Secondly, arguments may act as 'secondary' reasons for imposing strict liability: they are not as significant as key justifications but they still contribute in important ways to justifying strict liability. Like key arguments, secondary arguments may be juxtaposed or combined with other justifications, and the same line of reasoning may include one or more secondary arguments. Finally, arguments may be thrown in as 'extras' doing little or no work to support the imposition of strict liability; these have been called 'make-weight arguments',[5] as the 'true' reasons for imposing strict

---

[5] See Jane Stapleton, 'Tort, Insurance and Ideology' (1995) 58 MLR 820, 827.

liability must be identified in other arguments featuring in the same reasoning, whether by way of combination or juxtaposition.

The patterns of reasoning and the characterization of arguments presented above will provide both a map and a compass to navigate through the complexity of legal reasoning in strict liability. Even so, the justificatory value of arguments as well as their reciprocal relationship in the reasoning of a specific scholar or judge may remain unclear. This may be due to a lack of precision or sophistication of analysis within the materials, or to the fact that some of the arguments have fuzzy edges and may overlap. Furthermore, it may happen that an argument is presented as a certain argument but, in reality, it is a different one. I will acknowledge these kinds of difficulties while also providing, if possible, the interpretation of the argument that fits best the broader thinking of the relevant legal actor.

A further point which needs clarification concerns the *nature* of the arguments discussed in this work and, more particularly, the distinction (particularly evident in academic writings) between 'interpretive justifications' and 'normative justifications'. The first term refers to an argument which is used to interpret (or explain) the law, in our case strict liabilities, without the relevant legal actor taking a view as to the soundness of that argument. The second term, by contrast, refers to an argument which is relied upon to show why strict liability should be adopted, meaning that the relevant legal actor agrees with the argument in question, whether or not they also see it as a correct interpretation (or explanation) of the law.[6] My comparative analysis of arguments includes both types of justification, but I generally do not distinguish between these two usages for two reasons. First, it may be difficult to understand whether legal actors (and especially legal scholars) are putting forward an interpretive or normative justification, as they often do not clarify this point and their reasoning may be open to doubt (particularly in civil law systems). Secondly, it is doubtful whether reasoning which is being presented as merely interpretive does not include any normative dimension reflecting a prescriptive project of the relevant legal actor.[7]

Finally, a few words are necessary on the organization of the discussion that follows. This part of the book is organized by *arguments* and it includes seven sections, one for each argument. Within each section, there are six subsections. The first one introduces the relevant argument by explaining the core idea and its variations, while the final one provides a brief comparative conclusion on the significance of

---

[6] See Jules L Coleman, *The Practice of Principle: In Defence of a Pragmatist Approach to Legal Theory* (OUP 2001) 3 (distinguishing between justifications and explanations). cf John Gardner, 'What is Tort Law For? Part 1. The Place of Corrective Justice' (2011) 30(1) Law and Phil 1, 2–4(criticizing Coleman's distinction on the ground that all justifications are explanations and distinguishing between 'committal' and 'noncommittal' justificatory statements).

[7] See Peter Cane, 'Rights in Private Law' in Donal Nolan and Andrew Robertson (eds), *Rights and Private Law* (Hart Publishing 2012) 35, 41, 51 (arguing that, while presented as purely interpretive, rights-based theories of private law are prescriptive and driven by a desire to protect individual interests and autonomy).

that argument across the four jurisdictions. The four subsections in between form the heart of the discussion, as they explore the relevant argument in each of the four legal systems. In developing my analysis across these four subsections, the legal systems are not ordered in the same way for every argument but rather according to the prominence of the relevant argument in the systems. For this purpose by prominence I refer to a variety of factors, such as whether the argument is more heavily relied upon in one system than in others, whether it is still used or not, or in which system it was developed from an historical standpoint. When combined, these factors suggest that a particular argument is more prominent in some legal systems than in others, and it is on this basis that I have ordered their discussion. The practical advantages of this ordering are significant: discussing first the system where an argument is more prominent allows me to develop sooner rather than later a richer framework and vocabulary of analysis that will help the comparative discussion and it will also reduce repetitions. I am, however, conscious of the need to avoid bias when ordering the discussion. In this respect, I will take care to consider each argument as it is treated in each legal system, and in particular I will not superimpose on a discussion in one system a theoretical framework developed by legal actors for that argument in other jurisdictions. In other words, while feeding on the richer vocabulary of the legal system(s) where the argument is more prominent, the discussion will seek to be fair to each legal system and to its own reasoning in strict liability.

3.2
Risk

3.2.1 The Risk-based Justifications of Strict Liability

As a justification for imposing strict liability, the concept of 'risk' (*risque, rischio*) underlies and informs a variety of approaches. The widest of these suggests that a party should be liable because they created a risk of harm to another which then materialized ('risk creation', or 'theory of created risk'). On this view, the mere existence of a causal link between the risk created by a defendant and its materialization (ie the harm) is sufficient to trigger liability. A key feature of the theory of created risk is that it is broad enough to apply to any situation, as any action or even omission can contribute to a risk of harm to others.[1] Perhaps for this reason, more sophisticated versions of this theory distinguish according to the nature of the risk created. For example, liability may arise if the risk of harm was abnormal,[2] as where the defendant engages in dangerous activities such as blasting operations, nuclear installations, or toxic waste disposal ('abnormality of risk'). Or a person may be liable if they create and impose on another a 'nonreciprocal' risk of harm, that is a risk of harm 'greater in degree and different in order' from that created and imposed on them by the victim.[3] For example, airline companies and pilots create and impose a nonreciprocal risk of harm on homeowners by flying over their heads and are therefore liable strictly to them for the damage done on crashing ('nonreciprocity of risk').[4] Compared to risk creation, these two qualified approaches reduce considerably the scope of strict liability for created risk.

As will be seen, risk creation and its variants focus on the nature of the risk created by the defendant. By contrast, other risk-based arguments focus on the notion of gain and argue that a person who creates a risk of harm to others for the purpose of obtaining some gain must pay for the harm so caused. In this respect, two distinct theories of risk have been put forward depending on the meaning given to the notion of gain. The first adopts a very broad understanding of gain, with the result that any benefit derived from the creation of risk is enough to trigger liability

---

[1] Stephen Perry, 'Responsibility for Outcomes, Risk, and the Law of Torts' in Gerald Postema (ed), *Philosophy and the Law of Torts* (CUP 2001) 72, 86; Jenny Steele, *Risks and Legal Theory* (Hart Publishing 2004) 89.

[2] See Matthew Dyson and Sandy Steel, 'Risk and English Tort Law' in Matthew Dyson (ed), *Regulating Risk through Private Law* (Intersentia 2018) 23, 36.

[3] This theory has been proposed by George Fletcher, 'Fairness and Utility in Tort Theory' (1972) 85 Harv L Rev 537, 542.

[4] ibid 548.

Justifying Strict Liability. Marco Cappelletti, Oxford University Press. © Marco Cappelletti 2022.
DOI: 10.1093/oso/9780192859860.003.0004

74 JUSTIFYING STRICT LIABILITY

('risk–benefit'): for example, because riding a horse for pleasure in a park is an activity which gives the rider a benefit (pleasure), the rider should be strictly liable for the injury caused to a person innocently lying in the park. The second gain-based theory adopts a narrower understanding of gain so that only an economic benefit can justify the defendant's strict liability ('risk–profit'): for example, as operating an industrial plant is an activity which generates financial gain, the prospect of that gain justifies the firm being strictly liable for any damage caused to adjacent land.

An important point to note in relation to the terms 'benefit' and 'profit' is an ambiguity between the two which can make it difficult to understand whether the person using them (typically a legal scholar or judge) is referring to the theory of risk–benefit or to the theory of risk–profit. The ambiguity lies in the fact that, both in common and legal language (especially in French and Italian), the two terms 'benefit' and 'profit' can be used interchangeably and each can encompass both pecuniary and non-pecuniary gains.[5] Even so, it is often possible to see which gain-based theory of risk the scholar or judge refers to by the broader context.

Here, I shall explore how the various permutations of risk are used across the four legal systems and explain their significance as justifications for strict liability.

3.2.2 The Pervasive Nature of Risk in French Strict Liability

The influence of risk on French strict liability is remarkable and visible both in relation to the law of civil liability, whether included in the *Code civil* or in the numerous legislative measures introduced over the course of the twentieth century, and in relation to the law governing the liability of French public authorities. Except for nonreciprocity of risk,[6] the theories of risk presented above have all had considerable impact on French strict liability and, although they have varying levels of importance in the legal reasoning of scholars and courts, in general they reflect a broader effort to improve the position of victims of accidents.

Historically, the concept of risk has played a central role in the development of strict liability in French law. As a reaction to the growing number of accidents caused by industrialization in the second half of the nineteenth century, two prominent legal scholars, Saleilles and Josserand, spearheaded an intellectual revolution in civil liability which aimed to guarantee greater financial protection to the victims of accidents; in trying to secure this result, they called into question the 'sanctity' of fault and its adequacy to meet satisfactorily the new demands of social justice.[7] The value of social solidarity required the community to support those

---

[5] eg Florence Millet, *La notion de risque et ses fonctions en droit privé* (PUF 2001) [256], and Pietro Trimarchi, *La Responsabilità Civile: Atti Illeciti, Rischio, Danno* (Giuffrè 2017) 336, both using the term 'profit' as including non-pecuniary gains.

[6] cf n 13 in this section.

[7] Jean-Louis Halpérin, *Histoire du droit privé français depuis 1804* (PUF 2012) [128]–[129]. See also Patrice Jourdain, *Les principes de la responsabilité civile* (10th edn, Dalloz 2021) 10–11.

of its members who suffered some sort of harm, even if caused without fault.[8] Especially in cases of anonymous accidents in industrial contexts, a liability regime based on the fault of the defendant made it very difficult for the victim to prove the defendant's failure in conduct, with the result that the loss was systematically borne by the victim. To cure this situation and facilitate the compensation of victims, both Saleilles and Josserand appeal to the concept of risk. In 1894, Saleilles argues that justice required that a person who has the direction of an industrial activity and reaps its profits should bear the associated risk of harm and pay compensation under former article 1384(1) *Code civil* (Cc) (ie liability for the deeds of things), which he considers a crucial testing ground for his theory of risk and for ensuring greater protection to victims of accidents.[9] While at this stage he justifies the imposition of strict liability on risk–profit and confines its scope of application to the industrial context,[10] in later writings Saleilles goes further and argues that it is morally and socially desirable to link tort liability to the mere creation of risk on the basis of former article 1382 Cc,[11] advocating a generalized application of strict liability to 'the entire range of activities of individuals'.[12] Around the same time, Josserand puts forward a theory of 'created risk' (*risque-créé*) to justify liability for the deeds of things. In Josserand's view, whenever an accident occurs someone has to bear its costs. Since the victim of an accident is not only without fault but has no relationship with the thing which causes damage, the victim's loss should be borne by the person who directed the thing in their keeping for their own interest (be it pleasure or profit) and thus created a risk of harm.[13] Regardless of whether Josserand's view is best seen as referring to risk–benefit or risk creation, there is no doubt that his work, with Saleilles', made risk one of the conceptual cornerstones

[8] On the importance of social solidarity in France, see Léon Duguit, *L'état, le droit objectif et la loi positive* (Fontemoing 1901) 69–78.

[9] Raymond Saleilles, 'Rapport' Revue bourguignonne de l'enseignement supérieur 1894.647, 659 ff (hereafter Saleilles, 'Rapport'). See also Saleilles, D 1897.1.433.

[10] Saleilles, 'Rapport' (n 9) 661–62.

[11] Raymond Saleilles, 'Le risque professionnel dans le code civil' La réforme sociale 1898.633, 645–47 (hereafter Saleilles, 'Le risque professionnel'). Former article 1382 Cc founds civil liability on the defendant's fault, but Saleilles objects to this reading and argues that that provision sets a 'purely objective liability, based on the idea of risk and independent of any fault': ibid 645. See also Raymond Saleilles, *Les accidents de travail et la responsabilité civile* (Arthur Rousseau 1897) 74–75.

[12] Saleilles, 'Le risque professionnel' (n 11) 649 (and suggesting, at 647, the introduction of a compensation cap in situations where the claimant failed to prove the defendant's fault).

[13] Louis Josserand, *De la responsabilité du fait des choses inanimées* (Arthur Rousseau 1897) 106–09, 113–14. See also Louis Josserand, D 1925.1.97, 100. Interestingly, on a few occasions this leading scholar relied on nonreciprocity of risk as well: see Louis Josserand, *De l'esprit des droits et de leur relativité: théorie dite de l'abus des droits* (2nd edn, Dalloz 1939) [16] (concerning the justifications of liability for nuisance, on which see n 63 in this section); Louis Josserand, 'Les collisions entre véhicules et la responsabilité civile' D chron 1928.33; Louis Josserand, 'Les collisions entre véhicules et présomptions de responsabilité' D chron 1935.41, 42 (concerning traffic accidents). Nonreciprocity of risk has, however, never had meaningful significance in French reasoning on strict liability and, at least in the context of liability for the deeds of things, it is expressly rejected by both courts and legal scholars: see Patrice Jourdain in Geneviève Viney, Patrice Jourdain, and Suzanne Carval (eds), *Les conditions de la responsabilité. Traité de droit civil* (4th edn, LGDJ 2013) [640].

of French strict civil liability throughout the twentieth century.[14] Similarly, in the field of administrative liability, the notion of risk has featured prominently since the 1895 decision in *Cames*, a case concerning a worker who was injured while working in a state-owned munitions factory and who managed to obtain compensation from the state.[15] While the Conseil d'État did not expressly invoke the idea of risk, in hindsight French administrative law scholars have treated *Cames* as endorsing that very idea,[16] and as lying at the root of several other risk-based strict liabilities in administrative law.[17] To see the importance of risk in this area of French law, it suffices to consider that canonical works on the subject treat risk as an independent basis of liability, to be distinguished both from liability for fault and, within the realm of strict liability, from the principle of 'equality before public burdens' (*égalité devant les charges publiques*),[18] which can be seen as the French version, in the public law context, of loss spreading as proportionality of burdens and benefits.[19] In sum, the notion of risk has always played a very important role in the development of strict liability, both in civil and administrative law.

Before examining the impact of the various risk-based justifications on strict liability, it must be mentioned that the theories of risk have been challenged from their very inception. Many legal scholars criticize their desirability beyond strictly confined areas on a variety of grounds. For example, from a normative perspective it is suggested that imposing liability on grounds of risk would lead to social and moral injustices,[20] that it would cause 'senseless immobility' and therefore discourage all sorts of human activities,[21] and that it would generate legal uncertainty in the administration of the law;[22] others also criticize risk-based arguments for their failure to explain in a satisfactory way a variety of contexts of liability.[23]

---

[14] See Geneviève Viney, *Introduction à la responsabilité. Traité de droit civil* (4th edn, LGDJ 2019) [68]–[69]. See also Véronique Wester-Ouisse, Simon Taylor, and Duncan Fairgrieve, 'Risk and French Private Law' in Matthew Dyson (ed), *Regulating Risk Through Private Law* (Intersentia 2018) 55 (illustrating the role of risk in French private law more generally).

[15] CE 21.6.1895 (*Cames*), S 1897.3.33 note Hauriou.

[16] See the remarks of Maryse Deguergue, *Jurisprudence et doctrine dans l'élaboration du droit de la responsabilité administrative* (LGDJ 1994) 121–25.

[17] Marceau Long and others, *Les grands arrêts de la jurisprudence administrative* (22nd edn, Dalloz 2019) 45–46.

[18] See eg René Chapus, *Droit administratif général*, vol 1 (15th edn, Montchrestien 2001).

[19] This principle is therefore discussed in subsection 3.5.2 on loss spreading in French law (text accompanying nn 40–49 in that subsection). As to the meaning of burden–benefit proportionality, see subsection 3.5.1.

[20] Marcel Planiol, 'Études sur la responsabilité civile' RCLJ 1905.277, 278–79, 289 (on risk creation). See also Georges Ripert, *La règle morale dans les obligations civiles* (4th edn, LGDJ 1949) [123] (arguably on both risk creation and risk–benefit/profit).

[21] Planiol (n 20) 289. See also Georges Ripert, D 1930.1.57, 59–60 (on risk creation); Boris Starck, Henri Roland, and Laurent Boyer, *Obligations*, t. 1, *Responsabilité délictuelle* (5th edn, LITEC 1996) [48] (on risk–benefit and risk creation); François Terré and others, *Droits civil, Les obligations* (12th edn, Dalloz 2018) [908] (on risk–profit and risk creation).

[22] Henri Mazeaud, 'La faute dans la garde' RTD civ 1925.793, 801 (on risk–profit).

[23] See eg Starck, Roland, and Boyer (n 21) [46] (on risk–profit), [48] (on risk–benefit and risk creation); Jean-Sébastien Borghetti, 'La responsabilité du fait des choses, un régime qui a fait son temps' RTD civ 2010.1, [12]–[14] (on risk–profit and risk creation).

Notwithstanding these criticisms, risk has played a very important role in the development of French strict liability. It is widely acknowledged that the views of Saleilles and Josserand have influenced French courts, especially in the first few decades of the twentieth century.[24] For example, while it is true that in the *Jand'heur* litigation the Cour de Cassation did not clarify the substantive grounds on which it was abandoning a fault-based reading of liability for the deeds of things,[25] it is most likely that the court had been profoundly influenced by the theory of risk. Indeed, in that case the *procureur général* Matter emphatically advocated a broad and strict interpretation of article 1384(1) Cc,[26] and in doing so he expressly referred to the theory of risk by quoting[27] a passage from Saleilles' note to the Cour de Cassation's decision in *Teffaine* in 1896.[28] Nevertheless, it remains true that, in relation to any of the contexts where strict liability is imposed, it is very difficult to find judicial decisions expressly referring to any of the theories of risk as justifications for such imposition.[29] Therefore, it is more through the analysis of legal scholarship that the significance of risk-based justifications can be appreciated.

Starting with the theory of created risk, this argument features frequently in legal writings seeking to justify the imposition of strict liability. At least three patterns of risk creation are identifiable, each carrying its own justificatory weight.

First, the argument occasionally acts as a stand-alone and key justification: for example, leading authors consider that it is the risk created by putting the product on the market which explains the manufacturer's liability,[30] that it is the risk created by the thing which justifies the keeper's liability,[31] or that it is the risk generated by the kinetic energy of a vehicle which grounds the driver's or keeper's liability for traffic accidents.[32] This is not, though, the most frequent way in which risk creation

---

[24] eg Halpérin (n 7) [129]; Viney (n 14) [69].

[25] Ch réun 13.2.1930, D 1930.1.57 note Ripert. cf the decision in *Franck* (Ch réun 2.12.1941, S 1941.1.217 note H Mazeaud), where the Cour de Cassation defined *la garde* of the thing as the 'use, direction, and control' of it—a move widely seen as a partial return to fault.

[26] D 1930.1.57, 64ff.

[27] ibid 70.

[28] Civ 16.6.1896, D 1897.1.433, 439.

[29] One rare example is Trib Seine 2.4.1949, Gaz Pal 25–28.6.1949, 69, where an employee caused a traffic accident while driving the employer's vehicle. In that case, the court held the employer liable on the ground that, as owner and keeper of the vehicle, he 'assumed the risks of harm that could be caused by the vehicle in return for the profits he reaped from it'.

[30] Jacques Flour, Jean-Luc Aubert, and Eric Savaux, *Droit civil. Les obligations. 2. Le fait juridique* (14th edn, Dalloz 2011) [300] (but note the lack of any elaboration on this).

[31] Yvon Lambert-Faivre, 'L'évolution de la responsabilité civile d'une dette de responsabilité à une créance d'indemnisation' RTD civ 1987.1, 5. See also Fabrice Leduc, 'L'état actuel du principe général de responsabilité délictuelle du fait des choses' in Fabrice Leduc (ed), *La responsabilité du fait des choses, Réflexions autour d'un centenaire* (Economica 1997) 35, 44; Terré and others (n 21) [1000] (quoting Leduc); Lucien Charbonnier, 'Une notion-clé pour l'indemnisation des victimes d'accidents de la circulation: l' "implication" du véhicule (loi du 5 juillet 1985)' in Rapport de la Cour de cassation 1986, 96, 103 (though these lines of reasoning may be interpreted as being about abnormality of risk rather than risk creation, given their reference to danger or dangerousness).

[32] Starck, Roland, and Boyer (n 21) [54], but cf [642] (arguing that the *loi* Badinter on traffic accidents 'established an objective right of reparation to the benefit of the victims, thereby consecrating the theory of guarantee').

78   JUSTIFYING STRICT LIABILITY

is used in the French context, as the argument often forms part of a more complex reasoning which seeks to ensure the achievement of some particular goal.

Secondly, sometimes the conceptual distinctiveness of risk creation is preserved and the argument still does an important justificatory work, even if included within a broader reasoning. For example, when trying to identify the possible justifications for strict liability, Jourdain argues that (with the author's own emphasis)

> it seems natural to attribute liability to the party who is at the origin of the risk, to the party who *created* that risk. It is not a matter of sanctioning the creator of a risk but of ... pursuing a policy of accident avoidance which is based on the belief that the creator of a risk is in the best position to avoid its materialisation. The desire to *trace back liability to the creator of risk* features in all strict liabilities based on risk.[33]

Here, the focus is on avoiding accidents, and yet risk creation retains its conceptual distinctiveness and independence.[34] It seems as though the author is keeping the theory of created risk alive to perpetuate an idea which possesses the prestige of a tradition going back to Saleilles and Josserand and which, perhaps partly for this very reason, makes the imposition of strict liability more attractive and familiar. Similarly, in relation to the liability of French public bodies, influential legal scholars see the creation of risk as a reason for imposing strict liability, even though what is at times presented as *risque créé* hides, in reality, an argument based on the abnormality of risk, and the argument is sometimes juxtaposed with the principle of 'equality before public burdens'.[35]

This second pattern of reasoning can be distinguished from a third one, where the creation of risk again forms part of a broader reasoning but this time it does

---

[33] Jourdain (n 7) 30 (original emphasis). See also Patrice Jourdain, 'La reconnaissance d'une responsabilité du fait d'autrui en dehors des cas particuliers énoncés dans l'article 1384' RTD civ 1991.541 ('The idea of "social risk" linked to liberal therapies ... is no doubt what justifies the solution adopted by the Assemblée plénière. That *risk* is a valid basis of liability is understood above all through the essential role of insurance. All those whose activity is a source of risks are *well-suited to insure*, a circumstance which naturally designates them as responsible for the damage and which at the same time encourages them to insure against the risk of liability' (original emphasis)); Philippe Brun, *La responsabilité civile extracontractuelle* (5th edn, LexisNexis 2018) [675] (in relation to traffic accidents: 'it is because he participates in the creation of the risk (and he is consequently required to insure against it) that the driver or guardian of a vehicle can be ordered to pay compensation on the mere basis of an involvement [of the vehicle] in the accident').

[34] Note that Jourdain (n 7) 29–31 provides a long list of juxtaposed arguments to justify strict liability, and he starts off by saying that 'all of them are articulated around the notion of *risk*' (original emphasis).

[35] See, for example, Georges Berlia, 'Essai sur les fondements de la responsabilité en droit public français' RDP 1951.685, 688 (arguing that what goes under the banner of created risk are, typically, dangerous activities which by their very nature can cause harm); Duncan Fairgrieve and François Lichere, 'The Liability of Public Authorities in France' in Ken Oliphant (ed), *The Liability of Public Authorities in Comparative Perspective* (Intersentia 2016) 155, [68]–[69] (here risk creation seems to blur into abnormality of risk, as the two authors start off by referring to a generic creation of risk but then focus on risks that have 'the potential to cause mass harm').

not do any real justificatory work. For example, in relation to the vicarious liability of employers, Viney observes that while this liability is best seen 'as a means of attributing to firms the costs of the risks they create through their own activities', its 'objective ... is both to identify who must take out liability insurance for the protection of victims and to encourage firms to avoid accidents'.[36] Here, and in similar cases,[37] the impression is that the creation of risk merely stands for the possibility of occurrence of some harm, losing its conceptual distinctiveness as a justification and dissolving into other arguments.[38] In sum, risk creation in France is used in different ways and for each pattern of use it takes on a different significance.

Moving now to abnormality of risk, the argument plays a role in discussions regarding French strict liability either to support the introduction of a category of liability for dangerous activities,[39] or to explain contexts such as liability for defective products.[40] While the notion of abnormality of risk defies easy definitions[41] and may take on substantially different meanings across and within jurisdictions, French case law and academic writings embrace a particularly broad notion of abnormality of risk, one which encompasses ultra-hazardous activities, the abnormal position, state, or behaviour of a thing,[42] as well as the putting on

[36] Geneviève Viney in Viney, Jourdain, and Carval (eds) (n 13) [791–1]. Note that, in the same paragraph, she includes risk in the list of justifications which she sees as not providing by themselves adequate support to employers' vicarious liability.

[37] See Patrice Jourdain, D 1997.265, 267 (observing that, while there may be differences between parental liability and employers' vicarious liability—such as the absence of risk–profit among the reasons supporting parental liability—the two contexts have some common justifications: 'both parents and employers are creators of risks and the authority exercised over others puts them in the position to avoid accidents and to take out liability insurance, with the consequence that they are the most obvious parties to be liable'); Geneviève Viney and Anne Guégan-Lécuyer, 'The Development of Traffic Liability in France' in Wolfgang Ernst (ed), *The Development of Traffic Liability* (CUP 2010) 50, 71–72 (mentioning the risk of harm created by motor vehicles, but emphasizing victim protection and insurance spreading).

[38] In Viney's example, these are victim protection, loss spreading, and accident avoidance.

[39] eg Anne Guégan-Lécuyer, 'Vers un nouveau fait générateur de responsabilité civile: les activités dangereuses (Commentaire de l'article 1362 de l'Avant-projet Catala)' in *Etudes offertes à Geneviève Viney* (LGDJ 2008) 499; Jean-Sébastien Borghetti, 'La responsabilité du fait des choses et/ou du fait des activités dangereuses. Synthèse comparative' in *Le droit français de la responsabilité civile confronté aux projets européens d'harmonisation* (IRJS Éditions 2012) 279. The adoption of a specific liability for dangerous activities was included in two reform projects of French law: see Avant-projet Catala, article 1362; Avant-projet Terré, article 23. However, no particular urgency was felt for the adoption of this liability in light of the fact that the existing law, particularly in the form of liability for the deeds of things, is flexible enough to ensure that those injured in accidents caused by dangerous things or activities receive adequate financial protection. Indeed, in a discussion taking place within the group in charge of the Avant-projet Catala, it was observed that the existence of liability for the deeds of things made the introduction of a strict liability for dangerous activities pointless unless the latter were even stricter than the former, therefore achieving a greater degree of protection of victims: see Avant-projet Catala, fn 40 at 159 regarding article 1362 of the *projet*; and also ibid Viney, *Exposé des motifs*, (5), at 148.

[40] Jean-Sébastien Borghetti, *La Responsabilité du Fait des Produits: Etude de Droit Comparé* (LGDJ 2004) [616]ff (arguing that the foundational idea behind product liability is the *creation* of an *abnormal risk* of harm in the manufacturing and distribution of a product). Note that Borghetti develops his theory around the notion of cost internalization, which he seems to link tightly to risk–profit ([627]ff)).

[41] ibid [638]–[640].

[42] See Civ (2) 19.3.1980, D 1980.IR.414 note Larroumet. A fishing vessel lost a sunken winching mechanism in a harbour. Given that the *gardien*, the owner of the vessel, did not know the exact position of the mechanism, for safety reasons the harbour had to be closed to larger vessels. The Cour de

80 JUSTIFYING STRICT LIABILITY

the market of a product that, being defective, exceeds the risk of harm that society expects and is prepared for.[43] The idea of exposing others to an abnormal risk of harm seems particularly apt to attract or at least to explain the imposition of strict liability.[44] Due to its conceptual breadth, abnormality of risk is used in relation to many contexts of liability and, in keeping with the other risk-based arguments,[45] it is often deployed to achieve some specific goal which, in the French context, often means the compensation of victims.[46] For example, the existence of sources of increased risk of harm pushed the French law of civil liability to move away from the fault paradigm in relation to traffic accidents, first by devising judicially a general regime of strict liability for the deeds of things,[47] and then by enacting legislatively an even stricter special liability: the 'real and violent danger' posed by motor vehicles as well as the growing number of road victims made '[t]he imperative of compensating victims ... urgent',[48] a call finally met by the *loi* Badinter in

Cassation held that the presence somewhere of the sunken mechanism made the whole harbour unsafe and that the claimant was entitled to compensation for the purely economic loss suffered as a result of the closure of the harbour.

[43] Borghetti (n 40) [639].

[44] Note, however, that French civil courts are wary of embracing any formal distinction between dangerousness and non-dangerousness that may unduly restrict the scope of liability. The paramount example of this comes from the famous *Jand'heur* litigation in relation to liability for the deeds of things. In that case, the Chambre civile of the Cour de Cassation (Civ 21.2.1927, D 1927.1.97 note Ripert) sought to confine the operation of former article 1384(1) Cc to things that needed to be guarded in light of their dangerousness; three years later, however, the Chambres réunies (Ch réun 13.2.1930, D 1930.1.57 note Ripert) omitted any reference to the element of dangerousness, whit the consequence that any distinction between dangerous and non-dangerous things has been expelled from the liability for the deeds of things and not applied in later cases: see Viney (n 36) [634]. An exception to this judicial attitude is the distinction between *gardien de la structure* (responsible for harm caused by the thing's internal defects or characteristics) and *gardien du comportement* (responsible for harm caused by the thing's handling), first put forward by Bertold Goldman, *La détermination du gardien responsable du fait des choses inanimées* (Sirey 1947). The distinction has typically come into play where the harmful thing possessed 'its own dynamism capable of manifesting itself in a dangerous way', as in the case of bottled sparkling drinks, gas cylinders, fire extinguishers, and other flammable or corrosive products. See eg Civ (1) 12.11.1975, JCP 1976.II.18479 note Viney. For an overview and critical appraisal of the distinction, see Jourdain (n 13) [691]–[701].

[45] See text to nn 7–14, and text to n 66 in this section.

[46] Geneviève Schamps, *La mise en danger: un concept fondateur d'un principe général de responsabilité* (Bruylant/LGDJ 1998) 843ff (mentioning accident avoidance as well at 850, but overall giving far more importance to victim protection); Guégan-Lécuyer (n 39) 501–02 (mentioning loss spreading, victim protection, and accident avoidance); Jean-Sébastien Borghetti, 'La responsabilité de l'entreprise du fait des activités dangereuses' in Nicolas Ferrier and Anne Pélissier (eds), *L'entreprise face aux évolutions de la responsabilité civile* (Economica 2012) 59, 60 and 68 (mentioning victim protection). See also Louis Josserand, *Cours de droit civil positif français*, vol 1 (3rd edn, Sirey 1938) [1505] (on nuisance). cf Borghetti (n 40) [627]–[628] (combining abnormality of risk with risk–profit and cost internalization, although it is not entirely unclear what substantive goal, if any, he ascribes to this combination of ideas (which is probably due to the interpretive nature of his work); Borghetti (n 39) 279, 287 (seeing an appropriate balancing among the defendant's freedom of action, the claimant's right to safety, and the principle of 'legal certainty' (*sécurité juridique*), as the objective to be pursued through the creation of a liability for dangerous activities/things).

[47] André Tunc, 'Rapport sur les choses dangereuses et la responsabilité civile en droit français' in *Travaux de l'Association Henri-Capitant: Les choses dangereuses: journées néerlandaises* (Economica 1967) 50, 56.

[48] Viney and Guégan-Lécuyer (n 37) 60–61. See also Tunc (n 47) 56ff.

RISK 81

1985.[49] In addition, abnormality of risk plays a prominent role in the realm of public liability. Here, the key situations are those where public bodies cause harm by the operation of things or activities which, in the view of the Conseil d'État, qualify as dangerous.[50] This head of strict liability is justified by the idea that, if an activity undertaken by a public authority creates a significant risk of harm to another which then materializes, that authority should pay damages for the loss caused. Sometimes, this justification stands alone,[51] while at other times it features with other arguments, most notably victim protection and burden–benefit proportionality.[52] The impression one gets from these instances and patterns of reasoning is that, in the view of most French legal actors, the interests of the victim should not be sacrificed to the common good but, quite the opposite, the community in whose interest the public body created an increased risk of harm should compensate that person for the loss suffered.[53] Overall, then, abnormality of risk plays a significant role in the French debate on strict liability, whether public or private, especially by providing the starting point of a reasoning which seeks to justify strict liability on the basis of its ability to protect victims and spread losses.

As far as risk–benefit and risk–profit are concerned, the two arguments are used frequently. This may be due to the fact that in the French context, both risk–profit and risk–benefit are widely seen as arguments having their roots in a simple ideal of fairness (at times expressed as *justice*, other times as *équité*), suggesting that those who gain from their risk-creating activities should pay for the harm caused. Compared to risk creation and abnormality of risk, risk–benefit and risk–profit are deployed selectively depending on the context of liability. Risk–benefit is certainly more prominent than risk–profit in relation to, first, liability for the deeds of things and liability for animals. This may well be the case because these contexts of liability are not limited to things or animals as sources of economic profit but include also

---

[49] On which see text to nn 241–245 in section 2.4.

[50] For some examples, see n 267 in section 2.4. See also François Vincent, 'Responsabilité sans faute' JCl Admin, Fasc 824 (2015) [4]–[49]; Stéphanie Hennette-Vauchez, 'Responsabilité sans faute' in Répertoire de la responsabilité de la puissance publique (2017) [140]–[170].

[51] See eg CE 28.3.1919 (*Regnault-Desroziers*), S 1918–1919.3.25 note Hauriou; CE 3.2.1956 (*Thouzellier*), RDP 1956.854 (on escapes from open borstals); Yves Gaudemet, *Droit Administratif* (23rd edn, LGDJ 2020) [382]–[386].

[52] CE Ass 24.6.1949 (*Lecomte et Daramy*), D 1950.27 (holding that the administration is strictly liable 'where police officers use firearms or other equipment creating exceptional risks of harm to persons or property, and where the harm suffered in such circumstances exceeds, for its seriousness, the burdens that should be normally borne by citizens in exchange for the benefits of the public action'); Jacques Moreau, 'Rapport sur les choses dangereuses en droit administratif français' in *Travaux de l'Association Henri-Capitant: Les choses dangereuses: journées néerlandaises* (Dalloz 1971) 256, [4] (noting that the modern state must 'cure' and 'repair' everything, especially where the causes of accidents can be found in risks of exceptional frequency or of abnormal magnitude); Chapus (n 18) [1487] (arguing that liability for risk, which includes strict liability for abnormal risks of harm, is imposed in the name of social solidarity, so that the cost of compensating the victims is borne by the wider community).

[53] See Duncan Fairgrieve, *State Liability in Tort: A Comparative Law Study* (OUP 2003) 138 (arguing that the argument from abnormality of risk depends on another, fundamental justification of French public liability, that is the principle of 'equality before public burdens').

82 JUSTIFYING STRICT LIABILITY

those used for non-pecuniary purposes (eg a pet is typically a source of joy, not financial profit). Consistently with this, Savatier notes that the obligation to compensate for the harm caused by the thing or by the animal burdens the party who benefits from them;[54] similarly, more recently Jourdain argues that the benefits the keeper gets from the thing are one of the reasons why they should be designated as the liable party;[55] again, Carbonnier sees the theory of risk–benefit as the one most credited by legal scholars as explaining liability for the actions of animals.[56] Secondly, risk–benefit plays a greater role than risk–profit in the realm of administrative liability. Indeed, several legal scholars link the strict liability of public bodies to the benefit that these gain from, for example, employing their servants,[57] using things in their keeping,[58] or availing themselves of collaborators who are not public employees.[59] On this view, the theory of risk–benefit provides a 'moral justification' for the imposition of liability on public bodies, as it is only fair (*juste*) that the party who benefits from an activity should bear its correlative burdens.[60]

By contrast, in relation to other contexts of liability, such as private employers' vicarious liability, industrial nuisance, or defective products, it is the risk–profit justification that looms larger. This is because activities in these contexts involve some economic gain for the defendant. For example, it is widely thought that as an employer makes a gain from the activity of their employee, they should also bear the risk of harm resulting from that activity.[61] The distinctive importance of

---

[54] René Savatier, *Traité de la responsabilité civile*, vol 1 (2nd edn, LGDJ 1951) [337]. At [274], he absorbs risk–profit and risk–benefit in the theory of *risque-créé*, which he presents as involving some benefit or profit for the liable party. cf ibid [282], where the author emphasizes the importance of insurance for the sustainability and fairness of strict liability.

[55] Jourdain (n 7) 96 (juxtaposing risk–benefit with some idea of control (*maîtrise*), accident avoidance, and insurability).

[56] Jean Carbonnier, *Droit civil. Les biens, les obligations* (2nd edn, PUF 2017) [1166] (risk–benefit standing alone) (using the term 'profit', but likely including non-pecuniary benefits).

[57] See eg Charles Eisenmann, 'Sur le degré d'originalité du régime de la responsabilité extra-contractuelle des personnes publiques' JCP 1949.I.751, [10]; René Chapus, *Responsabilité publique et responsabilité privée: les influences réciproques des jurisprudences administrative et judiciaire* (LGDJ 1954) [245] (both authors drawing an analogy between the relationship between a private employer and its employees and the public administration and its servants, and arguing that both employers and the public administration are liable for the harm caused by their employees/servants because of the benefits they gain from their activities) (risk–benefit standing alone).

[58] Eisenmann (n 57) [10]; Chapus (n 57) [311]–[313] (both authors arguing that risk–benefit justifies both liability in the administration and liability in private individuals under article 1384(1) Cc, now article 1242(1)) (risk–benefit standing alone).

[59] Georges Vedel and Pierre Delvolvé, *Droit administratif*, vol 1 (12th edn, PUF 1992) 602–04.

[60] Jean-Paul Gilli, 'La "responsabilité d'équité" de la puissance publique' D chron 1971.125, 126.

[61] Marcel Planiol, 'Études sur la responsabilité civile' RCLJ 1909.282, 298–301 (risk–profit standing alone, and seen as 'the effect of an economic law which is both fair and reasonable'); René Demogue, *Traité des obligations en général—Tome V—Sources des obligations* (Rousseau 1925) [882] (risk–profit standing alone); Clothilde Grare, *Recherches sur la cohérence de la responsabilité délictuelle. L'influence des fondements de la responsabilité sur la reparation* (Dalloz 2005) [33]–[35] (giving credit to risk–profit), but cf [45]–[48] (where she emphasizes the importance of loss spreading for strict liability); Flour, Aubert, and Savaux (n 30) [205], [207] (juxtaposing risk–profit with victim protection to explain the employer's vicarious liability); Jourdain (n 7) 29–31 (juxtaposing risk–profit with accident avoidance (combined with risk creation), authority/control, insurability (combined with victim protection), and the deep-pockets argument), 105 (discussing risk–profit with accident avoidance, in juxtaposition

RISK   83

pecuniary gain for the liability of employers is emphasized by Viney, according to whom the element of profit may well recommend a stricter liability rule for employers than for other parties (eg parents) who are legally responsible for the harmful actions of others.[62] The same may hold true in relation to industrial nuisances and defective products, contexts where risk–profit is also sometimes relied upon as a justification for strict liability.[63]

Taking a step back, the significance in French reasoning of risk–profit and risk–benefit looks ambiguous. Sometimes, whether standing alone or featuring in a broader reasoning with other arguments, risk–profit and risk–benefit act as key justifications for strict liability.[64] At other times, though, their combination or juxtaposition with other arguments suggests that they are merely secondary or even make-weight arguments. To give one example, in identifying the rationale of employers' vicarious liability, Jourdain mentions arguments such as risk–profit, accident avoidance, and the deep-pockets rationale, but then concludes that the fundamental point is that employers are well suited to take out liability insurance.[65]

with the deep-pockets argument and insurability); Viney (n 36) [788-11], [868] (risk–profit standing alone), but cf [790], [791-1] (mentioning loss spreading, victim protection, and accident avoidance as well for the purpose of justifying employers' vicarious liability).

[62] Viney (n 36) [868].
[63] Louis Josserand, *De l'esprit des droits* (n 13) [16] (seeing risk–profit as key in the context of nuisance, but also relying on an argument based on nonreciprocity of risk); Henri Mazeaud, Léon Mazeaud, and André Tunc, *Traité théorique et pratique de la responsabilité civile délictuelle et contractuelle* (6th edn, Montchrestien 1965) [621-2] (here Tunc, though not Henri and Léon Mazeaud, invokes primarily the principle of equality before public burdens (and therefore an argument based on burden–benefit proportionality) to justify the imposition of strict liability for industrial nuisances, but he also attributes some significance to risk–profit). In relation to defective products, see eg Borghetti (n 40) [627]–[628] (combining risk–profit with abnormality of risk and cost internalization); Terré and others (n 21) [1228] (briefly mentioning, and arguably juxtaposing, risk–profit and risk creation); Brun (n 33) [763] (arguably attributing some importance to the fact that producers put their product on the market for a profit); Jean Calais-Auloy, 'Le risque de développement: une exonération contestable' in *Mélanges Michel Cabrillac* (Dalloz/Litec 1999) 81, 84–85 (juxtaposing risk–profit with accident avoidance, victim protection, and arguably loss spreading, for the purpose of justifying product liability for development risks).
[64] Planiol (n 61) 298–301; Demogue (n 61) [882] (both on employer's vicarious liability); Josserand, *De l'esprit des droits* (n 13) [16] (on nuisance); Eisenmann (n 57) [10], [23] (on public liability for the deeds of things and vicarious liability); Chapus (n 57) [245] (on the liability of public and private employers for the harmful conduct of their employees), [311]–[313] (on public liability for the deeds of things); Vedel and Delvolvé (n 59) 602–03 (on public liability for the actions of collaborators); Carbonnier (n 56) [1166] (on liability for animals); Borghetti (n 40) [627]ff (on product liability) (his interpretive theory of product liability is based on a logic of cost internalization where risk–profit and abnormality of risk (as reflected in the notion of defect) are both essential); Muriel Fabre-Magnan, *Droit des obligations. 2—Responsabilité civile et quasi-contrats* (4th edn, PUF 2019) [400] (on employers' vicarious liability); Terré and others (n 21) [1228] (on product liability). See also Patrice Jourdain 'La responsabilité du fait d'autrui à la recherche de ses fondements' in *Mélanges Lapoyade Deschamps* (PU Bordeaux 2003) 67, 73 (emphasizing risk–profit in relation to employers' vicarious liability) (but cf Jourdain (n 7) 105, where the emphasis is on insurability). In Viney (n 36) [788-11], risk–profit stands alone and acts as the key justification for employers' vicarious liability (but cf [790], [791-1], where the author mentions entirely different reasons, notably insurability, victim protection, and accident avoidance).
[65] Jourdain (n 7) 105. See also Jacques Ghestin, JCP 1991.II.169, n.21673, [7], [12] (in relation to a range of activities, mentioning risk–benefit/profit but giving more emphasis to loss spreading);

84   JUSTIFYING STRICT LIABILITY

One explanation for the limited importance that risk–benefit and risk–profit some-times show may be that other arguments are more suited to matching the social-ization of losses which has characterized the general evolution of French tort law. Nevertheless, even if of secondary or make-weight significance, gain-based the-ories of risk keep featuring in legal reasoning on strict liability because they carry the prestige of their original proponents, and therefore make strict liability (and its expansion) more attractive and familiar by linking it to the power of tradition. In sum, in an environment where the value of social solidarity and a sentiment of compassion for the victims of accidents are prominent, the risk–benefit and risk–profit arguments are, at least sometimes, exploited to 'help' other arguments justify the imposition of strict liability in the pursuit of goals such as the protection of vic-tims and the spreading of losses.[66]

3.2.3 Risk in Italian Law: The Varied Importance of its Permutations

The notion of risk (*rischio*) has become central to Italian tort law thanks to the sem-inal work of a few distinguished legal scholars in the 1960s,[67] as well as to the role played by courts and academics in interpreting certain provisions of the *Codice civile* as imposing liability on the basis of risk. As in French law, all risk-based ar-guments except nonreciprocity of risk feature in Italian reasoning. It will be seen, however, that the various arguments assume in Italy a different significance than in France.

To begin with, there is a stark difference in the patterns of use and importance of risk creation between the two legal systems. As already seen,[68] risk creation oc-casionally features as a stand-alone justification for strict liability in France and

Mireille Marteau-Petit, 'La dualité des critères de mise en œuvre de la responsabilité du fait d'autrui' RRJ 2002.1.255, [20] (arguing that the rationale of strict liability in situations where the defendant or-ganizes and controls the activity of another must be found in the profits gained through the exercise of the defendant's activity, but suggesting that this liability should be confined to firms or professionals on the ground that, unlike individuals, they take out liability insurance); Grare (n 61) [33]–[35] (arguing that risk–profit can justify strict liability for the deeds of things (at least when this liability was at its inception and in the early stages of its life) and the employer's vicarious liability), but cf [45]–[48] (ar-guing that the justification for strict liability must be identified in the value of social solidarity, which finds expression in the spreading of losses through insurance (quoting extensively the work of Viney)); Alain Bénabent, *Droit des obligations* (19th edn, LGDJ 2021) [557] (on liability for the action of another in general, juxtaposing risk–profit with several other justifications but seeing insurability as the most significant one).

[66] On the relationship between risk and loss spreading, see also text to nn 36–37 in subsection 3.5.2; on the relationship between risk and victim protection, see also text to and following n 25 in subsection 3.6.2. On the interplay between these three arguments in French law, see text to nn 30–40 in section 4.3.

[67] Most notably Pietro Trimarchi, *Rischio e responsabilità oggettiva* (Giuffrè 1961); Marco Comporti, *Esposizione al pericolo e responsabilità civile* (Morano editore 1965).

[68] See text to nn 30–32 and text following n 34 in this section.

RISK   85

it still enjoys currency and persuasiveness among French lawyers due at least in part to the prestige of figures such as Josserand and Saleilles. This sort of 'tribute to tradition' has not taken place in Italy for the simple reason that the mere creation of risk has never attracted meaningful support as a plausible justification for strict liability in the first place.[69] Indeed, generally risk creation is considered too vague and therefore unworkable: the argument goes that since every human activity creates a risk of harm to others, reliance on this risk-based justification does not allow any differentiation between human activities and, consequently, it would lead to the imposition of strict liability in all cases where a loss is suffered.[70]

This scepticism does not mean, though, that the creation of risk does not feature at all in Italian reasoning. In keeping with a pattern identified in France,[71] Italian legal scholars sometimes refer to the idea of 'created risk' (*rischio creato*) to signify the mere possibility of occurrence of some harm, while relying on other arguments to justify strict liability. For example, Salvi premises liability for traffic accidents on the 'statistical significance of the risk created by putting vehicles in motion',[72] but then identifies the rationale of this liability in the need to ensure protection to the victims of traffic accidents.[73] In examples like this, the impression is that the creation of a risk of harm does no real justificatory work.

Other times, the creation of risk is employed as a starting point within more complex theories seeking to justify strict liability. An important example of this may be found in the work of Trimarchi who, in 1961, puts forward an interpretive and normative economic theory of strict liability which he himself presents as premised on risk.[74] According to Trimarchi's theory, a defendant should be strictly liable if their activity is driven by economic decisions or decisions involving a cost–benefit

---

[69] cf Giovanni Motzo and Giovanni Duni, 'Rapport sur les choses dangereuses en droit public italien' in *Travaux de l'Association Henri-Capitant: Les choses dangereuses: journées néerlandaises* (Dalloz 1971) 291, 292, including fn 2 (advocating the adoption of a strict liability based on the mere creation of risk in both public and private law, although confining it to 'uncommon' human actions or activities and limiting it to a fair rather than full compensation). The two authors suggest that scholars such as Minervini, Trimarchi, and Comporti also advocated a liability based on risk creation but an analysis of these works suggests otherwise. In relation to the positions of Trimarchi and Comporti, see in this section n 70 and accompanying text (for their criticisms of risk creation) as well as text to nn 74–79 and to (and following) n 85 (regarding Trimarchi), and text to nn 93–95 and to n 98 (regarding Comporti). As regards Gustavo Minervini, 'Orientamenti in tema di responsabilità senza colpa' (1952) GC 626, he arguably finds persuasive arguments for strict liability based on risk–profit (644) and loss spreading (640, 644–45), but not risk creation. As to Duni himself, his main work on public liability (Giovanni Duni, *Lo Stato e la responsabilità patrimoniale* (Giuffrè 1968)) suggests that, while he refers multiple times to risk creation as a rationale, he also gives high importance to an efficient allocation of resources (9, 124–125) and to loss-spreading considerations (18, 573, 582), which are not easily reconcilable with a commitment to risk creation.

[70] eg Comporti (n 67) 166–68. See also Trimarchi (n 67) 92; Trimarchi (n 5) 277 (arguing that many human activities which create a risk of harm to others are justified by their social utility).

[71] See text to nn 36–38 in this section.

[72] Cesare Salvi, *La responsabilità civile* (3rd edn, Giuffrè 2019) 216.

[73] ibid 210.

[74] Trimarchi (n 67) refers many times to 'created risk' (*rischio creato*) when discussing strict liability in Italian tort law: see ibid 43, 51, 52, 161, 206, 208, 214, 218, 220, 226, 227, 268, 277, 307, 315, 320, 358, 371.

86   JUSTIFYING STRICT LIABILITY

analysis, if this activity is characterized by a minimum of continuity and organization,[75] and if the characteristic risk that such activity creates can be treated as one of its costs of operation and therefore be absorbed through self-insurance or some spreading mechanism.[76] These conditions reflect a very specific understanding of risk, as defendants are to be liable only where the risk they create is foreseeable, calculable, and spreadable.[77] If all these conditions are satisfied, strict liability can successfully and efficiently promote the avoidance of accidents.[78] In sum, Trimarchi restricts the type of risk which can trigger strict liability so tightly that the mere creation of a risk of harm cannot itself justify that very liability. In its heavily qualified form, Trimarchi's notion of risk is combined with accident avoidance, which acts as the key rationale of strict liability for *rischio di impresa* ('enterprise risk').[79]

The context where *rischio di impresa* has attracted the widest support among courts and scholars is employers' vicarious liability.[80] While the courts confine themselves to mentioning the theory of *rischio di impresa* without any meaningful elaboration on its constituent elements or goals,[81] legal scholars often use this theory as an 'empty box' which they fill with different and more elaborate

---

[75] Trimarchi (n 5) 285.

[76] ibid 280, 359–60.

[77] ibid 357–60. All these conditions typically—though not exclusively—obtain in relation to economic activities, with the consequence that the theory of *rischio di impresa* applies prevalently to firms. Furthermore, Trimarchi's theory applies across the distinct contexts of liability in articles 2049–2054 Cod civ, for the activities falling within the scope of *rischio di impresa* can be performed in a wide variety of situations involving employers, dangerous activities, things in one's keeping, actions of animals, ruinous buildings, and motor vehicles; to these, defective products should be also added.

[78] On the role of accident avoidance in Trimarchi's theory, see text to nn 54–59 in subsection 3.3.3. Trimarchi also mentions the compensation of victims as a function of tort liability (Trimarchi (n 5) 276), but the goal of protecting victims of accidents must not be overestimated in his theory: he makes clear that it would be wrong to infer from the widespread availability of insurance mechanisms that the fundamental goal of tort law is compensating victims; if that were the main goal, first-party insurance would be the answer. The reason why legal systems still retain tort law is that they seek to avoid the occurrence of accidents: ibid 279–80.

[79] It is on this basis that Trimarchi draws the boundaries of the various liability rules in Italian law. An example relates to product liability for development risks. As the relevant risk of harm cannot be calculated in any way, the imposition of strict liability would only serve objectives of victim protection without worrying about an optimal level of accident avoidance, which instead could be pursued through fault-based liability: see Trimarchi (n 5) 415–16.

[80] For a criticism of the theory of *rischio di impresa* with specific regard to employers' liability, see Renato Scognamiglio, 'Responsabilità per fatto altrui' Noviss Dig It (UTET 1968) XV, 691, 699–700. For further criticisms, see Comporti (n 67) 156–66; Cesare Salvi, 'Responsabilità extracontrattuale (dir. vig.)' Enc Dir XXXIX (Giuffrè 1988) 1186, 1220–21; Guido Alpa and Mario Bessone, *La responsabilità civile* (Giuffrè 2001) 528–44; Carlo Castronovo, *Responsabilità civile* (Giuffrè 2018) 483, 93.

[81] eg Civ (III) 27.3.1987 n.2994, (1988) 1 GI 1833 (confusing *rischio di impresa* with risk–benefit); Civ (III) 20.6.2001 n.8381; Civ (III) 6.3.2008 n.6033; Civ (sezione lavoro) 11.1.2010 n.215. cf Civ (III) 19.7.2012 n.12448, [6.1], (2012) 1 GC 2297. In relation to other contexts of liability, judicial decisions endorsing the theory of *rischio di impresa* are relatively rare and they can be found mostly in the context of liability for dangerous activities (Civ (III) 29.5.1989 n.2584, (1990) 1 GI 234; Civ (III) 10.10.2014 n.21426, [3.2], (2015) 1 Foro It 1303), where the general tendency, though, is for the courts to focus on the notion of dangerousness and to rely on other justifications. Decisions whose language resonates with Trimarchi's approach can be also found in the context of liability for things in one's keeping, although no express reference is made to *rischio di impresa*: see eg Civ (III) 10.8.2004 n.15429.

arguments. For example, some focus only on the avoidance of accidents,[82] others add to it the availability of insurance coverage,[83] and still others overlook accident avoidance while emphasizing the defendant's ability to absorb the costs of strict liability and spread them through price adjustments and insurance.[84] In all these discussions, the notion of risk is bent one way and then another to shape a variety of justificatory strategies, with the creation of risk as such receiving little or no emphasis. This is hardly surprising, for Trimarchi himself criticizes risk creation (as well as risk–benefit/profit) as unhelpful when trying to make sense of key aspects of employers' vicarious liability.[85] Overall, the idea of created risk drowns in a sea of other justifications so that what is put forward as the theory of *responsabilità per rischio* is not really based on risk creation but rather on a combination or juxtaposition of different justifications which receive varying emphasis according to the normative or interpretive views of their proponents. Paradoxically, then, what is presented as a theory of *responsabilità per rischio* puts forward justification(s) for strict liability that lie elsewhere than in risk creation.

An interesting contrast in the status of risk creation between the Italian and French systems therefore emerges. In France, this argument comes in three different shades. Sometimes, though not frequently, it acts as a stand-alone and key reason for imposing strict liability.[86] At other times, it is either combined or juxtaposed with other justifications within a broader reasoning,[87] but its conceptual distinctiveness from these other justifications is preserved and it remains a recognizable argument used to render the imposition of strict liability more attractive.[88] On yet other occasions, it again forms part of a broader reasoning but this time it merely stands for the possibility of occurrence of some harm, therefore dissolving into other justifications without retaining any conceptual independence

---

[82] Giovanna Visintini, *Trattato breve della responsabilità civile—Fatti illeciti. Inadempimento. Danno risarcibile* (3rd edn, Cedam 2005) 753–55 (juxtaposing accident avoidance with a combination between victim protection and the deep-pockets justification).

[83] See Pier Giuseppe Monateri, *La Responsabilità Civile. Trattato di Diritto Civile* (UTET 1998) 979; Mauro Sella, *La responsabilità civile nei nuovi orientamenti giurisprudenziali* (Giuffrè 2007) 1150–51.

[84] Salvi (n 72) 201–03 (juxtaposing this argument with victim protection and risk–benefit). For instancesof other lines of reasoning, see the following examples. In relation to liability for products, Guido Alpa, 'Prodotti difettosi, danno ingiusto, responsabilità del fabbricante' (1971) 1 GM 297, 303 (emphasizing loss spreading and accident avoidance); Ugo Carnevali, *La responsabilità del produttore* (Giuffrè 1974) 303, 47–49 (referring to accident avoidance, loss spreading, and administrative cost reduction). In relation to liability for dangerous activities (but also including liability for products), Gianmaria Volpe, 'Esercizio di attività pericolose, rischio d'impresa e controllo delle tecnologie' (1974) 4–5 GM 381, 382–83 (highlighting accident avoidance, victim protection, and loss spreading). In relation to article 2054 para 4 Cod civ (traffic accidents caused by defects of construction of vehicles), Guido Alpa, 'Costruzione di autoveicoli, clausole di esonero e responsabilità dell'impresa per una diversa lettura dell'articolo 2054, ultimo comma, codice civile' (1975) 4(1A) GI 751, 756, 759–62 (emphasizing accident avoidance in addition to victim protection) (hereafter Alpa, 'Costruzione di autoveicoli').

[85] Trimarchi (n 67) 92. The same point is made in Trimarchi (n 5) 293.

[86] Text to nn 30–32 in this section.

[87] Text to nn 33–34 in this section.

[88] One of the best examples is provided by Jourdain (n 7) 30, where the emphasis on risk creation is clear from the use of italicized words.

88 JUSTIFYING STRICT LIABILITY

and justificatory value.[89] In keeping with this last pattern, Italian legal scholars occasionally refer to the idea of created risk to signify merely that there is a possibility of some harm, in which case the creation of risk is not a justification for strict liability at all. At other times, the notion of risk is heavily qualified and accompanied by other justifications, with the result that again the mere creation of a risk of harm is not of itself a reason for imposing strict liability (as in Trimarchi's theory). This is all consistent with the widespread rejection that risk creation faces in the Italian context, where it is heavily criticized on grounds of vagueness and unworkability.[90]

However, other risk-based arguments, such as the argument from abnormality of risk, appear more significant as justifications for strict liability in the Italian context. In contrast with the French *Code civil*, the Italian *Codice civile* (Cod civ) expressly deals with harm caused by abnormal risks. Indeed, as already explained,[91] article 2050 Cod civ imposes liability for harm caused by the operation of dangerous activities, with dangerousness (ie abnormality of risk) being an express condition of liability. Furthermore, Italian courts consider motoring a dangerous activity and, in their view, it is this dangerousness which links the four rules contained in article 2054 Cod civ on liability for traffic accidents.[92] Besides featuring in the positive law, the notion of dangerousness has received considerable attention in Italian legal scholarship. For example, Comporti puts forward in 1964 an influential theory of strict liability based on 'exposure to danger' (*esposizione al pericolo*) to explain and justify strict liability in Italian tort law.[93] For Comporti, danger means a 'considerable potential for harm' and is to be inferred from the high frequency of accidents in a given period of time as well as from the magnitude/severity of accidents regardless of the frequency factor.[94] In his view, the party who carries on dangerous activities or otherwise creates situations involving a high probability of harm must be answerable for all losses caused to others by such activity or situation.[95]

In light of all this, it is not surprising to find abnormality of risk surfacing in Italian judicial decisions and academic writings which seek to justify or explain the imposition of strict liability especially—but not only—in relation to dangerous

---

[89] Text to nn 36–38 in this section.

[90] See text to n 70 in this section.

[91] See text to nn 291–301 in section 2.5.

[92] Civ sez un 29.4.2015 n.8620, [3.1]–[3.2], (2016) 1 RCP 205.

[93] Comporti (n 67). Exposure to danger would represent the rationale of, for example, liability for things in one's keeping (article 2051 Cod civ), liability for the action of animals (article 2052 Cod civ), liability for ruinous buildings (article 2053 Cod civ), liability for traffic accidents caused by defects in the manufacture or maintenance of the vehicle (article 2054, para 4 Cod civ), liability for nuclear installations (legge 31.12.1962 n.1860, D.P.R. 10.5.1975 n.519, and D.M. 20.3.1979), liability for accidents caused by airplanes (article 965 of *Codice della navigazione*), and liability for the exploitation of mines (article 31, r.d. 29.7.1927 n.1443): ibid 97, 99, 103, 107.

[94] Comporti (n 67) 173.

[95] ibid 175. For a criticism of Comporti's approach and, more generally, of the idea of justifying strict liability on the basis of an abnormal risk of harm, see Castronovo (n 80) 454–56.

activities under article 2050 and traffic accidents under article 2054 Cod civ.[96] As in France,[97] the typical pattern is that abnormality of risk forms part of a broader reasoning which supports or explains strict liability in the furtherance of some particular goal. For example, Comporti argues that 'the need to protect third parties ... constitutes the rationale for the rules of strict liability ... : he who creates and keeps sources of danger to the community, is equally obliged to compensate losses, regardless of any fault'.[98] Similarly, Sica observes that the rationale of articles 2050–2054 Cod civ may be 'intensifying the protection of victims in light of the particular dangerousness ... of the situations to which these provisions refer'.[99] These examples, to which others could be added,[100] show that, in keeping with the French attitude, there is in the Italian reasoning on strict liability a strong connection between abnormality of risk and the protection of victims as the ultimate goal which this liability pursues.

However, abnormality of risk can also be invoked in relation to different goals, most notably efficient accident avoidance, as is the case with the theories that engage with economic analysis. For example, in relation to dangerous activities, several Italian scholars conclude that strict liability is desirable because as between the operator of a dangerous activity and its potential victim, it is the former who has the technological expertise to reduce the accidents caused by that activity;[101] others argue that, since by definition dangerous activities entail a high risk of harm, strict liability is the best option because it would induce defendants to limit the intensity of their activity and therefore efficiently reduce the number of accidents.[102] In these economic elaborations, however, the link between abnormality of risk and strict liability seems more tenuous than in reasoning pursuing victim protection. In the latter, the creation of a high risk of harm triggers liability as soon as that risk has materialized to the detriment of the victim, for the occurrence of a loss, typically a personal injury, immediately determines the need for a compensatory response. By contrast, in an economic reasoning, what is crucial is the efficient avoidance of

---

[96] Comporti (n 67) 177 (on dangerous activities). On traffic accidents, Alpa, 'Costruzione di autoveicoli' (n 84) 774; Salvatore Sica, *Circolazione stradale e responsabilità: l'esperienza francese e italiana* (ESI 1990) 158–59, 193; Carlo G Terranova, 'Responsabilità da circolazione di veicoli' Dig Disc Priv (UTET 1998) XVII, 89, 90, 92, 101. Abnormality of risk is also seen as a reason for imposing strict liability in relation to other contexts of liability: see Comporti (n 67); Comporti, *Fatti Illeciti: le responsabilità oggettive—Artt. 2049-2053. Il Codice Civile—Commentario* (Giuffrè 2009) 302–04 (things in one's keeping), 355–56 (animals), 399 (ruinous buildings); Sica, ibid 162 (dangerous activities, things in one's keeping, animals, ruinous buildings, traffic accidents).

[97] See text to n 46 in this section.

[98] Comporti (n 67) 176 (therefore combining abnormality of risk with victim protection). This approach is sometimes described as pursuing 'aims of social solidarity': see Francesco D Busnelli and Salvatore Patti, *Danno e responsabilità civile* (3rd edn, Giappichelli 2013) 145–46.

[99] Sica (n 96) 162.

[100] See the references mentioned in n 96 in this section.

[101] Pier Giuseppe Monateri, 'Responsabilità civile' Dig Disc Priv (UTET 1998) XVII, 1, 10; Robert Cooter and others, *Il mercato delle regole—Analisi economica del diritto civile—I. Fondamenti* (Il Mulino 2006) 218.

[102] Enrico Baffi, 'Responsabilità "aggravata". Un'analisi giuseconomica' (2011) 4 DR 345, 355.

90 JUSTIFYING STRICT LIABILITY

accidents and the promotion of social welfare, with the consequence that in every situation—including those involving dangerous activities—strict liability may be rejected in favour of a fault-based rule if the latter were more conducive to those goals. In other words, abnormality of risk supports strict liability only if and to the extent that it aligns with the goals set out in the economic approach. In this way, the creation of an abnormal risk of harm seems to lose much of its justificatory role and it may be wondered whether, in Italian economic reasoning, it is seen as no justification at all but merely as a starting point of analysis when assessing liability rules in relation to dangerous activities. In any event, this 'economic' use of abnormality of risk puts the Italian reasoning in stark contrast with the French approach which, as earlier seen, typically links abnormality of risk to the need for victim compensation and finds its main source of inspiration in the value of social solidarity.[103]

Turning to risk–benefit and risk–profit, these are the most recurrent justifications for strict liability in Italian law among the various permutations of risk earlier identified. This may be due to their conceptual simplicity and moral attractiveness, as they are based on the view that it is inherently fair to make those who benefit from their harmful action pay for it.[104] Nevertheless, as we saw in relation to France,[105] these arguments are deployed selectively, depending on the context. First, risk–benefit and risk–profit are not invoked in relation to parental liability either in Italy or in France: as parents do not gain any benefit from the actions of their children, parental strict liability should be either rejected or based on other justifications.[106] Secondly, also similarly to the patterns of use in French law, risk–benefit looms larger in contexts where the benefit gained by the defendant can be of a non-pecuniary nature (such as in cases of vicarious liability where the defendant is not pursuing an economic interest,[107] liability for things in one's keeping,[108] for

---

[103] See text to nn 46–53 in this section.

[104] cf Trimarchi (n 5) 371–72 (criticizing the principle *cuius commoda eius et incommoda* on the ground that it can be justified only through 'a generic reference to a shapeless and undifferentiated sentiment of fairness [*equità*]'). Trimarchi rejects the theories of risk–profit and risk–benefit as too vague in relation to elements of the liability of employers and that of guardians/owners of things/animals: see Trimarchi (n 67) 92, 119–20 (on employers) and 246–47 (on things and animals); Trimarchi (n 5) 293, 302 (on employers) and 371–72 (on things and animals).

[105] See text to and preceding nn 54–63 in this section.

[106] Enrico Carbone, 'La responsabilità aquiliana del genitore tra rischio tipico e colpe fittizie' (2008) 1(2) Riv Dir Civ 1, 6–7; Maria Luisa Chiarella, 'Minore danneggiante e responsabilità vicaria' (2009) 10 DR 973, 979–80; Guido Alpa, *La responsabilità civile: principi* (2nd edn, UTET 2018) 444.

[107] eg Adriano De Cupis, *Il danno: teoria generale della responsabilità civile*, vol II (3rd edn, Giuffrè 1979) 162–65 (risk–benefit standing alone, which the author traces back to the value of social solidarity); Renato Alessi, *La responsabilità della pubblica amministrazione* (Giuffrè 1955) 69–70 (juxtaposing risk–benefit with victim protection, on the liability of public bodies for the actions of their employees under article 2049); Maria Pia Giracca, 'Responsabilità civile e pubblica amministrazione: quale spazio per l'art. 2049 c.c.?' (2001) 1 Foro It 3293, 3297 (juxtaposing risk–benefit with loss spreading and victim protection, in relation to the vicarious liability of public bodies).

[108] eg Alessandro Farolfi, 'Il danno cagionato da cose in custodia' in Paolo Cendon (ed), *Responsabilità civile*, vol III (2nd edn, UTET 2020) 3849, 3850 (risk–benefit standing alone); Alpa (n 106) 460–61; Civ (III) 19.5.2011 n.11016, [2.1], (2012) 1 DR 27; Civ (III) 12.5.2017 n.11785, [4], (2018) 1 DR 49.

the actions of animals,[109] for ruinous buildings,[110] and for traffic accidents[111]), whereas risk–profit is widely deployed in the entrepreneurial context of employers' vicarious liability for the harm caused by their employees.[112] Interestingly, though, risk–profit is only rarely mentioned in entrepreneurial contexts relating to defective products and dangerous activities, this marking a significant divergence from the French reasoning.[113] In these areas, in Italy liability is more often justified by relying on different arguments such as accident avoidance, loss spreading, or victim protection.

What, therefore, is the overall significance of gain-based theories of risk in relation to Italian strict liability? In discussing the French position, it was said that both

[109] Giuseppe Branca, 'Sulla responsabilità oggettiva per danni causati da animali' (1950) RTDPC 255, 260–61; Walter Ventrella, 'Danno cagionato da animali: fondamento della responsabilità e individuazione dei soggetti responsabili' (1978) 4(1) GC 741, 741, 744 (discussing risk–benefit with victim protection); Monateri (n 83) 1061 (risk–benefit standing alone); Visintini (n 82) 801–02 (risk–benefit standing alone); Massimo Franzoni, L'illecito. Trattato della responsabilità civile (2nd edn, Giuffrè 2010) 540–41 (risk–benefit standing alone); Valentina Cardani, 'Il danno cagionato da animali' in Cendon (n 108) 3869, 3871 (risk–benefit standing alone); Alpa (n 106) 467 (risk–benefit standing alone, and deriving from 'social needs'); Katia Mascia, 'Responsabilità per i danni cagionati dagli animali' (2020) 4 DR 538, 544 (noting that, coherently with the fact that the rationale of article 2052 lies in risk–benefit, public authorities cannot be held strictly liable for harm caused by wildlife, as they do not gain any benefit from these animals. See also Civ (III) 27.6.1997 n.5783; Civ (III) 11.6.2010 n.16023, [3.3]; Civ (III) 11.12.2012 n.22632, [6.3]; Civ (III) 9.4.2015 n.7093, [1.9.1], (2015) 5 GI 1062. cf Trimarchi's view at n 104 in this section.

[110] Giovanni Pugliese, 'Responsabilità per rovina di edificio in usufrutto' (1957) Temi 471, 473–74 (discussing risk–benefit with accident avoidance); Giuseppe Branca, 'Responsabilità dell'usufruttuario per rovina di edificio' (1958) 1 Foro It 1311, 1312–13 (risk–benefit standing alone); Civ (III) 29.1.1981 n.693, (1982) II Riv Dir Comm 47, 52 (arguably juxtaposing risk–benefit with accident avoidance); Franzoni (n 109) 564 (juxtaposing risk–benefit with abnormality of risk which, in turn, is discussed with the deep-pockets argument); Paolo Laghezza, 'Responsabilità per rovina di edificio e uso anomalo del bene' (2006) 10 DR 994, 996–97, including fn 6 (juxtaposing risk–benefit with efficient accident avoidance); Ugo Mattei, I Diritti Reali—2—La Proprietà. Trattato di Diritto Civile (UTET 2015) 351 (juxtaposing risk–benefit with the deep-pockets argument and with an efficiency argument based on cost internalization); Luca Leidi, 'La rovina e i difetti di edificio' in Cendon (n 108) 3880, 3882 (discussing risk–benefit with accident avoidance).

[111] eg Mario Griffey, La responsabilità civile derivante da circolazione dei veicoli e dei natanti (Giuffrè 1995) 91 (on liability under article 2054 para 3 Cod civ, combining risk–benefit with victim protection). See also the recent Civ sez un 29.4.2015 n.8620 (n 92) [3.3] (on liability under article 2054 paras 3–4 Cod civ, emphasizing risk–benefit).

[112] See eg Francesco Messineo, Manuale di diritto civile e commerciale, vol V (9th edn, Giuffrè 1957) 579 (juxtaposing risk–profit with the deep-pockets justification); Franzoni (n 109) 762–63, 767–69 (discussing risk–profit with loss spreading and efficient accident avoidance, in juxtaposition with victim protection); J Di Rosa, case note on Civ (III) 9.3.2017 n.6033, (2017) 6(1) Foro It 1986, 1987 (risk–profit standing alone); Civ (III) 9.6.2016 n.11816, [2.7].

[113] cf, for dangerous activities, Civ (III) 23.1.1962 n.95, (1962) 1 Foro It 2133; Guido Alpa, 'Attività pericolosa e responsabilità dell'ENEL. Verso la erosione dei privilegi della Pubblica Amministrazione?' (1982) 4(1) GC 919, 920; Giuseppe G Infantini, 'La responsabilità civile della pubblica amministrazione per danni causati nell'esercizio di attività pericolose e da cose in custodia' in Enrico Follieri (ed), La responsabilità civile della pubblica amministrazione (Giuffrè 2004) 297, 318–19 (although his reasoning arguably encompasses both risk–profit and risk–benefit). For defective products, see Trib Bari 12.12.2013, (2014) 11 DR 1070, 1071; Enzo Roppo, 'Sul danno causato da automobile difettose. Tutela dei danneggiati, regime di responsabilità e incidenza dell'assicurazione obbligatoria' (1978) 12(IV) GI 130, 132, 136, and 140 (on liability of producers for harm caused by defective motor vehicles under article 2054, para 4 Cod civ, juxtaposing risk–profit with victim protection and accident avoidance).

92 JUSTIFYING STRICT LIABILITY

risk–profit and risk–benefit act sometimes as key justifications for strict liability in a variety of contexts, and at other times as secondary or even make-weight arguments.[114] In Italy, risk–benefit undoubtedly acts as the leading justification for strict liability of owners or users of animals,[115] but in other contexts the role of the two gain-based theories of risk is more ambiguous. At times, whether standing alone or mentioned together with other arguments, risk–benefit and risk–profit act as key justifications in the mind of the relevant judge or scholar.[116] However, in other instances where they are either juxtaposed or combined with a variety of arguments, it is difficult to apprehend their exact significance in the reasoning put forward,[117] and they may at least sometimes look like either secondary or make-weight arguments.[118] Moreover, the fact that risk–benefit and risk–profit often appear together with justifications such as accident avoidance and victim protection,[119] which are

[114] See text to nn 64–66 in this section.

[115] See n 109 in this section.

[116] eg Francesco Carnelutti, 'La responsabilità civile per gli accidenti d'automobile' (1908) I Riv Dir Comm 401, 402 (on liability for traffic accidents); Lodovico Barassi, *La teoria generale delle obbligazioni*, vol 2 (Giuffrè 1946) 697–737, esp 710–30 (on several rules of strict liability); Branca (n 110) (on liability for ruinous buildings); Civ (III) 23.1.1962 n.95 (n 113) (on dangerous activities); De Cupis (n 107) 162–65 (on employers' vicarious liability); Francesca Degl'Innocenti, *Rischio di impresa e responsabilità civile—La tutela dell'ambiente tra prevenzione e riparazione dei danni* (Firenze University Press 2013) 28–29 (arguing that articles 2049, 2051–2053 Cod civ are widely seen as based on the principle *cuius commoda eius et incommoda*); Trib Bari 12.12.2013 (n 113) (on product liability).

[117] eg Lorena Fanelli, 'Fondo stradale dissestato per lavori ed esercizio di attività pericolosa: caratteri e limiti' (2001) 10 DR 925, text accompanying fns 4–7 (on dangerous activities, at first focusing on risk-benefit but then emphasizing victim protection and accident avoidance); Giovanni B Ferri, 'Garanzia, rischio e responsabilità oggettiva' (2005) 10–12(I) Riv Dir Comm 867, 870 (on the strict liability of firms, combining risk–profit with the theory of *rischio di impresa* in such a way that it is difficult to understand fully their respective justificatory role); Leidi (110) 3882 (in relation to ruinous buildings, discussing risk–benefit with accident avoidance); Civ sez un 29.4.2015 n.8620 (n 92) (arguing that liabilities under paras 3–4 of article 2054 Cod civ, concerning traffic accidents, are expression of the principle *cuius commoda eius et incommoda*, but then holding that liability under para 3 would not be strict but rather based on a presumption of fault!).

[118] Salvi (n 72) 201–03 (on employers' vicarious liability, mentioning very briefly risk–benefit after emphasizing the ability of defendants to spread losses); Franzoni (n 109) 762–63 and 767–69 (on employers' vicarious liability, mentioning risk–profit but arguably putting more emphasis on loss spreading, victim protection, and on an argument based on efficient accident avoidance); Alpa (n 113) 920 (on dangerous activities, mentioning risk–profit but adding that it is neither the only nor the most relevant justification for strict liability).

[119] See eg Fanelli (n 117) text accompanying fns 4–7 (on liability for dangerous activities, juxtaposing risk–benefit with victim protection and accident avoidance); Salvi (n 72) 202–03 (on employers' vicarious liability, juxtaposing risk–benefit with victim protection); Franzoni (n 109) 762–63, 767–69 (on employers' vicarious liability, discussing risk–profit with loss spreading and efficient accident avoidance, in juxtaposition with victim protection); Francesco Sangermano, 'La responsabilità dei padroni e dei committenti. La fattispecie del danno cagionato dal preposto al preponente' (2012) 4(2) RCP 1105, 1110 (on employers' vicarious liability, discussing risk–profit and victim protection); Civ (III) 19.5.2011 n.11016 (n 108) [2.1] (on liability for things in one's keeping, arguably combining risk–benefit with accident avoidance); Pugliese (n 110) 473–74 (on ruinous buildings, discussing risk–benefit with accident avoidance); Roppo (n 113) 132, 136, and 140 (on traffic accidents, juxtaposing risk–profit with victim protection and accident avoidance); Griffey (n 111) 91 (on traffic accidents, combining risk-benefit with victim protection); Aldo P Benedetti, 'Condotta del danneggiato e responsabilità da cose in custodia: spunti di riflessione' (2011) 3 DR 234, 237, fn 21 and text accompanying it (on product liability, employers' vicarious liability, and liability for nuclear installations, discussing risk–benefit with accident avoidance while warning against the excesses of victim protection). Occasionally, gain-based justifications are discussed with the deep-pockets argument as well: see Messineo (n 112) 579; Eugenio

abundantly relied upon in most contexts of liability,[120] further suggests that the significance of these risk-based arguments is ambiguous and therefore should not be exaggerated, in keeping with the position in France.[121] Finally, a cautious approach in estimating the significance of risk–benefit and risk–profit in Italy is also warranted in light of the various criticisms levelled against the two arguments, both in general terms and with reference to specific contexts of liability.[122] In sum, while the conspicuous reliance of Italian legal actors—especially scholars—on risk–benefit and risk–profit shows their attachment to an ideal of fairness that links gains to liabilities, the way these arguments are discussed, the criticisms they attract, and the concomitant presence of competing rationales suggest that the most significant justifications behind Italian strict liabilities often lie elsewhere.

3.2.4 Risk in the United States: All Five Permutations at Play

In keeping with the French and Italian approaches, risk features conspicuously in US tort reasoning as an argument for the imposition of strict liability. As will be seen, US legal actors deploy all the permutations of risk-based arguments, from risk creation and risk–benefit/profit to abnormality of risk and nonreciprocity of risk. Each of these variations has its own distinctive significance, with important similarities and differences as compared to the French and Italian approaches.

To begin with, risk creation is occasionally relied on by courts and scholars to justify the imposition of strict liability. For example, in the context of abnormally dangerous activities, in a case involving death caused by the explosion of a gas tank, the Supreme Court of Oregon holds that one 'factor which enters the picture is

Bonvicini, *La responsabilità civile*, vol I (Giuffrè 1971) 563 (both discussing employers' vicarious liability); Franzoni (n 109) 564 (on ruinous buildings, adding also abnormality of risk).

[120] See subsection 3.3.3 and subsection 3.6.3, respectively.

[121] Text to nn 64–66 in this section.

[122] In relation to parental liability, see n 106 in this section. In relation to employers' vicarious liability, see Trimarchi (n 5) 293, 302; Scognamiglio (n 80) 697ff; C Massimo Bianca, *Diritto civile. V—La responsabilità* (3rd edn, Giuffrè 2021) 706 at fn 13; Civ (III) 22.5.2001 n.6970, (2002) 1 NGCC 871 (expressly rejecting risk–profit as the rationale of employers' vicarious liability, holding that the requirement of *nesso di occasionalità necessaria* cannot be excluded on the ground that the employer did not gain any economic benefit from the actions of their employees). In relation to liability for dangerous activities, see Alpa (n 106) 459–60. In relation to liability for things in one's keeping, see Monateri (n 83) 1041; Paolo Laghezza, 'Quale causalità per l'art. 2051 c.c.? —Il commento' (2014) 3 DR 258, 266–67. In relation to liability for actions of animals, see Ventrella (n 109) 744 (rejecting risk–profit for unduly narrowing down the scope of article 2052 Cod civ). For a general criticism, see Comporti (n 67) 152–56; Castronovo (n 80) 28. In relation to the liability of public authorities, see eg Alberto Zito, *Il danno da illegittimo esercizio della funzione amministrativa. Riflessioni sulla tutela dell'interesse legittimo* (Editoriale Scientifica 2003) 161–62; Giulia Avanzini, 'Nuovi sviluppi nella responsabilità delle amministrazioni per danni derivanti da attività pericolose e da cose in custodia' (2010) 1 Diritto amministrativo 261, 268 (in relation to article 2050 Cod civ), 288 (in relation to article 2051 Cod civ); Alessandra Dominici, 'La responsabilità oggettiva in materia di appalti: il Consiglio di Stato si allinea alle pronunce del giudice comunitario'(2013) 1 Rivista amministrativa degli appalti 41, 63.

94 JUSTIFYING STRICT LIABILITY

the feeling that where one of two innocent persons must suffer, the loss should fall upon the one who created the risk causing the harm'.[123] Similarly, in relation to liability for defective products, there are cases where it has been held that one of the reasons for imposing strict liability is the creation of a risk of harm by placing defective products on the market.[124] The risk-creation argument appears in the reasoning of legal scholars too. For example, Keeton argues that '[i]t may be that most strict liabilities now recognized are illustrations of a single basis of liability—a principle that each activity is accountable for the distinctive risks it creates'.[125] In all these examples, the argument of risk creation may either stand alone, be combined, or be juxtaposed with other justifications, but it is always treated as conceptually distinct from the others and, as part of the reasoning in which it is included, it acts as a key justification for the imposition of strict liability.

At other times, however, the creation of risk merely acts as a starting point for more complex theories, and it is doubtful whether it works as a justification for strict liability at all. One example of this is provided by Keating's theory of enterprise liability, which suggests that firms should be strictly liable for their characteristic risks of harm.[126] In so holding, Keating often refers to the creation of risk but, similarly to Trimarchi with his *rischio di impresa* in the Italian context, he confines strict liability to conduct and activities in relation to which the relevant risk of harm can be predicted, priced into the operation of the activity, and therefore spread broadly.[127] What fuels Keating's theory is not the creation of risk as such but the belief that it is fair to spread the costs of accidents caused by firms in a way that achieves a proportional sharing of burdens and benefits across society.[128] In this and other cases where reference to risk-creating activities merely signifies the possibility of some harm in the future, the mere creation of a risk of harm does very little if no work at all as a justification for strict liability.[129] Indeed, in keeping with

---

[123] *McLane v Northwest Natural Gas*, 467 P.2d 635, 638 (Or.1970) (also mentioning abnormality of risk and nonreciprocity of risk). See also *Bierman v City of New York*, 60 Misc.2d 497, 498–99 (N.Y.1969) (juxtaposing risk creation with loss spreading and accident avoidance).

[124] eg *Dippel v Sciano*, 155 N.W.2d 55, 58 (Wis.1967) (juxtaposing risk creation with loss spreading, accident avoidance, and the protection of consumer expectations as further justifications); *Green v Smith & Nephew AHP, Inc*, 629 N.W.2d 727, 749–50 (Wis.2001) (juxtaposing risk creation with risk–profit, loss spreading, the protection of consumer expectations, and accident avoidance) (note at 750 the primary importance given to risk creation and to risk–profit, and the 'equitable' dimension attributed to risk creation).

[125] Robert E Keeton, *Venturing to Do Justice: Reforming Private Law* (HUP 1969) 162ff.

[126] Gregory C Keating, 'The Theory of Enterprise Liability and Common Law Strict Liability' (2001) 54 Vand L Rev 1285.

[127] See Gregory C Keating, 'The Idea of Fairness in the Law of Enterprise Liability' (1997) 95 Mich L Rev 1266. While Keating is committed to fairness and sees the spreading of losses as essential, Trimarchi is committed to economic efficiency and considers accident avoidance of paramount importance.

[128] This result is achieved by placing the financial burdens of accidents on those who benefited from the risk-imposing activity, namely the firm operating that activity as well as the users and consumers of the product or service provided by the firm. For more details on Keating's reliance upon burden–benefit proportionality, see subsection 3.5.3. Note that Keating juxtaposes this line of reasoning with an argument based on individual responsibility, on which see subsection 3.8.2.

[129] Besides Keating, see eg Young B Smith, 'Frolic and Detour' (1923) 23 Colum L Rev 444, 456–60 (loss spreading) (but cf Young B Smith, 'Frolic and Detour' (1923) 23 Colum L Rev 716, 725ff, where

patterns of reasoning that feature also in the French and Italian contexts,[130] the real justificatory work is done by other arguments such as loss spreading, accident avoidance, or victim protection, with the creation of risk dissolving into them.[131] Finally, there are cases where the creation of risk is mentioned but its significance remains ambiguous because of a lack of clarity in the relevant reasoning: here too, though, justifications other than risk creation seem to take over, so that it is difficult to understand whether risk creation retains any conceptual distinctiveness and separate justificatory weight.[132] To all this, two further considerations should be added. First, the development in US legal thought of complex economic and moral theories has led some legal scholars to reject, either implicitly or explicitly, risk creation on the ground of its moral indefensibility or practical unworkability.[133] Secondly, as will be seen below, the greater reliance of US scholars and courts on the qualified variants of risk creation (nonreciprocity of risk and abnormality of

he repeatedly emphasizes the creation of risk of injury in the context of *respondeat superior*); Mark Geistfeld, 'Should Enterprise Liability Replace the Rule of Strict Liability for Abnormally Dangerous Activities?' (1997) 45 UCLA L Rev 611, 658–60 (on abnormally dangerous activities, emphasizing accident avoidance) (the risk Geistfeld considers is not an abnormal one, for anything 'more than a negligible degree of risk' will be enough); Fowler V Harper, Fleming James Jr, and Oscar S Gray, *The Law of Torts*, vol 5 (2nd edn, Little, Brown and Company 1986) 20–21 (emphasizing accident avoidance, victim protection, and loss spreading, in the context of employers' vicarious liability); Virginia E Nolan and Edmund Ursin, 'Dean Leon Green and Enterprise (No-Fault) Liability: Origins, Strategies, and Prospects' (2001) 47 Wayne L Rev 91, 166–67 (suggesting the adoption of strict enterprise liability for supermarkets, which 'create specific types of hazards', so as to pursue compensation of victims, accident avoidance, and also an efficient administration of justice); Peter H Schuck, 'Municipal Liability under Section 1983: Some Lessons from Tort Law and Organizational Theory' (1989) 77 Geo LJ 1753, 1780 (in relation to the liability of municipalities under § 1983, emphasizing accident avoidance, which he juxtaposes with loss spreading, victim protection, reasons of morality, and (at 1781) a possible reduction in administrative costs).

[130] See text to nn 36–38 (France) and text following n 89 (Italy) in this section.
[131] See n 129 in this section.
[132] See eg Jed Handelsman Shugerman, 'The Floodgates of Strict Liability: Bursting Reservoirs and the Adoption of Fletcher v. Rylands in the Gilded Age' (2000) 110 Yale LJ 333, 374 (arguing that, when US courts adopted the rule in *Rylands v Fletcher*, 'they did have a basic sense that those who created risk had an ability to reduce risk and had a responsibility for the costs'); *Holland v Buckley*, 305 So.2d 113, 119 (La.1971): 'as between him who created the risk of harm and the innocent victim thereby injured, the risk creator should bear the loss. He maintains the animal for his own use or pleasure' (it could be argued that risk creation and risk–benefit are distinct and juxtaposed justifications here, but it could also be argued that the court is referring to someone who creates a risk of harm for their own benefit (use or pleasure), and therefore that the only argument put forward is in reality risk–benefit); *Peterson v Lou Bachrodt Chevrolet Co*, 329 N.E.2d 785, 786–87 (Ill.1975) (recognizing that risk–profit is 'one of the basic grounds supporting the imposition of strict liability upon manufacturers' but concluding with a statement on risk creation: 'the loss will ordinarily be ultimately borne by the party that created the risk') (if it is sufficient to create a risk of harm, then the profit element is irrelevant, which is very unlikely given the court's emphasis on risk–profit; if, on the other hand, risk–profit is necessary to justify strict liability, then it is unclear how risk creation can suffice to justify strict liability given that it does not include any profit element).
[133] eg Ernest J Weinrib, 'Right and Advantage in Private Law' (1989) 10 Cardozo L Rev 1283, 1305 (liability for mere creation of risk 'would be incompatible with the status of the [defendant] as a person'); Stephen R Perry, 'The Impossibility of General Strict Liability' (1988) 1 Can JL Juris 147, 154–58 (criticizing Epstein's causation-based theory of strict liability in a way that rejects, explicitly, risk–benefit and risk–profit and, implicitly, risk creation).

risk) and on the gain-based theories of risk (risk–profit and risk–benefit) provides a strong indication that most US legal actors do not see risk creation as a viable justification for strict liability.

Overall, therefore, it appears that the theory of created risk has limited significance in US legal reasoning. It is true that some scholars and courts treat this argument as a key justification for the imposition of strict liability. In this, the US position resembles the French one, with some scholars (and in United States judges) seeing the mere creation of risk as a plausible justification for strict liability. But compared to the French system, this is extremely rare given the enormous volume of existing academic writing and case law in the United States. The result is that the argument's impact is much weaker in the US context. Furthermore, as in Italy, in the United States risk creation does not enjoy the prestige which surrounds the argument in France from the time of Saleilles and Josserand. And indeed, in keeping with the Italian approach, in many examples of US reasoning the creation of risk dissolves into other arguments and loses any distinctiveness as a justification for strict liability. Relatedly, again resembling the Italian position,[134] risk creation attracts fierce criticism and its plausibility is doubted on grounds of immorality and unworkability. For all these reasons, the argument is of modest significance in the US context, especially when compared to France.

In contrast with the theory of created risk, other risk-based arguments have gained greater acceptance in the United States.

As far as nonreciprocity of risk is concerned, this argument was elaborated in detail by Fletcher in 1970. In Fletcher's view, fairness requires that losses should lie where they fall in situations of reciprocity of risk, that is where defendant and claimant impose on each other roughly the same degree of risk.[135] By contrast, liability would be appropriate where the defendant imposes a nonreciprocal risk of harm. As Fletcher puts it, 'a victim has a right to recover for injuries caused by a risk greater in degree and different in order from those created by the victim and imposed on the defendant—in short, for injuries resulting from nonreciprocal risks'.[136] This may happen in one of two situations. First, where a person behaves negligently, given that a negligently created risk is nonreciprocal relative to the risk of harm created by other people performing the same activity or action in a non-negligent way (eg negligent driver vs diligent driver); secondly, where a person engages reasonably (ie without any fault) in an activity which, by its very nature, imposes on others a particularly high or unusual, and therefore unreciprocated, risk of harm. The latter situation attracts the imposition of strict liability and applies to dangerous activities such as blasting, fumigating, or crop dusting,

---

[134] See text to n 70 in this section.

[135] Fletcher (n 3) 542.

[136] ibid. See also Mark A Geistfeld, 'Hidden in Plain Sight: The Normative Source of Modern Tort Law' (2016) 91 NYU L Rev 1517.

to the keeping of wild animals, to crashing airplanes, and certain types of nuisance.[137] Fletcher's theory has proved influential in US legal reasoning and it often surfaces in discussions seeking to justify the adoption of strict liability in a variety of contexts. For example, in relation to liability for abnormally dangerous activities, courts and especially legal scholars see the defendant's imposition of a nonreciprocal risk of harm on the claimant as a justification for strict liability, and typically juxtapose or combine it with arguments such as risk creation, abnormality of risk, risk–profit/benefit, accident avoidance, loss spreading, or the promotion of individual responsibility.[138] Similarly, in the context of liability for harm caused by wild animals, the Third Restatement LPEH considers nonreciprocity of risk as an argument supporting strict liability, and juxtaposes it with abnormality of risk and accident avoidance.[139] Again, in the context of liability for defective products, nonreciprocity of risk is occasionally mentioned as a possible justification for the imposition of strict liability.[140] In sum, in striking contrast with the French and Italian systems where nonreciprocity of risk does not feature meaningfully as an argument for strict liability, Fletcher's theory has had considerable influence in the United States. This does not mean, of course, that the argument has not been criticized and on a number of grounds, for example that it would be premised on morally shaky foundations, that it would lead to economic inefficiencies, or that

---

[137] Fletcher (n 3) 544, 547–48.

[138] *McLane* (n 123) 638 (discussing nonreciprocity of risk with abnormality of risk, in juxtaposition with risk creation); Second Restatement, § 522, comment *a* (arguably combining nonreciprocity of risk with risk–benefit); Virginia Nolan and Edmund Ursin, 'The Revitalization of Hazardous Activity Strict Liability' (1987) 65 NCL Rev 257, 290–93 (grouping nonreciprocity of risk with risk–profit under a fairness umbrella and then juxtaposing them with accident avoidance and loss spreading); William P Kratzke, 'Some Recommendations concerning Tort Liability of Government and Its Employees for Torts and Constitutional Torts' (1996) 9 Admin LJ Am U 1105, 1125–27 (criticizing the *Nelms* decision on government liability on grounds of nonreciprocity of risk); Mark Geistfeld, 'Negligence, Compensation, and the Coherence of Tort Law' (2003) 91 Geo LJ 585, 615–21 (juxtaposing nonreciprocity of risk with accident avoidance); Geistfeld (n 136) 1582ff (combining nonreciprocity of risk with an argument based on individual responsibility); John CP Goldberg and Benjamin C Zipursky, 'The Strict Liability in Fault and the Fault in Strict Liability' (2016) 85 Fordham L Rev 743, 763 (combining nonreciprocity of risk with risk–benefit and abnormality of risk, on grounds of fairness in the distribution of losses); Elias R Feldman, 'Strict Tort Liability for Police Misconduct' (2019) 53 Colum JL & Soc Probs 89 (proposing the introduction of strict liability for police misconduct, on the ground that policing creates abnormal and nonreciprocal risks of harm, with strict liability that would advance here the interests of justice, equality, and law enforcement).

[139] Third Restatement LPEH, § 22, comment *d* and the Reporters' Note to that comment (expressly referring to Fletcher's work).

[140] Dan B Dobbs, Paul T Hayden, and Ellen M Bublick, *Torts and Compensation—Personal Accountability and Social Responsibility for Injury* (8th edn, West Academic Publishing 2017) 748: 'the manufacturer imposes risks on the consumer that are quite different from any risks the consumer imposes on the manufacturer, and this fact justifies strict liability' (then juxtaposing this argument with other justifications such as the protection of consumer expectations, loss spreading, administrative cost reduction, risk–profit, and accident avoidance (ibid 747–50)) (note that the authors do not express any view as to the persuasiveness of these justifications). Interestingly, Fletcher himself casts doubt on the ability of the paradigm of reciprocity to account for strict product liability: see Fletcher (n 3) fn 24 ('Because of the market relationship between the manufacturer and the consumer, loss-shifting in products-liability cases becomes a mechanism of insurance, changing the question of fairness posed by imposing liability').

98 JUSTIFYING STRICT LIABILITY

it would be theoretically inconclusive or practically unworkable.[141] Although these criticisms may have eroded the credibility of nonreciprocity of risk as a justification for strict liability, the argument still enjoys considerable currency in US legal reasoning and it is often used, at least in relation to liability for abnormally dangerous activities and liability for wild animals, as a key justification for their imposition.

Turning now to abnormality of risk, this argument recurs in a variety of contexts of strict liability and shows remarkable flexibility as a justification for strict liability, being employed to serve several different purposes. Unsurprisingly, the context where abnormality of risk has gained wider currency is liability for abnormally dangerous activities because it constitutes a formal requirement for the application of the doctrine.[142] In this context, many courts and legal scholars see the abnormal character of the risk of harm created by the defendant's activity as a reason for imposing strict liability. As in France and in Italy,[143] abnormality of risk is typically either combined or juxtaposed with other arguments and used for the achievement of a variety of goals. For example, in their famous treatise, Harper and James argue that the harm caused by certain activities (eg blasting) 'is of such a serious nature that sound social policy demands that the actor assume the risk',[144] here that 'sound social policy' being loss spreading.[145] Another example can be found in *Cities Service Co v State*, where the District Court of Appeal of Florida observes that, given the 'still many hazardous activities' in society, 'it is too much to ask an innocent neighbor to bear the burden thrust upon him as a consequence of an abnormal use of the land next door',[146] thus showing a concern for victim protection. These instances of reasoning, to which many more could be added,[147]

---

[141] eg Richard A Posner, 'Strict Liability: A Comment' (1973) 2 J Legal Stud 205, 215–17; Jules L Coleman, 'Justice and Reciprocity in Tort Theory' (1975) 14 W Ontario L Rev 105; Stephen R Perry, 'The Moral Foundations of Tort Law' (1992) 77 Iowa L Rev 449, 469–72 (cf Perry (n 1) 114–15); Keating (n 127) 1320–25; John CP Goldberg and Benjamin C Zipursky, *The Oxford Introductions to U.S. Law: Torts* (OUP 2010) 261–62; James A Henderson Jr, Douglas A Kysar, and Richard N Pearson, *The Tort Process* (9th edn, Wolters Kluwer 2017) 503–04.

[142] See Second Restatement, § 520, and Third Restatement LPEH, § 20.

[143] Text to nn 46–53 (France) and to nn 98–103 (Italy) in this section.

[144] Fowler V Harper and Fleming James Jr, *The Law of Torts*, vol 2 (Little, Brown and Company 1956) 814.

[145] ibid 794–95 (drawing on Fleming James Jr, 'Accident Liability: Some Wartime Developments' (1946) 55 Yale LJ 365): 'there is a growing belief . . . that in this mechanical age the victims of accidents can, as a class, ill afford to bear the loss . . . and that better results will come from distributing such losses among all the beneficiaries of the mechanical process than by letting compensation turn upon an inquiry into fault'.

[146] 312 So.2d 799, 801 (Fla.1975).

[147] eg *Chavez v Southern Pacific Transportation*, 413 F.Supp. 1203, 1211 (Cal.1976) (combining abnormality of risk with loss spreading, which the court sees as a key rationale of strict liability throughout the judgment); *Yukon Equipment v Fireman's Fund Insurance*, 585 P.2d 1206, 1211–12 (1978) (juxtaposing abnormality of risk with risk–profit and accident avoidance). See also Jon G Anderson, 'The Rylands v. Fletcher Doctrine in America: Abnormally Dangerous, Ultrahazardous, or Absolute Nuisance?' (1978) Ariz St LJ 99, 135 (combining abnormality of risk with risk–profit and risk–benefit, with a view to compensating victims) (note the author's scepticism about the use of loss spreading in judicial reasoning, ibid fn 147); Gary T Schwartz, 'The Vitality of Negligence and the Ethics of Strict Liability' (1981) 15 Ga L Rev 963, 1003–04 (seeing the risky nature of the defendant's conduct as one of two situations where strict liability may be appropriate, on the basis of some unspecified 'moral

show that abnormality of risk is intended to support goals such as the spreading of losses or the compensation of victims. The strong connection between abnormality of risk and victim protection characterizes the French and Italian contexts too, highlighting a common trait among these three jurisdictions.[148] As in Italy, however, abnormality of risk can feature in reasoning seeking to promote primarily other goals, such as the avoidance of accidents or the reduction in administrative costs.[149] For example, Shavell notes that strict liability is more advantageous than negligence in relation to high-risk activities because the former 'will tend to reduce in a desirable way participation in these activities',[150] and that 'it is when an activity presents a significant danger that strict liability has the potential to meaningfully lower risk'.[151] To this, Posner adds that strict liability may be preferable to negligence in cases of abnormal risk of harm because of potentially lower administrative costs.[152] Therefore, in keeping with the Italian approach, US legal economists emphasize the minimization of the costs of accidents as the paramount goal of strict liability, including in cases of abnormal risk of harm. As already noted for Italy,[153] though, the move from abnormality of risk to the imposition of strict

judgment'); Geistfeld (n 129) 649 (arguing that, if compensation were the true rationale, dangerousness should be the only requirement of liability for abnormally dangerous activities, 'as the need for compensation is most pronounced when the risk-creating activity threatens widespread injury', but also arguing in this article that the justification which best explains the six factors in § 520 of the Second Restatement is accident avoidance); Goldberg and Zipursky (n 138) 763 (combining abnormality of risk with nonreciprocity of risk and risk–benefit, on grounds of fairness in the distribution of losses). See also Justice Stewart (dissenting, with whom Justice Brennan agreed) in *Laird v Nelms*, 406 US 797, 809–10 (1972) (arguing that strict liability for ultra-hazardous activities, based 'on the sound principle that he who creates such a hazard should make good the harm that results', should be applied to the government as it is applied to private entities; and juxtaposing this argument with a combination between loss spreading and victim protection insofar as public liability is concerned).

[148] See text to nn 46–53 (France) and nn 98–100 (Italy) in this section.

[149] To be sure, there are also instances of reasoning that aim simultaneously at a plurality of goals, including accident avoidance, victim protection, and loss spreading. An example is *Dyer v Maine Drilling & Blasting, Inc*, 984 A.2d 210 (Me.2009) where the Supreme Judicial Court of Maine rejects negligence for blasting operations and opts for a rule of strict liability on the following grounds: 'although blasting is a lawful and often beneficial activity, the costs should fall on those who benefit from the blasting, rather than on an unfortunate neighbor' ([19]); '[t]he negligence approach to abnormally dangerous activities initially taken by US courts was rooted in part in the idea that dangerous activities were essential to industrial development... But today, that attitude has changed, ... and strict liability seeks to encourage both cost-spreading and incentives for the utmost safety when engaging in dangerous activities' ([20]); and, '[a] person who creates a substantial risk of severe harm to others while acting for his own gain should bear the costs of that activity. Most of the courts of the nation have recognized this policy, and we now do as well' ([31]) (note the concern for the 'unfortunate' victim, the goals of loss spreading and accident avoidance, as well as the combination of abnormality of risk with risk–profit).

[150] Steven Shavell, *Economic Analysis of Accident Law* (HUP 1987) 31 (noting that 'the deterrent effect of strict liability on the level of participation in activities is not mentioned in the [Second] *Restatement* and is only infrequently noted in other places. Evidently, the mere creation of an unusual risk is seen as a justification for imposition of strict liability' (ibid 32, original emphasis)).

[151] Steven Shavell, 'The Mistaken Restriction of Strict Liability to Uncommon Activities' (2018) 10 Journal of Legal Analysis 1, 3.

[152] Richard A Posner, *Economic Analysis of Law* (9th edn, Wolters Kluwer 2014) 207–08 (while casting doubt on the compensatory function of tort law and, therefore, on any victim protection argument in favour of strict liability (ibid 208–09)).

[153] See text following n 102 in this section.

liability is immediate to a reasoning aiming at victim protection because the materialization of that abnormal risk demands compensation without further ado. By contrast, whenever the goal is the minimization of the costs of accidents, strict liability is constantly compared to negligence in terms of their respective costs to society and therefore rejected if it proves less efficient, whether or not an abnormal risk of harm is involved. In other words, in economic reasoning abnormality of risk leads to the imposition of strict liability only if such imposition is more conducive to efficient results than competing standards of liability. As a result, in keeping with Italian reasoning,[154] it is doubtful whether, in the view of US legal economists, abnormality of risk plays any real justificatory role or if it works instead merely as a starting point of analysis when considering activities involving a high risk of harm.

Finally, besides liability for abnormally dangerous activities, abnormality of risk features in discussions concerning other contexts as well. For example, in relation to liability for harm caused by wild animals, the high risk of harm involved in owning or possessing them is often put forward as one of the key reasons for imposing strict liability.[155] The argument is also used occasionally in the context of liability for defective products by pointing to the extraordinary risks of harm involved in such products,[156] although in this area other arguments are more significant.[157]

Overall, abnormality of risk plays an important role in the reasoning seeking to justify strict liability, particularly in the area of abnormally dangerous activities, where it is linked to a variety of societal goals such as victim protection, loss spreading, and accident avoidance.

As regards gain-based theories of risk, they attract prominent support among judges and legal scholars in the United States. Certainly, some criticisms have been levelled at both risk–benefit and risk–profit, for example because they may sound somewhat primitive justifications or because they may be practically unworkable or morally problematic.[158] Nevertheless, the view that imposing a risk

---

[154] See text following n 102 in this section.

[155] *Isaacs v Powell*, 267 So.2d 864, 865–66 (Fla.1972) (arguably combining abnormality of risk with risk–profit, but placing more emphasis on the former argument). See also Charles E Cantu, 'Distinguishing the Concept of Strict Liability in Tort from Strict Products Liability: Medusa Unveiled' (2003) 33 U Mem L Rev 823, 837–39; Third Restatement LPEH, § 22, comment *d* (juxtaposing abnormality of risk with nonreciprocity of risk and accident avoidance). Similarly, in relation to non-wild animals that present abnormally dangerous tendencies, Third Restatement LPEH, § 23, comment *b*, again focuses on abnormality of risk, nonreciprocity of risk, and accident avoidance.

[156] James A Henderson Jr, 'Coping with the Time Dimension in Products Liability' (1981) 69 Cal L Rev 919, fn 72: 'Another rationale frequently advanced is that because defective products present extraordinary risks, it is only fair that manufacturers should compensate injured victims' (citing as an example *Hoven v Kelble*, 256 N.W.2d 379, 391 (Wis.1977).

[157] See subsection 3.3.2 (accident avoidance) and subsection 3.5.3 (loss spreading).

[158] See eg Guido Calabresi, *The Costs of Accidents: A Legal and Economic Analysis* (YUP 1970) 5 ('phrases such as ... "let the party who benefits from a cost bear it" can no longer be accepted as sufficing to determine who ought to bear accident costs'); Perry (n 141) 464–65, and Perry (n 133) 154–58 (criticizing the moral persuasiveness of risk–benefit); Smith (n 129) 456 (rejecting risk–profit in relation to *respondeat superior*); Joseph H King Jr, 'A Goals-Oriented Approach to Strict Tort Liability for Abnormally Dangerous Activities' (1996) 48 Baylor L Rev 341, 359–60 (criticizing the fairness rationale

of harm on others for one's own gains should trigger liability upon materialization of that risk is alive and well in the United States. Undoubtedly, the US approach differs from what was observed in relation to France and Italy. In the two civil law systems, strict liability rules apply both to situations where a defendant earns a monetary gain from their conducts or activities and where the defendant's conducts or activities entail benefits of non-pecuniary nature (eg liability for things, for animals, or for traffic accidents).[159] Risk–profit is typically used to justify strict liabilities of the first type, and risk–benefit those of the second type.[160] Since in the United States many strict liabilities involve situations where the defendant is going to reap a monetary benefit from their potentially harmful conduct or activity, it is not surprising that risk–profit looms larger than risk–benefit in US reasoning. Indeed, while the latter is only occasionally mentioned, whether in general[161] or in relation to specific contexts such as liability for abnormally dangerous activities,[162] liability for animals,[163] and liability for private nuisance,[164] the former is heavily relied on by judges and scholars alike to justify several strict liabilities. The fairness of requiring defendants who profit from their harmful activities to compensate claimants for the losses suffered is invoked in the context of liability for abnormally dangerous activities,[165] liability for defective

of strict liability, which includes nonreciprocity of risk as well as 'a belief that between two innocent persons, the initiator who benefits from the ultimately injurious activity should be liable', on the ground that '[f]airness, whatever that term connotes, probably does not figure centrally among the goals of strict liability, at least as a conceptually distinct rationale').

[159] See section 2.4 (France) and section 2.5 (Italy).

[160] See text to nn 54–63 (France) and nn 106–113 (Italy) in this section.

[161] eg Richard A Epstein, *Modern Products Liability Law* (Quorum Books 1980) 27 (risk–benefit standing alone, in relation to cases involving strangers); Gregory C Keating, 'Strict Liability Wrongs' in John Oberdiek (ed), *Philosophical Foundations of the Law of Torts* (OUP 2014) 292, 306–07.

[162] Anderson (n 147) 135 (combining risk–benefit (and risk–profit) with abnormality of risk, with a view to compensating victims); Charles Cantu, 'Distinguishing the Concept of Strict Liability for Ultra-Hazardous Activities from Strict Products Liability under Section 402A of the Restatement (Second) of Torts: Two Parallel Lines of Reasoning That Should Never Meet' (2001) 35 Akron L Rev 31, 35–36 (combining risk–benefit with abnormality of risk); Goldberg and Zipursky (n 138) 763 (combining risk–benefit with abnormality of risk and nonreciprocity of risk, on grounds of fairness in the distribution of losses). See also Second Restatement, § 522, comment *a*.

[163] Anderson (n 147) 113 (referring to wild or abnormally dangerous animals, he endorses the arguments put forward in *Holland* (n 132) 119: 'as between him who created the risk of harm and the innocent victim thereby injured, the risk creator should bear the loss. *He maintains the animal for his own use or pleasure*') (emphasis added).

[164] Gregory C Keating, 'Nuisance as a Strict Liability Wrong' (2012) 4(3) JTL, article 2. Throughout his analysis, Keating focuses on productive activities, which suggests that he may actually have in mind risk–profit rather than risk–benefit. However, his fundamental claims are couched in such broad terms that he may well have in mind risk–benefit rather than risk–profit as the key justification for strict liability in nuisance law: '[t]he actor responsible for the nuisance reaps the benefits that come from conducting the activity that inflicts the nuisance; it is only fair for that actor to take the bitter with the sweet and bear the burdens of its conduct along with the benefits' (ibid 37) (see also ibid 8, 52).

[165] eg *Smith v Lockheed Propulsion Co*, 247 Cal.App.2d 774, 785 (Cal.1967) (combining risk–profit with loss spreading, with a view to compensating victims); *Langan v Valicopters*, 567 P.2d 218, 223 (Wash.1977) (mentioning the argument in the context of 'an equitable balancing of social interests');

102 JUSTIFYING STRICT LIABILITY

products,[166] employers' vicarious liability,[167] and—albeit more rarely—in the contexts of liability for animals[168] and of liability for nuisance.[169]

While at times risk–profit and risk–benefit stand alone to justify the imposition of strict liability, the most recurrent pattern is for these arguments to be either juxtaposed or combined with other justifications.[170] Here, risk–profit and risk–benefit are sometimes key in justifying strict liability;[171] at other times, they are given *some* significance but it is difficult to appreciate their exact justificatory weight.[172] Moreover, in keeping with the French and Italian positions,[173] the fact

---

Yukon (n 147) 1211-12 (juxtaposing risk–profit with abnormality of risk and accident avoidance); *Dyer* (n 149) [31], [19]-[20] (combining risk–profit with abnormality of risk, in juxtaposition with loss spreading and accident avoidance). See also Anderson (n 147) 135 (combining risk–profit (and risk–benefit) with abnormality of risk, with a view to compensating victims); Nolan and Ursin (n 138) 290–93 (grouping risk–profit with nonreciprocity of risk under a fairness umbrella and then juxtaposing them with accident avoidance and loss spreading). See also Jed Handelsman Shugerman, 'A Watershed Moment: Reversals of Tort Theory in the Nineteenth Century' (2008) 2(1) JTL article 2, 33–34.

[166] eg *Suvada v White Motor Co*, 210 N.E.2d 182, 186 (Ill.1965) (juxtaposing risk–profit with accident avoidance and an argument based on the protection of consumer expectations); *Peterson* (n 132) 786; *Beshada v Johns-Manville Prods Corp*, 447 A.2d 539, 547–49 (N.J.1982) (juxtaposing risk–profit with loss spreading, victim protection, accident avoidance, and administrative cost reduction); *Heath v Sears, Roebuck & Co*, 464 A.2d 288, 293 (N.H.1983) (juxtaposing risk–profit with accident avoidance); *Brooks v Beech Aircraft Corp*, 902 P.2d 54, 59 (N.M. 1995) (juxtaposing risk–profit with loss spreading and victim protection); *Green* (n 124) 749–50 (seeing risk–profit (together with risk creation) as the primary rationale of strict liability, although juxtaposing it with loss spreading, an argument based on the protection of consumer expectations, risk creation, and accident avoidance). See also Henderson Jr (n 156) fn 72 (though burying risk–profit in a footnote, together with abnormality of risk); James A Henderson Jr, 'Judicial Reliance on Public Policy: An Empirical Analysis of Products Liability Decisions' (1991) 59 Geo Wash L Rev 1570, 1576; Gregory C Keating, 'Products Liability as Enterprise Liability' (2017) 10(1) JTL 41, 47, 56–57, 63–64, 70–72 (grounding strict products liability in, inter alia, fairness, which includes risk–profit as far as the position of firms is concerned as well as the spreading of losses among those who benefit in any way from the harmful activity (users, consumers, participants in the activity itself)); Dobbs, Hayden, and Bublick (n 140) 747–50 (juxtaposing risk–profit with other justifications such as the protection of consumer expectations, loss spreading, administrative cost reduction, nonreciprocity of risk, and accident avoidance (ibid 747–50)).

[167] eg William L Prosser, *Handbook of the Law of Torts* (3rd edn, West Publishing Co 1964) 471 (discussing risk–profit with loss spreading and accident avoidance, with the latter being expressly defined as a 'makeweight argument') (the fourth and fifth editions of the handbook reiterate this approach); *Hinman v Westinghouse Electric Company*, 471 P.2d 988, 990 (Cal.1970) (quoting Prosser). See also *Becker v Interstate Properties*, 569 F.2d 1203, 1214 (3rd Cir.1977) (juxtaposing risk–profit with loss spreading, victim protection, and accident avoidance, in relation to the liability of an employer who hired a financially irresponsible independent contractor).

[168] *Isaacs* (n 155) 865-66 (combining risk–profit with abnormality of risk).

[169] See n 164 in this section.

[170] See nn 162, 165-168 in this section.

[171] See Prosser (n 167) 471; Epstein (n 161) 27; *Peterson* (n 132) 786; *Heath* (n 166) 293; *Beech Aircraft Corp* (n 166) 59, 63; *Green* (n 124) 750; *Hinman* (n 167) 990; Keating (n 161) 306–07.

[172] eg Fleming James Jr, 'Products Liability II' (1955) 34 Tex L Rev 192, 196, 227 (mentioning risk–profit, but then giving more significance to loss spreading so that risk–profit is either a secondary or make-weight argument; *Luth v Rogers & Babler Constr Co*, 507 P.2d 761, 764 (Alaska 1973) ('[w]hile the employer's benefit from the employee's activity is relevant to the existence of vicarious liability, benefit is not its sole determinant'); *Gossett v Simonson*, 411 P.2d 277, 279 (Or.1966) ('[t]he weight of authority elsewhere seems to support the view that mere benefit to the employer would not suffice to render the employer liable as a matter of law').

[173] See text to nn 64-66 (France) and text to nn 117-121 (Italy) in this section.

RISK   103

that both risk–benefit and risk–profit are often discussed with other and more
widespread justifications—most notably, loss spreading, victim protection, and accident avoidance—suggests that, at least in some cases, the two gain-based theories
of risk may well be thrown in the discussion as argumentative 'extras' and therefore
represent only make-weight arguments or arguments of secondary importance. In
sum, in the US context risk–profit (and to a lesser extent risk–benefit) certainly attract the support of many scholars and courts to justify strict liability in numerous
areas. At the same time, however, the overall significance of these arguments is difficult to pinpoint because it is hard to establish the extent to which at least some of
the scholars and judges employing them are committed to their underlying logic.
Finally, the importance of gain-based theories of risk should not be exaggerated
also because, as will be seen in subsequent sections, other justifications for strict
liability hold sway over the thinking of courts and especially scholars in the United
States.

3.2.5 Risk in English Law: Controversy and
Context-Dependence

As in the other three legal systems studied, the notion of risk has played a key role
in the development of strict liability in England. Except for nonreciprocity of risk,
which has attracted little attention and even less support, all the other permutations of risk feature visibly in the English legal reasoning. As will be seen, the patterns of use and the significance of the various risk-based justifications vary, with
interesting points of contact and contrasts to be drawn between England and the
other jurisdictions.

First, in the English context, risk creation has gained increased importance as a justification for strict liability, but its significance remains ambiguous.
Occasionally, it surfaces in the reasoning relating to defective products,[174]
breach of a non-delegable duty,[175] and the rule in *Rylands v Fletcher*,[176] either as

---

[174] Law Commission, *Liability for Defective Products* (Law Com No 82, 1977) [23], [37]–[38]
(juxtaposing risk creation with accident avoidance, loss spreading, victim protection, and administrative cost reduction); Peter Cane, *The Anatomy of Tort Law* (Hart Publishing 1997) 47–49 (risk creation
here stands alone and provides a possible explanation for the liability of distributors).

[175] John Murphy, 'Juridical foundations of common law non-delegable duties' in Jason W Neyers,
Erika Chamberlain, and Stephen GA Pitel (eds), *Emerging Issues in Tort Law* (Hart Publishing 2007)
369, 381–82 (arguing that '[i]n the earliest reported cases, the creation of risk seemed to be the driving
force behind the imposition of non-delegable duties' (381), that '[b]y the first half of the 20th century,
however, the tenor of the judgments had changed so that the idea of "exceptional" or "abnormal" risk
seemed to have replaced the bare requirement of "risk", "danger" or "peril"' (382), and finally that '[y]et,
notwithstanding the established case law that seemed to emphasise risk-creation, the middle of the 20th
century saw a second justificatory premise begin to gain prominence in non-delegable duty cases. This
was the assumption of responsibility' (382)).

[176] Cane (n 174) 49; Jenny Steele and Rob Merkin, 'Insurance Between Neighbours: *Stannard v Gore*
and Common Law Liability for Fire' (2013) 25 JEL 305, 306 (arguing that the rule in *Rylands* 'was at its

104   JUSTIFYING STRICT LIABILITY

a stand-alone justification (though very rarely) or together with other arguments. However, its use in these contexts is very limited and other justifications dominate. In contrast, in the context of vicarious liability the argument attracts more attention and, in several decisions of the highest courts, the creation of a risk of harm which is inherent in the nature of the defendant's activity is seen both as one of the rationales of vicarious liability,[177] and as one of the conditions for its application.[178] As a rationale, risk creation does not stand alone and it is put next to other justifications such as risk–benefit, loss spreading, the deep-pockets argument, or victim protection.[179] However, even if included within a broader reasoning, the emphasis placed on risk creation by judges stresses its conceptual distinctiveness and suggests that the argument does some justificatory work.[180]

This judicial approach also finds support in the work of a few legal scholars. For example, in considering the case law on vicarious liability, Brodie suggests that

inception justified by ideas of risk creation and loss bearing') (note that in the abstract of their article the same point is made but risk creation is juxtaposed with 'loss spreading' rather than with 'loss bearing').

[177] See *Dubai Aluminium Co Ltd v Salaam and Others*, [2003] 2 AC 366, [21]–[22] (Lord Nicholls); *Various Claimants v Catholic Child Welfare Society*, [2012] UKSC 56, [2013] 2 AC 1, [35], [73], [86] (Lord Phillips) [*CCWS*]; *Cox v Ministry of Justice*, [2016] UKSC 10, [2016] AC 660, [22]–[24]; *Armes v Nottinghamshire County Council*, [2017] UKSC 60, [2018] AC 355, [57]–[58]. More doubtful is the role of risk creation in *Lister v Hesley Hall Ltd*, [2002] 1 AC 215, [65] (Lord Millett) (arguably seeing in risk–benefit, not risk creation, the main rationale of vicarious liability, along with loss spreading); and in *Majrowski v Guy's and St Thomas's NHS Trust*, [2006] UKHL 34, [9] (Lord Nicholls) (whose language ('all forms of economic activity carry a risk of harm to others, and fairness requires that those responsible for such activities should be liable to persons suffering loss from wrongs committed in the conduct of the enterprise') may be interpreted as putting forward a risk-creation argument, which is then followed by arguments based on victim protection, the deep-pockets rationale, loss spreading, and accident avoidance).

[178] See *CCWS* (n 177) [35] and [47] (in relation to the first stage regarding the nature of the relationship between the defendant and the physical author of harm), [86]–[87] and [93] (in relation to the second stage, regarding the close connection that must link the relationship between defendant and physical author of harm with the latter's tortious conduct). (In the *CCWS* case, some brother teachers in a Roman Catholic residential school sexually or physically abused boys in their care. The UK Supreme Court held that the defendants diocesan bodies and the institute responsible for appointing the school headmaster and the other brothers were vicariously liable for the abuses. The court established that the relationship between the defendants and the abusers was of a nature to engage the former's vicarious liability, and that there was a sufficiently 'close connection' between that relationship and the abuser's tortious conduct on the ground that the placement of brother teachers in a residential school in which they also resided enhanced the risk that pupils may suffer from those abuses.) See also *Armes* (n 177) [61].

[179] See *CCWS* (n 177) [35] (discussing risk creation with the deep-pockets and loss-spreading rationales, as well as with arguments concerning the degree of control of the employer on the employee, the extent to which the latter's activity is part of the former's activity, and whether the tort was committed as a result of the employee's activity being taken on the employer's behalf), [73] (also identifying, by reference to the speech of Lord Hobhouse in *Lister* at [60], risk creation as a policy reason that justifies vicarious liability), [86]; *Cox* (n 177) [22]–[24] (combining risk creation with risk–benefit and with an argument concerning whether the tort was committed as a result of the employee's activity being taken on the employer's behalf); *Armes* (n 177) [57]–[58] (combining risk creation with risk–benefit and with an argument concerning whether the tort was committed as a result of the employee's activity being taken on the employer's behalf), [61] (discussing risk creation with loss spreading), [63] (referring to the deep pocket of the defendant and to insurance spreading, with a view to ensuring the compensation of victims). See also *Majrowski* (n 177) [9] (Lord Nicholls).

[180] See references in n 179 in this section.

'vicarious liability is ... seen as the corollary of the creation of risks by an enterprise',[181] and that '*Lister* is utterly consistent with the ultimate justification for the imposition of vicarious liability being the creation of enterprise risk'.[182] Similarly, Steele sees risk creation (and risk–benefit) as 'respectable justice arguments' which support vicarious liability on moral grounds, together with other justifications such as accident avoidance, victim protection, the deep-pockets rationale, and loss spreading.[183] As all these examples of judicial and academic reasoning show, the risk-creation rationale is typically put forward together with other justifications, including other risk-based arguments.[184] While this pattern of use may suggest that risk creation is not seen as a sufficient justification for the imposition of vicarious liability, it does not deny the increased attention and importance that the argument has gained in recent times.

Despite this, risk creation has been the target of numerous criticisms, with leading scholars casting doubts on its desirability or on its ability to explain the law. Some argue that imposing liability on grounds of pure risk creation would sacrifice too much in terms of individual freedom of action.[185] Others reject risk creation for its practical unworkability because it would lead to irresolvable problems of causal indeterminacy.[186] Still others find the argument 'puzzling' on the ground that, if risk creation were 'a *sufficient* justification for strict liability', English law would now feature a far greater number of strict liability torts.[187] Finally, similar criticisms sometimes target risk creation in specific contexts of liability, such as product liability,[188] and vicarious

---

[181] Douglas Brodie, 'Enterprise Liability: Justifying Vicarious Liability' (2007) 27 OJLS 493, 495.

[182] ibid 496. Note that both statements are immediately followed by a reference to the fairness inherent in the risk–profit argument, so that one is left wondering what is, in Brodie's view, the relative weight and the exact relationship between risk creation and risk–profit. Indeed, at various stages in his analysis, Brodie emphasizes either risk creation or risk–profit. See ibid 495, 497, 499, 500, 501 (emphasizing risk creation); 495, 496, 502, 507 (emphasizing risk–profit).

[183] Jenny Steele, *Tort Law, Text, Cases, and Materials* (4th edn, OUP 2017) 578–81.

[184] See text to, and references in, nn 179–183 in this section. See also *CCWS* (n 177) [87] (Lord Phillips) ('I do not think that it is right to say that creation of risk is simply a policy consideration and not one of the criteria [for imposing vicarious liability]. Creation of risk is not enough, of itself, to give rise to vicarious liability for abuse but it is always likely to be an important element in the facts that give rise to such liability'); Paula Giliker, 'Comparative Law and Legal Culture: Placing Vicarious Liability in Comparative Perspective' (2018) 6 Ch J Comp L 265, 277 (arguing that '[i]t is noticeable that the UK Supreme Court has proven reluctant to rely solely on this ground and, indeed, in *Armes*, the factors of control and deeper pockets were also influential in its analysis'); Dyson and Steel (n 2) 36 (suggesting that risk creation can be rescued as a justification for strict liability 'either by appealing to the *exceptional* or *abnormal* nature of the risk-imposition as a justification for such liability, or by recognising that the creation of risk is only part of a broader justification' (original emphasis)).

[185] Robert Stevens, *Torts and Rights* (OUP 2007) 99–100.

[186] Peter Cane and James Goudkamp, *Atiyah's Accidents, Compensation and the Law* (9th edn, CUP 2018) 400.

[187] Dyson and Steel (n 2) 36 (original emphasis).

[188] Jane Stapleton, 'Products Liability Reform—Real or Illusory?' (1986) 6 OJLS 392, 394 (doubting the appropriateness of risk creation on grounds of causal indeterminacy); Edwin Peel and James Goudkamp (eds), *Winfield & Jolowicz on Tort* (19th edn, Sweet & Maxwell 2014) fn 103 at [11-015] (noting that the risk-creation rationale cannot be reconciled with the requirement of defectiveness).

106 JUSTIFYING STRICT LIABILITY

liability.[189] Furthermore, as will be seen and in keeping with the US approach,[190] the greater reliance of English scholars and courts on abnormality of risk and on the gain-based theories of risk (risk–profit and risk–benefit) casts some doubt on the extent to which English legal actors are truly committed to risk creation as a persuasive justification for the imposition of strict liability.

Overall, then, the significance of risk creation in the English context is somewhat ambiguous. Compared to the French system, the argument certainly does not possess the prestige of a tradition going back to Saleilles and Josserand, but it still carries some weight. Where deployed, whether with other justifications or alone, the argument retains its distinctiveness and it does some work in justifying the imposition of strict liability. Especially in the field of vicarious liability, the reasoning of courts and some scholars has recently put particular emphasis on the creation of a risk of harm as one of the rationales of vicarious liability. At the same time, though, reliance on risk creation is modest outside that field. Furthermore, in keeping with the other three jurisdictions, risk creation is harshly criticized because seen as practically unworkable and morally problematic. Finally, as will be seen below, other and narrower risk-based arguments are certainly more prominent in the English context.

Moving now to the qualified variants of risk creation, nonreciprocity of risk has gained very little support in the English context. A rare example of support comes from McBride and Bagshaw, who draw directly on Fletcher's theory of nonreciprocity of risk and see it as one of the convincing justifications for product

---

[189] Some argue that risk creation cannot explain key features of the law of vicarious liability: see Stevens (n 185) 271–72 (arguing that the risk-creation rationale cannot explain why vicarious liability is confined 'to *torts* by *employees*') (original emphasis); Paula Giliker, *Vicarious Liability in Tort: A Comparative Perspective* (CUP 2010) 240 (noting that if liability were based on the theory of risk (this arguably including both risk creation and risk–benefit/profit), then it should 'extend to *all* harmful acts, including the acts of independent contractors') (original emphasis); John Bell, 'The Basis of Vicarious Liability' (2013) 72 CLJ 17, 20 (arguing that '[i]t is not risk creation as such that justifies vicarious liability'; '[r]ather, ... the potential danger may be something which happens in that kind of enterprise and which is a potential burden to be accepted alongside the benefits (not necessarily financial) to the enterprise'); Giliker (n 184) 277 ('[p]ure risk theory ... does not tell us why vicarious liability is placed on the employer (not just any risk creator) and why it is only the risk of tortious (as opposed to any harmful) behaviour that gives rise to responsibility for the injury suffered'). See also Phillip Morgan, 'Recasting Vicarious Liability' (2012) 71 CLJ 615, 634; James Goudkamp and James Plunkett, 'Vicarious Liability in Australia: On the Move?' (2017) 17 OUCLJ 162, 169. Others note that too generous an interpretation of risk creation may lead to an excessive expansion of vicarious liability: see eg James Plunkett, 'Taking Stock of Vicarious Liability' (2016) 132 LQR 556, 560–61 (criticizing the UK Supreme Court for adopting too broad a notion of risk creation and for its consequent failure to distinguish 'between risks that are *inherent in, incidental to or associated with* the employment relationship, as opposed to risks that are merely introduced by, or coincidental to the employment relationship') (original emphasis); Paula Giliker, 'A Revolution in Vicarious Liability: Lister, the Catholic Child Welfare Society Case and Beyond' in Sarah Worthington, Graham Virgo, and Andrew Robertson (eds), *Revolution and Evolution in Private Law* (Hart Publishing 2018) 121, 134ff (seeing as excessive the reliance placed by the UK Supreme Court on risk-based reasoning (in which risk creation is essential), which runs the risk of reducing the rationale of vicarious liability into a 'mere risk redistribution exercise' (ibid 139).

[190] Text following n 133 in this section.

RISK   107

liability under the Consumer Protection Act 1987.[191] But apart from this, the argument struggles to attract acceptance and indeed it is the target of various criticisms which have certainly weakened its appeal.[192] Therefore, in keeping with the French and Italian approaches, nonreciprocity of risk has failed to establish itself as a reason for imposing strict liability in the English context, this marking a striking contrast with the United States.

Far more important is instead abnormality of risk, even though it has had a troubled life in the English system. To begin with, the argument acts as a key justification for strict liability in a variety of contexts. For instance, it has always been a condition of application of the rule in *Rylands v Fletcher*,[193] and regularly put forward as one of its key justifications.[194] Other examples can be identified in relation to liability for dangerous animals,[195] to liability prescribed in statutes regulating

[191] Nicholas J McBride and Roderick Bagshaw, *Tort Law* (6th edn, Pearson Education 2018) 376–78 (juxtaposing nonreciprocity of risk with loss spreading, with accident avoidance, with an argument looking at the efficient allocation of resources (though presented as cost internalization), and with an argument resonating with victim protection). A further example resembling the argument of nonreciprocity of risk is Stevens' approach to the rule in *Rylands v Fletcher* and other pockets of strict liability included in legislation such as liability for dangerous animals and for nuclear installations. Stevens sees the gist of these liabilities in the notion of 'abnormal risk', which however means for him not an especially high risk of harm, but rather any risk which is outside of the normal risks that members of society impose on each other: Stevens (n 185) 113. This would represent, in his view, a sensible principle on which a rule of strict liability may be built in the English context.

[192] Peter Cane 'Justice and Justifications for Tort Liability' (1982) 2 OJLS 30, 45–46; Donal Nolan, 'The Distinctiveness of *Rylands v Fletcher*' (2005) 121 LQR 421, 448–49 (rejecting nonreciprocity of risk); Adam Slavny, 'Nonreciprocity and the Moral Basis of Liability to Compensate' (2014) 34 OJLS 417.

[193] See *Rylands v Fletcher*, (1866) LR 1 Ex 265, 279–80; *Gore v Stannard*, [2014] QB 1, [22].

[194] *Rylands* (n 193) 279–80. See *Jones v Festiniog Ry*, (1867-68) LR 3 QB 733, 736 (Blackburn J), 738 (Lush J) (abnormality of risk standing alone); *Powell v Fall*, (1880) 5 QBD 597, 601 (discussing abnormality of risk and an argument resonating with 'market deterrence'); Frederick Pollock, 'Duty of Insuring Safety: The Rule in Rylands v Fletcher' (1886) 2 LQR 52, 52 (emphasizing abnormality of risk, arguably in combination with victim protection); *Gunter v James*, (1907–1908) 24 Times L Rep 868 (combining abnormality of risk with risk–profit); *Rickards v Lothian*, [1913] AC 263, 280 (abnormality of risk standing alone); *Miles v Forest Rock Co Ltd*, (1918) 34 TLR 500, 501 (mentioning abnormality of risk and, arguably, risk–profit as well); *Noble v Harrison*, [1926] 2 KB 332, 342 (abnormality of risk standing alone); Carleton Kemp Allen, *Legal duties, and other essays in jurisprudence* (Clarendon Press 1931) 194 (combining abnormality of risk with risk–benefit); *Northwestern Utilities Ltd v London Guarantee & Accident Co Ltd*, [1936] AC 108, 118 (emphasizing abnormality of risk, though arguably mentioning risk–benefit/profit as well); *Hale v Jennings Bros*, [1938] 1 All ER 579, 585 (combining abnormality of risk with risk–profit); John M Eekelaar, 'Nuisance and Strict Liability' (1973) 8 Ir Jur 191, 205–06 (referring to abnormality of risk while approving of Baron Bramwell's approach in cases such as *Powell v Fall*); Jenny Steele, 'Private Law and the Environment: Nuisance in Context' (1995) 15 LS 236, 253 (note the fuzzy edges between risk creation and abnormality of risk); *Transco plc v Stockport MBC*, [2003] UKHL 61, [2004] 2 AC 1, [54]–[57], [60], [64] (Lord Hobhouse); *Stannard* (n 193) [156] (combining abnormality of risk with risk–benefit); Dyson and Steel (n 2) 37 (seeing the rule in *Rylands* as liability for exceptional risks); Cane and Goudkamp (n 186) 400 (abnormality of risk standing alone).

[195] *Filburn v People's Palace and Aquarium Co Ltd*, (1890) 25 QBD 258, 260 (combining abnormality of risk with accident avoidance); *Baker v Snell*, [1908] 2 KB 825, 833 (abnormality of risk standing alone); *Read v J Lyons*, [1947] AC 156, 171 (combining abnormality of risk with accident avoidance); *Behrens v Bertram Mills Circus Ltd*, [1957] 2 QB 1, 13–14 (combining abnormality of risk with accident avoidance); Law Commission, *Civil Liability for Animals* (Law Com No 13, 1967) [14]–[18], [20] (juxtaposing abnormality of risk with loss spreading and accident avoidance); John G Fleming, *The Law of Torts* (9th edn, LBC Information Services 1998) 399–400 (discussing abnormality of risk with accident avoidance and victim protection); *Mirvahedy v Henley*, [2003] 2 AC 491, [6]–[7], [13], [34] (Lord Nicholls) (abnormality of risk standing alone); Cristopher Sharp, 'Normal Abnormality? Liability

108   JUSTIFYING STRICT LIABILITY

certain dangerous activities,[196] and, rarely, even in relation to liability for nuisance.[197] Furthermore, insofar as activities of a dangerous character are involved, the *Honeywill* decision established that employers are under a non-delegable duty to ensure that their dangerous activity will not result in any damage, meaning that they are strictly liable for the harm negligently caused by the independent contractors to whom they entrusted such activity.[198] Here, it is precisely the abnormal character of the risk involved which justifies the imposition of strict liability.[199]

Abstracted from any specific context of liability, abnormality of risk has proved influential in the elaboration of theoretical approaches to strict liability and to proposals for reform. In particular, Honoré's famous theory of outcome responsibility identifies the 'extra element' needed to justify strict liability in the 'special risk of harm' involved in the defendant's activity.[200] Similarly, Fleming argues that '[t]he activities that qualify [for strict liability] are those entailing extraordinary risk to others, either in the seriousness or frequency of the harm threatened'.[201] In more recent times, Dyson and Steel argue that 'the *exceptional* or *abnormal* nature of the risk-imposition' can provide a justification for strict liability which is reconcilable 'with accepting negligence liability within its current limits'.[202] Finally, in terms of reform proposals, in its report on civil liability and compensation for personal injury, the Pearson Commission recommends the introduction of strict liability for exceptional risk,[203] seeking to implement by legislation the 'valuable principle ... of strict liability for personal injury caused by dangerous things or activities'.[204] These

for Straying Horses under the Animals Act 1971: Mirvahedy v. Henley [2003] UKHL 16' (2003) JPIL 172, 181; Simon Deakin and Zoe Adams, *Markesinis and Deakin's Tort Law* (8th edn, OUP 2019) 510 (combining abnormality of risk with risk–benefit and with an argument based on 'a duty to protect the public').

[196] Examples include: Nuclear Installations Act 1965, ss 7 and 12; Gas Act 1965, s 14; Environmental Protection Act 1990, s 73(6); Water Industry Act 1991, s 209. In relation to these, see the remarks in *Transco* (n 194) [42]–[45]; WV Horton Rogers, 'England' in Bernhard A Koch and Helmut Koziol (eds), *Unification of Tort Law: Strict Liability* (Kluwer Law International 2002) 101, 116. See also James Goudkamp and Donal Nolan, *Winfield & Jolowicz on Tort* (20th edn, Sweet and Maxwell 2020) [16-005]–[16-006].

[197] *Midwood v Manchester Corporation*, [1905] 2KB 597, 610 (arguably combining abnormality of risk with risk–profit); Maria Lee, 'What is Private Nuisance' (2003) 119 LQR 298, 323–25 (suggesting that strict liability should govern cases where the attendant risk of harm is abnormal).

[198] *Honeywill & Stein Ltd v Larkin Bros (London's Commercial Photographers) Ltd*, [1934] 1 KB 191.

[199] ibid 199 (arguably with a view to promoting the avoidance of accidents). See also Murphy (n 175) 382.

[200] Tony Honoré, 'Responsibility and Luck: The Moral Basis of Strict Liability' (1988) 104 LQR 530, 531, 542 (combining abnormality of risk with individual responsibility, and then adding an argument based on the avoidance of accidents, which 'reinforces the ... arguments for imposing outcome responsibility').

[201] Fleming (n 195) 369–70.

[202] Dyson and Steel (n 2) 36 (original emphasis).

[203] Pearson Commission, *Report of the Royal Commission on Civil Liability and Compensation for Personal Injury*, Cmnd 7054-I (1978), at ch 31.

[204] ibid [1642].

examples suggest that in the last 150 years many English scholars and judges have seen abnormality of risk as an important justification for strict liability.

As to its patterns of use, sometimes abnormality of risk stands alone and therefore acts as the fundamental justification for strict liability. In this type of reasoning, the relevant judge or scholar does not provide much elucidation on the nature of the argument, and one is therefore left to wonder whether abnormality of risk is really thought to be the end of the matter in justificatory terms or if instead it 'hides' a commitment to some ideal of fairness or to the achievement of some specific goal.[205] By contrast, at other times abnormality of risk forms part of a broader reasoning and it is either juxtaposed or combined with all sorts of justifications.[206] In these instances, the role of abnormality of risk is generally that of a means promoting broader goals. As in France and Italy, albeit less frequently, abnormality of risk is sometimes deployed for the purpose of compensating the victims of accidents.[207] At other times, as arguably in Italy and in the United States, it is linked to the avoidance of accidents, especially in relation to the keeping of dangerous animals.[208] Finally, in Honoré's theory of outcome responsibility, abnormality of risk is used to justify strict liability in combination with norms of individual responsibility,[209] giving rise to a pattern of reasoning which, at least in this form, could not be found in any of the other systems.

But despite all this, the argument from abnormality of risk has been harshly criticized and, as a result of this, its force has reduced over time. According to a frequent criticism, it is very difficult to identify a satisfying criterion to distinguish between dangerous and non-dangerous activities, and consequently to apply different liability regimes on that basis. To begin with, at a time when the rule in *Rylands v Fletcher* could have developed into something similar to the Italian or US liabilities for dangerous activities, the decision of the House of Lords in *Read v J Lyons* halted the expansion of the rule by, among other things, rejecting any sharp distinction between dangerous and non-dangerous activities/things on the ground that, since '[e]very activity in which man engages is fraught with some possible

---

[205] See examples of the argument standing alone in nn 194–195 in this section.

[206] See nn 194–200 in this section. These justifications include individual responsibility, risk–benefit/profit, the deep-pockets argument, loss spreading, victim protection, and accident avoidance.

[207] See eg Pearson Commission (n 203) [1641]–[1642], [1645], [1650], [1660], [1668] (recommending the imposition of strict liability on the controllers of dangerous things or operations, repeatedly emphasizing the point that it should be the controller and not the victim to bear the loss, especially given the availability of loss-spreading mechanisms). See also Alfred Thompson Denning, *What Next in the Law* (Butterworths 1982) 126–28 (combining abnormality of risk with victim protection). cf *J Lyons* (n 195) 173 (Lord Macmillan adopting a pro-firm stance and arguing that: if 'those who choose for their own ends to carry on [allegedly dangerous] operations ought to be held to do so at their peril', 'many industries would have a serious liability imposed on them').

[208] See eg *Filburn* (n 195) 260; *J Lyons* (n 195) 171; *Behrens* (n 195) 13–14. See also *Transco* (n 194) [54]–[57], [64] (Lord Hobhouse) (suggesting that defendants are strictly liable under the rule in *Rylands v Fletcher* because of the increased risk of harm they create to neighbouring land and because of their failure to control and confine the source of danger brought or kept on their land).

[209] Honoré (n 200).

110 JUSTIFYING STRICT LIABILITY

element of danger to others', it would be practically very difficult to decide which activities are dangerous and which are not.[210] A similar criticism is put forward by the Law Commission in its report on civil liability for dangerous things and activities,[211] by the Pearson Commission in its report on civil liability and compensation for personal injury,[212] and by the UK Supreme Court (then House of Lords) in *Cambridge Water*.[213] All these criticisms suggest that, in order to avoid uncertainties and practical difficulties, strict liability for dangerous activities should be introduced through statutory law.[214] The result of all this is that the rule in *Rylands* is now treated as a sub-species of the tort of private nuisance,[215] that there is no distinct category of liability for dangerous activities in English tort law, and that it is for the legislator to decide whether any particular activity or thing involves such a high degree of risk of harm that the adoption of a strict liability rule would be appropriate. Again, in the context of liability for breach of a non-delegable duty, in *Biffa Waste Services*, the Court of Appeal criticized the *Honeywill* decision for imposing strict liability on grounds of dangerousness,[216] and in *Woodland* the UK Supreme Court cast doubt on the future of *Honeywill* and similar decisions which, the court argued, 'may be ripe for re-examination' in the future.[217] Finally, the same type of criticism is popular among legal scholars. Key figures such as Cane, Goudkamp, Nolan, and Stanton all believe that the distinction between dangerous and non-dangerous activities or things is problematic, an approach which clearly undermines the credibility of abnormality of risk as a justification for imposing strict liability.[218] Here the difference with the other three legal systems is striking. Italian and US law both include a general liability for dangerous activities whose

---

[210] *J Lyons* (n 195) 172 (Lord Macmillan).

[211] Law Commission, *Civil Liability for Dangerous Things and Activities* (Law Com No 32, 1970) (Law Com No 32) [12]–[14] (arguing that a judicial reform of the rule in *Rylands* on the basis of the 'principle of special danger implicit in the rule' would have created considerable uncertainty, for it would have been 'relatively unpredictable' which activities would have qualified as ultra-hazardous).

[212] Pearson Commission (n 203) [1647].

[213] *Cambridge Water v Eastern Counties Leather*, [1994] 2 AC 264, 305 (Lord Goff) (arguing that, considering 'the uncertainties and practical difficulties of its application', courts should refrain from developing a general strict liability rule on the basis of concepts such as 'especially dangerous' or 'ultra-hazardous' activity).

[214] Law Com No 32 (n 211) [17]; Pearson Commission (n 203) [1649]–[1651]; *Cambridge Water* (n 213) 305. See also *Transco* (n 194) [7] (Lord Bingham).

[215] *Transco* (n 194) [9] (Lord Bingham).

[216] *Biffa Waste Services v Maschinenfabrik Ernst Hese GmbH*, [2008] EWCA Civ 1257, [69]–[78].

[217] *Woodland v Swimming Teachers Association*, [2013] UKSC 66, [2014] AC 537, [6] (Lord Sumption).

[218] Cane (n 174) 50; Peter Cane, 'Fault and Strict Liability for Harm in Tort Law' in William Swadling and Gareth Jones (eds), *The Search for Principle: Essays in Honour of Lord Goff of Chieveley* (OUP 1999) 171, 187; Cane and Goudkamp (n 186) 92–93; Keith M Stanton, 'The Legacy of Rylands v Fletcher' in Nicholas J Mullany and Allen M Linden (eds), *Tort Tomorrow, a Tribute to John Fleming* (LBC Information Services 1998) 84, 90–91; Nolan (n 192) 448. See also Jane Stapleton, *Product Liability* (Butterworths 1994) 185–86 (finding abnormality of risk 'unconvincing both descriptively and normatively'); Anthony Gray, *Vicarious Liability: Critique and Reform* (Hart Publishing 2018) 142–45 (suggesting that it is difficult to decide 'when a risk crosses the line between 'normal' or even 'hazardous' to 'extra-hazardous').

development is in the hands of the courts; in France, even if the *Code civil* does not (yet) include a strict liability for dangerous activities, its introduction has been proposed twice.[219] This shows that legal actors from these three jurisdictions believe that the distinction between dangerous and non-dangerous activities is a workable and meaningful one. In this respect, a further contrast emerges between English and US law. In both common law systems the degree of risk of harm is a relevant factor when conducting the negligence calculus in the tort of negligence, but US courts believe that there are substantive reasons to make room for a distinct and strict liability for activities involving an especially high risk of harm. This suggests that English courts reject this type of liability not only because they see the distinction between dangerous and non-dangerous activities as unworkable but also because they think it is undesirable to expand strict liability to activities involving a substantial risk of harm.[220]

Overall, then, the significance of abnormality of risk in English legal reasoning is ambiguous. On the one hand, the argument features visibly as a justification for the imposition of strict liability in a variety of contexts. On the other hand, especially in more recent times courts and scholars entertain a sceptical view about the argument's conceptual foundation, that is the distinction between what is dangerous and what is not, therefore removing a potent justification for strict liability.

Moving now to gain-based theories of risk, the significance of both risk–benefit and risk–profit in English legal reasoning would be limited if it were not for the lively discussions taking place in relation to vicarious liability. To be sure, risk–benefit and risk–profit feature in a variety of contexts. For example, they have been occasionally used to justify the rule in *Rylands v Fletcher*,[221] liability for nuisance,[222] liability for animals,[223] employers' liability to their employees for breach

---

[219] See Avant-projet Catala, article 1362; Avant-projet Terré, article 23.

[220] See eg *J Lyons* (n 195) 173 (Lord Macmillan).

[221] *Rylands* (n 193) 279–80 (combining risk–benefit with abnormality of risk); Allen (n 194) 194 (combining risk–benefit with abnormality of risk); *Gunter* (n 194) 868 (combining risk–profit with abnormality of risk); *Jennings Bros* (n 194) 585; (combining risk–profit with abnormality of risk); Cane (n 192) 54 (seeing risk–benefit as the basis for the rule in *Rylands*); *Stannard* (n 193) [156] (combining risk–benefit with abnormality of risk). See also John Rason Spencer, 'Motor-cars and the Rule in *Rylands v Fletcher*: A Chapter of Accidents in the History of Law and Motoring' (1983) CLJ 65, 76 (interpreting *Powell v Fall* as based on a combination of risk–profit and abnormality of risk); John Murphy, 'The Merits of Rylands v Fletcher' (2004) 24 OJLS 643, 663 (seeing risk–benefit as 'absolutely fundamental to the justification for imposing strict liability' under *Rylands*). For a criticism of risk–profit as a rationale of *Rylands*, see Stevens (n 185) 111–12.

[222] *Midwood* (n 197) 610–11 (arguably combining risk–profit with abnormality of risk); *Allen v Gulf Oil Refining Ltd*, [1980] QB 156, 169 (maintaining that undertakers acting with statutory authority 'ought not to be allowed—for their own profit—to damage innocent people or property without paying compensation'). Gerry Cross, 'Does Only the Careless Polluter Pay? A Fresh Examination of the Nature of Private Nuisance' (1995) 111 LQR 445, 473–74 (juxtaposing risk–benefit with accident avoidance).

[223] Patrick S Atiyah, *Accidents, Compensation and the Law* (3rd edn, Weidenfeld & Nicholson 1980) 544 (combining risk–benefit with abnormality of risk); Kumaralingam Amirthalingam, 'Animal Liability: Equine, Canine and Asinine' (2003) 119 LQR 563, 564 (juxtaposing risk–benefit/profit with insurability); Deakin and Adams (n 195) 510 (combining risk–benefit with abnormality of risk and with an argument based on 'a duty to protect the public').

112   JUSTIFYING STRICT LIABILITY

of statutory duty,[224] and liability for defective products.[225] Furthermore, they also feature as attractive arguments in the reasoning of a few scholars who seek to justify strict liability on grounds of individual responsibility.[226] Whether combined or juxtaposed with other arguments, in all these instances risk–benefit and risk–profit are key justifications in the reasoning put forward by the relevant judge or scholar, but the fact remains that their use in these contexts of liability is occasional. In this respect, there is a marked contrast with the French, Italian, and US approaches, where risk–benefit and risk–profit are used more frequently but not always as key arguments.[227]

The situation is however different in relation to vicarious liability, where risk–profit and especially risk–benefit are particularly significant in the English context. Here, despite some criticisms,[228] these two arguments are widely relied upon and their justificatory significance is great. As far as risk–profit is concerned, several scholars deploy this argument to justify vicarious liability,[229] and some judicial

---

[224] *Smith v Northamptonshire CC*, [2009] UKHL 27, [2009] ICR 734, [41] (Baroness Hale). See also Douglas Brodie, 'Employers' Liability and Allocation of Risk' (2018) 47 ILJ 431, 433, 438 (advocating for a common law expansion of employers' liability to their employees).

[225] Stapleton (n 218) 186–87 (combining risk–profit with Honoré's theory of outcome responsibility). Murphy (n 221) 659 (combining risk–profit with the deep-pockets argument in relation to liability for defective products and, more generally, to the liability of commercial industrial enterprises).

[226] See Stapleton (n 218) 186ff (providing a 'moral enterprise liability' theory which is based on risk-profit and on notions of individual responsibility); Cane (n 174) 50 (seeing risk–profit as normatively attractive though descriptively inaccurate as to the then-current state of English tort law); Cane (n 218) 202–06 (recognizing the ethical force of risk–profit but seeing it as too broad a principle, and concluding that the argument is the 'most ethically satisfying explanation of (strict) vicarious liability'). See also Cane and Goudkamp (n 186) 174–75, 453 (linking risk–benefit/profit to ideas of fairness and morality both in public and private law contexts, though it is not entirely clear to what extent the two authors support this argument). See also Slavny (n 192), who identifies the moral basis of liability to compensate in two principles, namely the 'avoidability principle' and the 'benefit principle'. On the former, see text to n 116 in subsection 3.3.4. The latter posits that '[w]henever A harms B, there is a stronger reason to let the cost fall on the party that benefits more from the risk-creating activity' (at 428). While this principle clearly overlaps with risk–benefit, Slavny's focus is on cases where the main beneficiary of the risk-imposing activity is someone other than the defendant/risk-imposer, and therefore on cases where risk–benefit is not necessarily involved.

[227] Text to nn 64–66 (France), to nn 117–121 (Italy), to and following nn 170–173 (United States) in this section.

[228] See Patrick S Atiyah, 'Personal Injuries in the Twenty-First Century: Thinking the Unthinkable' in Peter Birks (ed), *Wrongs and Remedies in the Twenty-First Century* (Clarendon Press 1996) 1, 16; Stevens (n 185) 258–59; Goudkamp and Plunkett (n 189) 169; Dyson and Steel (n 2) 40.

[229] eg Fleming (n 195) 410 (arguably juxtaposing risk–profit with the deep-pockets argument, loss spreading, and accident avoidance); Stapleton (n 218) 190–93; Tony Honoré, 'The Morality of Tort Law—Questions and Answers' in David G Owen (ed), *Philosophical Foundations of Tort Law* (OUP 1995) 73, 85, 88–89 (putting forward an argument that resonates strongly with risk–profit and combining it with loss spreading); Murphy (n 221) 659; Brodie (n 181) 495, 496, 502, 507 (emphasizing risk–profit), but cf 495, 497, 499, 500, 501 (mentioning risk creation too), and cf Douglas Brodie, *Enterprise Liability and the Common Law* (CUP 2010) 11, where he seems to prefer, at least interpretively, risk–benefit over risk–profit, for the former can accommodate the vicarious liability of 'non-profit making bodies such as charities'; Cane (n 218) 206 (arguing that risk–profit is the 'most ethically satisfying explanation of (strict) vicarious liability'); Cane and Goudkamp (n 186) 400 (seeing vicarious liability as resting on the risk–profit idea); Plunkett (n 189) 560 (preferring risk–profit over risk–benefit, but it is unclear to what extent he would support the former); Christian Witting, 'Breach of the Non-Delegable Duty: Defending Limited Strict Liability in Tort' (2006) 29 UNSWLJ 33, 46 (recognizing risk–profit as a frequent justification for vicarious liability).

opinions as well emphasize it.[230] The idea that someone who avails themselves of another's actions for their own profit should pay compensation if the latter harms a third party is seen as a morally attractive justification for imposing vicarious liability. Even where discussed with other reasons such as the deep-pockets rationale, loss spreading, or accident avoidance, risk–profit appears to be particularly relevant in the reasoning put forward, especially in the academic literature.[231] Over time, however, English courts have started to see risk–profit as inadequate to justify vicarious liability, because too narrow, and to place increasing reliance on risk–benefit for justificatory purposes. While in older cases the focus was on the traditional profit-seeking defendant employers, in recent times the doctrine of vicarious liability has been invoked in relation to entities that do not pursue economic interests.[232] English courts have therefore shifted the emphasis from risk–profit to risk–benefit so as to make sure that entities not pursuing financial profit could be caught in the net of vicarious liability and that victims, especially if suffering from very serious misconduct such as sexual abuses or racist assaults, were adequately compensated. As a result, in leading cases such as *Lister*, *Cox*, and *Armes*, risk–benefit features very prominently. To be sure, the argument does not stand alone in these and other judgments and is instead discussed with justifications such as risk creation, the deep-pockets rationale, loss spreading, and victim protection. But as was seen for risk creation itself, this does not reduce the importance of the argument. Indeed, not only is risk–benefit recognized as 'the most influential idea in modern times'[233] for the purpose of justifying vicarious liability, but its importance has grown at the expense of risk–profit. As Lord Reed observes:

> The defendant need not be carrying on activities of a commercial nature …. It need not therefore be a business or enterprise in any ordinary sense. Nor need the benefit which it derives from the tortfeasor's activities take the form of a profit. It is sufficient that there is a defendant which is carrying on activities in the furtherance of its own interests. The individual for whose conduct it may be vicariously liable must carry on activities assigned to him by the defendant as an integral part of its operation and for its benefit.[234]

---

[230] *Limpus v London General Omnibus Co*, (1862) 1 H & C 526, 537 (Williams J), 539–40 (Willes J); *Romford Ice and Cold Storage v Lister*, [1956] 2 QB 180, 186 (Denning LJ, dissenting); *Morris v Ford Motor Co Ltd*, [1973] QB 792, 798 (Lord Denning MR); *Viasystems (Tyneside) Ltd v Thermal Transfer (Northern) Ltd*, [2006] QB 510, [55] (Rix LJ); *Weddall v Barchester Healthcare Ltd*, [2012] EWCA Civ 25, [63] (Aikens LJ).

[231] See references mentioned in nn 229–230 in this section.

[232] See *CCWS* (n 177); *Armes* (n 177); *Lister* (n 177).

[233] *Armes* (n 177) [67].

[234] *Cox* (n 177) [30]. For similar remarks, see *Lister* (n 177) [65] (Lord Millett).

114 JUSTIFYING STRICT LIABILITY

Therefore, despite some criticisms,[235] risk–benefit is very prominent in recent judicial attempts to justify vicarious liability,[236] and its importance cannot be exaggerated in light of the fact that the argument contributes to defining the boundaries of the doctrine by including in its scope of application entities not pursuing financial profit.[237]

In sum, the significance of gain-based theories of risk in the English context is mixed. On the one hand, compared to the other three systems studied, generally they are less heavily relied on across the spectrum of the strict liabilities recognized in the law of torts. On the other hand, when they *are* used, and even if combined or juxtaposed with other justifications, both risk–benefit and risk–profit constitute key reasons for the imposition of strict liability in England, whereas in the other three jurisdictions—but especially in France and Italy—they appear in some cases at least to act as secondary or even make-weight arguments. Furthermore, while in all four legal systems risk–benefit and risk–profit appeal to an ideal of fairness, in the English context and especially in the academic literature this connection emerges with particular force, with several legal scholars putting forward moral theories of responsibility which emphasize the fairness of making strictly liable gain-seeking parties. Put another way, in English legal reasoning the link between gain-based theories of risk and norms of responsibility is particularly strong, a pattern not at all evident in the other three jurisdictions.

3.2.6 Concluding Remarks

This section has shown that risk represents a widespread and significant argument in legal reasoning seeking to justify the imposition of strict liability in the four legal systems studied. Compared to other arguments which will be analysed in this book, risk has a particular feature: it cannot be described as a unitary argument because it consists of several different permutations (risk creation, nonreciprocity of risk, abnormality of risk, risk–benefit, and risk–profit). Each permutation possesses its own conceptual distinctiveness, which is reflected in the way strict

---

[235] Stapleton (n 218) 190 (arguing that risk–profit is descriptively superior to risk–benefit); Plunkett (n 189) 560 (criticizing the UK Supreme Court in *Cox* for reducing to 'little more than semantics' the difference between a profit-seeking firm and a non-profit body, for 'only the former receives a form of gain from which they can be fairly said to be able to offset their losses').

[236] Few scholars support this approach: see Steele (n 183) 578–81 (juxtaposing risk–benefit (and risk creation) with other justifications such as accident avoidance, victim protection, the deep-pockets argument, and loss spreading). See also Bell (n 189) 20 (preferring risk–benefit over risk creation, though it is not entirely clear whether his position is only interpretive or also normative); Brodie (n 229) 11, but cf Brodie (n 181) 495, 497, 499, 500, 501, and then 495, 496, 502, 507, where he emphasizes risk creation and risk–profit, respectively.

[237] This expansion of the boundaries of vicarious liability is one of the reasons why several legal scholars reject the descriptive accuracy of risk–profit as a justification for the doctrine: see eg Stevens (n 185) 258–59; Morgan (n 189) 618; McBride and Bagshaw (n 191) 854–55.

liability is justified, and follows its own patterns of use. As a result, the significance of risk as a justification for strict liability is better assessed if its permutations are evaluated one by one.

Starting with risk creation, the idea that a party should be liable because they created a risk of harm which then materialized is treated in markedly different ways across the four jurisdictions. In all of them, the argument is criticized on various grounds, most notably because seen as morally unpersuasive or as practically unworkable. Consistently with this, risk creation is flatly rejected in the Italian context and, where mentioned, the creation of risk is generally deployed as the starting point of a broader reasoning that seeks to justify strict liability on entirely different grounds.[238] Therefore, the creation of risk loses its conceptual distinctiveness as a justification and, as will be seen in subsequent sections, the real reasons for strict liability in the Italian context lie elsewhere. Similarly, in the United States, it is true that some scholars and courts rely on risk creation as a key reason to justify strict liability, but again in many instances the creation of risk loses any justificatory value and strict liability is justified on the basis of other arguments. In yet other cases, it is very difficult to pinpoint the significance of the argument because of a lack of clarity in the relevant reasoning. As a result, the overall significance of risk creation in the United States is modest.[239] The situation looks different in France and in England, where the theory of created risk has gained comparatively more acceptance. In France, from the time of Saleilles and Josserand risk creation has enjoyed a prestige which, perhaps, renders strict liability more acceptable and familiar in the French context. This does not mean, though, that French legal actors think that risk creation does much justificatory work when it comes to supporting the imposition of strict liability. While occasionally standing alone and therefore acting as a key justification, the creation of risk is in many cases discussed with other arguments[240] which, as will be seen in subsequent sections, dominate the scene and explain better the heavy reliance on strict liability in France. Finally, in England, risk creation has gained increasing acceptance in recent times, essentially because of the justificatory role it has taken on in the context of vicarious liability.[241] However, because of the criticisms received, of its modest use outside the law of vicarious liability, and of the greater prominence of abnormality of risk and risk–benefit/ profit, the significance of risk creation must be assessed cautiously in the English context.[242]

As far as nonreciprocity of risk is concerned, the different significance of this argument across the four legal systems is striking. In the United States, the argument has proved influential among courts and scholars, with numerous contexts of strict

---

[238] See text to and following nn 70–85 in this section.
[239] See text to and following nn 123–134 in this section.
[240] See text to nn 30–38 in this section.
[241] See text to nn 177–184 in this section.
[242] See text to and following nn 185–190 in this section.

116 JUSTIFYING STRICT LIABILITY

liability often justified on this basis (even if in combination or juxtaposition with other arguments).[243] By contrast, in the other three legal systems nonreciprocity of risk cannot be found except for very few mentions.[244] Different reasons may be at play across the three jurisdictions to explain this absence. The theory of nonreciprocity of risk is based on an interpersonal and bilateral understanding of tort law, with an avowed rejection of collective goals as acceptable bases for imposing liability in tort. In light of this, it is not surprising that the argument has not attracted support in France and Italy, where tort law is widely perceived as a system geared towards the achievement of broader goals, whether victim protection, loss spreading, or accident avoidance. Furthermore, it is doubtful that the theory of nonreciprocity of risk would accommodate contexts of strict liability such as strict liability for things or for non-dangerous animals, whose core elements would be hardly reconcilable with the postulates of Fletcher's approach. As to England, by contrast, the little support gained by nonreciprocity of risk is harder to explain. Infused as it is with a rhetoric of morality, responsibility, and bilateral justice, nonreciprocity of risk would be attuned to the way in which English tort law is often portrayed by its own legal actors (and especially legal scholars).

In relation to abnormality of risk, this argument features prominently in the Italian and US systems, which both include a distinct category of liability for dangerous activities (albeit with robust differences in terms of their formal requirements and respective scope of application). In these jurisdictions, the creation of an abnormal risk of harm is perceived as an important justification for the imposition of strict liability, and in many instances it is linked to broader societal ends such as victim protection, loss spreading, or accident avoidance.[245] The French approach contrasts, at least in part, with the Italian and US ones. In France, there is no distinct legal category of civil (ie private law) liability for dangerous activities but, despite this, abnormality of risk is alive and well. On the one hand, the argument is mentioned in proposals to introduce a specific and very strict liability rule for dangerous activities so as to ensure even greater protection to the victims of accidents. On the other hand, the notion of abnormality of risk is understood very broadly and, as such, as capable of justifying, together with other arguments, a variety of existing strict liabilities, from liability for the deeds of things to liability for traffic accidents and liability for defective products.[246] Moreover, in the realm of French administrative law, there exists a head of liability for dangerous things or activities which, while not enjoying as much importance as in the past,[247] still testifies to the continuing role that abnormality of risk plays in justifying strict liability and in satisfying the pressing moral imperative of social solidarity.[248] In the English system,

---

[243] See text to nn 136–140 in this section.

[244] See n 13, and n 191 and accompanying text in this section.

[245] For Italy, see text to nn 98–103; for the United States, see text to nn 143–154 in this section.

[246] See text to nn 39–49 in this section.

[247] See Simon Whittaker, *Liability for Products* (OUP 2005) 121.

[248] See text to nn 50–53 in this section.

the argument from abnormality of risk occupies a peculiar position. On the one hand, it is seen as a prominent justification in a variety of contexts, where it can be used either as a stand-alone justification for strict liability or in combination/juxtaposition with other arguments. In the latter case, abnormality of risk is either deployed to serve goals such as the compensation of victims or the avoidance of accidents (similarly to the other three legal systems) or to support and promote norms of individual responsibility (a pattern of use which seems specific to English law).[249] On the other hand, its prominence in English reasoning is greatly diminished in light of judicial and academic criticisms which consider unconvincing the distinction between dangerous and non-dangerous activities/things. Given that this scepticism directly undermines the conceptual foundation of the argument, it has contributed to the demise of the rule in *Rylands* and promises to do the same in relation to the *Honeywill* doctrine, therefore making the future of abnormality of risk in England uncertain.[250]

Finally, as regards risk–benefit and risk–profit, the idea that it is fair or otherwise desirable to link gains to liabilities attracts support in all four legal systems. In France, Italy, and the United States the two gain-based theories of risk are used conspicuously to justify a wide range of strict liabilities. Their overall significance, however, is ambiguous: sometimes they are seen as key justifications, while at other times their justificatory weight is unclear and they behave more like either secondary or make-weight arguments.[251] The English approach is different insofar as the two gain-based arguments are used less frequently but, where relied upon, they act as key justifications in most instances of reasoning[252] (such as in the law of vicarious liability).[253]

The section, therefore, provides a picture of complexity in which risk-based arguments are patterned in all sorts of different ways and in which their role varies within and across the four legal systems. What is clear is the degree of flexibility that the various permutations of risk reveal across the four jurisdictions. Sometimes, they retain their full distinctiveness and constitute in themselves fundamental reasons for the imposition of strict liability. At other times, they can be put to serve a range of distinct goals, such as meeting the demands of social justice by ensuring compensation and the spreading of losses, promoting some understanding of morality and individual responsibility, or pursuing the minimization of the risk of accidents.

---

[249] See text to nn 206–209 in this section.
[250] See text to nn 210–220 in this section.
[251] For France, see text to nn 64–66; for Italy, see text to nn 114–122; for the United States, see text to and following nn 170–173 in this section.
[252] See text to nn 221–227 in this section.
[253] See text to nn 229–237 in this section.

3.3

Accident Avoidance

3.3.1 Accident Avoidance as a Justification for Strict Liability

It is widely accepted that avoiding (or preventing) accidents is better than having to deal with their tragic consequences. Can the law of tort contribute to the avoidance of death, personal injury, or damage to property? This question often receives an affirmative answer, and it is not difficult to find legal actors who, across the four legal systems studied, invoke accident avoidance as a justification for the imposition of liability in tort. In particular, it is argued that the threat of a legal sanction, typically the payment of damages, provides people with incentives to modify their behaviour and thereby reduce the risk of harm. The potential of tort for reducing such risk is often invoked in relation to intentional or negligent conduct, but an argument based on the avoidance of accidents is also deployed to justify strict liability. In broad terms, this argument suggests that losses should be borne by the party who is best suited to avoid or reduce the number or severity of accidents ('accident avoidance'). So understood, accident avoidance can support the imposition of strict liability in a variety of ways which are best explained by considering how strict liability may be better than fault at reducing the risk of accidents.

First, strict liability can more effectively stimulate an improvement in the safety of potentially harmful activities. Fault keeps defendants merely to the standard of the reasonable person, but strict liability puts more pressure on them to change the way they organize and run their activities. Furthermore, while in the fault model consideration is often given only to the precautions adopted very near or at the time of the accident ('situational safety'), strict liability ignores the level of precautions adopted in any particular situation; rather, it leaves it to the defendant to find a way to avoid accidents or reduce their likelihood by, for example, investing in research and development or by making (even structural or organizational) changes that can render the relevant activity safer ('background safety'[1]).

Another way in which strict liability may promote the avoidance of accidents more effectively than fault is by preventing or reducing the operation of harmful activities or by inducing a shift to other, safer activities. The idea is that, faced with the costs of liability for the accidents caused (even if non-negligently), the party carrying on a particular activity will decide either to reduce the intensity of that

---

[1] I owe this term to Lewis Sargentich, who used it in the Tort course at the Harvard Law School during the autumn of 2013.

Justifying Strict Liability. Marco Cappelletti, Oxford University Press. © Marco Cappelletti 2022.
DOI: 10.1093/oso/9780192859860.003.0005

activity, that is to engage less in it, or to shift to safer activities. For example, if driving a certain number of kilometres per month causes a certain number of accidents *even if without negligence*, the hope is that the adoption of strict liability will induce a reduction in the number of kilometres driven and, consequently, in the number of non-negligently caused accidents; or, if shipping goods by truck causes *even if without negligence* more accidents than shipping goods by air, the adoption of strict liability may induce the shipper to shift to the latter activity and reduce the number of accidents.[2] As this strategy to avoid accidents impacts on the intensity, or level, of the potentially harmful activity, I will call it 'activity modification'.

Background safety and activity modification can overlap, though. On a broad understanding of the former, reducing the intensity of an activity (eg the number of kilometres driven) may well be seen as part of a background-safety strategy insofar as such reduction of intensity can be described as a structural or organizational change in the way activities are carried on. Given this overlap, in the following discussion I do not distinguish sharply between these two ways of avoiding accidents.

As I will show, the significance of accident avoidance as a justification for strict liability and the way in which this argument is used vary considerably across the four legal systems studied.

3.3.2 The Pervasive Nature of Accident Avoidance in the United States

Among the four legal systems studied, the law of the United States is where accident avoidance looms largest as a justification for the imposition of strict liability. The ability to prevent accidents forms one of the primary criteria for evaluating the desirability of different tort rules, with the result that accident avoidance features conspicuously in discussions regarding strict liability. The importance of accident avoidance is due partly to the prominence of the economic analysis of law, which has profoundly influenced US legal thought since the 1960s, and partly to the belief that, irrespective of any commitment to economic analysis, preventing accidents is a commendable goal as it removes the need to compensate the losses they cause. As a result, accident avoidance thrives as a justification for strict liability in a wide variety of contexts of strict liability in US tort law.

Since the second half of the twentieth century, several legal scholars have put forward economic analyses of tort law in the belief that the ultimate goal of this area of law is the minimization of the costs of accidents. In the context of accident avoidance, this means that potential defendants and claimants should be induced to adopt cost-justified precautions to the point where additional avoidance

---

[2] Kenneth S Abraham, *The Forms and Functions of Tort Law* (5th edn, Foundation Press 2017) 201–02.

measures would cost more than the costs of accidents they would avoid. Which type of liability rule, strict or fault-based, achieves this goal more effectively is an issue that has sparked a lively debate among legal economists, receiving strikingly different answers. As will be seen, the economic theories put forward disagree as to the ability of strict liability to reduce accidents efficiently and therefore accord to it a different role in tort law.

To begin with, Calabresi's famous 'cheapest cost avoider' theory suggests that liability should be imposed on the party who is in the better position 'to make the cost–benefit analysis between accident costs and accident avoidance costs and to act on that decision once it is made'.[3] A key element in Calabresi's theory is that the search for the cheapest cost avoider is influenced by what he terms 'market' or 'general' deterrence.[4] According to this approach, whose theoretical basis can be found in the 'resource allocation' theory studied in welfare economics,[5] it is key that all accident-causing activities internalize their full social costs, including the costs of accidents they cause to third parties (with or without negligence). If the costs of accidents of (say) car driving were not included in the 'price' of this activity, people would ignore its true cost; as a result, drivers would not adopt precautions that they would instead take if they knew (and had to pay for) the true cost of driving, and there would be too much car driving in society at the expense of safer substitutes available on the market (eg trains or buses). By forcing a full internalization of costs through the market, the general deterrence approach provides incentives either to move to safer activities or to make activities safer, for example by adopting further precautions or investing in research and development.[6] The search for the cheapest cost avoider within the relevant accident-causing activity is no easy task, as a variety of factors ought to be taken into account,[7] but if successful it selects as liable in tort the party who can avoid accidents most cheaply, and therefore it promises to minimize the risk of accidents more efficiently than the fault system.[8] Ultimately, then, this approach proposes a regime of liability which rejects entirely fault as a

---

[3] Guido Calabresi and Jon T Hirschoff, 'Toward a Test for Strict Liability in Torts' (1971) 81 Yale LJ 1055, 1060; Guido Calabresi, 'Optimal Deterrence and Accidents' (1974) 84 Yale LJ 656, 666 (hereafter Calabresi, 'Optimal Deterrence'); Guido Calabresi and Alvin K Klevorick, 'Four Tests for Liability in Torts' (1985) 14 J Legal Stud 585, 588, 591. See also Guido Calabresi, *The Costs of Accidents: A Legal and Economic Analysis* (YUP 1970) 135ff (hereafter Calabresi, *Costs*).

[4] Calabresi, *Costs* (n 3) 69–73.

[5] ibid.

[6] ibid 70–71, 74–75.

[7] ibid 135–73.

[8] See eg Calabresi, *Costs* (n 3) 237–73; Calabresi, 'Optimal Deterrence' (n 3) 657–64, 666–70. Note that the paramount goal of Calabresi's approach is to minimize the sum of three types of costs: 'primary costs', which are the direct accident costs (ie the loss itself) and the costs of avoiding accidents; 'secondary costs', which include the social costs of leaving victims of accidents uncompensated; and 'tertiary costs', which include the costs of running any system that seeks to reduce primary and/or secondary costs (Calabresi, *Costs* (n 3) 26–28). Therefore, in Calabresi's theory, accident avoidance is combined with the loss-spreading and deep-pockets arguments (as means to reduce secondary costs), as well as with a reduction in administrative costs (ie the costs of administering tort claims), which are part of the tertiary costs incurred to reduce primary and/or secondary costs.

criterion for the attribution of losses and which replaces the negligent person with the cheapest cost avoider as the liable party.[9]

A very different approach is put forward by Posner. For him, while negligence is generally superior to strict liability, there are specific situations where pursuing efficient accident avoidance requires a decrease in the level of the defendant's activity.[10] For example, having a pet tiger is sooner or later likely to cause grave injury to others, given the nature of tigers and given that 'there is only so much the owner can do, in the way of being careful, to keep the tiger under control' (situational and background safety); therefore, '[t]he most promising precaution may simply be not to have a tiger—an activity-level change' (activity modification).[11] Besides wild animals, other contexts of liability which Posner considers as appropriately subjected to strict liability and justified by efficient accident avoidance are employers' vicarious liability,[12] liability for abnormally dangerous activities,[13] and product liability for manufacturing defects.[14] Clearly, in Posner's view, efficient accident avoidance leads to the imposition of strict liability only in specific contexts.

A still different approach to efficient accident avoidance, featuring in the work of scholars such as Shavell, Cooter, and Ulen, focuses on whether accidents are unilateral or bilateral as well as on the adoption of safety-enhancement precautions and changes in activity levels.[15] In unilateral accidents, only the injurer's behaviour can reduce the probability or gravity of losses, whereas in bilateral accidents the conduct of both injurers and victims are relevant for the purposes of accident avoidance.[16] As a result, the choice of the most appropriate rule will depend on whether the type of accident is unilateral or bilateral and on what the parties (or the injurer if the accident is unilateral) can do to take precautions or modify the

---

[9] According to Calabresi, the 'general' deterrence approach suffers from some limitations as a result of which it is highly undesirable to rely exclusively on the market to reach decisions about accident costs: see Calabresi, *Costs* (n 3) 78–94. For this reason, he suggests that market-driven choices should be supplemented by collective decisions about accident-causing activities, for example by prohibiting them altogether or by regulating the way in which they should be performed (see ibid 95ff, 174ff). This approach, which is called 'specific deterrence', has its own limitations too (see ibid 107–13). As a result, in Calabresi's view, a good system of accident law is very likely to include both general and specific deterrence methods.

[10] William M Landes and Richard A Posner, 'The Positive Economic Theory of Tort Law' (1980) 15 Ga L Rev 851, 904.

[11] Richard A Posner, *Economic Analysis of Law* (9th edn, Wolters Kluwer 2014) 207. See also *GJ Leasing Co, Inc v Union Elec Co*, 54 F.3d 379, 386 (7th Cir.1995) (Circuit Judge Posner) (treating the keeping of a tiger in one's possession as an abnormally dangerous activity).

[12] Posner (n 11) 218–19; Landes and Posner (n 10) 914–15 (mentioning background-safety measures in addition to activity-modification adjustments).

[13] Posner (n 11) 207–08. See also Richard A Posner, 'A Theory of Negligence' (1972) 1 J Legal Stud 29, 76.

[14] Posner (n 11) 210–11; William M Landes and Richard A Posner, 'A Positive Economic Analysis of Products Liability' (1985) 14 J Legal Stud 535.

[15] See Steven Shavell, 'Strict Liability versus Negligence' (1980) 9 J Legal Stud 1 (hereafter Shavell, 'Strict Liability versus Negligence'); Steven Shavell, *Economic Analysis of Accident Law* (HUP 1987) 5–31 (hereafter Shavell, *Economic Analysis*); Robert Cooter and Thomas Ulen, *Law & Economics* (6th edn, Pearson 2012) 199–213.

[16] Shavell, 'Strict Liability versus Negligence' (n 15) 1, 6.

level of their activity. On this basis, if the focus is on taking precautions to reduce accidents, strict liability is desirable in cases of unilateral accidents;[17] by contrast, in cases of bilateral accidents, fault and strict liability would be equally efficient because both parties are in a position to take precautions.[18] If, instead, efficient accident avoidance requires a change in the level of activity, strict liability will be desirable in cases of unilateral accidents,[19] whereas in cases of bilateral accidents it will be desirable only where it is more important to reduce the level of the injurer's activity than the level of the victim's activity.[20] On this approach, then, efficient accident avoidance justifies the imposition of strict liability in a variety of contexts, such as abnormally dangerous activities,[21] wild animals,[22] defective products,[23] or employers' vicarious liability.[24]

All these economic approaches share the view that avoiding accidents is key. However, they differ in important respects because they disagree as to strict liability's potential in reducing accidents efficiently and therefore they expand or shrink its role in tort law accordingly.[25] In this sense, then, accident avoidance is a two-edged sword that can either promote or undermine strict liability: sometimes, the prevention of accidents is used an argument that supports a wide reliance on strict liability, other times it is an argument that marginalizes strict liability and favours negligence-based rules.[26]

While the impact of economic analysis on US legal reasoning cannot be exaggerated and has produced an enormous volume of literature in the field, the importance of accident avoidance is not confined to theories based on law and economics. In relation to most contexts of strict liability, there are many examples of

---

[17] Cooter and Ulen (n 15) 204.

[18] ibid 204–11.

[19] Shavell, *Economic Analysis* (n 15) 23–25.

[20] ibid 29; Cooter and Ulen (n 15) 211–213.

[21] Steven Shavell, 'The Mistaken Restriction of Strict Liability to Uncommon Activities' (2018) 10 Journal of Legal Analysis 1.

[22] Shavell, *Economic Analysis* (n 15) 31.

[23] Cooter and Ulen (n 15) 251–53.

[24] Shavell, *Economic Analysis* (n 15) 172–73, cf 174 (warning that '[t]he administrative costs associated with imposition of vicarious liability may outweigh the beneficial effects on incentives').

[25] The approaches considered in the text differ in other respects too. For example, while they all give relevance to administrative costs, they attribute a very different role to distributional concerns (and therefore to arguments based on the spreading of losses or the existence of a 'deep pocket'): both Calabresi, *Costs* (n 3) 39–67, and Louis Kaplow and Steven Shavell, *Fairness v Welfare* (HUP 2002) 28ff, 86ff recognize their importance in assessing legal rules, while Posner is more sceptical about their role in tort law (see eg Richard A Posner, 'Strict Liability: A Comment' (1973) 2 J Legal Studies 205, 210; Richard A Posner, 'Book Review (reviewing Guido Calabresi, *The Costs of Accidents: A Legal and Economic Analysis* (1970))' (1970) 37 U Chi L Rev 636, 638–39, 646). See also subsection 3.4.4 (on the deep-pockets justification) and subsection 3.5.3 (on loss spreading), for further discussion. On the differences between Calabresi and Posner, see also George L Priest, *The Rise of Law and Economics* (Routledge 2020) 61–80.

[26] cf Alan O Sykes, 'Strict Liability versus Negligence in Indiana Harbor' (2007) 74 U Chi L Rev 1911, 1919 ('[i]n general, it is difficult to say which rule is superior from an economic standpoint purely as a matter of theory, and the empirical information necessary to determine which rule is superior across important classes of cases is often unavailable').

124 JUSTIFYING STRICT LIABILITY

judges and scholars who, while possibly influenced by the views of legal economists, rely on accident avoidance without showing any strong commitment to economic efficiency. For example, in the context of liability for abnormally dangerous activities, the Supreme Court of Iowa observes that operators of dangerous activities should be found strictly liable because, compared to potential victims, they are 'in a superior position to develop safety technology to prevent ... accidents';[27] similarly, among legal scholars, the avoidance of accidents is seen either as a good reason for imposing strict liability for hazardous activities or as the rationale that fits best all the requirements set out in § 520 of the Second Restatement.[28] In the context of product liability, references to accident avoidance are even more frequent, not least because this is the area where the most intense and lively discussions on the justifications for the imposition of liability take place. As early as 1944, in his landmark concurring opinion in *Escola v Coca Cola Bottling Co of Fresno*, Justice Traynor observes that 'public policy demands that responsibility be fixed wherever it will most effectively reduce the hazards to life and health inherent in defective products that reach the market', and that '[i]t is evident that the manufacturer can anticipate some hazards and guard against the recurrence of others, as the public cannot'.[29] In more recent times, a plethora of courts and scholars have similarly stressed the importance of avoiding accidents and shared the view that strict liability would induce manufacturers (and other suppliers of products) to reduce the risk of accidents.[30] Another context where accident avoidance features

---

[27] *National Steel Service Center v Gibbons*, 319 N.W.2d 269, 272–73 (Iowa 1982) (quoting at length Richard Posner, *Economic Analysis of Law* (2nd edn, Little, Brown 1977)) (juxtaposing accident avoidance with loss spreading). See also *Bierman v City of New York*, 60 Misc.2d 497, 498–99 (N.Y.1969) (citing Calabresi) (juxtaposing accident avoidance with loss spreading and risk creation); *Dyer v Maine Drilling & Blasting, Inc*, 984 A.2d 210 (Me.2009) [19]–[20], [31] (juxtaposing accident avoidance with loss spreading and with a combination of arguments featuring abnormality of risk and risk–profit).

[28] See, respectively, Virginia Nolan and Edmund Ursin, 'The Revitalization of Hazardous Activity Strict Liability' (1987) 65 NCL Rev 257, 292 (citing Posner as well as Calabresi and Hirschoff) 290–93 (juxtaposing accident avoidance with loss spreading and fairness (which consists of nonreciprocity of risk and of risk–profit)), and Mark Geistfeld, 'Should Enterprise Liability Replace the Rule of Strict Liability for Abnormally Dangerous Activities?' (1997) 45 UCLA L Rev 611, 652–58. See also Joseph H King Jr, 'A Goals-Oriented Approach to Strict Tort Liability for Abnormally Dangerous Activities' (1996) 48 Baylor L Rev 341, 352–56 (recognizing that accident avoidance is a goal of strict liability—with several references to Calabresi's work—but giving it only secondary importance); Danielle Keats Citron, 'Reservoirs of Danger: Evolution of Public and Private Law at the Dawn of the Information Age' (2007) 80 S Cal L Rev 241 (drawing on Posner's and Calabresi's analysis in her discussion of accident avoidance, and juxtaposing this argument with a variety of other justifications, including loss spreading and the promotion of individual responsibility).

[29] *Escola v Coca Cola Bottling Co of Fresno*, 150 P.2d 436, 440–41 (Cal.1944) (juxtaposing accident avoidance with loss spreading, victim protection, and administrative cost reduction).

[30] eg *Francioni v Gibsonia Truck Corp*, 372 A.2d 736, 739 (Pa.1977) (juxtaposing accident avoidance with victim protection and loss spreading); *Leichtamer v Am Motors Corp*, 424 N.E.2d 568, 575 (Ohio 1981) (accident avoidance standing alone); *Heath v Sears, Roebuck & Co*, 464 A.2d 288, 293 (N.H.1983) (juxtaposing accident avoidance with risk–profit); *Queen City Terminals, Inc v Gen Am Transp Corp*, 653 N.E.2d 661, 671–672 (Ohio 1995) (juxtaposing accident avoidance with loss spreading and administrative cost reduction); *Gantes v Kason Corp*, 679 A.2d 106, 111–12 (N.J. 1996) (accident avoidance standing alone). As to legal scholars, see eg William L Prosser, 'The Fall of the Citadel' (1966) 50 Minn L Rev 791, 799–800, 816 (juxtaposing accident avoidance with victim protection, administrative cost reduction, an argument based on consumer expectations, and loss spreading (though the last one 'appears

ACCIDENT AVOIDANCE   125

prominently is employers' vicarious liability. Scholars and courts argue that a regime of strict liability would induce employers to take a variety of actions to reduce the risk of accidents, such as by monitoring more intensely their employees' conduct, assigning simpler tasks to accident-prone employees, or rethinking the way of performing their activities.[31] Again, a concern to prevent accidents is also visible in relation to other contexts such as liability for the harm caused by animals,[32] statutory strict parental liability,[33] and liability for traffic accidents.[34] Finally, in relation to public bodies in the exercise of their 'administrative' functions, accident avoidance is relied upon in a variety of situations, for example to call for a reform of the 'discretionary function' exception protecting public bodies from liability[35] or,

to play only the part of a makeweight argument', at 800)); Abraham (n 2) 226–27 (on manufacturing defects) (juxtaposing accident avoidance with administrative cost reduction and loss spreading). See also Gregory C Keating, 'Products Liability as Enterprise Liability' (2017) 10(1) JTL 41, 46ff (juxtaposing accident avoidance with spreading-based and fairness arguments, although attributing only limited significance to accident avoidance).

[31] See *Gossett v Simonson*, 411 P.2d 277, 279–80 (Or.1966) (juxtaposing accident avoidance with risk–profit and with an argument based on 'risk-distribution'); *Mary M v City of Los Angeles*, 814 P.2d 1341, 1347–49 (Cal.1991) (juxtaposing accident avoidance with victim protection and loss spreading); *Lisa M v Henry Mayo Newhall Mem Hosp*, 907 P.2d 358, 366–67 (Cal.1995) (juxtaposing accident avoidance with victim protection and loss spreading); Fowler V Harper, Fleming James Jr, and Oscar S Gray, *The Law of Torts*, vol 5 (2nd edn, Little, Brown and Company 1986) 21 (juxtaposing accident avoidance with victim protection and loss spreading); Gary T Schwartz, 'The Hidden and Fundamental Issue of Employer Vicarious Liability' (1996) 69 S Cal L Rev 1739, 1763–64 (juxtaposing accident avoidance with administrative cost reduction), 1756, fn 91 (combining accident avoidance with the deep-pockets argument); Abraham (n 2) 213 (juxtaposing accident avoidance with administrative cost reduction and loss spreading). See also *Becker v Interstate Properties*, 569 F.2d 1203, 1210–12, 1214 (3rd Cir.1977) (juxtaposing accident avoidance with loss spreading, victim protection, and risk–profit, in relation to the liability of an employer who hired a financially irresponsible independent contractor); *Anderson v Marathon Petroleum Company*, 801 F.2d 936, 938–39 (7th Cir.1986) (emphasizing accident avoidance as a reason to impose vicarious liability on the hirers of independent contractors in situations involving the performance of abnormally dangerous activities, and also briefly mentioning an argument based on victim protection).
[32] See Third Restatement LPEH, comment *d* to § 22 and the Reporters' Note to that comment (juxtaposing accident avoidance with abnormality of risk and nonreciprocity of risk).
[33] See *Curry v Superior Court*, 20 Cal.App.4th 180, 187–89 (Cal.1993) (arguably juxtaposing accident avoidance with victim protection); Pamela K Graham, 'Parental Responsibility Laws: Let the Punishment Fit the Crime' (2000) 33 Loy LA L Rev 1719, 1727 (juxtaposing accident avoidance with victim protection, with the former being seen of primary significance).
[34] See eg Kenneth S Abraham and Robert L Rabin, 'Automated Vehicles and Manufacturer Liability for Accidents: A New Legal Regime for New Era' (2019) 105 Va L Rev 127; Kyle Logue, 'The Deterrence Case for Comprehensive Automaker Enterprise Liability' (2019) 1 J L & Mob 1.
[35] See eg Barry R Goldman, 'Can the King do no Wrong? A New Look at the Discretionary Function Exception to the Federal Tort Claims Act' (1992) 26 Ga L Rev 837, 856–58 (juxtaposing accident avoidance with loss spreading and victim protection as the reasons militating against the 'discretionary function' exception); Bruce A Peterson and Mark E Van Der Weide, 'Susceptible to Faulty Analysis: United States v. Gaubert and the Resurrection of Federal Sovereign Immunity' (1997) 72 Notre Dame L Rev 447, 484–86 (criticizing an excessively broad 'discretionary function' exception and arguing that it may be theoretically possible to remove it and impose strict liability on the federal government whether or not discretion was exercised, on grounds of (efficient) accident avoidance in juxtaposition with nonreciprocity of risk and loss spreading). See also Judge Keating's dissenting opinion in *Riss v City of New York*, 240 N.E.2d 860 (N.Y.1968), where the majority found the city of New York not liable for deciding not to accord police protection to a woman threatened and then injured by a former suitor, on the ground that the city was exercising its discretion as to how its limited resources should be allocated and

126   JUSTIFYING STRICT LIABILITY

more generally, to support an expansion of government liability on the basis of the doctrine of *respondeat superior.*[36]

In sum, US courts and scholars make widespread use of accident avoidance in their attempt to justify the imposition of strict liability in a variety of contexts, regardless of whether they adhere to economic approaches to the law. What is the *significance* of the accident-avoidance argument in the US reasoning? Occasionally, accident avoidance stands alone as an argument for imposing strict liability and is therefore seen as the fundamental reason for such imposition,[37] but this is rare because in most cases the argument is either combined or (more often) juxtaposed with other justifications and can therefore assume varying significance.[38] In legal reasoning committed to economic analysis, accident avoidance is typically discussed together with arguments such as loss spreading (and/or the deep-pockets justification) and administrative cost reduction, all acting as a means to the greater end of increasing social welfare. Here, depending on the view of the single scholar or judge, the concern to avoid accidents may be equally if not more important than

that a court should not interfere with such determinations. At 865–66, Judge Keating disagrees with the majority view and relies on accident avoidance to argue that the city should be vicariously liable for the negligence of members of the police department. See also Peter H Schuck, *Suing Government: Citizen Remedies for Official Wrongs* (YUP 1983) ch 5, esp 113–15.

[36] See eg Schuck (n 35) ch 5 (advocating the vicarious liability of government 'for every harmful act or omission committed by its agents within the scope of their employment that is tortious under applicable law' (at 111), on grounds of accident avoidance, victim protection, loss spreading, compliance with moral norms, and administrative cost reduction). See also Kenneth Culp Davis and Richard J Pierce, *Administrative Law Treatise* (3rd edn, Little, Brown and Company 1994) ch 19 at 206, 208, 228, 256–57 (juxtaposing accident avoidance with victim protection); William P Kratzke, 'Some Recommendations concerning Tort Liability of Government and Its Employees for Torts and Constitutional Torts' (1996) 9 Admin LJ Am U 1105, 1164–67 (juxtaposing accident avoidance with loss spreading); Richard J Pierce and Kristin E Hickman, *Administrative Law Treatise* (6th edn, Wolters Kluwer 2019) vol 3, 2262, 2268, 2307 (juxtaposing accident avoidance with victim protection). Other public law areas where accident avoidance is deployed involve the violation of federal or constitutional rights, either to justify the liability of municipalities under § 1983 or to advocate a change in the *Bivens* doctrine so that liability is imposed on the federal government rather than on its agents. On the former, see eg *Owen v City of Independence*, 445 US 622 (1980) [16,17], [20] (juxtaposing accident avoidance with loss spreading and victim protection, even though the latter two arguments seem more significant in the court's reasoning); Susanah M Mead, '42 U.S.C. § 1983 Municipal Liability: The Monell Sketch Becomes a Distorted Picture' (1987) 65 NCL Rev 517, 538–40 (arguing that victim protection, accident avoidance, and loss spreading (as proportionality of burdens and as taxation spreading) are the most pressing reasons for seeing *respondeat superior* as the basis of liability under § 1983); Peter H Schuck, 'Municipal Liability under Section 1983: Some Lessons from Tort Law and Organizational Theory' (1989) 77 Geo LJ 1753, 1779–80 (relying on accident avoidance, victim protection, taxation spreading, administrative cost reduction, and considerations of morality, to reject the 'official policy' requirement under § 1983 and support the adoption of a type of municipal liability which is, in essence, strict); Schuck (n 35) ch 5, esp 119. On the latter situation (ie change to the *Bivens* doctrine) see eg Susan Bandes, 'Reinventing *Bivens*: The Self-Executing Constitution' (1995) 68 S Cal L Rev 289, 341 (juxtaposing accident avoidance with victim protection, loss spreading, the promotion of moral norms, and administrative cost reduction); Diana Hassel, 'A Missed Opportunity: The Federal Tort Claims Act and Civil Rights Actions' (1996) 49 Okla L Rev 455, 474–75 (juxtaposing accident avoidance with victim protection).

[37] eg *Gantes* (n 30) 111–12; *Leichtamer* (n 30) 575.

[38] See nn 27–36 in this section.

other arguments,[39] but its pivotal role is completely clear. To have a sense of this, the words of Calabresi are particularly illuminating when he warns legal scholars (including himself) that they 'fail at times to keep in mind that it is minimization of total accident costs, not minimization of accidents, which is the goal'.[40] In other words, accident avoidance is so central in economic analysis that legal economists sometimes treat it as if it were the ultimate goal, forgetting that instead it is only a means to a further goal. This discussion provides two important insights. On the one hand, accident avoidance is central to economic analysis and constitutes an essential reason for imposing strict liability (or, for that matter, any type of liability). On the other hand, the importance of this argument lies in its role in promoting social welfare; here, it is a means to an end, not an end in itself.

Where, instead, it is discussed by scholars and judges who do not profess any adherence to economic analysis, the avoidance of accidents represents an end in itself which can be pursued regardless of economic theories. As Schwartz points out, '[t]here is no reason why all analysts who care about deterrence as an important social goal should be classified as economists or required to accept the complete methodology of an economic analysis, and all the arguably artificial assumptions tied to that analysis'.[41] Outside economic reasoning, accident avoidance is typically juxtaposed with a variety of other arguments and in this way it can assume different justificatory weight. In some cases, the prevention of accidents acts as a key justification for the imposition of strict liability. For example, a court may describe accident avoidance as the 'first and foremost objective of strict liability', with other arguments such as loss spreading or administrative cost reduction being of secondary importance.[42] In other cases, the reverse happens, with accident avoidance being of secondary importance and other arguments acting as key justifications. In *Green*, for example, the prevention of accidents is given some consideration, but the 'primary rationale underlying the imposition of strict [products] liability' is seen as lying in creating a risk of harm by manufacturing a product and profiting from it.[43] In still other cases, accident avoidance acts as a make-weight argument. For instance, at one point in his discussion of product liability as an example of enterprise liability, Keating seems to suggest that one of the reasons for imposing strict liability is accident avoidance,[44] but elsewhere he either omits any reference

---

[39] Compare the approaches of Calabresi, *Costs* (n 3) 26–28 (seeing the reduction in secondary and tertiary costs as no less important than a reduction in primary costs) and of Kaplow and Shavell (n 25) 86ff (similarly recognizing an important role to distributive and administrative concerns in addition to the avoidance of accidents), with that of Posner (n 11) ch 6 (focusing on avoiding inefficient accidents and reducing tertiary costs while largely ignoring distributive concerns).

[40] Guido Calabresi, 'Fault, Accidents and the Wonderful World of Blum and Kalven' (1965) 75 Yale LJ 216, 218 at fn 7.

[41] Schwartz (n 31) 1764.

[42] eg *Queen City Terminals* (n 30) 671–72.

[43] eg *Green v Smith & Nephew AHP, Inc*, 629 N.W.2d 727, 750 (Wis.2001). See also King Jr (n 28) 350, 353 (seeing loss spreading as more important than accident avoidance in relation to strict liability in general).

[44] Keating (n 30) 96–97.

128   JUSTIFYING STRICT LIABILITY

to this rationale[45] or openly criticizes it.[46] The impression is that in the context of product liability he is using accident avoidance to make his overall reasoning look more attractive, even though the argument adds very little to it. Finally, in many cases where the relevant reasoning does not allow us to pinpoint the exact justificatory weight of accident avoidance compared to other, juxtaposed rationales, the impression is that it is still recognized as a respectable justification for the imposition of strict liability.[47] In sum, even outside the realm of economic reasoning, accident avoidance features conspicuously as a justification for the imposition of strict liability. However, in contrast with what happens in economic reasoning, the avoidance of accidents is not treated as a means to wider ends but as an end in itself that is worth pursuing, regardless of other objectives.

All this makes clear that accident avoidance is an argument that permeates US legal reasoning in strict liability. This does not mean, of course, that it has remained unchallenged. To begin with, accident avoidance is rejected by those who think that tort liability can be justified only by considerations pertaining to the bilateral interaction between claimant and defendant. In this framework of analysis, accident avoidance is unacceptable, as it embodies a collective goal that disregards both the relationship between claimant and defendant and the doing of interpersonal justice between them.[48] Secondly, sometimes accident avoidance is criticized even by those who do not rule out justifications pursuing societal goals. For example, Keating vigorously argues for the recognition of a broad theory of enterprise liability in US tort law and, in seeing a key element of his theory in the fairness of distributing losses among all those who benefit from the harmful activity, he underlines the 'enterprise liability doctrine's relative indifference to optimal precaution', this signalling the author's scepticism towards accident avoidance as a persuasive reason for imposing strict liability.[49] Thirdly, some legal scholars argue that, while tort liability (whether strict or fault-based) can achieve some level of accident prevention, it does not do so to the extent suggested by many legal economists.[50] Finally, it must be remembered that, as already seen when discussing

---

[45] ibid 56–57.

[46] ibid 62. See also Gregory C Keating, 'The Idea of Fairness in the Law of Enterprise Liability' (1997) 95 Mich L Rev 1266, 1373–74.

[47] eg *Mary M* (n 31) 1347–49; *Lisa M* (n 31) 366–67; Harper, James, and Gray (n 31) 21.

[48] See eg Ernest J Weinrib, 'The Special Morality of Tort Law' (1989) 34 McGill LJ 403, 408; George Fletcher, 'Fairness and Utility in Tort Theory' (1972) 85 Harv L Rev 537, 537–43. The same treatment is therefore reserved to any other justification that embodies goals transcending the bilateral interaction between claimant and defendant (eg loss spreading, victim protection, administrative cost reduction, and the deep-pockets argument).

[49] Keating (n 46) 1277, 1378. See also ibid 1373–74. Note that in Keating's theory, the beneficiaries of a harmful activity who, as such, must bear some share in the cost of accidents include not only the defendant (typically the firm gaining monetary profits from the harmful activity), but also third parties who nonetheless benefited from it (such as the firm's customers and the users of the product or service provided).

[50] Gary T Schwartz, 'Reality in the Economic Analysis of Tort Law: Does Tort Law Really Deter?' (1994) 42 UCLA L Rev 377.

accident avoidance in economic reasoning,[51] the goal of preventing accidents may militate not only in favour but also against the adoption of strict liability.

Notwithstanding these criticisms, in the United States the presence of accident avoidance as a reason for imposing liability in tort is pervasive. As far as strict liability is concerned, accident avoidance attracts the attention of many courts and legal scholars and it features conspicuously in discussions seeking to justify this type of liability. The argument is either used in the context of economic reasoning as a means to wider ends or considered as a goal worth pursuing in itself. Either way, it plays an essential role in US legal reasoning and it certainly constitutes a very significant justification for the imposition of strict liability.

3.3.3 Accident Avoidance in Italy: A Leading Justification

In several respects, the significance of accident avoidance as a justification for the imposition of strict liability in the Italian context resembles the US position and contrasts sharply with the way in which accident avoidance is seen in the English and French contexts. The idea that strict liability can lead to a reduction in the number or severity of accidents features prominently in many Italian scholarly works and, strikingly, also in judicial decisions to support or explain strict liability.

The prominence of accident avoidance as a justification for strict liability in Italy is in large part due to the role played by law and economics in Italian legal scholarship. This approach to the study of tort law first appeared in Trimarchi's work *Rischio e responsabilità oggettiva*,[52] and then grew in importance under the influence of US legal economists, such as Calabresi, Posner, and Shavell. Calabresi in particular has influenced Italian scholars in a variety of ways,[53] and his towering legacy can be easily appreciated as soon as one engages with the Italian tort scholarship of the last fifty years. Unsurprisingly, then, while accident avoidance may be also invoked by scholars not committed to an economic analysis, it is in the efforts of those working from the perspective of law and economics that this argument assumes major importance. These efforts have, in turn, affected the thinking of Italian courts, whose reasoning often shows a marked—though by no means exclusive—concern for the avoidance of accidents in numerous contexts of liability. As this

---

[51] See text to nn 3–26 in this section.

[52] Pietro Trimarchi, *Rischio e responsabilità oggettiva* (Giuffrè 1961).

[53] Calabresi's writings have attracted so much attention in Italy that they have been frequently translated into Italian, a notable example being the translation of *The Costs of Accidents* (Guido Calabresi, *Costi degli incidenti e responsabilità civile. Analisi economico-giuridica* (A De Vita, V Varano, V Vigoriti (trs), Giuffrè 1975)). Moreover, over the years Calabresi has participated in countless conferences in Italy, and he has himself published various contributions in Italian, such as Guido Calabresi and Enrico Al Mureden, '*Driverless* car e responsabilità civile' (2020) 1 Rivista di diritto bancario 7. Finally, during his sixty years of law teaching at Yale, Calabresi has taught many Italian jurists who went there for their postgraduate studies, a notable example being Carlo Castronovo, a leading private and tort law scholar.

judicial attitude is the result of academic debates, I will first consider the work of legal scholars and then its reception in judicial reasoning.

Since the 1960s, justifications of strict liability based on accident avoidance have featured constantly in Italian legal scholarship reflecting the fact that Italian scholars started to develop a keen interest in law and economics around that time. To begin with, in the work of Trimarchi tort liability is seen as providing incentives to reduce efficiently the risk of accidents and therefore to increase social welfare.[54] In Trimarchi's view, strict liability can induce either background-safety measures, such as the adoption of further precautions or changes in productive methods, or activity-modification strategies, such as shutting down one's own activity in whole or in part.[55] Importantly, Trimarchi subjects the imposition of strict liability to the condition that the defendant's activity presents a minimum of continuity and organization,[56] and that the risk of harm created can be calculated and therefore be absorbed through spreading mechanisms or, if possible, even self-insurance.[57] Otherwise, he argues, strict liability would not be an effective economic pressure but only a blow which would undermine the defendant's finances while not advancing the goal of efficient accident avoidance.[58] Nevertheless, he expressly notes that distributing losses (eg through insurance or self-insurance) and compensating victims must be considered secondary goals and justifications of liability as compared to the efficient avoidance of accidents.[59]

A second approach followed by Italian law and economics scholars shares Trimarchi's view that the essential objective of tort liability is the achievement of efficient accident avoidance, but prioritizes different aspects of economic reasoning. For example, Monateri embraces the view that fault-based liability should be adopted in situations where both parties are in a position to take precautions to avoid accidents (bilateral accidents), while strict liability, even with no defence based on the victim's fault, should be adopted in situations where only the defendant can do something to avoid the accident (unilateral accidents).[60] A straightforward application of this approach is in the context of dangerous activities, for it is only the operator of such activities and not the victim that has the technological

---

[54] Pietro Trimarchi, *La Responsabilità Civile: Atti Illeciti, Rischio, Danno* (Giuffrè 2017) 3–4, 275–79. Note that Trimarchi's theory contemplates victim protection as another goal of tort liability: ibid 3–4, 276.

[55] ibid 278 and 283 (on strict liability in general), 296 (on employers' vicarious liability), 374 (on liability for things in one's keeping and for the actions of animals).

[56] ibid 285. Therefore, Trimarchi's theory applies strict liability to contexts such as product liability, employers' vicarious liability, liability for abnormally dangerous activities, and even liability for things/animals and liability for traffic accidents.

[57] ibid 280–81, 359–60.

[58] ibid 352, 359–60, 280. cf the position of Tunc in France, at n 157 in this section.

[59] Trimarchi (n 54) 8, 279–80. See also Trimarchi (n 52) 31–34.

[60] Pier Giuseppe Monateri, 'Responsabilità civile' Dig Disc Priv (UTET 1998) XVII, 1, 6–10; See also Robert Cooter and others, *Il mercato delle regole—Analisi economica del diritto civile—I. Fondamenti* (Il Mulino 2006) 210–18.

expertise to prevent accidents; therefore, strict liability should apply.[61] A further example is provided by product liability. In many cases the manufacturer is the only party who can act so as to minimize the number of accidents or their magnitude. But there are situations where the consumer is also in a position to take precautions, for example by not using a lawn mower to trim hedges.[62] Given this, the goal of efficient accident avoidance suggests that producers should be subjected to a regime of strict liability unless the victim negligently misused the product or voluntarily exposed themselves to the risk of harm.[63] This approach takes into account not only what precautions the parties can adopt to improve situational or background safety but also the intensity of the defendant's and claimant's respective activities. Indeed, if the intensity of the defendant's activity impacts on the number or magnitude of accidents more than the intensity of the claimant's activity, strict liability should apply so as to induce the defendant to reduce that intensity and therefore cause fewer accidents.[64] Fundamentally, therefore, the desirability of strict liability depends on the nature, bilateral or unilateral, of accidents and on how the intensity of activity influences such accidents; also, unlike in Trimarchi's approach,[65] the availability of spreading mechanisms is not key, and distributive concerns are treated with caution because seen as potentially hindering the efficient avoidance of accidents.[66]

Different again but equally influential is Castronovo's view, which sees strict liability as pursuing, first and foremost, the avoidance of accidents and considers distributive concerns less essential because only applicable to situations where firms, as opposed to physical individuals, cause harm to others.[67] In the pursuit of accident avoidance, strict liability induces those involved in potentially harmful activities either to abstain from engaging in those very activities or to adopt safety measures suitable to prevent accidents.[68] Directly influenced by Calabresi since his studies at Yale in the late 1970s,[69] Castronovo embraces the 'cheapest cost avoider' approach, arguing that

---

[61] Monateri (n 60) 9–10; Pier Giuseppe Monateri, 'Responsabilità del produttore di sigarette per danni da fumo attivo' (2005) 12 DR 1210, 1223.

[62] Robert Cooter and others, *Il mercato delle regole – Analisi economica del diritto civile – II. Applicazioni* (Il Mulino 2006) 204.

[63] ibid.

[64] Cooter and others (n 60) 220–22. See also Pier Giuseppe Monateri, *La Responsabilità Civile. Trattato di Diritto Civile* (UTET 1998) 979 (on employers' vicarious liability) (hereafter Monateri, *La Responsabilità Civile*); Giuseppe Monateri, *Illecito e responsabilità civile—Tomo II. Trattato di diritto privato* (UTET 2002) 246–47 (on product liability); Enrico Baffi and Dario Nardi, 'La responsabilità da custodia della P.A.: prospettive di analisi economica del diritto' (2016) 4 DR 337 (on liability for things in one's keeping).

[65] See text to nn 57–58 in this section, and text to and following nn 118–119 in subsection 3.5.4.

[66] Cooter and others (n 60) 222–23.

[67] Carlo Castronovo, *Responsabilità civile* (Giuffrè 2018) 23–24.

[68] ibid 24–26.

[69] ibid 496; Guido Calabresi, 'L'allievo Carlo Castronovo e le parole del diritto, da Yale a Milano. Spunti e ricordi' in *Scritto in onore di Carlo Castronovo* (Jovene 2018) 1–8.

132   JUSTIFYING STRICT LIABILITY

[t]he person who is made answerable for a certain harm must bear liability because he was found, before its occurrence, in the most adequate position to evaluate the opportunity to avoid it and the way to avoid it in the most convenient way, so that the occurrence of the harm descends by an option for it, taken as an alternative to the contrary decision; and because each of these [decisions] has a cost, bearing the cost of the harm means paying for the choice made.[70]

In treating the 'cheapest cost avoider' approach as based on an element of choice, Castronovo does not see it as belonging exclusively to economic reasoning but instead as 'rooted in a human dimension' which, together with its considerable precision, makes it superior to any other previous attempt to justify strict liability.[71] Furthermore, unlike Trimarchi's approach based on *rischio di impresa* and Monateri's approach focusing on the bilateral/unilateral nature of accidents, the 'cheapest cost avoider' approach is 'universal', in the sense that it could replace altogether the fault paradigm and be the sole criterion for the attribution of liability in respect of all accidents.[72]

In sum, and in keeping with the United States, there is a spectrum of economic approaches which emphasize the importance of accident avoidance as a key factor in assessing the appropriateness of liability rules. Inevitably, different economic theories yield different results in terms of the desirability of strict liability. As was seen in relation to the United States,[73] economic analysis deploys accident avoidance as a means to cost minimization and therefore the argument constitutes a two-edged sword that can either support or weaken the case for strict liability, depending on the economic theory which the scholar (or judge) adopts. The same holds true in the Italian context, with Trimarchi, Castronovo, and Monateri each providing strikingly different recipes for choosing between strict liability and fault.

The adoption of an economic perspective by leading Italian scholars has had a remarkable impact on the reasoning of many academics and, albeit to a lesser extent, on that of courts. Examples from the academic literature can be found with reference to numerous contexts of liability. For instance, in relation to employers' vicarious liability, Sella argues that this liability is based on Trimarchi's *rischio di impresa* and suggests that strict liability constitutes an incentive for employers not to underestimate the risks of harm (citing Monateri).[74] Similarly, in the context of

---

[70] Castronovo (n 67) 492–93. See also Carlo Castronovo, *Problema e sistema nel danno da prodotti* (Giuffrè 1979) 595ff.

[71] Castronovo (n 67) 493–94.

[72] ibid 493. The emphasis this author puts on the element of choice and the language he adopts more generally in these pages of his book suggest that his reasoning contains an argument based on individual responsibility as a justification for strict liability: see text to nn 116–118 in subsection 3.8.4.

[73] See text to nn 25–26, and text to and following n 40 in this section.

[74] Mauro Sella, *La responsabilità civile nei nuovi orientamenti giurisprudenziali* (Giuffrè 2007) 1150–51 (adding an argument based on insurability). See also Federico Gustavo Pizzetti, 'Responsabilità civile del datore di lavoro, occasionalità necessaria e stato soggettivo del danneggiato' (1999) 4 DR 430, text to fns 15–19; Massimo Franzoni, *L'illecito. Trattato della responsabilità civile* (2nd edn, Giuffrè 2010) 762–63.

ACCIDENT AVOIDANCE 133

product liability, Pardolesi argues that a regime of strict liability with a defence of contributory negligence constitutes the best approach because it would minimize the costs of accidents by giving both producers and consumers incentives to take efficient precautions.[75] Comparable reasoning can be found in many other contexts, such as liability for dangerous activities,[76] liability for things in one's keeping,[77] liability for the actions of animals,[78] liability for ruinous buildings,[79] liability for nuisance,[80] and liability for administrative activities.[81] All these examples show that, in keeping with US legal economists, many Italian scholars value the tools of

[75] Paolo Pardolesi, 'Riflessioni sulla responsabilità da prodotto difettoso in chiave di analisi economica del diritto' (2017) 2 Riv Dir Priv 87. For other examples in this context, see Guido Alpa, 'Prodotti difettosi, danno ingiusto, responsabilità del fabbricante' (1971) I GM 297, 299, 303 (discussing accident avoidance and loss spreading); Ugo Carnevali, *La responsabilità del produttore* (Giuffrè 1974) 47–50 (combining accident avoidance with loss spreading and administrative cost reduction, clearly drawing on Calabresi); Cooter and others (n 62) 203–04 (focusing on efficient accident avoidance); Annalisa Bitetto, 'Responsabilità da prodotto difettoso: strict liability o negligence rule?' (2006) 3 DR 259, 266–67 (providing an efficiency-based analysis of accident avoidance); Antonio Davola and Roberto Pardolesi, 'In viaggio col robot: verso nuovi orizzonti della r.c. auto ("driverless")?' (2017) 5 DR 616, 628–29, text to and following fn 47 (juxtaposing accident avoidance with victim protection).

[76] Monateri, *La Responsabilità Civile* (n 64) 1011 (agreeing with Trimarchi's approach), 1031 (seeing efficient accident avoidance as the goal of article 2050 Cod civ); Trimarchi (n 60) 9–10; Dario Covucci, 'Attività pericolosa e responsabilità oggettiva del produttore di sigarette' (2010) 6 NGCC 667, [2.2] (drawing on Calabresi's approach to justify the imposition of strict liability on the manufacturers of tobacco products).

[77] Monateri, *La Responsabilità Civile* (n 64) 1050–51, including fn 9 (seeing Italian case law as perfectly consistent with economic analysis and the goal of avoiding accidents); Paolo Laghezza, 'La responsabilità della P.A. per omessa manutenzione delle strade' (2002) 12 DR 1201; Maria Paola Serra, 'La natura oggettiva della responsabilità per danni da cose in custodia: le ragioni di una scelta' (2009) 7 DR 751, esp 757ff; Enrico Baffi and Dario Nardi, 'Analisi economica del diritto e danno cagionato da cose in custodia' (2018) 3 DR 327; Enzo Vincenti, 'La dottrina in dialogo con la giurisprudenza: il pensiero di Pietro Trimarchi in taluni orientamenti della Cassazione civile' (2018) 4 RCP 1396 (arguing that some decisions of the Corte di Cassazione are aligned with Trimarchi's emphasis on accident avoidance).

[78] Annalisa Bitetto, 'Danni provocati da animali selvatici: chi ne risponde e perché?' (2003) 3 DR 275, text to fns 26–28 and to fns 31–32 (discussing accident avoidance with loss spreading and the deep-pockets argument, with a view to minimizing the social costs of accidents); Trimarchi (n 54) 369–82 (focusing on efficient accident avoidance while rejecting risk–benefit and risk–profit).

[79] Monateri, *La Responsabilità Civile* (n 64) 1079; Enrico Baffi, 'La responsabilità del proprietario per danni da rovina di edificio come forma di responsabilità vicaria: analisi giuseconomica' (2017) 6 DR 657.

[80] See eg Trimarchi (n 52) 4–5, 348, 358–59; Giovanna Visintini, 'Immissioni e tutela dell'ambiente' (1976) RTDPC 689, 690; Roberto Pardolesi, 'Azione reale e azione di danni nell'art. 844 c.c. —Logica economica e logica giuridica nella composizione del conflitto tra usi incompatibili delle proprietà vicine' (1977) 1 Foro It 1144, 1150–53. For an extended treatment of liability for nuisance through the lenses of economic analysis, see also Ugo Mattei, *Tutela inibitoria e tutela risarcitoria: contributo alla teoria dei diritti sui beni* (Giuffrè 1987) 345–403.

[81] Gian Domenico Comporti, 'Il cittadino viandante tra insidie e trabocchetti: viaggio alla ricerca di una tutela risarcitoria praticabile' (2009) 3 Diritto Amministrativo 663, 676–77 (focusing on efficient accident avoidance); Elisa Scotti, 'Appunti per una lettura della responsabilità dell'amministrazione tra realtà e uguaglianza' (2009) 3 Diritto amministrativo 521, 591–92 (seeing accident avoidance through the lenses of economic analysis, and juxtaposing it with loss spreading); Sara Valaguzza, 'Percorsi verso una "responsabilità oggettiva" della pubblica amministrazione' (2009) 1 Diritto processuale amministrativo 50, 96–97 (juxtaposing accident avoidance with loss spreading, again by adopting a perspective of law and economics).

economic analysis and consider accident avoidance a persuasive justification for strict liability as it plays a key role in the pursuit of greater social welfare.

Though less common, it is also possible to find judicial decisions engaging with accident avoidance from the perspective of law and economics. The most interesting examples concern liability for dangerous activities and liability for things in one's keeping.[82] As regards the former, in 2005 and 2009 two first-instance judges relied on the difference between unilateral and bilateral accidents to deny the application of article 2050 Cod civ to the production of cigarettes. As the smokers involved were aware of the health risk connected with tobacco consumption and voluntarily decided to smoke and run that risk instead of quitting altogether or reducing the number of cigarettes per day, their injuries constituted a bilateral accident and therefore strict liability could not apply.[83] In 2009, however, the Corte di Cassazione rejected this line of argument and applied article 2050 to a manufacturer of tobacco products.[84] First, the court considered the 'cheapest cost avoider' approach by doing a 'copy and paste' operation from Castronovo's work.[85] Secondly, the court rejected the view that strict liability should apply only in cases of unilateral accidents on the ground, first, that there are cases of unilateral accidents where the legislator opted for a fault-based liability rule,[86] and secondly, that article 1227 Cod civ provides for a general duty on potential victims to avoid or minimize the risk of harm, irrespective of whether the standard of liability chosen by the legislator is strict or fault-based.[87] The fact that one or both parties can avoid or reduce the risk of harm cannot therefore determine which liability rule applies.[88] Again in the context of tobacco litigation, a lower court has recently relied on Calabresi's 'cheapest cost avoider' approach to identify the rationale of article 2050.[89] Finally, in cases concerning liability for things in one's keeping, the Corte di Cassazione again mentions the 'cheapest cost avoider' theory as a justification for this liability,[90] and a decision from a lower court provides a sophisticated economic analysis based on the incentives to be given to the keeper of the thing for purposes of efficient accident avoidance.[91] In sum, similarly to the United States

---

[82] Examples may be found also in relation to employers' vicarious liability, where on several occasions the Corte di Cassazione stated that the rationale of this liability is *rischio di impresa*, therefore drawing on the elaborations of Trimarchi: Civ (III) 20.6.2001 n.8381; Civ (III) 6.3.2008 n.6033; Civ (sezione lavoro) 11.1.2010 n.215; Civ (III) 19.7.2012 n.12448, (2012) 1 GC 2297.

[83] Trib Brescia 10.8.2005, (2005) 12 DR 1210; Trib Roma 28.1.2009 n.1828, (2009) 11 DR 1084.

[84] Civ (III) 17.12.2009 n.26516, (2010) 6 DR 569.

[85] ibid [3.10].

[86] ibid [3.14] (car passengers cannot do anything to avoid accidents and yet, under article 2054 Cod civ, the driver is liable only if at fault).

[87] ibid.

[88] ibid [3.13]–[3.14].

[89] Trib Milano 11.7.2014 n.9235, (2015) 2 LRC 579, 580. cf Civ (III) 10.10.2014 n.21426, [3.2], (2015) 1 Foro It 1303 (identifying the rationale of article 2050 in *rischio di impresa*).

[90] eg Civ (III) 6.7.2006 n.15383, [5.6], (2006) 11 DR 1145; Civ (III) 19.2.2008 n.4279, [4.2], (2008) 11 DR 1112.

[91] Trib Monza 22.10.2001, (2002) 12 DR 1201.

but in striking contrast with what will be seen for England and France, efficient accident avoidance features very prominently in the work of Italian legal scholars and, through them, it has spilled into the reasoning of the courts.

As was seen in relation to the United States, though, economic analysis does not exhaust the significance of accident avoidance as a justification for strict liability in the Italian system. Indeed, while Italian reasoning reveals a strong connection between economic analysis and accident avoidance, judicial decisions or scholarly work that refer to accident avoidance without linking this to broader theories of economic efficiency are not unusual. As regards the courts, there are many examples of rulings that treat accident avoidance as important without resorting to economic analysis. In particular, in relation to article 2051 Cod civ, on several occasions the Corte di Cassazione has stated that 'the function of [strict liability for things in one's keeping] is to attribute liability to the party who is in the position to control the risks stemming from the thing',[92] and that the notion of *custodia* refers to the 'power of governing' the thing, which consists of 'the power to control the thing, to remove situations of danger that may have materialised, and to exclude others from coming into contact with the thing'.[93] The expressions 'to control the risks' and 'to remove situations of danger' resonate strongly with a commitment to avoiding accidents.[94] Decisions where preventing accidents is seen as key are also found outside the context of liability for things in one's keeping, although less frequently. To give an example in relation to the liability of parents, on a few occasions the Corte di Cassazione has suggested that imposing strict parental liability is desirable because it provides parents with an incentive to raise their children in a way that minimizes the risk of dangerous conduct on their part.[95] In sum, the reasoning of these courts suggests that preventing accidents constitutes a key justification for strict liability.

As regards scholarly works not drawing on economic analysis, the typical pattern is that accident avoidance is referred to in a generic way as a reason for adopting

---

[92] Civ sez un 11.11.1991 n.12019, [2.b], (1993) 1 Foro It 922; Civ (III) 25.7.2008 n.20427, [3.2], (2008) 1 Foro It 3461; Civ (III) 8.2.2012 n.1769, [4.1.1], (2012) 9 GC 2047B; Civ (III) 13.1.2015 n.295, (2015) 1 Foro It 460; Civ (III) 29.9.2017 n.22839, [1.2].

[93] Civ (III) 12.7.2006 n.15779, [2.2], (2006) Rep Foro It , voce *Responsabilità civile*, n.481; Civ (VI) 4.10.2013 n.22684, [4.1], (2014) 6 DR 616; Civ (III) 29.9.2017 n.22839, [1.2]; Civ (III) 14.3.2018 n.6141, [6].

[94] Trimarchi himself argues that liability for things in one's keeping should be attributed to the party who could 'intervene on the general conditions of risk' stemming from the thing, primarily because in this way it would be possible to promote a reduction in the risk of accidents: see Trimarchi (n 54) 374–75.

[95] Civ (III) 20.3.2012 n.4395, [2.4], (2012) 12 DR 1218 (accident avoidance standing alone); Civ (III) 19.2.2014 n.3964, [4.4], DR 2014.11.1052 (accident avoidance standing alone). For further examples, see: in relation to the liability of schools, Civ (I) 9.5.2016 n.9337, [1.2.2]–[1.2.3], (2017) 2 DR 212 (accident avoidance standing alone); in relation to employers' vicarious liability, Civ (III) 25.2.2008 n.4718, (2008) 1 NGCC 926 (accident avoidance standing alone); in relation to liability for animals, Civ (III) 11.12.2012 n.22632, [6.3] (discussing accident avoidance with risk–benefit/profit); in relation to liability for ruinous buildings, Civ (III) 29.1.1981 n.693, (1982) II Riv Dir Comm 47, 52 (arguably juxtaposing accident avoidance with risk–benefit).

136 JUSTIFYING STRICT LIABILITY

strict liability, without any further elaboration. In these cases, it is difficult to say how relevant accident avoidance is, but it looks as though it acts at times as either a secondary or make-weight argument, while at other times as a key justification. An example of the first attitude is provided by Comporti who, in expounding his theory based on exposition to danger, considers the protection of victims as paramount and strict liability as fundamentally geared towards that goal;[96] he devotes very little attention to the circumstance that the defendant may be able to control or avoid the created dangers,[97] this suggesting that preventing losses is not a particularly significant factor in his reasoning justifying strict liability. In cases like this, then, the key reason for strict liability lies elsewhere than in accident avoidance, often in a willingness to see victims compensated for their losses.[98] By contrast, at other times accident avoidance looks more significant. For example, in relation to liability for the harm caused by construction defects in motor vehicles, Roppo argues that strict liability should be imposed not on the owners of defective vehicles but on their manufacturers, for they are best suited to avoid or correct the defects which can cause harm—and also for being those who profit most from the car industry.[99] In this case, accident avoidance plays a key role on the face of the reasoning considered or, at least, it does not look less important than other considerations (such as risk–profit, in the present example).[100]

Overall, then, the emerging picture suggests that, in keeping with the approach in the United States, avoiding accidents is a very important reason for imposing strict liability in the Italian context. In discussions based on economic reasoning, accident avoidance constitutes the focal point of analysis and the single most important objective to be accomplished in view of greater social welfare. In

---

[96] Marco Comporti, *Esposizione al pericolo e responsabilità civile* (Morano editore 1965) 24–25, 27, 174–76, 255ff. See also the interpretation of Comporti's approach given by Francesco D Busnelli and Salvatore Patti, *Danno e responsabilità civile* (3rd edn, Giappichelli 2013) 145–46.

[97] Comporti (n 96) 175.

[98] See eg Giovanni Facci, 'L'illecito del figlio minore, la prova liberatoria dei genitori e la responsabilità oggettiva' (2005) 2 LRC 162, text to fns 18–20 (briefly mentioning the avoidance of accidents but interpreting the rigorous attitude of the courts vis-à-vis parental liability as based on the desire to ensure the compensation of victims).

[99] Enzo Roppo, 'Sul danno causato da automobile difettose. Tutela dei danneggiati, regime di responsabilità e incidenza dell'assicurazione obbligatoria' (1978) 12(IV) GI 130, 136, 140 (adding victim protection as well).

[100] For similar examples, all providing interpretive views on liability for things in one's keeping, see Cesare Salvi, *La responsabilità civile* (3rd edn, Giuffrè 2019) 177, 182 (juxtaposing accident avoidance with victim protection); Paolo Garraffa, 'La responsabilità del gestore di un impianto di calcio "saponato"' (2018) 7–8 NGCC 1052, 1059 (accident avoidance standing alone); Franco Anelli and Carlo Granelli, *Manuale di diritto privato Torrente Schlesinger* (24th edn, Giuffrè 2019) 911 (arguing that keeper of the thing is the person who is in a position to monitor the thing or to keep it under control so as to avoid the causation of harm). For a prescriptive statement regarding the liability of public bodies for things in their keeping, see Giuseppe G Infantini, 'La responsabilità civile della pubblica amministrazione per danni causati nell'esercizio di attività pericolose e da cose in custodia' in Enrico Follieri (ed), *La responsabilità civile della pubblica amministrazione* (Giuffrè 2004) 297, 344–45 (juxtaposing accident avoidance with victim protection).

discussions not engaging with economic analysis, many judges and scholars similarly consider accident avoidance to be an important reason for imposing strict liability.

Of course, all this does not mean that accident avoidance has never been challenged. Some Italian scholars seem to consider it axiomatic that strict liability focuses only on compensatory goals and that the fault paradigm would more naturally and effectively pursue the goal of preventing accidents on the ground that, unlike strict liability, it scrutinizes the defendant's conduct.[101] Similarly, in discussions regarding product liability, in the 1970s some academics cast doubt on the ability of strict liability to pursue accident avoidance on the ground that, for many firms, the potential costs of liability are insignificant compared to the profits they make and that, therefore, the imposition of strict liability would have no effect on their choices or methods of production.[102] Again, some doubts have been raised in relation to the deterrent potential of the liability of public authorities in a variety of situations, whether strict or based on fault.[103] It is possible that, to some extent, these criticisms have attenuated the influence of accident avoidance as a reason for adopting strict liability, but they have not undermined its attractiveness in the eyes of many scholars and courts. Indeed, an analysis of the Italian reasoning suggests that the vitality of this argument has remained largely intact and that it is widely seen as a key justification today. Most likely because of the growing influence exercised by approaches based on law and economics, the idea that strict liability may contribute to preventing losses has thrived and become one of the most frequently rehearsed arguments for imposing strict liability in the Italian context.

3.3.4 Accident Avoidance in English Law: Not (Yet?) a Leading Justification

Compared to the US and Italian approaches, accident avoidance has less appeal as a justification for strict liability in England. To be sure, the argument appears in the reasoning of many English legal actors who see the avoidance of accidents as

---

[101] Salvatore Patti, *Famiglia e responsabilità civile* (Giuffrè 1984) 275, 292–93; Luigi Corsaro, 'Funzione e ragioni della responsabilità del genitore per il fatto illecito del figlio minore' (1988) IV GI 225 (on parental liability). See also Enrico Carbone, 'La responsabilità aquiliana del genitore tra rischio tipico e colpe fittizie' (2008) 1(2) Riv Dir Civ 1, 14–16.

[102] Mario Bessone, 'Prodotti dannosi e responsabilità dell'impresa' (1971) 1 RTDPC 97, 138–39; Mario Bessone, 'Progresso tecnologico, prodotti dannosi e controlli sull'impresa' (1972) 2 Pol dir 203, 227–30. cf Mario Bessone, 'Profili della responsabilità del produttore nell'esperienza italiana' in Guido Alpa and Mario Bessone (eds), *Danno da prodotti e responsabilità dell'impresa—Diritto italiano ed esperienze straniere* (Giuffrè 1980) 9, 27–28 (seeing strict liability as desirable for its loss-spreading potential in situations where firms are involved).

[103] See Giovanni Comandé and Luca Nocco, 'The Liability of Public Authorities in Italy' in Ken Oliphant (ed), *The Liability of Public Authorities in Comparative Perspective* (Intersentia 2016) 251, [204] (arguing that 'the deterrence effect of such condemnations for the Italian state is null').

138 JUSTIFYING STRICT LIABILITY

a plausible reason for imposing strict liability. However, it is also met with broad scepticism and lacks the theoretical support that economic analysis provides to it in the United States and Italy. As a result, it seems fair to say that accident avoidance struggles to establish itself as a leading justification for the imposition of strict liability in the English context.

The idea that imposing strict liability may be justified by appealing to the desirability of avoiding accidents features in the reasoning of several English legal actors. For example, in relation to the rule in *Rylands v Fletcher*, Salmond argues that an occupier of land is strictly liable 'not merely for *causing* the escape of deleterious things from his land into that of his neighbours, but also for *failing to prevent* such an escape'.[104] In *Transco*, Lord Hobhouse repeatedly observes that the rule in *Rylands* stems from the failure to control and confine the risk created by the dangerous use of land.[105] Similar statements can be found in relation to liability for the harm caused by dangerous animals, where since the famous *Filburn* case several judges have emphasized that the person who keeps a dangerous animal is strictly liable if they fail to prevent it from doing harm.[106] Similarly, the Law Commission's report on civil liability for animals, on which the Animals Act 1971 is based, observes that one of the reasons for imposing strict liability for a dangerous activity (which includes keeping dangerous animals) is that the person carrying it on is in the best position to avoid accidents.[107] Consistently with this, recent cases such as *Mirvahedy* and *Welsh* show that accident avoidance is in the mind of judges when interpreting some provisions of the Animals Act 1971: arguing that the keeper of an animal can decide whether 'to run the unavoidable risks involved in keeping [it]' means inducing them to make a cost–benefit analysis and decide whether it makes more sense to stop engaging in that activity or to continue it and pay compensation, this embodying an activity-modification argument.[108] Again, in the field of

[104] John W Salmond, *The Law of Torts: a Treatise on the English Law of Liability for Civil Injuries* (1st edn, Stevens and Haynes 1907) 191 (original emphasis), but cf 199–201 (providing an interpretation of the Act of God defence which leads to think that, for Salmond, liability under *Rylands* was merely a specific rule of vicarious liability for the negligence of another, on which see Mark Lunney, 'Professor Sir John Salmond (1862–1924): An Englishman Abroad' in James Goudkamp and Donal Nolan (eds), *Scholars of Tort Law* (Hart Publishing 2019) 103, 115–16).

[105] *Transco plc v Stockport MBC*, [2003] UKHL 61, [2004] 2 AC 1, [54]–[57], [64] (also emphasizing the abnormality of the risk of harm so created) (mentioned with approval by Stelios Tofaris, 'Rylands v Fletcher Restricted Further' (2013) 72 CLJ 11, 13). See also *Perry v Kendricks Transport Ltd*, [1956] 1 WLR 85, 90 (Jenkins LJ) (suggesting that 'defendants were under an obligation under the rule to prevent it [ie the thing], or the dangerous element in it, escaping on to a neighbour's land and doing damage there'); John Murphy, 'The Merits of Rylands v Fletcher' (2004) 24 OJLS 643, 665ff (suggesting that the rule in *Rylands* may foster environmental protection).

[106] See eg *Filburn v People's Palace and Aquarium Co Ltd*, (1890) 25 QBD 258, 260; *Read v J Lyons*, [1947] AC 156, 171; *Behrens v Bertram Mills Circus Ltd*, [1957] 2 QB 1, 13–14 (therefore all combining accident avoidance with abnormality of risk).

[107] Law Commission, *Civil Liability for Animals* (Law Com No 13, 1967) [14]–[18], [20] (juxtaposing accident avoidance with loss spreading and abnormality of risk).

[108] *Mirvahedy v Henley*, [2003] 2 AC 491, [157] (Lord Walker); *Welsh v Stokes*, [2007] EWCA Civ 796, [47] (Dyson LJ) (both adding that the defendants could decide 'whether or not to insure against those risks'). See also David Howarth, 'The House of Lords and the Animals Act: closing the stable door' (2003) 62 CLJ 548, 548–49.

nuisance, *Rapier v London Tramways Company* reveals a willingness to take into account accident avoidance, again in the form of activity modification:[109] if the defendants 'cannot have 200 horses together, even when they take proper precautions, without committing a nuisance, all [the judge] can say is, they cannot have so many horses together'.[110] Further references to accident avoidance can be identified in the context of product liability. In the 1970s, both the Law Commission and the Pearson Commission argue that strict liability may encourage manufacturers to 'ensure the highest possible standards of safety',[111] and therefore 'reduce the risk of further accidents'.[112] In more recent times, several English legal actors have interpreted the Product Liability Directive as based on a variety of justifications, including the manufacturer's ability to avoid accidents.[113] In the field of vicarious liability, accident avoidance features in the reasoning of some courts and of several legal scholars, typically on the ground that the defendant is in a position to control the physical author of harm and take a variety of steps that can help reduce the risk of accidents.[114] Finally, in relation to employers' liability to their employees

---

[109] [1893] 2 Ch 588.

[110] ibid 602. See also Gerry Cross, 'Does Only the Careless Polluter Pay? A Fresh Examination of the Nature of Private Nuisance' (1995) 111 LQR 445, 473–74 (juxtaposing accident avoidance with risk–benefit).

[111] Pearson Commission, *Report of the Royal Commission on Civil Liability and Compensation for Personal Injury*, Cmnd 7054-I (1978) [1234]–[1235] (juxtaposing accident avoidance with several other arguments, including loss spreading and victim protection (the latter is mentioned at [1259] in relation to the exclusion of the development risk defence)).

[112] Law Commission, *Liability for Defective Products* (Law Com No 82, 1977) [23], [37]–[38] (juxtaposing accident avoidance with risk creation, loss spreading, victim protection, and administrative cost reduction).

[113] Department of Trade and Industry, *Implementation of European community directive on product liability: an explanatory and consultative note* (1985) [37], [39] (juxtaposing accident avoidance with victim protection). Matthew Dyson and Sandy Steel, 'Risk and English Tort Law' in Matthew Dyson (ed), *Regulating Risk through Private Law* (Intersentia 2018) 23, 42 (referring to efficient accident avoidance); *Gee v DePuy International Ltd*, [2018] EWHC 1208, [167] (arguably juxtaposing accident avoidance with loss spreading); Nicholas J McBride and Roderick Bagshaw, *Tort Law* (6th edn, Pearson Education 2018) 376–78 (juxtaposing accident avoidance with nonreciprocity of risk, loss spreading, with an argument looking at the efficient allocation of resources (though presented as cost internalization), and with an argument resonating with victim protection).

[114] *Majrowski v Guy's and St Thomas's NHS Trust*, [2006] UKHL 34, [9] (Lord Nicholls) (juxtaposing accident avoidance with victim protection, the deep-pockets argument, loss spreading and, perhaps, risk creation); *Viasystems (Tyneside) Ltd v Thermal Transfer (Northern) Ltd*, [2006] QB 510, [55] (Rix LJ) (discussing accident avoidance with loss spreading, in juxtaposition with risk–profit); Malcom A Clarke, *Policies and Perceptions of Insurance Law in the Twenty-First Century* (OUP 2005) 310 (arguing that '[a]ny recent expansion of vicarious liability seems to have been driven less by desire for loss distribution ... than by the goal of loss prevention (and safety at work), or by respect for the logical development of legal principle'); Jonathan Morgan, 'Vicarious Liability For Independent Contractors' (2016) 31 PN 235, 249–51 (suggesting that accident avoidance 'seems to justify the core feature of vicarious liability—ie making one (typically solvent) person strictly liable for the torts of another (typically impecunious) party, when he has some degree of authority and control over that other'); Jenny Steele, *Tort Law, Text, Cases, and Materials* (4th edn, OUP 2017) 578–81 (juxtaposing accident avoidance with risk–benefit, risk creation, victim protection, the deep-pockets argument, and loss spreading); Christian Witting, 'Modelling Organisational Vicarious Liability' (2019) 39(4) LS 1, 7–9 (juxtaposing accident avoidance with victim protection, and devoting most of his article to discussing the potential of vicarious liability for reducing accidents); Christian Witting, *Street on Torts* (16th edn, OUP 2021) 631. See also John G Fleming, *The Law of Torts* (9th edn, LBC Information Services 1998) 410, and Douglas

140 JUSTIFYING STRICT LIABILITY

for breach of statutory duty, judges and scholars have on various occasions emphasized that the imposition of strict liability promotes the preventive purpose of health and safety regulations by inducing good practice in workplaces and, therefore, a reduction in the risk of injury.[115]

In addition to all this, accident avoidance features in the work of some legal scholars discussing liability regardless of any specific tort, with varying degrees of prominence. For example, Slavny identifies the 'moral basis of liability to compensate', which encompasses both fault-based and strict liability, in two principles, one of which is the 'avoidability principle': '[w]henever A harms B, there is a stronger reason to let the cost fall on the party who had a better opportunity to avoid the risk'.[116] Another example is Gardner's approach, which justifies tort law by reference to the role it plays in securing conformity to a moral norm of corrective justice, and yet it sees the avoidance of accidents as part of what tort law is for.[117] Again, Stapleton seems to recognize as legitimate 'the interest in deterring certain conduct by requiring injurers to pay the full social costs of the injuries they cause'.[118] Finally, Honoré's early attempt to justify strict liability on the basis of outcome responsibility and abnormality of risk adds a 'consequentialist argument for avoiding serious harm',[119] and Cane sees the avoidance of losses as one of the responsibility-based justifications for the imposition of strict liability.[120]

Brodie, 'Enterprise Liability: Justifying Vicarious Liability' (2007) 27 OJLS 493, 495 (both seeing accident avoidance as a secondary justification). In relation to liability for breach of a non-delegable duty, see Christian Witting, 'Breach of the Non-Delegable Duty: Defending Limited Strict Liability in Tort' (2006) 29 UNSWLJ 33, 58–60; Stelios Tofaris, 'Vicarious Liability and Non-Delegable Duty for Child Abuse in Foster Care: A Step too Far?' (2016) 79 MLR 884, 896.

[115] See eg *Dugmore v Swansea NHS Trust*, [2002] EWCA Civ 1689; [2003] ICR 574, [27] (Hale LJ) (concerning s 7(1) of the Control of Substances Hazardous to Health Regulations 1988 and 1994); Nigel Tomkins, 'Civil Health and Safety Law after the Enterprise and Regulatory Reform Act 2013' [2013] JPIL 203, 205 (quoting Lord Drummond Young's reasoning in the Scottish case *Cairns v Northern Lighthouse Board*, [2013] CSOH 22, 2013 SLT 645, at para [37], which discusses accident avoidance together with loss spreading (from an efficiency as well as moral perspective), and arguably victim protection); Michael A Jones (ed), *Clerk & Lindsell on Torts* (23rd edn, Sweet & Maxwell 2020) [12-02] (again referring to Lord Drummond Young's reasoning in *Cairns v Northern Lighthouse Board* at paras [37], [38], and [43], which emphasize the importance of avoiding accidents together with an efficient and fair spreading of losses); *Smith v Northamptonshire CC*, [2009] UKHL 27, [2009] ICR 734, [4], [20], [24], [27]–[29] (Lord Hope); [48] (Lord Carswell) (concerning the Provision and Use of Work Equipment Regulations 1998).

[116] Adam Slavny, 'Nonreciprocity and the Moral Basis of Liability to Compensate' (2014) 34 OJLS 417, 425–28. The other principle, juxtaposed with accident avoidance, is the 'benefit principle', on which see n 226 in subsection 3.2.5.

[117] John Gardner, 'What is Tort Law For? Part 1. The Place of Corrective Justice' (2011) 30(1) Law and Phil 1, 25 (accident avoidance, however, 'cannot be the *whole* story of what tort law is for') (original emphasis).

[118] Jane Stapleton, 'Tort, Insurance and Ideology' (1995) 58 MLR 820, 843.

[119] Tony Honoré, 'Responsibility and Luck: The Moral Basis of Strict Liability' (1988) 104 LQR 530, 542. cf Stephen R Perry, 'The Moral Foundations of Tort Law' (1992) 77 Iowa L Rev 449, 495 (doubting that Honoré has in mind deterrence).

[120] Peter Cane, 'Responsibility and Fault: A Relational and Functional Approach to Responsibility' in Peter Cane and John Gardner (eds), *Relating to Responsibility: Essays in Honour of Tony Honoré on his 80th Birthday* (Hart Publishing 2001) 81, 109–10.

The emerging picture may suggest that accident avoidance is a central justification for the imposition of strict liability in England: it features in a wide variety of contexts of liability and, in many of the examples seen above, it is accorded considerable justificatory weight, even where it is combined or juxtaposed with other justifications. However, this is only part of the picture, and there are several reasons to be cautious when assessing the argument's overall significance in England.

First, in none of the contexts of liability where it appears accident avoidance stands out as the dominant justification and, in contexts such as vicarious liability or the rule in *Rylands v Fletcher*, it is clearly less prominent than arguments such as loss spreading or risk.[121] Secondly, accident avoidance is the target of numerous criticisms, both with reference to specific contexts of liability and in general. For example, in relation to product liability, leading scholars such as Stapleton criticize efficient accident avoidance on the grounds that the argument would be normatively undesirable and descriptively inaccurate,[122] and that it would be unworkable, for it would be very difficult to identify the cheapest cost avoider and determine the range of compensable losses.[123] Similarly, several scholars criticize accident avoidance as a plausible justification for vicarious liability on the grounds that it cannot explain some key features of the law,[124] that strict liability is unlikely to deter,[125] or, quite the opposite, that it would end up causing over-deterrence![126] Most importantly, in this field of English law the role of accident avoidance has been sidelined by the UK Supreme Court. In *Armes*, Lord Reed criticizes a decision of the Canadian Supreme Court[127] where liability of a local authority for the abuse of children by foster parents was denied on the ground that 'the imposition of vicarious liability

---

[121] See subsection 3.2.5 (risk) and subsection 3.5.5 (loss spreading).

[122] Jane Stapleton, *Product Liability* (Butterworths 1994) 137–62.

[123] Jane Stapleton, 'Products Liability Reform—Real or Illusory?' (1986) 6 OJLS 392, 397–99. See also John A Jolowicz, 'The Protection of the Consumer and Purchaser of Goods under English Law' (1969) 32 MLR 1, 1–2, 9 (admitting his scepticism about the law's ability to contribute effectively to the avoidance of accidents, and suggesting that preventing accidents 'is the business of the criminal law'); (Lord) Griffiths, Peter De Val and R J Dormer, 'Developments in English Product Liability Law: A Comparison with the American System' (1988) 62 Tul LR 353, 373 (commenting on the Product Liability Directive and arguing that arguments from accident avoidance 'do not seem wholly convincing', for '[i]t may, perhaps, be doubted whether manufacturers' perceptions of the extent of their potential liability directly affect the design and manufacturing process').

[124] Glanville Williams, 'Vicarious Liability and the Master's Indemnity' (1957) 20 MLR 437, 439.

[125] Paula Giliker, *Vicarious Liability in Tort: A Comparative Perspective* (CUP 2010) 242–43; John Murphy, 'Juridical foundations of common law non-delegable duties' in Jason W Neyers, Erika Chamberlain, and Stephen GA Pitel, *Emerging Issues in Tort Law* (Hart Publishing 2007) 369, 373–74. See also McBride and Bagshaw (n 113) 854 (arguably making the same point).

[126] Donal Nolan, 'Review of "Douglas Brodie, *Enterprise Liability and the Common Law* (CUP 2010)"' (2012) 41(3) ILJ 370, 371–72; James Goudkamp and James Plunkett, 'Vicarious liability in Australia: on the move?' (2017) 17 OUCLJ 162, 168–69. See also Anthony Gray, *Vicarious Liability: Critique and Reform* (Hart Publishing 2018) 145–48 (criticizing the 'deterrence' prong of the 'enterprise risk theory', which he rejects and sees as largely based on ideas such as cost internalization, the spreading of losses, and the avoidance of accidents); James Goudkamp and Donal Nolan, *Winfield & Jolowicz on Tort* (20th edn, Sweet and Maxwell 2020) [21-006] (arguing that, 'as elsewhere in tort law, it is questionable whether deterrence is a justification for tort liability or merely a beneficial effect of its imposition').

[127] *KLB v British Columbia*, 2003 SCC 51, [2003] 2 SCR 403.

142   JUSTIFYING STRICT LIABILITY

would not result in the deterrence of such abuse'.[128] After noting that the Canadian decision 'reflects the view taken in that jurisdiction that the deterrence of tortious behaviour is one of the principal justifications for the imposition of vicarious liability', Lord Reed observes that 'a number of justifications for the imposition of vicarious liability have been advanced in the British case law, but deterrence has not been prominent among them', being 'not mentioned in either the *Christian Brothers* [*CCWS*] case or *Cox*'s case'.[129] In the view of the UK Supreme Court, then, the argument from accident avoidance has little or no significance as a justification for vicarious liability, which is instead dominated by risk-based arguments and, perhaps to a lesser extent, by arguments based on loss spreading.[130]

Regardless of any specific context of liability, several English legal scholars question the ability of tort law to reduce meaningfully the number or severity of accidents. For example, entertaining a radical position about tort law's deterrent function, Jolowicz maintains that 'prevention, in so far as it is the business of the law, is the business of the criminal law', while the civil law should mainly 'decide who shall bear the financial consequences when things have gone wrong'.[131] Less drastic is Atiyah, who argues that tort liability may be effective 'in preventing a surgeon [from] operating on a patient without his consent', or 'in deterring newspapers from publishing much which could be defamatory',[132] but then adds that '[t]he effectiveness of tort actions ... as a deterrent in the field of accidents ... is much more dubious'.[133] In sum, many English legal scholars doubt the ability of tort law to induce a reduction in the number or severity of accidents, and at most they concede that tort law may have some deterrent potential in relation to intentional or seriously negligent conduct. Therefore, it is not surprising that these scholars give little or no credit to accident avoidance as a possible justification for the imposition of strict liability.

This tendency to link accident avoidance to fault-based liability leads some scholar to discuss the argument only from the perspective of what can be expected of the reasonable person, forgetting that accident avoidance measures can go beyond ordinary care. An example of this can be identified in Stevens' refutation of accident avoidance as a justification for the imposition of vicarious liability:

---

[128] *Armes v Nottinghamshire County Council*, [2017] UKSC 60, [2018] AC 355, [66].

[129] ibid [67]. Afterwards, Lord Reed labels risk–benefit as the 'most influential idea' grounding vicarious liability.

[130] See subsection 3.2.5 (risk) and subsection 3.5.5 (loss spreading).

[131] Jolowicz (n 123) 9. See also Robert Stevens, *Torts and Rights* (OUP 2007) 321–23 (showing considerable scepticism about tort law's ability to regulate human conduct).

[132] Patrick S Atiyah, *Accidents, Compensation and the Law* (3rd edn, Weidenfeld & Nicholson 1980) 557.

[133] ibid 558. See also Glanville Williams, 'The Aims of the Law of Tort' (1951) 4 CLP 137, 172 (arguing that '[t]he tendency ... is to choose the deterrent purpose for torts of intention, and the compensatory purpose for other torts'); Peter Cane and James Goudkamp, *Atiyah's Accidents, Compensation and the Law* (9th edn, CUP 2018) 405–30.

it is commonly said that holding an employer liable for the torts of his employees will encourage the employer to be careful. The employer has control and is in a position to reduce the harm caused by employees by the selection, supervision, and organization of staff. However, this argument fails to explain why the employer is liable even where he has taken due care in these matters. When the employer has done all that he can, what further encouragement is there in imposing liability in any event?[134]

Here, Stevens links accident avoidance tightly to careless conduct and does not seem to consider the possibility that strict liability may put an additional economic pressure on employers to find ways of reducing accidents. In other words, the strategies which strict liability can deploy to avoid accidents, namely background safety and activity modification, are not explored.

A further reason why accident avoidance struggles to establish itself as a prominent justification for strict liability (and tort liability more generally) relates to the English scepticism about the economic analysis of law. It was seen that both in the United States and in Italy the ascendancy of law and economics provided a formidable framework where accident avoidance could flourish in the reasoning of legal scholars (and of judges, to a lesser extent). In sharp contrast with this approach, in England efficiency-based reasoning has received very little support, with the result that accident avoidance lacks an important theoretical basis. An early notable exception to this is Baron Bramwell, whose judicial opinions in the second half of the nineteenth century make use of welfare economics to justify the imposition of strict liability for nuisance and under the rule in *Rylands v Fletcher*. In Bramwell's view, either the defendant's activity is profitable enough to pay compensation for the harm caused and still survive, or it cannot, in which case it is in the public interest that they should discontinue their activity.[135] This position is reminiscent of the approaches of Trimarchi in Italy and Calabresi in the United States.[136] Once a firm is forced to internalize the full social costs of its activity, which include compensation for the harm caused to third parties (even if without fault), the firm may try to find a way of reducing accidents, for example by lowering the level of its activity or by making it safer. If the firm decides not to do this, it will have to raise the price of its product or service, with the result that consumers/users will buy less of that product or service (preferring safer alternatives); as a result, the firm's product or service will be used less and the overall number of accidents it causes will diminish. To make all this work, though, it is necessary that the 'price' of the firm's activity reflects its true social cost, meaning that as far as tort liability is concerned,

---

[134] Stevens (n 131) 258.

[135] In relation to nuisance, see *Hammersmith and City Railway Co v Brand*, (1866-67) LR 2 QB 223, 231 (for similar remarks, see also *Bamford v Turnley*, (1862) 3 B & S 66, 84–85). In relation to the rule in *Rylands v Fletcher*, see *Powell v Fall*, (1880) 5 QBD 597, 601.

[136] See text to nn 54–55 (Trimarchi) and to nn 3–6 (Calabresi) in this section.

144   JUSTIFYING STRICT LIABILITY

the firm should be strictly liable. A possible outcome of this approach, and the one envisaged by Baron Bramwell, is that if the social wealth a firm creates is less than what it costs to society, and if the firm does not find a solution to this, then it should be driven out of the market because its existence does more harm than good to society.

This way of thinking, though, has never gained acceptance in England and those scholars who have engaged with economic analysis (mostly in its Calabresian version), have shown a good deal of scepticism about the workability and desirability of this approach. For example, in discussing Calabresi's theory of 'general' (or 'market') deterrence,[137] Atiyah argues that 'there is undoubtedly an attraction in the use of the market mechanism in certain situations,[138] but adds that this approach has important limitations and 'the details of the argument seem to depend too much on forms of "fine tuning" which are inappropriate to the circumstances.[139] In *Transco*, Lord Hoffmann comments on Baron Bramwell's interpretation of the rule in *Rylands* and rejects it. In doing so, he observes that while '[i]t is tempting to see, beneath the surface of the rule, a policy of requiring the costs of a commercial enterprise to be internalised', the fear of imposing too much liability on firms has brought the law in another direction, that of a negligence-dominated tort law.[140]

Finally, in keeping with the position of part of US legal scholarship, some English legal scholars reject accident avoidance, especially in its efficiency-based version, on the ground that it embodies an instrumentalist approach which, by seeing tort rules purely as a function of broader social goals, conflicts with the vision of tort law as a system of interpersonal justice. For example, Cane argues that both Posner's and Calabresi's approaches (to negligence and strict liability, respectively) do not fit tort law because they are at odds with the backward-looking nature of the latter and because, where applied to a bilateral relationship as that between claimant and defendant, economic analysis undermines its own logic by subjecting itself to the constraints of the tort system.[141] Perhaps even more fundamentally, though, efficient accident avoidance conflicts with Cane's understanding of tort law as a 'system of ethical rules and principles of personal responsibility.[142]

In sum, an assessment of the overall significance of accident avoidance suggests that the argument struggles to establish itself as a leading justification for the imposition of strict liability. To be sure, it receives the support of many English legal

---

[137] See Calabresi, *Costs* (n 3) 135–73.

[138] Atiyah (n 132) 579–80.

[139] ibid 609–11. See also Patrick S Atiyah, 'Personal Injuries in the Twenty-First Century: Thinking the Unthinkable' in Peter Birks (ed), *Wrongs and Remedies in the Twenty-First Century* (Clarendon Press 1996) 1, 27–30; Cane and Goudkamp (n 133) 420–30.

[140] *Transco* (n 105) [29].

[141] Peter Cane, 'Justice and Justifications for Tort Liability' (1982) 2 OJLS 30, 42–45, 48.

[142] Peter Cane, *The Anatomy of Tort Law* (Hart Publishing 1997) 27; Peter Cane, 'Tort Law as Regulation' (2002) 31 CLWR 305. See also Donal Nolan, 'Causation and the Goals of Tort Law' in Andrew Robertson and Hang Wu Tang (eds), *The Goals of Private Law* (Hart Publishing 2009) 165, 189.

actors across a wide spectrum of contexts of liability, and from time to time legal scholars put renewed effort in endorsing it as a viable justification for tort liability (whether fault-based, strict, or both). On the other hand, accident avoidance is not the leading argument in any of the contexts of liability where it appears, it is usually discussed in relation to intentional or negligent conduct, and it is often criticized, especially in its version based on economic efficiency, which has never attracted particular sympathies among English judges and, especially, legal scholars.

3.3.5 Avoiding Accidents: (Not) a Concern of French Strict Liability?

The concern to prevent accidents features conspicuously in the French context, with leading authors identifying accident avoidance as one of the goals pursued by French tort law.[143] While more emphasis is put on the deterrent potential of tort law in respect of intentional or negligent conduct, accident avoidance is also discussed in relation to strict liability. However, in striking contrast with the US and Italian approaches, this argument has modest significance in the French context as a justification for strict liability, with other arguments dominating the scene. In this respect, the situation in France bears some resemblance to that in England where, as discussed, accident avoidance struggles to become a central justification for the imposition of strict liability. As for many other arguments in the French context, we must look at academic writings rather than judicial decisions to appreciate the role of accident avoidance in the French reasoning in strict liability.

On the premise that 'prevention is better than cure', several French legal scholars acknowledge the role of strict liability in avoiding accidents and maintain that this goal must not be left to fault-based liability. In particular, it is emphasized that *prévention* should not be seen as coterminous with *dissuasion*.[144] While the latter only targets intentional or negligent behaviour, *prévention* also includes the avoidance of accidents caused without negligence. On this basis, accident avoidance features in legal reasoning relating to a variety of contexts of liability. For example, Malaurie, Aynès, and Stoffel-Munck argue that 'the modern foundation of liability for the deeds of things is the idea to impose on everyone the risks of the thing he uses', and that 'generally it is the person who makes use of the thing [*exploitant*] who is best able to prevent and calculate the risks and therefore to insure against

---

[143] eg André Tunc, 'Responsabilité civile et dissuasion des comportements antisociaux' in *Aspects nouveaux de la pensée juridique: recueil d'études en hommage à Marc Ancel*, vol 1 (Pedone 1975) 407. See also Philippe Brun, *La responsabilité civile extracontractuelle* (5th edn, LexisNexis 2018) [156]. cf Geneviève Viney, *Introduction à la responsabilité. Traité de droit civil* (4th edn, LGDJ 2019) [53]–[55] (critically assessing tort law's potential for accident avoidance) and Mireille Bacache-Gibeili, *Les obligations, La responsabilité civile extracontractuelle* (3rd edn, Economica 2016) [47] (arguably seeing the protection of victims as the primary goal of tort law and the avoidance of accidents as a secondary goal).

[144] Florence Millet, *La notion de risque et ses fonctions en droit privé* (PUF 2001) [511]–[512].

146   JUSTIFYING STRICT LIABILITY

them'.[145] Similarly, in relation to employers' vicarious liability, Viney argues that its goal is 'to identify who must take out liability insurance for the protection of victims and to encourage firms to avoid accidents'.[146] In relation to liability for traffic accidents, Viney and Guégan-Lécuyer argue that in identifying the keeper and the driver of the vehicle as the potentially liable parties, the *loi* Badinter designates 'the persons who are best placed and able to *master the potentially damage-creating activity*, and consequently the better able to obtain insurance to cover the risks to which their activity gives rise'.[147] Again, in the context of product liability, Calais-Auloy criticizes the development risk defence on several grounds, including that such defence would dissuade manufacturers from engaging seriously in their research and development efforts or, even worse, it would encourage them to keep the results of their research secret.[148] Finally, and perhaps most strikingly, in relation to parental liability Radé supports the *Bertrand* decision by relying heavily on accident avoidance and by suggesting that, faced with the prospect of such a rigorous regime of liability, parents will be encouraged to put in place a 'global prevention policy' which is wider and more effective than what it would be under a regime of liability based on fault.[149] The basic idea in these examples is that the ability of keepers, employers, parents, drivers, and producers to avoid accidents is a reason for holding them strictly liable.

[145] Philippe Malaurie, Laurent Aynès, and Philippe Stoffel-Munck, *Droit des obligations* (11th edn, LGDJ 2020) [107]. See also Patrice Jourdain, *Les principes de la responsabilité civile* (10th edn, Dalloz 2021) 96; Noël Dejean de La Bâtie, *Aubry et Rau, Droit civil français, t. VI-2, Responsabilité delictuelle* (8th edn, Litec 1989) 273ff (basing liability for the deeds of things and for animals on the notion of 'authority', but emphasizing the importance of the defendant's ability to prevent the damage); Brun (n 143) [289] (making clear that liability for the deeds of things is not based on fault), [377] and [387] (arguing that the *gardien* is the person who can, at the time of the accident, avoid the damage), [401]-[406] (arguing that liability for animals largely follows the regime of liability for the deeds of things). French courts too have occasionally mentioned the power to avoid accidents in setting out the conditions of liability for the deeds of things: see eg Civ (2) 5.1.1956, Bull civ II no 2, 1956; Civ (1) 9.6.1993, JCP G 1994.II.22202, 2.2.1994 no 5 note Viney. Today, the notion of *garde* is defined as the 'use, direction, and control' of the thing, on which see also text to n 162 in this section.
[146] Geneviève Viney in Geneviève Viney, Patrice Jourdain, and Suzanne Carval (eds), *Les conditions de la responsabilité. Traité de droit civil* (4th edn, LGDJ 2013) [791-1], [813]. See also Jourdain (n 145) 105; François Terré and others, *Droits civil, Les obligations* (12th edn, Dalloz 2018) [1069].
[147] Geneviève Viney and Anne Guégan-Lécuyer, 'The Development of Traffic Liability in France' in Wolfgang Ernst (ed), *The Development of Traffic Liability* (CUP 2010) 50, 71 (emphasis added).
[148] Jean Calais-Auloy, 'Le risque de développement: une exonération contestable' in *Mélanges Michel Cabrillac* (Dalloz/Litec 1999) 81, 85. cf Christian Gollier, 'Le risque de développement est-il assurable?' Risques, 1993, no 14, 49 (supporting a regime of strict liability with a development risk defence on grounds of, inter alia, efficient accident avoidance).
[149] Cristophe Radé, 'Le renouveau de la responsabilité du fait d'autrui (apologie de l'arrêt Bertrand)' D 1997.279, [13]. See also Pierre-Dominique Ollier, *La responsabilité civile des père et mère* (LGDJ 1961) [232] and [236] (juxtaposing accident avoidance and the deep-pockets argument (with the latter being linked to victim protection)); Geneviève Viney, JCP 2002.I.124, [20]-[21] (arguing that the *Levert* decision seeks to promote greater authority and responsibility of parents, 'the only effective barrier against a growing juvenile violence'; but note the author's concern for the availability of insurance and the sustainability of the insurance market in the text following fn 57); Jourdain (n 145) 112 (juxtaposing accident avoidance with an argument based on authority, the deep-pockets rationale, loss spreading, and victim protection).

In addition to this, accident avoidance features in the work of some legal scholars discussing liability regardless of any specific context of liability. For example, Tunc argues that strict liability encourages firms to improve the behaviour of their employees, the equipment used in their plants, the quality of their products, and their organization more generally.[150] Others such as Millet observe that strict liability provides incentives to invest in research and new technologies and that, if the firm is insured, insurers will play an important role in reducing the risk of accidents by advising and monitoring the choices and behaviour of the firm.[151] In applying these strategies of accident avoidance to firms, the proposed reasoning applies across recognized contexts of liability and typically encompasses rules such as liability for products or the vicarious liability of employers for the harm caused by their employees.

The picture emerging from all this may suggest that accident avoidance constitutes a prominent reason for imposing strict liability in the French context, but this impression would be misleading. Indeed, a variety of reasons suggest that accidence avoidance has limited significance among French legal actors.

First, the argument is treated as a key justification only occasionally.[152] In most examples of reasoning seeking to justify strict liability, accident avoidance is omitted and, where invoked, it is mentioned together with justifications which are given far more prominence in French reasoning.[153] Moreover, contrary to the approach in the other three legal systems, accident avoidance is often discussed without any elaboration or clarification as to the measures which could be taken to avoid accidents and, in particular, the activity-modification strategy is largely neglected.[154] The vast majority of authors either refer to the adoption of background-safety measures[155] or generically mention the goal of preventing accidents without fuller explanation.[156] Even the comparatively more developed discussions—such

---

[150] Tunc (n 143) 414; André Tunc, *La responsabilité civile* (2nd edn, Economica 1989) [165], [153].

[151] Millet (n 144) [531]–[537].

[152] See eg Radé (n 149); Viney (n 149).

[153] On liability for the deeds of things, see Jourdain (n 145) 96 (juxtaposing accident avoidance with risk–benefit, loss spreading, and some idea of control (*maîtrise*)); Malaurie, Aynès, and Stoffel-Munck (n 145) [107] (discussing accident avoidance with loss spreading). On employers' vicarious liability, see Viney (n 146) [791-1], [813] (discussing accident avoidance with a combination between loss spreading and victim protection); Jourdain (n 145) 29–31 (combining accident avoidance with risk creation, in juxtaposition with risk–profit, authority/control, insurability, victim protection, and the deep-pockets argument), 105 (discussing accident avoidance with risk–profit, in juxtaposition with the deep-pockets rationale and insurability); Terré and others (n 146) [1069] (quoting Viney above). On traffic accidents, see Viney and Guégan-Lécuyer (n 147) 71–72 (discussing accident avoidance with loss spreading and victim protection). On product liability, see Calais-Auloy (n 148) 84–85 (juxtaposing accident avoidance with risk–profit, victim protection, and arguably loss spreading, for the purpose of justifying product liability for development risks).

[154] cf Jacques Flour, Jean-Luc Aubert, and Eric Savaux, *Droit civil. Les obligations. 2. Le fait juridique* (14th edn, Dalloz 2011) [70] (explaining the theory of risk by reference to fairness as well as to the idea that 'the threat of a more extended liability will prevent or reduce the operation of dangerous activities').

[155] See eg Millet (n 144) [531]–[532]; Tunc (n 143) 414; Calais-Auloy (n 148) 85.

[156] See eg Jourdain (n 145) 105; Viney (n 146) [791-1]; Malaurie, Aynès, and Stoffel-Munck (n 145) [107]. A striking exception is Radé (n 149) (discussing parental liability).

148   JUSTIFYING STRICT LIABILITY

as those of Tunc and Radé—do not compare with the sophistication of analysis featuring in the other three legal systems, particularly where accident avoidance is seen through the lenses of economic analysis (mostly in the United States and in Italy).

Secondly, preventing accidents as a justification for strict liability is often either seen as acceptable only as long as spreading mechanisms mitigate the effects of strict liability on defendants, or is deployed merely as a make-weight argument. For example, Tunc himself thinks that strict liability should operate to avoid accidents only in relation to those classes of defendants who are expected to be insured, or who are subjected to a regime of compulsory insurance, or again who can spread the costs of liability in other ways (eg by passing them on to consumers); otherwise, strict liability would be too 'harsh'.[157] Other scholars acknowledge that strict liability contributes to accident avoidance while promoting the protection of victims,[158] but then suggest that 'what should be promoted is a system which makes liable those who, because of the control they have on the harmful activity, are able to resort to liability insurance, whether or not they are in a position to avoid accidents'.[159] Overall, the impression is that preventing accidents is a concern that strict liability may seek to address, but only to the extent that pursuing this goal conforms to the spreading of losses and the protection of victims.

Arguments from accident avoidance and loss spreading can even conflict, reflecting a contrast between fault-based and strict liability. This typically happens when accident avoidance is taken to refer only to situational safety, that is to precautions that could be adopted at the time of the accident rather than safety measures to be taken in the background. Indeed, in relation to liability for the deeds of things or the action of animals, Jourdain observes that:

> [i]f one sees [this] liability ... as completely divorced from the idea of fault and as linked to insurance, one will naturally designate as the party liable, ie as *gardien*, the person placed in the best position to take out insurance, that is, in the vast majority of cases, the owner of the thing or animal, without worrying too much

---

[157] Tunc (n 143) 414. Tunc's view is in some respects reminiscent of Trimarchi's approach in Italy, for the latter too subjects the application of strict liability to the availability of loss-spreading mechanisms: see Trimarchi (n 54) 280–81, 359–60. Nevertheless, the two authors hold very different views as to the role and main purposes of strict liability, with Tunc prioritizing victim protection and loss spreading, and Trimarchi focusing on the efficient avoidance of accidents. This explains why in the latter's approach, but not in the former's, distributional concerns are of secondary importance: see Trimarchi (n 54) 8.

[158] Chantal Russo, *De l'assurance de responsabilité à l'assurance directe: contribution à l'étude d'une mutation de la couverture des risques* (Dalloz 2001) [742].

[159] ibid [756]. See also Samuel Rétif, 'Un critère unique de la garde de la chose: la faculté de prévenir le préjudice qu'elle peut causer?' RCA November 2004, 7, [6]; Viney and Guégan-Lécuyer (n 147) 71–72 (mentioning accident avoidance but clearly seeing insurance spreading and victim protection as the key justifications for liability for traffic accidents); Jourdain (n 145) 105 (including accident avoidance among the justifications for employers' vicarious liability but concluding that the key reason is insurability).

about the powers he exercised when the harm materialised or about whether he had at that time any chance to avoid the occurrence of that harm. By contrast, if one tries to put liability for the deeds of things in the context of liability for fault, then one is pushed to attribute the capacity of *gardien* to the person who actually had, when the harmful event occurred, the chance to avoid it, notably by controlling the thing or the animal better.[160]

Here, therefore, Jourdain suggests a close relationship between, on the one hand, strict liability and loss spreading and, on the other hand, fault and accident avoidance. The result of this is that, in keeping with the approach of some Italian and English scholars,[161] the goal of preventing accidents is seen as being more naturally achieved through fault-based liability than through strict liability.

The intimate relationship between fault and accident avoidance should be by no means surprising. Indeed, a further reason to be cautious when assessing the importance of accident avoidance as a justification for strict liability in French law relates to its perceived effect on the strictness of liability. As seen above, it is true that many authors see the goal of preventing accidents as consistent with strict liability and believe that no-fault liabilities will encourage the adoption of background measures that can enhance the safety of their activities and hence reduce the likelihood or severity of accidents. However, other scholars tend to associate accident avoidance with fault and, as a result, consider it as a factor that reduces the degree of strictness of liability rules. The best examples of this are again provided by discussions relating to the notion of *la garde* in the liability for the deeds of things, judicially defined as the 'use, direction, and control' of the thing at the time of the accident.[162] In discussing this condition of liability, Carbonnier first equates *la garde* with the power to avoid damage,[163] and then adds that, by identifying the keeper by reference to such power, French law operates a 'shift towards fault' in the liability rule.[164] Again, in an effort to assess the importance of accident avoidance in relation to this context of liability, Rétif observes that, while accident avoidance is only rarely a concern for the courts,[165] the consideration they give to it confirms that this liability rule is not as strict as it is often thought to be.[166] Put another way, preventing harm is a goal that relates to what the defendant should have done at

---

[160] Patrice Jourdain in Viney, Jourdain, and Carval (eds), *Les conditions de la responsabilité. Traité de droit civil* (n 146) [675]. The reference to 'powers' refers to the classic definition of *gardien*, on which see text to n 197 in section 2.4.

[161] See text to n 101 (Italy), and text to and following nn 132–134 (England) in this section.

[162] eg Ch réun 2.12.1941, D chron 1942.25 note Ripert (*Franck*); Civ (2) 22.2.1984, D 1985.2.19; Civ (1) 9.6.1993, JCP 1994.II.22202, 2.2.1994 no 5 note Viney.

[163] Jean Carbonnier, *Droit civil. Les biens, les obligations* (2nd edn, PUF 2017) [1173].

[164] ibid [1176].

[165] Rétif (n 159) [6].

[166] ibid [22].

150   JUSTIFYING STRICT LIABILITY

the time of the accident and, therefore, it is seen as naturally relevant to liability for fault rather than strict liability.

A final reason suggesting that accident avoidance is not a prominent justification in the French reasoning on strict liability relates to the very marginal role that economic theory plays in French legal scholarship. As seen in relation to the US and Italian contexts, the economic analysis of tort law is widespread and avoiding accidents is a key element from the perspective of economic efficiency. By contrast, and in keeping with the English approach, French academics are reluctant to engage with economic analysis,[167] though for (partly) different reasons. In England, economic analysis is criticized mainly on the grounds that it would be practically unworkable as well as incompatible with a vision of tort law as a system of interpersonal justice;[168] in France, besides its problems of practical workability, economic analysis is criticized on the ground that it would be at odds with the value of social solidarity.[169] As a result, a key intellectual underpinning of the accident avoidance argument is missing from the French context, and it is therefore not surprising to see that, in keeping with the English approach, this argument plays a far less significant role in French reasoning than in the US and Italian ones. Relatedly, as the discussion of accident avoidance in the United States and Italy has made clear, the view of some legal economists is that there are situations where fault (or even a rule of no liability) may achieve efficient accident avoidance better than strict liability. This view would reduce the room for strict liability, with a consequent diminution in the degree of protection afforded to the victims of accidents, an outcome that French lawyers do not seem prepared to accept.

To conclude, accident avoidance is clearly part of French legal reasoning, as demonstrated by those few scholars who take seriously the ability of strict liability to reduce the risks of accidents. However, this is a rare pattern of reasoning and, in stark contrast with the US and Italian approaches, the overall significance of accident avoidance as a justification for strict liability is modest. This relates to the prominence of other justifications in the French context as well as to the fact that, as also seen in relation to England, accident avoidance lacks the theoretical support provided by the economic analysis of law. In sum, it is ironic if not surprising that while French law is the 'home' of strict liability, avoiding accidents through it is really not one of its main concerns.

---

[167] cf Grégory Maitre, *La responsabilité civile à l'épreuve de l'analyse économique du droit* (LGDJ 2005) esp [168]–[187] (discussing strict liability's ability to induce an efficient reduction of accidents).

[168] See text to nn 137–142 in this section.

[169] Muriel Fabre-Magnan, *Droit des obligations. 2—Responsabilité civile et quasi-contrats* (4th edn, PUF 2019) [40] at 57–58.

3.3.6 Concluding Remarks

Overall, the patterns of use and the significance of accident avoidance as a justification for strict liability vary substantially across the four legal systems. These variations relate to the way in which tort law and its functions are perceived, as well as to the role that the economic analysis of law plays in the four legal systems.

In both the United States and Italy, accident avoidance constitutes a very prominent justification for the imposition of strict liability. In both jurisdictions, several leading scholars (and some courts) use accident avoidance to justify strict liability in a wide variety of contexts, such as dangerous activities, defective products, traffic accidents, animals, and the harmful actions of employees or children.[170] The ascendancy of accident avoidance as a justification for strict liability is largely due to the emergence of law and economics as one of the main approaches to legal studies. Since 1960s, the economic analysis of law has reshaped the intellectual foundations of tort law in the two systems (but especially in the United States) and has made the avoidance of accidents an important consideration in tort theory. Legal scholars adhering to this approach have attributed increasing importance to tort law as a way of regulating conduct and of providing potential defendants and victims with incentives to take efficient avoidance measures. While distributive arguments such as the deep-pockets justification and loss spreading may or may not feature in the reasoning of legal economists, the goal of avoiding accidents efficiently is a constant element of analysis, as it provides the main criterion for assessing the desirability of legal rules.[171] In this respect, accident avoidance justifies strict liability whenever it is thought that strict liability is better than fault at reducing efficiently the number or severity of accidents.[172] Relatedly, it is important to note that accident avoidance is, for legal economists, a means to a achieve a more fundamental end, which is the promotion of social welfare.[173] Accident avoidance cannot, however, be reduced merely to a matter of economic analysis in either legal system. Again in a wide variety of contexts of liability, many US and Italian legal actors use this argument without adhering to economic reasoning: they are content to acknowledge that avoiding accidents is an important social goal in itself and that strict liability can usefully contribute to it.[174] Where used without a commitment to economic analysis, accident avoidance is placed under fewer theoretical constraints and therefore it is sometimes discussed with justifications which seldom feature in economic analysis, as for example victim protection or the various risk-based arguments. Having said this, both in the United States and Italy accident avoidance

---

[170] See subsection 3.3.2 (United States) and subsection 3.3.3 (Italy).

[171] See text to nn 3–26 (United States), and text to nn 55–72 (Italy) in this section.

[172] See text to nn 25–26 (United States), and text preceding and following n 73 (Italy) in this section.

[173] See text to and following n 40 (United States), and text following n 81 (Italy) in this section.

[174] See nn 27–36 and nn 41–43 and accompanying text (the United States) as well as nn 92–100 and accompanying text (Italy) in this section.

152   JUSTIFYING STRICT LIABILITY

attracts a variety of criticisms,[175] as doubts are cast on strict liability's (and tort law's) potential for reducing the risk of accidents, and (in the United States) the argument is seen as incompatible with a vision of tort law as a system of individual responsibility and justice.

This picture contrasts sharply with the approaches of English and French law. In both jurisdictions, some legal actors use accident avoidance as a justification for the imposition of strict liability in many contexts of liability. For example, in England the argument is sometimes used in contexts such as the rule in *Rylands*, liability for nuisance, for dangerous animals, for defective products, for breach of statutory duty, and vicarious liability.[176] Similarly, in France the argument is deployed in contexts such as liability for the deeds of things, liability for products, parental liability, and liability for traffic accidents.[177] Importantly, this takes place without the support of economic analysis, which is frowned upon in both legal systems, and this is reflected in the patterns of use of the argument: in keeping with those US and Italian courts and scholars who do not engage with economic efficiency, accident avoidance is often mentioned together with justifications which are not very popular in economic reasoning, such as victim protection, loss spreading, or the various permutations of risk.[178] However, despite the fact that accident avoidance is put forward as a key justification by some legal scholars (and, in England, judges), it has limited significance in both legal systems. In part, this is due to perceived 'intrinsic' limits of the argument. In both systems, it is often thought that accident avoidance is more naturally achieved through fault-based liability on the grounds that only intentional or negligent conduct is receptive to the threat of civil liability; as a result, the goal of avoiding accidents is typically associated with fault-based liability.[179] Furthermore, in England accident avoidance is seen as opposed to the promotion of interpersonal justice,[180] while in France the potential clash is perceived to be with goals such as the spreading of losses or the protection of victims.[181] A further, essential reason why accident avoidance has failed to develop into a leading justification for the imposition of strict liability (or, for that matter, of tort liability more generally) in England and France relates to the antipathy that legal actors have for the economic analysis of law.[182] Whether this is because law and economics is thought to entail a fine-tuning which is too abstract and divorced from reality, or because

---

[175] See text to and following nn 48–51 (United States), and text to and following nn 101–103 (Italy) in this section.

[176] See text to nn 104–115 in this section.

[177] See text to nn 145–151 in this section.

[178] See eg nn 105–108, nn 110–116, and text to n 119 (England), text to nn 145–148 as well as n 149 and n 153 (France) in this section.

[179] See text to nn 132–134 (England), and text to and following nn 160–166 (France) in this section.

[180] See text to and preceding nn 141–142 in this section.

[181] See text to nn 157–160 in this section.

[182] See text to nn 137–142 (England), and text to and following n 169 (France) in this section.

it may clash with the principles of individual responsibility (in England)[183] or with the value of social solidarity (in France),[184] the end result is that in both legal systems accident avoidance lacks the intellectual support which has instead allowed the argument to thrive in the United States and Italy.

[183] See text to n 139 and to nn 141–142 in this section.
[184] See text to and following n 169 in this section.

3.4

Deep Pockets

3.4.1 The Deep-Pockets Justification of Strict Liability

One of the most traditional justifications put forward to support the imposition of strict liability is the so-called deep-pockets argument, according to which the costs of an accident should be placed on those who, because of their wealth, are better able to shoulder them. This argument can proceed on either economic or moral grounds. From an economic point of view, it is thought that, in general and subject to certain caveats, a sum of money taken from a wealthier person causes less economic dislocation than the same amount taken from a poorer person.[1] From a moral point of view, it is seen as inherently fairer to ask a sacrifice to those who, having greater financial means, are likely to suffer less from bearing the costs of an accident.[2]

The deep-pockets justification can certainly apply to cases where both claimant and defendant are individuals, but the most common situation, almost a cliché, to which the argument is associated is where the claimant is an individual and the defendant a large firm with very extensive financial resources. Paradoxically, though, it is precisely where a firm is involved that the deep-pockets argument tends to lose its distinctiveness and be absorbed (at least to some extent) in spreading mechanisms, because no matter how deep the pockets of the firm are, it will typically spread the costs of liability in a variety of ways.[3] Nevertheless, the deep-pockets justification deserves a separate treatment from loss spreading, for two reasons. First, it is conceptually distinct from it: a party may be found liable on the ground that they have deep pockets, regardless of whether they are able to spread losses; or, quite the opposite, they may be found liable because they can spread losses (eg because insured against the risk of their own liability), even if they have empty pockets. Secondly, distinguishing the deep-pockets argument from loss spreading will provide an interesting perspective on the evolution of legal reasoning in strict liability across the four legal systems.

---

[1] Guido Calabresi, *The Costs of Accidents: A Legal and Economic Analysis* (YUP 1970) 41.

[2] Jean-Sébastien Borghetti, *La Responsabilité du Fait des Produits: Etude de Droit Comparé* (LGDJ 2004) [620].

[3] See subsection 3.5.1.

Justifying Strict Liability. Marco Cappelletti, Oxford University Press. © Marco Cappelletti 2022.
DOI: 10.1093/oso/9780192859860.003.0006

156   JUSTIFYING STRICT LIABILITY

3.4.2 Deep Pockets in France: On the Way Towards the Socialization of Losses

In France, the concern to ensure that victims of accidents could find someone with deep pockets to sue and receive compensation from was considered a valuable justification for strict liability especially in the first half of the twentieth century. As Esmein (a leading tort jurist of the time) notes when describing the attitude of French law, and of courts in particular:

> We like to satisfy the claim of the victim of an accident and, by putting the compensation of the damage on the shoulders of a person able to pay, involved in any way in the [harmful] event, we take a first step towards the socialization of risk, the ideal of solidarity.[4]

This thinking reflects a paradigm shift in the way tort law should deal with accidents that occurred in France in the late nineteenth century. Accidents were no longer seen as a matter of individual responsibility but rather as a *social* problem: their widespread occurrence was linked to life in modern society and, as a result, society had to start *socializing* their costs through policies of redistribution.[5] In France, this way of thinking has been always intertwined with a pro-victim stance that, in many cases, has resulted from a combination of left-wing politics with the Christian commitment to protecting the poor and the unlucky.[6] From this perspective, it may be seen as perfectly fine to shift losses onto wealthy defendants, as their pockets would not be affected too much by the imposition of liability and the victims of accidents would be duly compensated. This is seen as an attractive approach in the French context in a variety of situations, especially in older academic writing. For example, in relation to employers' vicarious liability, Rodière argues that 'often the employee ... does not have the financial resources to stand the magnitude of harm which he can cause to others while doing his job', and, as a result, 'fairness [*équité*] leads to provide the victim with the assets of the employer as a general guarantee'.[7] Similarly, in relation to the liability of parents, Ollier argues that strict liability is justified on the ground that it is desirable to give victims a solvent defendant.[8] More recently, references to the deep-pockets justification can

---

[4] Paul Esmein, 'Prendre l'argent là où il est' Gaz Pal 1958.2.46, 46.

[5] François Ewald, *L'État providence* (Bernard Grasset 1986).

[6] See Jean-Sébastien Borghetti, 'The Culture of Tort Law in France' (2012) 3 JETL 158, 173–74, including fn 51 (linking this pro-victim position to prominent jurists such as Saleilles, Josserand, Tunc, and Viney, whom he labels 'Social Christians').

[7] René Rodière, *La responsabilité civile* (Rousseau 1952) [1472] (combining the deep-pockets argument with victim protection, the two providing content to 'social interest' and 'fairness' (*utilité sociale* and *équité*), and adding risk-based arguments as well as an 'attribution' theory as possible justifications).

[8] Pierre-Dominique Ollier, *La responsabilité civile des père et mère* (LGDJ 1961) [232] and [235] (juxtaposing the deep-pockets argument (geared towards victim protection) with accident avoidance).

be found occasionally in academic works and even in judicial decisions. For example, leading authors as well as the criminal chamber of the Cour de cassation explain employers' vicarious liability by reference to the law's willingness to help victims by giving them a target (the employer) that is more solvent than the employee;[9] others mention the deep-pockets argument when explaining certain judicial decisions in the context of liability for defective products.[10]

Nevertheless, while the deep-pockets argument has played an important role in the past in supporting some of the strict liability rules recognized in French law,[11] this argument has not carried the day as a significant justification for strict liability. Imposing liability on the ground that the defendant has extensive financial resources is today widely seen either as an out of date approach or as a halfway house towards a broader socialization of the costs of accidents that finds its most significant expression in insurance-based mechanisms of distribution of losses.[12] These propositions find direct support in the reasoning of some of the most influential French legal scholars, where the deep-pockets justification is critically assessed and replaced with more sophisticated arguments for the imposition of liability, most notably loss spreading. For example, in discussing the justifications of employers' vicarious liability, Viney argues that the idea of offering a solvent defendant to the victim is no longer adequate to meet contemporary social needs, and that it should be replaced by the idea of charging firms for the losses they cause so that they can take out liability insurance and try to avoid accidents.[13] Similarly, while speaking of the justifications of liability for the action of another in general, Jourdain observes that 'the guarantee of solvency allows the victim to bring an action against someone who is more solvent than the physical author of harm (employers for the torts of their employees, parents for the harmful action of their children, artisans for the torts of their apprentices)', but then adds that [t]his justification is to be linked to the aptitude for insurance, which gives it all its meaning'.[14]

---

[9] Philippe Malaurie, Laurent Aynès, and Philippe Stoffel-Munck, *Droit des obligations* (11th edn, LGDJ 2020) [97] (combining the deep-pockets argument with victim protection, in juxtaposition with various risk-based arguments); Alain Bénabent, *Droit des obligations* (19th edn, LGDJ 2021) [572] (juxtaposing the deep-pockets argument (with a view to victim protection) with risk creation, loss spreading, as well as an 'attribution' theory and a presumption of fault in the employer's supervision of, and instructions to, their employee); Cass crim 29.6.2011, JCP G 2012.530 no 3, para 5, at pp 864–65, note Bloch ('the sole purpose of the civil liability of employers is to protect third parties against the insolvency of the author of the crime and not to relieve the latter of any liability').

[10] Borghetti (n 2) [646] (arguing that French courts sometimes find a defendant liable even if they did not exercise their activity for an economic gain and explaining this phenomenon by reference to the deep-pockets argument (*richesse oblige*) and to actual insurance coverage (*assurance oblige*)).

[11] Geneviève Viney in Geneviève Viney, Patrice Jourdain, and Suzanne Carval (eds), *Les conditions de la responsabilité. Traité de droit civil* (4th edn, LGDJ 2013) [791-1]; Christophe Radé, 'Art. 1382 à 1386— Fasc. 143: DROIT À RÉPARATION. —Responsabilité du fait d'autrui. —Domaine: responsabilité des commettants' JCl Civil Code (updated to 16 May 2016) [5] (both authors discussing employers' vicarious liability).

[12] See subsection 3.5.2.

[13] Viney (n 11) [791-1].

[14] Patrice Jourdain, *Les principes de la responsabilité civile* (10th edn, Dalloz 2021) 31.

158 JUSTIFYING STRICT LIABILITY

Here, the deep-pockets argument loses all its distinctiveness and dissolves into the socialization of risk, that is into a broad spreading of the costs of accidents. What is key, therefore, is not so much the depth of the pocket of the party designated as liable but the circumstance that this party is in a suitable position to dilute the costs of liability via insurance or other spreading mechanisms,[15] while achieving the goal of compensating victims.

In sum, even if historically important and still occasionally relied upon to support or explain strict liability, the deep-pockets argument has lost much of its significance either because it appears as in itself outdated, or because it is made redundant by the availability of spreading mechanisms.

3.4.3 Deep Pockets in Italy: A Justification Belonging to the Past?

As in France, the deep-pockets justification for strict liability surfaces in the Italian reasoning. Occasionally used in the past, especially in the course of the 1960s and 1970s, this argument is today of limited significance and, even in the contexts where it is more frequently used, its status appears controversial. To grasp the significance of this argument in the Italian context, one needs to turn to the work of academics, for judicial reasoning almost ignores it.

In the early second part of the twentieth century, Italian academics occasionally included the deep-pockets argument in their explanations of a variety of strict liabilities. For example, in discussing the liability of guardians for the harm caused by individuals lacking mental capacity and the employers' vicarious liability, Messineo argues that the rationale of these liabilities lies in the circumstance that guardians and employers are normally better equipped than the physical author of harm to pay compensation.[16] Similarly, Majello identifies the rationale of parental liability in the need to obviate the predictable condition of insolvency of the child.[17] Again, in relation to traffic accidents, Forchielli thinks that the liability of owners for the harm caused by their motor vehicles was explained by the legislator's fear that their driver could be insolvent or uninsured;[18] as insurance became compulsory only in the late 1960s, imposing liability on vehicle owners was seen as the best

---

[15] See subsection 3.5.2.

[16] Francesco Messineo, *Manuale di diritto civile e commerciale*, vol V (9th edn, Giuffrè 1957) 579 (juxtaposing the deep-pockets argument with risk–profit in relation to employers' vicarious liability). On this context of liability, see also Paolo Forchielli, *Responsabilità civile*, vol II (CEDAM 1969) 56–60; Eugenio Bonvicini, *La responsabilità civile*, vol I (Giuffrè 1971) 563.

[17] Ugo Majello, 'Responsabilità dei genitori per il fatto illeciti del figlio minore e valutazione del comportamento del danneggiato ai fini della determinazione del contenuto della prova liberatoria' (1960) Dir giur 43, 45–46 (combining the deep-pockets argument with victim protection, in juxtaposition with an argument based on the parental duty of upbringing).

[18] Forchielli (n 16) 59–60.

solution to ensure the compensation of victims, for owners were usually thought to be relatively wealthy.[19]

More recently, we can still find occasional reference to the deep-pockets argument in legal scholarship, particularly with respect to the liability of parents for the harmful action of their children. In this context, academics explain the very rigorous approach with which some Italian courts in effect impose strict liability on parents by noting that parents would typically have the deeper pocket and would therefore guarantee compensation to claimants.[20] At times, the same argument is also used to explain employers' vicarious liability[21] or the liability of owners of ruinous buildings.[22] In all these cases, the idea is that strict liability is imposed because the party designated as liable is presumed solvent and can therefore ensure that the claimant will be compensated for the loss suffered. Hence, rather as in France, the deep-pockets argument is a means towards the goal of compensating the victims of accidents and, as a result, it is almost always either combined or juxtaposed with the victim protection argument. Finally, in very few cases the deep-pockets argument is grounded in economic reasoning and seen as consistent with economic efficiency: for example, in supporting the imposition of strict liability on the public administration for harm caused by wildlife to third parties, it is suggested that 'burdening the deeper pocket [ie the administration] with the costs of liability is efficient whenever one or more individuals come into contact with a richer, stronger, more informed, and more organised party'.[23]

---

[19] Gianguido Scalfi, 'Responsabilità per vizi e per difetti dell'autoveicolo' (1974) RCP 323, 339; Alfonso Alibrandi, 'Note sulla responsabilità civile del proprietario del veicolo coinvolto in sinistro stradale' (1991) 7–8 Archivio giuridico della circolazione e dei sinistri stradali 545, [2].

[20] eg Salvatore Patti, *Famiglia e responsabilità civile* (Giuffrè 1984) 258 (combining the deep-pockets argument with victim protection). See also Giovanni Facci, 'La responsabilità dei genitori in caso di incidente stradale del figlio minore: per colpa od oggettiva?' (2006) 2 Fam Dir 138, 140 (combining the deep-pockets argument with victim protection); Maria Luisa Chiarella, 'Minore danneggiante e responsabilità vicaria' (2009) 10 DR 973, 986; Monica Crovetto, 'La responsabilità oggettiva dei genitori' in Paolo Cendon (ed), *Responsabilità civile*, vol III (2nd edn, UTET 2020) 3706, 3718 (combining the deep-pockets argument with victim protection).

[21] Giuseppe Leotta, 'Sulla responsabilità del datore di lavoro ex art. 2049 cod. civ' (2001) 2 Rivista giuridica del lavoro e della previdenza sociale 399, 402 (though recognizing that this argument cannot provide a complete explanation of the liability rule); Marco Comporti, *Fatti Illeciti: le responsabilità oggettive—Artt. 2049-2053. Il Codice Civile—Commentario* (Giuffrè 2009) 91 (juxtaposing the deep-pockets justification with risk–benefit/profit); Giovanna Visintini, *Trattato breve della responsabilità civile—Fatti illeciti. Inadempimento. Danno risarcibile* (3rd edn, Cedam 2005) 753–55 (combining the deep-pockets argument with victim protection, in juxtaposition with efficient accident avoidance).

[22] Massimo Franzoni, *L'illecito. Trattato della responsabilità civile* (2nd edn, Giuffrè 2010) 564 (discussing the deep-pockets justification with abnormality of risk, in juxtaposition with risk–benefit); Ugo Mattei, *I Diritti Reali—2—La Proprietà. Trattato di Diritto Civile* (UTET 2015) 351 (juxtaposing the deep-pockets justification with risk–benefit and with an efficiency argument based on cost internalisation).

[23] Annalisa Bitetto, 'Danni provocati da animali selvatici: chi ne risponde e perché?' (2003) 3 DR 275, text to fns 26–32 (seeing the liability of a deep pocket as a spreading method, and discussing it with accident avoidance and loss spreading, with a view to minimizing the social costs of accidents). See also Enrico Carbone, 'La responsabilità aquiliana del genitore tra rischio tipico e colpe fittizie' (2008) 1(2) Riv Dir Civ 1, 12–13 (on parental liability, linking the deep-pockets argument to Calabresi's work).

160 JUSTIFYING STRICT LIABILITY

Despite the occasional reliance on the deep-pockets argument in academic discussions, the current significance of this justification is limited. To begin with, it almost never features in judicial reasoning and, when it does, it is criticized. In a number of recent decisions, the Corte di Cassazione seeks to explain the rationale of strict liability and, in doing so, it considers a variety of academic theories; when referring to 'deep pocket[s]' in common law systems and '*richesse oblige*' in the French tradition, the court appears to suggest that this rationale belongs to the past and that other, more refined theoretical elaborations deserve greater attention.[24] As far as legal scholarship is concerned, the idea of basing liability on the financial capabilities of defendants is subjected to criticisms such as that of Trimarchi, who argues that imposing liability on the deeper pocket would constitute a haphazard and irrational system of compulsory charity that shifts wealth from the richer to the poorer.[25]

The limited significance of the deep-pockets arguments in Italy also emerges if one moves to specific contexts of liability, where it is clear that the argument recurs far less frequently than other justifications. Particularly in contexts of liability where the defendant is typically a firm, as in employers' vicarious liability, liability for dangerous activities, and liability for products, reliance on the deep-pockets argument is limited. This is not surprising because distributive concerns are usually (and better) resolved through spreading mechanisms, with the result that, in terms of legal reasoning, the deep-pockets justification gives way to loss spreading.[26] This may appear to resonate with what was observed in relation to the French system, where it was noted that historically the deep-pockets argument has acted as a halfway house towards the socialization of risk,[27] but this similarity should not be overemphasized, given the broader picture in both systems. As will be seen in the section 3.5, while in France the loss-spreading justification is very prominent in relation to most contexts of liability, in Italy it is largely confined to situations where firms are involved.

In Italy, the status of the deep-pockets argument also looks similarly weakened in contexts where physical individuals are designated as the liable parties. For instance, as regards traffic accidents, the argument lost its force when vehicles became subjected to compulsory insurance in the 1960s. Today, therefore, compensation is paid by insurers and the depth of the vehicle owner's pockets has become immaterial.[28] Again, in relation to parental liability, many authors criticize the idea that parents should be liable because they may be assumed to have the resources to pay

---

[24] eg Civ (III) 6.7.2006 n.15383, [5.6], (2006) 11 DR 1145 (things in one's keeping); Civ (III) 19.2.2008 n.4279, [4.2], (2008) 11 DR 1112 (things in one's keeping); Civ (III) 17.12.2009 n.26516, [3.11], (2010) 6 DR 569 (dangerous activities).

[25] Pietro Trimarchi, *Rischio e responsabilità oggettiva* (Giuffrè 1961) 29–30.

[26] See subsection 3.5.4.

[27] See subsection 3.4.2.

[28] See n 19 in this section.

compensation: this assumption may well not be right;[29] moreover, if the objective is to protect victims of accidents while not crushing parents financially, then either strict liability should be combined with compulsory insurance[30] or courts should apply a standard of liability that takes into account the parent's conduct.[31]

Rather paradoxically, the deep-pockets argument may have slowed down the development of strict liability precisely in the context where it is most frequently used, that is liability of parents. To illustrate this point, a comparison with the French system is particularly useful. In France, parental liability is strict and this strictness is today justified not on grounds of deep-pockets but typically on grounds of insurability;[32] unsurprisingly, the use of household insurance, which covers liability for harms caused by children, is widespread.[33] The result is that in most cases where a child causes harm to someone, the victim gets compensation and the parents, thanks to their insurance coverage, are not crushed by the costs of liability. In Italy, by contrast, insurability is not used as a justification to support the adoption of parental liability and, unsurprisingly, liability insurance against the harm caused by children is much less used,[34] with the consequence that the distributive result seen above for France cannot be attained in the Italian context; significantly, the very nature of parental liability is still controversial, with views oscillating between strict liability and fault-based liability.[35] In this picture, the deep-pockets argument may play a role in explaining why some scholars and courts are not prepared to accept the adoption of strict parental liability.[36] While offering an explanation for that portion of the case law that reads the liability of parents as strict, the deep-pockets argument does not help parental liability to become a full-blown strict liability because of the potentially haphazard allocation of losses it could generate on a large scale. Indeed, imposing strict liability on parents on the ground that they are (assumed to be) solvent may be undesirable, both because it may be very

---

[29] Patti (n 20) 269.

[30] Silvia Taccini, 'Il sistema della responsabilità civile dei genitori: tra profili di protezione e di garanzia' (2008) 1 DR 5, 11; Paolo Pardolesi and Marina Dimattia, 'Responsabilità dei genitori per l'illecito dei minori: un esercizio di precomprensione?' (2010) 2 DR 168, 174–75; Silvia Monti, 'Responsabilità dei genitori: alcune riflessioni' (2014) 11 DR 1054, 1060–61.

[31] See Patti (n 20) 329–31; Carbone (n 23) 14–16. See also Chiarella (n 20) 986–87.

[32] See text to n 18 in subsection 3.5.2.

[33] See Borghetti (n 6) 166–67. See also text to nn 19–20 in subsection 3.5.2.

[34] While in France the household insurance is widespread, in Italy it is relatively uncommon: as of 2016, only 24.6 per cent of the Italian families benefited from that type of insurance policy. See Luisa Anderloni, Alessandra Tanda, and Daniela Vandone, *Vulnerabilità e benessere delle famiglie italiane*, available at http://www.forumaniaconsumatori.it/images/pdf/rapporto_vulnerabilit_unimi_2016.pdf, at 23.

[35] For an overview of this clash, see Franzoni (n 22) 722–37.

[36] Another reason for this may be identified in that strict liability would entail a relationship between parents and children similar to that typical of patriarchal societies, where parents (but especially fathers) were perceived to be almost owners of their children and therefore in complete control of their actions. By contrast, in a perspective that takes into account the particularities of parenting in the modern society, and that seeks to help minors develop autonomously their personalities and behave more responsibly, it is thought that a regime of fault-based parental liability may be more appropriate: see Franzoni (n 22) 736–37.

162 JUSTIFYING STRICT LIABILITY

difficult to ascertain whether they really have deep pockets[37] and because, in the absence of insurance cover, the loss would be left concentrated on their shoulders. Unsurprisingly, then, some courts are reluctant to see parental liability as strict and prefer to base it on a presumption of fault,[38] while many scholars propose the introduction of strict parental liability coupled with a regime of compulsory insurance.[39] In other words, to be socially sustainable the strict liability in parents needs to be combined with spreading mechanisms and, if parents are to be held strictly liable in a consistent way, the deep-pockets argument will need to be abandoned in favour of justifications based on loss spreading. This is, of course, what happened in France.

To conclude, while used in the past in a variety contexts of liability, today the deep-pockets argument appears only very occasionally in Italian legal reasoning. Furthermore, in the context where it still retains some significance, that is parental liability, its role is ambiguous and, ironically, its usage may have contributed to hindering the development of strict liability in the area. With the passing of time, the deep-pockets argument has lost much of its force, partly because of the criticisms levelled at it, partly because of the emergence of spreading mechanisms.

3.4.4 The Minor Significance of the Deep-Pockets Argument in the United States

Compared to the other justifications for strict liability discussed in this work, the deep-pockets argument has the least appeal in the United States. While it occasionally surfaces in the case law and academic writing, the argument has very limited significance today because it is much criticized and often seen as redundant given the availability of more convincing justifications. In keeping with the French and Italian approach, the status of the deep-pockets argument in the United States looks only minor.[40]

The availability of deep pockets is sometimes put forward as a justification for strict liability in contexts such as liability for abnormally dangerous activities and employers' vicarious liability. For example, Shugerman argues that the judicial reception of *Rylands v Fletcher* from the 1890s across the United States stemmed from a variety of reasons, primarily the ability to 'control ... the hazardous activity and the choice to reduce or move it', but also the 'deeper pockets' of industrialists who were responsible for the activity.[41] It is however in the context of employers'

---

[37] See n 29 in this section.
[38] See Franzoni (n 22) 729–31, 736–37.
[39] See n 30 in this section.
[40] The same conclusion holds true for the English context: see subsection 3.4.5.
[41] Jed Handelsman Shugerman, 'The Floodgates of Strict Liability: Bursting Reservoirs and the Adoption of Fletcher v. Rylands in the Gilded Age' (2000) 110 Yale LJ 333, 373–74; Jed Handelsman Shugerman, 'A Watershed Moment: Reversals of Tort Theory in the Nineteenth Century' (2008) 2(1)

vicarious liability that the deep-pockets argument recurs more often as a justifica-tion for strict liability,[42] and the existence of a 'deep pocket' may be invoked to ac-complish a variety of goals, including victim protection or accident avoidance. For example, the Supreme Court of Minnesota observes that

> [p]robably the most popular reason [for vicarious liability] is to provide the in-jured person with a 'deep pocket.' In other words, vicarious liability is attached to the master-servant relationship, providing the injured person with a defendant who in all likelihood can respond in damages if he establishes a right thereto.[43]

In this passage, the deep pockets of the employer act as a means to the goal of pro-tecting the victims of accidents, but this combination is not the only pattern of use of this argument. Indeed, in contrast with the approach of French and most Italian scholars, the idea of making the wealthier pay is not necessarily always tied to the protection of victims and may be used for entirely different purposes. For instance, Schwartz observes that 'the employer's "deep pockets" come in as a factor favoring liability because "deep pockets" are conducive to deterrence—not because the "deep pocket" employer can conveniently serve as a source of compensation for accident victims'.[44] Here, therefore, the deep-pockets argument is instrumental to the avoidance of accidents. Similarly, this time from the standpoint of economic analysis, Shavell argues that the liability of employers can better advance the avoid-ance of accidents 'the higher the [employer's] assets are'.[45]

The proposition that losses may be placed on someone on the basis of their ability to pay has also received attention regardless of any specific context of li-ability, especially in the work of legal economists. For example, in his pioneering analysis on the costs of accidents, Calabresi considers the imposition of liability on the deeper pockets as a viable means to reduce the social costs of leaving losses concentrated on victims (Calabresi's 'secondary costs').[46] Similarly, Kaplow and

---

JTL article 2, 34 (mentioning the deep pockets of firms as entailing a moral duty to pay for the costs of their activities) (here this argument (which is merged with risk–profit) is juxtaposed with other justifi-cations such as victim protection and individual responsibility).

[42] See eg Bryant Smith, 'Cumulative Reasons and Legal Method' (1949) 27 Tex L Rev 454, 458–59; *Riviello v Waldron*, 391 N.E.2d 1278, 1281 (N.Y.1979); John L Hanks, 'Franchisor Liability for the Torts of Its Franchisees: The Case for Substituting Liability as a Guarantor for the Current Vicarious Liability' (1999) 24 Okla City U L Rev 1, 17, fn 24. cf William L Prosser, *Handbook of the Law of Torts* (2nd edn, West Publishing Co 1955) 351 (seeing the deep-pockets rationale as a 'scarcely convincing reason').

[43] *Weber v Stokely-Van Camp, Inc*, 144 N.W.2d 540, 542 (Minn.1966).

[44] Gary T Schwartz, 'The Hidden and Fundamental Issue of Employer Vicarious Liability' (1996) 69 S Cal L Rev 1739, 1756, fn 91.

[45] Steven Shavell, *Economic Analysis of Accident Law* (HUP 1987) 172 (adding that another im-portant factor is the employer's ability to control the employee's behaviour, as this also impacts on the ability to avoid accidents).

[46] Calabresi (n 1) 39ff. This does not mean that Calabresi would impose liability solely on the basis of the deep-pockets argument or, more generally, of a reduction in secondary costs. As Calabresi himself makes clear, the reduction of secondary costs 'cannot be the only aim of a system of accident law' (ibid

Shavell acknowledge that the distribution of income is an important factor in evaluating the desirability of different liability rules and that their distributive effects should be taken into account as much as their effects on the reduction of accident costs.[47] Therefore, on the assumption that the same loss is heavier on the poor than on the rich, strict liability may be superior to negligence because it would minimize the adverse effects of accidents on the formers' well-being.[48]

Although the deep-pockets justification is occasionally used both in academic and judicial reasoning, its overall significance in the United States should not be exaggerated. To begin with, the deep-pockets argument is rejected by those who consider tort law purely as a system of interpersonal justice and therefore see any argument rooted in the pursuit of broader social goals as inadequate to justify the imposition of liability. From this perspective, the deep-pockets argument is unacceptable because it does not focus on the doing of justice between defendant and claimant but rather on a collective concern that losses should be shifted to more affluent parties as better able to bear them.[49] Secondly, the shifting of a loss on the ground of wealth does not take into account that defendants may be as worthy of compassion as injured claimants, and that if the reason for imposing liability is 'wealth-equalization' (ie the shifting of wealth from the more affluent to the less affluent), then this policy decision ought to be made by the legislator, not by judges.[50] Thirdly, a particular strand in economic thinking, whose main proponent is Posner, does not give serious consideration to the deep-pockets argument for strict liability. In contrast with the views of Shavell, Kaplow, and Calabresi,[51] Posner's focus is almost exclusively on providing appropriate incentives for an efficient avoidance of accidents, with distributive concerns and associated notions such as deep-pockets (or loss spreading) being largely ignored or rejected.[52] To give one

43). As already explained, the aim is instead to minimize the sum of primary, secondary, and tertiary costs (see n 8 in subsection 3.3.2).

[47] Louis Kaplow and Steven Shavell, *Fairness v Welfare* (HUP 2002) 28ff, 86ff. In their work, the two scholars argue that 'social welfare' should be the only source of inspiration of legal rules, to the exclusion of fairness concerns: ibid 3–13. In their view, social welfare is based on individuals' well-being, this including anything that a person may value, whereas fairness concerns are those which 'are not reducible to concerns about individuals' well-being' (ibid 4–5).

[48] ibid 119. The situations Kaplow and Shavell have in mind are those involving nonreciprocal accidents: here injurers and victims belong to separate categories, meaning that those who are victims can never be injurers and that those who are injurers can never be victims of the same type of accident. Conversely, reciprocal accidents occur 'when those who are injurers in some instances are victims in other instances (such as when drivers can strike pedestrians, but the same individuals sometimes drive and sometimes walk)' (ibid 99).

[49] See eg Ernest J Weinrib, 'The Insurance Justification and Private Law' (1985) 14 J Legal Stud 681, 684; Ernest J Weinrib, 'The Special Morality of Tort Law' (1989) 34 McGill LJ 403, 408–09; Jules L Coleman, 'The Structure of Tort Law' (1988) 97 Yale LJ 1233, 1248.

[50] David G Owen, 'Rethinking the Policies of Strict Products Liability' (1980) 33 Vand L Rev 681, 703–06.

[51] See nn 46–48 in this section.

[52] eg Richard A Posner, 'Book Review (reviewing Guido Calabresi, The Costs of Accidents: A Legal and Economic Analysis (1970))' (1970) 37 U Chi L Rev 636, 638–39, 646 (showing scepticism for the proposition that tort law should be worried with the consequences of leaving losses concentrated on

example, Landes and Posner consider the deep-pockets argument (with a view to protecting victims) 'an unsatisfactory explanation' for the liability of employers and instead find accident avoidance as its convincing justification.[53] Fourthly and finally, even if strict liability is deemed desirable on distributional grounds, whether for 'moral' or 'economic' reasons, loss spreading looms much larger than the deep-pockets argument in US legal reasoning.[54] Quite tellingly, it is even possible to find judicial and academic statements which, in considering both the deep-pockets and loss-spreading justifications, dismiss the former while approving of the latter.[55] In keeping with the French and Italian approaches,[56] it appears that US courts and scholars believe that distributive concerns are better dealt with through spreading mechanisms than by imposing liability on the wealthier.

Because of all this, attempts to justify strict liability on the basis of a deep-pockets argument are not a common feature in US legal reasoning. Even so, some judges and perhaps even more some juries may from time to time covertly consider the defendants' financial means (and perhaps their ability to spread losses) when deciding tort disputes. Strikingly, a former justice and chief justice of the West Virginia Supreme Court of Appeals admits:

As a state court judge, much of my time is devoted to designing elaborate new ways to make business pay for everyone else's bad luck. I may not always congratulate myself at the end of the day on the brilliance of my legal reasoning, but when I do such things as allow a paraplegic to collect a few hundred thousand dollars from the Michelin Tire—thanks to a one-car crash of unexplainable cause—I at least sleep well at night. Michelin will somehow survive (and if they don't, only the French will care), but my disabled constituent won't make it the rest of her life without Michelin's money.[57]

victims). See also Kaplow and Shavell (n 47) 31–38 (explaining why legal economists may wish to ignore distributional considerations in their analysis).

[53] William M Landes and Richard A Posner, 'The Positive Economic Theory of Tort Law' (1980) 15 Ga L Rev 851, 914–15. See also Richard A Posner, 'Utilitarianism, Economics, and Legal Theory' (1979) 8 J Legal Stud 103; Richard A Posner, 'The Ethical and Political Basis of the Efficiency Norm in Common Law Adjudication' (1980) 8 Hofstra L Rev 487 (both showing Posner's emphasis on wealth maximization); Richard A Posner, *Economic Analysis of Law* (9th edn, Wolters Kluwer 2014) 205ff (comparing negligence with strict liability by reference to the efficient avoidance of accidents and to administrative costs).

[54] See subsection 3.5.3.

[55] *Hinman v Westinghouse Electric Company*, 471 P.2d 988, 990 (Cal.1970) (quoting William L Prosser, *Handbook of the Law of Torts* (3rd edn, West Publishing Co 1964) 471) (on employers' vicarious liability); *Bowling v Heil Co*, 511 N.E.2d 373, 379 (Ohio 1987) (quoting W Page Keeton, Dan D Dobbs, Robert E Keeton, and David G Owen, *Prosser and Keeton on the Law of Torts* (5th edn, West Publishing Co 1984) 692–93) (on liability for defective products); Young B Smith, 'Frolic and Detour' (1923) 23 Colum L Rev 444, 460 (on employers' vicarious liability).

[56] See text to nn 12–15 (France) and to n 26 (Italy) in this section.

[57] Richard Neely, *The Product Liability Mess. How Business Can Be Rescued From the Politics of State Courts* (Free Press 1988) 1.

Failure to include explicitly the deep-pockets argument in their reasoning suggests that judges may not see it as a good 'official' justification and may think that it is better not to refer to it in their opinions. Rare as they may be, in such cases the deep-pockets argument works as a 'crypto-justification' and suggests that judges may be more attracted by it than their reasoning shows. It is no easy task to estimate the exact impact of this phenomenon, given that a crypto-justification typically remains hidden and that it may be at work no less in the tort of negligence or other fault-based liability rules than in contexts of strict liability. On the other hand, given that courts (and scholars) often hold views in direct opposition to the idea of imposing liability on the basis of the defendant's wealth,[58] it seems very unlikely that the deep-pockets argument works as a crypto-justification on a large scale.

In sum, in the United States the significance of the deep-pockets argument is limited. It is occasionally relied upon in both judicial and academic reasoning to serve a variety of goals, most notably the compensation of victims, but also the avoidance of accidents or the promotion of social welfare. However, the vast majority of courts and scholars either ignore this argument or criticize it, and other justifications are seen as more convincing rationales for the imposition of strict liability.

3.4.5 Deep Pockets in England: A Justification of Modest Significance, with an Exception

As in the other three legal systems studied, the significance of the deep-pockets argument as a justification for strict liability is very limited in the English context, where legal actors largely ignore this argument in most contexts of liability. The only, though significant exception is vicarious liability, and here there is a clash of views as to its proper role.

One rare example of the deep-pockets argument being used outside the context of vicarious liability is in Murphy's 2004 article on 'the merits of Rylands v Fletcher', where he argues that

> the factory owner with deep pockets who stands to profit from his industrial enterprise should also be strictly liable for any mishaps occasioned by the escape of any dangerous element stored there. And while this argument can be applied with ease to a commercial industrial enterprise—just as it applies, *mutatis mutandis*, to commercial producers of defective consumer products—it does not lend itself

---

[58] Examples are provided by the pervasive nature of accident avoidance in the United States, as seen in subsection 3.3.2, as well as by the emphasis that many legal scholars put on norms of individual responsibility, as will be seen in subsection 3.8.2.

at all well to a private house-dwelling neighbour: a very common defendant in nuisance cases.[59]

Here, the deep-pockets justification is combined with risk–profit to justify the imposition of strict liability for the losses caused by the escape of harmful substances. It is however difficult to pinpoint the exact significance of the argument, for it is discussed with several other justifications,[60] and in a later work Murphy himself rejects it (at least in the context of vicarious liability and liability for breach of a non-delegable duty).[61]

The paucity of references to a deep pocket in most areas of English tort law contrasts with the pattern identified in the law of vicarious liability, which many scholars and judges justify on the basis of a deep-pockets argument. For example, both Baty and Williams think that this argument provides a sound explanation for the existence of vicarious liability. In his book on vicarious liability published in 1916, Baty identifies nine different bases for it, concluding that 'in hard fact, the real reason for employers' liability is [that] the damages are taken from a deep pocket'.[62] Similarly, forty years later Williams argues that vicarious liability would have not developed but for the scarce financial resources of employees,[63] and adds that '[h]owever distasteful the theory may be, we have to admit that vicarious liability owes its explanation, if not its justification, to the search for a solvent defendant'.[64] Other scholars go beyond mere explanation and appear to support the deep-pockets argument. For example, today Steele argues that vicarious liability is justified by a cumulation of reasons, which include the depth of an employer's pockets.[65]

Courts have also invoked this argument on several occasions, again together with other ones. For example, in *CCWS* Lord Phillips states that one of the 'policy reasons' which 'make it fair, just and reasonable to impose vicarious liability' is that 'the employer is more likely to have the means to compensate the victim than

---

[59] John Murphy, 'The Merits of Rylands v Fletcher' (2004) 24 OJLS 643, 659. Murphy's reference to a 'dangerous element' can hardly be seen as an argument based on abnormality of risk, as he seems to reject the idea that strict liability under the rule in *Rylands v Fletcher* should be limited to high-risk activities: see ibid 663–64, including fn 112.

[60] See ibid 665ff.

[61] John Murphy, 'Juridical foundations of common law non-delegable duties' in Jason W Neyers, Erika Chamberlain, and Stephen GA Pitel, *Emerging Issues in Tort Law* (Hart Publishing 2007) 369, 372–74.

[62] Thomas Baty, *Vicarious Liability* (Clarendon Press 1916) 154.

[63] Glanville Williams, 'Liability for Independent Contractors' (1956) 14 CLJ 180, 195.

[64] Glanville Williams, 'Vicarious Liability and the Master's Indemnity' (1957) 20 MLR 220, 232.

[65] Jenny Steele, *Tort Law, Text, Cases, and Materials* (4th edn, OUP 2017) 578–81 (combining the deep-pockets argument with loss spreading and victim protection, and juxtaposing them with risk creation, risk–benefit, and accident avoidance). See also John G Fleming, *The Law of Torts* (9th edn, LBC Information Services 1998) 410 (juxtaposing the deep-pockets justification with risk–profit, loss spreading, and accident avoidance).

the employee'.[66] The defendant's ability to pay an award of damages is one of the reasons that in the *Armes* case pushes the UK Supreme Court to impose vicarious liability on the defendant local authority for the sexual abuse that a child suffered as a result of the acts of her foster parents, in whose care the child had been placed by the local authority. In particular, the court observes that '[m]ost foster parents have insufficient means to be able to meet a substantial award of damages', while 'local authorities which engage them can more easily compensate the victims of injuries which are often serious and long-lasting'.[67]

All these examples from English reasoning show that the typical pattern for the deep-pockets argument is to be either combined or juxtaposed with many other justifications, most notably loss spreading, victim protection, and the risk-based arguments. Given the great emphasis placed on these other arguments both within and outside the law of vicarious liability, it is most likely that the deep-pockets argument, where used, is not seen as a sufficient reason for imposing strict liability especially in more recent times. Furthermore, in keeping with the other three legal systems studied, the deep-pockets argument is typically used as a means to ensure that victims of accidents are adequately compensated.[68] On the other hand, it is difficult to identify examples where the argument is deployed on the basis of economic reasoning,[69] this marking a clear difference with the US approach.[70] This happens because English legal actors see the aim of the deep-pockets argument as the pursuit of victim protection rather than the minimization of the costs of accidents. This may be partly due to the fact that when English scholars discuss US theories of economic analysis they tend to focus on accident avoidance only and they ignore what legal economists say about tort law's role in reducing the social costs of accidents through distributive mechanisms.

In the context of vicarious liability, where it is mostly used, the deep-pockets argument has also attracted much criticism, with many legal scholars and, on one occasion, the UK Supreme Court casting serious doubt on it.[71] For example, Atiyah

---

[66] *Various Claimants v Catholic Child Welfare Society*, [2012] UKSC 56, [2013] 2 AC 1, [35] [*CCWS*]. See also *Majrowski v Guy's and St Thomas's NHS Trust*, [2006] UKHL 34, [9] (Lord Nicholls) (combining the deep-pockets rationale with victim protection, in juxtaposition with loss spreading, accident avoidance and, perhaps, risk creation); *Viasystems (Tyneside) Ltd v Thermal Transfer (Northern) Ltd*, [2006] QB 510, [52] (May LJ) (arguing that 'vicarious liability is a policy device of the law to redistribute the incidence of loss from a supposedly impecunious employee, who is personally at fault, to one or more supposedly *solvent* and *insured* employers, who are not personally at fault' (emphasis added)).

[67] *Armes v Nottinghamshire County Council*, [2017] UKSC 60, [2018] AC 355, [63]. Another example can be found in *Various Claimants v Barclays Bank plc*, [2017] EWHC 1929 (QB) [45].

[68] See eg Paula Giliker, *Vicarious Liability in Tort: A Comparative Perspective* (CUP 2010) 230.

[69] cf Jonathan Morgan, 'Vicarious Liability for Independent Contractors' (2016) 31 PN 235, 249 ('The fact that the employer is more likely to satisfy judgment justifies making him liable for the torts of those over whom he has some kind of authority or control. But *not* to ensure compensation for the victim. Rather because by holding such assets (or insurance), the employer is amenable to tort deterrence (including reactions by insurers, eg raising premiums)—ie responsive to liability in a way that the (judgment-proof) employee simply is not') (original emphasis).

[70] See text to nn 45–48 in this section.

[71] See also Jane Stapleton, *Product Liability* (Butterworths 1994) 93–94, 187 (rejecting this argument in relation to product liability).

believes that the deep-pockets argument is hardly satisfying in terms of fairness and that, at any rate, it is unreliable because it simply assumes that potential defendants such as company shareholders are wealthier than victims.[72] Similarly, Cane argues that the 'fairness of vicarious liability depends on who [the employers] are and what they have done, not on what they can afford'.[73] Moreover, several scholars suggest that the deep-pockets argument does not fit important features of the law of vicarious liability and that it ought to be rejected. Stevens, for instance, maintains that the argument 'fails to explain why this particular employer, rather than another body with an equally deep or deeper pocket, should compensate the claimant', and that, '[i]f taken seriously, this rationale collapses into an argument that in order to ensure compensation, liability for losses should be imposed upon the deepest pocket of all: the state'.[74] McBride and Bagshaw are also very critical of the deep-pockets argument, arguing that '[t]his theory does not work: there is nothing "fair, just and reasonable" about giving effect to a principle of "can pay, will pay"'.[75] And in the *Cox* case the Supreme Court considers all the five policy rationales that Lord Phillips put forward in *CCWS*, suggesting that the deep-pockets (as well as the loss-spreading) argument is not 'a principled justification for imposing vicarious liability' and that '[t]he mere possession of wealth is not in itself any ground for imposing liability'.[76] This judicial about-turn on the relevance of the deep-pockets argument has been welcomed by scholars such as Plunkett, who defines it as 'refreshing'.[77]

The message all these criticisms convey is that making defendants pay on the ground that they are wealthier than claimants is morally unpalatable.[78] In a way, it seems as though many English legal actors see the deep-pockets argument as somewhat 'primitive' in that it penalizes the wealthy without providing a good reason for doing so. Relatedly, and in keeping with the approach of the other three legal systems studied,[79] loss spreading is seen as more acceptable than the

---

[72] Patrick S Atiyah, 'Personal Injuries in the Twenty-First Century: Thinking the Unthinkable' in Peter Birks (ed), *Wrongs and Remedies in the Twenty-First Century* (Clarendon Press 1996) 1, 25–26.

[73] Peter Cane, 'Vicarious Liability for Sexual Abuse' (2000) 116 LQR 21, 26.

[74] Robert Stevens, *Torts and Rights* (OUP 2007) 258. For similar remarks, see also Patrick S Atiyah, *Vicarious Liability in the Law of Torts* (Butterworths 1967) 22 (though cf p 334, arguably suggesting that where employers hire independent contractors of limited financial resources, there is no 'real injustice in imposing liability on the employer'); Morgan (n 69) fn 84 and accompanying text as well as text following fn 94 (targeting the deep-pockets rationale as linked to victim protection); James Goudkamp and James Plunkett, 'Vicarious liability in Australia: On the Move?' (2017) 17 OUCLJ 162, 168.

[75] Nicholas J McBride and Roderick Bagshaw, *Tort Law* (6th edn, Pearson Education 2018) 852–853. Other scholars who are sceptical about the deep-pockets justification include: John Bell, 'The Basis of Vicarious Liability' (2013) 72 CLJ 17, 19; Peter Cane, 'Fault and Strict Liability for Harm in Tort Law' in William Swadling and Gareth Jones (eds), *The Search for Principle: Essays in Honour of Lord Goff of Chieveley* (OUP 1999) 171, 187–88; Murphy (n 61) 372–74; Anthony Gray, *Vicarious Liability: Critique and Reform* (Hart Publishing 2018) 151–53.

[76] *Cox v Ministry of Justice*, [2016] UKSC 10, [2016] AC 660, [20].

[77] James Plunkett, 'Taking Stock of Vicarious Liability' (2016) 132 LQR 556, 559.

[78] See John A Jolowicz, 'Liability for Accidents' (1968) 26 CLJ 50, 57–58 (implicitly rejecting the deep-pockets argument).

[79] See text to nn 12–15 (France), to n 26 (Italy), and to nn 54–56 (United States) in this section.

170 JUSTIFYING STRICT LIABILITY

deep-pockets argument because it ignores the depth of the parties' pockets and be-cause, by relying on a variety of spreading mechanisms, it shelters everyone from heavy financial burdens. For Jolowicz, '[i]f it were really the case that a person held liable to pay damages actually paid them out of his own pocket', then sticking to the fault paradigm 'would not be an unreasonable position to adopt', but the wide-spread availability of 'channels of distribution' changes everything.[80] Similarly, in reflecting on vicarious liability Steele argues that 'introducing *insurance* into the equation makes [the deep-pockets justification] into a more modern argument',[81] and Giliker recognizes that '[i]t is the development of insurance ... which argu-ably rendered vicarious liability both workable and acceptable to employers'.[82] In sum, it is not surprising that, similar to the position in France, Italy, and the United States, loss spreading is more attractive than the deep-pockets argument and that it therefore looms much larger than the former in English legal reasoning.[83]

Overall, then, the significance of the deep-pockets argument in the English con-text is very limited. First, in most contexts of liability the argument is simply not used. Furthermore, while it is true that it is occasionally relied on in the context of vicarious liability, its position looks very unstable because of the contrasting views that members of the UK Supreme Court have expressed in recent times and because of the plethora of criticisms that legal scholars have levelled at it. Finally, the status of the argument is further weakened by the loss-spreading justification, which provides a more modern and acceptable solution than merely taking money from a deep pocket.

3.4.6 Concluding Remarks

Overall, therefore, while the deep-pockets justification possesses its own particular features across the four legal systems studied, it ultimately has a modest signifi-cance in all of them.

First, its use in all four jurisdictions is very limited, with other justifications dominating the legal reasoning around strict liability. In the four systems the ar-gument is used in relation to employers' vicarious liability, which constitutes the only significant context in England;[84] by contrast, in the other three legal systems the argument features in further contexts such as, for example, liability for abnor-mally dangerous activities in the United States,[85] liability for products in France,[86]

---

[80] Jolowicz (n 78) 57–58.
[81] Steele (n 65) 580 (original emphasis).
[82] Giliker (n 68) 235.
[83] See subsection 3.5.5.
[84] See text to nn 62–67 in this section.
[85] See text to n 41 in this section.
[86] See text to n 10 in this section.

parental liability and liability for ruinous buildings in Italy.[87] Nevertheless, it must be remembered that reliance on the deep-pockets argument is scant. Moreover, in all four systems the argument is generally deployed in combination or juxtaposition with other justifications. What emerges is that it is typically used as a means towards broader ends and that, in this respect, it can serve various goals. Often, it is used to ensure that victims of accidents get compensation, especially if doing so would save a person of modest financial means from ruin while demanding only a relatively small sacrifice from a wealthy defendant. Pursuing victim protection by resorting to the deep-pockets argument is a common and widespread pattern in all four jurisdictions, and in the French system stands out as the only way in which the argument is used. By contrast, in the United States, England, and Italy, though only very rarely in the latter two,[88] the deep-pockets argument is sometimes grounded in economic reasoning and invoked either to avoid accidents or to reduce the socio-economic dislocation caused by leaving losses concentrated on victims.[89] But even if the deep-pockets argument can stem from economic reasoning, its most natural and frequent collocation is in the context of a desire to ensure adequate relief to the victims of accidents, even in the United States.

Finally, and especially in modern times, the deep-pockets argument has fallen into disfavour in all four jurisdictions. This is due in part to its perceived inherent unfairness or to the economic problems that its application may determine. In part, however, its demise is also due to the availability of another justification which, based on the availability of spreading mechanisms, can achieve distributive goals without all the (moral and economic) difficulties implicated in the idea of determining liability purely on grounds of wealth. This justification, which is the focus of the next section, is widely thought to be an evolution of the deep-pockets argument and to be capable of rendering the imposition of strict liability more acceptable and convenient. Spreading the cost is better than imposing the burden on a single person, even if they can bear it.

---

[87] See text to nn 20 and 22 in this section.
[88] See, respectively, text to n 23 and n 69 in this section.
[89] See text to nn 44–48 in this section.

3.5

Loss Spreading

3.5.1 The Loss-Spreading Justification of Strict Liability

Losses hurt less if their burden is spread rather than being concentrated on any particular individual. This proposition can be couched either in terms of economic cost or social solidarity. From an economic perspective, 'taking a large sum of money from one person is more likely to result in economic dislocation ... than taking a series of small sums from many people'.[1] From a perspective of social solidarity, the provision of collective sources of compensation shelters the victims of accidents from their sufferings so as to reduce the adverse impact on their lives.[2] Losses may be spread through different channels of distribution, some involving potential defendants (as with third-party insurance) and others involving potential claimants (as with first-party insurance). As the present work analyses arguments for strict liability as opposed to arguments favouring fault or no liability,[3] the focus of this section is on spreading losses via defendants rather than via claimants.[4]

Regardless of whether we see it through the lenses of economics or solidarity, the 'loss-spreading' justification for strict liability can be supported in various ways. According to a first approach, strict liability should be imposed on defendants because they can spread its costs through insurance. This spreading mechanism, which is here labelled 'insurance spreading', applies to firms or individuals, as they can both take out liability insurance for the risk of harm they impose on others. Within insurance spreading a further subdivision of approaches is in order: if, as between two parties in tort litigation, the defendant carries insurance coverage while the claimant does not, liability should be imposed on the former because they are better able to spread the costs of accidents as a matter of fact ('actual insurance coverage'); or, liability should be placed on the defendant if, regardless of actual insurance coverage, they are well positioned to spread the costs of accidents by taking out liability insurance ('insurability').

---

[1] Guido Calabresi, *The Costs of Accidents: A Legal and Economic Analysis* (YUP 1970) 39. See also Richard Posner, 'The Concept of Corrective Justice in Recent Theories of Tort Law' (1981) 10 J Legal Stud 187, fn 3.

[2] André Tunc, 'Foreword' in Geneviève Viney, *Le déclin de la responsabilité individuelle* (LGDJ 1965) ii; André Tunc, 'Les causes d'exonération de la responsabilité de plein droit de l'art. 1384, al. 1er du Code civil' D chron 1975.83, 85 (hereafter Tunc, 'Les causes d'exonération').

[3] See section 1.1.

[4] A discussion of the second type would involve consideration of a range of further and different types of arguments which cannot be entered into here.

Justifying Strict Liability. Marco Cappelletti, Oxford University Press. © Marco Cappelletti 2022.
DOI: 10.1093/oso/9780192859860.003.0007

According to a second approach, liability should be placed on firms because they are able to pass the loss on to consumers or to factor in the relevant costs in other ways such as by decreasing wages or shares of profits. This type of spreading, more limited in its scope of application as it refers only to firms, is here called 'enterprise spreading'. Where firms are involved, in practice there is often a synergy between enterprise and insurance spreading, and this is reflected in the reasoning of legal actors seeking to justify strict liability. Indeed, it is well known that firms often take out liability insurance to protect themselves against the costs of potential tort liability. In this case, the direct costs of liability are paid by the insurer; what the firm pays are the insurance premiums and the increases in those premiums, typically through price adjustments and/or a reduction in wages and/or in the shares of profit accruing to the shareholders. These two aspects of loss spreading overlap, but nonetheless they should be kept distinct because they refer to different methods of spreading losses and they allow us to identify important differences across the four laws in terms of the justifications for the imposition of strict liability.

A third approach to loss spreading, which applies only to public bodies, suggests that they should be liable for the harm caused by their activities on the ground that they can spread the costs of liability among taxpayers, who therefore act as the ultimate bearers of such costs. This spreading-based argument, focused as it is on taxation as the key channel of distribution of losses, is here called 'taxation spreading'. Moreover, public bodies may be protected by liability insurance and, whenever they provide services or goods to the public, they may be in a position to pass the costs of liability on to the users or consumers of such services or goods. Here again, therefore, there is a potential synergy among various channels of distribution of losses and a possible overlap among insurance, enterprise, and taxation spreading.

The picture is further complicated by the existence of a fourth approach to loss spreading, which cuts across the other three. This fourth approach seeks to promote a proportional sharing of burdens and benefits deriving from harmful activities. Unlike the other approaches seen above, which focus on the particular methods of distributing losses (eg insurance, price adjustments, or taxation), 'loss spreading as proportionality of burdens and benefits' (or 'burden–benefit proportionality') is concerned with selecting the persons over whom such costs should be spread, and these are all those who benefit from the harmful activity, regardless of whether the distribution of losses occurs through insurance mechanisms, enterprise spreading, or taxation. For example, in the case of losses caused by the tortious action of an employee or by a defective product, the defendant firm should be liable because it can spread the loss among all those who benefit from its activity, that is the firm itself (comprising the shareholders, the employees etc) as well as all the users and consumers of the service or activity provided. Similarly, if a public body harms an individual while performing an activity for the benefit of the wider community, liability should be imposed on that public body and ultimately paid for by that community; in this way, the person harmed will be compensated and will not bear a disproportionate burden compared to that shouldered by the other members of society. In sum, according to the 'burden–benefit proportionality' argument, the ultimate bearers of the loss will be all those who gained some benefit from the harmful activity. It is clear, therefore, that this approach to loss spreading cuts across the others in that it focuses on making the 'right' people pay via spreading, no matter what mechanisms are used to distribute the burden.

As will be seen in this section, there are substantial variations across the four laws in the way all these approaches to loss spreading are used and in the significance they have in each legal system studied.

3.5.2 Loss Spreading in France: A Panacea?

Among the four systems under consideration, French law is where loss spreading looms largest as a justification for the imposition of strict liability, with insurance spreading in civil liability and proportionality of burdens and benefits in public liability dominating the scene. While it is difficult, though not impossible,[5] to find judicial statements expressly couched in spreading terms, it is the academic literature that shows fully the extent to which spreading-based arguments act as key justifications for strict liability in France.

French law has undergone a profound transformation from a system of individual liability to a system based on the socialization (or collectivization) of losses.[6] With industrialization and the scientific and technological progress there was a steep increase in the number of accidents in the second half of the nineteenth century. These were not seen as fatalities that had to be accepted, but rather as misfortunes that required compassion and cure in a spirit of social solidarity. The fundamental function of tort law became the protection of the victims of accidents and the fault paradigm was seen as unfit for the job in a many contexts.[7] To make the objective of compensation attainable it was necessary to realize a socialization of the costs of liability, for particular individuals could not bear them in full.[8]

---

[5] cf Geneviève Viney, *Introduction à la responsabilité. Traité de droit civil* (4th edn, LGDJ 2019) [25].

[6] See Geneviève Viney, *Le déclin de la responsabilité individuelle* (LGDJ 1965); Yvon Lambert-Faivre, 'L'évolution de la responsabilité civile d'une dette de responsabilité à une créance d'indemnisation' RTD civ 1987.1; Loic Cadiet, 'Sur les faits et les méfaits de l'idéologie de la réparation' in *Le juge entre deux millénaires—Mélange offerts à Pierre Drai* (Dalloz 2000) 495; Régis de Gouttes, 'À propos des métamorphoses du droit de la responsabilité civile: à la recherche d'une remise en ordre dans le désordre actuel des normes' Gaz Pal 16.2.2012 n.47.

[7] See Jean-Louis Halpérin, *Histoire du droit privé français depuis 1804* (PUF 2012) [128]-[129]; Patrice Jourdain, *Les principes de la responsabilité civile* (10th edn, Dalloz 2021) 10–14.

[8] Geneviève Viney, 'De la responsabilité personnelle à la répartition des risques' Arch phil dr 1977.5, 11.

176 JUSTIFYING STRICT LIABILITY

Therefore, despite some isolated criticism,[9] the availability of liability insurance has long been seen as the answer, a panacea capable of justifying the imposition of strict liability in a wide variety of contexts.

To begin with, insurance spreading surfaces in the liability for the deeds of things. As early as 1897, Josserand identifies the rationale of this type of liability in the theory of risk, which he sees as allowing for the compensation of all who suffered due to the deeds of others' things.[10] Crucially, when challenged by the counterargument that his theory of risk would detrimentally affect the economy by imposing too great a cost on firms, Josserand replies that this potential drawback can be easily neutralized through liability insurance.[11] Similarly, Savatier relies on risk to explain the liability for the deeds of things,[12] but he regards insurance spreading as what really drives the judicial expansion of strict liability (for the deeds of things and beyond) and as the element which makes strict liability 'bearable'.[13] Again, in an article discussing liability for the deeds of things at a time when motor accidents were not yet dealt with by special legislation, Tunc argues that the cost of compensation should not be borne by an individual but by a collective source,[14] and he suggests that a good liability system should, when deciding how to distribute losses, take into account insurability, actual insurance coverage, and whether either party is under compulsory insurance arrangements.[15] Finally, today insurance spreading is sometimes relied upon to justify the presumption of guardianship in the owner of the thing, for the owner is seen as the party best placed to take out insurance against the risks of accidents which may be caused by the thing.[16]

Besides liability for the deeds of things, insurance spreading is very important in numerous other areas of French tort law. In the context of liability for the action of another, insurability is indicated as one of the key reasons for the imposition of strict liability.[17] For example, in the case of parental liability, Viney describes parents as 'guarantors' for the damage caused by the fact of their offspring and as

---

[9] eg Jean-Sébastien Borghetti, 'The Development of Product Liability in France' in Simon Whittaker (ed), *The Development of Product Liability* (CUP 2010) 87, 102–03 (suggesting that loss spreading 'should not by itself be sufficient to justify the imposition of liability').

[10] Louis Josserand, *De la responsabilité du fait des choses inanimées* (Arthur Rousseau 1897) 105–06.

[11] ibid 115–16.

[12] René Savatier, *Traité de la responsabilité civile*, vol 1 (2nd edn, LGDJ 1951) [337].

[13] ibid [282].

[14] Tunc, 'Les causes d'exonération' (n 2) 85.

[15] ibid 85–86 (combining insurance spreading with victim protection). See also Jourdain (n 7) 96 (juxtaposing insurability with risk–benefit, control (*maîtrise*), and accident avoidance); Philippe Malaurie, Laurent Aynès, and Philippe Stoffel-Munck, *Droit des obligations* (11th edn, LGDJ 2020) [107] (discussing insurability with accident avoidance).

[16] See eg Patrice Jourdain in Geneviève Viney, Patrice Jourdain, and Suzanne Carval (eds), *Les conditions de la responsabilité. Traité de droit civil* (4th edn, LGDJ 2013) [701]; Jourdain (n 7) 92 (combining insurability with victim protection, and adding an argument based on accident avoidance as well).

[17] eg Jourdain (n 7) 29–31 (discussing liability for the action of another in general and combining insurability with victim protection, in juxtaposition with risk–profit, accident avoidance (combined with risk creation), authority/control, and the deep-pockets argument).

the 'most naturally designated' party to bear the relevant costs and the best able to spread them through liability insurance.[18] The increase in rigour of strict parental liability that the Cour de cassation brought about with the *Levert* decision,[19] which held parents liable even if there was no failure in the harmful conduct of their child, is explained in the literature as a consequence of the widespread use of household insurance in France.[20] As to the employers' vicarious liability for the tort of their employees, again insurance spreading is often identified as a leading justification.[21] For example, after listing multiple rationales for this type of liability, Jourdain concludes that ultimately employers are held vicariously liable because they are, in most cases, very well positioned to take out liability insurance;[22] others, while putting forward different justifications, most notably risk-based arguments, do not reject the idea that the courts may consider the insurance status of the parties as a decisive factor in allocating the costs of accidents.[23] A significant indication of the French approach is also embodied in the rule laid down by the Cour de cassation in a 2007 decision, where it was established that the employee's general immunity from liability does not apply if the employee himself is insured against liability, with the consequence that the employee's insurer is exposed to a recourse action from either the employer or the employer's insurer.[24] This rule suggests that the

---

[18] Geneviève Viney in Viney, Jourdain, and Carval (eds), *Les conditions de la responsabilité. Traité de droit civil* (n 16) [877] (a view she extends to liability for the deeds of things), [870] at 1186 (seeing parental liability as pursuing the goal of victim protection). See also André Tunc, 'L'enfant et la balle' JCP 1966.I.1983. It was in the *arrêt Bertrand* that the Cour de cassation turned parental liability into an instance of strict liability: Civ (2) 19.2.1997, D 1997.265, 266 note Jourdain. See also Bernard Puill, 'Vers une réforme de la responsabilité des parents' D chron 1988.185, [24]–[28] (recommending the introduction of compulsory insurance to support strict parental liability); Geneviève Viney, JCP 1997.II n.22848, 252 (adding that, should the *Bertrand* decision increase the costs of the insurance premiums, these extra costs would be offset by the savings secured by the disappearance of the fault element from the range of issues to be assessed at trial); Yvonne Lambert-Faivre, 'L'éthique de la responsabilité' RTD civ 1998.1, 11–13 (emphasizing the importance of liability insurance for strict parental liability); Jourdain (n 7) 112 (combining insurability with victim protection (in turn combined with the deep-pockets rationale as well), in juxtaposition with accident avoidance and with an argument based on authority); Mireille Bacache-Gibeili, *Les obligations, La responsabilité civile extracontractuelle* (3rd edn, Economica 2016) [331] (seeing parental liability as a means to ensure victim protection and arguing that the *Bertrand* decision is acceptable in light of liability insurance); Alain Bénabent, *Droit des obligations* (19th edn, LGDJ 2021) [564] (identifying the rationale of strict parental liability in the idea of risk creation and in the ability of parents to take out liability insurance, but putting more emphasis on the latter argument).

[19] Civ (2) 10.5.2001 (*Levert*), D 2002.1315 note Denis Mazeaud.

[20] Jean-Sébastien Borghetti, 'The Culture of Tort Law in France' (2012) 3 JETL 158, 166–67.

[21] While for convenience I refer to employers and employees, article 1242 of the *Code civil* refers to the wider notions of *commettants* and *préposés*.

[22] Jourdain (n 7) 105. See also Geneviève Viney, JCP 2000.I.241, 1244, [19] (emphasizing the importance of insurance spreading); Viney (n 18) [790], [791-1], [813] (combining insurability with victim protection, and adding an argument based on accident avoidance); Bénabent (n 18) [572] (juxtaposing insurability with an argument based on a presumption of fault, with an *ad hoc* attribution theory, as well as with risk creation, victim protection, and the deep-pockets rationale).

[23] eg Savatier (n 12) [282].

[24] Civ (1) 12.7.2007, JCP 2007.II.10162 note Hocquet-Berg. The immunity does not apply also where the employee acted intentionally, even if with the assent or under the instructions of their employer (Ass plén 14.12.2001, JCP 2002.II.10026 note Billiau).

178   JUSTIFYING STRICT LIABILITY

courts pay particular attention to insurance spreading and to the insurance status of the parties in devising the functioning mechanisms of tort rules.

Again in the context of liability for the action of another, the French courts have on occasion considered the actual insurance coverage of the defendant as a justification for the imposition of strict liability. In the *Blieck* case, the Court of Appeal of Limoges held liable a private centre for occupational therapy for the damage caused by a mentally disabled person to the property of the claimant. After holding that every risk-generating activity must pay for the losses caused on the ground that the 'compensation of victims is a principle embedded in [French] political and social morality', the court mentions the actual insurance coverage enjoyed by the centre as a relevant factor supporting a finding of liability.[25] Similarly, a number of legal scholars mention insurance spreading, whether in the form of insurability or of actual insurance coverage, as one of the main rationales for the imposition of strict liability in this type of situation.[26]

Further examples of legal reasoning including insurance spreading can be found in relation to liability for defective products and liability for traffic accidents. In the context of product liability, academic writings appearing both before and after the implementation of the Product Liability Directive justify the imposition of strict liability on the ground that, by relying on liability insurance, the manufacturer is in a position to spread the costs of accidents caused by their defective products.[27] As regards traffic accidents, both before and after the enactment of the *loi* Badinter,[28] there are abundant references to the importance of insurance spreading as an argument supporting the imposition of strict liability. In the *Desmares* case,[29]

---

[25] CA Limoges 23.3.1989, RCA November 1989, comm n.361.

[26] Jacques Ghestin, JCP 1991.II.169, n.21673, [7], [12] (referring to risk-based arguments as well); Patrice Jourdain, RTD civ 1995.890, 901 (juxtaposing insurance spreading with an argument based either on risk creation or abnormality of risk); Patrice Jourdain, D 1997.496, 497 (juxtaposing insurability with an argument based on authority and with victim protection (arguably supported by the idea of risk creation)); Olivier Gout, 'Le droit français positif et prospectif de la responsabilité du fait d'autrui' in *Le droit français de la responsabilité civile confronté aux projets européens d'harmonisation* (IRJS Éditions 2012) 291, 294 (combining actual insurance coverage with victim protection).

[27] eg Jean-Francis Overstake, 'La responsabilité du fabricant de produits dangereux' RTD civ 1972.485, [80]; Ghestin (n 26) [7]; Geneviève Viney, 'La mise en place du système français de responsabilité des producteurs pour le défaut de sécurité de leurs produits' in *Mélanges offerts à Jean-Luc Aubert—Propos sur les obligations et quelque autres thèmes fondamentaux du droit* (Dalloz 2005) 329, 356–58 (arguing that one of the objectives of strict product liability is to compensate victims quickly and effectively and that, if the available insurance mechanisms are not reinforced so as to deal with certain types of losses (eg catastrophic losses), the need for the protection of victims of products will not be met). cf Jean-Sébastien Borghetti, *La Responsabilité du Fait des Produits: Etude de Droit Comparé* (LGDJ 2004) [622]–[623] (rejecting loss spreading, understood as a combination of insurance and enterprise spreading, as a persuasive explanation of product liability), [644]–[645] (arguing though that loss spreading may contribute to the determination of the liable party where the theory of cost internalization does not provide an answer), [646] (arguing that loss spreading, together with the deep-pockets rationale, may explain the imposition of liability on not-for-profit entities); Borghetti (n 9) 102–03 (critically noting that, for many French legal actors, insurance coverage makes the case for strict product liability compelling in view of the ultimate goal of victim protection).

[28] See text to nn 242–245 in section 2.4.

[29] Civ (2) 21.7.1982, D 1982.449 note Larroumet, concl Charbonnier.

the Avocat général Charbonnier argued that the availability of insurance is a formidable means to ensure the complete protection of victims without exposing the responsible party to burdensome liabilities and that therefore both the values of social solidarity and individual well-being can be served at the same time.[30] Enacted in 1985 as a reaction to the Cour de cassation's activism in *Desmares*, the *loi* Badinter constitutes a 'law for the compensation of victims by means of insurance'[31] and it is typically justified by reference to insurance spreading.[32]

The widespread use and significance of this argument should not surprise if account is taken of the extraordinary development of the French insurance market. As emphasized by Borghetti, most potential defendants are, one way or another, protected by liability insurance and it is therefore very rare that tort damages will come out of their own pockets; aware of this, French courts are happy to expand the scope of tort liability by, for example, introducing new strict liabilities or by augmenting the strictness of those already in existence.[33]

In sum, the emerging picture strongly suggests that insurance spreading is an essential justification for strict liability in France. Even if discussed with other arguments, the frequency with which it is used as well as the emphasis put on it confirm this view.[34] Importantly, insurance spreading and victim protection appear

---

[30] ibid 450. See also Geneviève Viney, 'L'indemnisation des victimes de dommages causes par le "fait d'une chose" après l'arrêt de la Cour de cassation' D chron 1982.201 (supporting *Desmares* on the ground that it is based on the assumption that motor vehicles are insured (at 206), and suggesting that it would not promote negligent behaviour and that it may bring about a reduction in the volume of litigation (at 205)).

[31] André Tunc, *La responsabilité civile* (2nd edn, Economica 1989) Postface, [4], at 166.

[32] See eg Geneviève Viney and Anne Guégan-Lécuyer, 'The Development of Traffic Liability in France' in Wolfgang Ernst (ed), *The Development of Traffic Liability* (CUP 2010) 50, 71–72 (seeing insurance spreading as a key justification for this liability regime); Geneviève Viney, 'Les trentes ans de la loi Badinter: bilan et perspectives. Propos introductifs' in *Les trentes ans de la loi Badinter—Bilan et perspectives*, RCA September 2015, dossier 12, 7, [40]–[42] (juxtaposing insurance spreading with victim protection and administrative cost reduction); Bacache-Gibeili (n 18) [673] (seeing the availability of insurance and the need to protect victims as the reasons for the decision in *Desmares* and the adoption of the *loi* Badinter); François Terré and others, *Droits civil, Les obligations* (12th edn, Dalloz 2018) [1165] (recognizing the pivotal role of insurance in the *loi* Badinter but doubting that the *loi* is really part of French tort law because of its departure from traditional notions of causation).

[33] See eg Borghetti (n 20) 166–67; text to nn 19–20 in this section. See also Muriel Fabre-Magnan, *Droit des obligations. 2—Responsabilité civile et quasi-contrats* (4th edn, PUF 2019) [45] (arguing that the actual insurance coverage of defendants exerts considerable influence on French judges).

[34] eg Chantal Russo, *De l'assurance de responsabilité à l'assurance directe: contribution à l'étude d'une mutation de la couverture des risques* (Dalloz 2001) [742] (mentioning accident avoidance as an argument for strict liability), but cf [756] (emphasizing the importance of insurance spreading, even at the expense of accident avoidance); Clothilde Grare, *Recherches sur la cohérence de la responsabilité délictuelle. L'influence des fondements de la responsabilité sur la reparation* (Dalloz 2005) [33]–[35] (mentioning risk–profit), but cf [45]–[48] (emphasizing the importance of insurance spreading); Borghetti (n 20) 166–67 (explaining strict parental liability on the basis of insurance spreading); Jourdain (n 7) 105 (seeing insurability as the single most important justification for employers' vicarious liability). See also André Tunc, 'Responsabilité civile et dissuasion des comportements antisociaux' in *Aspects nouveaux de la pensée juridique: recueil d'études en hommage à Marc Ancel*, vol 1 (Pedone 1975) 407, 414 (suggesting that accident avoidance is an acceptable justification for strict liability only if the effects of this liability on defendants are mitigated through spreading mechanisms).

together very often in French reasoning,[35] and the relationship between the two is important to shed further light on the significance of the former. As shown throughout this section, insurance spreading is frequently used as a means to the end of victim protection. By being imposed on the party who is insured or who can more conveniently insure, strict liability provides victims of accidents with the target that is most likely to meet their claim, given the presence of an insurance company behind the defendant. In other words, insurance spreading attracts widespread consensus among French legal actors because it is conducive to the realization of the fundamental objective of compensating the victims of accidents.

A further point which emerges from French discussions concerns the relationship between loss spreading and risk-based arguments. As seen in a variety of examples set out in this subsection,[36] some legal scholars (and even courts in at least one case) justify strict lability on the basis of risk and then add an insurance spreading argument. The impression one gets is that while arguments such as risk creation or risk–benefit/profit can *theoretically* support strict liability, it is the possibility for defendants to resort to spreading mechanisms such as insurance which makes strict liability acceptable and which, therefore, provides considerable support for its imposition. As a result, it seems that the emergence and continuing vitality of risk-based justifications is made possible, at least in part, by the availability of spreading mechanisms and that, therefore, besides being an independent argument, loss spreading is also deployed to buttress other arguments, reinforcing their appeal. At the same time, as seen in our discussion of risk, risk-based justifications may sometimes be 'exploited' in light of their prestige to help other arguments such as loss spreading support the imposition of strict liability and make the latter more attractive and familiar.[37] In sum, it appears that, at least to some extent, risk and loss spreading are mutually reinforcing justifications of strict liability in France.

Finally, but very importantly, insurance spreading marks the boundaries of the French willingness to impose strict liability. As is now very clear, from a French perspective the great merit of combining strict liability with liability insurance is that the costs of accidents will be spread widely rather than left concentrated on any one person, whether the claimant, the defendant, or a third party. By contrast, without spreading mechanisms cushioning its impact on defendants, strict liability would be too harsh for them and therefore much less attractive to the French legal system. In this respect, then, insurance spreading works as a 'safety valve' against excessive reliance on strict liability, because the latter remains attractive so long as its full costs are removed from the defendant and spread via liability insurance. Excellent examples are provided in the context of liability for traffic accidents. In

[35] See references relying on both arguments in nn 15–18, n 22, nn 26–27, and n 32, as well as the text to n 31 in this section.
[36] See text to nn 10–13 and to n 25, as well as n 26 in this section.
[37] See subsection 3.2.2.

LOSS SPREADING   181

1951, when these accidents were still governed by liability for the deeds of things, Savatier argues that

> [t]he courts could never have said in fairness that every motorist is answerable for the harm caused by his car, even without his fault, if all conscientious motorists had not been insured. It is only insurance that makes such liability bearable, without unfairly substituting, in the person of the motorist not at fault, one victim to another.[38]

Similarly, today some leading scholars argue that what makes the extreme rigour of the *loi* Badinter morally acceptable is compulsory insurance: 'to apply the strict regime of compensation envisaged in the statute to individuals not covered by insurance, for example pedestrians or cyclists, would have led to grave injustices'.[39] In sum, insurance spreading is an attractive argument in France because it ensures, through the imposition of strict liability, the compensation of victims while at the same time avoiding anyone in society being financially crushed by that very imposition. In this way, the value of social solidarity represents a safeguard which ensures that the interests of both victims and defendants are adequately protected.

The very same idea of distributing losses widely also permeates discussions relating to the strict liability of French public authorities. In this area, it is however a different spreading-based argument that dominates the scene, namely proportionality of burdens and benefits, with taxation spreading being also relied upon, though less frequently. At the turn of the twentieth century, as legal scholars working in the field of civil liability showed a growing confidence in insurance mechanisms and insurance-based arguments, so French public lawyers started to see in the principle of 'equality before public burdens' (*égalité devant les charges publiques*) a persuasive reason for imposing strict liability on the state for the harm caused to its citizens.[40] According to this principle, thought to derive from article

[38] Savatier (n 12) [282].

[39] eg Patrice Jourdain in Geneviève Viney, Patrice Jourdain, and Suzanne Carval (eds), *Les régimes spéciaux et l'assurance de responsabilité* (4th edn, LGDJ 2017) [123]. See also Josserand (n 10) 115–16; Charbonnier (n 29) 450. cf Boris Starck, Henri Roland, and Laurent Boyer, *Obligations*, t. 1, *Responsabilité délictuelle* (5th edn, LITEC 1996) [84]–[85], [89] (arguing that what makes it fair to shift the loss from an innocent claimant to an innocent defendant is the availability of liability insurance, but then adding that strict liability should apply regardless of insurance for the purpose of 'guaranteeing' compensation to anyone who suffered from personal injuries or damage to property). On the 'guarantee theory', see Boris Starck, *Essai d'une théorie générale de la responsabilité civile considérée en sa double fonction de garantie et de peine privée* (L Rodstein 1947); Boris Starck, 'Domaine et fondement de la responsabilité sans faute' RTD civ 1958.475, 515. For a critique of Starck's theory, see Eugène Louis Bach, 'Réflexions sur le problème du fondement de la responsabilité civile en droit français' RTD civ 1977.221, [111]–[119].

[40] Maurice Hauriou, 'Les actions en indemnité contre l'Etat pour préjudices causés dans l'administration publique' RDP 1896.51; George Teissier, *La responsabilité de la puissance publique* (Chez Paul Dupont 1906, reprinted Editions La Mémoire du Droit 2009) [147] (on administrative liability in general), [175]–[177] (in relation to public works); Gaston Jèze, *Éléments du droit public et administratif* (V Giard & E Brière 1910) 99; Léon Duguit, *Traité de Droit Constitutionnel*, vol 3 (3rd edn, Fontemoing 1930) 469 (on administrative liability in general); Pierre Delvolvé, *Le principe d'égalité*

182   JUSTIFYING STRICT LIABILITY

13 of the *Déclaration des droits de l'homme et du citoyen*,[41] no individual should bear a disproportionate burden compared to that shouldered by the other members of society as a result of an activity that a public body performs for the common good. When such an activity causes, even without any fault, substantial harm to a specific member of the public, the unlucky individual should be entitled to compensation from the benefited community (via the state or other public entity having standing as defendant).[42] This line of thinking, a clear example of loss spreading as proportionality of burdens and benefits, has been used to justify the imposition of strict liability in a wide variety of contexts, as where harm is caused by a legislative act,[43] a lawful administrative decision,[44] or by the carrying out of public works.[45] For example, in the famous *La Fleurette* case, a statute forbade manufacturers to call a product 'cream' if it was not made entirely from milk. As a consequence of this legislation, the firm *La Fleurette* was forced to discontinue the manufacture of one of its products. It therefore sought relief before the Conseil d'État, which considered that

devant les charges publiques (LGDJ 1969). See also Maryse Deguergue, *Jurisprudence et doctrine dans l'élaboration du droit de la responsabilité administrative* (LGDJ 1994) 138–42; Duncan Fairgrieve, *State Liability in Tort: A Comparative Law Study* (OUP 2003) 137–38, 144–50; John Bell, 'Administrative Law' in John Bell and others, *Principles of French Law* (2nd edn, OUP 2008) 168, 188–89, 193–95 (hereafter Bell, 'Administrative Law'); John Bell, 'The Reform of Delict in the Civil Code and Liability in Administrative Law' in Jean-Sébastien Borghetti and Simon Whittaker (eds), *French Civil Liability in Comparative Perspective* (Hart Publishing 2019) 425, 426–28, 437–40. For an (infrequent) example of this approach to private parties, see Henri Mazeaud, Léon Mazeaud, and André Tunc, *Traité théorique et pratique de la responsabilité civile délictuelle et contractuelle* (6th edn, Montchrestien 1965) [621-2] (here Tunc, though not Henri and Léon Mazeaud, draws on the public law principle of equality before public burdens to develop a 'burden–benefit proportionality' argument in the context of liability for private nuisance).

[41] 'For the maintenance of the forces of law and order and for the expenses of administration a general contribution is indispensable; it must be equally shared between citizens according to their means' (translation by Fairgrieve (n 40) 137, fn 6).
[42] The exact scope of the principle of 'equality before public burdens' is controversial, with some French scholars arguing that it may constitute the basis of all French public liability: for a discussion of this issue, see eg Thierry Debard, 'L'égalité des citoyens devant les charges publiques: fondement incertain de la responsabilité administrative' D chron 1987.157; Roger Errera, 'The Scope and Meaning of No-Fault Liability in French Administrative Law' (1986) 39 CLP 157, 171–73; Marie-Aimée de Latournerie, 'The Law of France' in John Bell and Anthony W Bradley (eds), *Governmental Liability: A Comparative Study* (United Kingdom National Committee of Comparative Law 1991) 200, 225–27; Fairgrieve (n 40) 144, and fn 71; Bell, 'Administrative Law' (n 40) 195.
[43] See eg CE Ass 14.1.1938 (*La Fleurette*), D 1938.3.41; Olivier Gohin, 'La Responsabilite de l'État en tant que Legislateur' (1998) 50(2) RIDC 595; René Chapus, *Droit administratif général*, vol 1 (15th edn, Montchrestien 2001) [1516]–[1518].
[44] See eg CE 30.11.1923 (*Couitéas*), D 1923.3.59 concl Rivet; Jean-Paul Gilli, 'La "responsabilité d'équité" de la puissance publique' D chron 1971.125, 128; Georges Vedel and Pierre Delvolvé, *Droit administratif*, vol 1 (12th edn, PUF 1992) 605–09; L Neville Brown and John S Bell, *French Administrative Law* (5th edn, OUP 1998) 198–99.
[45] See eg Charles Eisenmann, 'Sur le degré d'originalité du régime de la responsabilité extracontractuelle des personnes publiques' JCP 1949.I.751, [11]; Chapus (n 43) [1506]–[1509].

Nothing ... gives reason to think that the legislator intended to put on the claimant a burden which would not normally fall upon it; that this burden, created in the public interest, must be borne by society; that it follows that the firm 'La Fleurette' is entitled to claim that the State should be ordered to pay compensation for the loss it suffered.[46]

As it is assumed that the cost of liability is ultimately borne by French taxpayers, each contributing a tiny fraction of the total loss, it can be readily seen that proportionality of burdens and benefits goes hand in hand with taxation spreading; and indeed, the two arguments are sometimes combined together when justifying strict public liability.[47] However, proportionality of burdens and benefits recurs far more frequently than taxation spreading in French reasoning. Why is this so? Probably because the former argument contains a clear *moral* directive prescribing a collective, proportional sharing of losses, which embodies an ideal of justice and fairness rooted in the value of social solidarity. This moral content is not, by contrast, immediately visible within the argument based on taxation spreading, which therefore may be perceived as less potent (and therefore appealing) at a justificatory level. On the other hand, taxation is essential from a practical perspective, as it is the actual conduit for redistributing the costs of 'public accidents'; therefore, it must be an implicit assumption in the minds of those French public lawyers who justify strict public liability by reference to proportionality of burdens and benefits. As a result, even if taxation spreading is not heavily relied upon in the express reasoning of French legal actors, it would be wrong to think that distributing losses through taxes does not play a role in supporting the strict liability of public bodies.

Finally, besides being combined with taxation spreading, proportionality of burdens and benefits is sometimes put forward as the sole justification for the entire body of public liability,[48] and at other times it is mentioned together with other justifications such as risk or victim protection.[49] What all these instances and patterns

---

[46] *La Fleurette* (n 43).

[47] See eg Maurice Hauriou, S 1897.3.33; Teissier (n 40) [147]; Marcel Waline, 'Cinquante ans de jurisprudence administrative' D chron 1950.21, 22–23; Fairgrieve (n 40) 137; Duncan Fairgrieve and François Lichere, 'The Liability of Public Authorities in France' in Ken Oliphant (ed), *The Liability of Public Authorities in Comparative Perspective* (Intersentia 2016) 155, [68].

[48] See Jean Waline, 'L'évolution de la responsabilité extracontractuelle des personnes publiques' EDCE 1994.459, 470–71; Dominique Philipp, 'De la responsabilité à la solidarité des personnes publiques' RDP 1999.593, esp 615 and 631. cf Bell, 'Administrative Law' (n 40) 195 (noting that this approach would hide the difference between the distinct instances of French public liability).

[49] See eg Maxime Mignon, 'La socialisation du risque' D chron 1947.37 (discussing burden–benefit proportionality with the 'theory of risk'); CE Ass 24.6.1949 (*Lecomte et Daramy*), D 1950.27 (combining burden–benefit proportionality with abnormality of risk); Delvolvé (n 40) [636]–[638] (combining burden–benefit proportionality with victim protection to explain the emergence of public liability *sans faute*); Waline (n 48) 470–71 (arguing that the whole of administrative liability finds its justification in the principle of equality before public burdens), 477 (reading the expansion of liability without fault (and the objectivization of fault) as means to protect the victims of accidents); Deguergue (n 40) 119–20 (reading Laferrière's theory of liability for public works as a juxtaposition between burden–benefit proportionality and abnormality of risk).

184   JUSTIFYING STRICT LIABILITY

of reasoning suggest is that proportionality of burdens and benefits is a key reason for imposing strict liability on French public bodies in a variety of contexts. It is so attractive because, by prescribing members of the public to share equally in the positive and negative effects of the public action, it avoids any concentration of losses and therefore gives expression to the value of social solidarity.

Given the reliance that the French reasoning places on spreading-based arguments as sound justifications for the imposition of strict liability, it is surprising to see how marginal the role of enterprise spreading is whenever firms are involved. To be sure, the argument sporadically appears in the context of liability for defective products[50] as well as in relation to professional activities,[51] but if compared to insurance spreading its frequency, and therefore significance, is infinitely smaller. This is striking, given that from a loss-spreading perspective it would be natural to argue that firms should be liable because they can pass the costs of liability on to consumers or factor in such costs in other ways, regardless of whether they have insurance coverage or not. The fact that firms can take out liability insurance and thus bring about an even broader spreading of losses is certainly significant and yet of somewhat secondary importance when compared to enterprise spreading, which may well be alone sufficient to accomplish a meaningful dispersion of losses where the defendant is a firm. Why, then, are French legal actors so reluctant to rely on enterprise spreading? One explanation for this may be that, while well aware of and sympathetic with the practical operation of enterprise spreading mechanisms, they do not want to inject into the legal debate, dominated as it is by a rhetoric of social solidarity, ideas resonating with the economic analysis of law.[52] Indeed, as it will be seen while discussing the US and Italian approaches to loss spreading, enterprise spreading is often put forward in the context of theories based on economic analysis.

In conclusion, the importance (both theoretical and practical) of loss spreading in France cannot be exaggerated. In many cases, the spreading of losses is readily identified as an essential reason for imposing strict liability. At other times, it may not receive particular emphasis or be presented as a central justification, as where

---

[50] Overstake (n 27) [80] (combining enterprise spreading with insurability and adding an argument based on burden–benefit proportionality as well); Ghestin (n 26) [7] (juxtaposing enterprise spreading with insurability); Jean Calais-Auloy, 'Le risque de développement: une exonération contestable' in *Mélanges Michel Cabrillac* (Dalloz/Litec 1999) 81, 85 (arguably seeing enterprise spreading as a reason to forbid the development risk defence, together with other arguments such as risk–profit, accident avoidance, and victim protection).

[51] Viney (n 6) [324]ff. cf Viney (n 18) [791-1], [813] (in discussing the rationale of employers' vicarious liability, she refers to insurability and accident avoidance as key justifications without mentioning enterprise spreading at all), [790] (omitting accident avoidance altogether and focusing only on liability insurance as a means for 'guaranteeing the victims' of the employee's harmful conduct).

[52] While recently there has been some interest in law and economics (see Grégory Maitre, *La responsabilité civile à l'épreuve de l'analyse économique du droit* (LGDJ 2005)), it seems fair to say that French legal actors are still reluctant to give credit to the insights of economics. See also Fabre-Magnan (n 33) [40] (critically appraising the application of economic thinking to tort law).

the relevant theory is founded on risk-based arguments or on the desire to 'guarantee' victims; but even in these instances, the idea that the costs of accidents will be distributed widely through spreading mechanisms rather than left concentrated on a particular person plays an important role and it is often seen as what renders strict liability an attractive and acceptable solution. The fundamental significance of loss spreading reflects the paramount importance of social solidarity, a value which imbues the French reasoning on strict liability and which constitutes a safeguard for the interests of all.

3.5.3 Loss Spreading in the United States: A Leading and Flexible Justification

In the United States loss spreading is a prominent justification for the imposition of strict liability even though, in comparison with France, it features in a less pervasive way and it is handled very differently. As the following discussion will make clear, this argument is exposed to a variety of approaches which show its great flexibility, but also to several criticisms which have weakened its status even if only slightly. Moreover, in striking contrast with the French approach, there is no imbalance in significance between insurance spreading and enterprise spreading, with both featuring conspicuously in US reasoning.

To begin with, unlike the French position, the actual insurance coverage of the defendant is generally not seen in the United States as an attractive justification for the imposition of strict liability. For example, in a case of liability for abnormally dangerous activities, the Supreme Court of Iowa maintains that the choice of the party that is going to bear the loss must not be made 'on the basis of the parties' relative abilities to spread the risk of loss *in a particular case*'.[53] Similarly, leading scholars from the law and economics movement point out that liability rules must be chosen having in mind *categories* of defendants and claimants, and not the *particular* defendant and claimant to the case being litigated, with the consequence that 'there should [not] be one liability rule for insured persons and another for the uninsured'.[54] Again, those who see tort law as a system of interpersonal justice refuse to accord any relevance whatsoever to the 'actual insurance coverage' argument, for this is seen as wholly incompatible with any notion of individual responsibility.[55] Having said this, it is however possible that judges or juries occasionally and covertly take into account the insurance realities of the case being litigated; but

---

[53] *National Steel Service Center v Gibbons*, 319 N.W.2d 269, 272 (Iowa 1982) (emphasis added).

[54] See Guido Calabresi and Jon T Hirschoff, 'Toward a Test for Strict Liability in Torts' (1971) 81 Yale LJ 1055, 1070, fn 54.

[55] See eg Ernest J Weinrib, 'The Insurance Justification and Private Law' (1985) 14 J Legal Stud 681, 683. As will be seen below, the same criticism is levelled at insurability and enterprise spreading: see text to nn 87–89 in this section.

186 JUSTIFYING STRICT LIABILITY

even so, it seems unlikely that this phenomenon would occur on a large scale, for US reasoning regards highly goals and values (eg accident avoidance, individual responsibility) which are at odds with the idea of finding liability on the basis of actual insurance coverage. Moreover, the insurance status of the parties may be taken into account in decisions as to the imposition of liability for fault as much as strict liability.

The rejection of actual insurance coverage contrasts with the prominent role that insurability and enterprise spreading play in the United States. These two arguments feature frequently in the case law and academic writings as justifications for strict liability in contexts such as product liability, liability for abnormally dangerous activities, and employers' vicarious liability.[56] In this respect, insurability and enterprise spreading are both seen as means to achieve a wide distribution of losses, particularly where firms are involved: firms can not only take out liability insurance, they can also absorb the costs of liability by passing them on to consumers through price adjustments. Therefore, both arguments contribute significantly to shaping the loss-spreading justification for strict liability in the US context and, in striking contrast with the French approach, insurability does not loom larger than enterprise spreading.

In the United States, the spreading of losses has been a fundamental theme in tort theory throughout the twentieth century, it has come into contact with a variety of approaches, and it has been used in different ways and for different purposes. To begin with, loss spreading was strongly connected to victim protection in the work of numerous tort scholars from the 1920s to the 1950s which, in conjunction with Justice Traynor's famous concurring opinion in *Escola v Coca Cola Bottling Co*,[57] paved the way towards an increased significance of strict liability in US tort law.[58] For example, in a well-known article published in 1948, James criticizes a bilateral and fault-based conception of tort law for its failure to decrease 'the

---

[56] In relation to product liability, see eg *Escola v Coca Cola Bottling Co of Fresno*, 150 P.2d 436, 441 (Cal.1944); *Codling v Paglia*, 298 N.E.2d 622, 627–28 (N.Y.1973); *Blankenship v Gen Motors Corp*, 406 S.E.2d 781, 784 (W.Va.1991); Second Restatement, §402A, comment *c*. In relation to employers' vicarious liability, see eg *Johnston v Long*, 181 P.2d 645, 651 (Cal.1947); *Hinman v Westinghouse Electric Company*, 471 P.2d 988, 990 (Cal.1970); *Fruit v Schreiner*, 502 P.2d 133, 141 (Alaska 1972). In relation to liability for abnormally dangerous activities, see eg *Chavez v Southern Pacific Transportation*, 413 F.Supp. 1203, 1208–09 (Cal.1976); *Hutchinson v Capeletti Brothers, Inc.*, 297 So.2d 952, 953–54 (Fla.1981).

[57] *Escola* (n 56) 441.

[58] See eg Leon Green, 'The Duty Problem in Negligence Cases' (1928) 28 Colum L Rev 1014, and (1929) 29 Colum L Rev 255; Lester W Feezer, 'Capacity to Bear Loss as a Factor in the Decision of Certain Types of Tort Cases' (1930) 78 U Pa L Rev 805, and (1931) 79 U Pa L Rev 742; Fleming James Jr, 'Accident Liability Reconsidered: The Impact of Liability Insurance' (1948) 57 Yale LJ 549; Fowler V Harper and Fleming James Jr, *The Law of Torts*, vol 2 (Little, Brown and Company 1956) ch XIII. For an overview of these developments, see Virginia E Nolan and Edmund Ursin, *Understanding Enterprise Liability: Rethinking Tort Reform for the Twenty-first Century* (Temple University Press 1995) 21–124; Edmund Ursin, 'Judicial Creativity and Tort Law' (1981) 49 Geo Wash L Rev 229. cf George L Priest, 'The Invention of Enterprise Liability: A Critical History of the Intellectual Foundations of Modern Tort Law' (1985) 14 J Legal Stud 461.

toll of life, limb, and property' typical of the 'machine age'.[59] In James' view, it is the 'principal job of tort law ... to deal with these losses' and '[t]he best and most efficient way to do this is to assure accident victims of compensation, and to distribute the losses involved over society as a whole or some very large segment of it'.[60] In *Escola*, a case concerned with product liability, Justice Traynor argues that

> [t]hose who suffer injury from defective products are unprepared to meet its consequences. The cost of an injury and the loss of time or health may be an overwhelming misfortune to the person injured, and a needless one, for the risk of injury can be insured by the manufacturer and distributed among the public as a cost of doing business.[61]

In this type of reasoning, judges and scholars are committed to ensuring that the victims of accidents receive compensation and they acknowledge that the spreading of losses achieves this result with the great advantage of avoiding any disruption to the life or business of anyone.[62] Here, then, besides being a goal worth pursuing in itself, loss spreading is used as a means to support strict liability and, through it, greater victim protection. This way of looking at loss spreading and combining it with victim protection is reminiscent of the French approach which, as seen above,[63] puts particular emphasis on loss spreading as a way of supporting strict liability for purposes of compensation.

In contrast to France, though, in the United States the loss-spreading argument can often be found in reasoning not driven by the value of social solidarity and by the desire to ensure victim protection, and an important reason for this is the emergence of law and economics in the second part of the twentieth century. While some legal economists quickly dismiss loss spreading and prefer to focus on other issues,[64] leading figures in the field such as Calabresi, Kaplow, and Shavell, think differently. For example, Calabresi takes loss spreading very seriously and sees it as a means to reduce the 'secondary costs' of accidents (ie the negative effects of leaving a loss concentrated rather than spread).[65] Here loss spreading is no

---

[59] James (n 58) 549.

[60] ibid 550. See Guido Calabresi, 'Professor Fleming James Jr (1904–1981)' in James Goudkamp and Donal Nolan (eds), *Scholars of Tort Law* (Hart Publishing 2019) 259, 264–65 (noting that, for James, 'spreading ... meant meeting the, broadly defined, *needs* of victims') (original emphasis).

[61] *Escola* (n 56) 441 (juxtaposing this argument with accident avoidance and administrative cost reduction).

[62] See also *Seely v White Motor Co*, 403 P.2d 145, 151 (Cal.1965); *Price v Shell Oil Co*, 466 P.2d 722, 725–26 (Cal.1970); *Chavez* (n 56) 1214; *Mahowald v Minnesota Gas Co*, 344 N.W.2d 856, 868 (Minn.1984) (Todd J dissenting, with whom Scott J and Wahl J agreed); *Beshada v Johns-Manville Prods Corp*, 447 A.2d 539, 547 (N.J.1982). See also Roger Traynor, 'The Ways and Meanings of Defective Products and Strict Liability' (1965) 32 Tenn L Rev 363, 366–67 (in relation to product liability, combining loss spreading with victim protection, in juxtaposition with accident avoidance).

[63] See subsection 3.5.2.

[64] See text to nn 85–86 in this section.

[65] Calabresi (n 1) 39ff. See also Calabresi and Hirschoff (n 54) 1076ff (seeing 'distributional' considerations, which include the spreading of losses, as potentially decisive in the choice of liability rules).

longer merely a gateway to victim protection, but rather one of the '*methods* or *approaches*' for achieving the fundamental '*subgoal*' of a reduction in secondary costs which, in turn, serves the 'broadest aim' of minimizing the total sum of the costs of accidents.[66] Similarly, Shavell and Kaplow acknowledge that if liability rules are to be judged from the standpoint of their effects on individuals' well-being, distribution of income matters, and therefore loss spreading (as well as the availability of a deep pocket) become relevant factors that must be balanced with the effects that the same liability rules have on accident avoidance and administrative costs.[67] It is on this basis that it will then be possible to decide between different types of liability, whether strict or based on fault. In sum, in the works of these legal economists, the distribution of losses is certainly important but it constitutes only one aspect of a broader and complex 'calculus', and it cannot therefore have the same centrality that it enjoys in the reasoning of scholars who, like James, see loss spreading as the fuel of strict liability (and perhaps of tort law more generally).[68]

A further recognizable pattern of use of loss spreading in US reasoning is rooted in an ideal of fairness understood as proportionality of burdens and benefits, and it suggests that losses should be distributed among the *beneficiaries* of the harmful activity. This approach, whose main proponent today is Keating, is clearly distinct from those seen so far and it maintains that a party who 'is capable of spreading the costs of accidental harm *across those who benefit from the creation of the relevant risks*', should be strictly liable for that harm.[69] First, and in keeping with the position in France, this argument is relied upon in relation to public bodies: where the federal government, the states, or other local authorities harm a citizen in the performance of their administrative activities, the loss should not be left concentrated on the unlucky victim but should instead be distributed across the whole community as the ultimate beneficiary of the activity which has caused the harm.[70]

---

[66] Calabresi (n 1) 16 (original emphasis) (therefore combining loss spreading with accident avoidance and administrative cost reduction). To understand the importance of loss spreading in Calabresi's view, consider Guido Calabresi and Kenneth C III Bass, 'Right Approach, Wrong Implications: A Critique of McKean on Products Liability' (1970) 38 U Chi L Rev 74, 90 (arguing that 'where the case in terms of primary cost avoidance is close we will opt for the loss allocation which effectuates significant secondary cost reductions').

[67] Louis Kaplow and Steven Shavell, *Fairness v Welfare* (HUP 2002) 119. See n 48 in subsection 3.4.4, explaining the type of situation to which this reasoning applies.

[68] On the influence of James on Calabresi's thinking, see Guido Calabresi (n 60).

[69] Gregory C Keating, 'The Idea of Fairness in the Law of Enterprise Liability' (1997) 95 Mich L Rev 1266, 1329 (original emphasis) (hereafter Keating, 'The Idea of Fairness'). See also Gregory C Keating, 'Distributive and Corrective Justice in the Tort Law of Accidents' (2000) 74 S Cal L Rev 193; Gregory C Keating, 'The Theory of Enterprise Liability and Common Law Strict Liability' (2001) 54 Vand L Rev 1285; Gregory C Keating, 'Strict Liability Wrongs' in John Oberdiek (ed), *Philosophical Foundations of the Law of Torts* (OUP 2014) 292 (hereafter Keating, 'Strict Liability Wrongs'); Gregory C Keating, 'Products Liability as Enterprise Liability' (2017) 10(1) JTL 41 (hereafter Keating, 'Products Liability'). See also Francis H Bohlen, 'The Rule in Rylands v. Fletcher: Part III' (1911) 59 U Pa L Rev 423, 444 ff.

[70] See eg Fleming James Jr, 'Tort Liability of Governmental Units and Their Officers' (1955) 22 U Chi L Rev 610, 614–15, 653–55 (relying on proportionality of burdens and benefits with a view to compensating victims and spreading losses among the taxpayers, in relation to all governmental activities other than legislative and political decisions); Kenneth Culp Davis, 'Administrative Officers' Tort Liability' (1956–1957) 55 Mich L Rev 201, 227, 232–34 (combining proportionality of burdens and benefits with

Besides public authorities, in the United States the same argument is put forward in relation to firms and physical individuals as well. Proportionality of burdens and benefits leads to the imposition of strict liability on firms because they can distribute the costs of accidents across all the beneficiaries of their activity, these including the firm itself as well as the consumers and users of the product or service provided.[71] Equally, strict liability should apply to physical individuals if their activities, though diffuse and disorganized, are actuarially significant when taken in the aggregate, so that those carrying out such activities can insure against the attendant risk of harm and therefore spread the loss among their beneficiaries:[72] for example, dog owners should be strictly liable for the harm caused by their dogs to

---

victim protection, arguably in juxtaposition with accident avoidance, to advocate the vicarious liability of government for its officers' exercise of discretionary functions); *Johnson v State of California*, 447 P.2d 352, 363 (Cal.1968) (relying on proportionality of burdens and benefits to justify the imposition of vicarious liability on the state of California for the failure of one of its Youth Authority officials to disclose the homicidal tendencies of youthful parolee to foster parents); Cornelius J Peck, 'Laird v. Nelms: A Call for Review and Revision of the Federal Tort Claims Act' (1973) 48 Wash L Rev 391, 411–12, 420–21 (seeing proportionality of burdens and benefits as a persuasive reason to impose strict liability on the federal government in *Nelms* itself, arguably in combination with a concern for the compensation of victims); Osborne M Reynolds Jr, 'Strict Liability under the Federal Tort Claims Act: Does "Wrongful" Cover a Few Sins, No Sins, or Non-Sins?' (1974) Am U L Rev 813, esp 833–35 (emphasizing loss spreading as burden–benefit proportionality among the reasons in support of the inclusion of strict liability in the FTCA); Barry R Goldman, 'Can the King Do No Wrong? A New Look at the Discretionary Function Exception to the Federal Tort Claims Act' (1992) 26 Ga L Rev 837, 856–58 (combining proportionality of burdens and benefits with taxation spreading, in juxtaposition with accident avoidance and victim protection as the reasons militating against the 'discretionary function' exception under the FTCA); William P Kratzke, 'Some Recommendations Concerning Tort Liability of Government and Its Employees for Torts and Constitutional Torts' (1996) 9 Admin LJ Am U 1105, 1164–67 (combining proportionality of burdens and benefits with taxation spreading, in juxtaposition with accident avoidance, to support the vicarious liability of government for the negligent implementation of its policies). See also Justice Stewart's dissenting opinion (with whom Justice Brennan agreed) in *Laird v Nelms*, 406 US 797, 809–10 (1972) (discussing proportionality of burdens and benefits with taxation spreading, arguably in combination with victim protection, and in juxtaposition with abnormality of risk, to justify governmental strict liability for ultra-hazardous activities); *Owen v City of Independence*, 445 US 622 (1980) [20], [16,17] (juxtaposing proportionality of burdens and benefits with accident avoidance and victim protection, to justify the liability of a municipality under § 1983); Susanah M Mead, ''42 U.S.C. § 1983 Municipal Liability: The Monell Sketch Becomes a Distorted Picture' (1987) 65 NCL Rev 517, 538–40 (combining proportionality of burdens and benefits with taxation spreading, in juxtaposition with accident avoidance and victim protection, to criticize *Monell's* rejection of *respondeat superior* as the basis of municipal liability under § 1983).

[71] Keating, 'Products Liability' (n 69) 47, 56 (discussing product liability and the liability of private firms more generally). Given its focus on the spreading of losses and on the beneficiaries of the harmful activity as the ultimate bearers of the costs of accidents, this argument must not be confused with risk–benefit or risk–profit. These latter arguments, to which any spreading logic is irrelevant, suggest that liability should be imposed on the party who benefits or profits from the risk of harm that *they created* (which is not the case of, say, the consumers of a harmful product). Therefore, while the element of benefit/profit is clearly decisive in the risk–benefit/profit arguments for the determination of the party liable, this is not the case for the argument based on burden–benefit proportionality; here, the element of benefit/profit identifies the parties across whom the loss must be spread, whether or not these created the risk of harm which then occurred. Keating uses both types of justifications to support strict liability in US tort law, together with an argument based on individual responsibility: see Gregory C Keating, 'Strict Liability Wrongs' (n 69) 301–08.

[72] Keating, 'The Idea of Fairness' (n 69) 1331–39.

190 JUSTIFYING STRICT LIABILITY

third parties because, combined with insurance, strict liability 'should ... be able to spread the costs of dogfights across all dog owners, thereby aligning the benefits and burdens of dog ownership as far as the infliction of accidental injuries on strangers is concerned'.[73] Several examples of this approach can be identified in contexts such as liability for abnormally dangerous activities,[74] employers' vicarious liability,[75] and product liability.[76]

A further spreading-based argument surfacing in the reasoning of US judges and scholars is taxation spreading. Confined to the realm of public liability, this argument is typically put forward to explain the strict liability of public bodies and/or to support its expansion, usually by means of vicarious liability, on the ground that the losses charged to the public purse are in fact distributed among taxpayers, for whom the resulting burden is slight. This justification is frequently put forward together with proportionality of burdens and benefits and/or with victim protection, although further arguments may also feature in the same reasoning.[77] Interestingly, we earlier saw that in France the significance of taxation spreading is clearly lesser

---

[73] ibid 1334.

[74] See eg *Lubin v Iowa City*, 131 N.W.2d 765, 770 (Iowa 1964); *Siegler v Kuhlman*, 502 P.2d 1181, 1188 (Wash.1972) (Rosellini J, concurring) (in a case concerning the transportation of a highly flammable material, maintaining that a good reason for imposing strict liability is that the defendant can spread the loss among its customers—who benefit from this extrahazardous use of the highways').

[75] See eg *Montague v AMN Healthcare, Inc*, 223 Cal.App.4th 1515, 1523–24 (Cal.2014) (juxtaposing burden–benefit proportionality with accident avoidance and victim protection); Fowler V Harper, Fleming James Jr, and Oscar S Gray, *The Law of Torts*, vol 5 (2nd edn, Little, Brown and Company 1986) 21, including fn 15 (juxtaposing burden–benefit proportionality with accident avoidance and victim protection); Rhett B Franklin, 'Pouring New Wine into an Old Bottle: A Recommendation for Determining Liability of an Employer under Respondeat Superior' (1994) 39 SD L Rev 570, 575–76 (juxtaposing burden–benefit proportionality with accident avoidance and victim protection).

[76] See eg Keating, 'Products Liability' (n 69); *Richman v Charter Arms Corp*, 571 F.Supp. 192, 203 (La.1983) (juxtaposing burden–benefit proportionality with reasons of 'economic efficiency'); *Schump v Firestone Tire and Rubber Co*, 541 N.E.2d 1040, 1049 (Ohio 1989) (Sweeney J, dissenting) (arguing that strict product liability is based upon the idea that losses should be spread over those who benefit from the product).

[77] See n 70 as well as Bohlen (n 69) fn 136; *Rayonier, Inc v United States*, 352 US 315, 319–20 (1957) (relying on taxation spreading, burden–benefit proportionality and, arguably, victim protection, to justify the federal government's vicarious liability for the negligence of its Forest Service in fighting a fire); Peter H Schuck, 'Suing Our Servants: The Court, Congress, and the Liability of Public Officials for Damages' (1980) 1980 Sup Ct Rev 281, 347–51 (juxtaposing taxation spreading with victim protection, morality, wealth redistribution, and (secondarily) accident avoidance, to argue for an expanded government liability based on *respondeat superior*); Peter H Schuck, 'Municipal Liability under Section 1983: Some Lessons from Tort Law and Organizational Theory' (1989) 77 Geo LJ 1753, 1779–80 (combining taxation spreading with insurability, in juxtaposition with accident avoidance, victim protection, reasons of morality, and administrative cost reduction, to reject the 'official policy' requirement under § 1983 and support the adoption of a type of municipal liability which is, in essence, strict); Kenneth Culp Davis, *Administrative Law. Cases—Text—Problems* (West Publishing 1973) [182] (noting that, because 'supported by taxation', governmental units 'may be the best of all possible loss spreaders', a fact that 'may lead us to see that the basis for governmental liability should not be fault but should be equitable loss spreading'); Bruce A Peterson and Mark E Van Der Weide, 'Susceptible to Faulty Analysis: United States v. Gaubert and the Resurrection of Federal Sovereign Immunity' (1997) 72 Notre Dame L Rev 447, 484–86 (juxtaposing taxation spreading with (efficient) accident avoidance and nonreciprocity of risk, to criticize the excessive breadth of the 'discretionary function' exception and to argue that it may be possible to remove it and to impose strict liability on the federal government).

than that of burden–benefit proportionality, at least at the level of overt reasoning, probably because the French see the latter argument as more easily connected to the (very much cherished) value of social solidarity. In the United States, by contrast, the position is different: no dramatic imbalance seems to emerge in the use of the two arguments, suggesting that the idea of sharing losses proportionately among the beneficiaries of public activities attracts no greater support than the idea of spreading the same losses across taxpayers. An explanation for this may be that the practical result of the two arguments is the same: the beneficiaries of a public activity are indeed the taxpayers, and therefore roughly the same people are the ultimate bearers of the costs of liability under both approaches. In sum, short of any special attachment to one argument or the other (as instead happens in France), there is no practical reason why US lawyers should prioritize either proportionality of burdens and benefits or taxation spreading at a justificatory level, and in fact they do not do so. What matters is only that the loss caused by the administration is distributed widely rather than left to rest on a few individuals.

Finally, in US reasoning loss spreading can sometimes feature, typically in judicial opinions, as an objective worth pursuing regardless of other goals and without any particular connotation, acting either as a stand-alone justification or in juxtaposition with a variety of other arguments. For example, in relation to employers' vicarious liability, in *Lisa M*, where a hospital is held not liable for torts committed by an ultrasound technician against a patient, the Supreme Court of California maintains that this is the most appropriate conclusion in the light of the 'three policy goals of the respondeat superior doctrine—preventing future injuries, assuring compensation to victims, and spreading the losses caused by an enterprise equitably'.[78] Similarly, in a case involving liability for abnormally dangerous activities, the New Jersey Supreme Court juxtaposes two distinct policy rationales for this type liability, arguing that firms should internalize the external costs of their unusually dangerous activities, and that they are in 'a better position to administer the unusual risk by passing it onto the public'.[79] Again, in the context of product liability, in *US Airways v Elliott Equipment Co*, the United States District Court for the Eastern District of Pennsylvania justifies the imposition of strict liability on the grounds that manufacturers are encouraged to increase product safety and that they can distribute the cost of injuries by charging it in their businesses.[80] In this

---

[78] *Lisa M v Henry Mayo Newhall Mem Hosp*, 907 P.2d 358, 366–67 (Cal.1995). See also *Johnston* (n 56) 651 (loss spreading standing alone); *Hinman* (n 56) 990 (juxtaposing loss spreading with risk-profit); *Schreiner* (n 56) 141 (loss spreading standing alone).

[79] *T & E Industries, Inc v Safety Light Corp*, 587 A.2d 1249, 1257 (N.J.1991) (the somewhat cryptic argument from cost internalization is perhaps linked to abnormality of risk and risk–benefit). See also *Hutchinson* (n 56) 953–54 (juxtaposing loss spreading with reasons of 'logic and fundamental fairness' which look like a combination between abnormality of risk and victim protection); *Dyer v Maine Drilling & Blasting, Inc*, 984 A.2d 210 (Me.2009) [19]–[20], [31] (juxtaposing loss spreading with accident avoidance and with a combination of arguments featuring abnormality of risk and risk–profit).

[80] No. CIV.A. 06-1481, 2008 WL 4461849 (Pa.2008) at *5 [sic]. See also *Codling* (n 56) 628 (juxtaposing loss spreading with accident avoidance); *Francioni v Gibsonia Truck Corp*, 372 A.2d 736,

192   JUSTIFYING STRICT LIABILITY

type of reasoning, it is not easy to pinpoint the exact significance of loss spreading vis-à-vis the other arguments included in the same reasoning, but the emphasis put on it suggests that the courts usually keep it in high regard or that at least they do not see it as less important than other arguments.

What emerges is therefore a complex picture, where loss spreading proves to be a flexible argument which, depending on the relevant scholar or judge, may be seen as an independent objective worth pursuing in itself, as a means to promote the protection of victims or the minimization of the costs of accidents, or as a notion embodying an ideal of fairness as proportionality of burdens and benefits. Or it could even be all (or some of) these things at once, a particularly striking example of this being *Chavez v Southern Pacific Transportation*, where an action was successfully brought for property destruction and personal injuries caused by the explosion of bomb loaded boxcars.[81] According to the United States District Court for the Eastern District of California:

> One public policy now recognized in California as justifying the imposition of strict liability for the miscarriage of an ultrahazardous activity is the social and economic *desirability of distributing the losses*, resulting from such activity, among the general public.[82]
>
> [T]he risk distribution justification for imposing strict liability is well suited to claims arising out of the conduct of ultrahazardous activity. The *victims* of such activity are *defenseless*. Due to the very nature of the activity, the losses suffered as a result of such activity are likely to be substantial—an 'overwhelming misfortune to the person injured.' ... By indirectly imposing liability on *those that benefit from the dangerous activity*, risk distribution benefits the social-economic body in two ways: (1) the *adverse impact of any particular misfortune* is lessened by spreading its cost over a greater population and over a larger time period, and (2) social and economic *resources can be more efficiently allocated* when the actual costs of goods and services (including the losses they entail) are reflected in their price to the consumer.[83]

739 (Pa.1977) (juxtaposing loss spreading with accident avoidance and victim protection); *Bell v Jet Wheel Blast*, 462 So.2d 166, 171 (La.1985) (juxtaposing loss spreading with accident avoidance); *Bowling v Heil Co*, 511 N.E.2d 373, 378–79 (Ohio 1987) (clearly seeing loss spreading as the fundamental rationale of product liability); *Promaulayko v Johns Manville Sales Corp*, 562 A.2d 202, 204 (N.J.1989) (juxtaposing loss spreading with accident avoidance); *Queen City Terminals, Inc v Gen Am Transp Corp*, 653 N.E.2d 661, 671–72 (Ohio 1995) (juxtaposing loss spreading with accident avoidance and administrative cost reduction); *Brooks v Beech Aircraft Corp*, 902 P.2d 54, 59 (N.M. 1995) (juxtaposing loss spreading with victim protection and risk–profit); *Green v Smith & Nephew AHP, Inc*, 629 N.W.2d 727, 749–50 (Wis.2001) (juxtaposing loss spreading with accident avoidance, with the protection of consumer expectations, with risk creation and risk–profit) (note, though, the primary importance given to risk creation and to risk–profit).

[81]   *Chavez* (n 56).
[82]   ibid 1208 (emphasis added).
[83]   ibid 1209 (emphasis added).

[The defendant] is in a position to pass along the loss to the public.... [T]he social and economic benefits which are ordinarily derived from imposing strict liability are achieved. *Those which benefit* from the dangerous activity bear the inherent costs. The *harsh impact of inevitable disasters* is softened by *spreading* the cost among a greater population and over a larger time period. A more *efficient allocation of resources* results.[84]

In the quoted passages, the court makes use of all the flexibility that loss spreading possesses: it recognizes that loss spreading is a desirable goal to pursue; it notes that the losses should be distributed among those who benefit from the harmful activity, so that a proportional sharing of benefits and burdens is achieved; it treats loss spreading as a means to soften the misfortunes or disasters afflicting the victims, but also as a means to bring about a more efficient allocation of resources. In reasoning like this, it is difficult to discern the relative weight of all the ideas put forward, but what is clear is that loss spreading is given the utmost importance.

In sum, subjected to a variety of approaches and used in different ways and for different purposes, loss spreading constitutes a leading justification for the imposition of strict liability in the United States. However, this does not mean that the argument has remained unchallenged. First, while it is true that legal economists such as Calabresi, Kaplow, and Shavell recognize the importance of distributing losses through tort rules, others working in the same field do not. An influential figure such as Posner dismisses loss spreading by arguing that 'there is little to this argument' and that the claimant 'can avoid a concentrated loss by insuring',[85] and he prefers to focus on tort law's ability to promote the adoption of efficient precautions and the maximization of wealth.[86] Secondly, as already mentioned in relation to actual insurance coverage, theories of tort law based on interpersonal justice marginalize or reject any 'collective' concerns such as those reflected into loss-spreading arguments. For example, according to Weinrib, loss spreading is unacceptable because, by identifying the party liable on grounds of spreading abilities, it makes determinations of liability depend on factors entirely external to the claimant/defendant relationship.[87] Thirdly, as Keeton puts it, loss spreading should not supplant concepts of 'individual responsibility, with moral content', which 're-main vital to an understanding of tort decisions and trends'.[88] An illustration of this type of criticism appears to be in action to counteract the New Jersey Supreme Court's decision in *Beshada*, according to which strict product liability applies even

---

[84] ibid 1214 (emphasis added).

[85] Richard A Posner, 'Strict Liability: A Comment' (1973) 2 J Legal Stud 205, 210.

[86] See Richard A Posner, 'Book Review (reviewing Guido Calabresi, The Costs of Accidents: A Legal and Economic Analysis (1970))' (1970) 37 U Chi L Rev 636.

[87] Weinrib (n 55). See also Ernest J Weinrib, 'The Special Morality of Tort Law' (1989) 34 McGill LJ 403, 408; George Fletcher, 'Fairness and Utility in Tort Theory' (1972) 85 Harv L Rev 537, 547, fn 40.

[88] Robert E Keeton, 'Conditional Fault in the Law of Torts' (1959) 72 Harv L Rev 401, 444.

194   JUSTIFYING STRICT LIABILITY

to unknowable risks of harm, in rejection of any 'state of the art' (or development risk) defence. While the decision may be on 'solid ground' from the perspective of accident avoidance and loss spreading, which both feature prominently in the court's reasoning, 'fairness considerations cut strongly the other way', for it is unjust to hold someone liable for risks that they did not have reason to know about when the product was put into circulation.[89] Fourthly and finally, some legal scholars argue that tort adjudication is a poor tool for making decisions about the distribution of losses in society. For Epstein, for example, these require the balancing of a wide range of considerations which cannot be properly assessed in judicial opinions and which should be left to the legislator; furthermore, if what matters is ensuring that everyone is protected from accidents and other misfortunes in life, 'then the most appropriate response is a comprehensive system of first party insurance', not the tort system; '[t]o allow loss spreading issues covertly to dominate the structure of the tort law will only produce unsound results and bad general principles'.[90]

All these criticisms have certainly affected the attractiveness of loss spreading and have induced greater caution in deploying this argument to develop or expand rules of strict liability,[91] despite the existence of a well-developed insurance market and the widespread use of liability insurance.[92] In this respect, there is a striking contrast with French law, where loss spreading goes almost unchallenged and is widely used to justify all sorts of strict liabilities, buttressed as they are by a heavy reliance on insurance. But even so, and whether deployed to protect victims, to minimize the costs of accidents, or to bring about a proportional sharing of burdens and benefits, loss spreading is part and parcel of US tort reasoning and it

[89]   Robert Rabin, 'Some Thoughts on the Ideology of Enterprise Liability' (1996) 55 Md L Rev 1190, 1205–06.

[90]   Richard A Epstein, 'Products Liability: The Search for the Middle Ground' (1978) 56 NCL Rev 643, 660–61. See also Richard A Epstein, 'Products Liability as an Insurance Market' (1985) 14 J Legal Stud 645; Gary T Schwartz, 'Foreword: Understanding Products Liability' (1979) 67 Cal L Rev 435, 445–46; David G Owen, 'Rethinking the Policies of Strict Products Liability' (1980) 33 Vand L Rev 681, 706–07. For an interesting debate on the effects of loss spreading on product liability and the insurance market, see George Priest, 'Understanding the Liability Crisis' in Walter Olson (ed), *New Directions in Liability Law* (Academy of Political Science 1988) 196 (arguing that all the reliance placed on strict product liability as a loss-spreading device caused the insurance crisis that hit the United States in the mid-1980s and which resulted in a steep increase in insurance premiums, in the unavailability of insurance coverage for certain products or activities, and in the further consequence that some manufacturers or service providers curtailed their operations); cf Steven P Croley and Jon D Hanson, 'What Liability Crisis? An Alternative Explanation for Recent Events in Products Liability' (1991) 8 Yale J Reg 1 (challenging Priest's reconstruction and arguing that what Priest calls 'insurance crisis' was 'a welcome consequence of efficiency-enhancing changes in the law' (at 11)).

[91]   Nolan and Ursin (n 58) 138–51.

[92]   For example, the so-called homeowner's insurance provides both property and personal liability insurance to 93 per cent of homeowners in the United States: for an overview of the development of this type of insurance, see Kenneth Abraham, *The Liability Century. Insurance and Tort Law from the Progressive Era to 9/11* (HUP 2008) 174–78; for statistical data, see Insurance Information Institute, *2021 Insurance Fact Book*, 90ff.

still constitutes one of the main arguments put forward to justify the imposition of strict liability in this legal system.[93]

3.5.4 Loss Spreading in Italy: A Neglected Argument?

Fuelled by both the value of social solidarity and the economic analysis of law in the 1970s, loss spreading had the potential to become a dominant argument in the Italian context. However, due to a variety of criticisms which were levelled at it and at certain theories which featured it, legal scholars became increasingly dubious about its appropriateness as a justification for strict liability, with the result that the argument failed to become as prominent as it is in France or even in the United States. Today, loss spreading is mostly used in contexts of liability where firms are involved but, even there, it does not appear as conspicuously as other arguments.

To begin with, while there are abundant discussions about the interplay between Italian tort law and insurance practices,[94] insurance spreading does not loom large as a justification for strict liability in Italy. As in the United States, leading academics argue that the actual insurance coverage of the parties should not affect the outcome of tort disputes because otherwise tort law would become an economically and socially irrational, a case-by-case 'good Samaritan' system where the insured pays damages for the simple reason that they happened to carry liability insurance.[95] Consistently with this position, legal scholars do not encourage the courts to take into account the insurance status of the parties when deciding how to allocate the costs of accidents. In the light of this, it is surprising to find statements in the literature according to which the courts would be in fact influenced by the insurance cover of the parties, with the consequence that if the defendant took out liability insurance the court would find liability more easily than it would have been otherwise.[96] These scholars, though, are unable to point to a single judicial decision which expressly takes into account the insurance cover of the parties and the few studies dealing with this issue contradict their claim.[97] Furthermore,

---

[93] See Croley and Hanson (n 90) 4, fn 10 (arguing that '[d]eterrence and insurance have been widely accepted as the twin goals of products liability, indeed, of tort law in general').

[94] See eg Aurelio Donato Candian, *Responsabilità civile e assicurazione* (EGEA 1993).

[95] eg Pietro Trimarchi, *Rischio e responsabilità oggettiva* (Giuffrè 1961) 30–31; Stefano Rodotà, 'Modelli e funzioni della responsabilità civile' (1984) RCDP 595, 602.

[96] eg Ugo Carassale, *Assicurazione Danni e Responsabilità civile: Guida alla lettura della giurisprudenza* (Giuffrè 2005) 2–3; Cesare Salvi, *La responsabilità civile* (3rd edn, Giuffrè 2019) 319. See also Enrico Quadri, 'Indennizzo e assicurazione' in Marco Comporti and Gianguido Scalfi (eds), *Responsabilità civile e assicurazione obbligatoria* (Giuffrè 1988) 97, 103; Candian (n 94) 6–7; Dianora Poletti, 'Le regole di (de)limitazione del danno risarcibile' in Nicolò Lipari e Pietro Rescigno (eds), *Diritto civile, Volume IV, Attuazione e tutela dei diritti. Tomo III, La responsabilità e il danno* (Giuffrè 2009) 291, 300–01, 318; Andrea Parziale, 'Il "caso dell'amaca", danno alla persona e costi assicurativi' (2013) 6 DR 688, 691.

[97] See Ugo Natoli, Francesco D Busnelli, and Annamaria Galoppini, 'Responsabilità, assicurazione e solidarietà sociale nel risarcimento dei danni' (1970) 45 Annuario di diritto comparato 55–57 (arguing that, as to product liability, liability for traffic accidents, and employers' vicarious liability, insurance

196   JUSTIFYING STRICT LIABILITY

in keeping with the US approach, a hidden judicial reliance on actual insurance coverage would sit uneasily with other justifications for strict liability. For example, accident avoidance features conspicuously as a justification in Italian judicial reasoning, and any reliance on actual insurance coverage is likely to remove safety incentives from the parties and therefore hinder the goal of preventing accidents.

Turning to insurability as a justification for the imposition of strict liability, this argument is far from enjoying the same status that it has in the French context. There, insurability features very frequently in a wide variety of contexts, from liability for the deeds of things or the actions of animals, to vicarious liability, product liability, and liability for traffic accidents.[98] In Italy, the situation is very different. As far as liability for things in one's keeping is concerned, it is true that the 1942 Report of the Ministry of Justice to the *Codice civile* states that 'the harshness of this regime can be corrected via contracts of insurance'.[99] However, courts and scholars do not use insurability as a justification for this liability and prefer other arguments such as accident avoidance, risk, or victim protection.[100] Moreover, in striking contrast with the French approach, insurability is all but absent from discussions concerning liability for animals,[101] which is widely justified on the basis of risk–benefit,[102] and from discussions concerning parental liability, which are dominated by generic statements concerning the protection of victims and by occasional references to the deep-pockets argument.[103] On the rare occasions where insurability is discussed in the context of parental liability, the effects of insurance spreading are treated with scepticism.[104] Indeed, it is remarked that

does not determine the outcome of tort disputes). See also the study of Giovanni Iudica and Alessandro P Scarso, 'Tort Liability and Insurance: Italy' in Gerhard Wagner (ed), *Tort Law and Liability Insurance* (Springer 2005) 119, [45]–[69]. After observing that insurability and the actual insurance coverage of the parties are not significant in the resolution of tort disputes, Iudica and Scarso interestingly add that 'no distinction is drawn between compulsory liability insurance and—in the relatively few cases in which it can be considered as being widespread—voluntary liability insurance' ([61]). Thus, even where one or both parties are under compulsory insurance arrangements, it is unlikely that the courts will take that into account, at least on the face of the judgment; for product liability, see Nadia Coggiola, 'The Development of Product Liability in Italy' in Simon Whittaker (ed), *The Development of Product Liability* (CUP 2010) 192, 228 ('Italian courts never seem to take into account the availability, existence or incidence of liability or first party insurance when compensating the damage arising out of the defective products, either when they apply D.P.R. 224/1988 or when they apply other laws').

[98] See subsection 3.5.2.

[99] n.794: '[L]a durezza di tale situazione … può essere corretta mercè contratti di assicurazione'.

[100] The rationale of this liability remains very controversial both for courts and for scholars. For an overview of the various positions, see Marco Comporti, *Fatti Illeciti: le responsabilità oggettive—Artt. 2049-2053. Il Codice Civile—Commentario* (Giuffrè 2009) 294–98.

[101] cf Annalisa Bitetto, 'Danni provocati da animali selvatici: chi ne risponde e perché?' (2003) 3 DR 275, text to fns 26–32; Pietro Trimarchi, *La Responsabilità Civile: Atti Illeciti, Rischio, Danno* (Giuffrè 2017) 276–86, 336ff, but see text to nn 117–123 in this section.

[102] See text to n 115 in subsection 3.2.3.

[103] See text to n 20 in subsection 3.4.3 and n 38 in subsection 3.6.3. In addition to this, it must also be remembered that the views of Italian courts as to the nature of parental liability still oscillate between fault and strict liability: see text to nn 289–290 in section 2.5 and to n 35 in subsection 3.4.3.

[104] Salvatore Patti, *Famiglia e responsabilità civile* (Giuffrè 1984) 328ff. cf Pier Giuseppe Monateri, *La Responsabilità Civile. Trattato di Diritto Civile* (UTET 1998) 974 (suggesting that parents must be held

greater recourse to spreading via voluntary insurance and strict liability may exacerbate economic inequalities between wealthier and poorer families, as the latter are concerned first with meeting basic needs and only secondarily with taking out insurance coverage.[105] A solution may be the introduction of compulsory insurance,[106] which would therefore become widespread and more easily accessible by the population at large.[107] However, this arrangement is criticized, as it would be likely to increase the volume of litigation and remove safety incentives from the parents.[108] Given how little attention insurability has attracted in the context of parental liability, it is not surprising to find no evidence of courts employing such an argument. More generally, while some scholars argue that insurability would nudge Italian judges to find defendants liable in a variety of contexts, no case law is offered to support this claim.[109] The picture which emerges suggests that, in striking contrast with France, insurability (let alone the actual insurance coverage of the parties) is not an argument frequently used to justify the imposition of strict liability in contexts where defendants are often physical individuals. This may well reflect the fact that, compared to France, liability insurance is not very common in Italy outside the business context.[110]

The role of insurability becomes more significant, though, if we move to situations where defendants are typically firms, as in the contexts of employers' vicarious liability and product liability. Here, loss spreading features in the legal reasoning on strict liability in the form of insurability and/or enterprise spreading, and it is clear that both spreading strategies are well entrenched in the minds of Italian legal actors. Couched in these terms, the loss-spreading argument acquired considerable force in Italy in the 1970s as a result of the convergence of two quite distinct intellectual commitments, one rooted in the value of social solidarity, the other in law and economics. At the same time, though, a wide range of doubts were

---

strictly liable for the damage caused by their children and 'must take out liability insurance', juxtaposing this argument with accident avoidance and victim protection); it is however unclear what weight the author attaches to insurability, especially because his approach seems to focus primarily on accident avoidance and only secondarily on victim protection (ibid 946–47).

[105] Patti (n 104) 328–29. See also Maria Luisa Chiarella, 'Minore danneggiante e responsabilità vicaria' (2009) 10 DR 973, 986.

[106] Silvia Taccini, 'Il sistema della responsabilità civile dei genitori: tra profili di protezione e di garanzia' (2008) 1 DR 5, 11; Paolo Pardolesi and Marina Dimattia, 'Responsabilità dei genitori per l'illecito dei minori: un esercizio di precomprensione?' (2010) 2 DR.168, 175; Silvia Monti, 'Responsabilità dei genitori: alcune riflessioni' (2014) 11 DR 1054, 1060–61.

[107] Patti (n 104) 329.

[108] ibid 329–30. Warning against the negative effects of compulsory insurance on the goal of avoiding accidents, see also Chiarella (n 105) 986. cf Monti (n 106).

[109] Antonio La Torre, L'assicurazione nella storia delle idee. La risposta giuridica al bisogno di sicurezza economica: ieri e oggi (Giuffrè 2000) 276–77 and fns 659–660 (referring to liability for things in one's keeping and to liability for dangerous activities). cf Coggiola (n 97) 228 (excluding that insurability influences courts in product liability cases).

[110] See eg n 34 and accompanying text in subsection 3.4.3.

198   JUSTIFYING STRICT LIABILITY

cast on loss spreading, with the result that the significance of this argument looks weaker in Italy than in the French or even in the US context.

From the 1960s, Italian tort law (and private law more generally) has undergone a process of profound transformation under the guidance of legal scholars.[111] Taking the constitutional principle of social solidarity as a source of inspiration,[112] legal scholars started to reframe the fundamental question of tort law, which shifted from 'why the harm-doer should be held liable [to] why the victim should bear the loss'.[113] This new approach went hand in hand with an expansion of the list of legally protected interests[114] and with a reassessment of the role of fault, which lost its primacy within the system and became one of the many criteria laid down in the *Codice civile* for imposing liability.[115] In this new framework, tort law was seen as one of the instruments available to protect citizens from the 'adversities of life', and firms as able to 'contribute to a project for the "global" protection of individuals against harms connected to life in society'.[116] In this intellectual climate, distributive issues moved to the forefront, and the spreading of losses became key, especially in relation to the strict liability of firms, as a means to protect victims.

In parallel with these developments, the economic analysis of tort law emerged and gained ground in Italy, with two main approaches proving particularly influential. First, as already discussed,[117] Trimarchi's theory of *responsabilità per rischio di impresa* suggests that strict liability should apply wherever the defendant's activity presents a minimum of continuity and organization and the relevant risk of harm can be calculated and therefore absorbed through spreading mechanisms.[118] If this were not the case, strict liability would not promote accident avoidance and social welfare and would simply inflict hard blows on unprepared defendants.[119] For Trimarchi, the availability of insurance or other spreading devices is key because it helps to decide which categories of defendants should be held strictly liable and which not. However, his avowed primary goal of strict liability is the efficient avoidance of accidents,[120] with the distribution of losses being expressly seen as

---

[111] For a recent account of these developments, see Francesco D Busnelli and Salvatore Patti, *Danno e responsabilità civile* (3rd edn, Giappichelli 2013) 138 ff; Giovanni Marini, 'Gli anni settanta della responsabilità civile. Uno studio sulla relazione pubblico/privato (parte I)' (2008) 1 RCDP 23, 27–29.

[112] Article 2 of the Italian Constitution reads as follows: 'The Republic recognises and guarantees the inviolable rights of the person, both as an individual and in the social groups where human personality is expressed. The Republic expects that the fundamental duties of political, economic, and social solidarity be fulfilled' (translation available at https://www.senato.it/documenti/repository/istituzione/costituzione_inglese.pdf). See Stefano Rodotà, *Il Problema della Responsabilità Civile* (Giuffrè 1964) 105ff.

[113] Marini (n 111) 27.

[114] See eg Francesco D Busnelli, *La lesione del credito da parte di terzi* (Giuffrè 1964); Rodotà (n 112); Renato Scognamiglio, 'Illecito (diritto vigente)' Noviss Dig It (UTET 1962) VIII, 164.

[115] Rodotà (n 112) 127 ff.

[116] Rodotà (n 95) 599.

[117] See text to nn 74–79 in subsection 3.2.3 and text to nn 54–59 in subsection 3.3.3.

[118] Trimarchi (n 95) 36, 44; Trimarchi (n 101) 280, 285, 359–60.

[119] Trimarchi (n 101) 359.

[120] ibid 275–80.

subordinated to it.[121] Along with Trimarchi's theory of *rischio di impresa*, the work of Calabresi in the United States has had a great influence on Italian scholars. As has been seen,[122] in Calabresi's work the spreading of losses plays a fundamental role in seeking to minimize the secondary costs of accidents and, in turn, the total sum of the costs of accidents. In both Trimarchi's and Calabresi's view, compensating victims and spreading losses cannot be the sole concern, for otherwise solutions such as a comprehensive system of social security or first-party insurance would score far better than tort law and all its costly procedures; if there is a law of torts, it is because the legal system wishes to reduce the risks of accidents.[123]

As a result of the convergence of these intellectual movements—one stressing the importance of social solidarity and the other elaborating on the insights of law and economics—loss spreading emerged as an important justification for strict liability during the 1970s. All this is particularly evident in relation to employers' vicarious liability and strict product liability, for it is in these contexts that firms were typically involved and that the need to protect weaker parties as well as to accomplish a rational distribution of losses was felt more acutely.

As already seen,[124] Trimarchi's theory was and is frequently invoked to justify employers' vicarious liability. While different scholars interpret the theory in different ways, many of them consider the ability to spread losses as one of the reasons for imposing vicarious liability on employers,[125] and at times accord to it even more importance than what Trimarchi himself does. By prescribing that employers internalize the costs of accidents caused by their employees, the theory of *rischio di impresa* leads them to rely on insurance and enterprise spreading, therefore achieving a distribution of losses which aligns with economic rationality and the principle of social solidarity.[126] More difficult to disentangle is the position of judges: occasionally, they refer to *rischio di impresa* and state that the damage caused by the employees must be treated as a cost of the employer's business;

---

[121] ibid 8, 279–80. See also Trimarchi (n 95) 30–38.

[122] See text to nn 65–66 in this section.

[123] Trimarchi (n 101) 279; Calabresi (n 1) 43–44.

[124] See text to nn 80–84 in subsection 3.2.3.

[125] See eg Monateri (n 104) 979 but cf 1003 (observing that the primary goal of all tort doctrines and rules should be providing incentives for an efficient avoidance of accidents); Salvi (n 96) 201–03; Mauro Sella, *La responsabilità civile nei nuovi orientamenti giurisprudenziali* (Giuffrè 2007) 1150–51; Massimo Franzoni, *L'illecito. Trattato della responsabilità civile* (2nd edn, Giuffrè 2010) 762–63, 767–69. cf Paolo Forchielli, *Responsabilità civile*, vol II (CEDAM 1969) 56–60 (rejecting both insurability and enterprise spreading as proper justifications for employers' vicarious liability); Guido Alpa, *La responsabilità civile: principi* (2nd edn, UTET 2018) 448 (suggesting that loss spreading, as any other justification, cannot by itself justify employers' vicarious liability).

[126] Guido Alpa, *Responsabilità dell'impresa e tutela del consumatore* (Giuffrè 1975) 397 (arguing that, by founding article 2049 on the theory of *rischio di impresa*, and therefore by giving to it a broad interpretation, 'it would be possible to meet the demands of "social solidarity" which the Constitutional Chart features among the "fundamental principles" of the [Italian] system'). See also Civ (III) 22.10.2004 n.20588, [4], which, in reconstructing the academic views as to the foundation of article 2049 Cod civ, refers both to *rischio di impresa* and to the constitutional principle of social solidarity, emphasizing their loss-spreading implications.

200   JUSTIFYING STRICT LIABILITY

however, they do not provide any further clarification, with the result that it is difficult to pinpoint their reading of Trimarchi's theory and to understand whether there is any concern in particular, be it accident avoidance, the spreading of losses, or victim protection, which drives their reasoning.[127] True, one may argue that the courts are fully aware of the loss-spreading component of Trimarchi's theory, and yet it is noteworthy that they virtually never make any direct reference to it.[128]

It is, however, in the context of product liability in the 1970s that the convergence between social solidarity and law and economics became more evident and that legal scholars engaged in a lively discussion on loss spreading. At a time when there was no dedicated law governing the extra-contractual liability of manufacturers (the Product Liability Directive coming into force only a decade later), individual scholars differed as to the provisions of the *Codice civile* to which they appealed to find a ground for strict product liability, such as article 2049 on employers' vicarious liability, article 2050 on liability for dangerous activities, or article 2051 on liability for things in one's keeping. Regardless of the provisions relied upon, major works in the field such as those by Alpa and Castronovo devoted considerable attention to loss spreading and to the idea that firms would have the ability to distribute the costs of accidents via insurance and higher prices.[129] Particularly supportive of loss spreading was Castronovo who, in embracing Calabresi's approach, argued in his early writings that the spreading of losses was a fundamental concern of tort law,[130] that such concern found expression in the constitutional principle of social solidarity,[131] and that loss spreading could even be the settling criterion in allocating losses where it was difficult to identify the cheapest cost avoider.[132]

Given all this, one would have expected loss spreading to thrive in Italian legal reasoning and establish itself as a truly dominant justification, but in fact the argument did not manage to break through and today it looks less significant than justifications such as risk, accident avoidance, or victim protection. How has this

---

[127] See eg Civ (III) 20.6.2001 n.8381, [2.1]; Civ (sezione lavoro) 11.1.2010 n.215, [5]. On rare occasions the courts refer to *rischio di impresa* in relation to liability for dangerous activities: see Civ (III) 10.10.2014 n.21426, (2015) 1 Foro It 1303; Civ (III) 29.5.1989 n.2584, [2], (1990) 1 GI 234.

[128] cf Civ (III) 19.7.2012 n.12448, (2012) 1 GC 2297 (mentioning insurance as one of the options available to the defendant in order to handle risks of harm in a 'more effective, rational and less expensive way' than the victims of the torts of their employees).

[129] See Alpa (n 126) 70–84, 294–309, 334–40, 453–59; Carlo Castronovo, *Problema e sistema nel danno da prodotti* (Giuffrè 1979) ch 5. See also Ugo Carnevali, *La responsabilità del produttore* (Giuffrè 1974) 47–50; Gustavo Ghidini, 'Prevenzione e risarcimento nella responsabilità del produttore' (1975) Rivista delle società 530, 532–33, 545; Gianmaria Volpe, 'Esercizio di attività pericolose, rischio d'impresa e controllo delle tecnologie' (1974) 4–5 GM 381, 382–83. More recently, see Massimo Franzoni, 'La responsabilità del produttore di beni di consumo' (1993) 1 Diritto ed economia delle assicurazioni 3, 6–7; Franzoni (n 125) 652–53 (arguing that strict product liability performs an exclusively compensatory function and adding, by referring to both Trimarchi and Calabresi at fn 11, that it is appropriate to attribute the costs of accidents to manufacturers because they are in the best position to spread such costs, through insurance and pricing).

[130] Castronovo (n 129) 628–29, 634–35.

[131] ibid 595ff.

[132] ibid 654–55 (including fn 218), 797–98.

happened? The explanation must be found in the criticisms made against the argument and in the turn which economic analysis has taken in Italy. First, some of the same scholars who mentioned loss spreading as a reason for imposing strict liability on firms cast doubt on the idea that they are always in a position to spread the costs of their liabilities: on the one hand, adjusting prices to reflect these costs may not be possible because of the specific conditions of market competition and of consumers demand, or because of the costs of raw materials and workforce; on the other hand, insurance cover may not be available for certain types of risks, and there may be indemnity ceilings as well as other terms in insurance policies which in effect prevent a meaningful spreading of losses.[133] Secondly, scholars such as Ponzanelli warned that an excessive reliance on the combination of strict liability and liability insurance could distort the dynamics of the insurance market, increase the administrative costs of the tort system, undermine the protection of the weaker parties (with poorer consumers cross-subsidizing richer ones), and hinder the avoidance of accidents.[134] Thirdly, the whole idea of making consumers or other third parties the ultimate payers of firms' liability was seen as the product of a market logic which translated liability into a subsidy to firms[135] and encouraged firms to carry on 'morally repugnant' cost–benefit analyses.[136] Fourthly, as Marini suggests in his reconstruction of the development of Italian tort theory of the 1970s, legal scholars (especially from the left) failed to appreciate to the full the significance of Calabresi's theory and its distributive implications: they distrusted Calabresi's emphasis on the market as a mechanism to avoid accidents ('market deterrence') and failed to realize that he put collective decision-making ('specific deterrence') next to it as a complementary strategy for the avoidance of accidents;[137] at the same time, legal scholars did not realize the fundamental role that distributive concerns played in Calabresi's approach and his constant balancing exercise between the two goals of avoiding accidents and spreading losses.[138] Fifthly, in the field of law and economics, accident avoidance and allocative efficiency receive

---

[133] Alpa (n 126) 454–58; Mario Bessone, 'Profili della responsabilità del produttore nell'esperienza italiana' in Guido Alpa and Mario Bessone (eds), *Danno da prodotti e responsabilità dell'impresa— Diritto italiano ed esperienze straniere* (Giuffrè 1980) 9, 11, 37–38 (perhaps partly for this reason, Bessone makes clear that firms should be liable regardless of insurance, for they can anyway pass the cost of liability on to consumers through pricing or otherwise absorb it); Marino Bin, 'L'assicurazione della responsabilità civile da prodotti' in Guido Alpa, Marino Bin, and Paolo Cendon (eds), *Trattato di diritto commerciale e diritto pubblico dell'economia. La responsabilità del produttore* (CEDAM 1989) 273.

[134] Giulio Ponzanelli, 'Nuove figure di danno alla persona e tecniche assicurative' (1989) RCP 409, 405–06, 421; Giulio Ponzanelli, *La responsabilità civile. Profili di diritto comparato* (Il Mulino 1992) 103–04 (criticizing the approaches of James and Calabresi).

[135] Alpa (n 126) 302–03; Marini (n 111) 59.

[136] Marini (n 111) 60 (adding that, in 1970s, some legal scholars thought that if manufacturers could systematically resort to insurance, then the ability of tort law to reduce the risk of accidents would be frustrated).

[137] Giovanni Marini, 'Gli anni settanta della responsabilità civile. Uno studio sulla relazione pubblico/privato (parte II)' (2008) 2 RCDP 229, 234–44.

[138] ibid 234, 240.

more attention than loss spreading today. Certainly, the influence of Calabresi is visible in the work of a high number of Italian legal scholars, and even courts,[139] but not many of either have put particular emphasis on the spreading of losses. A notable exception is Castronovo: besides espousing the model of the 'cheapest cost avoider' for purposes of accident avoidance, he keeps recognizing the importance of diluting the costs of accidents and thinks that loss-spreading considerations may be decisive when devising the strict liability of *firms or other professional entities*, for these can generally pass the costs of liability on to consumers/users.[140] And we earlier saw that Trimarchi recognizes a role, even if subordinated, to distributive concerns, and that he considers the ability to spread losses as a condition for imposing strict liability.[141] Apart from these scholars, however, other leading Italian academics working in the field of law and economics either marginalize or treat with caution distributional considerations (and hence spreading-based arguments), on the basis that these may be in potential conflict with the primary goal of avoiding accidents efficiently.[142]

As a result of all this, the role of loss spreading in Italy is not as prominent as in France or even as in the United States. Whether out of fear for the undesirable effects that an excessive reliance on loss spreading may have on accident avoidance, or because of the perverse results to which it may lead in terms of subsidizing firms and of cross-subsidizing richer consumers, in the Italian context loss spreading is approached with some caution. This is true even for instances of reasoning where the protection of victims is central and which, as such, may be thought to have everything to gain by relying on loss spreading. In this respect, the contrast with France is striking, for there the paramount goal of victim protection finds an indispensable buttress in loss spreading, which is therefore widely relied upon. In Italy, victim protection is also one of the most common arguments for the imposition of strict liability,[143] but the loss-spreading justification is not used as frequently to support it. In addition to this, many of the legal scholars currently engaging with

---

[139] See Roberto Pardolesi and Bruno Tassone, 'Guido Calabresi on Torts: Italian Courts and the Cheapest Cost Avoider' (2008) 4 Erasmus Law Review 7.

[140] Carlo Castronovo, *Responsabilità civile* (Giuffrè 2018) 23–24. The same does not hold true, however, for contexts of liability where physical individuals are typically involved, such as liability for things in one's keeping or for the actions of animals, liability for ruinous buildings and liability for traffic accidents. In these contexts, potential defendants and potential claimants are in a similar position from the perspective of their spreading abilities, and therefore the key justification of such strict liabilities lies not in loss spreading but rather in accident avoidance: see ibid 24. See also Carlo Castronovo, 'Danno da prodotti (dir. it. e stran.)' Enc Giur (Treccani 1995) X, 1, [9.2] at 12 (criticizing the adoption of the development risk defence in the Product Liability Directive and in the Italian implementing law also on the ground that, ultimately, 'a better distribution of losses would be achieved if the cost of the accident were allocated to the manufacturer').

[141] See text to nn 118–121 in this section.

[142] See Robert Cooter and others, *Il mercato delle regole—Analisi economica del diritto civile—I. Fondamenti* (Il Mulino 2006) 222–23; Enrico Baffi and Dario Nardi, 'Colpa e livelli di attività: il contributo della Law and Economics' (2014) 1 RCDP 137, 138–39; Enrico Baffi and Dario Nardi, 'L'analisi economica del diritto e la giurisprudenza' (2016) 10 DR 1012, 1017, text to fn 9.

[143] See subsection 3.6.3.

the economic analysis of law ignore loss spreading and prefer focusing on the effects that tort rules have on the efficient avoidance of accidents. In this respect, the Italian reasoning departs to some extent from the approach adopted in the United States, where a higher number of prominent legal economists attach weight to the spreading of losses (and other distributive considerations).

In addition to all this, Italian legal actors do not give any consideration to burden–benefit proportionality in discussing the liability of private persons or bodies, marking a striking contrast with the approach of several US scholars and courts.[144] The position is somewhat different in relation to the strict liability of public bodies, as here Italian legal actors do occasionally rely upon proportionality of burdens and benefits as well as on taxation spreading, sometimes in combination together and sometimes in juxtaposition with accident avoidance and/or victim protection. As far as proportionality of burdens and benefits is concerned, the main thrust of the reasoning here is that when the public administration achieves its objectives by sacrificing the interests of a particular person, the individual so affected should be compensated and their loss proportionately borne by all members of society.[145] Especially when compared to the French approach, though, the overall significance of this argument in Italy should not be exaggerated: in Italian law, the contexts of liability for which this argument is invoked are far fewer and justifications of an entirely different nature (eg accident avoidance, victim protection) are seen as more attractive.

Similar remarks are in order in relation taxation spreading. This argument features occasionally in the reasoning of Italian legal actors as an express reason for imposing strict liability on public bodies, sometimes in combination with proportionality of benefits and burdens, at other times in juxtaposition with victim protection and/or accident avoidance.[146] The impression is that, while taxation

---

[144] See subsection 3.5.3.

[145] See Renato Alessi, *La responsabilità della pubblica amministrazione* (Giuffrè 1955) 120ff (in relation to, for example, lawful administrative acts such as takings, the destruction or occupation of private property, the killing of animals for reasons of public health, or the imposition of easements in the public interest); Giovanni Duni, *Lo Stato e la responsabilità patrimoniale* (Giuffrè 1968) 18, 573, 582; Guido Corso, 'La responsabilità della pubblica amministrazione da attività lecita' (2009) 2 Diritto amministrativo 203, 224–26 (juxtaposing proportionality of burdens and benefits with victim protection and accident avoidance to explain the expansion of public liability, for both physical and administrative activities); Elisa Scotti, 'Appunti per una lettura della responsabilità dell'amministrazione tra realtà e uguaglianza' (2009) 3 Diritto amministrativo 521, 591–92 (juxtaposing proportionality of burdens and benefits with accident avoidance, in relation to administrative activities); Alessandra Dominici, 'La responsabilità oggettiva in materia di appalti: il Consiglio di Stato si allinea alle pronunce del giudice comunitario' (2013) 1 Rivista amministrativa degli appalti 41, 65 (combining proportionality of burdens and benefits with taxation spreading, in juxtaposition with accident avoidance, for the purpose of justifying a generalized strict liability for administrative activity). For a general discussion of the evolution of the principle of social solidarity in the law of accidents, see also Andrea Crismani, *Le indennità nel diritto amministrativo* (Giappichelli 2012) 96–125, esp 110–15 (emphasizing the importance of the principles of social solidarity and equality among citizens, and therefore of proportionality of burdens and benefits, as the basis of the state's obligation to make monetary reparation for the harm caused by lawful public actions or activities).

[146] See eg Federico Cammeo, *Corso di diritto amministrativo*, vol III (La Litotipo 1914) 1359–60 (combining taxation spreading with victim protection); Alberto Romano, *Giurisdizione amministrativa*

204 JUSTIFYING STRICT LIABILITY

spreading may feature in the Italian reasoning less often than proportionality of benefits and burdens as a rationale of strict public liability, redistributing losses through taxation is perceived as key if public bodies are to compensate the victims of accidents by the imposition of strict liability and therefore give effect to the constitutional principle of social solidarity. In this respect, there seems to be some resemblance to the French position.[147] On the other hand, the fear that imposing too much liability on public bodies may endanger the public purse, which could be used more beneficially to improve public services,[148] may help to explain why spreading-based arguments have been used with a degree of prudence in the public field.

To conclude, in the 1970s loss spreading received considerable attention among Italian legal scholars, both because of the ethos of social solidarity which had been imbuing Italian law since the intellectual revolution initiated in the 1960s, and because of the emphasis placed on it by some prominent figures in the law and economics movements around the same years. However, the argument was also met with several criticisms and, perhaps reflecting doubts about market deterrence, many Italian scholars refrained from supporting Calabresi's view of loss spreading with any conviction. All this scepticism hampered the ascendancy of the argument as a dominant justification in the Italian context, and while it is possible that it lives covertly in generic invocations of social solidarity and more explicitly in references to Trimarchi's *rischio di impresa* (particularly in relation to vicarious liability), the argument is handled with care, especially if compared to the treatment it receives in the French and US reasoning. In some of its variants, loss spreading appears to be of some (and perhaps even growing) significance in relation to the strict liability of public bodies, but it does not currently have the status it enjoys in France and perhaps even in the United States, at least at the level of overt reasoning.

---

e limiti della giurisdizione ordinaria (Giuffrè 1975) 289–90 (discussing taxation spreading in relation to the compensability of losses due to the violation of *interessi legittimi*, though it is unclear whether he sees liability as strict or based on fault); Dominici (n 145) 65 (combining taxation spreading with proportionality of burdens and benefits, in juxtaposition with accident avoidance); Chiara Feliziani, 'L'elemento soggettivo della responsabilità amministrativa. Dialogo a-sincrono tra Corte di giustizia e giudici nazionali' (2018) 6 federalismi.it 1, 27, fn 140 (juxtaposing taxation spreading with accident avoidance and victim protection). See also Maria Pia Giracca, 'Responsabilità civile e pubblica amministrazione: quale spazio per l'art. 2049 c.c.?' (2001) 1 Foro It 3293, 3297 (juxtaposing loss spreading with risk–benefit and victim protection, in relation to the vicarious liability of public bodies); Sara Valaguzza, 'Percorsi verso una "responsabilità oggettiva" della pubblica amministrazione' (2009) 1 Diritto processuale amministrativo 50, 96–97 (juxtaposing loss spreading with accident avoidance, from a perspective of law and economics): while both authors do not expressly refer to any specific variant of loss spreading, the wording they choose points in the direction of taxation spreading.

[147] See text to and following n 47 in this section.

[148] See eg Giovanni Comandé and Luca Nocco, 'The Liability of Public Authorities in Italy' in Ken Oliphant (ed), *The Liability of Public Authorities in Comparative Perspective* (Intersentia 2016) 251, [201]–[204] (questioning whether imposing liability on public bodies can really advance the goals of compensation and deterrence, and suggesting that it would be much better 'to use that money to ameliorate the situation, rather than to distribute it as a sort of windfall, so to speak, "like the rain"').

3.5.5 Loss Spreading in England: The Most Controversial Argument of All?

Compared to the other three systems, English law is the one where loss spreading proves more controversial. In most contexts of liability, the argument is relied upon only sporadically, though with the important exception of vicarious liability, where the argument is often seen in academic and especially judicial reasoning as a key reason for strict liability. At the same time, though, several criticisms target loss spreading both within and outside the context of vicarious liability, with the result that the argument struggles to become a dominant justification for the imposition of strict liability.

A clear starting point is that, in keeping with the United States and Italy, insurance coverage is generally not considered an attractive justification for the imposition of strict liability in England. To be sure, prominent figures such as Honoré and Lord Denning rely on it: the former argues that 'there seems no moral reason to require fault as a condition of tort liability' if the defendant is insured or likely to be insured (eg because required by the law to take out insurance) and if 'the insurance premium is modest';[149] the latter, in considering motor vehicle owners' vicarious liability for traffic accidents, notes the existence of compulsory insurance and refers to the actual insurance coverage of the defendant owner as a reason for imposing strict liability on them.[150] These, however, are very rare examples of actual insurance coverage being used to support strict liability. This fact, coupled with the plethora of criticisms levelled at the loss-spreading argument in general (which include actual insurance coverage),[151] suggests that the significance of the latter is extremely limited.

---

[149] Tony Honoré, 'The Morality of Tort Law—Questions and Answers' in David G Owen (ed), *Philosophical Foundations of Tort Law* (OUP 1995) 73, 88.

[150] See *Launchbury v Morgans*, [1971] 2 QB 245, 253–55 (combining this argument (and insurability) with victim protection); *Nettleship v Weston*, [1971] 2 QB 691, 700 (using here actual insurance coverage in the tort of negligence, noting that 'morally the learner driver is not at fault; but legally she is liable to be because she is insured and the risk should fall on her'). See also Lord Denning's remarks in *Morris v Ford Motor Co Ltd*, [1973] QB 792, 798 (juxtaposing actual insurance coverage with risk–profit); *Lamb v Camden LBC*, [1981] 1 QB 625, 637–38. Another example is in Rob Merkin, 'Tort, Insurance and Ideology: Further Thoughts' (2012) 75 MLR 301, 304 (arguing that if the insurance position of the parties is known to the court, then it may be perfectly appropriate to take it into account, so as to further private intentions or statutory requirements (as in the case of compulsory insurance)). While Merkin's discussion focuses primarily on fault-based liability, his analysis should apply to strict liability as well (to which he expressly refers at 317). See also Rob Merkin and Sheila Dziobon, 'Tort Law and Compulsory Insurance' in TT Arvind and Jenny Steele (eds), *Tort Law and the Legislature: Common Law, Statute and the Dynamics of Legal Change* (Hart Publishing 2013) 303, 315. In the case of Lord Denning and of Merkin, the significance of actual insurance coverage as a justification for strict liability looks somewhat limited, as it is not entirely clear to what extent they would support the argument beyond situations where compulsory insurance arrangements are in place. By contrast, Honoré holds a more generous view as to the scope of application of the 'actual insurance coverage' argument, as he takes compulsory insurance merely as an example of when the defendant would be able to spread losses and avoid too heavy a burden on themselves: see Honoré (n 149) 88–90.

[151] See text to nn 194–210 in this section.

206 JUSTIFYING STRICT LIABILITY

By contrast, a very different picture emerges in relation to the use and significance of both insurability and enterprise spreading. As will be seen, these arguments surface in English reasoning as justifications for strict liability and, especially where firms or other large entities are involved, they are often put forward together and seen as equally important ways of spreading losses. In this respect, English reasoning resembles the US and Italian approaches where, in contrast with France, enterprise spreading is no less important than insurability.

To begin with, either or both of these two arguments are sometimes relied upon regardless of any specific context of liability. For example, Jolowicz argues that '[t]he proliferation of large enterprises and the prevalence of liability insurance have produced the result that the losses suffered by successful plaintiffs are most frequently placed in the so-called channels of distribution', most notably insurance and higher prices for consumers.[152] In his view, courts should consider the existence of these spreading mechanisms and the victims of accidents should not be refused compensation.[153] Loss spreading also features prominently in the 1978 Pearson Commission's report on civil liability and compensation for personal injuries, particularly in the part concerning the protection of individuals exposed to exceptional risks of harm.[154] In the Pearson Commission's view, the legislative introduction of strict liability would be appropriate because firms can charge 'the incidental cost of personal injuries ... to the cost of the business, and so ultimately spread [it] over all consumers of the goods or services in question',[155] adding that compulsory insurance would be 'appropriate in most cases'.[156] Finally, Honoré maintains that if there are loss-spreading mechanisms available to cushion the effects of strict liability on defendants, especially insurance, there is no moral objection to this type of liability in tort law.[157]

Turning to specific liabilities, insurability and/or enterprise spreading surface with varying frequency in a number of contexts. For example, in relation to liability for animals, the Law Commission identifies the ability of keepers of dangerous animals to insure against the risk of harm as a reason for recommending the statutory introduction of strict liability.[158] In the context of the rule in *Rylands v Fletcher*, some scholars see loss spreading as one of the reasons which led to

[152] John A Jolowicz, 'Liability for Accidents' (1968) 26 CLJ 50, 58, 61.
[153] ibid 59–63.
[154] Pearson Commission, *Report of the Royal Commission on Civil Liability and Compensation for Personal Injury*, Cmnd 7054-I (1978) ch 31.
[155] ibid [1641]–[1645] (combining loss spreading with abnormality of risk and victim protection).
[156] ibid [1668].
[157] Honoré (n 149) 89–90.
[158] Law Commission, *Civil Liability for Animals* (Law Com No 13, 1967) [14]–[18], [20] (juxtaposing insurability with abnormality of risk and accident avoidance). See also John G Fleming, *The Law of Torts* (9th edn, LBC Information Services 1998) 406 (arguing that insurability, along with abnormality of risk, justifies the exclusion of a defence based on act of a stranger); *Mirvahedy v Henley*, [2003] 2 AC 491, [157] (Lord Walker); *Welsh v Stokes*, [2007] EWCA Civ 796, [47] (Dyson LJ) (both adding accident avoidance considerations).

the establishment of the rule,[159] and which should support the rule nowadays as well.[160] Again, in relation to employers' liability to employees for breach of statutory duty, some legal scholars emphasize the ability of employers to pass the costs of workplace accidents on to consumers/users and insurers as an attractive justification for strict liability.[161] More frequent is the reliance placed on these spreading-based arguments in the context of product liability. Both the Law Commission and the Pearson Commission identify one of the reasons in favour of adopting strict liability in the producer's ability to insure against the risk of harm and pass the relevant costs on to consumers.[162] Among legal scholars, Jolowicz argues that whether or not liability insurance is taken out, the cost of manufacturers' and sellers' liability will 'be reflected in the prices that they charge' and ultimately borne by consumers and users.[163] Similarly, today scholars such as McBride and Bagshaw justify strict product liability on the basis of manufacturers' spreading abilities.[164]

It is, however, in the context of vicarious liability that insurability and/or enterprise spreading emerge most often as rationales for the imposition of strict liability, finding support in the work of several leading scholars and in many judgments of the highest judicial authorities. As early as the 1950s, Williams argues that firms may be appropriately held vicariously liable because they can insure against liability

[159] John Murphy, 'The Merits of Rylands v Fletcher' (2004) 24 OJLS 643, 665 ('the growth of large-scale industry during the latter part of that [nineteenth] century, coupled with its ability to distribute the cost of accident via insurance and higher prices, weakened the kinds of *laissez-faire* arguments that were being advanced in favour of an increasingly pervasive fault principle'). See also Jenny Steele and Rob Merkin, 'Insurance Between Neighbours: *Stannard v Gore* and Common Law Liability for Fire' (2013) 25 JEL 305, 305–06.

[160] Murphy (n 159) 665.

[161] Nigel Tomkins, 'Civil Health and Safety Law after the Enterprise and Regulatory Reform Act 2013' [2013] JPIL 203, 205 (quoting Lord Drummond Young's reasoning in the Scottish case *Cairns v Northern Lighthouse Board* [2013] CSOH 22, 2013 SLT 645, at para [37], which discusses loss spreading (from an efficiency as well as moral perspective) together with accident avoidance and, arguably, victim protection); Michael A Jones (ed), *Clerk & Lindsell on Torts* (23rd edn, Sweet & Maxwell 2020) [12-02] (again referring to Lord Drummond Young's reasoning at paras [37], [38], and [43] of his judgment, which emphasizes the importance of an efficient and fair spreading of losses, together with accident avoidance). Note that employers have the obligation to insure against their liability for personal injury to their employees: see the Employers' Liability (Compulsory Insurance) Act 1969, which came into force on 1 January 1972.

[162] Law Commission, *Liability for Defective Products* (Law Com No 82, 1977) [23], [37]–[38] (juxtaposing loss spreading with accident avoidance, risk creation, administrative cost reduction, and victim protection); Pearson Commission (n 154) [1235] (using insurability and enterprise spreading in combination with proportionality of burdens and benefits, in juxtaposition with several other arguments, including accident avoidance (mentioned at [1234]) and victim protection (mentioned at [1259] in relation to the exclusion of the development risk defence)).

[163] John A Jolowicz, 'The Protection of the Consumer and Purchaser of Goods under English Law' (1969) 32 MLR 1, 12, 14 (mentioning proportionality of burdens and benefits as well, in relation to goods that are not as advertised by the manufacturer, on which see n 177 in this section).

[164] Nicholas J McBride and Roderick Bagshaw, *Tort Law* (6th edn, Pearson Education 2018) 376–78 (juxtaposing loss spreading with accident avoidance, with nonreciprocity of risk, with an argument looking at the efficient allocation of resources (though presented as cost internalization), and with an argument resonating with victim protection). See also Christopher Newdick, 'The Future of Negligence in Product Liability' (1987) 103 LQR 288, 288 (discussing insurability and enterprise spreading, in juxtaposition with risk–profit and, arguably, victim protection).

208 JUSTIFYING STRICT LIABILITY

and, above all, because they can pass all the attendant costs on to consumers; therefore, '[t]o turn the undeserved loss of the individual into the loss of the community may accord with sound social and economic policy'.[165] Similarly, Atiyah observes that 'the primary justification of vicarious liability lies in the distribution of costs and losses throughout the customers of an industry, generally by means of insurance'.[166] More recently, Steele highlights the merits of insurance and identifies the spreading abilities of defendant employers as a key reason for imposing vicarious liability, which she considers 'the most promising route for compensation'.[167] Next to the reasoning of academics, a high number of judicial statements, mostly from the UK Supreme Court (or House of Lords), suggests that loss spreading is a key rationale of vicarious liability. In *Lister*, Lord Millet defines vicarious liability 'as a loss-distribution device',[168] adding in *Dubai Aluminium* that this device is 'based on grounds of social and economic policy'.[169] Again, in *Majrowski*, Lord Nicholls maintains that 'the financial loss from the wrongs can be spread more widely, by liability insurance and higher prices'.[170] Finally, in *CCWS*, Lord Phillips states that corporate entities 'can usually be expected to insure against the risk of such liability, so that this risk is more widely spread',[171] and that, compared to the employee, 'the employer ... can be expected to have insured against' the risk of liability.[172] In sum,

---

[165] Glanville Williams, 'Vicarious Liability and the Master's Indemnity' (1957) 20 MLR 437, 440–41 (adding that this is a 'persuasive and in some ways a satisfactory theory' except that it 'fails to explain the present law [in that] ... it is necessary to prove the servant's negligence').

[166] Patrick S Atiyah, *Vicarious Liability in the Law of Torts* (Butterworths 1967) 172, 22–28. See also Patrick S Atiyah, 'Personal Injuries in the Twenty-First Century: Thinking the Unthinkable' in Peter Birks (ed), *Wrongs and Remedies in the Twenty-First Century* (Clarendon Press 1996) 1, 16 (not expressly endorsing loss spreading but arguing that vicarious liability 'appears ... to rest on ideas of distributive justice and not of corrective justice').

[167] Jenny Steele, *Tort Law, Text, Cases, and Materials* (4th edn, OUP 2017) 578–81 (combining loss spreading with the deep-pockets rationale and victim protection, and juxtaposing them with accident avoidance, risk creation, and risk–benefit). See also Ewan McKendrick, 'Vicarious Liability and Independent Contractors: A Re-Examination' (1990) 53 MLR 770, 784 (arguably combining loss spreading with victim protection); Fleming (n 158) 410 (juxtaposing loss spreading with risk–profit, the deep-pockets argument, and accident avoidance).

[168] *Lister v Hesley Hall Ltd*, [2002] 1 AC 215, [65] (also mentioning risk–benefit).

[169] *Dubai Aluminium Co Ltd v Salaam and Others*, [2003] 2 AC 366, [107].

[170] *Majrowski v Guy's and St Thomas's NHS Trust*, [2006] UKHL 34, [9] (juxtaposing loss spreading with victim protection, the deep-pockets rationale, accident avoidance and, perhaps, risk creation).

[171] *Various Claimants v Catholic Child Welfare Society*, [2012] UKSC 56, [2013] 2 AC 1, [34] [*CCWS*].

[172] ibid [35]. See also *Various Claimants v Barclays Bank plc*, [2017] EWHC 1929 (QB), [45] (applying all the five factors indicated by Lord Phillips in *CCWS*, including insurability). In *WM Morrison Supermarkets plc v Various Claimants*, [2018] EWCA Civ 2339, [78], the Court of Appeal observes that, faced with the possibility of massive data breaches resulting in a large number of claims for potentially ruinous amounts, the solution is for companies 'to insure against such catastrophes ... and losses caused by dishonest or malicious employees'. On the other hand, the court rejects the 'actual insurance coverage' argument: 'We have not been told what the insurance position is in the present case, and of course it cannot affect the result. The fact of a defendant being insured is not a reason for imposing liability, but the availability of insurance is a valid answer to the Doomsday or Armageddon arguments put forward ... on behalf of Morrisons': ibid [78]. Note, however, that the UK Supreme Court reversed this decision, although it did not consider at all the Court of Appeal's remarks on insurability: see *WM Morrison Supermarkets plc v Various Claimants*, [2020] UKSC 12, [2020] 2 WLR 941. For another example from the Court of Appeal, see *Viasystems (Tyneside) Ltd v Thermal Transfer (Northern) Ltd*, [2006] QB 510, [55] (Rix LJ) (observing that '[l]iability is extended to the employer on the practical

in the law of vicarious liability there is widespread reliance on loss spreading in the form of insurability and/or enterprise spreading and, while these arguments are invariably combined or juxtaposed with many others (above all the various permutations of risk), English scholars and especially courts appear to hold them in very high regard.

Taking a step back from the materials discussed above, some interesting points emerge regarding the use of insurability and enterprise spreading as justifications for strict liability in English tort law. First, there are substantial variations in the frequency with which these arguments are used across the various strict liabilities. While rarely invoked in a majority of contexts, they occasionally surface in discussions on product liability and, more importantly, they are used on a regular basis in legal reasoning (especially judicial) regarding the law of vicarious liability. In this respect, there is some resemblance with the US approach, for there too loss spreading is used more conspicuously in contexts of this type, where firms or other large entities are involved. Secondly, we saw that in Italy and especially in the United States insurability and enterprise spreading are sometimes put forward by legal scholars working in the field of law and economics. This way of looking at loss spreading is difficult to find in the English context, a rare example being the support in *Clerk and Lindsell* and in a scholarly article by Tomkins of economic reasoning to criticize the Enterprise and Regulatory Reform Act 2013 for abolishing employers' strict liability for breach of statutory duty.[173] An explanation for the scarce frequency of this pattern is that, apart from Atiyah, English scholars show scant interest in law and economics. And even Atiyah, who has always paid attention to Calabresi's approach, is very cautious about its usefulness for English law. In particular, he argues that the goals of avoiding accidents and spreading losses may conflict and be difficult to reconcile.[174] Moreover, given the inherent difficulties in operating the complex approach envisaged by Calabresi, Atiyah suggests that 'it is not easy to see why—in the field of personal injuries and sickness—the loss distribution function should not be undertaken by a social security system paid for out of taxation'.[175]

A further spreading-based justification which features in the reasoning of English legal actors is proportionality of burdens and benefits. A pattern that emerges is the tendency to use this argument in contexts where public bodies

---

assumption that, inter alia, because he can spread the risk through pricing and insurance, he is better organised and able to bear that risk than the employee') (also putting forward accident avoidance and risk–profit justifications).

[173] See n 161. A further example may, perhaps, be Lord Millett's definition of vicarious liability as 'a loss distribution device based on grounds of social and *economic* policy': see *Dubai Aluminium* (n 169) [107] (emphasis added).

[174] Patrick S Atiyah, *Accidents, Compensation and the Law* (3rd edn, Weidenfeld & Nicholson 1980) 603–06.

[175] ibid 612.

rather than private entities are the defendants. As regards the latter, whether they are physical individuals or firms, it is certainly possible to come across burden–benefit proportionality. For example, in maintaining that the imposition of strict liability is justified so long as its costs are spread rather than left concentrated on the defendant, Honoré argues for a 'system that redistributes losses among those who benefit from the activities that cause them'.[176] Similarly, in its recommendations on the reform of product liability the Pearson Commission states that 'it [is] justifiable and sensible that consumers as a whole should pay for the cost of insuring against injuries caused by a *product from which they benefit*, just as they pay for its other costs'.[177] However, examples of this type which deploy burden–benefit proportionality to justify strict liability in private parties are rare and relatively old. As a result, this pattern of reasoning appears to have modest significance in the English context, especially when compared to the US approach;[178] instead, other spreading-based arguments are more popular.

The picture looks different, though, when we turn to the liability of public authorities. In this area, there are very prominent legal scholars who advocate the adoption of rules of strict liability on the basis of a proportional sharing of burdens and benefits. For example, Craig argues that the normative foundations of the case law on nuisance are questionable, that '[i]t is harsh to make the individual bear the loss arising from socially beneficial activities', and that '[t]here is a strong argument for placing the cost on those who take the benefit of the relevant activity'.[179] Similarly, Bell (who has worked extensively on French law) maintains that where the harm caused by an administrative activity is planned, as in cases of expropriation, or it is a foreseeable though unintended result of an activity, as in the case of experimental medical techniques, the ideal of burden–benefit proportionality suggests that the administration should compensate the victim of the loss.[180]

---

[176] Honoré (n 149) 90. He also provides a specific example concerning traffic accidents: 'Loss spreading is indeed often achieved by a form of distributive justice that allocates burdens roughly in proportion to benefits. Those who benefit from some activity, say motoring, are made to bear a proportionate share of the losses that the activity causes, for example through compulsory third-party insurance' (89). Note, however, that for Honoré '[t]his does not entail that loss spreading is an aim of the tort system as such, merely that some form of insurance is essential if a system of corrective justice is to operate fairly in modem conditions' (90).

[177] Pearson Commission (n 154) [1235] (emphasis added). See also *Hammersmith and City Railway Co v Brand*, (1866-67) LR 2 QB 223, 231 (Baron Bramwell observing that compensation for losses caused by running locomotives 'comes from the public which gets the benefit'); Jolowicz (n 163) 14 (arguing that 'to pass on to purchasers as a whole the cost of carrying the risk that the goods may not always measure up to the claims made for them by their advertisements is only to require them to take the rough with the smooth. If advertising helps to keep down prices by promoting sales, then those who benefit from that should carry the financial risks that are involved').

[178] See text to nn 71–76 in this section.

[179] Paul Craig, *Administrative Law* (9th edn, Sweet & Maxwell 2021) [30–055]. The author makes a similar point in relation to the rule in *Rylands v Fletcher* (at [30–060]) and recognizes burden–benefit proportionality as the rationale of compensatory arrangements such as those laid down in the Land Compensation Act 1973 and in the Vaccine Damage Payment Act 1979 (at [30–072]).

[180] John Bell, 'Governmental Liability in Tort' (1995) 6 NJCL 85, 88–89, 99–100 (discussing proportionality of burdens and benefits together with Honoré's theory of outcome responsibility, on which see subsection 3.8.3).

LOSS SPREADING   211

Many other examples of proportionality of burdens and benefits being seen as a persuasive argument to justify the strict liability of public authorities can be found in the English academic literature.[181] This argument is, by contrast, approached with caution by judges. Certainly, there are examples of judicial reasoning using burden–benefit proportionality. For instance, in cases involving claims in nuisance and under the Human Rights Act 1998, English courts have relied on this argument to hold the defendant public body liable for losses caused by an activity carried on in the general interest, as where a public authority decides for reasons of expense not to prevent the continuance of periodic sewerage flooding of private premises,[182] or where the operations of an RAF station caused noise and disturbance to neighbouring landowners.[183] Similarly, in *Armes*, Lord Reed suggests that by finding the defendant local authority vicariously liable for the sexual abuse committed by foster parents to the detriment of their child, 'the burden of a risk

---

[181] See Harry Street, *Governmental Liability* (CUP 1953) 66ff, 78 (relying on proportionality of burdens and benefits to support the imposition of strict liability at least wherever exceptional harm is caused to an individual in the exercise of a physical activity by the administration); John DB Mitchell, 'Administrative Law and Parliamentary Control' (1967) 38 The Political Quarterly 360, 372 (showing appreciation for proportionality of burdens and benefits: if 'properly handled', the principle of *égalité devant les charges publiques* 'can produce a wealth of remedy of which we are not in sight'); Charles J Hamson, 'Escaping Borstal Boys and the Immunity of Office' (1969) 27 CLJ 273, esp 276–80 (seeing proportionality of burdens and benefits as attractive in relation to the public administration's deliberate imposition of a risk of harm on specific members of the public); Sue Arrowsmith, *Civil Liability and Public Authorities* (Earlsgate Press 1992) 217 (seeing proportionality of burdens and benefits as a common justification for the compensatory scheme provided for in the Land Compensation Act 1973 as well as for other instances where losses result from lawful administrative activities), 115–16 (again discussing this argument in relation to lawful administrative action, arguably in combination with victim protection); Tom Cornford, *Towards a Public Law of Tort* (Taylor and Francis 2008) ch 5, esp 51–52 including fn 21 (seeing the French version of proportionality of burdens and benefits (the principle of *égalité devant les charges publiques*) as a reason to support the imposition of strict liability on the administration wherever both the loss inflicted is exceptional if compared to the risks to which the average citizen is exposed and the relevant administrative action is undertaken in the public interest); Henry WR Wade and Christopher F Forsyth, *Administrative Law* (11th edn, OUP 2014) 660 (in relation to the rule in *Rylands v Fletcher*, arguing that 'where the [defendants] are acting for the benefit of the community, it would be altogether fairer to require them to bear liability for accidents irrespective of fault, for then the cost would be spread equitably over the users of the service instead of being charged wholly upon the unfortunate person injured'), 648 (in relation to the vicarious liability of public authorities, arguing that in *Dorset v Home Office*, [1970] AC 1004 the House of Lords 'took a noteworthy step towards spreading over the whole community the price that has to be paid for experimental penal policies, rather than requiring it to be borne by the individual victim', though this statement may refer to spreading-based arguments other than burden–benefit proportionality).

[182] *Marcic v Thames Water Utilities Ltd*, [2002] QB 929, [113]-[117]. The House of Lords reversed this decision in *Marcic v Thames Water Utilities Ltd*, [2003] UKHL 66, [2004] 2 AC 42, and held, inter alia, that there was neither an actionable nuisance, as this would have been incompatible with the statutory scheme regulating the relevant sewerage system, nor a good claim under the Human Rights Act 1998, as the statutory scheme was compatible with the claimant's rights under the European Convention on Human Rights. Note however that, at [45], Lord Nicholls refers to the Court of Appeal's invocation of proportionality of burdens and benefits and argues that this type of consideration should be taken into account by the relevant administrative authorities, for 'those who enjoy the benefit of effective drainage should bear the cost of paying some compensation to those whose properties are situated lower down in the catchment area and who, in consequence, have to endure intolerable sewer flooding'.

[183] *Dennis v Ministry of Defence*, [2003] EWHC 793 (QB), esp [46]-[47] (discussing the claim in nuisance), [63] (discussing the claim under the Human Rights Act 1998).

borne in the general interest is shared, rather than being borne solely by the victims'.[184] However, instances of judicial reasoning of this kind are sporadic and, at least for the time being, proportionality of burdens and benefits is unlikely to take hold among English judges,[185] despite the support it attracts among legal scholars. This is not surprising given the continuing centrality of fault in the realm of public liability as well as the existence of a conflicting and influential approach to the allocation of losses: as Lord Scott puts it in *Transco* in speaking about activities authorized or required by statute, 'members of the public are expected to put up with any adverse side-effects of such an activity provided always that it is carried on with due care'.[186] Here, then, there is a striking contrast with the French position, where the principle of 'equality before public burdens' has important consequences for the liability of public bodies.[187]

Finally, again in the field of public liability, taxation spreading is an argument rarely invoked in the English context.[188] Certainly, those who justify the strict liability of public authorities on grounds of loss spreading are aware that taxation mechanisms are key to sustaining financially the imposition of such liability, and yet, in keeping with the French approach,[189] they prefer to rely instead upon burden–benefit proportionality. The likely reason for this is that the latter argument is rooted in an ideal of fairness which taxation spreading lacks and which is thought therefore to provide a more appealing basis of strict public liability. In other words, while taxpayers are the obvious ultimate bearers of the costs of accidents caused by 'public' activities, the mere fact of their existence is seen as an unpalatable reason for imposing strict liability on English public bodies.

So far, this discussion has provided a picture of the uses and significance of the various permutations of loss spreading in English reasoning. A further, important pattern that emerges from the materials is the use of loss spreading as a means to facilitate compensation. Examples of this pattern can be found in Jolowicz's article

---

[184] *Armes v Nottinghamshire County Council*, [2017] UKSC 60, [2018] AC 355, [61]. See ibid [57]–[63] (putting forward a variety of further arguments, including other spreading-based justifications, the deep-pockets rationale, risk creation, risk–benefit, victim protection, an argument based on the defendant's control over the tortfeasor and an argument based on whether the tort was committed as a result of activity being taken by the tortfeasor on behalf of the defendant).

[185] See Basil Markesinis, 'Plaintiff's Tort Law or Defendant's Tort Law? Is the House of Lords Moving towards a Synthesis?' (2001) 9 Torts LJ 168, 179; Duncan Fairgrieve and Daniel Squires, *The Negligence Liability of Public Authorities* (2nd edn, OUP 2019) [5.51].

[186] *Transco plc v Stockport MBC*, [2003] UKHL 61, [2004] 2 AC 1, [89].

[187] See text to and following nn 40–49 in this section.

[188] Examples can be found in the speech of Viscount Dilhorne in *Dorset* (n 181) 1045 (arguing that 'it is wrong that those who suffer loss or damage at the hands of those who have escaped from custody as a result of negligence on the part of the custodians should have no redress save against the persons who inflicted the loss or damage who are unlikely to be able to pay'; and that 'they should not have to bear the loss themselves, whereas, if there is such a duty [of care], liability might fall on the Home Office and the burden on the general body of taxpayers'); and in Pearson Commission (n 154) [1641] (arguing that it would be the taxpayers or ratepayers who pay the costs of strict liability for the accidental harm caused by a public service involving an exceptional risk of harm).

[189] See text to and following n 47 in this section.

on liability for accidents,[190] in the Pearson Commission's report,[191] and in a variety of academic and judicial statements on vicarious liability.[192] In these instances, the court or legal scholar finds loss spreading attractive because the imposition of strict liability on someone who can spread the loss over a wider community of payers ensures that the victims of accidents will be compensated without crushing financially anyone. However, this pattern is not as widespread in England as it is in legal systems where victim protection is given a higher priority, and here the contrast with France is again particularly marked: the first and foremost concern of French law is to ensure that victims of accidents get compensation, and this result is achieved without penalizing financially the defendants thanks to spreading mechanisms. By contrast, many scholars and judges in England think that there is more to tort law than merely the compensation of victims,[193] with the result that any attempt to promote a broad and deep socialization of losses through tort law is handled with care.

It is not surprising, therefore, to see that loss spreading is met with several criticisms, especially in legal scholarship, either in general or in relation to specific contexts of strict liability.

At the level of general criticisms, many legal scholars oppose loss spreading on the ground that it is at odds with the structure and functions of tort law. For example, Cane points out that tort law is best understood as an ethical system of personal responsibility, and that any spreading function would be incompatible with its underpinning principles, backward-looking nature, and bilateral structure.[194] In a similar vein, Stapleton argues that 'so long as tort ... is viewed and structured as a system of individual responsibility, we cannot convincingly draw a moral

---

[190] Jolowicz (n 152) esp 57–61.

[191] Pearson Commission (n 154) ch 31 (on 'exceptional risks').

[192] See eg *CCWS* (n 171) [34]–[35]; *Armes* (n 184) [61], [63]; McKendrick (n 167) 784; Steele (n 167) 580.

[193] See subsection 3.6.5.

[194] See Peter Cane, 'Justice and Justifications for Tort Liability' (1982) 2 OJLS 30, 53 ('[i]nsurance and personal responsibility are incompatible ideas'); Peter Cane, 'Corrective Justice and Correlativity in Private Law' (1996) 16 OJLS 471, 480 ('to determine the incidence of tort liability on the basis of whether one or other of the parties was or could have been insured does indeed seem inconsistent with the whole notion of personal responsibility which underlies the law of tort and the concept of corrective justice'); Peter Cane, *The Anatomy of Tort Law* (Hart Publishing 1997) 228–31 (hereafter Cane, *Anatomy*); Peter Cane, 'Fault and Strict Liability for Harm in Tort Law' in William Swadling and Gareth Jones (eds), *The Search for Principle: Essays in Honour of Lord Goff of Chieveley* (OUP 1999) 171, 200–01 (rejecting Honoré's reliance on loss spreading to justify strict liability); Peter Cane, *Responsibility in Law and Morality* (Hart Publishing 2002) 247 (arguing that while 'liability insurance is a positively desirable adjunct to civil law responsibility rules and principles because it enables injurers to fulfil obligations of repair that would otherwise be beyond their resources', tort law 'should [not] take account of whether the defendant was insured against liability or could have bought such insurance'); Peter Cane and James Goudkamp, *Atiyah's Accidents, Compensation and the Law* (9th edn, CUP 2018) 238 ('tort law is, at bottom, a system of rules and principles of personal responsibility for conduct and its consequences; and, although tort law could not operate as effectively as it does as a compensation system, and would probably not have developed as it has, without widespread liability insurance, the basis of tort liability is personal responsibility, not the availability of insurance').

214 JUSTIFYING STRICT LIABILITY

distinction between defendants merely on the basis of their capacity to share or offload that responsibility onto others in an insurance pool'.[195] And Morgan warns courts not to bend tort law to serve the purposes of victim protection and loss spreading, and encourages them to 'reaffirm their commitment to the principle of individual responsibility and corrective justice, which alone can explain the law of tort'.[196] Again, Nolan suggests that using a 'mechanism of corrective justice' such as tort law 'to pursue broader social goals of compensation [ie loss spreading] and deterrence will inevitably lead to incoherence'.[197] Finally, McBride puts forward a rights-based approach to tort law in which reasons of public interest, which include the spreading of losses, can never be reasons for imposing liability, but only for denying it.[198] Moreover, while legal scholars recognize that insurance has an enormous impact on the practical operation of the tort system,[199] and do not exclude that courts are sometimes influenced by the actual insurance coverage of the parties,[200] they warn that judges are ill-equipped to decide tort cases based on mechanisms (eg insurance) about which they know relatively little, especially where the insurance position of the parties is unknown.[201]

Turning now to specific contexts of strict liability, criticisms of loss spreading can be identified in relation to the rule in *Rylands v Fletcher* and to strict product liability, although the vast majority of them is concentrated in the law of vicarious liability, which is hardly surprising as vicarious liability is the context in which loss spreading is most forcefully supported. As regards the rule in *Rylands*, Lord Hoffmann in *Transco* considers Baron Bramwell's approach in *Rylands* itself (and in some nuisance cases) and argues that '[i]t is tempting to see, beneath the surface of the rule, a policy of requiring the costs of a commercial enterprise to be internalised; to require the entrepreneur to provide, *by insurance or otherwise*, for the risks to others which his enterprise creates'; however, he continues, the fear of hindering economic growth prevented the development of any broad principle of

---

[195] Jane Stapleton, 'Tort, Insurance and Ideology' (1995) 58 MLR 820, 825. See also *Romford Ice and Cold Storage v Lister*, [1957] AC 555, 576–77 (Viscount Simonds); *Hunter v Severs*, [1994] 2 AC 350, 363 (Lord Bridge).

[196] Jonathan Morgan, 'Tort, Insurance and Incoherence' (2004) 67 MLR 384, 400 (and worriedly acknowledging, at 386, that insurance spreading is sometimes seen by the courts as a 'positive reason for imposing liability in negligence').

[197] Donal Nolan, 'Causation and the Goals of Tort Law' in Andrew Robertson and Hang Wu Tang (eds), *The Goals of Private Law* (Hart Publishing 2009) 165, 189.

[198] Nicholas McBride, 'Rights and the Basis of Tort Law' in Donal Nolan and Andrew Robertson (eds), *Rights and Private Law* (Hart Publishing 2012) 331, 364–65.

[199] Richard Lewis, 'The Relationship between Tort Law and Insurance in England and Wales' in Gerhard Wagner (ed), *Tort Law and Liability Insurance* (Springer 2005) 47.

[200] See eg Malcom A Clarke, *Policies and Perceptions of Insurance Law in the Twenty-First Century* (OUP 2005) 319–20 (noting that '[a]s regards the ... the magnetic effect of available insurance, at one level the influence of insurance may be general and almost subliminal'). See also n 150 in this section, and cf Stapleton (n 195) 826–27.

[201] Clarke (n 200) 322–23, 330, 333. See also Stapleton (n 195) 829–32; Merkin (n 150) 308–10. cf Merkin and Dziobon (n 150) 315 (arguing that the argument against insurance spreading may break down 'where there is a requirement for compulsory liability insurance').

strict liability and, '[o]n the whole', it is 'no liability without fault ... which gained the ascendancy'.[202] As to strict product liability, Stapleton suggests that merely focusing on compensation and on the spreading ability of manufacturers does not provide a solid theoretical basis to the Product Liability Directive, and that it leads to serious problems of uncertainty in the attribution of liability.[203] Finally, as far as vicarious liability is concerned, many legal scholars see the loss-spreading rationale as descriptively inaccurate or normatively undesirable.[204] In particular, it is argued that this rationale cannot explain why liability attaches to 'employers of domestic staff who are without customers or insurance' and why liability is limited to cases where employees committed a tort in the course of their employment.[205] Furthermore, it is argued that the bilateral structure of tort law makes it a poor loss-spreading device and that, '[i]f the court were allowed to go beyond those two parties, it might identify a much better loss spreader than either of them'.[206] Finally, it is warned that 'there is a danger of placing too much faith in the general panacea of insurance cover' in the field of vicarious liability, for this may eventually impact adversely the insurance market and the level of premiums.[207] In addition to scholarly objections, the appropriateness of loss spreading was called into question by the UK Supreme Court's decision in *Cox*. In considering the five policy factors which in *CCWS* Lord Phillips regarded as inspiring vicarious liability,[208] the court in *Cox* discusses together the deep-pockets and loss-spreading rationales, holding that '[n]either of these is a principled justification for imposing liability',[209] and that '[a]s for insurance, employers insure themselves because they are liable: they are not liable because they have insured themselves'.[210] On the other hand, the force of this judicial statement should not be exaggerated, for several earlier as well as

---

[202] *Transco* (n 186) [29] (emphasis added).

[203] Jane Stapleton, 'Products Liability Reform—Real or Illusory?' (1986) 6 OJLS 392, 394; Jane Stapleton, *Product Liability* (Butterworths 1994) 93–95.

[204] eg Stapleton (n 195) 827–829; Cane, *Anatomy* (n 194) 228–31; Robert Stevens, 'A Servant of Two Masters' (2006) 122 LQR 201, 202; Anthony Gray, *Vicarious Liability: Critique and Reform* (Hart Publishing 2018) 139–41.

[205] Robert Stevens, *Torts and Rights* (OUP 2007) 258–59; McBride and Bagshaw (n 164) 853 (adding that '[t]here seems nothing "fair, just and reasonable" about shifting a loss onto someone else simply because he or she can absorb and spread it more easily than the person currently suffering that loss'). See also Jonathan Morgan, 'Vicarious Liability for Independent Contractors' (2016) 31 PN 235, 247–48; James Goudkamp and Donal Nolan, *Winfield & Jolowicz on Tort* (20th edn, Sweet and Maxwell 2020) [21-006].

[206] Cane, *Anatomy* (n 194) 231, 229–30. See also Birke Häcker, '*Fait d'autrui* in Comparative Perspective' in Jean-Sébastien Borghetti and Simon Whittaker (eds), *French Civil Liability in Comparative Perspective* (Hart Publishing 2019) 143, 173 (arguing that '[s]ince a defendant insures against liability, it would lead to a vicious logical circle to maintain that his liability depends on whether or not insurance will ultimately cover it').

[207] Paula Giliker, *Vicarious Liability in Tort: A Comparative Perspective* (CUP 2010) 239–40. See also Paula Giliker, 'Vicarious Liability, Non-delegable Duties and Teachers: Can You Outsource Liability for Lessons?' (2015) 31 PN 259 (discussing non-delegable duties and vicarious liability, and criticizing the tendency to see tort law merely as a loss-distribution device aiming at the compensation of victims).

[208] *CCWS* (n 171) [35].

[209] *Cox v Ministry of Justice*, [2016] UKSC 10, [2016] AC 660, [20].

[210] ibid.

subsequent judgments (such as the Supreme Court's decision in *Armes* and the Court of Appeal's decision in *Morrison Supermarkets*) suggest that the spreading ability of defendants constitutes a very important consideration in judicial reasoning.[211] More generally, therefore, in the field of vicarious liability there seems to be a profound disagreement between a majority of legal scholars, who show a clear antipathy against loss spreading, and the highest judicial authorities which see loss spreading as an important reason buttressing the imposition of vicarious liability.

Given all this, then, what is the significance of loss spreading as a justification for strict liability in English law? The overall picture is a complex one and the argument is probably the most controversial of all. In a legal milieu where the tort system is often reconstructed on the basis of principles of individual responsibility or corrective justice, loss spreading attracts many criticisms and therefore struggles to become a dominant argument. The scarcity of its use in contexts such as the rule in *Rylands*, liability for nuisance, and liability for animals, attests to this impression. However, the position changes somewhat in relation to liability for products and certain liabilities of public bodies and is dramatically different in the context of vicarious liability, where widespread reliance is placed on loss spreading (along with other arguments) to justify strict liability. Today, vicarious liability constitutes the battlefield for the clash between supporters and opponents of loss spreading; while a majority of legal scholars frown upon this argument and object to it in several ways, many other scholars do not and, perhaps more importantly, English courts seem perfectly comfortable with it as a key rationale for this liability.

3.5.6 Concluding Remarks

Overall, the patterns of use and significance of arguments based on loss spreading present marked variations across the four systems studied. These differences are inextricably linked to the ways in which the debate on the functions of tort law has unfolded and, in this respect, there are two key elements. First, the degree to which the four legal systems are committed to the idea that tort law should be concerned only with considerations of interpersonal justice, to the exclusion of broader, collective concerns. Secondly, and relatedly, the extent to which values such as social solidarity and burden–benefit proportionality or goals such as the protection of victims or the minimization of the costs of accidents influence decisions as to the allocation of losses.

In France, through the relentless work of jurists, supported in a more discreet way by the courts and the occasional intervention of the legislator, tort law has developed as a markedly socialized system for the allocation of losses, the paramount

---

[211] On *Armes* (n 184), see text to n 184 in this section; on *Morrison Supermarkets*, see n 172.

objective being the protection of victims. The value of social solidarity is highly regarded and it finds expression in the concern of ensuring that the financial costs of accidents are spread widely rather than left concentrated on any particular individual. In all this, little if any resistance comes from concerns about interpersonal justice. Since the community should stand ready to shelter the unlucky victim of an accident, abundant reliance on strict liability is natural and loss spreading appears to be a key justification for the imposition of strict liability in a wide range of contexts, whether defendants are physical individuals, firms, or public bodies.[212] Particularly prominent are insurance spreading and burden–benefit proportionality (in the form of the principle of 'equality before public burdens'), while little trace of enterprise spreading can be identified in the reasoning of French legal actors. This may be due at least in part to the general French antipathy towards the economic analysis of law, given that in other legal systems enterprise spreading is often put forward in theories rooted in law and economics.[213] It is therefore possible that French legal actors deliberately choose to steer clear of a terminology and of ideas reminiscent of economic analysis, while perfectly aware of the existence and operation of enterprise spreading. Similarly, attempts to justify the strict liability of public bodies do not often refer expressly to taxation spreading. While practically indispensable for the implementation of the principle of 'equality before public burdens', the spreading of losses through taxation is not as prominent an argument for strict liability as the proportionality of burdens and benefits. Taxation spreading lacks the immediate moral appeal which burden–benefit proportionality enjoys by its being based on an ideal of *fair* sharing of losses. In sum, inspired by the value of social solidarity, loss spreading is one of the most fundamental justifications for strict liability in French law.

In the United States, loss spreading is also a prominent justification for the imposition of strict liability but, in comparison with France, it is less pervasive, it is handled differently, and it is met with several criticisms. In common with France, the ascendancy of loss spreading is related to the effort of several scholars and courts in the first half of the twentieth century to ensure that, in situations where firms were involved, victims of accidents received adequate compensation, for firms could easily spread the costs of liabilities through insurance and pricing.[214] However, the impact of this approach has diminished over time and it is not comparable to the French experience. Moreover, in sharp contrast with French law, the emergence of law and economics has profoundly influenced the intellectual foundations of US tort law and, at least in the view of some legal economists, the spreading of losses is very important (though still subservient to the minimization of the costs of accidents or to the increase of individuals' well-being).[215]

---

[212] See generally subsection 3.5.2.
[213] See text to and preceding n 52 in this section.
[214] See text to nn 57–62 in this section.
[215] See text to nn 65–68 in this section.

218   JUSTIFYING STRICT LIABILITY

Furthermore, some legal scholars and courts entertain an understanding of loss spreading as a strategy to achieve a proportional sharing of burdens and benefits across society, in keeping with the French principle of 'equality before public burdens',[216] even though in France this argument is specific to administrative liability whereas in the United States it is put forward in relation to both private parties and public bodies. Finally, taxation spreading is conspicuously relied upon by US judges and especially scholars to explain the imposition of strict liability on public authorities or to advocate its expansion, typically on a vicarious basis.[217] The existence of these different patterns and ways of understanding loss spreading is clearly reproduced at the level of judgments, where loss spreading may be put forward alternatively or cumulatively on the basis of economic efficiency, of burden–benefit proportionality, of a desire to protect the victims of accidents, or without any of these connotations. Moreover, while in France loss spreading is regularly used regardless of the nature of the defendant (whether an individual, a firm, or a public body), in the United States loss spreading is typically—though not always—advocated in contexts of liability where firms or public bodies are involved. Furthermore, again in contrast with the French approach, insurability and enterprise spreading feature both conspicuously in US reasoning, whereas actual insurance coverage is rejected.[218] Finally, loss spreading is met in the United States with a variety of criticisms, which seek to show its perceived incompatibility with notions of corrective justice and personal responsibility, its irrelevance to issues of economic efficiency, or the inappropriateness for courts to decide distributive matters.[219]

Compared to the French and US approach, in Italian law loss spreading plays a less significant role as a justification for strict liability. The intellectual revolution which affected tort law principles and doctrines from the 1960s brought to the forefront of the discussion the need to protect victims in a spirit of social solidarity as well as the insights of the economic analysis of law, with a complete emancipation from an understanding of tort law as a system of interpersonal justice.[220] Notwithstanding the existence of such ideal conditions for its emergence as a leading argument, loss spreading has failed to thrive as one would have expected. In relation to contexts where defendants typically are physical individuals, loss spreading is all but absent,[221] while in relation to firms the argument features in discussions concerning employers' vicarious liability and product liability,[222] though not as prominently as in France or the United States. The likely explanation

---

[216] See text to nn 69–76 in this section.
[217] See text to, preceding, and following n 77 in this section.
[218] See text to nn 53–55 in this section.
[219] See text to nn 85–90 in this section.
[220] See text to nn 111–123 in this section.
[221] See text to nn 99–110 in this section.
[222] See text to nn 124–132 in this section.

for the failure of loss spreading to become a dominant justification (even where firms are involved) lies in a variety of factors: the belief that an excessive reliance on tort liability as a spreading device may have detrimental effects such as distorting the insurance market or hindering the goal of avoiding accidents, the distrust for the market logic which underlies loss spreading as put forward in the law and economics movement, and the tendency of many legal scholars influenced by the economic analysis of law to neglect distributive considerations.[223] Unsurprisingly, and perhaps as a result of this 'silence' from legal scholars, Italian courts do not mention loss spreading as a reason for imposing strict liability; whether they are influenced as a matter of fact by it (and particularly by the actual insurance coverage of the parties) is not possible to say.[224] Certainly, courts do sometimes mention Trimarchi's theory of *rischio di impresa*, mostly in relation to the employer's vicarious liability, but given their generic references to the theory it is difficult to understand their position in relation to loss spreading.[225] Finally, loss-spreading arguments are used to justify the imposition of strict liability on public bodies, whether in the form of proportionality of burdens and benefits or in the form of taxation spreading.[226] But again, their significance in Italy is not as marked as that which these arguments possess in France or even in the United States, sometimes because of a fear of undermining the financial resources of public bodies and sometimes because arguments of a different nature are seen as more attractive. In sum, overall loss spreading features less prominently in Italian reasoning than in the French or US contexts.

Finally, in English law loss spreading is surrounded by controversy and caution. The idea that tort law should be concerned with the spreading of losses is firmly rejected by all those legal scholars who see the tort system as based on notions of corrective justice or personal responsibility. Given that loss spreading embodies distributive concerns and entails considering factors that are wider than 'doing of justice' between claimant and defendant, the argument is usually seen as irreconcilable with the bilateral structure and backward-looking nature of tort law.[227] Despite these and other criticisms, though, the argument features conspicuously in academic and especially judicial reasoning as a key reason for imposing vicarious liability[228] and, though less frequently, it also surfaces in discussions concerning other contexts as well.[229] In relation to its patterns of use in English reasoning, the loss-spreading justification takes usually the form of insurability and/or enterprise spreading, whereas actual insurance coverage is widely rejected. In this respect, the

---

[223] See text to nn 133–142 in this section.
[224] See text to nn 96–97 in this section.
[225] See text to nn 127–128 in this section.
[226] See text to nn 145–147 in this section.
[227] See text to nn 194–198 in this section.
[228] See text to and following nn 165–172 in this section.
[229] See text to nn 152–164 in this section.

220   JUSTIFYING STRICT LIABILITY

English approach resembles the Italian and the US ones, while it marks a clear contrast with French law. Moreover, the use of loss spreading in the English context is at least sometimes guided by a concern to ensure that victims of accidents get compensation for their losses,[230] therefore replicating a pattern which also features in the other three legal systems. In addition, loss spreading is occasionally understood as rooted in an ideal of fairness as the proportionality of burdens and benefits,[231] especially in relation to the liability of public bodies, although this pattern is less significant than in France and in the United States. Finally, in contrast with the US and Italian approaches, loss spreading lacks the support of the economic analysis of law,[232] which has never developed in England. All this, combined with a predilection for fault-based liability, has prevented loss spreading from prospering as an argument in favour of strict liability. Even in the only context where loss spreading finds considerable support—the law of vicarious liability—many legal scholars and the UK Supreme Court's remarks in *Cox* cast doubt on its significance.

---

[230] See text to and following nn 190–192 in this section.
[231] See text to nn 176–187 in this section.
[232] See text to nn 173–175 in this section.

3.6

Victim Protection

3.6.1 Victim Protection as a Justification for Strict Liability

Protecting the victims of accidents through compensation for the harm suffered can be easily described as what tort law *does*. Indeed, whenever a judge finds a defendant liable in tort and orders them to pay compensation, the interests of the claimant are protected by means of monetary reparation. However, compensating victims may be also described not just as what tort law does but as what it *seeks to achieve*.[1]

As a goal, the protection of victims is a recurrent justification for the imposition of strict liability because the victim of an accident will more easily obtain compensation under a regime of strict liability than under a regime based on fault. In some jurisdictions, the concern to compensate victims is so prominent that judicial decisions and even more academic writings sometimes justify strict liability merely by reference to it.[2] More often, though, sheltering victims from the financial consequences of accidents constitutes the ultimate objective of a more elaborate reasoning in which arguments such as risk, the deep-pockets justification, or loss spreading are deployed to serve this paramount goal. With victim protection as the goal, these arguments can work as criteria for identifying the person liable, whether the risk creator, the risk gainer, the deeper pocket, or the best loss spreader. Once identified, the person liable (or their insurer) will pay and the goal of protecting victims through compensation can be achieved. In this sense, then, most of the justifications discussed so far—notably risk, the deep-pockets argument, and loss spreading—may be seen as means for removing losses from the victims.

In this section, I shall illustrate how the victim protection argument is used across the four systems under consideration and explore its significance as a justification for strict liability.

---

[1] Geneviève Viney, *Introduction à la responsabilité. Traité de droit civil* (4th edn, LGDJ 2019) [48]; Guido Alpa, *La responsabilità civile: principi* (2nd edn, UTET 2018) 49–50; Peter Cane, *The Anatomy of Tort Law* (Hart Publishing 1997) 206, 213; John CP Goldberg, 'Twentieth-Century Tort Theory' (2002) 91 Geo LJ 513, 521ff.

[2] See text to nn 14–18 (France) and to nn 29–31 (Italy) in this section.

Justifying Strict Liability. Marco Cappelletti, Oxford University Press. © Marco Cappelletti 2022.
DOI: 10.1093/oso/9780192859860.003.0008

3.6.2 The Ultimate Reason for Strict Liability in France?

Compared to the other three legal systems, France is the jurisdiction where the protection of victims features most prominently as a justification for the imposition of strict liability. Since the last quarter of the nineteenth century, making sure that victims of accidents receive compensation has become 'a true social imperative' stemming from the value of social solidarity,[3] which drove the expansion of tort law in general and of strict liability in particular throughout the twentieth century. This pro-victim attitude has been so strong and overwhelming in the French discourse that the expression 'compensation ideology' (*idéologie de la réparation*) has been coined to describe the phenomenon,[4] with the protection of victims acting as the yardstick of the desirability and effectiveness of liability rules.[5]

To be sure, especially in more recent times some leading, if somewhat isolated voices have been raised against the idea of reducing tort liability to an instrument of victim protection. For example, Borghetti identifies a variety of objections to this reductionist tendency: first, if compensation was all that mattered, then other systems for the redistribution of losses (such as universal no-fault plans) could do the job better than tort law; secondly, focusing exclusively on the interests of victims leads to neglect those of defendants and of society more generally; and finally, the rhetoric of compensation risks putting bodily injuries and economic losses on the same level of importance, a practice not in line with the very humanitarianism that inspires the pro-victim attitude.[6]

Despite these attempts to question the dominance of the compensation ideology, improving the position of victims remains a fundamental preoccupation of French legal actors and it informs the whole debate on the justifications of strict liability. This key role of victim protection is reflected in the breadth and degree of strictness of French strict liabilities in the law itself. For example, in relation to traffic accidents liability is extremely strict in France,[7] while it depends in some measure on the assessment of the driver's conduct in Italy and it is generally governed by fault in the United States and England.[8] Again, strict liability for the action of another is particularly broad in French law compared to the other three jurisdictions,[9] and this is especially true after the judicial interpretation of article 1384(1) (now article

---

[3] Geneviève Viney, 'De la responsabilité personnelle à la répartition des risques' Arch phil dr 1977.5, 6.

[4] Loic Cadiet, 'Sur les faits et les méfaits de l'idéologie de la réparation' in *Le juge entre deux millénaires—Mélange offerts à Pierre Drai* (Dalloz 2000) 495.

[5] Jean-Sébastien Borghetti, 'The Culture of Tort Law in France' (2012) 3 JETL 158, 173.

[6] ibid 174–75. See also Philippe Rémy, 'Critique du système français de responsabilité civile' Revue juridique de l'USEK 1997.5.49.

[7] See text to nn 243–245 in section 2.4.

[8] See text to nn 60–61 in section 2.2 (England), text to nn 156–159, including n 158 in section 2.3 (United States), and text to nn 302–306 in section 2.5 (Italy).

[9] See text to nn 51–71 in section 2.2 (England), text to nn 147–159 in section 2.3 (United States), text to nn 289–290 and nn 321–325 in section 2.5 (Italy).

1242(1)) Cc extended strict liability to defendants who have the power to organize and control the way of life of another, and to defendants who supervise or organize the activity of another.[10] Again, compared to the other three legal systems,[11] the liability of parents for the harm caused by their children is particularly strict in France.[12] Finally, in the case of public bodies, French law imposes strict liability in situations where the other three legal systems (and especially the English and the US one) would adopt a fault-based standard or even impose no liability at all.[13] What emerges from these contrasts is a strong commitment of French courts and legislator to guarantee a very high degree of protection to the victims of accidents, a concern that in the other three systems is present but is not of the same intensity as in the French context.

In order to appreciate the significance of victim protection in strict liability, attention must be now turned to the work of legal scholars. To begin with, compensating victims is so central that sometimes French strict liability is justified or explained by reference to the protection of victims without more. For example, in relation to parental liability, Viney argues that 'what justifies [this] liability is not the concern to sanction a poor upbringing or inadequate monitoring [of children], but the desire to make sure that the victim of a harm caused by the minor receives compensation.'[14] Statements to the same effect can be found in relation to many other contexts of strict liability, such as employers' vicarious liability,[15] the liability for the action of animals,[16] the liability for the damage caused by ruinous buildings,[17] and the liability for the deeds of things.[18]

---

[10] See text to nn 207–212 in section 2.4.

[11] See text to nn 154–159 in section 2.3 (England and the United States), text to nn 289–290 in section 2.5 (Italy), and text to n 38 in subsection 3.4.3 (Italy).

[12] See text to nn 215–218 in section 2.4.

[13] On public liability, see generally text to nn 87–108 in section 2.2 (England), text to nn 175–185 in section 2.3 (United States), text to nn 255–279 in section 2.4 (France), and text to nn 339–357 in section 2.5 (Italy).

[14] Geneviève Viney in Geneviève Viney, Patrice Jourdain, and Suzanne Carval (eds), *Les conditions de la responsabilité. Traité de droit civil* (4th edn, LGDJ 2013) [870] at p 1186.

[15] Georges Ripert, *La règle morale dans les obligations civiles* (4th edn, LGDJ 1949) [126] (arguing that liability for the action of another is based on the idea of guaranteeing the victims of accidents, and noting that many judicial decisions are inspired by a sentiment of commiseration for them); Nicola Molfessis, 'La jurisprudence relative à la responsabilité des commettants du fait de leurs préposés ou l'irrésistible enlisement de la Cour de cassation' in *Ruptures, movements et continuité du droit, Autour de Michelle Gobert* (Economica 2004) 495, [60] (arguing that the interest of the victim is the only justification that can explain the criteria adopted by the courts to define the doctrine of employee's abuse of functions).

[16] eg Boris Starck, Henri Roland, and Laurent Boyer, *Obligations*, t. 1, *Responsabilité délictuelle* (5th edn, LITEC 1996) [657] (arguing that the objective of this liability rule is to protect third parties from the harmful actions of animals).

[17] eg Christine Desnoyer, 'La jurisprudence relative à l'articulation des articles 1386 et 1384, alinéa 1er du Code civil. L'instrumentalisation de la règle *Specialia generalibus derogant*' RTD civ 2012.461, [40]–[41] (criticizing the way in which the Cour de Cassation interprets the rule on ruinous buildings but expressly agreeing with the view that such rule is about the protection of victims).

[18] Starck, Roland, and Boyer (n 16) [641] (again deploying their 'guarantee theory' to provide a justification for this liability rule) (see also Jérôme Julien, 'Les régimes de responsabilité du fait d'une chose' in Philippe le Tourneau (ed), *Droit de la responsabilité et des contrats. Régimes d'indemnisation*

224   JUSTIFYING STRICT LIABILITY

Much more often victim protection is discussed with other justifications. Occasionally, it is juxtaposed with arguments which enshrine goals alternative or additional to the protection of victims, as for example the avoidance of accidents or the reduction of administrative costs.[19] In these cases, however, the impression is that victim protection plays a more important role, with these other arguments acting as secondary or even make-weight justifications.[20] A second, more frequent and significant pattern consists in combining victim protection with justifications such as risk, loss spreading, or the deep-pockets argument, in this way giving rise to a more elaborate argumentation. The typical pattern of reasoning works in the following way: the party designated as liable to bear the costs of accidents is either the risk creator, the risk gainer, the deeper pocket, or the loss spreader; these criteria for determining the person liable are typically (if not always) put forward with a very specific goal in mind, which is facilitating the compensation of victims. For example, the theories of risk elaborated by Saleilles and Josserand at the turn of the twentieth century in relation to liability for the deeds of things were driven by an explicit desire to protect the victims of accidents, especially those arising in the industrial context.[21] Similarly, the deep-pockets justification often invoked in relation to the vicarious liability of employers and parents was based on the need to provide victims with a solvent defendant.[22] Again, and in more recent times, loss spreading is put forward as the mechanism that, through the imposition of strict liability, can ensure a smooth compensation of victims in a wide range of contexts of liability.[23] In all these cases, then, arguments such as risk, loss spreading,

(12th edn, Dalloz 2021) 951, [2221.13] adhering to this approach). cf Jean-Sébastien Borghetti, 'La responsabilité du fait des choses, un régime qui a fait son temps' RTD civ 2010.1, [5] (criticizing victim protection as 'too short a justification' for the imposition of strict liability).

[19] See eg Patrice Jourdain, *Les principes de la responsabilité civile* (10th edn, Dalloz 2021) 29–31 (on various rules of strict liability); Jean Calais-Auloy, 'Le risque de développement: une exonération contestable' in *Mélanges Michel Cabrillac* (Dalloz/Litec 1999) 81, 84–85 (on product liability); Geneviève Viney, 'L'indemnisation des victimes de dommages causes par le "fait d'une chose" après l'arrêt de la Cour de cassation' D chron 1982.201, 204, 205–06 (on traffic accidents).

[20] On the limited importance of accident avoidance and administrative cost reduction in France, see subsections 3.3.5 and 3.7.5, respectively.

[21] See text to nn 7–14 in subsection 3.2.2. See also Jacques Moreau, 'Rapport sur les choses dangereuses en droit administratif français' in *Travaux de l'Association Henri-Capitant: Les choses dangereuses: journées néerlandaises* (Dalloz 1971) 256, [3]–[4] (combining risk-based arguments with victim protection in relation to the liability of public bodies).

[22] René Rodière, *La responsabilité civile* (Rousseau 1952) [1472]–[1473], relying on CA Paris 20.10.1934, DH 1934.529 (the same idea is expressed in Cass crim 29.6.2011, JCP G 2012.530 no 3, para 5, at pp 864–65, note Bloch).

[23] See eg Pierre Delvolvé, *Le principe d'égalité devant les charges publiques* (LGDJ 1969) [636]–[638]; Jean-Paul Gilli, 'La "responsabilité d'équité" de la puissance publique' D chron 1971.125, 125; Jean Waline, 'L'évolution de la responsabilité extracontractuelle des personnes publiques' EDCE 1994.459, 470–71, 477 (all three scholars discussing the liability of public bodies); André Tunc, 'L'insertion de la loi Badinter dans le droit commun de la responsabilité civile' in *Mélanges Roger O. Dalcq—Responsabilité et assurances* (Larcier 1994) 557, 559 (on traffic accidents); Viney (n 14) [791-1], [813] (on employers' vicarious liability), [877] at p 1199 (on parental liability and liability for the deeds of things); Jourdain (n 19) 92 (on liability for the deeds of things). cf Jean-Sébastien Borghetti, 'The Development of Product Liability in France' in Simon Whittaker (ed), *The Development of Product Liability* (CUP 2010) 87,

or the deep-pockets one act as means to guarantee compensation and show that protecting the victims of accidents is considered the paramount goal in French law.

Overall, therefore, what is the significance of victim protection in the French reasoning? Protecting victims through compensation is probably the single most important reason put forward to justify strict liability in French law. In a sense, then, one could argue that victim protection is so important that it makes a search for further justifications superfluous: as Borghetti puts it in depicting the French approach, 'justification is not so important provided that victims are compensated'.[24] In another sense, however, looking at the role of other justifications is extremely important because this reveals the exact extent of the French commitment to the protection of victims. As already seen, in modern discussions the deep-pockets justification is of limited importance, essentially because it has been made redundant by the emergence of insurance. As to the arguments based on risk, they are certainly important especially at a theoretical level because they provide reasons to take away certain types of accidents from the fault paradigm, and therefore they constitute an attractive buttress to justify the imposition of strict liability;[25] on the other hand, they do not and cannot provide what it takes to rely as heavily on strict liability as French law in fact does. In this respect, the job is done by another extremely powerful justification, loss spreading. This argument takes on a double, crucial role in French law: like risk-based arguments, it provides theoretical support to strict liability by pointing out that the costs of accidents will be diluted across society to the point that no-one will feel a significant financial effect as a result of such accidents. At the same time, loss spreading provides practical support to strict liability by making it financially and socially sustainable, even if adopted in a wide range of contexts and if possessing great rigour. In other words, the defendant's ability to distribute widely the costs of accidents is essential to the functioning of French strict liability and to its attractiveness, and if spreading mechanisms—especially cheap insurance coverage—were not available it is very unlikely that the French commitment to protecting victims would be as passionate.[26] Therefore, it appears that the victim protection argument is very much dependent both theoretically and practically on the distribution of losses, and that the availability of spreading mechanisms draws the limits of the French willingness to resort to strict liability as a means to compensate victims.

102–03 (recognizing the interplay between the protection of victims and the spreading of losses but suggesting that the latter 'should not by itself be sufficient to justify the imposition of liability').

[24] Borghetti (n 5) 178.
[25] See generally subsection 3.2.2.
[26] See text to and following nn 34–35 and text to, preceding, and following nn 38–39 in subsection 3.5.2.

3.6.3 An Essential Justification, but Not All that Matters in Italian Reasoning

As in France, compensating the victims of accidents is one of the fundamental goals of Italian tort law and it constitutes one of the most significant justifications for the imposition of strict liability. Compared to the French position, however, the Italian approach is less single-minded. Indeed, the patterns of use of victim protection as well as the importance attributed to other goals such as the avoidance of accidents show that the protection of victims is not as overwhelming in the Italian context as it is in the French one.

As seen in the section on loss spreading, since the 1960s legal scholars spearheaded a 'revolution' in tort law which shifted the focus from sanctioning the defendant's wrongful conduct to protecting the victims of accidents.[27] This new approach, which was fuelled by the constitutional principle of social solidarity, challenged the primacy of fault in the law of extra-contractual liability[28] and paved the way towards a broad recognition of strict liability as a regime more conducive to the protection of victims than the fault paradigm. In this context, victim protection became the most important justification for imposing strict liability and even today it remains an extremely significant argument.

How does this prominence manifest itself in the reasoning of courts and scholars? As far as judicial decisions are concerned, it is possible to find occasional statements that expressly recognize the protection of victims as a reason for imposing strict liability. For example, the Corte di Cassazione observes that the rationale of articles 2051, 2052, 2053, and 2054 Cod civ 'lies in the need to increase the protection of victims for the primary purpose of securing the compensation of losses'.[29] But judicial statements of this sort are not common and the significance of victim protection emerges with greater force in the work of academics than in the reasoning of courts. To begin with, as in France, there are cases where strict liability is justified by a bare reference to victim protection, as if a concern for victims could by itself support a finding of liability. For example, in relation to traffic accidents, Bianca suggests that the strict liability of vehicle owners under article 2054 para 3 Cod civ finds its rationale in the need to guarantee the compensation to victims.[30] Similarly, in relation to the vicarious liability of employers for the harm caused by their employees, Ferrari argues that the function of article 2049 Cod civ is to

---

[27] eg Stefano Rodotà, *Il Problema della Responsabilità Civile* (Giuffrè 1964) 107; Marco Comporti, *Esposizione al pericolo e responsabilità civile* (Morano editore 1965).

[28] Rodotà (n 27) 127ff.

[29] Civ (III) 26.10.1998 n.10629, (1998) 1 Foro It 3109. See also Civ (III) 21.5.2014 n.11270, [1.1].

[30] C Massimo Bianca, *Diritto civile. V—La responsabilità* (3rd edn, Giuffrè 2021) 733; Civ (III) 21.5.2014 n.11270, [1.1]. See also Giuseppe Campeis and Arrigo De Pauli, 'La responsabilità per vizi di costruzione dei veicoli' (1990) Riv giur circolaz e trasp 140, 141 (on the liability for traffic accidents under article 2054, para 4 Cod civ).

ensure compensation to the victims of accidents.[31] This use of victim protection as a stand-alone justification for strict liability appears only sporadically, though, because in the vast majority of cases it is either combined or juxtaposed with other justifications.

In keeping with the French approach, the typical pattern is that arguments such as the deep-pockets one, loss spreading, or risk-based justifications are combined with victim protection and provide the criteria to identify the party strictly liable (the deeper pocket, the loss spreader, the risk gainer, or the creator of abnormal risks), hence acting as means to protect victims.[32] Therefore, inspired by the constitutional principle of social solidarity, these arguments buttress victim protection as a reason for, and a goal of, strict liability. From these patterns of argumentation, it emerges that giving financial relief to the victims of accidents constitutes a key justification for the adoption of strict liability. But while its importance as a reason for strict liability is clear, victim protection is less significant than in France. While the French approach is single-minded in seeing the compensation of victims as the ultimate goal and crucial justification of strict liability, in Italy victim protection is often juxtaposed with goals additional or alternative to it, such as the avoidance of accidents, the promotion of social welfare, or (less frequently) the spreading of losses.[33] For example, it is argued that in entrepreneurial contexts strict liability 'offers greater protection to the victims of accidents while also *marginalising accident-prone firms* from the market.'[34] Similarly, in relation to the position of parents for the harm caused by their children, it is suggested that strict

---

[31] Vincenzo Ferrari, 'Una ipotesi di responsabilità civile in funzione di garanzia' (2011) 1(1) Foro It 203, 204.

[32] eg Comporti (n 27) 174–76 (on the need to protect victims of harms caused by abnormal risks); Mario Bessone, 'Profili della responsabilità del produttore nell'esperienza italiana' in Guido Alpa and Mario Bessone (eds), *Danno da prodotti e responsabilità dell'impresa—Diritto italiano ed esperienze straniere* (Giuffrè 1980) 9, 26–28 (seeing the spreading abilities of firms as a reason to impose strict liability, with a view to ensuring a swift and certain compensation to victims of defective products); Luigi La Battaglia, 'Danno da prodotto farmaceutico difettoso e prova liberatoria' (2002) 10 DR 986, [1] (arguing that, in relation to high risk activities, it is consistent with the constitutional principle of social solidarity to allocate the loss to the best cost-bearer (here arguably referring to the deep-pockets argument and/or loss spreading); Caterina Murgo, 'La responsabilità dei genitori per fatto illecito dei figli minori: una conferma che invita alla riflessione' (2016) 2 RCP.541, 549 (on parents as deep-pockets guaranteeing compensation); Andrea Parziale, 'Il "caso dell'amaca", danno alla persona e costi assicurativi' (2013) 6 DR 688, 691 (on insurance and deep-pockets as means to victim protection in relation to ruinous buildings); Mario Griffey, *La responsabilità civile derivante da circolazione dei veicoli e dei natanti* (Giuffrè 1995) 91 (on risk–benefit as the principle behind liability for traffic accidents (article 2054 para 3 Cod civ), to be read in the framework of the legislator's willingness to protect victims); Federico Cammeo, *Corso di diritto amministrativo*, vol III (La Litotipo 1914) 1359–60 (arguing that where the public administration's lawful action significantly sacrifices the interests of a particular individual, the victim should be compensated by the public purse, as the money come from the wider community through taxation).

[33] This pattern of reasoning features only occasionally in the French context: see n 19 and accompanying text in this section.

[34] Gianmaria Volpe, 'Esercizio di attività pericolose, rischio d'impresa e controllo delle tecnologie' (1974) 4–5 GM 381, 382 (emphasis added) (relying on the theory of *rischio di impresa* and emphasizing the firms' ability to spread the costs of liability through insurance and price adjustments (ibid 383)).

228   JUSTIFYING STRICT LIABILITY

liability 'is about *efficient accident avoidance* and the certainty of compensation in favour of third parties coming into contact with the minor'.[35] Again, the imposition of strict liability on the public administration is often justified on the ground that it can both induce public bodies to take adequate precautions and financially protect the victims of administrative failures or other accidents.[36] In sum, and regardless of whether the particular scholar's reasoning places victim protection on an equal, less, or more important footing than other aims, what emerges is a belief that strict

---

[35] Pier Giuseppe Monateri, *La Responsabilità Civile. Trattato di Diritto Civile* (UTET 1998) 947 (emphasis added). For further examples on parental liability, see also Enrico Carbone, 'La responsabilità aquiliana del genitore tra rischio tipico e colpe fittizie' (2008) 1(2) Riv Dir Civ 1, 5–6; Maria Luisa Chiarella, 'Minore danneggiante e responsabilità vicaria' (2009) 10 DR 973, 985–86; and Paolo Pardolesi and Marina Dimattia, 'Responsabilità dei genitori per l'illecito dei minori: un esercizio di precomprensione?' (2010) 2 DR 168, 174, all mentioning accident avoidance and victim protection (Pardolesi and Dimattia, ibid 175, add that strict liability would reduce the burden on judicial activity and promote the adoption of compulsory insurance). On employers' vicarious liability, see Giovanna Visintini, *Trattato breve della responsabilità civile—Fatti illeciti. Inadempimento. Danno risarcibile* (3rd edn, Cedam 2005) 753–55 (combining victim protection with the deep-pockets rationale, in juxtaposition with efficient accident avoidance); Massimo Franzoni, *L'illecito. Trattato della responsabilità civile* (2nd edn, Giuffrè 2010) 762–63 and 767–69 (juxtaposing victim protection with a cluster of other arguments including loss spreading, risk–profit, and efficient accident avoidance); Cesare Salvi, *La responsabilità civile* (3rd edn, Giuffrè 2019) 201–03 (juxtaposing victim protection with risk–benefit and loss spreading). On liability for dangerous activities, see eg Lorena Fanelli, 'Fondo stradale dissestato per lavori ed esercizio di attività pericolosa: caratteri e limiti' (2001) 10 DR 925, text accompanying fns 4–7 (juxtaposing victim protection with accident avoidance and risk–benefit). On liability for things in one's keeping, see eg Salvi, ibid 177, 182 (juxtaposing victim protection with accident avoidance). For traffic accidents under article 2054, para 4 Cod civ, see eg Enzo Roppo, 'Sul danno causato da automobile difettose. Tutela dei danneggiati, regime di responsabilità e incidenza dell'assicurazione obbligatoria' (1978) 12(IV) GI 130, 132 (mentioning victim protection), 136, 140 (juxtaposing victim protection with accident avoidance and risk–profit). On product liability, see Mario Bessone, 'Prodotti dannosi e responsabilità dell'impresa' (1971) 1 RTDPC 97, 100 (discussing victim protection and efficient accident avoidance); Giulio Ponzanelli, 'Il produttore è responsabile del danno cagionato da difetti del suo prodotto' in Roberto Pardolesi and Giulio Ponzanelli (eds), 'La responsabilità per danno da prodotti difettosi' (1989) 3 Le nuove leggi civili commentate 497, 506, 508 (juxtaposing victim protection with accident avoidance and loss spreading); Alessandro Stoppa, 'Responsabilità del produttore' Dig Disc Priv (UTET 1998) XVII, 119, 124 (juxtaposing victim protection with accident avoidance and loss spreading). On liability for industrial nuisances, the judicially created remedy of indemnity finds its justification, on the one hand, in the protection of the party harmed by the emissions from the diminution in the value of their property and, on the other hand, in the need to internalize the costs of the emissions to the firm that causes the nuisance: see Rosario Petruso, 'Immissioni' Dig Disc Priv (UTET 2012 agg) 546, 553.

[36] See Giuseppe G Infantini, 'La responsabilità civile della pubblica amministrazione per danni causati nell'esercizio di attività pericolose e da cose in custodia' in Enrico Follieri (ed), *La responsabilità civile della pubblica amministrazione* (Giuffrè 2004) 297, 344–45 (juxtaposing victim protection with accident avoidance in relation to liability for things in one's keeping); Guido Corso, 'La responsabilità della pubblica amministrazione da attività lecita' (2009) 2 Diritto amministrativo 203, 224–26 (juxtaposing victim protection with accident avoidance and loss spreading to explain the expansion of public liability, for both physical and administrative activities); Giulia Avanzini, 'Nuovi sviluppi nella responsabilità delle amministrazioni per danni derivanti da attività pericolose e da cose in custodia' (2010) 1 Diritto amministrativo 261, 261–62 (juxtaposing victim protection with accident avoidance in relation to the liability of public bodies for dangerous activities and for things in one's keeping); Chiara Feliziani, 'L'elemento soggettivo della responsabilità amministrativa. Dialogo a-sincrono tra Corte di giustizia e giudici nazionali' (2018) 6 federalismi.it 1, 27, fn 140 (juxtaposing victim protection with accident avoidance and loss spreading, for the purpose of justifying a broader strict liability of the public administration for the exercise of its administrative functions).

liability can pursue a variety of goals and that victim protection alone is too brief a justification for it.[37]

This approach is further confirmed by the position of many authors who disagree with any single-minded pursuit of victim protection and call into question the appropriateness of strict liability. For example, Patti, in line with Trimarchi's view, argues that strict liability should be confined to economic activities presenting a minimum of organization and continuity (eg all entrepreneurial activities) and therefore criticizes the pro-victim stance that pushed many Italian courts to read parental liability as strict.[38] Similarly, in relation to liability for things in one's keeping, Benedetti argues that too much emphasis on strict liability and the protection of victims undermines other functions of tort law, first and foremost the prevention of accidents.[39] Finally, but very importantly, the view that victim protection would be the ultimate goal of tort liability is frowned upon in the Italian literature influenced by law and economics. Here it is regularly argued that the aim of tort liability (both strict and fault-based) is not to protect the victims of accidents but to increase social welfare, with the result that compensating losses is appropriate only if it can advance this goal.[40] All this suggests that compensation is not the only concern emerging from the Italian reasoning and that, compared to the French approach, it is a comparatively less significant justification for strict liability.

Overall, therefore, compensating the victims of accidents is certainly an essential justification for strict liability in the Italian context, but the legal reasoning of

---

[37] For a critical appraisal of victim protection in French law, see Borghetti (n 18) [5]–[6] (arguing that all liability rules should be determined only after considering and balancing a variety of goals, which include—besides compensating victims—sanctioning reprehensible behaviour, avoiding accidents, guaranteeing the rights of citizens, and protecting the interests of those whose actions are likely to cause harm to others). Borghetti's approach seems, however, somewhat isolated in the French context.

[38] Salvatore Patti, 'Responsabilità dei genitori: una sentenza in linea con l'evoluzione europea' (2001) 4 Familia 1174, 1177–78. On parental liability, see also Luigi Corsaro, 'Funzione e ragioni della responsabilità del genitore per il fatto illecito del figlio minore' (1988) IV GI 225, 226ff; Carbone (n 35) 14–16; Aldo P Benedetti, 'La responsabilità dei genitori per il trasporto in motorino di un passeggero da parte del figlio minorenne' (2012) 3 DR 267, 271.

[39] Aldo P Benedetti, 'La caduta di un alunno durante una gita scolastica: chi risponde?' (2012) 7 DR 755, 764. See also eg Arianna Fusaro, 'Attività pericolose e dintorni. Nuove applicazioni dell'art. 2050 c.c.' (2013) (6) Riv Dir Civ 1337, text following fn 103 (criticizing the judicial tendency to interpret too broadly the notion of dangerousness in the liability for dangerous activities (article 2050 Cod civ), and adding that 'in some extreme applications [of the provision], the rationale seems to lie entirely in a logic of protecting the injured party'); Carlotta De Menech, 'Il progressivo (ed irriflessivo) dilagare della responsabilità per fatto dei dipendenti' in Carlo Granelli (ed), *I nuovi orientamenti della Cassazione civile* (Giuffrè 2017) 456, 470–71 (criticizing the courts for not providing coherent justifications for the strict liability of employers and for being merely guided by a desire to ensure that victims receive compensation).

[40] Paolo Pardolesi, *Profili comparatistici di analisi economica del diritto* (Cacucci 2015) 20 (citing John G Fleming, Carolyn Sappideen, and Prue Vines, *Fleming's The Law of Torts* (10th edn, Pyrmont 2011) 180ff); Annalisa Bitetto, ' "Nuisance" e danni non patrimoniali' (2018) 4 DR 478, text to fn 13. See also Pier Giuseppe Monateri, 'Responsabilità civile' Dig Disc Priv (UTET 1998) XVII, 1, 2–3. cf Alpa (n 1) 46–50 (arguing that the role of accident avoidance in tort law is confined to marginal situations, that the consequences of economic theories are problematic, and that the fundamental goal of liability rules is compensation).

courts and scholars shows considerable attentiveness for other goals too, such as accident avoidance. This reflects an openness to considerations other than victim protection that is not seen in the French context and that ultimately weakens, if only moderately, the importance of victim protection as a justification for Italian strict liability.

3.6.4 The Protection of Victims in the United States: A Falling Star?

Compensating the victims of accidents for the losses they have suffered is often described as one of the primary goals of US tort law,[41] and one which also features in academic discussions and judicial opinions seeking to justify the imposition of strict liability. As will be seen, the argument from victim protection was especially popular from the 1920s to the 1970s among legal scholars supporting the strict liability of firms, but since then it has lost some of its force due to the ascendancy of law and economics and of theories of interpersonal justice. While the footprint of this pro-victim stance is still clearly visible in US legal reasoning, victim protection enjoys less currency than in the past and it is less significant than in the French or even the Italian context.

As seen in our discussion of loss spreading, since the 1920s and until the 1970s, many scholars in the United States suggested that accidental losses should be seen as the by-product of the industrial age and that fault was wholly inadequate to care for the victims of accidents.[42] In order to make sure that victims received compensation, they argued for the imposition of strict liability on those who were in a position to spread losses through a variety of spreading mechanisms. This approach targeted both situations involving firms, as these would typically be excellent loss spreaders via insurance and/or enterprise spreading, and situations where firms were not involved and yet the financial consequences of accidents could be either spread via insurance,[43] as in traffic accidents, or be distributed among the taxpayers/beneficiaries of governmental activities.[44]

---

[41] See Louis Kaplow and Steven Shavell, *Fairness v Welfare* (HUP 2002) 88, fn 6.

[42] See text to nn 57–62 in subsection 3.5.3.

[43] See references in n 58 in subsection 3.5.3. The solutions envisaged ranged from changes in the common law to the enactment of compensation plans targeting specific types of accidents. See eg Leon Green, 'The Duty Problem in Negligence Cases' (1928) 28 Colum L Rev 1014, and (1929) 29 Colum L Rev 255, 275–79 (proposing legislative compensation schemes for traffic accidents, railroad crossing accidents, and for accidents on landowners' land which occurred to 'intruders'). For a detailed discussion of both common law and legislative strategies, see Virginia E Nolan and Edmund Ursin, *Understanding Enterprise Liability: Rethinking Tort Reform for the Twenty-first Century* (Temple University Press 1995) 21–122.

[44] See eg Fleming James Jr, 'Tort Liability of Governmental Units and Their Officers' (1955) 22 U Chi L Rev 610, 614–15, 653–55; Kenneth Culp Davis, 'Administrative Officers' Tort Liability' (1956–1957) 55 Mich L Rev 201, 232–33; *Rayonier, Inc v United States*, 352 US 315, 319–20 (1957).

It is largely by this route that victim protection has come to constitute an important justification for strict liability in the United States. Unsurprisingly, then, where victim protection is deployed to support strict liability, the relevant reasoning typically includes arguments from loss spreading. In some cases, victim protection and loss spreading are presented as distinct and juxtaposed goals.[45] In this pattern, it is difficult to discern any specific interplay between the two arguments as well as their respective significance; all that can be said is that they constitute important and independent reasons for imposing strict liability. At other times, loss spreading acts both as an independent goal and as a means to achieve victim protection, with the two justifications being therefore combined.[46] In this pattern, the goal of compensating victims is achieved, at least in theory, by imposing strict liability on the loss spreader, meaning that loss spreading provides the criterion to identify the party strictly liable. Here the interplay (and strong connection) between victim protection and loss spreading is clear: the existence of spreading mechanisms makes it possible to afford protection to the victims of accidents by imposing the loss on someone who is able to dilute it across society and who therefore will not be crushed by a finding of liability. Absent spreading mechanisms, the case for strict liability in the furtherance of victim protection would be weakened.

While there is a special link between victim protection and the spreading of losses, victim protection can also feature in reasoning that involve other justifications. Arguments such as risk (abnormality of risk, risk–benefit, or risk–profit), the deep-pockets justification or accident avoidance can, alternatively or cumulatively,[47] be either combined or juxtaposed with victim protection in contexts such as liability for abnormally dangerous activities,[48] product liability,[49] vicarious

---

[45] eg *Mary M v City of Los Angeles*, 814 P.2d 1341, 1348–49 (Cal.1991); *Lisa M v Henry Mayo Newhall Mem Hosp*, 907 P.2d 358, 366–67 (Cal.1995).

[46] eg Lester W Feezer, 'Capacity to Bear Loss as a Factor in the Decision of Certain Types of Tort Cases' (1930) 78 U Pa L Rev 805, 808–10; *Escola v Coca Cola Bottling Co of Fresno*, 150 P.2d 436, 441 (Cal.1944); Fleming James Jr, 'Products Liability II' (1955) 34 Tex L Rev 192, 226–28; *Beshada v Johns-Manville Prods Corp*, 447 A.2d 539, 546–47 (N.J.1982); *Seely v White Motor Co*, 403 P.2d 145, 151 (Cal.1965).

[47] This does not mean that loss spreading cannot feature in these instances of reasoning, as shown in nn 48–50 in this section.

[48] *Cities Service Co v State*, 312 So.2d 799, 801 (Fla.1975) (combining victim protection with abnormality of risk); *Chavez v Southern Pacific Transportation*, 413 F.Supp. 1203, 1209, 1214 (Cal.1976) (combining (as well as juxtaposing) victim protection with loss spreading, also in juxtaposition with an argument based on efficient resource allocation); *Mahowald v Minnesota Gas Co*, 344 N.W.2d 856, 868 (Minn.1984) (Justice Todd, dissenting, with whom Justices Scott and Wahl agreed) (combining victim protection with loss spreading, in juxtaposition with risk creation); *In State Department of Environmental Protection v Ventron Corp*, 468 A.2d 150, 160 (N.J.1983) (combining victim protection with abnormality of risk); Jon G Anderson, 'The Rylands v. Fletcher Doctrine in America: Abnormally Dangerous, Ultrahazardous, or Absolute Nuisance?' (1978) Ariz St LJ 99, 135 (combining victim protection with abnormality of risk and with risk–benefit/profit, but also saying that liability cannot be excessive and therefore calling for a balancing exercise between competing interests).

[49] eg *Escola* (n 46) 440–41 (combining victim protection with loss spreading, in juxtaposition with accident avoidance and administrative cost reduction); Roger Traynor, 'The Ways and Meanings of Defective Products and Strict Liability' (1965) 32 Tenn L Rev 363, 366–67 (combining victim protection

232 JUSTIFYING STRICT LIABILITY

liability,[50] strict parental liability,[51] liability for traffic accidents,[52] and liability of public authorities for their administrative activities.[53] Here two main patterns emerge. First, in keeping with both the French and Italian approaches, victim protection is combined with arguments that identify the party strictly liable (the creator of abnormal risk, the risk gainer, the deeper pocket).[54] By being put to such a use, these arguments act as means to ensure the compensation of victims

with loss spreading, in juxtaposition with accident avoidance); *Vandermark v Ford Motor Co*, 391 P.2d 168, 171–72 (Cal.1964) (in relation to retailers, juxtaposing victim protection with accident avoidance); *Francioni v Gibsonia Truck Corp*, 372 A.2d 736, 739 (Pa.1977) (juxtaposing victim protection with accident avoidance and loss spreading); *Beshada* (n 46) 547–49 (combining victim protection with loss spreading, in juxtaposition with accident avoidance, administrative cost reduction, and risk–profit).

[50] *Mary M* (n 45) 1347–49 (juxtaposing victim protection with accident avoidance and loss spreading); *Elias v Unisys Corp*, 573 N.E.2d 946, 948 (Mass.1991) (combining victim protection with the deep-pockets argument); *Lisa M* (n 45) 367 (juxtaposing victim protection with accident avoidance and loss spreading); *Farmers Ins Group v County of Santa Clara*, 906 P.2d 440, 454–55 (Cal.1995) (juxtaposing victim protection with accident avoidance and loss spreading); *Montague v AMN Healthcare, Inc*, 223 Cal.App.4th 1515, 1523–24 (Cal.2014) (juxtaposing victim protection with accident avoidance and loss spreading); Lewis A Kornhauser, 'An Economic Analysis of the Choice between Enterprise and Personal Liability for Accidents' (1982) 70 Cal LR 1345, at fn 4 (mentioning victim protection as a potentially relevant factor in deciding the most appropriate regime of liability); Fowler V Harper, Fleming James Jr, and Oscar S Gray, *The Law of Torts*, vol 5 (2nd edn, Little, Brown and Company 1986) 21 (juxtaposing victim protection with accident avoidance and loss spreading); Rhett B Franklin, 'Pouring New Wine into an Old Bottle: A Recommendation for Determining Liability of an Employer under Respondeat Superior' (1994) 39 SD L Rev 570, 575–76 (juxtaposing victim protection with accident avoidance and loss spreading).
[51] Pamela K Graham, 'Parental Responsibility Laws: Let the Punishment Fit the Crime' (2000) 33 Loy LA L Rev 1719, 1727 (juxtaposing victim protection with accident avoidance).
[52] *Michaelsohn v Smith*, 113 N.W.2d 571, 573–74 (ND.1962) (combining victim protection with the deep-pockets/loss-spreading rationales, in relation to the 'family purpose' doctrine); *Young v Beck*, 251 P.3d 380, 385–86 (Ariz.2011) (juxtaposing victim protection with accident avoidance and arguably risk–benefit, again in relation to the 'family purpose' doctrine, and giving primary significance to the former argument). See also Green (n 43) 276 (discussing victim protection with risk–profit and loss spreading in relation to railway crossing cases), 278 (discussing victim protection with risk–benefit and loss spreading in relation to general traffic accidents), as well as all the proposals for reforming the law of accidents discussed in Nolan and Ursin (n 43) 21–68.
[53] See eg Peter H Schuck, *Suing Government: Citizen Remedies for Official Wrongs* (Yale University Press 1983) ch 5 (advocating the vicarious liability of government 'for every harmful act or omission committed by its agents within the scope of their employment that is tortious under applicable law' (at 111), on grounds of victim protection, accident avoidance, loss spreading, compliance with certain moral norms, and a reduction in administrative costs); Richard J Pierce and Kristin E Hickman, *Administrative Law Treatise*, vol 3 (6th edn, Wolters Kluwer 2019) 2262, 2268, 2307 (juxtaposing victim protection with accident avoidance, to advocate an expanded government liability). See also, in relation to the violation of federal or constitutional rights, *Owen v City of Independence*, 445 US 622 (1980) [16,17], [20] (juxtaposing victim protection with loss spreading and accident avoidance, to justify the liability of a municipality under § 1983); Susanah M Mead, '42 U.S.C. § 1983 Municipal Liability: The Monell Sketch Becomes a Distorted Picture' (1987) 65 NCL Rev 517, 538–40 (juxtaposing victim protection with loss spreading and accident avoidance, to criticize *Monell's* rejection of *respondeat superior* as the basis of municipal liability under § 1983); Susan Bandes, 'Reinventing *Bivens*: The Self-Executing Constitution' (1995) 68 S Cal L Rev 289, 341 (juxtaposing victim protection with accident avoidance, loss spreading, the promotion of moral norms, and administrative cost reduction, to advocate a change in the *Bivens* doctrine so that liability is imposed on the federal government rather than on its agents for the violation of a citizen's constitutional rights).
[54] See eg *Ventron Corp* (n 48) 160 (abnormality of risk); *Unisys Corp* (n 50) 948 (the deep-pockets argument); Anderson (n 48) 135 (risk–benefit/profit).

and, in this way, they reinforce the case for imposing strict liability on grounds of victim protection. Secondly, resembling a pattern already discussed in relation to Italy, victim protection can be juxtaposed with arguments indicating further and potentially conflicting goals of strict liability, such as accident avoidance or loss spreading (when presented as distinct from victim protection).[55] This pattern shows an awareness in US legal actors that the goal of strict liability cannot be reduced to victim protection and cannot be the only, or even the more important, justification for the imposition of strict liability. Unfortunately, in many cases the relevant court or scholar does not elaborate on the interplay between victim protection and other goals, with the result that it is difficult to pinpoint their relative significance. What is clear, however, is that, in keeping with the Italian approach,[56] this type of reasoning shows an attentiveness to goals other than victim protection in justifying strict liability.

This tendency to shun any single-minded attachment to victim protection finds support in the open criticisms that several US scholars level at the idea of justifying tort liability on merely compensatory grounds. First, those who put forward an interpersonal understanding of tort law consider victim protection an unsatisfactory argument because it focuses only on the claimant and their needs, breaking the nexus between claimant and defendant from which any justification for liability (strict or fault-based) should be derived.[57] Secondly, it is argued that victim protection cannot be the sole determinant of liability, for '[o]therwise, the award will be an arbitrary shifting of loss from one person to another at a net loss to society due to the economic and sociological costs of adjudication.'[58] Thirdly, at least insofar as legal scholars are concerned, economic reasoning can often clash with an argument from victim protection. Indeed, if the goal of tort law is to minimize the costs of accidents and if the main way to achieve this goal is to provide incentives for efficient precautions, a commitment to compensation via strict liability will be unwarranted whenever it gives inappropriate incentives to potential victims.[59] In

[55] On liability for abnormally dangerous activities, see eg *Chavez* (n 48) 1209. On product liability see eg *Escola* (n 46) 440–41; *Vandermark* (n 49) 171–72; *Beshada* (n 46) 547–49. On employers' vicarious liability, see eg *Mary M* (n 45) 1347–49; *Lisa M* (n 45) 366–67; *Farmers* (n 50) 454–55; *Montague* (n 50) 1523–24; Harper, James, and Gray (n 50) 21; Franklin (n 50) 574–76. On strict parental liability, see Graham (n 51) 1727. On the liability of public authorities, see eg *Owen v City of Independence* (n 53) [16,17], [20]; Mead (n 53) 538–40; Bandes (n 53) 341.

[56] See text to nn 33–40 in this section.

[57] Ernest J Weinrib, 'The Special Morality of Tort Law' (1989) 34 McGill LJ 403, 408–09. See also Jules L Coleman, *Risks and Wrongs* (CUP 1992) 209.

[58] Robert E Keeton and Jeffrey O'Connell, *Basic Protection for Traffic Victim* (Little, Brown and Company 1965) 242. See also Richard A Epstein, 'Products Liability: The Search for the Middle Ground' (1978) 56 NCL Rev 643, 644–45; Richard A Epstein, *Modern Products Liability Law* (Quorum Books 1980) 29. For an extended criticism of victim protection in the context of liability for products, see David G Owen, 'Rethinking the Policies of Strict Products Liability' (1980) 33 Vand L Rev 681, 703–07.

[59] For example, where the intensity of the potential victim's activity impacts on the accident rate more than the intensity of the potential injurer's activity: see Robert Cooter and Thomas Ulen, *Law & Economics* (6th edn, Pearson 2012) 204, 212–13; Richard A Posner, *Economic Analysis of Law* (9th edn, Wolters Kluwer 2014) 207. See also Guido Calabresi, *The Costs of Accidents: A Legal and Economic Analysis* (YUP 1970) 43–44 (rejecting the view that compensation is the sole aim of accident law).

sum, there are a variety of reasons why victim protection is seen as an unpalatable argument for the imposition of liability, whether strict or based on fault, and it is clear that, compared to the French and even Italian approach, overall this argument is less significant as a justification for the imposition of strict liability.

To conclude, victim protection is a particularly prominent justification among those scholars and judges advocating the strict liability of firms in the first half of the twentieth century in the United States. In this context, the paramount goal of protecting victims is intertwined with loss spreading, the latter reinforcing the case for strict liability by promising a wide distribution of losses while making tort a viable system of compensation. The footprint of this approach is clearly visible in the reasoning of more recent courts and scholars, especially in relation to situations involving firms or public bodies rather than physical individuals as potential defendants. At the same time, however, due to the ascendancy of law and economics and of interpersonal theories of tort law as well as to the establishment of competing justifications, the victim protection argument has been met with increasing scepticism and its use as a justification for strict liability has correspondingly diminished. Here, therefore, we can see a striking contrast with the French and Italian approaches.

3.6.5 Victim Protection in English Law: An Argument to Be Handled with Care

Among the four legal systems studied, English law is where victim protection features less prominently as a justification for strict liability. While this argument is occasionally relied upon, particularly in specific contexts such as the law of vicarious liability, it is also met with broad scepticism and it is often considered at odds with the values and goals that many legal scholars see as inspiring English tort law.

As seen in our discussion of loss spreading,[60] there is a clear connection between this argument and victim protection. The possibility of diluting the costs of accidents is seen as an attractive way of ensuring that victims receive compensation while avoiding that anyone else, whether the defendant or other third parties, be excessively burdened by the costs of liability. It is therefore not surprising to see that, in instances of reasoning seeking to justify strict liability in English law, victim protection is sometimes combined with loss spreading. Examples of this pattern were already illustrated when discussing loss spreading itself, and they include both academic and judicial reasoning in a variety of contexts, especially—though not only—the law of vicarious liability.[61] The upshot is that, in keeping with the

---

[60] See text to and following nn 190–192 in subsection 3.5.5.

[61] See Ewan McKendrick, 'Vicarious Liability and Independent Contractors: A Re-Examination' (1990) 53 MLR 770, 784; *Various Claimants v Catholic Child Welfare Society*, [2012] UKSC 56, [2013] 2

other three legal systems, the availability of insurance and other spreading mechanisms encourages the adoption of strict liability and hence the compensation of victims at little social cost; without such channels of distribution, the case for strict liability would be weakened and any commitment to protect victims would likely be less enthusiastic.

The link between victim protection and loss spreading does not mean, however, that the former is necessarily presented only in combination with the latter, for other justifications may accompany it, for example accident avoidance, the deep-pockets argument, or the various permutations of risk. In these instances, and again in keeping with the approach followed in the other three jurisdictions,[62] two main patterns emerge. First, victim protection may be combined with arguments which have the function of identifying the party strictly liable: besides the loss spreader, this could be the deeper pocket, the risk gainer, or the creator of (abnormal) risks, in contexts such as the rule in *Rylands v Fletcher*,[63] the operation of dangerous activities,[64] traffic accidents,[65] or vicarious liability.[66] Where this

---

AC 1, [34]–[35] [*CCWS*]; *Armes v Nottinghamshire County Council*, [2017] UKSC 60, [2018] AC 355, [61], [63]; Jenny Steele, *Tort Law, Text, Cases, and Materials* (4th edn, OUP 2017) 580. See also John A Jolowicz, 'Liability for Accidents' (1968) 26 CLJ 50, esp 57–61 (on liability in general for accident losses); *Launchbury v Morgans*, [1971] 2 QB 245, 253–55 (on traffic accidents); Pearson Commission, *Report of the Royal Commission on Civil Liability and Compensation for Personal Injury*, Cmnd 7054-I (1978) ch 31 (on liability for 'exceptional risks').

[62] See text to nn 19–23 (France), to nn 32–36 (Italy), to nn 47–55 (United States) in this section.

[63] Frederick Pollock, 'Duty of Insuring Safety: The Rule in Rylands v Fletcher' (1886) 2 LQR 52, 52 (maintaining that '[t]he law takes notice that certain things are a source of extraordinary risk, and a man who exposes his neighbour to such risk is held, although his act is not of itself wrongful, to insure his neighbour against any consequent harm not due to some cause beyond human foresight and control'). See also *Hoare & Co v McAlpine*, [1923] 1 Ch 167) 175 (arguably sharing the claimant's view that 'when a man releases some force brought by him on to his own property which gets beyond his control and injures his neighbour, . . . he is in the position of an insurer and liable for the damage he may cause').

[64] Pearson Commission (n 61) ch 31 (on liability for 'exceptional risks') esp [1641]–[1645] (combining victim protection with abnormality of risk and loss spreading).

[65] Alfred Thompson Denning, *What Next in the Law* (Butterworths 1982) 126–28 (combining victim protection with abnormality of risk).

[66] See eg John A Jolowicz, 'The Right to Indemnity between Master and Servant' (1956) 14 CLJ 101, 106 ('[t]he whole purpose of the master's vicarious liability is to ensure that the innocent third party, injured by the negligence of a servant acting in the course of his employment, can look to a worthwhile defendant'); *Majrowski v Guy's and St Thomas's NHS Trust*, [2006] UKHL 34, [9] (Lord Nicholls) (maintaining that vicarious liability is fair 'because it means injured persons can look for recompense to a source better placed financially than individual wrongdoing employees'); *CCWS* (n 61) [34] ('[t]he policy objective underlying vicarious liability is to ensure, insofar as it is fair, just and reasonable, that liability for tortious wrong is borne by a defendant with the means to compensate the victim'), [35] (seeing as one of the reasons justifying vicarious liability that 'the employer is more likely to have the means to compensate the victim than the employee and can be expected to have insured against that liability'); Steele (n 61) 580 (combining victim protection with the deep-pockets argument and loss spreading); Paula Giliker, 'A Revolution in Vicarious Liability: Lister, the Catholic Child Welfare Society Case and Beyond' in Sarah Worthington, Graham Virgo, and Andrew Robertson (eds), *Revolution and Evolution in Private Law* (Hart Publishing 2018) 121, 132–33, 136 (hereafter Giliker, 'A Revolution in Vicarious Liability'); Paula Giliker, 'Comparative Law and Legal Culture: Placing Vicarious Liability in Comparative Perspective' (2018) 6 Ch J Comp L 265, 278 (in both works interpreting the English case law as committed to victim protection via risk-based reasoning) (hereafter Giliker, 'Comparative Law and Legal Culture'). See, for an example in the field of breach of a non-delegable duty, Stelios Tofaris,

happens, these arguments support the imposition of strict liability and the pursuit of victim protection as its goal.

A second pattern consists instead in juxtaposing victim protection with arguments that embody goals different from ensuring compensation, in most cases accident avoidance, but also loss spreading (where presented as distinct from victim protection) as well as (rarely) a reduction in administrative costs. Examples of this pattern involve contexts of liability such as product liability,[67] vicarious liability,[68] liability for breach of a statutory duty,[69] or even liability for accidents in general.[70] In these instances, then, victim protection is put next to competing goals which may be pursued alternatively or in addition to it. At times, it may be possible to infer from the overall reasoning the relative weight given to victim protection in comparison with these other arguments, as in the *NBA* case, where Burton J clearly attaches paramount importance to victim protection in interpreting and applying the Product Liability Directive.[71] At other times, by contrast, it may be difficult to pinpoint or rank the arguments' relative weight. For example, in a couple of cases following the *NBA* decision, English courts departed from Burton J's focus on victim protection and stated that 'the Directive is not driven solely by [consumers'] interests',[72] or that 'whilst the effective protection of consumers is a key objective of the Directive, it is not the main or overriding objective. It has equal status with the other objectives'.[73] In these examples, victim protection is not judged as more important than other arguments, and this type of reasoning suggests that, in keeping with the Italian and US approaches,[74] English legal actors who see victim protection as a goal of strict liability are however open to recognize that strict liability can serve other goals as well.

'Vicarious Liability and Non-Delegable Duty for Child Abuse in Foster Care: A Step too Far?' (2016) 79 MLR 884, 895 (combining victim protection with risk creation, and suggesting that this should be the basis of liability in the *Armes* case).

[67] Department of Trade and Industry, *Implementation of European community directive on product liability: an explanatory and consultative note* (1985) [37], [39] (juxtaposing victim protection with accident avoidance); *A v National Blood Authority*, [2001] 3 All ER 289 [*NBA*], [75] (juxtaposing victim protection with accident avoidance); *Gee v DePuy International Ltd*, [2018] EWHC 1208, [72]–[73] (juxtaposing victim protection with all the objectives stated in the Recitals of the Product Liability Directive).

[68] Steele (n 61) 578–81 (juxtaposing victim protection (which is combined with the loss-spreading and deep-pockets rationales) with accident avoidance, and adding risk–benefit and risk creation as well under the banner of 'justice arguments').

[69] eg Steele (n 61) 880, 882 (juxtaposing victim protection with administrative cost reduction, in relation to employers' liability for breach of health and safety regulations).

[70] Jolowicz (n 61) 62–63 (juxtaposing victim protection with administrative cost reduction and loss spreading).

[71] *NBA* (n 67) [13], [31], [75], [178](v).

[72] *Wilkes v Depuy International Ltd*, [2016] EWHC 3096, [54].

[73] *Gee* (n 67) [73].

[74] See text to nn 55–56 (United States), and to nn 33–37 (Italy) in this section.

Finally, victim protection is occasionally put forward as a stand-alone argument. The desire to compensate injured workers has sometimes been seen as the fundamental reason for imposing strict liability on employers for breach of statutory duty;[75] outside this area, examples of victim protection as a stand-alone justification are rarer, and they typically feature in attempts to explain the imposition of strict liability in the Product Liability Directive.[76] As a result, it seems fair to say that this specific pattern of reasoning has very limited significance in the English context.

Overall, the emerging picture suggests that the patterns of use of victim protection in English law resemble those characterizing the other three jurisdictions studied. There is, however, a fundamental difference because reliance on victim protection is far less frequent in English law than in the other systems, at least at the level of overt reasoning. The explanation for this seems to lie in the reluctance of many English legal actors to reduce strict liability (or, for that matter, tort liability in general) to a compensatory device. This reluctance manifests itself in two quite different ways. First, victim protection as a goal of tort liability is harshly criticized. Particularly illustrative is Stapleton's thinking, according to which

> it is as banal and misleading to say that the 'function' or 'purpose' of tort is compensation as it is to say that the 'function' or 'purpose' of a petrol station is to dispense petrol: the question of interest is who is entitled to have the benefit dispensed and why.[77]

In other words, Stapleton is denying that compensating victims may be in itself a purpose of tort law, which is probably the strongest criticism that can be formulated against victim protection as a justification for strict liability. But even conceding that the protection of victims may conceivably constitute an intelligible goal of tort law, such a goal would enshrine a needs-based approach to the allocation

---

[75] See eg *Groves v Wimborne (Lord)*, [1898] 2 QB 402, 408 (AL Smith LJ), 414–15 (Rigby LJ), 416 (Vaughan Williams LJ) (concerning the Factory and Workshop Act 1878); *Coltman v Bibby Tankers*, [1988] AC 276, 295–96, 301 (Lord Oliver); *Knowles v Liverpool City Council*, [1993] 1 WLR 1428, 1432 (Lord Jauncey) (both cases concerning the Employer's Liability (Defective Equipment) Act 1969). See also *Craner v Dorset CC*, [2008] EWCA Civ 1323, [2009] ICR 56, [8] (Longmore LJ) (implying that the Workplace (Health, Safety and Welfare) Regulations 1992 and the Provision and Use of Work Equipment Regulations 1998 are expression of a 'compensation culture'). Note that, following changes made by the Enterprise and Regulatory Reform Act 2013, negligence is now generally required to trigger liability for the breach of health and safety regulations and that, therefore, strict liability is now exceptional in this area: see n 71 and accompanying text in section 2.2.

[76] See eg Simon Whittaker, 'The EEC Directive on Product Liability' (1985) 5 YEL 233, 235; Elspeth Deards and Christian Twigg-Flesner, 'The Consumer Protection Act: Proof at Last that it is Protecting Consumers?' (2001) 10 Nottingham LJ 1, 18–19.

[77] Jane Stapleton, 'Tort, Insurance and Ideology' (1995) 58 MLR 820, fn 24. See also John W Salmond, *The Law of Torts: a Treatise on the English Law of Liability for Civil Injuries* (1st edn, Stevens and Haynes 1907) 10 ('[p]ecuniary compensation is not in itself the ultimate object or a sufficient justification of legal liability'); Donal Nolan, 'Causation and the Goals of Tort Law' in Andrew Robertson and Hang Wu Tang (eds), *The Goals of Private Law* (Hart Publishing 2009) 165, 166.

238   JUSTIFYING STRICT LIABILITY

of losses which, as such, is incompatible with English tort law as a bilateral system of individual responsibility or corrective justice.[78] Descending to specific contexts of liability, the tendency of courts to use vicarious liability as a compensatory tool in favour of vulnerable individuals has stirred considerable controversy, and the tension between this judicial approach and norms of responsibility is a source of concern among legal scholars.[79] Similarly, in relation to product liability, Stapleton is very critical of the *NBA* decision and of the judge's single-minded pro-victim approach which disregards other goals set out in the Product Liability Directive.[80] Finally, speaking generally about the liability of public bodies, Bell maintains that it is 'not enough to say that the victim should not have to shoulder the burden of her or his loss', and that it is necessary to 'provide positive reasons why the state should be held responsible for that loss'.[81]

Moreover, the English scepticism for victim protection as a justification for strict liability is also reflected in the formulation of theories of strict liability which are perceived as being in accordance with norms of individual responsibility. Very interestingly, these justificatory attempts often draw on risk-based arguments: for example, Honoré combines his theory of outcome responsibility with abnormality of risk in seeking to justify strict liability in general;[82] Stapleton combines outcome responsibility with risk–profit to provide a sound justification for strict product liability;[83] Cane sees the 'most ethically satisfying explanation' of vicarious liability again in the risk–profit argument.[84] In these instances of reasoning, risk-based justifications are key because, contrary to victim protection or any other argument focusing on collective and forward-looking concerns (eg loss spreading or accident avoidance), they are seen as capable of reconciling strict liability with principles of personal responsibility and corrective justice.[85] This may also explain a specific pattern of judicial reasoning taking place in the law of vicarious liability: while English courts see this type of liability as conducive to ensuring that victims receive

---

[78]   Peter Cane, 'Justice and Justifications for Tort Liability' (1982) 2 OJLS 30, 52–53. See also Jonathan Morgan, 'Tort, Insurance and Incoherence' (2004) 67 MLR 384, 394–400.

[79]   See eg Giliker, 'Comparative Law and Legal Culture' (n 66) 277–78. See also Giliker, 'A Revolution in Vicarious Liability' (n 66) 139; Peter Cane, 'Vicarious Liability for Sexual Abuse' (2000) 116 LQR 21, 23–26 (commenting on two Canadian cases).

[80]   Jane Stapleton, 'Bugs in Anglo-American products liability' in Duncan Fairgrieve (ed), *Product Liability in Comparative Perspective* (CUP 2005) 295, 325–30, 332–33. See also Jane Stapleton, *Product Liability* (Butterworths 1994) 93 (hereafter Stapleton, *Product Liability*).

[81]   John Bell, 'Governmental Liability in Tort' (1995) 6 NJCL 85, 103.

[82]   Tony Honoré, 'Responsibility and Luck: The Moral Basis of Strict Liability' (1988) 104 LQR 530.

[83]   Stapleton, *Product Liability* (n 80) 185ff.

[84]   Peter Cane, 'Fault and Strict Liability for Harm in Tort Law' in William Swadling and Gareth Jones (eds), *The Search for Principle: Essays in Honour of Lord Goff of Chieveley* (OUP 1999) 171, 202, 206 (even though recognizing its own limitations); cf Peter Cane, *Responsibility in Law and Morality* (Hart Publishing 2002) 40 (arguing that one of the functions of vicarious liability is to increase the chances of obtaining compensation by providing victims with an additional target for their claims).

[85]   Peter Cane and James Goudkamp, *Atiyah's Accidents, Compensation and the Law* (9th edn, CUP 2018) 453.

compensation for the harm suffered,[86] they invariably rely on risk-based reasoning, to the point of recognizing risk–benefit as 'the most influential idea in modern times' for the purpose of justifying vicarious liability.[87] This reliance on risk-based arguments, focused as they are on the defendant's side, may signify a desire to bring in some notion of individual responsibility with a view to counterbalancing, at the level of reasoning if not of practical results, the overall effort to protect victims.

In sum, especially if compared to the French and Italian approaches, victim protection is handled in England more cautiously when it comes to justifying the imposition of liability in tort. This finding is further buttressed by a comparison of the positive laws in these jurisdictions. If the extent to which strict liability is relied upon were a function of the tort system's commitment to the protection of victims, then one would be led to conclude that victim protection in England is considerably less prominent than in the two civil law systems.

To conclude, victim protection is treated prudently as a justification for strict liability in English law. The argument is occasionally relied upon in a variety of contexts, and it seems particularly important in judicial reasoning characterizing the law of vicarious liability. On the other hand, several legal scholars criticize it vigorously, mainly on the ground that compensation is not a goal of tort law at all, or that it is not compatible with the underlying structure and principles of the tort system. In this respect, then, English reasoning contrasts strikingly with the French and Italian approaches and, even if less dramatically, with the US one too.

3.6.6 Concluding Remarks

Overall, the patterns of use and significance of the victim protection argument present interesting similarities and contrasts across the four legal systems studied.

In France, ensuring that victims of accidents receive adequate compensation is the most important goal attributed to strict liability and a variety of arguments accompany victim protection to bolster the case for strict liability.[88] Among these, particularly important are, at a theoretical level, risk-based arguments and, both theoretically and practically, arguments based on loss spreading.[89] Indeed, it is the availability of mechanisms allowing for a wide distribution of losses that makes it acceptable and possible to rely on broad and rigorous strict liabilities so as to ensure maximum protection to the victims of accidents.[90] In Italy, victim protection is also a very important justification for the imposition of strict liability. In keeping

---

[86] Giliker, 'A Revolution in Vicarious Liability' (n 66) 133, 136; Giliker, 'Comparative Law and Legal Culture' (n 66) 277–78.

[87] *Armes* (n 61) [67].

[88] See text to nn 3–5 in this section.

[89] See text to nn 24–26 in this section.

[90] See text to n 26 in this section.

with the French approach, it is combined with justifications such as the various permutations of risk, the deep-pockets argument, and loss spreading (though less frequently than in France).[91] However, the reasoning put forward by Italian legal actors suggests that, unlike France, strict liability may be usefully deployed to achieve goals additional or alternative to victim protection. In line with this, several Italian legal scholars—especially those influenced by law and economics—criticize an overemphasis on victim protection and warn against the effects that a systematic recourse to strict liability for such purpose may have on other goals, such as the avoidance of accidents.[92] Therefore, while victim protection is a very important argument, Italian law is not as committed to the 'compensation ideology' as French law. In the United States too, victim protection is an important justification for the imposition of strict liability. This argument is often combined or juxtaposed with many other justifications,[93] but it presents particularly strong links with loss spreading,[94] in this resembling the French approach. It must be noted, however, that while the argument was particularly important in the middle part of the twentieth century, its significance has somewhat diminished since then due to the concurrent ascendancy of law and economics and of theories of inter-personal justice.[95] Both approaches call into question the appropriateness of victim protection as a reason for imposing liability in tort and suggest that goals other than compensating victims may be served by strict liability. Given the force that these intellectual movements enjoy in the United States today, it is not surprising that victim protection is less prominent than in the French or the Italian contexts. In England, the *patterns* of use do not differ from those characterizing the other three legal systems: indeed, where used, the argument is sometimes combined with loss spreading, while at other times it is accompanied by justifications such as risk or (more rarely) the deep-pockets rationale.[96] However, the argument is relied upon far less frequently than in the other three legal systems, and it is rejected by several leading scholars who seek to show its incompatibility with tort law as a system of individual responsibility and justice.[97] Given this, and despite its current popularity in the law of vicarious liability—where protecting the vulnerable has become a priority—victim protection remains highly controversial in English law.

---

[91] See text to n 32 in this section.
[92] See text to nn 38–40 in this section.
[93] See text to nn 47–55 in this section.
[94] See text to and following nn 42–46 in this section.
[95] See text to nn 57–59 in this section.
[96] See text to nn 60–73 in this section.
[97] See text to and following nn 77–87 in this section.

3.7
Reduction in Administrative Costs

3.7.1 Reduction in Administrative Costs as a Justification for Strict Liability

Strict liability is sometimes justified on the ground that, compared to fault-based liability, it entails lower costs in administering tort claims. Under the latter regime, it is necessary to investigate the defendant's conduct and assess whether they were negligent. Dealing with this issue can be difficult, time-consuming, and costly, for example where expert testimony or witness interviews are necessary, or where other complex factual determinations must be made (eg because the evidence is destroyed or unavailable). Strict liability avoids all these inconveniences and costs by removing the need to assess the defendant's conduct.[1] Furthermore, in these circumstances there is less room for disagreement between the parties, and therefore there are greater chances of settlement, with a consequent further saving of money.[2] In sum, according to this argument, under a regime of strict liability fewer private and public resources will be spent on tort claims than under a regime based on fault ('administrative cost reduction'). This argument, though, can be turned on its head and be used to question the desirability of strict liability. In particular, it is sometimes argued that, by avoiding the negligence issue and increasing the chances for the claimant to be compensated, the adoption of strict liability could encourage the filing of lawsuits and therefore augment the overall administrative costs of the tort system.[3] This ambiguity in the argument inevitably affects its justificatory weight.

Moreover, as will be apparent from the following discussion, the concern to reduce administrative costs features mostly in the reasoning of those applying an economic thinking to tort liability, therefore drawing a marked distinction between legal systems where 'law and economics' has taken hold and those where it has not. As a result, both the significance of administrative cost

---

[1] Joseph H King Jr, 'A Goals-Oriented Approach to Strict Tort Liability for Abnormally Dangerous Activities' (1996) 48 Baylor L Rev 341, 358. The argument based on a reduction in administrative costs must not be confused with a different one according to which the difficulty of providing evidence should not penalize victims and should therefore lead to the adoption of strict liability rules. This latter argument is part of a strategy to help victims secure compensation, not to reduce administrative costs.

[2] Steven Shavell, *Economic Analysis of Accident Law* (HUP 1987) 264.

[3] See eg n 12 and accompanying text in this section.

Justifying Strict Liability. Marco Cappelletti, Oxford University Press. © Marco Cappelletti 2022.
DOI: 10.1093/oso/9780192859860.003.0009

242   JUSTIFYING STRICT LIABILITY

reduction and the way in which this argument is used vary considerably across the four legal systems studied.

3.7.2 The Ambiguous Significance of Reducing Administrative Costs in the United States

Of the four systems considered, more emphasis is placed in the United States on the reduction of administrative costs as a justification for adopting strict liability. The argument features in the reasoning of both legal scholars and, to a lesser extent, courts, but its significance must not be exaggerated. For reasons that will be explored below, the role it plays as a justification for strict liability is rather ambiguous.

Administrative costs have attracted considerable attention in the United States since the emergence of law and economics as an influential approach to the study of law. The balancing of costs and benefits typical of approaches rooted in economic theory has rendered administrative costs an important factor in choosing a regime of liability.[4] But the concern to reduce administrative costs is not the exclusive province of economic reasoning, as some scholars and courts who justify strict liability on other grounds also show concern for administrative costs as well, and in a variety of contexts. For example, in relation to abnormally dangerous activities, it is suggested that ultrahazardous operations often destroy the evidence necessary to prove the defendant's negligence, and so strict liability resolves the problem by rendering the issue of negligence irrelevant, with a consequent reduction in administrative costs.[5] Similarly, in relation to defective products, several legal scholars and courts emphasize the savings strict liability can secure both in terms of the time and money involved in the fact finding process,[6] and in terms of avoiding multiple

---

[4] eg Guido Calabresi, *The Costs of Accidents: A Legal and Economic Analysis* (YUP 1970) 28. The cost of administering tort claims is part of what Calabresi terms 'tertiary costs', these including all costs involved in seeking to reduce accidents and to spread losses. For Calabresi, the best regime of liability is that which minimizes the sum of all accident costs, ie primary, secondary, *and* tertiary costs, on which see the remarks made in n 8 in subsection 3.3.2. See also Louis Kaplow and Steven Shavell, *Fairness v Welfare* (HUP 2002) 86, 99–133 (consistently considering administrative costs in assessing the effect of legal rules on social welfare); and Richard A Posner, *Economic Analysis of Law* (9th edn, Wolters Kluwer 2014) 208 (comparing negligence and strict liability by reference to the administrative costs they entail).

[5] Kenneth S Abraham, *The Forms and Functions of Tort Law* (5th edn, Foundation Press 2017) 208–09 (juxtaposing administrative cost reduction with accident avoidance). See also King Jr (n 1) 350–61 (juxtaposing administrative cost reduction with loss spreading, accident avoidance, an argument presented as 'loss allocation' (which can be recast as accident avoidance via the 'market deterrence' approach), fairness as nonreciprocity of risk and risk–benefit (though showing scepticism for fairness-based rationales), and an argument based on the protection of individual autonomy).

[6] Richard A Epstein, *Modern Products Liability Law* (Quorum Books 1980) 48; James A Henderson Jr, 'Coping with the Time Dimension in Products Liability' (1981) 69 Cal L Rev 919, 931–39 (juxtaposing administrative cost reduction with accident avoidance, loss spreading, and fairness (this including disparate arguments, from risk–profit and abnormality of risk, to the protection of consumers' expectations, the manufacturer's deliberate taking of the physical well-being of victims, and loss spreading as burden–benefit proportionality)); *Beshada v Johns-Manville Prods Corp*, 447 A.2d 539, 547–49

unnecessary actions along the chain of distribution.[7] Again, as regards *respondeat superior*, some leading scholars justify the strict liability of employers by arguing that it may be very difficult to identify the failures of large firms or the identity of the negligent employee and that, even if such difficulties are overcome, providing the relevant evidence can be costly and time-consuming.[8]

By taking a step back and considering how administrative cost reduction is used in the US reasoning, one can see that its significance is ambiguous. To begin with, whether in academic writing or in the case law, the reduction of administrative costs does not feature as a stand-alone argument, suggesting that it is not in itself seen as capable of justifying the imposition of strict liability. Consistently, the concern to decrease administrative costs is regularly either juxtaposed or combined with other justifications, from accident avoidance or loss spreading to risk-based arguments or victim protection.[9] Here, the significance of a reduction in administrative costs varies depending on whether or not the argument is part of an economic reasoning. In the former case, the potential for decreasing administrative costs is prima facie highly significant, at least at a theoretical level.[10] Indeed, in combination with accident avoidance, a reduction in administrative costs is constantly taken into account as one of the key factors in choosing between negligence and strict liability.[11] If, by hypothesis, negligence were more efficient than strict

(N.J.1982) (juxtaposing administrative cost reduction with loss spreading, accident avoidance, risk-profit, and victim protection); *Halphen v Johns-Manville Sales Corp*, 484 So.2d 110, 116–19 (La.1986) (juxtaposing administrative cost reduction with risk creation, loss spreading, accident avoidance, and 'justice' (the latter acting as a constraint)); Products Liability Restatement, § 2, comment *a* (in relation to manufacturing defects, juxtaposing administrative cost reduction with accident avoidance, an argument based on the protection of consumer expectations, the manufacturer's deliberate taking of the physical well-being of victims, and loss spreading); Dan B Dobbs, Paul T Hayden, and Ellen M Bublick, *Torts and Compensation—Personal Accountability and Social Responsibility for Injury* (8th edn, West Academic Publishing 2017) 747–50 (juxtaposing administrative cost reduction with consumer expectations, loss spreading, risk–profit, nonreciprocity of risk, and accident avoidance).

[7] *Escola v Coca Cola Bottling Co of Fresno*, 150 P.2d 436, 441–42 (Cal.1944) (juxtaposing administrative cost reduction with accident avoidance, victim protection, and loss spreading); William L Prosser, 'The Assault upon the Citadel (Strict Liability to the Consumer)' (1960) 69 Yale LJ 1099, 1123–24; Epstein (n 6) 48.

[8] See eg Gary T Schwartz, 'The Hidden and Fundamental Issue of Employer Vicarious Liability' (1996) 69 S Cal L Rev 1739, 1763–64 (juxtaposing administrative cost reduction with accident avoidance); Abraham (n 5) 213 (juxtaposing administrative cost reduction with accident avoidance and loss spreading). See also, in relation to the liability of public authorities, Peter H Schuck, *Suing Government: Citizen Remedies for Official Wrongs* (YUP 1983) ch 5 (putting forward a reduction in administrative costs (at 102) as one of the reasons why it would be desirable to adopt a broad government liability based on *respondeat superior*, together with arguments such as victim protection, accident avoidance, loss spreading, and morality).

[9] See nn 5–8 in this section.

[10] By contrast, some legal economists ignore or reject the relevance of the economic dislocation caused by letting losses concentrated on the victims of accidents: see text to nn 51–52 in subsection 3.4.4.

[11] See eg Calabresi (n 4) 143–44 ('[t]he first guideline for picking the cheapest cost avoider is to seek the optimal relationship between avoidance costs and administrative costs'); Guido Calabresi and Alvin K Klevorick, 'Four Tests for Liability in Torts' (1985) 14 J Legal Stud 585, 626 (focusing their analysis on efficient accident avoidance, but acknowledging that administrative costs 'are quite likely to be

liability at avoiding accidents but strict liability entailed lower administrative costs, the choice between them would depend on the size of the savings as between the two rules: if the savings secured through strict liability in terms of administrative costs were greater than the savings secured through negligence in terms of accident avoidance, strict liability would be the better rule. Complicating the picture, however, is the difficulty inherent in determining with certainty which liability rule reduces administrative costs more. In particular, scholars sometimes doubt the superiority of strict liability on the ground that, by making proof of negligence unnecessary and hence recovery easier, the adoption of strict liability rules may encourage the bringing of claims, therefore increasing the volume of litigation and, with it, the overall administrative costs of the tort system.[12] This sort of discussion shows that, for legal economists, administrative costs are an important element of analysis, for their reduction may tilt the balance in favour of the rule which can be administered more cheaply. At the same time, however, they also show that, on closer inspection, the significance of administrative cost reduction as an argument for strict liability should not be exaggerated. Indeed, the speculative character of the comparisons between negligence and strict liability in their impact on administrative costs leaves largely unresolved the issue of which rule is better at lowering such costs.[13] As a result, while a reduction in administrative costs is *potentially* a powerful argument for strict liability, it can be just as easily used to support liability based on negligence. Furthermore, whether because of the paucity of empirical data or the inherent difficulty in giving accurate estimates, economic analyses of tort law discuss administrative costs under different liability rules only briefly, preferring instead to focus on the ability of these rules to provide safety incentives and avoid accidents. In sum, while a reduction in administrative costs appears at first sight to be key in the promotion of social welfare, its significance as

extremely important' in determining which rule of liability, whether strict or based on fault, is most appropriate).

[12] See Louis Kaplow and Steven Shavell, 'Property Rules Versus Liability Rules: An Economic Analysis' (1996) 109 Harv L Rev 713, 754, including fn 131; King Jr (n 1) 358; Posner (n 4) 208 (cf William M Landes and Richard A Posner, 'A Positive Economic Analysis of Products Liability' (1985) 14 J Legal Stud 535, 550 (arguing that the 'volume of litigation' concern may be alleviated in the context of products liability if most accidents could be prevented 'because [the manufacturer] had better information than consumers on expected injuries')); Shavell (n 2) 174 (on vicarious liability); David Rosenberg, 'The Judicial Posner on Negligence versus Strict Liability: Indiana Harbor Belt Railroad Co. v. American Cyanamid Co.' (2007) 120 Harv L Rev 1210, 1215–19 (showing, among other things, the difficulty of estimating the administrative costs involved in negligence actions as opposed to those involved in strict liability actions).

[13] Shavell (n 2) 264–65 (arguing that, '[i]n sum, then, the comparison of the size of administrative costs under the two forms of liability is ambiguous as a theoretical matter', and adding that the role of insurers in litigation may diminish the difference in administrative costs between negligence and strict liability).

a justification for imposing strict liability (or, for that matter, any type of liability) looks attenuated.[14]

A different picture emerges when considering the use of this argument outside of economic theory. To begin with, in many cases administrative cost reduction is ignored, arguably because the relevant judge or scholar deems it irrelevant in itself or not connected to the justifications for strict liability that they put forward. Moreover, paying attention to administrative costs is in conflict with certain ways of theorizing about tort law, for instance where tort liability is seen as based on interpersonal justice. Here, depending on the flexibility of the relevant theory, arguments rooted in collective concerns such as reducing administrative costs are either marginalized because they do not conform to norms of individual responsibility,[15] or flatly rejected because they are divorced from notions of corrective justice.[16]

But even where mentioned to support strict liability, administrative cost reduction is given a justificatory weight that differs from what we see in economic reasoning. Indeed, while in economic theories the argument is generally presented in combination with other arguments (notably accident avoidance and distributional considerations) and used as a means to minimize the overall costs of accidents, beyond this type of analysis the reduction of administrative costs is typically juxtaposed, rather than combined, with a variety of justifications.[17] Here the impression is that in most cases administrative cost reduction is not a key argument for the imposition of strict liability. To give just one example, in *Beshada* the Supreme Court of New Jersey identifies a number of reasons for imposing strict liability for asbestos exposure without a development risk defence, one of these being the high administrative costs that would be involved in assessing the scientific knowability of the dangerousness of asbestos.[18] The order of discussion of all the reasons given and the general tone of the decision strongly suggest that the driving justifications for strict liability lay elsewhere, most likely in victim protection and loss spreading, and that a reduction in administrative costs was probably seen as a secondary justification.[19] There is, however, a point of convergence between legal economists

[14] Henderson Jr (n 6) 1591 (providing empirical evidence for the proposition that administrative costs are rarely mentioned in judicial opinions on product liability cases, whether decided on theories of strict liability or not).

[15] See eg John CP Goldberg and Benjamin C Zipursky, 'The Strict Liability in Fault and the Fault in Strict Liability' (2016) 85 Fordham L Rev 743, esp 784ff.

[16] If liability must depend entirely on reasons pertaining to the bilateral relationship between defendant and claimant, any collective consideration such as a reduction in administrative costs is clearly unacceptable: see eg Ernest J Weinrib, 'The Special Morality of Tort Law' (1989) 34 McGill LJ 403, 408, 410 (his rejection of 'wealth maximization' as a goal of tort law necessarily extends to all its constituent elements, including reducing the administrative costs of the tort system).

[17] See nn 5–8 in this section.

[18] *Beshada* (n 6) 547–49.

[19] ibid 548. See also King Jr (n 1) 350–61 (seeing loss spreading as more significant than administrative cost reduction (which he presents in terms of 'administrative efficiency')); Schwartz (n 8) 1763–64 (seeing accident avoidance as more significant than administrative cost reduction); Gregory C Keating, 'The Idea of Fairness in the Law of Enterprise Liability' (1997) 95 Mich L Rev 1266 (supporting strict

and scholars not committed to economic theory: like the former, the latter can also see administrative costs as potentially militating against the imposition of strict liability. For example, Keating argues that whenever strict liability can merely shift the loss without spreading it, strict liability is not justified because it 'incurs administrative costs without delivering substantive benefits'.[20] In sum, administrative cost reduction does not look particularly significant for those who justify strict liability on grounds other than minimizing the costs of accidents and, even where the argument is mentioned, it is likely to act as a secondary or make-weight argument, or even to be used as a reason to reject strict liability.

To conclude, it is clear that reducing administrative costs is a significant argument, at least in principle, for economic theory. In this context, however, the acute uncertainty surrounding administrative costs under different regimes of liability makes this argument a wild card, which can either support strict liability or undermine it. Outside economic analysis, the argument from administrative costs is often neglected. Where used, it is typically overshadowed by other justifications for strict liability, met with the scepticism of those entertaining an interpersonal vision of tort law, or again turned on its head and used to reject or marginalize strict liability.

3.7.3 Reducing Administrative Costs in Italy: A Concern for the Legal Economists Only?

In keeping with the US approach, a justification for strict liability based on reducing administrative costs features in the Italian reasoning, and it shows the same ambiguity and uncertainty that characterize it in the US context. However, unlike in the United States, in Italy this argument is basically ignored by Italian judges and, as far as legal scholars are concerned, it is almost exclusively invoked by those who approach strict liability (and tort law more generally) through the lenses of law and economics.

---

enterprise liability on the basis of a fair distribution of losses and arguing that no defence based on victim's negligence should be allowed, for otherwise the administrative advantages of strict liability would be jeopardized by requiring an investigation into the victim's (and at times even into the defendant's) conduct: see ibid 1369).

[20] Keating (n 19) 1353. See also Oliver Wendell Holmes, *The Common Law* (Little, Brown and Company 1923) 96 ('[t]he undertaking to redistribute losses simply on the ground that they resulted from the defendant's act would ... be open' to a variety of objections, including the fact that the '[state's] cumbrous and expensive machinery ought not to be set in motion unless some clear benefit is to be derived from disturbing the *status quo*'); Clarence Morris, 'Hazardous Enterprises and Risk Bearing Capacity' (1952) 61 Yale LJ 1172, 1176 ('if a defendant's superior risk bearing capacity is a good reason for shifting a loss to him, a plaintiff's superior risk bearing capacity provides an even better reason to let the loss lie where it has fallen, *for the administrative and legal expenses of shifting the loss may be saved*') (emphasis added).

Given the special attention that economic theory pays to the impact of liability rules on social welfare, it is only natural that the concern to reduce administrative costs is more acutely felt by those working in the field of law and economics. After all, administrative costs are no less real than any other cost caused by accidents, and therefore they are taken into account when it comes to evaluating the cost-minimizing ability of different liability rules. On the other hand, as noted when discussing the United States, the effects of liability rules on administrative costs are especially difficult to ascertain and it therefore remains unsettled which liability rule is better at reducing such costs. This uncertainty is clearly visible in Italy as well. In theorizing about tort liability, both Trimarchi, on the one hand, and Mattei, Monateri, and Pardolesi (in their book co-authored with Cooter and Ulen), on the other, point out that strict liability should bring down the cost of litigating individual claims by removing the need to assess the defendant's conduct, but that it may well increase the overall number of claims because of the greater chances to obtain compensation than under a regime based on fault.[21] The result is that it is unclear which rule is cheaper in terms of overall administrative costs. Uncertainty transpires in relation to specific contexts of liability as well. For example, as far as the liability for things in one's keeping is concerned, Baffi and Nardi suggest on one occasion that it may be difficult for the judge to determine the efficient level of precautions that the parties should have adopted and that, at least in some circumstances, a rule of strict liability coupled with a defence of contributory negligence may desirably simplify the court's assessment of the parties' conduct and hence reduce administrative costs.[22] However, on another occasion, the two authors emphasize that while strict liability may reduce administrative costs by streamlining the activity of judges, this regime still entails a costly procedure for shifting the loss from the claimant to the defendant; if these remaining administrative costs are not offset by a reduction in the number or severity of accidents, then it may be cheaper—and therefore better—to let the loss lie where it fell.[23] This balancing between savings and administrative costs appears to be difficult to carry out in practice and it is therefore conducive to uncertainties when it comes to choosing among strict liability, liability for fault, and no liability. Again, in relation to liability for ruinous buildings, Baffi provides the usual statement that it is difficult to choose between strict liability and fault on the basis of their effects on administrative costs, and concludes that in many cases the former regime would be better than the latter

---

[21] Pietro Trimarchi, 'Transfers, Uncertainty and The Cost of Disruption' (2003) 23 Int Rev Law Econ 49, 60; Robert Cooter and others, *Il mercato delle regole—Analisi economica del diritto civile—I. Fondamenti* (Il Mulino 2006) 223.

[22] Enrico Baffi and Dario Nardi, 'L'analisi economica del diritto e la giurisprudenza' (2016) 10 DR 1012, 1018.

[23] Enrico Baffi and Dario Nardi, 'Analisi economica del diritto e danno cagionato da cose in custodia' (2018) 3 DR 327, 333. For a similar point, see Pietro Trimarchi, *La Responsabilità Civile: Atti Illeciti, Rischio, Danno* (Giuffrè 2017) 352.

248   JUSTIFYING STRICT LIABILITY

on grounds of efficient accident avoidance.[24] Finally, in relation to liability for products, a number of Italian scholars refer to the reduction of the Calabresian 'tertiary' costs, which include the costs of administering tort claims, as a reason for adopting strict liability;[25] others, by contrast, point to the potential effects on administrative costs as one of the reasons for qualifying strict product liability with a defence based on the user/consumer's fault,[26] or for not adopting a regime of strict liability for certain avoidable accidents and for development risks.[27]

The upshot is that, in keeping with the US approach, in Italian economic reasoning administrative costs are part of a broader 'calculus' which seeks to identify the liability rule which minimizes the overall costs of accidents. In this respect, then, a reduction in administrative costs is seen as theoretically relevant as a reduction in the number of accidents or as the spreading of the attendant losses, and it is therefore combined with these considerations for the purpose of choosing the most cost-minimizing liability rule. On the other hand, as explained above,[28] the precise effects of different liability rules on administrative costs are often unclear and it is therefore difficult to choose between fault and strict liability on this ground. Probably because of this, and in keeping with their colleagues in the United States, Italian legal economists devote most of their effort and thinking to the efficient avoidance of accidents. In sum, in Italian economic reasoning as well the significance of reducing administrative costs as an argument for strict liability looks initially great, but it then diminishes considerably when we consider that relatively little is known about the effects of liability rules on administrative costs and that, hence, the same argument may be used either to support or to reject strict liability.

Outside of the realm of law and economics, the picture is dramatically different. Here, it is far less frequent to come across instances of reasoning that consider a reduction in administrative costs, with most of them concerning the liability of parents for the action of their offspring. In advocating strict parental liability, Pardolesi and Dimattia argue that this regime would have a number of beneficial

---

[24] Enrico Baffi, 'La responsabilità del proprietario per danni da rovina di edificio come forma di responsabilità vicaria: analisi giuseconomica' (2017) 6 DR 657, 663, 666–67.

[25] See Ugo Carnevali, *La responsabilità del produttore* (Giuffrè 1974) 47–50; Carlo Castronovo, *Problema e sistema nel danno da prodotti* (Giuffrè 1979) 651 (discussing strict liability in general, but clearly extending his remarks to product liability as well, given the focus of the author's book); Giulio Ponzanelli, 'Causa probabile del danno e responsabilità del produttore' (2004) 5 DR 527, [3] (arguing that strict product liability is meant to help the claimant by removing the need to prove the defendant's fault, and that its function is also to achieve a better allocation of economic resources by reducing administrative costs, securing a better level of deterrence, and acting as a tool for the internalization of costs). See also Dario Covucci, 'Attività pericolosa e responsabilità oggettiva del produttore di sigarette' (2010) 6 NGCC 667, [2.2] (arguing that the manufacturing of tobacco products constitutes a dangerous activity for the purposes of article 2050 Cod civ and that the imposition of strict liability for the harm caused to smokers would be desirable because it would, among other things, reduce administrative costs).

[26] Cooter and others (n 21) 234–35; Cooter and others, *Il mercato delle regole—Analisi economica del diritto civile—II. Applicazioni* (Il Mulino 2006) 204.

[27] Trimarchi (n 23) 410–12, 415–16.

[28] See text to nn 21–27 in this section.

effects, including the fact that judges would no longer be involved in a 'tiresome search for almost impalpable faults'.[29] Similarly, Monti argues that a regime of strict (or quasi-strict) liability would, if coupled with compulsory insurance, provide a series of advantages, including a substantial reduction in tort litigation.[30] Further examples may be found in other areas as well, but again they are very rare, and perhaps open to being reclassified as arguments of a different nature.[31] Moreover, even where mentioned, administrative cost reduction is typically juxtaposed with a variety of other arguments, and here the impression is that it acts as a justification of secondary importance. Going back to the examples considered above, Pardolesi and Dimattia would adopt a regime of strict parental liability to avoid irreconcilable judicial decisions as well as discriminations against poorer parents, to compensate victims and avoid accidents, *to relieve judges from the difficult task of assessing the parents' conduct*, and to promote the adoption of compulsory insurance;[32] Monti, on her part, argues that a regime of strict (or quasi-strict) parental liability plus compulsory insurance would protect both the victims of the harmful action of the minor as well as the latter's parents, *it would reduce the volume of litigation* at least as far as accidents of modest magnitude are concerned, and it would simplify the quantification of pecuniary damages.[33] In these examples, the order of discussion of the arguments put forward but especially the varying emphasis placed on them suggest that reducing administrative costs is not a key justification for strict liability. In sum, in keeping with the US approach, this argument gets a cold reception in the legal reasoning outside of law and economics, even though in Italy it receives even less attention that in the United States. A plausible explanation for the Italian approach is that the many legal scholars who are not into law and economics see no reason to consider a reduction in administrative costs as an attractive justification for strict liability, and indeed they typically justify it on the basis of entirely different arguments which may well conflict with administrative cost reduction, such as risk, loss spreading, victim protection, or accident avoidance (where not linked to the promotion of social welfare). A final, related point

---

[29] Paolo Pardolesi and Marina Dimattia, 'Responsabilità dei genitori per l'illecito dei minori: un esercizio di precomprensione?' (2010) 2 DR 168, 175.

[30] Silvia Monti, 'Responsabilità dei genitori: alcune riflessioni' (2014) 11 DR 1054, 1061. See also Salvatore Patti, *Famiglia e responsabilità civile* (Giuffrè 1984) 285 (while not supporting strict parental liability, he admits that its adoption would 'allow considerable savings in judicial activity').

[31] See App Brescia 4.5.1958 (as reported in Vinicio Geri, *La R.C. da cose in custodia, animali e rovina di edificio* (Giuffrè 1974) 342, fn 136) ('the reason why the law places the liability for the harm caused by a ruinous building on its owner is due, in part, to the great practical difficulty of identifying the party truly responsible for the construction defect or the maintenance defect'); Renato Scognamiglio, 'Responsabilità civile' Noviss Dig It (UTET 1968) XV, 628, 646 (arguing that the building's owner can provide evidence of the real cause of the accident more easily than the claimant). While these statements can be seen as relating to a reduction in administrative costs, they can just as easily be interpreted as concerned with facilitating the compensation of victims, which is an entirely different argument: see n 1 in this section.

[32] Pardolesi and Dimattia (n 29) 174–75.

[33] Monti (n 30) 1060–61.

250 JUSTIFYING STRICT LIABILITY

concerns the use of the argument in judicial reasoning. As seen above, US courts do occasionally refer to administrative costs in their effort to justify strict liability.[34] This is not the case in Italy, however, and the very little consideration given to administrative costs in academic writings may help explain their neglect in judicial reasoning.

All in all, then, the significance of this argument in the Italian context is rather limited. Reducing administrative costs is certainly a concern for economic theory, which is interested in identifying the effects of liability rules on all the types of costs generated by accidents. However, the extreme difficulty in gauging with precision the relative impact of fault and strict liability on administrative costs renders the choice between the two regimes a very difficult one, with the result that an argument based on administrative costs may be used either to support strict liability or to reject it. Outside of economic reasoning, this argument is relied upon only very rarely to justify strict liability and, where it is, it does not carry much justificatory weight.

3.7.4 The Modest Significance of Administrative Cost Reduction in England

While legal actors in England pay attention to the costs of administering the tort system, particularly as compared to other compensation systems,[35] the idea of justifying strict liability on grounds of administrative savings fails to attract any meaningful support, especially if compared to the US and Italian approaches. As will be seen below, in English law this argument lacks the theoretical support that it enjoys, at least to some extent, in those two legal systems.

As a justification for strict liability, administrative cost reduction is not unknown in English reasoning, and examples of this argument can be found in various contexts. For instance, in relation to accidents in general, Jolowicz argues that the adoption of strict liability instead of fault would increase the predictability of the outcome of future cases, therefore encouraging settlements and reducing the volume of litigation.[36] In the context of liability for products, the Law Commission believes that one of the reasons for adopting strict liability lies in the need to 'discourage unnecessary litigation'.[37] Similarly, in relation to liability for animals, the

---

[34] See subsection 3.7.2.

[35] See eg the Pearson Commission, *Report of the Royal Commission on Civil Liability and Compensation for Personal Injury*, Cmnd 7054-I (1978); Patrick S Atiyah, *Accidents, Compensation and the Law* (3rd edn, Weidenfeld & Nicholson 1980) 509–19; Peter Cane and James Goudkamp, *Atiyah's Accidents, Compensation and the Law* (9th edn, CUP 2018) 375–82.

[36] John A Jolowicz, 'Liability for Accidents' (1968) 26 CLJ 50, 62–63. See also James Goudkamp and Donal Nolan, *Winfield & Jolowicz on Tort* (20th edn, Sweet and Maxwell 2020) [1–045] (mentioning a reduction in administrative costs as one of the advantages of strict liability over fault).

[37] Law Commission, *Liability for Defective Products* (Law Com No 82, 1977) [23](f), [38](f).

same legal actor emphasizes that strict liability for harm caused by straying live-stock 'can only be justified if it provides a clear rule as to liability [...], enabling disputes to be settled normally without recourse to litigation'.[38] Again, in respect of traffic accidents, Spencer maintains that English law's decision to let fault govern this area 'added enormously to the cost of litigating and settling' claims because of the difficult and time-consuming question of whether the driver was at fault, while a regime of strict liability would have avoided this issue almost completely and therefore would have resolved such cases in a quick and cheap way.[39] Finally, in relation to the liability of employers for breach of statutory duty, Steele criticizes the 2013 legislative reform of health and safety regulations by noting that, in the course of Parliamentary debates, 'it was pointed out that the strict liability provisions generally avoided costly litigation over whether there had been any lack of care'.[40] Further examples may be identified in English reasoning,[41] but overall it is clear that administrative cost reduction is by far the rarest argument put forward to justify strict liability in England, at least among the justifications explored in this book.

Reflecting further on the patterns of use of the argument in question and on its broader significance in English reasoning, a number of additional points can be made. First, in the few cases in which it is relied upon, administrative cost reduction almost never stands alone, a notable exception being the Law Commission's statement on strict liability for straying livestock, where administrative savings constitute *the* reason for the retention of strict liability.[42] Otherwise, administrative cost reduction is in most cases juxtaposed with other arguments such as victim protection, loss spreading, risk, or accident avoidance.[43] In light of the varying

---

[38] Law Commission, *Civil Liability for Animals* (Law Com No 13, 1967) [63], [64].

[39] John Rason Spencer, 'Motor-cars and the Rule in *Rylands v Fletcher*: A Chapter of Accidents in the History of Law and Motoring' (1983) CLJ 65, 80. See also the Pearson Commission (n 35) [995] (proposing a no-fault plan for injuries caused by motor vehicles, also on the ground that a liability system based on negligence is 'unduly slow, and expensive to administer'), but cf [1062], [1067] (rejecting the additional adoption of strict tort liability for these accidents because such a regime 'might result in considerable uncertainty and a good deal of litigation', and because it would 'place an unfair financial burden on the motorist').

[40] Jenny Steele, *Tort Law, Text, Cases, and Materials* (4th edn, OUP 2017) 882.

[41] See James Goudkamp, *Tort Law Defences* (Hart Publishing 2013) 168 (arguing that 'the main reason why strict liability is imposed for harm resulting from abnormally dangerous activities is that, typically, those who cause harm while engaged in such activities will be at fault. The imposition of strict liability saves the effort and expense of inquiring as to fault when fault will normally be present').

[42] See n 38 in this section.

[43] Jolowicz (n 36) 57–58, 61–63 (on accidents in general, juxtaposing administrative cost reduction with loss spreading and victim protection); Law Com No 82 (n 37) [23], [37]–[38] (on product liability, juxtaposing administrative cost reduction with risk creation, accident avoidance, loss spreading, and victim protection); Spencer (n 39) 80–81 (on traffic accidents, juxtaposing administrative cost reduction with victim protection, with the need to avoid distorting the law of negligence, and with abnormality of risk); Steele (n 40) 882 (on employers' liability for breach of statutory duty, juxtaposing administrative cost reduction with victim protection); Goudkamp and Nolan (n 36) [1-045] (on strict liability in general, juxtaposing administrative cost reduction with victim protection, although it is not entirely clear whether the two authors see these as reasons for strict liability or as effects of its imposition).

emphasis placed on these arguments and on the way in which they are discussed by the relevant legal actor, the impression is that a reduction in administrative costs is typically seen as carrying less justificatory weight than the other arguments and that, in any event, it never appears to be more important than them. To give one example, in his article on liability for accidents, Jolowicz supports a general regime of strict liability on the basis of loss-spreading considerations for the most part of his analysis, and it is only towards the end of the article that he mentions a reduction in administrative costs as a clear advantage of adopting such a regime.[44] In sum, administrative cost reduction does not typically constitute a key reason for imposing strict liability in English law, but it rather acts as an argument of secondary significance.

What are, then, the reasons for the very limited significance of administrative cost reduction in England? A number of them can be put forward. First, the absence of 'law and economics' as a way of approaching the law deprives this argument of an essential theoretical buttress. We saw that both in the Unites States and in Italy the effect of liability rules on the cost of litigation is a relevant factor in assessing their ability to minimize the overall costs of accidents, together with a concern to avoid accidents in the first place and to diffuse their social impact.[45] It is indeed in the context of economic reasoning that administrative cost reduction assumes considerable significance in these two legal systems, as otherwise it receives little support even there. As any 'law and economics' intellectual movement is lacking in the context of English tort law, it is understandable that an argument based on administrative costs receives little attention and even less support among English legal actors. Secondly, the argument itself can be turned on its head and be used to undermine the adoption of strict liability rather than support it. As seen above,[46] a point routinely made by legal economists is that while strict liability may bring down the cost of litigating individual claims, it may on the other hand increase the total number of cases, therefore augmenting rather than reducing the overall administrative costs of the tort system as compared to fault liability. Along similar lines, Cane and Goudkamp criticize the Pearson Commission's proposals to adopt a regime of strict liability for dangerous things and activities on various grounds, including the possibility that 'their implementation could trigger a huge amount of litigation';[47] and the Pearson Commission itself, in proposing a reform in the area of motor vehicle accidents, rejected the idea of adopting a system of strict tort liability (in addition to a no-fault scheme) on the ground that such a regime 'might result in considerable uncertainty and a good deal of litigation'.[48] Thirdly, we saw that in the United States an argument such as administrative cost

[44] Jolowicz (n 36).
[45] See subsections 3.7.2 and 3.7.3, respectively.
[46] See text to n 12 and to n 21 in this section.
[47] Cane and Goudkamp (n 35) 92.
[48] Pearson Commission (n 35) [1062].

reduction conflicts openly with theories of tort liability based on norms of inter-personal justice,[49] as that argument embodies a collective, forward-looking concern that is divorced from the doing of justice between the particular claimant and the particular defendant. Because of this, the idea of justifying strict liability with a possible reduction in administrative costs has no appeal among the many English legal scholars who see tort law as a system concerned with the doing of individual justice.[50] And even for those legal actors who are not wedded to this particular approach to tort law, a reduction in administrative costs may simply be an irrelevant consideration, as where strict liability is justified on grounds of accident avoidance, loss spreading, or victim protection. Finally, given the modest use of administrative cost reduction among legal scholars, it comes as no surprise that the argument is neglected in English judicial reasoning, in this respect resembling the Italian approach.[51]

To conclude, an argument for strict liability based on administrative savings is only rarely used in England and, even where mentioned, it is generally of secondary importance compared to other justifications. Given the English overall scepticism for 'law and economics' and the tendency to theorize about tort law on the basis of notions of interpersonal justice, it is not surprising at all that administrative cost reduction bears very little significance in the English reasoning on strict liability.

3.7.5 Reducing Administrative Costs in France: An Insignificant Argument

While aware of the possible effects of different liability rules on administrative costs, French legal actors pay scarce attention to the reduction of these costs as a justification for strict liability. In this respect, French reasoning contrasts markedly with the US and Italian approaches, while bearing some resemblance with the English one, where, as discussed, the argument in question has little significance as well.

Looking at the French reasoning on strict liability, it is possible to come across instances of administrative savings being used as a reason in favour of strict liability. For example, while discussing strict liability in general and its deterrent potential, Tunc notes that this type of liability 'saves long and sometimes costly disputes'.[52] In relation to specific contexts of liability, other leading scholars as well take into account administrative costs to justify or defend the adoption of (sometimes

---

[49] See text to nn 15–16 in this section.
[50] See subsection 3.8.3.
[51] See subsection 3.7.3.
[52] André Tunc, 'Responsabilité civile et dissuasion des comportements antisociaux' in *Aspects nouveaux de la pensée juridique: recueil d'études en hommage à Marc Ancel*, vol 1 (Pedone 1975) 407, 414 (juxtaposing administrative cost reduction with accident avoidance).

254 JUSTIFYING STRICT LIABILITY

extremely) strict liabilities. In the context of parental liability, Viney defends the *Bertrand* decision on various grounds, including the fact that, should *Bertrand* increase the costs of insurance premiums, these extra costs would be offset by the savings secured by removing fault as an issue to be assessed at trial.[53] Similarly, in relation to traffic accidents, in *Desmares* the Avocat général Charbonnier supports a regime of strict liability *without* a defence of contributory negligence on the ground that this development would simplify litigation, for it would be no longer necessary to assess the victim's fault;[54] Viney herself agrees with this,[55] and in addition defends *Desmares* from the objection that it would augment insurance costs because, even if this were true, such increases would be alleviated by a reduction in the volume of litigation.[56] Finally, after the enactment of the *loi* Badinter, Viney and also Jourdain explain a regime of liability as strict as that implemented by the *loi* for traffic accidents on various grounds, including the fact that its drafters wanted to encourage settlements and therefore reduce the volume of litigation.[57]

These instances of reasoning show that, to some extent, French legal actors are aware of the effects of liability rules on administrative costs and that they may refer to the reduction of these costs to support strict liability or to defend it from a variety of objections. However, this pattern of reasoning is *very* rare, providing a first strong indication that the argument fails to attract any meaningful support among French legal actors. Moreover, administrative cost reduction does not act as a stand-alone justification, as it is invariably juxtaposed with other arguments, generally victim protection, loss spreading and, at times, even accident avoidance.[58] In the examples discussed, reducing the number of claims or the length or complexity of litigation is a concern that receives far less attention or emphasis than the other arguments put forward; this is not surprising, for these other arguments—especially victim protection and loss spreading—constitute the most significant justifications for strict liability in France.[59] This is so true that, in some instances at

---

[53] Geneviève Viney, JCP 1997.II n.22848, 252. cf Patrice Jourdain, 'La responsabilité des père et mère: une responsabilité principale et directe, indépendante de celle du mineur' D 2003.4.231 (note to Ass plén 13.12.2002) [8]–[9] (arguing that one of the possible explanations for the *Levert* decision is the simplification of liability determinations that follows from removing the need to assess the minor's fault, but concluding that there are countervailing reasons to reject such developments).

[54] Civ (2) 21.7.1982, D 1982.449 note Larroumet, concl Charbonnier, 450–52 (juxtaposing administrative cost reduction with victim protection and insurance spreading).

[55] Geneviève Viney, 'L'indemnisation des victimes de dommages causes par le "fait d'une chose" après l'arrêt de la Cour de cassation' D chron 1982.201, 204, 205–06 (juxtaposing administrative cost reduction with victim protection and insurance spreading).

[56] ibid 205.

[57] Geneviève Viney, 'Les trentes ans de la loi Badinter: bilan et perspectives. Propos introductifs' in *Les trentes ans de la loi Badinter—Bilan et perspectives*, RCA September 2015, dossier 12, 7, [40]–[42]; Patrice Jourdain in Geneviève Viney, Patrice Jourdain, and Suzanne Carval (eds), *Les régimes spéciaux et l'assurance de responsabilité* (4th edn, LGDJ 2017) [85] (both authors juxtaposing administrative cost reduction with victim protection). See also Jean-Sébastien Borghetti, 'Extra-Strict Liability for Traffic Accidents in France' (2018) 53 Wake Forest L Rev 265, 282, 286–89, 291.

[58] See references in nn 52–57 in this section.

[59] See subsections 3.5.2 and 3.6.2.

least, simplifying litigation is seen as conducive to improving the position of victims, who will be able to receive compensation more easily and quickly thanks to streamlined trials, at which point one could even wonder whether reducing administrative costs retains any distinctiveness as an argument for strict liability.[60] In sum, the patterns of use of administrative cost reduction suggest that this argument is almost impalpable in the French reasoning on strict liability and that, even where used, its significance is modest. In this respect, then, the French position bears some resemblance with the English approach while differing markedly from what happens in the United States and Italy.

Why, then, is administrative cost reduction largely neglected in France? As already explained,[61] in the United States and in Italy this argument owes much of its significance to its being one of the elements taken into account by legal economists, with a view to minimizing the overall costs of accidents. In France, however, economic analysis has never attracted meaningful support, and it is frowned upon because its focus on cost-benefit analysis is far removed from the French imperative of social solidarity and its overt commitment to protecting the victims of accidents.[62] It is therefore inevitable that the French rejection of 'law and economics' reduces drastically any room for administrative savings as a significant consideration in choosing between liability rules and as an argument for justifying strict liability. In this respect, then, the French approach resembles the English one, as in both legal systems the modest role of administrative cost reduction has much to do with the scepticism for 'law and economics', even though in the two jurisdictions this critical stance is based on profoundly different reasons, social solidarity in France and a taste for principles of individual responsibility in England.

Relatedly, giving too much credit to an argument based on administrative savings (whether or not from an efficiency perspective) may lead to results that would be seen as unpalatable in France because not favourable enough to the victims of accidents and, therefore, in dissonance with social solidarity. If, say, it was proven that the costs of administering fault were lower than the costs of administering strict liability, would French law shift to fault in contexts where it had previously decided to impose strict liability? In all likelihood, the answer would be negative, for the higher administrative costs of strict liability would merely mean that a greater amount of money would have to be spread across society so as to avoid that any one person was financially crushed by the costs of accidents. In other words, the only idea of choosing fault over strict liability because of the former's (hypothetically) lower administrative costs would be likely seen as immoral because it

---

[60] See Viney (n 55) 204 (arguing that assessing the victim's fault in traffic accidents is one of the main causes of the excessive length of trials and that endless litigation is one of the most serious problems of the compensation system dealing with traffic accidents).

[61] See subsections 3.7.2 and 3.7.3.

[62] See also text to and following n 169 in subsection 3.3.5 and text to n 52 in subsection 3.5.2.

256 JUSTIFYING STRICT LIABILITY

would undermine the wellbeing of the victims of accidents for no adequate reason, given that the costs it would save could anyway be spread widely. So long as the job of strict liability is thought to be about ensuring compensation and spreading losses, French legal actors will most likely keep ignoring administrative savings as a justification for this type of liability.

Overall, then, administrative cost reduction is almost impalpable in the French context, as it is very rarely used and, even where it is, it does not act as a key justification. The absence of 'law and economics' can certainly account for this, as also seen in relation to England. More generally, the impression is that the idea of justifying strict liability on the basis of administrative savings is seen as irrelevant to, if not in potential conflict with, the key concerns of and justifications for strict liability in France, namely the protection of victims and the spreading of losses, in a true spirit of social solidarity.

3.7.6 Concluding Remarks

Reducing administrative costs by way of imposing strict liability is a concern that is not shared in the same way and to the same degree in the four legal systems considered. As a result, the patterns of use and the significance of administrative cost reduction as an argument for strict liability vary markedly across the four jurisdictions. These variations relate to the degree of development of 'law and economics' as a way of approaching tort law and, more generally, to what the main functions of strict liability (and of tort law more broadly) are perceived to be.

In both the United States and Italy, administrative cost reduction has a meaningful role to play in the reasoning of legal economists. For them, administrative costs are as real and therefore as worthy of consideration as any other cost generated by the occurrence of accidents and by the allocation of the attendant losses. Therefore, economic approaches assess liability rules not only for their ability to avoid accidents or spread their consequent losses, but also for how costly they are to administer. From the reasoning of US and Italian scholars, what emerges is that it is difficult to settle whether overall it is cheaper to administer a rule of strict liability or one based on the defendant's fault. What it is generally maintained is that strict liability may bring down the cost of individual claims, while fault may reduce the overall number of claims; as a result, it is unclear which one reduces more effectively the overall administrative costs of the tort system. Hence, an argument based on administrative costs looks like a wild card, which can be easily used either to support or to reject strict liability. Moreover, this uncertainty arguably pushes legal economists in both legal systems to focus their works on the effects of liability rules on accident avoidance and, albeit less so, on loss distribution, and instead to deal rather briefly with administrative savings. As a result of all this, the significance of administrative cost reduction is somewhat ambiguous in 'law and economics'.[63] Outside economic theory, the picture is rather different. First, the argument is used far less frequently, both in the United States and (particularly so) in Italy, though featuring in a variety of contexts of liability. Moreover, in both systems its justificatory weight is reduced because the argument is usually juxtaposed with justifications that, for the legal actor who is speaking, are far more important.[64] Finally, in the United States, the idea of justifying strict liability (or any other tort liability) on the basis of a possible reduction in administrative costs attracts the criticism of those who, by seeing tort law as a system of interpersonal justice, reject forward-looking, collective concerns as good reasons for imposing liability.[65] This type of criticism, by contrast, is not visible in Italy, where legal actors do not see any problem with justifying strict liability, and tort liability more generally, by reference to forward-looking considerations.[66]

The picture is radically different in England and France. In both jurisdictions, administrative cost reduction can be seen at play in the reasoning of some legal actor seeking to justify the imposition of strict liability. For example, in England this argument is used in contexts such as liability for traffic accidents, animals, defective products, or breach of statutory duty, and even in relation to strict liability in general.[67] Similarly, in France it is invoked in contexts such as liability of parents for the action of their children, liability for traffic accidents, or again strict liability in general.[68] However, this argument is only very rarely relied upon in both legal systems. Moreover, even where used, it is typically juxtaposed with a variety of other justifications which enjoy greater justificatory weight, most notably risk, loss spreading, or victim protection.[69] In sum, administrative cost reduction appears to have very little significance in both legal systems, for partly the same reasons. The common trait here is the absence of 'law and economics', which therefore cannot provide the type of theoretical support that the argument enjoys in the United States and Italy.[70] Besides this common ground, we saw that the English tendency to theorize tort law as a system of interpersonal justice clashes with a forward-looking justification such as administrative cost reduction,[71] in this respect showing a concern that is acutely felt by a strand of legal scholarship in the United States as well. By contrast, in France this type of criticism does not surfaces in legal reasoning. In keeping with Italy, the approach of French legal actors is

---

[63] See text to nn 10–14 (United States), and text to and following nn 21–28 (Italy) in this section.

[64] See text to nn 17–19 (United States), and text to and following nn 29–33 (Italy) in this section.

[65] See text to nn 15–16 in this section.

[66] See especially subsections 3.3.3 (accident avoidance), 3.5.4 (loss spreading), and 3.6.3 (victim protection).

[67] See text to nn 36–41 in this section.

[68] See text to nn 52–57 in this section.

[69] See nn 43–44 and accompanying text (England), nn 52–57 and text to nn 58–60 (France) in this section.

[70] See text to and following n 45 (England), and text to and following nn 61–62 (France) in this section.

[71] See text to nn 49–50 in this section.

profoundly forward-looking, especially when it comes to justifying strict liability,[72] and little attention is paid to the concerns of interpersonal justice which instead characterize English and US legal reasoning.[73]

[72] See subsections 3.5.2 (loss spreading) and 3.6.2 (victim protection).
[73] See section 3.8.

3.8

Individual Responsibility

3.8.1 Individual Responsibility as a Justification for Strict Liability

It is often said that people ought to take responsibility for their actions and for the outcomes they bring about in the world. Depending on numerous factors, such as the nature of the action or outcome in question, the identity of the agent and of the party demanding a response from them, and the relationship between the parties, responsibility for actions or outcomes may take a variety of forms.[1] For example, in some circumstances an apology or some other showing of contrition may be enough, while at other times more institutionalized responses such as civil liability or criminal punishment may be more appropriate. Insofar as accidents attracting a possible tort response are concerned, liability is sometimes justified on the basis of (what I will label here) 'individual responsibility'. In this respect the term 'responsibility' is not a synonym for legal (tort) liability; instead, it involves a moral judgment about whether the defendant ought to be answerable in some way to the claimant for the harm caused to him or her. A considerable number of theories have been devised which see tort law as an ethical system of responsibility and which seek to justify tort liability accordingly. Generally each of these theories articulates its own conception of responsibility on the basis of concepts such as agency, autonomy, choice, duty, or wrong, but the theories play with these ideas in different ways, with the result that they produce a number of (sometimes very) different conceptions of individual responsibility and, therefore, different possible justifications for strict liability. Given these variations, it would not be helpful (or indeed practically possible) to discuss here these various particular theories. For now, it suffices to say that these theories see strict liability as embodying some norm of responsibility which governs the relationship between (potential) claimants and (potential) defendants and which defines their reciprocal rights and duties. As one would expect, most responsibility-based theories happily accommodate liability based on fault because fault is generally seen as providing a morally satisfactory justification for ascribing responsibility to a defendant and, therefore, for finding them liable in tort. But the imposition of strict liability is more problematic, with the result that most—though not all—of these theories tend to restrict its role in

---

[1] Christopher Kutz, 'Responsibility' in Jules L Coleman, Kenneth Einar Himma, and Scott J Shapiro (eds), *The Oxford Handbook of Jurisprudence and Philosophy of Law* (OUP 2004) 548, 550.

Justifying Strict Liability. Marco Cappelletti, Oxford University Press. © Marco Cappelletti 2022.
DOI: 10.1093/oso/9780192859860.003.0010

260   JUSTIFYING STRICT LIABILITY

tort law. As each conception of individual responsibility treats strict liability in its own way, I will illustrate the key elements of each and explain their distinctive features vis-à-vis strict liability in the course of the following discussion. However, it is helpful to say at the outset that what I will show is that the significance of individual responsibility as a justification for strict liability and the way in which it is used vary considerably across the four legal systems studied. And in this respect, and for the first time in my comparative discussion of legal reasoning, there is a dramatic contrast between the common law and civil law systems.

3.8.2 Individual Responsibility in the United States: An Argument of Moderate Significance

As a justification for the imposition of strict liability in the United States, we can see that individual responsibility is part of the reasoning of US legal actors, and especially of those legal scholars who see tort law through the lens of moral philosophy. Generally speaking, though, most US responsibility-based approaches tend to favour fault as a proper basis of tort liability, and their proponents typically avoid contaminating their theories with the very arguments that in the US context are most often deployed to justify the imposition of strict liability. As a result, individual responsibility does not seem to constitute a prominent justification for strict liability in the United States.

As a reaction to the emergence and growing influence of theories seeing tort law as an instrument of socio-economic policy, from the 1970s several US scholars have appealed to notions such as duty, right, wrong, harm, or responsibility as key to understanding the meaning and functions of tort law. This intellectual effort has sought to emphasize the 'morality' of tort law:[2] its goal is to achieve some form of relational, interpersonal justice between claimant and defendant, not some societal goal extraneous to the claimant–defendant nexus as, for example, the reduction of accidents or the spreading of losses. A multitude of such theories have been put forward in the United States and, with one notable exception,[3] each of the theories discussed below is portrayed by its proponent as a theory of corrective justice.[4] All these theories share the view that some conception of responsibility is key to understanding tort law and liability, but each of them puts forward its own understanding of responsibility, which may be more or less favourable to the imposition of strict liability. In other words, depending on the specific conception of

---

[2] See Gregory C Keating, 'Strict Liability Wrongs' in John Oberdiek (ed), *Philosophical Foundations of the Law of Torts* (OUP 2014) 292, fn 1.

[3] See text to nn 43–48 in this section.

[4] As noted by Peter Cane, 'Rights in Private Law' in Donal Nolan and Andrew Robertson (eds), *Rights and Private Law* (Hart Publishing 2012) 35, 40, all corrective justice theorists 'adopt a backward-looking, responsibility-based perspective on law'.

responsibility adopted, strict liability is treated in a different and sometimes a very different way.

Let us start with Epstein's famous approach to strict liability which seeks 'to develop a normative theory of torts that takes into account common sense notions of individual responsibility'.[5] Epstein's approach is frequently labelled as 'libertarian' because it argues that each person has dominion over themselves and that they own the good and bad they bring about in the world.[6] In tort law, this means that if a person's conduct can be causally linked to the harm suffered by another, corrective justice requires the former to be liable to the latter, regardless of fault. As Epstein himself puts it, 'the principles of strict liability say that the liberty of one person ends when he causes harm to another',[7] and '[t]he major premise of the theory of strict liability is that, prima facie, [the defendant] should not be allowed to help himself by taking or destroying the plaintiff's person or property'.[8] In Epstein's view, there are four causal paradigms which 'fasten[] responsibility upon the defendant',[9] namely force, fright, compulsion, and dangerous conditions. In particular, if the defendant causes harm to the claimant by using force against them, by frightening (or shocking) them, by compelling someone else to harm them, or by creating dangerous conditions that result in harm to them, then there is a prima facie case for imposing liability on the defendant.[10] It can be seen, then, that Epstein's theory argues for a general imposition of strict liability but, in light of the harsh criticisms it has attracted partly for this very reason, it enjoys little currency today.[11]

---

[5] Richard A Epstein, 'A Theory of Strict Liability' (1973) 2 J Legal Stud 151, 151.

[6] See John CP Goldberg, 'Twentieth-Century Tort Theory' (2002) 91 Geo LJ 513, 564–65.

[7] Epstein (n 5) 203–04. See also Richard A Epstein, 'Causation and Corrective Justice: A Reply to Two Critics' (1979) 8 J Legal Stud 477, 479.

[8] Richard A Epstein, 'Intentional Harms' (1975) 4 J Legal Stud 391, 398.

[9] Epstein (n 5) 169.

[10] ibid 166–89. The 'prima facie' qualification follows from Epstein's recognition of a number of defences which may allow the defendant to escape liability. To do so, the defendant must either disprove causation or show that the claimant assumed the risk of harm or trespassed the defendant's own person or land: see Richard A Epstein, 'Defenses and Subsequent Pleas in a System of Strict Liability' (1974) 3 J Legal Stud 165, esp 174–85, 185–201, and 201–13. For an application of Epstein's approach to the law of private nuisance, see Richard A Epstein, 'Nuisance Law: Corrective Justice and Its Utilitarian Constraints' (1979) 8 J Legal Stud 49, 50–73 (hereafter Epstein, 'Nuisance Law').

[11] For criticisms of Epstein's approach, see eg John Borgo, 'Causal Paradigms' (1979) 8 J Legal Stud 419; Richard A Posner, 'Epstein's Tort Theory: A Critique' (1979) 8 J Legal Stud 457; Jules Coleman, 'Moral Theories of Torts: Their Scope and Limits: Part 1' (1982) Law & Phil 371, 379–80; Stephen R Perry, 'The Impossibility of General Strict Liability' (1988) 1 Can JL Juris 147; Jane Stapleton, *Product Liability* (Butterworths 1994) 165–73; Ernest Weinrib, *The Idea of Private Law* (OUP 2013) ch 7 (arguing that strict liability cannot be reconciled with principles of corrective justice, and criticizing Epstein's attempt to show the opposite). See also Richard A Epstein, 'Toward a General Theory of Tort Law: Strict Liability in Context' (2010) 3 JTL, article 6 (responding to some of the criticisms levelled at his theory, refining his own views and reaffirming at p 5 that, in situations 'involving bodily injury or property damage in stranger cases', 'the strict liability system remains preferable to the negligence one'). Note that Epstein's own thinking has evolved towards economic considerations, and his pro-market stance has led him to factor in reasons of economic efficiency when choosing between liability rules: see eg Richard A Epstein, 'Causation in Context: An Afterword' (1987) 63 Chi-Kent L Rev 653, 661; Epstein, 'Nuisance Law' (n 10) 74–102.

262 JUSTIFYING STRICT LIABILITY

A completely different approach is that of Keating, whose conception of individual responsibility seeks to justify strict liability and to show that it is and must be an important part of US tort law. In his view, two types of strict liability can be identified: right-based strict liability and harm-based strict liability. The former lies outside the scope of the present work, as it involves 'boundary crossings that may *both* do no harm and be entirely free of fault',[12] that is torts actionable *per se* (eg conversion, trespass to land, and some batteries).[13] By contrast, harm-based strict liability concerns the justifiable infliction of harm on another, examples being some nuisances, product liability, liability for abnormally dangerous activities, and the employer's vicarious liability for the torts of their employees.[14] Keating believes that tort law seeks to reconcile freedom of action with security from harm in a way that gives to everyone 'the most favorable circumstances to pursue her ends or aspirations, consistent with a like freedom for others'.[15] Harm-based strict liability achieves this result by imposing on the defendant an obligation not to inflict reasonable harm without repairing it.[16] While the defendant may harm the claimant by way of a justifiable (ie reasonable) conduct, and in so doing their conduct is not wrongful, the defendant cannot cause harm, even justifiably, without paying for it. In other words, 'harming justifiably without repairing' is the wrong that grounds responsibility and therefore the imposition of strict liability, as the defendant must not benefit from the reasonable infliction of harm on another at the latter's expense.[17] Understood in this way, strict liability embodies corrective justice as 'it undoes interactions that involve one person who benefits herself by reasonably harming another person'.[18] But Keating's theory does not stop here because he then juxtaposes his wrong-based conception of responsibility with a broader notion of fairness which requires that the burdens and benefits of human activities are fairly apportioned across society.[19] Keating's idea of a fair distribution of losses means both that defendants ought to bear the risk of harm they impose on others for their own advantage (risk–benefit) and that all those who benefit from

---

[12] Keating (n 2) 297 (original emphasis). This type of strict liability is imposed, in Keating's view, 'for the simple reason that the right itself would be fatally compromised by tolerating all reasonable (or justified) boundary crossings without regard to whether consent was given to those crossings' (ibid 298). In this type of situation, then, the defendant's responsibility goes so far as to coincide with a failure to respect another's right, however innocent or reasonable the violation is.

[13] See section 1.2.

[14] Keating (n 2) 296–97.

[15] Gregory C Keating, 'Distributive and Corrective Justice in the Tort Law of Accidents' (2000) 74 S Cal L Rev 193, 197 (hereafter Keating, 'Distributive and Corrective Justice'). See also Gregory C Keating, 'The Idea of Fairness in the Law of Enterprise Liability' (1997) 95 Mich L Rev 1266, 1312–17 (hereafter Keating, 'The Idea of Fairness').

[16] Keating (n 2) 306.

[17] ibid 296–97, 301–06. A similar argument was already put forward by Robert E Keeton, 'Conditional Fault in the Law of Torts' (1959) 72 Harv L Rev 401, 427–30.

[18] Keating (n 2) 306.

[19] ibid 306–08. See also Keating, 'Distributive and Corrective Justice' (n 15) 200, 219–21; Keating, 'The Idea of Fairness' (n 15) 1328–39.

the harmful activity ought to bear a proportional share of the loss (burden–benefit proportionality).[20] As can be seen, there is a complex pattern of reasoning at play here justifying strict liability: an understanding of wrong as 'harming justifiably without repairing' produces a certain conception of responsibility which is then juxtaposed with risk–benefit and burden–benefit proportionality. On this basis, Keating's approach justifies several key contexts of strict liability in US tort law and accords to strict liability a key role in the United States.

While both Epstein's and Keating's understandings of individual responsibility show a distinct taste for strict liability, the picture changes considerably as soon as one turns to other responsibility-based theories of US tort law. These differ quite substantially among themselves in many respects, but one aspect they have in common is a clear preference for fault over strict liability.

In subsection 3.2.4 of the book,[21] I discussed Fletcher's reciprocity paradigm as an example of a risk-based justification for strict liability, as the argument is typically characterized as justifying strict liability on the basis of the imposition of a nonreciprocal risk of harm. In propounding this argument, Fletcher does not provide any articulated conception of individual responsibility but merely suggests that the reciprocity paradigm accords with corrective justice and that it strikes a correct balance between freedom of action and security from harm.[22] By contrast, in a recent article providing a revised understanding of the reciprocity paradigm, Geistfeld sets out a more elaborate conception of individual responsibility based on liberal egalitarianism as underlying and justifying that paradigm within tort law.[23] According to Geistfeld, reciprocity is best seen not as a theory of tort law but as a behavioural norm which shapes key features of US tort law,[24] including negligence and strict liability rules.[25] In his view, the reciprocity norm ordinarily generates a norm of conduct of reasonable care and therefore requires negligence as the default rule of tort liability; as to strict liability, this should be limited to situations where individuals engage in conduct that poses risks of harm exceeding the ordinary or background level of risk in the community, as is the case with abnormally dangerous activities or the keeping of wild animals.[26] According to Geistfeld's account, strict liability plays only a secondary role, with fault being the primary form of liability in tort. Importantly, though, for Geistfeld the reciprocity norm cannot provide a complete justification for tort law and for the way in which the norm itself is enforced in this area,[27] including the imposition of strict liability. Such a

---

[20] See Keating (n 2) 306–08; Keating, 'The Idea of Fairness' (n 15) 1328–39; Gregory C Keating, 'Products Liability as Enterprise Liability' (2017) 10(1) JTL 41, 47, 56–57, 70–72.

[21] See text to nn 135–140 in subsection 3.2.4.

[22] George Fletcher, 'Fairness and Utility in Tort Theory' (1972) 85 Harv L Rev 537, 569, 550–51.

[23] Mark A Geistfeld, 'Hidden in Plain Sight: The Normative Source of Modern Tort Law' (2016) 91 NYU L Rev 1517.

[24] ibid 1571–72.

[25] ibid 1568.

[26] ibid 1560, 1572–82.

[27] ibid 1583, 1592.

justification is instead provided by values of liberal egalitarianism, according to which each individual has an equal right to autonomy and self-determination and is responsible for the consequences of their autonomous choices.[28] It is this conception of individual responsibility that justifies tort rules governing liability for nonreciprocal risks of harm, whether liability is strict or based on fault, and that ensures the striking of a proper balance between autonomy and security from harm. In sum, 'the substantive rationale for modern tort law extends far beyond the behavioral norm of reciprocity,'[29] and it can be identified in a specific conception of individual responsibility as deriving from the liberal egalitarian values of autonomy and self-determination. In combination with nonreciprocity of risk, this argument justifies the imposition of liability in tort, whether strict or based on fault. In this framework, though, strict liability applies only where the risk of harm exceeds the ordinary or background level of risk in the community, therefore playing only a secondary role as compared to fault.

A similarly reduced domain for strict liability is recognized in Coleman's and Perry's distinct conceptions of individual responsibility. For Coleman, one of the most prominent corrective justice theorists, the party who is responsible for the *wrongful* loss of another must repair that loss.[30] In this framework, there is room for both fault and strict liability, as they both follow the defendant's wrong consisting in the breach of a duty owed to the claimant. Where fault and strict liability differ is in the fact that they constitute 'different ways of articulating the content of one's duty to others'.[31] In fault-based liability, the duty is not to harm another through fault (eg negligent or reckless driving), whereas in strict liability the duty is not to harm full stop (eg while conducting blasting operations).[32] In either case, corrective justice demands that the person breaching their duty to another be liable in tort. This principle of corrective justice gives content to, and is constrained by, a specific conception of individual responsibility which requires persons' lives to reflect as much as possible their choices and agency and as little as possible other circumstances and (mis)fortunes.[33] Both fault and strict liability are consistent with this understanding of responsibility because they both link losses to human agency by holding liable the person whose wrongful conduct is responsible for such losses. There is, then, room for strict liability in Coleman's approach, but not as much as it may seem at first. Indeed, in drawing the boundaries of his theory, Coleman argues that corrective justice can explain only the core of tort law, of which important

---

[28] ibid 1588.

[29] ibid 1592.

[30] Jules L Coleman, *The Practice of Principle: In Defence of a Pragmatist Approach to Legal Theory* (OUP 2001) 22.

[31] Jules L Coleman, 'Facts, Fictions, and the Grounds of Law' in Joseph Keim Campbell, Michael O'Rourke, and David Shier (eds), *Law and Social Justice* (MIT Press 2005) 327, 329.

[32] ibid 329–30; Coleman (n 30) 35, fn 19.

[33] Coleman (n 30) 59–63.

areas such as vicarious liability or product liability do not, in his view, form part.[34] In sum, while in principle recognizing a role to strict liability in tort law, notably in the form of liability for abnormally dangerous activities, as he admits himself, Coleman's version of corrective justice and individual responsibility cannot explain key and well-established contexts of strict tort liability.[35]

Still from the perspective of corrective justice, Perry develops an entirely different conception of responsibility to justify tort liability, although a similarly modest role is recognized to strict liability. In Perry's view, an individual must take moral responsibility for the outcomes, good and bad, that they bring about in the world.[36] Crucially, if the bad outcome consists of a harm to someone, responsibility for it attaches only on condition that the individual in question had the capacity to *foresee* and *avoid* the harm,[37] in which case that individual is the moral 'author' of the adverse outcome.[38] This 'avoidability-based conception' of outcome responsibility is 'a plateau of responsibility that singles out the outcome-responsible agent as a *potential* cost-bearer', but more is required to convert this moral responsibility into legal responsibility.[39] This can occur in two distinct ways. First, if two individuals participate in an activity where they 'jointly create risks to which they are all vulnerable' (eg driving), liability will fall on the party who acted carelessly.[40] This corresponds to fault-based liability and, more specifically, to negligence. Secondly, moral outcome responsibility can, regardless of fault, become legal responsibility where an individual *unilaterally* imposes a risk of harm on the victim, as 'where the defendant's activity is very uncommon' (eg blasting), 'or when the likely victim is simply not in a position to know about the risk or to take any steps to avoid it if he does know about it' (eg falling airplanes).[41] The element of unilaterality is therefore key to justifying the imposition of strict liability in situations involving abnormally dangerous activities or the like.[42] In sum, Perry's view of strict liability in tort

---

[34] ibid 36. In his earlier writings, Coleman held a more radical view vis-a-vis strict liability: see Jules L Coleman, *Risks and Wrongs* (CUP 1992) 368–69 (reconstructing the rule in *Rylands v Fletcher* as well as liability for abnormally dangerous activities as arguably based on fault), endnote 8 to chapter 18 (claiming that strict liability is not part of the core of tort law).

[35] A further example of strict liability that Coleman provides in his earlier work regards situations where a defendant, without the claimant's prior consent, damages the latter's property for reasons of necessity (eg to avoid some more serious harm to their own property or bodily integrity). In doing so, the defendant acts justifiably, but nonetheless commits a wrong by invading the claimant's right and can therefore be found strictly liable: see Coleman (n 34) 371–72 (using as an illustration of this point the famous case *Vincent v Lake Erie*, 124 N.W. 221 (Minn.1910)).

[36] Stephen Perry, 'Responsibility for Outcomes, Risk, and the Law of Torts' in Gerald Postema (ed), *Philosophy and the Law of Torts* (CUP 2001) 72, 80.

[37] ibid 81, 88, 92.

[38] ibid 92, 119.

[39] ibid 73–74 (original emphasis).

[40] ibid 110, 112, 119–20.

[41] ibid 114–15. By contrast, at 96 Perry admits that his theory of outcome responsibility cannot explain vicarious liability.

[42] ibid 115. See also Stephen Perry, 'Torts, Rights, and Risk' in John Oberdiek (ed), *Philosophical Foundations of the Law of Torts* (OUP 2014) 38, 51–53.

law is rather restrictive, as his reasoning suggests that strict liability is appropriate only if both his moral conception of individual responsibility and the element of unilaterality in risk imposition are present. If either of these is missing, then strict liability is unwarranted.

A further, responsibility-based approach to tort that deserves attention for the way it treats strict liability is Goldberg and Zipursky's theory of civil recourse. On their account, tort law is best understood as a repository of relational norms of conduct and, therefore, as a body of law based on notions of wrongdoing and responsibility.[43] Goldberg and Zipursky's interpretation of tort law draws a distinction between 'wrongs-based liability' and 'licensing-based liability', which they justify on profoundly different grounds. Wrongs-based liability attaches to a defendant who wrongfully, that is by not complying with some relational rule of conduct, harms the claimant.[44] Wrongs-based liability is sometimes imposed for negligent conduct, and at other times for conduct beyond or apart from diligent or reasonable conduct and therefore encompassing several instances of strict liability such as nuisance, vicarious liability, or products liability (as well as trespass, battery, or defamation).[45] What justifies the imposition of liability, whether in these contexts of strict liability or in the tort of negligence, is the defendant's harmful violation of a relational norm of conduct. Even if strict, therefore, wrongs-based liability is in line with Goldberg and Zipursky's vision of tort law as a law of wrongs, for it finds its justification in the defendant's wrongful interference with the claimant's legally protected rights. For these two scholars, strict liability is certainly acceptable to the extent that it embodies wrongs-based liability. The other type of liability, licensing-based liability, is liability which attaches to a defendant merely because some harm flows from their activity to the claimant's person or property, without there being any violation of some relational norm of conduct. This type of liability, which finds an example in the liability for abnormally dangerous activities,[46] is acceptable

---

[43] John CP Goldberg and Benjamin C Zipursky, 'The Strict Liability in Fault and the Fault in Strict Liability' (2016) 85 Fordham L Rev 743, 785–88 (hereafter Goldberg and Zipursky, 'The Strict Liability in Fault and the Fault in Strict Liability'). Goldberg and Zipursky have developed a fresh way of looking at tort law, labelled 'civil recourse theory', on the details of which see eg John CP Goldberg and Benjamin C Zipursky, 'Torts as Wrongs' (2010) 88 Tex L Rev 917 (hereafter Goldberg and Zipursky, 'Torts as Wrongs'); John CP Goldberg and Benjamin C Zipursky, 'Civil Recourse Revisited' (2011) 39 Fla St U L Rev 341; John CP Goldberg and Benjamin C Zipursky, 'Rights and Responsibility in the Law of Torts' in Donal Nolan and Andrew Robertson (eds), *Rights and Private Law* (Hart Publishing 2012) 251; John CP Goldberg and Benjamin C Zipursky, 'Civil Recourse Defended: A Reply to Posner, Calabresi, Rustad, Chamallas, and Robinette' (2013) 88 Ind LJ 569; John CP Goldberg and Benjamin C Zipursky, *Recognizing Wrongs* (HUP 2020) (hereafter, Goldberg and Zipursky, *Recognizing Wrongs*).

[44] Goldberg and Zipursky, 'The Strict Liability in Fault and the Fault in Strict Liability' (n 43) 755: 'each wrongs-based tort contains a rule that sets a standard of conduct by identifying a way of acting upon another that one is enjoined from doing'. Note that, in their view, both injury and violation of a norm of conduct constitute essential elements of wrongdoing: see Goldberg and Zipursky, 'Torts as Wrongs' (n 43) 941–45.

[45] Goldberg and Zipursky, 'The Strict Liability in Fault and the Fault in Strict Liability' (n 43) 748–57, 771–75.

[46] ibid 762–65 (at 763, explaining this context of liability by combining nonreciprocity of risk, abnormality of risk, and risk–benefit, on the basis of 'an idea of fair distribution' in the allocation of losses).

INDIVIDUAL RESPONSIBILITY   267

insofar as it 'plays a minor supporting role' in US tort law, with wrongs-based liability being instead the 'lead actor'.[47] The predominant role of wrongs-based liability, including its strict permutations, is necessary to preserve tort law as a body of relational norms of conduct which can establish what we owe to each other and therefore set our spheres of reciprocal liberties and responsibilities. Importantly, Goldberg and Zipursky believe that, within the realm of wrongs-based liability, strict liability norms should not be too many or too rigorous, as otherwise the assignment of liability may be too far removed from genuine wrongdoing, individual liberties may be excessively restricted, and the law may set standards of conduct that are unattainable and therefore not suitable to work as a guidance for the behaviour of individuals.[48] In sum, Goldberg and Zipursky do not reject strict liability *tout court*, but they want it to be in the form of wrongs-based liability and not too harsh on defendants in terms of the prescribed standard of conduct.

The responsibility-based theories discussed so far are an important part of tort reasoning in the United States, and they all recognize that strict liability has a role to play within tort law. At the same time, though, their conceptions of responsibility can vary, even dramatically, with a consequent divergence in the way they view strict liability. In this respect, only a very few responsibility-based theories support a broad imposition of strict liability, namely Epstein's libertarian approach (which has been much criticized)[49] and the responsibility-based prong of Keating's theory of harm-based strict liability (which has also been criticized[50] and has not yet attracted widespread support). As to the other leading responsibility-based theories, they accord strict liability a more limited role. As mentioned above, Geistfeld's liberal egalitarian understanding of the reciprocity paradigm sees negligence as the default rule in US tort law and confines strict liability to uncommon activities that generate an especially high risk of harm.[51] Coleman admits that his version of corrective justice may well fail to explain important contexts of strict liability such as product liability and vicarious liability.[52] Perry's avoidability-based conception of responsibility confines strict liability to uncommon situations where the imposition of risk is unilateral, and it is unable to explain vicarious liability.[53] Finally,

---

See also Goldberg and Zipursky, *Recognizing Wrongs* (n 43) 191–92 (discussing *Rylands* and its progeny), but also 192–96 (arguing that strict product liability is wrongs-based, even though admitting that liability for manufacturing defects 'sometimes comes close to the line between strict liability wrongs and licensing-based liability without wrongdoing', at fn 23).

[47] Goldberg and Zipursky, 'The Strict Liability in Fault and the Fault in Strict Liability' (n 43) 785.

[48] See John CP Goldberg and Benjamin C Zipursky, 'Tort Law and Moral Luck' (2007) 92 Cornell L Rev 1123, 1160.

[49] See n 11 in this section.

[50] See eg Goldberg and Zipursky, 'The Strict Liability in Fault and the Fault in Strict Liability' (n 43) 765–67.

[51] See text to n 26 in this section.

[52] See text to n 34 in this section.

[53] See n 41 and text to and following n 42 in this section.

Goldberg and Zipursky's theory of civil recourse suggests that strict liability has a role to play in tort law, but possibly only in the form of wrongs-based liability, and it casts doubt on the appropriateness of treating liability for abnormally dangerous activities as really part of US tort law.[54] Overall, the centrality which these theories give to moral concepts such as autonomy, choice, duty, wrong, or wrongdoing results in an increase in the persuasiveness of fault as the proper basis of liability and therefore curbs significantly the role of strict liability in tort law.[55] Moreover, the emphasis that these tort theorists put on the relationship between claimant and defendant makes most of the arguments analysed in this book look unpersuasive for the imposition of tort liability. Arguments such as accident avoidance, loss spreading, victim protection, administrative cost reduction, or the deep-pockets justification aim to achieve broader societal goals which are at odds with the claimant–defendant nexus and which, therefore, are generally unattractive to legal scholars who see tort law as based on individual responsibility. As a result, the menu of justifications from which *these* scholars can choose in order to justify strict liability is typically rather limited.

All this does not mean, though, that it is not possible to use individual responsibility together with other arguments in order to justify strict liability. An example of this pattern can be found, exceptionally, among the 'moral' tort theorists themselves: as we have seen, in seeking to justify several contexts of strict liability and to advocate a general regime of strict enterprise liability, Keating juxtaposes his conception of individual responsibility with loss spreading as burden–benefit proportionality (and with risk–benefit as well). By doing so, Keating's approach generates a broader justificatory basis which is able to support strict liability to a greater extent than most of the other responsibility-based approaches. Further examples may be found in the work of legal scholars who do not draw as heavily on moral philosophy. For example, in a well-known article encouraging the elaboration of mixed theories of tort law, Schwartz suggests that numerous tort law doctrines, including strict liability torts, can be concurrently justified by rationales based on accident avoidance and corrective justice.[56] Also, in a work advocating the imposition of strict liability for bursting cyber-reservoirs of personal data, Citron juxtaposes Calabresi's approach to efficient accident avoidance, 'enterprise liability' understood as loss spreading plus accident avoidance, Epstein's libertarian conception of strict liability, Fletcher's reciprocity paradigm, Keating's invocation of a proportional distribution of losses, corrective justice as understood by Coleman,

---

[54] See text to nn 46–48 in this section.

[55] A context-specific example of this can be found in David G Owen, 'Moral Foundations of Products Liability Law: Toward First Principles' (1993) 68 Notre Dame L Rev 427, 453 (arguing that 'the ideals of freedom and especially of equality support a scheme of responsibility containing pockets of strict liability but basically built on fault'). See also Keating, 'Distributive and Corrective Justice' (n 15) 195.

[56] Gary T Schwartz, 'Mixed Theories of Tort Law: Affirming Both Deterrence and Corrective Justice' (1997) 75 Texas L Rev 1801, 1821.

Perry, and Weinrib, and, finally, Goldberg and Zipursky's civil recourse theory.[57] As this potpourri of arguments shows, justifications of profoundly different nature may be used together, particularly if it is thought that this is what it takes to support in a more convincing way the adoption of strict liability. Despite these examples, though, the general impression is that, for legal scholars, the connection between individual responsibility and strict liability is not seen as strong. On the one hand, those who use the tools of moral philosophy are generally not sympathetic to strict liability, or at least they think it is appropriate to curb it in some way or to confine it to specific circumstances. As to other legal scholars, individual responsibility does not seem to be one of the first arguments which comes to mind when thinking about the justifications for strict liability, with other arguments such as loss spreading, accident avoidance, or victim protection dominating the scene, as shown in earlier sections of Part 3 of this book.

How, though, do US courts handle the idea of individual responsibility? First, they do not put forward or reproduce any sophisticated responsibility-based theory in their judgments, at least for the purpose of justifying strict liability. This is not surprising, as judges are not moral philosophers and therefore may not feel comfortable in engaging with that type of reasoning. However, we can find occasional references to responsibility that arguably appeal to some notion of justice or morality, even though they are very generic and therefore cannot be easily assimilated to any particular conception of individual responsibility. An example of this is Judge Friendly's oft-cited opinion in *Ira S Bushey & Sons, Inc v United States*, a case involving the vicarious liability of the United States for property damage caused by a drunken sailor of the Coast Guard to the drydock owner.[58] After rejecting a number of policy-driven rationales for *respondeat superior* such as accident avoidance and loss spreading, Judge Friendly maintains that this doctrine 'rests ... in a deeply rooted sentiment that a business enterprise cannot justly disclaim responsibility for accidents which may fairly be said to be characteristic of its activities'.[59] Other examples as well may be identified in the reasoning of US courts,[60] but overall it is clear that they do not rely very much on individual responsibility

---

[57] Danielle Keats Citron, 'Reservoirs of Danger: Evolution of Public and Private Law at the Dawn of the Information Age' (2007) 80 S Cal L Rev 241, 283–93. Note, though, that as far as corrective justice and civil recourse are concerned, Citron argues that these 'theories sit uncomfortably with strict liability' but that a reconciliation would be possible if fault or wrongdoing were presumed (292–93). On this point, it must be noted that a regime based on presumed fault does not correspond to strict liability, given that the defendant can escape liability by providing evidence of absence of fault.

[58] 398 F.2d 167 (2d Cir.1968).

[59] ibid [5]. For other judicial opinions sharing the same view in relation to vicarious liability, see *Rodgers v Kemper Constr Co*, 50 Cal.App.3d 608, 618 (Cal.1975) (adding loss spreading and an argument based on 'optimal resource allocation'); *Essig v United States*, 675 F.Supp. 84, 88 (N.Y.1987); *Harris v Trojan Fireworks Co*, 120 Cal.App.3d 157, 163 (Cal.1981) (adding loss spreading); *Toyota Motor Sales U.S.A., Inc v Superior Court*, 220 Cal.App.3d 864, 878 (Cal.1990) fn 10 (arguably adding risk–profit).

[60] See Jed Handelsman Shugerman, 'A Watershed Moment: Reversals of Tort Theory in the Nineteenth Century' (2008) 2(1) JTL article 2, 22–36 (showing that the rule in *Rylands v Fletcher* started to gain judicial support in the United States in the 1890s not on the basis of economic reasoning but

270 JUSTIFYING STRICT LIABILITY

as a justification for strict liability. Moreover, as we have seen in the case of legal scholars, courts may also link responsibility-based theories of tort law to fault rather than to strict liability. For example, in *Kenney v Liston* the Supreme Court of Appeals of West Virginia observes that '[t]he primary unifying principle of tort law is one of *corrective justice*, that is, the law establishes a legal duty for a tortfeasor to repair any damage or losses *carelessly* inflicted upon a victim'.[61] In sum, US courts can certainly invoke some morality-oriented notion of responsibility but, at least as far as strict liability is concerned, they do so only occasionally and, as has been shown throughout this book, they rely far more often on arguments such as risk, loss spreading, accident avoidance, or victim protection. In this respect, the behaviour of US courts looks similar to that of legal scholars.

More generally, the fact that individual responsibility has not flourished as a justification for strict liability in the United States may well relate to the place that responsibility-based approaches have had in US tort law. Over the course of the twentieth century, the law of torts has been dominated by approaches that see its purpose as to achieve a variety of societal goals, such as the (efficient) avoidance of accidents, the compensation of victims, or the spreading of losses.[62] Adherents to these approaches see moral concepts such as right, wrong, duty, or responsibility as superfluous, unable to make sense of tort law, or unfit for the challenges posed by modernity in the form of accidental injuries.[63] In this intellectual climate, a responsibility-based conception of tort law which is rooted in those moral concepts and which prioritizes the relational dimension of tort law is embraced by only a minority of legal actors. As a result, arguments such as accident avoidance, victim protection, or loss spreading feature far more prominently than any conception of individual responsibility in the US reasoning seeking to justify strict liability (and, perhaps, tort liability more generally).

To conclude, individual responsibility has had a moderate significance in the United States as a justification for strict liability. Several legal scholars have put forward conceptions of individual responsibility which, depending on their specific content, accord varying importance to strict liability. Most of them, however, show a predilection for fault and, one way or another, they routinely confine strict liability to specific situations such as those involving dangerous activities. For their part, US courts do not seem particularly attracted by individual responsibility as a justification for strict liability, and they certainly do not engage in sophisticated moral reasoning. In a legal milieu dominated by an inclination to see tort law as a tool for the achievement of societal goals wider than the claimant–defendant

---

rather on moral grounds, all showing an emphasis on responsibility and accountability for business choices that caused harm to others).

[61] 760 S.E.2d 434, 445 (W.Va.2014) (emphasis added).
[62] See generally Goldberg (n 6).
[63] ibid 519–21, 563–64.

relationship, individual responsibility cannot be at the forefront of discussions seeking to justify strict liability.

3.8.3 The Limited Significance of Individual Responsibility in English Law

English tort law is often associated with ideas of interpersonal morality and justice, and it is therefore not surprising to see that individual responsibility surfaces in the reasoning justifying the imposition of strict liability. In keeping with the US approach, this is especially true as far as legal scholars are concerned. At the same time, though, the existence of competing 'moral' views of tort law as well as the predominance of other arguments in the reasoning surrounding strict liability suggest that individual responsibility carries only a limited significance as a justification for strict liability in the English context.

Unlike in the United States, tort reasoning is not dominated in England by views that see tort law as an instrument of socio-economic policy. On the contrary, considerable emphasis is placed on principles of corrective justice and norms of individual responsibility. In this setting, a variety of 'moral' approaches to tort law have been devised and, in keeping with equivalent theories in the United States, their focus tends to be on the relationship between claimant and defendant and not on broader societal goals that tort liability may be thought to serve. Within this mode of thinking, or at least overlapping with it, a variety of responsibility-based theories have been put forward in England with a view to justifying strict liability. As will be seen, these theories may adopt distinct conceptions of individual responsibility, or they may share the same conception but add further arguments, the overall result being that strict liability is treated and justified in a variety of different ways.

Our discussion of English responsibility-based theories must start with Honoré's famous conception of outcome responsibility. In Honoré's view, by choosing a course of action, a person 'bets' on it: if the outcome of their chosen actions is good, they will receive credit for it; if it is bad, they will incur discredit for it. Either way, that person will be responsible for the outcome of their action (outcome responsibility).[64] Crucially, outcome responsibility is prior to legal responsibility, meaning that something additional to outcome responsibility is required before someone can be held liable in tort for the harm caused to another. The needed extra element can either be fault, leading to fault-based liability, or an especially high risk of harm, leading to the imposition of strict liability.[65] As a result, strict liability should

---

[64] Tony Honoré, 'Responsibility and Luck: The Moral Basis of Strict Liability' (1988) 104 LQR 530, 530ff.

[65] ibid 537–42. The moral basis of outcome responsibility lies in a principle of distributive justice according to which a person who reaps the benefit of their own risk-taking should also bear the losses that may result from it: see Tony Honoré, 'The Morality of Tort Law—Questions and Answers' in David G Owen (ed), *Philosophical Foundations of Tort Law* (OUP 1995) 73, 83–84. This principle is similar to the

272   JUSTIFYING STRICT LIABILITY

apply only to high-risk activities such as 'storing explosives, running nuclear power stations, keeping wild animals, marketing drugs or other dangerous products'.[66] To this combination of outcome responsibility with abnormality of risk, Honoré adds a further argument, noting that outcome responsibility would be also justified by 'a consequentialist argument for avoiding serious harm'.[67] The weight of this accident avoidance justification is however unclear, although it seems to be of secondary significance given how very little emphasis Honoré places on it. Overall, therefore, it can be seen that, given its reliance on abnormality of risk, Honoré's first formulation of his approach to strict liability is quite restrictive, in effect limiting this form of liability to the operation of dangerous things and activities.

In his later writings, though, Honoré drops the abnormality of risk argument as a companion to outcome responsibility and replaces it with loss spreading as proportionality of burdens and benefits. This move is explained by the fact that, for Honoré, tort law must ensure that the financial burden imposed on defendants via a finding of liability is not out of proportion with the gravity of their conduct. To achieve this result, there are two options: a requirement of fault, so that the burden of liability is proportional to and justified by the intentional or negligent nature of the defendant's conduct; or, secondly, the spreading of losses among those who benefit from the harmful activity (eg through insurance mechanisms), so that the burden of strict liability 'is tempered by loss distribution'.[68] In this reasoning, outcome responsibility is combined with loss spreading, so that the imposition of strict liability would be justified wherever outcome responsibility obtains *and* losses can be spread in a meaningful way across the beneficiaries of the harmful activity.[69] In this later version of Honoré's theory, the imposition of strict liability can certainly go beyond the operation of dangerous things and activities, provided that the conditions spelled out above are met.

Honoré's theory of outcome responsibility has proved influential in England, attracting the attention of several leading tort scholars. For example, in seeking to defend strict liability from a variety of objections, Gardner adopts Honoré's

---

risk–benefit argument identified in section 3.2, with one key difference: Honoré's principle of distributive justice grounds outcome responsibility, whereas risk–benefit grounds directly legal responsibility in the form of tort liability.

[66] Honoré (n 64) 537.

[67] ibid 542.

[68] See Honoré (n 65) 88–90. For a criticism of Honoré's reliance on loss spreading, see eg Peter Cane, 'Fault and Strict Liability for Harm in Tort Law' in William Swadling and Gareth Jones (eds), *The Search for Principle: Essays in Honour of Lord Goff of Chieveley* (OUP 1999) 171, 201 (arguing that this argument 'has nothing to do with personal responsibility for the outcome of conduct').

[69] As far as vicarious liability is concerned, Honoré rules out outcome responsibility as a possible justification, given that it is the employee's conduct, and not the employer's, that causes harm to another. What justifies the employer's vicarious liability is the fact that the employer has control over the business and stands to gain if the business goes well (this argument resonating strongly with the risk–benefit/profit justifications identified in section 3.2), in combination with the availability of loss-spreading mechanisms: see Honoré (n 65) 85, 88–90.

approach and further develops it to show that there can be a persuasive account of moral agency that does not oppose the imposition of strict liability: in this account, 'we are authors of our accomplishments as well as pursuers of our purposes', 'we are conceived in terms of our successes and failures as well as our attempts and neglects', 'it is sometimes the achievement and not just the thought, or effort, that counts', and 'the problem of private law is not just the problem of how to make the will of one compatible with the will of others, but also the problem of how to co-ordinate those many aspects of our conflicting activities which are not reducible to the input of our wills at all'.[70] In Gardner's view, such an account of moral agency 'gives rise to the really strong case for strict liability in many areas of private law, including the law of torts'.[71] Similarly, in relation to governmental liability in tort, Bell supports the imposition of strict liability on the basis of Honoré's theory of outcome responsibility wherever harm is a planned consequence of governmental activity or where, though not planned, it is a known or foreseeable occurrence.[72] Indeed, if the government undertakes certain policies and these have the intended or known/foreseeable effect of harming someone, then principles of responsibility require that the government is held liable for the bad outcome it caused.

Another leading scholar who draws on Honoré's conception of outcome responsibility is Stapleton who, however, adheres to Honoré's approach only to a certain extent. In Stapleton's view, Honoré's theory is an attractive starting point to justifying strict liability, as it debunks various philosophical objections to the morality of strict liability.[73] At the same time, though, Stapleton criticizes Honoré's reliance on abnormality of risk as the extra element justifying the imposition of strict liability and thinks that 'this argument is unconvincing both descriptively and normatively'.[74] To resolve this problem, Stapleton proposes to sever outcome responsibility from abnormality of risk and to combine it with risk–profit, so as to provide 'a new theory of strict moral enterprise liability'.[75] In particular, she maintains that

> There *is* a coherent theme which does link most existing pockets of tortious strict liability ... It is the taking of risk *in pursuit of financial profit*. A non-consequentialist basis of these liabilities might be expressed in terms of a moral argument that if, in seeking to secure financial profit, an enterprise causes certain types of loss, it should be legally obliged to pay compensation to the victim.[76]

---

[70] John Gardner, 'The Purity and Priority of Private Law' (1996) 46 U Toronto LJ 459, 492 (hereafter Gardner, 'Purity'). See also John Gardner, 'Obligations and Outcomes in the Law of Torts' in Peter Cane and John Gardner (eds), *Relating to Responsibility* (Hart Publishing 2001) 111, 133–34.

[71] Gardner, 'Purity' (n 70) 492.

[72] John Bell, 'Governmental Liability in Tort' (1995) 6 NJCL 85, 89 (discussing this argument together with proportionality of burdens and benefits), 99–100.

[73] See Stapleton (n 11) 184.

[74] ibid 185–86.

[75] ibid 185.

[76] ibid 186 (original emphasis).

274 JUSTIFYING STRICT LIABILITY

This argument, Stapleton explains, constitutes an 'extension' of Honoré's approach and applies to only a limited set of situations, namely those involving financial profit.[77] Firms bet on whether their products or services will be profitable or not, and in the process they impose a risk of harm on others, such as users or consumers. If their bet is successful and therefore their product/service causes no harm, firms get social credit as well as financial profit. If, however, harm is caused, they get social discredit but they still retain the financial profits they have previously made by selling/providing their product/service. In the latter scenario, it is morally justifiable to hold the firms strictly liable on the ground that they brought about a bad outcome in the world while being entitled to retain the financial profits of their harmful activity.[78] An approach that combines outcome responsibility with risk–profit can, in Stapleton's view, justify a variety of contexts of strict liability, such as product liability, vicarious liability, or the US liability for abnormally dangerous activities.[79]

A responsibility-based approach that departs in a more radical way from Honoré's theory of outcome responsibility is propounded by Cane. As regards accidental harm, in his earlier writings Cane notes that, taken alone, outcome responsibility would end up by favouring a generalized regime of strict liability and that, therefore, it cannot explain why the law often requires fault before imposing tort liability.[80] In search of a sound limitation to outcome-based strict liability, Cane rejects abnormality of risk and, similarly to Stapleton, sees the idea of imposing strict liability on those who stand to make a financial profit from risk-imposition as 'a normatively attractive proposal', even though of limited descriptive value as far as modern tort law is concerned.[81] Cane's approval of the idea of risk–profit is confirmed in his later work, where he maintains that 'the most ethically satisfying explanation for strict liability for harm is that those who create risks of harm in pursuit of profit should bear the costs when such risks materialize';[82] but while this rationale accords with ethical principles of personal responsibility, Cane suggests that it also has its own limitations, as it focuses too much on the defendant's conduct and too little on the claimant's interests, forgetting that tort law is a two-sided affair which looks at both parties.[83] In subsequent works, Cane builds on this idea and provides a more elaborate conception of responsibility. In his view, Honoré's theory of outcome responsibility is too agent-focused and for this reason it fails to capture adequately important aspects of tort law, including strict liability. By contrast, Cane's approach maintains that moral and legal responsibility must be

---

[77] ibid 187.
[78] ibid 186–88.
[79] ibid 188–93.
[80] Peter Cane, *The Anatomy of Tort Law* (Hart Publishing 1997) 50.
[81] ibid.
[82] Cane (n 68) 202.
[83] ibid 202–03.

viewed in a more relational way, which stresses both the defendant's conduct and its outcomes as well as the impact of these outcomes on the victim.[84] In addition to this, Cane believes that responsibility practices promote broader social values as well, for society at large is interested in the way its members behave.[85] In sum, moral and legal responsibility involve a three-way relationship among defendants, claimants, and society. Paying attention to all three sides of the relationship is key to justifying the various forms of legal responsibility,[86] and this is especially true as far as strict liability is concerned.[87] First, responsibility for bad outcomes in the form of strict liability helps define an agent's identity: this identity can exist if the person in question feels they can 'act purposively' and bring about some change in the world; to instil this feeling, it may be necessary to allocate to them the 'owner-ship' of a bad outcome they caused, even if without fault.[88] Secondly, in seeking to strike a balance between the interests of agents/defendants and those of victims/claimants, strict liability prioritizes the latter and protects them by reducing via compensation the impact on them of the defendant's harmful conduct.[89] Thirdly, and finally, strict liability is beneficial to the wider community as it induces po-tential defendants to choose safer activities in the future.[90] As can be seen, the second and third arguments Cane puts forward to justify strict liability resonate very strongly with the victim protection and accident avoidance arguments we saw earlier in the book, even though he portrays them as springing directly from his conception of responsibility.[91] Interestingly, Cane himself ranks these distinct ar-guments and sees the second and third as key, for he suggests that 'the ultimate jus-tification for strict responsibility will be found in the benefits it brings to individual potential victims and to society, not in ideas about agency and the ownership of outcomes'.[92] In sum, Cane's conception of responsibility is particularly broad and

---

[84] Peter Cane, 'Responsibility and Fault: A Relational and Functional Approach to Responsibility' in Peter Cane and John Gardner (eds), *Relating to Responsibility: Essays in Honour of Tony Honoré on his 80th Birthday* (Hart Publishing 2001) 81, 103 (hereafter Cane, 'Responsibility and Fault'); Peter Cane, *Responsibility in Law and Morality* (Hart Publishing 2002) 49–53, 184–86 (hereafter Cane, *Responsibility in Law and Morality*).

[85] Cane, 'Responsibility and Fault' (n 84) 103, 108–09; Cane, *Responsibility in Law and Morality* (n 84) 53–56, 107–09.

[86] Cane, *Responsibility in Law and Morality* (n 84) 56, 108.

[87] Cane, 'Responsibility and Fault' (n 84) 109.

[88] ibid 91, 93, 109.

[89] ibid 109. See also Cane, *Responsibility in Law and Morality* (n 84) 40 (arguing that one of the func-tions of vicarious liability, which he distinguishes from liability for bad outcomes, is to 'promote[] the reparative function of civil law by providing an injured person with an additional target for a compensa-tion claim').

[90] Cane, 'Responsibility and Fault' (n 84) 109–10.

[91] Arguably, it is the three-directional nature of Cane's conception of responsibility that allows for this move. See also Cane, *Responsibility in Law and Morality* (n 84) 204 (making a similar point in sug-gesting that 'ideas about the fair social distribution of risks and costs of harm' are necessary to explain strict liability and that, although these ideas are removed from notions of agency and will, strict liability is nevertheless a form of responsibility).

[92] Cane, 'Responsibility and Fault' (n 84) 110. Note that, in relation to vicarious liability, he seems to incorporate an argument based on risk–benefit/profit into his conception of responsibility: see Cane, *Responsibility in Law and Morality* (n 84) 176.

accommodates a range of arguments that justify strict liability for causing bad outcomes regardless of fault.

Apparently somewhat similar is Witting's approach to liability for breach of non-delegable duty not involving lack of reasonable care. First, Witting adopts Cane's conception of responsibility as a three-way relationship between agent, victim, and the wider community, this meaning that 'courts might legitimately take into account the interests of those who are injured and the need to distribute risks of harm and costs of injury'.[93] At least in some cases, it would be appropriate to give precedence to the victim's interest in bodily integrity over the defendant's interest in autonomy, as protecting the former is key to the flourishing of all human beings.[94] This provides, in Witting's view, an argument for accepting 'a responsibility base in tort law independent of fault' and, ultimately, a responsibility for bad outcomes which 'rests ... upon an ordering of protected interests'.[95] In specific relation to breach of non-delegable duty, Witting focuses on accidents arising out of ongoing activities (as opposed to isolated acts) and combines the line of reasoning sketched above with an argument resonating with accident avoidance.[96] Institutions such as hospitals and schools engage in repetitive activities whose performance is delegated to a high number of persons; as these activities will, over time, give rise to a predictable number of accidents, the relevant institution is in a position to foresee them and, therefore, to take steps to minimize the risk of their occurrence.[97] This is why, in Witting's view, strict liability is warranted for breach of non-delegable duty wherever the duty-holder engages in ongoing activities.

These responsibility-based theories represent an important feature of English tort reasoning, and they each recognize some role to strict liability in tort law, whether in general or with reference to specific contexts of liability. In this respect, the English approach resembles the US one, even though in the United States such theories are higher in number and more diversified in nature.[98] In England, as illustrated above, the influence of Honoré's theory of outcome responsibility is considerable and a number of legal scholars draw on it to justify strict liability (even though other approaches as well can be identified, as that of Cane). On the other hand, this does not mean that the views of these English scholars as to strict liability coincide, even if they share the same conception of responsibility. To give one example from above, Stapleton relies on Honoré's theory of outcome responsibility, but while Honoré himself combines this conception of responsibility with abnormality of risk (in his 1988 article) or loss spreading (in his subsequent work),

---

[93] Christian Witting, 'Breach of the Non-Delegable Duty: Defending Limited Strict Liability in Tort' (2006) 29 UNSWLJ 33, 53.

[94] ibid 53–56.

[95] ibid 56.

[96] ibid 57.

[97] ibid 58–59.

[98] See subsection 3.8.2.

Stapleton prefers to tie it to risk–profit. In other words, while their respective lines of reasoning share the same argument as a starting point, that is outcome responsibility, they subsequently part ways by selecting different additional arguments. They therefore end up by producing a very different justificatory reasoning for strict liability.

A further point concerns the nature of the English responsibility-based theories considered above. We saw that most of the US 'moral' theories are framed in a way that constrains the types of admissible justification for strict liability: they see the claimant–defendant nexus as key and, as a result, they are typically reluctant to take on board arguments which are divorced from that nexus. The same pattern cannot be identified for most of the English responsibility-based theories, as their proponents happily deploy additional arguments which go beyond the claimant–defendant nexus and which embody broader societal goals. As already seen, Honoré, Cane, and Witting refer (with varying emphasis) to the avoidance of accidents; Honoré himself as well as Bell in his discussion of governmental liability emphasize loss spreading as proportionality of burdens and benefits; and Cane puts forward an argument resonating with victim protection. In the hands of these English scholars, then, individual responsibility appears to be compatible with a wider range of arguments than those allowed in US 'moral' reasoning and, when it comes to justifying strict liability, they see nothing wrong with injecting into their reasoning arguments that reflect broader societal concerns, in the belief that these do not undermine the merits and coherence of their responsibility-based approaches. In sum, the English conceptions of individual responsibility are structurally more malleable and therefore more open to recognizing a key role to strict liability than many of their US counterparts.[99]

Despite all this, though, it would be a mistake to portray individual responsibility as a leading justification for strict liability in the English context and for a variety of reasons. First, the relationship between strict liability and morality has been a difficult one for a long time. As early as 1907, the first edition of *Salmond on Torts* observes that

> Reason demands that a loss shall lie where it falls, unless some good purpose is to be served by changing its incidence; and in general the only purpose so served is that of punishment for wrongful intent or negligence.[100]

This passage offers significant indications as to the perceived immorality of strict liability, which ought to be confined to exceptional circumstances such as where

---

[99] A possible exception to this is, in the United States, the position of Keating: see text to nn 14–20 in this section.

[100] John W Salmond, *The Law of Torts: a Treatise on the English Law of Liability for Civil Injuries* (1st edn, Stevens and Haynes 1907) 10.

278 JUSTIFYING STRICT LIABILITY

damage is caused by wild animals or by the escape of water or other dangerous sub-stances.[101] This antipathy towards strict liability gained growing support among judges in the first part of the twentieth century,[102] finding a striking example in the House of Lords in *Read v J Lyons*, which restricted the significance of the rule in *Rylands v Fletcher*.[103] What is most interesting for present purposes is that, in that case, Lord Macmillan defines strict liability as a 'primitive rule' and regards fault as morally superior on the ground that 'a man's freedom of action is subject only to the obligation not to infringe any duty of care which he owes to others'.[104] Scepticism about the morality of strict liability is still visible today, despite the efforts of theor-ists such as Honoré and Cane to show otherwise. Indeed, a number of influential legal scholars see tort law as linked to norms of interpersonal morality or of indi-vidual responsibility and hold views that sit more comfortably with fault than with strict liability.[105] The existence of these approaches within the strand of 'moral' thinking has the effect of reducing, or at least casting doubt on, the moral persua-siveness of individual responsibility as a justification for imposing strict liability. In addition to this, these 'moral' approaches are often sceptical about or opposed to the belief that societal goals should play a role in determining the imposition of tort liability, whether strict or based on fault.[106] As a result, the attractiveness of

[101] ibid 12.

[102] For an account of this development see John Rason Spencer, 'Motor-cars and the Rule in *Rylands v Fletcher*: A Chapter of Accidents in the History of Law and Motoring' (1983) CLJ 65, 73–74.

[103] See text to nn 14–16 in section 2.2.

[104] *Read v J Lyons*, [1947] AC 156, 171.

[105] Nicholas McBride, 'Rights and the Basis of Tort Law' in Donal Nolan and Andrew Robertson (eds), *Rights and Private Law* (Hart Publishing 2012) 331, 364–65 (arguing that it would be wrong to hold liable on policy grounds (eg accident avoidance, victim protection, or loss spreading) a driver who runs down a pedestrian without any fault, and that the driver should not be held liable at all) (hereafter McBride, 'Rights and the Basis of Tort Law'); Nicholas McBride, *The Humanity of Private Law. Part I: Explanation* (Hart Publishing 2019) 247–50, 254 (arguing that, in their current state, both vicarious li-ability and liability for defective products are not wrong-based and therefore are at odds with the rest of English private law); Allan Beever, *A Theory of Tort Liability* (Hart Publishing 2016) (whose discussion of tort liability does not engage in a meaningful way with contexts of strict liability such as the rule in *Rylands v Fletcher*, vicarious liability, liability for defective products, and liability for animals). See also Paula Giliker, *Vicarious Liability in Tort: A Comparative Perspective* (CUP 2010) 223–24 (in contrasting the English regime of parental liability with the French one, she notes that 'English law continues to ad-here to a system based on fault and to prioritise principles of individual responsibility'); Paula Giliker, 'Vicarious Liability, Non-delegable Duties and Teachers: Can You Outsource Liability for Lessons?' (2015) 31 PN 259, 260 (arguing that '[c]laims [in tort] must have a legal basis and in a system framed fundamentally around the idea of corrective justice—defendants being held accountable for their fault which foreseeably harms others—strict liability is regarded as exceptional'). cf Robert Stevens, *Torts and Rights* (OUP 2007) 111–13 (recognizing a potentially significant role to strict liability on the basis of an argument that straddles nonreciprocity of risk and abnormality of risk, which should lead to the adop-tion of a general rule of liability modelled after the US liability for abnormally dangerous activities), 97–98 (recognizing that Honoré's theory of outcome responsibility is a morally powerful argument, but adding that it 'has little explanatory power in relation to the world as we find it'); note, however, that Stevens's theory is not based on any clear notion of responsibility, and it is instead based on the view that tort law is about the infringement of rights: ibid 1–19.

[106] See eg Stevens (n 105) 306–40; McBride, 'Rights and the Basis of Tort Law' (n 105) 339–41, 364–65. See also Donal Nolan, 'Causation and the Goals of Tort Law' in Andrew Robertson and Hang Wu Tang (eds), *The Goals of Private Law* (Hart Publishing 2009) 165, 189 (rejecting compensation and de-terrence as proper functions of the law of torts); Jonathan Morgan, 'Tort, Insurance and Incoherence'

responsibility-based theories such as those of Honoré and Cane, reliant as they are on arguments such as loss spreading or accident avoidance, is diminished.

As in the United States, the significance of individual responsibility in England is also weakened by the fact that strict liability is, in all the contexts in which it applies, far more often justified on the basis of other arguments, whether in the form of justifications embodying societal goals such as loss spreading, accident avoidance, and victim protection, or in the form of the various risk-based arguments. Moreover, the relationship between individual responsibility and these arguments looks different and offers significant indications as to the role of individual responsibility itself in English law. As far as the justifications reflecting broader societal goals are concerned, these, on the one hand, and individual responsibility, on the other, are widely perceived as belonging to different and conflicting ways of seeing and theorizing tort law in general and strict liability in particular. It is therefore relatively rare to see instances of reasoning relying on both types of argument.[107] By contrast, risk-based justifications are more easily seen as aligned with norms of individual responsibility. As we have seen, leading scholars such as Stapleton and Cane (in his earlier writings) see risk–profit as rooted in norms of individual responsibility.[108] Also, in the most recent edition of *Atiyah's Accidents, Compensation and the Law*, Cane and Goudkamp argue that, as a system of corrective justice, tort law is at least to some extent based on ideas of responsibility for conduct and its consequences,[109] and they suggest that strict liability may fit this system on the ground that 'the person who reaps the *benefit* of engaging in a *risky* activity ought in fairness to bear the cost of any loss or damage caused by the activity'.[110] On this basis, some instances of reasoning deploying risk-based justifications may be interpreted as including an implicit responsibility-based argument. To give one example, it was famously stated by Blackburn J in *Rylands v Fletcher* that,

> We think that the true rule of law is, that the person who for his own purposes brings on his lands and collects and keeps there anything likely to do mischief if

(2004) 67 MLR 384, 392–400 (rejecting victim protection and loss spreading as valid justifications for imposing liability in tort). In relation to loss spreading, a similar view is shared by Jane Stapleton, 'Tort, Insurance and Ideology' (1995) 58 MLR 820.

[107] For examples, see text to nn 68–69, to nn 84–92, to nn 93–97 in this section.

[108] See text to nn 75–82 in this section.

[109] Peter Cane and James Goudkamp, *Atiyah's Accidents, Compensation and the Law* (9th edn, CUP 2018) 238, 401–02.

[110] ibid 453 (emphasis added). See also n 226 in subsection 3.2.5 and nn 82–85 in subsection 3.6.5 and accompanying text; John G Fleming, *The Law of Torts* (9th edn, LBC Information Services 1998) 369 (arguing that '[t]he prevailing opposition to strict liability is linked to the view that the essence of tort law is corrective justice, that is, to impose an obligation to repair only on a wrongdoer', but also that '[t]he continuing vitality of corrective justice in tort theory explains why common law (though not all statutory) applications of strict liability have been linked to the few situations of creating "abnormal risks" ').

it escapes, must keep it in at his peril, and, if he does not do so, is prima facie answerable for all the damage which is the natural consequence of its escape.[111]

While this passage (and the whole case) may be read in a variety of ways, one possible interpretation is that Blackburn J had in mind some conception of individual responsibility which would attach tort liability to bad consequences brought about when pursuing some benefit by way of an unusually risky conduct.[112] Having said that, though, it must be emphasized, first, that the instances of reasoning referring expressly to both risk and individual responsibility are not many. Secondly, it cannot simply be assumed that those who invoke risk-based arguments (without mentioning individual responsibility) necessarily do so on the basis of a further responsibility-based justification operating at the back of their mind: as we have seen, arguments based on risk may be used to foster not some principle of responsibility, but instead goals such as the avoidance of accidents or the protection of victims.[113] In sum, while many English legal actors see risk and individual responsibility as compatible justifications, the two remain clearly distinct and the former is far more prominent than the latter in the English reasoning on strict liability.

A final reason why individual responsibility cannot be said to shine brightly in English law as a justification for strict liability is its treatment in judicial reasoning. In keeping with the US approach, English judges do not put forward sophisticated moral theories of strict liability, most likely because they see it as unnecessary and probably not straightforward. To be sure, they do often rely on the terms 'responsibility' or 'responsible', but the impression one gets is that they generally do so to indicate nothing more than legal (tort) responsibility. In some cases, it may be that something more is at play, as when, in *JGE*, Ward LJ in the Court of Appeal reflects on a combination of rationales for vicarious liability (arguably without any express endorsement) and suggests that 'a business enterprise cannot justly disclaim responsibility for accidents that may fairly be said to be characteristic of its activities'.[114] But even assuming that this argument was truly about some norm of individual responsibility and that the court was sympathetic with it, instances of judicial reasoning of this kind are likely to be very rare.

---

[111] (1866) LR 1 Ex 265, 279.

[112] See also text to and following nn 86–87 in subsection 3.6.5 (suggesting that the judicial reliance on risk-based reasoning in the law of vicarious liability may signify a desire to stress norms of individual responsibility).

[113] See eg nn 195 and 207–208 and accompanying text as well as text following n 232 in subsection 3.2.5.

[114] *JGE v English Province of Our Lady of Charity*, [2013] QB 722, [52]. This passage arguably borrows from Judge Friendly's opinion in *Ira S Bushey & Sons, Inc v United States*, on which see text to nn 58–59 in this section. See also *Chester v Afshar*, [2004] UKHL 41, [2005] 1 AC 134, [22] (Lord Steyn) (quoting with approval Tony Honoré, 'Medical Non-disclosure: Causation and Risk: Chappel v Hart' (1999) 7 Torts LJ 1, in the part where Honoré argues that, in imposing strict liability on a doctor for the harm caused to a patient, the High Court of Australia in *Chappel v Hart*, [1999] 2 LRC 341, (1998) 72 ALJR 1344, was giving 'legal sanction to an underlying moral responsibility for causing injury').

Overall, individual responsibility has only limited significance as a justification for strict liability in the English context. Several leading scholars put forward 'moral' theories that rely heavily on the argument and also recognize an important role to strict liability, whether in general or in relation to specific contexts. Several others, however, suggest 'moral' approaches that, for various reasons, either marginalize strict liability or hinder the flourishing of individual responsibility as a justification for it. As to the courts, they seem to attribute little or no significance to individual responsibility, at least at the level of express reasoning. As shown earlier in this book, arguments other than individual responsibility are far more common justifications for strict liability in the English context.

3.8.4 Individual Responsibility in Italian Law: An Insignificant Argument

In striking contrast with US law and English law, individual responsibility is really not part of the Italian reasoning on strict liability. The evolution of Italian tort law and the main ways of theorizing about it show that this argument has limited relevance in this area of Italian law and that, where used, it is more closely associated with fault than with strict liability.

Italian legal scholars are well aware of the philosophical debates surrounding the notion of responsibility as well as of the US and English responsibility-based theories of tort law, and yet they are reluctant to rely on individual responsibility as a justification for strict liability. An exception to this approach is probably Castronovo's reinterpretation of Calabresi's theory based on the cheapest cost avoider. As already seen,[115] Castronovo sees Calabresi's approach as turning on the element of choice: a person is made answerable for harm on the ground that, before its occurrence, they were in the best position to assess the opportunity to avoid it and how to avoid it in the most convenient way, so that it can be said that that person chose the occurrence of that harm instead of its avoidance and that, for this reason, they are responsible, and therefore liable, for it.[116] While recognizing that Calabresi's approach was originally developed from an economic perspective, Castronovo believes that it is also 'rooted in a human dimension', adding that the cheapest cost avoider and the reasonable person we find in the fault paradigm are 'expressive of the same human reality',[117] but that the former is preferable because the choice implicated in the cost-benefit analysis is more considered and conscious than that involved in the abstract standard of conduct required of the reasonable

---

[115] See text to nn 70–72 in subsection 3.3.3.
[116] Carlo Castronovo, *Responsabilità civile* (Giuffrè 2018) 492–94.
[117] ibid 493.

282   JUSTIFYING STRICT LIABILITY

person.[118] But Castronovo's attempt to justify strict liability goes farther than this, as he adds to this choice-based conception of responsibility other arguments such as the avoidance of accidents and the spreading of losses,[119] suggesting that strict liability is about reaching the socially most useful or adequate result.[120] Therefore, while some conception of individual responsibility may be part of Castronovo's reasoning on strict liability, it remains somewhat unclear what its exact justificatory weight is and how its relationship with those other arguments plays out.

Apart from Castronovo, though, it is very difficult to find other Italian scholars relying on individual responsibility as a justification for strict liability. In this respect, a point that needs to be made concerns risk. We saw that, in the United States and in England, risk-based justifications are seen as compatible with certain conceptions of individual responsibility, and that their combinations are sometimes put forward to justify the imposition of strict liability.[121] The picture is, in Italy, very different. There, the most significant risk-based arguments, namely abnormality of risk and risk–profit/benefit, are not overtly associated with norms of individual responsibility. As far as abnormality of risk is concerned, this is typically linked to victim protection or accident avoidance.[122] As to the gain-based theories of risk, in rare cases these may be used to pursue goals such as the protection of victims;[123] much more commonly, though, there are only generic statements emphasizing the fairness of requiring the person who benefits or profits from their actions or activities to bear the attendant losses. In other words, contrary to their US and English counterparts, Italian legal actors do not express a view of risk-based justifications that is premised on any clearly articulated conception of individual responsibility. Finally, and quite significantly, some Italian philosophers such as Abbagnano vigorously reject the compatibility of arguments based on risk–profit/benefit with norms of moral and legal responsibility, arguing that the former stem instead from considerations of social policy.[124]

Why, then, is individual responsibility so insignificant in the Italian context as a justification for strict liability? The evolution of Italian tort law shows that this argument has always been associated with fault and that strict liability has been based on very different justifications. To begin with, in the first part of nineteenth century, tort law was largely based on an ethical notion of 'fault' (*colpa*) which entailed the imposition of liability on the basis of the defendant's reprehensible

---

[118] See Maria Antonietta Foddai, *Sulle tracce della responsabilità. Idee e norme dell'agire responsabile* (Giappichelli 2005) 335.

[119] Castronovo (n 116) 23–26.

[120] ibid 21–22.

[121] See, in this section, text to and following nn 23–29, to and following nn 41–42 (United States); text to nn 64–66, to nn 75–82, to nn 108–110 (England).

[122] See text to nn 98–103 in subsection 3.2.3.

[123] Mario Griffey, *La responsabilità civile derivante da circolazione dei veicoli e dei natanti* (Giuffrè 1995) 91.

[124] See eg Nicola Abbagnano, 'Il giudizio di responsabilità nella morale e nel diritto' (1957) 1 Rivista di filosofia 30, 45.

behaviour and culpable state of mind.[125] Moral responsibility and civil liability were seen as, in essence, the same, as they were both concerned with the free moral agency of individuals, and tort liability performed a compensatory as well as moralizing function.[126] With the process of industrialization, the number of accidents increased dramatically, and in this new reality the ethical understanding of fault and responsibility was seen as no longer capable by itself of striking the proper balance between freedom of action and security from harm.[127] With the change in the social and economic dynamics that the machine age brought about in the second part of nineteenth century, a new, more socially oriented understanding of tort law emerged.[128] In particular, fault was no longer exclusively concerned with principles of moral agency, and it acquired a 'socio-economic' dimension in the sense that it was seen as serving the interests of nascent industry by limiting liability for accidents to cases of negligent (or intentional) conduct.[129] Moreover, increasing attention started being paid to the claimant's interests and, since the fault paradigm was sometimes seen as inadequate to meet the social challenges of modern life, strict liability started to gain ground in the view of several legal scholars.[130] In this scenario, the overall emphasis on norms of moral agency and individual responsibility progressively diminished, though these were still relied upon by many of those who saw fault as the linchpin of tort law: in their view, only faulty, morally objectionable conduct could justify the attribution of liability, and any deviation from this approach would constitute too much of an invasion of an individual's freedom of action.[131] At this stage, therefore, arguments based on a rhetoric of individual responsibility were, at most, compatible with fault but they were certainly not seen as providing a plausible or attractive rationale for the imposition of strict liability.

---

[125] Cesare Salvi, *La responsabilità civile* (3rd edn, Giuffrè 2019) 18–19.

[126] Michele Graziadei, 'Liability for Fault in Italian Law: The Development of Legal Doctrine from 1865 to the End of the Twentieth Century' in Nils Jansen (ed), *The Development and Making of Legal Doctrine* (CUP 2010) 126, 136, 140.

[127] Salvi (n 125) 19–20.

[128] Guido Alpa and Mario Bessone, *La responsabilità civile* (Giuffrè 2001) 132ff.

[129] ibid 101–02.

[130] See Vittorio Emanuele Orlando, 'Saggio di una nuova teorica sul fondamento giuridico della responsabilità civile' (1893) Arch dir pubbl 241; Lodovico Barassi, 'Contributo alla teoria della responsabilità per fatto non proprio in ispecial modo a mezzo di animali' (1897) Rivista italiana per le scienze giuridiche 325, 174, 379, and (1898) Rivista italiana per le scienze giuridiche 56; Nicola Coviello, 'La responsabilità senza colpa' (1897) Riv It Sc Giur 188; Giacomo Venezian, 'Danno e risarcimento fuori dei contratti' in *Opere giuridiche, vol 1—Studi sulle obbligazioni* (Athenaeum 1919); Pietro Cogliolo, 'La responsabilità riflessa' in *Scritti varii di diritto privato*, vol 1 (4th edn, UTET 1914) 215, 217–18; Giovanni Pacchioni, *Elementi di diritto civile* (2nd edn, UTET 1921) 361–64; Roberto de Ruggiero, *Istituzioni di diritto civile*, vol III (6th edn, Principato 1930) 499–502.

[131] See the historical reconstruction provided in Alpa and Bessone (n 128) 101–02, 132–40; and in Castronovo (n 116) 13–17. See also Guido Alpa, *La responsabilità civile: principi* (2nd edn, UTET 2018) 44 (noting that the traditional, fault-based understanding of tort liability focused on authorship of harm).

284　JUSTIFYING STRICT LIABILITY

As Italian tort law developed following the enactment of the new *Codice civile* in 1942, its intellectual foundations developed in several ways, but the role of individual responsibility remained very limited. As already mentioned,[132] since the 1960s several leading Italian scholars criticized the view that fault (under article 2043 Cod civ) should be the centre of gravity of Italian tort law and suggested that the liability rules envisaged in articles 2047–2054 should be given the same importance as article 2043, even if departing from the fault paradigm. For example, Rodotà reorganized Italian tort law around the constitutional principle of solidarity and argued that the purpose of all these liability rules is not to reflect some moral conception of responsibility and impose liability on the person who may be seen as the author of harm on the basis of their free agency and choice; rather, its purpose is to make a comparative assessment of the interests of the parties and, on that basis, to decide who should bear the loss.[133] Trimarchi also rationalized Italian tort law in a way that is far removed from individual responsibility, but he did so from an entirely different perspective. For him, the point of tort liability, whether strict or based on fault, is not to reflect some moral judgment about the defendant's conduct and responsibility but rather to minimize efficiently the risk of accidents.[134] The intellectual revolution initiated with the work of Rodotà and Trimarchi paved the way to a shared understanding of tort law as an instrument of social engineering and policy,[135] in which the rationale of liability for accidents must be found in broader societal concerns rather than in some norms of free moral agency. Moreover, in this context, fault is widely understood as a deviation from an abstract standard of conduct, that of the reasonable person; it is not the basis of an ethical assessment of behaviours or outcomes but one of the technical criteria established in the *Codice civile* for the attribution of liability.[136] While this approach waters down the connection between fault and individual responsibility, it does not sever it entirely, as liability based on fault still depends on a human failure to comply with prescribed duties of behaviour, even if measured against an abstract standard.[137] Moreover, some Italian philosophers studying the concept of responsibility emphasize the importance of duties of behaviour and suggest that

---

[132]　See eg text to nn 111–123 in subsection 3.5.4.

[133]　Stefano Rodotà, *Il Problema della Responsabilità Civile* (Giuffrè 1964) 58–75.

[134]　See Pietro Trimarchi, *Rischio e responsabilità oggettiva* (Giuffrè 1961).

[135]　Pier Giuseppe Monateri, 'Responsabilità civile' Dig Disc Priv (UTET 1998) XVII, 1.

[136]　Rodotà (n 133) esp 164ff; Stefano Rodotà, 'Modelli e funzioni della responsabilità civile' (1984) RCDP 595, 599; Massimo Franzoni, *L'illecito. Trattato della responsabilità civile* (2nd edn, Giuffrè 2010) 395; Andreina Occhipinti, 'La colpevolezza' in Paolo Cendon (ed), *Responsabilità civile*, vol 1 (2nd edn, UTET 2020) 255, 269–70.

[137]　See Francesco Donato Busnelli, 'Nuove frontiere della responsabilità civile' (1976) 1–2 Jus 41, 49–50; cf Salvi (n 125) 29–30. For a reconstruction of the debate on the meanings of *colpa* and on the relationship between 'moral fault' (*colpa morale*) and 'legal fault' (*colpa giuridica*), see Alpa and Bessone (n 128) 239–71; Renato Scognamiglio, 'Responsabilità civile' Noviss Dig It (UTET 1968) XV, 628, 632–36. When it comes to intentional conduct, norms of responsibility and morality are certainly part of the picture, as the disvalue of the defendant's conduct attracts a moral judgment calling for a legal sanction, sometimes in the form of more-than-compensatory damages: see eg Occhipinti (n 136) 252.

INDIVIDUAL RESPONSIBILITY 285

any form of legal liability which is divorced from such a duty is no responsibility at all; in their view, therefore, fault is compatible with responsibility while strict liability does not involve any responsibility at all, and therefore it would be better to stop using the term *responsabilità* to refer to strict liability (*responsabilità oggettiva*) and to develop a new language and conceptual framework for it.[138] In sum, principles of free moral agency and individual responsibility belong to fault liability and only there are seen as playing a possible justificatory role. These principles do not influence the reasoning of Italian legal scholars and courts on strict liability which, as earlier discussion in this book has shown, rests on very different ideas.[139] In this respect, then, the picture is strikingly different from that found in US law and in English law, where influential responsibility-based theories have been put forward to explain or support the imposition of fault liability as well as of strict liability.

A further, closely related reason that may explain the absence of individual responsibility as an argument for strict liability in the Italian context is that, unlike in the United States and England, Italian tort reasoning shuns any 'interpersonal justice' approach to tort law, at least as far as the reasons for imposing liability in tort, whether strict or based on fault, are concerned. For example, Salvi argues that theories appealing to the doing of justice between claimant and defendant are not convincing to the extent that they exclude broader societal interests from the menu of acceptable justifications for the imposition of liability, and therefore fail to make sense of vicarious liability.[140] While explicit criticisms of this type are not common, the Italian way of theorizing about tort law and justifying liability— with a good deal of weight being given to societal interests—strongly suggests that Salvi's scepticism is shared by most Italian legal actors and that theories focusing on 'interpersonal justice' are rejected in this legal system. Given the close relationship between the demands of 'interpersonal justice' and arguments based on individual responsibility,[141] it is no wonder that a rejection of the former goes hand in hand with a rejection (or neglect) of the latter.

In conclusion, individual responsibility is really not part of the reasoning seeking to justify strict liability in the Italian context. Here, the evolution of tort law has constantly associated this argument with liability for fault, while strict liability has been invariably justified by a number of different arguments drawn from wider

---

[138] See Abbagnano (n 124) 45; Uberto Scarpelli, 'Riflessioni sulla responsabilità politica. Responsabilità, libertà, visione dell'uomo' in Rinaldo Orecchia (ed), *La responsabilità politica. Diritto e tempo* (Giuffrè 1982) 41, 47, 52, 70–71. cf Castronovo (n 116) 10–11 (noting on this point the disagreement between legal scholars and philosophers).

[139] See mainly subsections 3.2.3 (risk), 3.3.3 (accident avoidance), 3.5.4 (loss spreading), and 3.6.3 (victim protection).

[140] Salvi (n 125) 30–31. See also Giulio Ponzanelli, *La responsabilità civile. Profili di diritto comparato* (Il Mulino 1992) 101–02.

[141] See subsections 3.8.2 (United States) and 3.8.3 (England).

286   JUSTIFYING STRICT LIABILITY

societal values or concerns, such as the principle of social solidarity, the compensation of victims, or the avoidance of accidents.

3.8.5 Individual Responsibility, an Argument at Odds with French Strict Liability

In France, strict liability is justified on grounds entirely different from individual responsibility. The evolution of French tort law and of its intellectual foundations show that individual responsibility has been traditionally linked to liability based on fault, where this argument still appears to have some significance. As regards individual responsibility, then, the French approach resembles the Italian and contrasts sharply with the US and English.

As in Italy, it is very difficult to find in France instances of reasoning deploying individual responsibility as an argument in favour of strict liability. One rare example is Tunc's criticism of the idea that fault should be a necessary criterion of liability in order to promote human dignity. In expressing his view, Tunc quotes a 'moral theorist and Catholic priest' as follows:

> Everyone is responsible for their own destiny, and this entails two things jointly. On one side, each person bears the consequences of their actions, and therefore makes reparation of the damage that they cause to others, even without fault. On the other side, no one is hindered in the accomplishment of their destiny by the actions of others, even where not at fault; because if the actions of others prevent me from leading the life of my own choosing, I can no longer take responsibility for my destiny; the guarantee they give me that they will, if necessary, make reparation for the losses that they cause to me, on the contrary, leaves me at least a margin of real autonomy.[142]

This reasoning can be certainly interpreted as putting forward a responsibility-based argument for strict liability. On the other hand, in Tunc's view this is not the most pressing reason for imposing strict liability: as his writings make clear, strict liability is all about compensating the victims of accidents and distributing the attendant financial burdens as widely as possible.[143] These are the true justifications for strict liability and, while the responsibility-based argument quoted above shows that Tunc was aware of the philosophical debate surrounding the choice

---

[142] André Tunc, *La responsabilité civile* (2nd edn, Economica 1989) [157] (quoting Louis de Naurois, 'Juriste et moraliste en présence des obligations inter-personnelles de justice' Nouvelle revue théologique 1963.598, 604).

[143] See references to André Tunc's work in nn 2, 14, 18, 31, 34 in subsection 3.5.2, and in n 23 in subsection 3.6.2.

between fault and strict liability, we should not exaggerate its importance, which remains minimal.[144]

The reasons for this lie in the way French tort law has evolved and in the way in which the debate on tort liability has unfolded. Certainly, norms of free moral agency and responsibility were key until the mid-nineteenth century. Before the advent of the machine age and the socio-economic changes that came with it, each person was considered as able to choose and control their own conduct and the results of their actions (or those of their children, pupils, employees, or animals), and accidents typically involved a few, easily identifiable parties. At this stage, as understood by the drafters of the *Code civil*, tort law embraced an individualistic and moralizing approach whose purpose was to ensure, on the one hand, that the claimant was compensated for their loss and, on the other, that the defendant took responsibility for their own misconduct.[145] In this framework, liability could only be imposed on the basis of fault, which was perceived as the true and necessary yardstick of the moral and social inadequacy of human behaviour, and tort disputes were perceived as involving justice between the particular claimant and the particular defendant.[146]

With the process of industrialization, all this started to change. In many cases, accidents were no longer the immediate result of the physical act of a particular individual but were linked to some failure of new technologies and activities. This resulted in more frequent and severe injuries and in the inability to find out the cause of the accident, let alone the person whose (faulty) conduct may have played a role in its causation.[147] In this new reality, a reversal in moral outlook occurred: morality required the victims of accidents to gain compensation, not to hold someone liable only on the basis of their fault. From this perspective, it soon became clear that fault could not provide an appropriate response to the needs of victims and of society more generally, and strict liability was adopted in a variety of contexts, even though it faced vigorous opposition from some leading scholars throughout the first half of the twentieth century[148] who saw fault as the only, or at least the

---

[144] French legal scholars are generally aware of philosophical discussions on the concept of responsibility (see eg Muriel Fabre-Magnan, *Droit des obligations. 2—Responsabilité civile et quasi-contrats* (4th edn, PUF 2019) [49]–[55]), but they do not bring the insights of these discussions to bear on the reasoning concerning strict liability.

[145] See Geneviève Viney, 'De la responsabilité personnelle à la répartition des risques' Arch phil dr 1977.5, 5–6; Geneviève Viney, *Introduction à la responsabilité. Traité de droit civil* (4th edn, LGDJ 2019) [15]–[16]; Judith Rochfeld, 'La responsabilité' in Judith Rochfeld (ed), *Les grandes notions du droit privé* (2nd edn, PUF 2013) 481, [4].

[146] Rochfeld (n 145) [4].

[147] ibid [8].

[148] See eg Marcel Planiol, 'Études sur la responsabilité civile' RCLJ 1905.277 279 (arguing that 'liability without fault would, if admitted, be a social injustice. It would be, in the civil law, the equivalent of convicting an innocent in the criminal law.... There is only one adjective for this solution: monstruous'); Georges Ripert, *La règle morale dans les obligations civiles* (4th edn, LGDJ 1949) [112]–[123] (arguing that tort liability is the legal implementation of moral responsibility and that strict liability, as based on the theory of risk, dismantles the very idea of responsibility); René Savatier, *Les métamorphoses économiques et sociales du droit civil d'aujourd'hui* (2nd edn, Dalloz 1952) [292] (criticizing the process

most credible, moral justification for shifting a loss from a person who suffers it to another person.[149] On this account, tort liability (*la responsabilité civile*) should be based on fault, as otherwise it would involve no responsibility at all.

Notwithstanding this opposition, strict liability and other mechanisms for the distribution of losses expanded in French law inexorably over the course of the twentieth century and, particularly over its second half, liability for accidents has been widely no longer seen as a matter of justice between two parties, but rather as a collective problem of the rational apportionment of the inevitable burdens of socially useful activities.[150] In this respect, more than any other, it is the value of solidarity that has inspired the distribution of accidental losses and the expansion of strict liability, with a view to protecting the victims of accidents and to spreading their attendant costs.[151] To accomplish these goals, the development of liability insurance and other spreading mechanisms have been particularly important as they have made the expansion of tort liability, especially strict tort liability, financially sustainable. At the level of reasoning this has meant that, as I have earlier explained, it is arguments such as risk, loss spreading, and victim protection that have always dominated the scene. These arguments (to which we could add the 'deep-pockets' justification) share a common source, for they all stem from a commitment to solidarity. This is obvious as far as loss spreading and victim protection are concerned, but it is also true—though less obviously—for risk-based justifications. As noted above in relation to the United States and England,[152] risk can be combined with a conception of individual responsibility in order to justify the imposition of strict liability. In France, however, this does not happen: since the time of Saleilles and Josserand, justifications such as risk creation and risk–benefit/profit have been typically put forward with a view to protecting victims and to 'socializing' losses, and the same is true for abnormality of risk especially as regards the liability of public bodies.[153] In the words of Brun, 'no theory symbolises better [than risk] the rise of the philosophy of solidarity and the correlative decline of individual responsibility'.[154] Given all this, it is only natural that individual responsibility plays

---

of socialization of losses and the expansion of strict liability for, inter alia, the gradual elimination of the idea of fault they entail, and arguing that, 'so distorted, civil liability turns against moral responsibility and destroys it'). See also René Savatier, 'Personnalité et dépersonnalisation de la responsabilité civile' in *Mélanges de droit, d'histoire et d'économie offerts à Marcel Laborde-Lacoste par ses collègues, ses élèves et ses amis* (Éditions Bière 1963) 321ff.

[149] See eg Ripert (n 148) [117].

[150] Tunc (n 142) [153] at 122.

[151] Yvon Lambert-Faivre, 'L'évolution de la responsabilité civile d'une dette de responsabilité à une créance d'indemnisation' RTD civ 1987.1 (outlining the evolution of civil liability from fault to strict liability to compensation schemes).

[152] See, in this section, text to and following nn 23–29, to and following nn 41–42 (United States); text to nn 64–66, to nn 75–82, to nn 108–110 (England).

[153] See subsection 3.2.2.

[154] Philippe Brun, *La responsabilité civile extracontractuelle* (5th edn, LexisNexis 2018) [156]. On the decline of individual, personal responsibility, see generally Geneviève Viney, *Le déclin de la responsabilité individuelle* (LGDJ 1965).

no role as a justification for strict liability in France: any insistence on norms of responsibility that focused on the defendant's agency would be seen as pointless, for the burden of liability is shouldered by insurers and ultimately spread across (and borne by) a wider portion of the community. Here, then, the French approach contrasts strikingly with the US and English ones, as responsibility-based theories are not part of the French reasoning on strict liability.

A further likely reason for the absence of individual responsibility from the French context is that, in keeping with the Italian position,[155] French legal actors do not appear to value approaches which see tort law as a matter of interpersonal justice between the particular claimant and the particular defendant. Indeed, we have seen in the US and English contexts that there is an intimate connection between this 'relational' (or interpersonal) approach to tort law and the use of justifications for liability (whether strict or fault-based) which are premised on norms of individual responsibility.[156] By contrast, French legal actors (especially scholars) happily rely on justifications reflecting broader societal concerns which go beyond the claimant–defendant nexus, such as the compensation of victims or the spreading of losses, or even the avoidance of accidents though mostly in connection with fault liability. In light of this, then, it should not be surprising that individual responsibility is largely ignored in the French legal reasoning as an argument in favour of strict liability.

Instead, norms of individual responsibility have retained significance in relation to liability for fault: indeed, throughout the twentieth century there have been legal scholars who have put forward a moral, fault-based conception of individual responsibility which constitutes, in their view, an attractive justification for the imposition of civil liability. As Bacache-Gibeili puts it, 'moral duty requires of a person who has adopted a reprehensible course of action to take responsibility for the harmful consequences caused to others';[157] in addition to this, she continues, 'fault allows tort law to perform a deterrent function', as 'individuals are encouraged to be diligent and prudent so as to avoid all liability'.[158] 'In doing so', she concludes, 'fault makes it possible to link civil liability to moral responsibility and to attribute to it two functions', one compensatory and one deterrent.[159] According

---

[155] See text to, preceding and following nn 140–141 in this section.

[156] See subsections 3.8.2 (United States) and 3.8.3 (England).

[157] Mireille Bacache-Gibeili, *Les obligations, La responsabilité civile extracontractuelle* (3rd edn, Economica 2016) [7]. See also the references mentioned in n 148 in this section as well as Philippe le Tourneau, 'La verdeur de la faute dans la responsabilité civile (ou la relativité de son déclin)' RTD civ 1988.505, 506–07, 509–10 (providing a subjective understanding of fault which considers the agent's shortcomings and other idiosyncrasies when assessing their conduct).

[158] Bacache-Gibeili (n 157) [7].

[159] ibid. On the punitive and deterrent functions of French tort law, see eg Boris Starck, *Essai d'une théorie générale de la responsabilité civile considérée en sa double fonction de garantie et de peine privée* (L Rodstein 1947); Suzanne Carval, *La responsabilité civile dans sa fonction de peine privée* (LGDJ 1995); Alexis Jault, *La notion de peine privée* (LGDJ 2005); Bacache-Gibeili (n 157) [47], [60]–[64]; Fabre-Magnan (n 144) [37]–[40], [454]; Marco Cappelletti, 'Comparative Reflections on Punishment in Tort

to this way of thinking, it is the defendant's free agency and the defective character of their conduct that justify a judgment of moral responsibility as well as the imposition of legal liability, especially when it comes to particularly reprehensible courses of action. But while this reasoning plays a justificatory role in relation to fault liability, it is at odds with the way in which French scholars and courts understand strict liability which is instead viewed as an instrument of social policy based on a morality of solidarity which is geared towards the achievement of compensatory and spreading goals.

To conclude, individual responsibility is far from the minds of French legal actors when it comes to justifying strict liability. The evolution of French tort law and the development of its intellectual foundations have relegated norms of individual responsibility to fault, while strict liability is justified on entirely different grounds. In this respect, the French position resembles the Italian one while showing a marked difference with the US and the English approaches.

3.8.6 Concluding Remarks

As an argument for strict liability, individual responsibility creates a sharp distinction between, on the one hand, England and the United States and, on the other hand, Italy and France. In the two common law systems, many legal scholars look at tort law through the lenses of moral philosophy and tend to investigate tort liability by considering very carefully whether a defendant should be held responsible and consequently liable to a claimant for the harmful consequences of their actions. As a result, we find in both systems (but especially in the United States) a wide variety of theories that seek to justify the imposition of tort liability, whether fault-based or strict, on the basis of norms of individual responsibility. These theories vary considerably in their own conception of responsibility and put forward different lines of reasoning to justify tort liability. In the United States, a few of these theories recognize a key role to strict liability,[160] but most of them seem to sit much more comfortably with liability for fault, arguably because of their focus on notions such as autonomy, choice, duty, or wrong(doing).[161] Relatedly, these responsibility-based theories take the view that tort liability should be mostly, if not exclusively, concerned with the doing of justice between the particular claimant and the particular defendant, and therefore they typically steer clear of justifications that reflect broader societal concerns such as the avoidance of accidents, the spreading

---

Law' in Jean-Sébastien Borghetti and Simon Whittaker (eds), *French Civil Liability in Comparative Perspective* (Hart Publishing 2019) 329, 343–49.

[160] See text to and following nn 5–20 in this section.
[161] See text to nn 23–55 in this section.

of losses, or the protection of victims.[162] As these (and other) forward-looking considerations constitute the leading justifications for the imposition of strict liability (or, for that matter, of liability in general) in US tort law, it can readily be seen that the overall significance of individual responsibility in the tort reasoning concerning strict liability should not be exaggerated.

If we look at English law, we see that the situation is similar in some respects but different in others. As in the United States, responsibility-based approaches to tort law represent an important feature of English legal reasoning, and there are influential theories based on their own conceptions of responsibility that seek to justify the imposition of strict liability.[163] Compared to their US counterparts, these theories are more flexible in that they make room for arguments that reflect broader societal concerns and, therefore, they look more equipped to recognizing an important role to strict liability in tort law.[164] At the same time, though, the appeal of these theories is weakened by the existence of competing moral approaches that both show a predilection for fault and cast doubt on the appropriateness of justifying tort liability by reference to societal goals removed from the claimant–defendant nexus.[165] In addition to this, strict liability is far more commonly justified on the basis of arguments other than some conception of individual responsibility. As a result of all this, it is fair to say that the significance of individual responsibility as a justification for strict liability is, in the English context, rather limited.

The US and English pictures contrast sharply with the approaches in Italian and French law. In these two civil law systems, norms of individual responsibility have traditionally played a justificatory role in relation to fault liability. From the late nineteenth century and throughout the twentieth century, the fault paradigm has embodied an attractive norm of responsibility according to which a person who adopts a defective course of action is responsible for the loss thereby inflicted on someone else and must therefore 'repair' the loss.[166] By contrast, except for rare and truly exceptional instances,[167] norms of individual responsibility do not feature in the reasoning seeking to justify strict liability. In both Italy and France, any insistence on such norms has always been seen as irrelevant to, and arguably in conflict with, the emergence and development of strict liability. The arguments routinely deployed to justify this type of liability embody broader societal concerns, such as the compensation of victims, the spreading of losses, or the avoidance of accidents. This is entirely consistent with the widespread belief that tort law is a tool of social engineering and that tort disputes should not be reduced to the relationship

---

[162] See text following n 55 in this section.

[163] See text to nn 64–97 in this section.

[164] See text to and preceding n 99 in this section.

[165] See text to nn 100–106 in this section.

[166] See text to nn 125–127, to n 131, to and following nn 137–138 (Italy) text to nn 145–146, to and following nn 157–159 (France) in this section.

[167] See text to nn 115–120 (Italy), and text to and preceding n 142 (France) in this section.

292 JUSTIFYING STRICT LIABILITY

between the particular claimant and the particular defendant. While this way of theorizing about tort law has certainly influenced the discussion on the foundations of fault liability as well, it is in connection with strict liability that it has shown all its force. Not only is the reasoning on Italian and French strict liability dominated by forward-looking considerations, but the very justifications which in the United States and (especially) England are perceived as compatible with norms of individual responsibility, namely the risk-based justifications, are often seen in Italy and in France as subservient to social policy and solidarity.[168] In sum, while in England and in the United States strict liability is sometimes seen as expressive of norms of individual responsibility, and these are therefore relied upon to underline a moral dimension to strict liability itself, the same does not happen in Italy and France. There, strict liability gives expression to radically different moral values and goals, usually associated with the need to compensate victims, the spreading of losses, or the avoidance of accidents. Against this backdrop, the belief is that there is no room—and perhaps no need—for individual responsibility as a justification of strict liability.

---

[168] See subsection 3.2.3 as well as text to n 124 (Italy) in this section; subsection 3.2.2 as well as text to nn 153–154 (France) in this section.

4

Concluding Reflections

This book has sought to provide a comparative analysis of the most significant substantive arguments put forward in England, the United States, France, and Italy to justify strict liability: risk, accident avoidance, the deep-pockets justification, loss spreading, victim protection, administrative cost reduction, and individual responsibility. These arguments have been identified, explained, and analysed comparatively, focusing on how they are used across the four laws and on the significance that they have borne in each of them. In this way, my analysis has painted a complex picture in relation to each argument. In this final Part of the book, I will instead comment on the patterns of arguments across the four laws as well as on the relationship between the arguments and the different values and goals which characterize and inspire the reasoning in strict liability in these systems. I will conclude by providing some remarks on the complexity of legal reasoning in strict liability from a comparative perspective.

4.1 Justifications and Contexts of Liability

Before discussing the patterns of reasoning in detail, it is useful to consider a preliminary point about the relationship between the contexts of liability (such as liability for animals, vicarious liability, or product liability) and the arguments which emerges from the analysis in Part 3. While paying attention to the contexts of liability is clearly very important in understanding the role and significance of arguments in each legal system, it is difficult to identify any special connection which links particular arguments to one or more specific contexts of liability but not to others. In other words, the same particular argument may be used to justify the imposition of strict liability in a plurality of contexts and a particular context may attract a multitude of arguments, both within and across legal systems. A possible explanation for this phenomenon lies in the nature of the arguments themselves. Arguments such as accident avoidance, loss spreading (if understood as insurance spreading or as proportionality of burdens and benefits), victim protection, administrative cost reduction, and individual responsibility are extremely general and malleable, meaning that they can be used to justify strict liability (and, in some cases, fault liability as well) in all sorts of situations, no matter what type of activity or conduct the defendant is engaged in. The picture starts to look different, though, if we look at two specific permutations of loss spreading, namely

Justifying Strict Liability. Marco Cappelletti, Oxford University Press. © Marco Cappelletti 2022.
DOI: 10.1093/oso/9780192859860.003.0011

taxation spreading and enterprise spreading. These arguments refer to particular channels of distribution and therefore involve specific classes of defendant: taxation spreading relies on the imposition of taxes as a means of loss distribution and therefore applies only to situations involving public entities; similarly, enterprise spreading relies on price adjustments or a decrease in wages/profits, and it therefore applies only to situations where firms are involved. Clearly then, while these two arguments also have a wide reach, they are bound by the nature of defendants and therefore cannot apply wherever public entities or firms are not involved. This feature is confirmed by their use in the four laws we have considered.

If we move on to arguments from risk, the picture changes again as we consider its different permutations. Risk creation and risk–benefit look extremely flexible, for most (if not all) human activities may be characterized as involving the creation of a risk of harm or the accruing of some sort of benefit (even if purely emotional or psychological) to the party engaging in them. Therefore, these risk-based arguments may be used to justify a wide variety of strict liabilities, and this is reflected in how they are used across the four legal systems. By contrast, the other risk-based arguments (nonreciprocity of risk, abnormality of risk, and risk–profit) are more selective in the criteria which are attracted by them. Appealing to the creation of a nonreciprocal or abnormal risk of harm or to the taking of risk for a financial profit provides not only a justification for the imposition of liability but also a well-defined condition of liability, in the form of a criterion for identifying the party liable. In particular, liability can be justified on the basis of these arguments only in situations involving, respectively, a defendant imposing a nonreciprocal risk of harm, an abnormal risk of harm, or any risk of harm with a view to a profit, and again this all emerges from the way in which these arguments are used in the four jurisdictions.[1]

Finally, some remarks should be made in relation to the deep-pockets justification, which is a highly adaptable argument given that it fits any situation in which the defendant is likely to have enough financial resources to shoulder someone else's loss. Consistently with this versatility, the argument has been used over time to justify a variety of disparate strict liabilities across the four legal systems,[2] even though one context of liability, namely the vicarious liability of employers, has significantly attracted the deep-pockets justification in all of them, especially earlier in its development. This is understandable, as employers have traditionally been seen as the party best equipped to sustain the financial consequences of accidents caused by their employees.

Overall, some arguments are malleable enough to fit most factual situations and, therefore, to justify the imposition of strict liability in a very wide variety of contexts. Other arguments, by contrast, have some built-in elements that restrict the

---

[1] See section 3.2.
[2] See section 3.4.

range of situations which can attract them and, therefore, the contexts of strict liability they may justify. Despite their differing flexibility, though, each of the arguments examined in this book is seen as capable of justifying multiple contexts of strict liability, as has been seen throughout each section of Part 3; conversely, it is also true that more than one argument may be used to justify the same context of liability. To give just one example, risk–profit may be invoked to justify product liability or the vicarious liability of employers; at the same time, each of these contexts of liability may be justified on the basis of *additional* arguments such as accident avoidance, loss spreading, or victim protection. In other words, there seems to be no one-to-one relation between any particular context of strict liability and any particular substantive justification considered in the book.

4.2 Some Reflections on the Patterns of Reasoning in Strict Liability

As we saw in Part 2 of the book, strict liability is generally defined negatively as 'liability without fault'. And, unless we are given further elucidation, all we can say is that strict liability does not rest on fault, but we do not know on *what it rests*. In trying to answer this question, this study has suggested that there are as many ways of justifying strict liability as there are distinct structures of reasoning that may be put forward for that purpose. In this respect, it may be helpful to think of the reasoning on strict liability as an edifice whose building blocks are the substantive arguments used to erect it. As shown throughout Part 3, legal actors across the four legal systems cherry-pick the most attractive building blocks for their own edifice, the overall result being many different building types, that is many different justificatory structures for strict liability. These building blocks can be used in many different ways. In particular, arguments may be put forward as stand-alone justifications, or they may be combined or juxtaposed with other arguments. Distinguishing among these patterns allows us to understand how legal actors in the four legal systems structure their own thinking about strict liability, and also provides us with useful information regarding the role (and sometimes the justificatory weight) that these legal actors give to the arguments used.

A good starting-point for reflection is provided by stand-alone arguments. Where an argument stands alone, it is put forward as the only justification for strict liability, and it obviously constitutes *the* single reason for imposing strict liability in the view of its proponent. As shown in Part 3, this pattern can be identified in relation to most of the arguments discussed, particularly as regards the various permutations of risk,[3] but also (though less frequently) accident

---

[3] See eg references to risk as a stand-alone argument in nn 30–32, nn 56–58 and n 61 in subsection 3.2.2, nn 107–109 in subsection 3.2.3, text to n 125 and n 161 in subsection 3.2.4, and nn 194–195 in subsection 3.2.5.

296   JUSTIFYING STRICT LIABILITY

avoidance,[4] victim protection,[5] loss spreading,[6] and individual responsibility.[7] Where a stand-alone argument does not embody any goal, as for example is the case for arguments based on risk, one is left to speculate if there is something else behind the relevant argument which is actually driving it. For instance, abnormality of risk features in English reasoning as a stand-alone justification in a few contexts of strict liability,[8] but it is unclear in such cases whether strict liability seeks to protect victims, to avoid accidents, to promote norms of individual responsibility, or to achieve a plurality of goals all at once. Similarly, risk–benefit or risk–profit are used in the other three legal systems as stand-alone arguments in contexts such as liability for animals, employers' vicarious liability, or product liability:[9] are these arguments an attempt to promote some conception of individual responsibility, or is an undisclosed 'societal' goal being pursued, for example an increased protection of victims? In sum, in the few instances where arguments which do not embody any goal are used as stand-alone justifications, one is left feeling dissatisfied because there appears to be more going on 'behind the curtains' than it is revealed to the reader. But more generally, and very significantly, reliance on stand-alone justifications is rare in all the four jurisdictions studied. This reveals that strict liability is generally perceived as requiring a reinforced justificatory basis which cannot be provided by resorting to a single argument; indeed, as I will explain, legal actors in the four laws typically link strict liability to a constellation of arguments which are usually put together either in juxtaposition or in combination.

As I explained in the introduction to Part 3,[10] a juxtaposition of arguments consists of a list of independent justifications which point to strict liability from different directions. Juxtaposed arguments do not show any meaningful integration or interconnectedness among themselves and are instead simply thrown in the mix one after another. Precisely because of this, any argument can be juxtaposed with any one or more of the others and, as our discussion in Part 3 has shown, there are really no limits to the inventiveness with which legal actors across the four laws juxtapose arguments, regardless of their nature! First, in all four systems there are juxtapositions among arguments which embody some specific goal, such as victim protection, loss spreading, accident avoidance, administrative cost reduction, or the promotion of individual responsibility.[11] Secondly, even if sporadically,

---

[4] See eg text to n 37 in subsection 3.3.2 as well as references to accident avoidance as a stand-alone argument in n 95 in subsection 3.3.3.

[5] See text to nn 14–18 in subsection 3.6.2, to nn 29–31 in subsection 3.6.3, and to nn 75–76 in subsection 3.6.5.

[6] See eg references to loss spreading as a stand-alone argument in n 78 in subsection 3.5.3.

[7] See eg text to nn 5–10, to nn 30–35, to and following nn 43–45 in subsection 3.8.2.

[8] See text to n 205 as well as the references to the argument as a stand-alone justification in nn 194–195 in subsection 3.2.5.

[9] See references to stand-alone arguments in n 56 in subsection 3.2.2, nn 108–110 and n 112 in subsection 3.2.3, and n 161 in subsection 3.2.4.

[10] See section 3.1.

[11] See eg André Tunc, 'Responsabilité civile et dissuasion des comportements antisociaux' in *Aspects nouveaux de la pensée juridique: recueil d'études en hommage à Marc Ancel*, vol 1 (Pedone 1975) 407, 414

CONCLUDING REFLECTIONS 297

juxtapositions may involve only arguments which do not embody any goal, as where the deep-pockets justification is put next to any of the risk-based permutations, or where some of the latter are juxtaposed among themselves.[12] Finally, juxtapositions frequently take place between arguments which embody some specific goal and arguments which do not do so, as where accident avoidance, victim protection, or loss spreading are juxtaposed with the deep-pockets rationale or the risk-based arguments.[13]

Most of these juxtapositions reveal a common problem, though, which is a deficit of clarity in legal reasoning, especially where lots of justifications feature together. In particular, it is often difficult to understand the interplay, if there is any, among the arguments put forward and to pinpoint their relative significance within any broader reasoning. This may be acceptable where a legal actor (typically a legal scholar) simply presents or summarizes the arguments that other legal actors from the same jurisdiction have used to justify strict liability. However, where instead legal actors are in effect providing their own justifications for strict liability, a greater elaboration on the arguments used is desirable to achieve sufficient clarity. For example, in a reasoning which juxtaposes (say) victim protection and accident avoidance, what is the relative justificatory weight of each of these goals? Do they have the same weight or does either of them take priority over the other? And if there is a conflict between them, meaning that (for example) in a set of situations victim protection would require strict liability while accident avoidance would not, how should the conflict be resolved? Occasionally it is possible to answer this type of questions, for example where the arguments involved in the juxtaposition are expressly ranked, or some other information helps to shed light on the legal actor's thinking (eg one particular argument is mentioned multiple times, or it is given clearly more emphasis than other justifications).[14] In a majority of cases, however,

(on strict liability in general); Pier Giuseppe Monateri, *La Responsabilità Civile. Trattato di Diritto Civile* (UTET 1998) 947 (on parental liability); Fowler V Harper, Fleming James Jr, and Oscar S Gray, *The Law of Torts*, vol 5 (2nd edn, Little, Brown and Company 1986) 21 (on employers' vicarious liability); Joseph H King Jr, 'A Goals-Oriented Approach to Strict Tort Liability for Abnormally Dangerous Activities' (1996) 48 Baylor L Rev 341, 350–61 (on strict liability in general, with a view to identifying the justifications that should guide liability for abnormally dangerous activities); Christian Witting, 'Modelling Organisational Vicarious Liability' (2019) 39(4) LS 1, 7–9 (on vicarious liability).

[12] See eg Francesco Messineo, *Manuale di diritto civile e commerciale*, vol V (9th edn, Giuffrè 1957) 579 (on employers' vicarious liability); *McLane v Northwest Natural Gas*, 467 P.2d 635, 638 (Or.1970) (on abnormally dangerous activities); François Terré and others, *Droits civil, Les obligations* (12th edn, Dalloz 2018)[1228] (on product liability).

[13] *Green v Smith & Nephew AHP, Inc*, 629 N.W.2d 727, 749–50 (Wis.2001) (on liability for defective products); Patrice Jourdain, *Les principes de la responsabilité civile* (10th edn, Dalloz 2021) 96 (on liability for the deeds of things); Enzo Roppo, 'Sul danno causato da automobile difettose. Tutela dei danneggiati, regime di responsabilità e incidenza dell'assicurazione obbligatoria' (1978) 12(IV) GI 130, 140 (on liability of producers for harm caused by defective motor vehicles); Nicholas J McBride and Roderick Bagshaw, *Tort Law* (6th edn, Pearson Education 2018) 376–78 (on product liability).

[14] King Jr (n 11) 353 (on strict liability in general, arguing that accident avoidance 'should be accorded less weight than loss spreading considerations'); *Queen City Terminals, Inc v Gen Am Transp Corp*, 653 N.E.2d 661, 671–72 (Ohio 1995) (on product liability, treating accident avoidance as more

the reasoning put forward is quite opaque and one is left to speculate about the significance of each argument relative to the others in the list and about their exact role in any broader reasoning. Where this happens, strict liability rests on shaky foundations: here, then, scholars such as Stevens may have a point when they argue that '[j]ustifications for legal rules are not like the ingredients of vegetable soup', as '[w]e cannot simply add together a number of disparate ingredients and expect to get a satisfactory result'.[15]

Different considerations come into play with respect to combinations of arguments. Where a legal actor combines two or more arguments, they are not put forward as separate, independent rationales, but are instead presented with some level of integration or interconnectedness.[16] This means that the justificatory role and significance of each argument depends on the other arguments featuring in the combination; or that, even if not interdependent, combined arguments are presented as working together and as shaping together the reasoning justifying strict liability, so that if one of the arguments were removed, the relevant reasoning would not stand up and would look very different, for example by leading to the imposition of strict liability in an entirely different type of situation.

In contrast with the juxtaposition pattern, clearer trends can be identified in relation to combinations of arguments. First, arguments from victim protection and accident avoidance are typically not combined in the four legal systems studied. Why is this so? A plausible explanation is that these two justifications are often seen as ultimate goals of strict liability that neither fuel each other nor work together for the achievement of some other, further goal. In other words, their paths never cross and therefore, while they can be juxtaposed, they do not seem capable of being combined. Secondly, there are combinations in which none of the arguments embody some specific goal, as where the various permutations of risk are combined together,[17] or where risk-based arguments are combined with the deep-pockets rationale.[18] This type of combination, however, is relatively rare and the reason for this appears to be that legal actors generally seek to justify strict liability by linking it to the achievement of some goal. This finds direct confirmation in the fact that, as

important than other arguments such as loss spreading); *Green* (n 13) 749–50 (on product liability, seeing risk–profit, together with risk creation, as the primary rationale of strict liability and adding to them loss spreading, the protection of consumer expectations, and accident avoidance); Jourdain (n 13) 105 (on employers' vicarious liability, mentioning risk–profit, accident avoidance, and the deep-pockets argument, but concluding that the fundamental point is insurability); Douglas Brodie, 'Enterprise Liability: Justifying Vicarious Liability' (2007) 27 OJLS 493, 495 (suggesting that accident avoidance is a justification of secondary importance compared to risk); and see text to and following nn 32–33 in subsection 3.7.3 in relation to administrative cost reduction.

[15] See Robert Stevens, *Torts and Rights* (OUP 2007) 259 (discussing the justifications for vicarious liability in English law).

[16] See section 3.1.

[17] See eg *Rylands v Fletcher*, (1866) LR 1 Ex 265, 279–80; *Isaacs v Powell*, 267 So.2d 864, 865–66 (Fla.1972); *Gore v Stannard*, [2014] QB 1, [156].

[18] See John Murphy, 'The Merits of Rylands v Fletcher' (2004) 24 OJLS 643, 659.

CONCLUDING REFLECTIONS 299

shown throughout Part 3, the most frequent combinations are those where one or more arguments act as goals of strict liability and one or more others act as means to achieve them.

This last type of combination, ie that involving means and goals, is illuminating insofar as the nature of legal arguments and the relationship among them are concerned. Indeed, a point which emerges from the analysis in Part 3 is that the same argument may be used as a means to pursue a variety of different goals. For example, the deep-pockets and the loss-spreading arguments may be relied upon to pursue victim protection (as happens in all four systems), or, quite differently, to avoid accidents or minimize their social costs (as happens in the United States and, more rarely, in Italy and England).[19] Similarly, the gain-based theories of risk may be used to promote norms of individual responsibility (especially in common law quarters),[20] or, rather differently, to ensure that victims of accidents receive compensation (especially in France and Italy).[21] Again, abnormality of risk may be invoked to promote norms of individual responsibility,[22] to accomplish the compensation of victims or the spreading of losses,[23] or to pursue the avoidance of accidents.[24] Moreover, two of the arguments discussed, namely accident avoidance and loss spreading, constitute for some legal actors goals worth pursuing in themselves[25] while, in the view of others, they are linked to the achievement of further goals such as the increase in social welfare or (but this is true only for loss spreading) the compensation of victims.[26] In sum, in contrast with the juxtaposition pattern, an analysis of the combination pattern allows us to appreciate the chameleonic nature of the arguments examined and to see how these, where combined with certain justifications, can take on distinct justificatory roles and create a variety of lines of argumentation to justify strict liability.

A further, key point is that the problems of clarity in legal argumentation which occur in relation to the juxtaposition pattern fade away in most instances of combinations of arguments. This is especially true in more sophisticated reasoning,

---

[19] See subsections 3.4.2 and 3.5.2 (France), subsections 3.4.3 and 3.5.4 (Italy), subsections 3.4.5 and 3.5.5 (England), subsections 3.4.4 and 3.5.3 (United States).

[20] See eg Jane Stapleton, *Product Liability* (Butterworths 1994) 186–87; Peter Cane and James Goudkamp, *Atiyah's Accidents, Compensation and the Law* (9th edn, CUP 2018) 453.

[21] Saleilles and Josserand (see nn 9–13 in subsection 3.2.2 for references); Mario Griffey, *La responsabilità civile derivante da circolazione dei veicoli e dei natanti* (Giuffrè 1995) 91.

[22] See text to n 209 in subsection 3.2.5.

[23] See text to nn 46–53 in subsection 3.2.2, to and following nn 97–100 in subsection 3.2.3, to nn 143–148 in subsection 3.2.4, and to n 207 in subsection 3.2.5.

[24] See eg Geneviève Schamps, *La mise en danger: un concept fondateur d'un principe général de responsabilité* (Bruylant/LGDJ 1998) 849–50 (though giving priority to the compensation of victims). See also text to nn 101–103 in subsection 3.2.3, to and following nn 149–154 in subsection 3.2.4, and to n 208 in subsection 3.2.5.

[25] See eg text to n 41 in subsection 3.3.2 and text to, preceding and following nn 78–80 in subsection 3.5.3.

[26] See eg text to, preceding and following nn 39–40 in subsection 3.3.2, text to nn 54–58 and text following n 81 in subsection 3.3.3, text to and following n 35 in subsection 3.5.2, text to, preceding and following nn 190–192 in subsection 3.5.5.

300 JUSTIFYING STRICT LIABILITY

where combined arguments work harmoniously together towards the achievement of an overarching goal, with each of them playing a well-defined role and having its own significance depending, at least in part, on the other arguments featuring in the same reasoning. Particularly striking examples of this have been discussed in relation to the reasoning put forward in the law and economics literature in the United States and Italy. In combining arguments such as accident avoidance, loss spreading, and a reduction in administrative costs, legal economists explain how each of these arguments (and goals) relate to one another and to strict liability, whether or not they conflict with one another and how they should be balanced with each other.[27] Similarly, though from an entirely different perspective, several legal scholars in England and in the United States combine arguments such as abnormality of risk, nonreciprocity of risk, risk–profit or risk–benefit, with theories of individual responsibility (which may vary according to the scholar's preferred normative or interpretive view). Used in this way, such arguments acquire a specific 'moral' connotation and their aim is to render strict liability consistent with norms of individual responsibility.[28]

The situation is somewhat different in relation to less elaborate combinations of arguments, where problems of clarity may occasionally emerge. In many cases, the reasoning justifying strict liability is simple and the relationship among the arguments used is clear: for example, where the deep-pockets argument is combined with (say) victim protection, the former act as the means and the latter as the goal to be pursued through strict liability. However, there are combinations which, despite being prima facie straightforward, present some difficulties when one tries to understand the relative role and significance of the various arguments put forward.[29] Where this is the case and the relevant legal actor fails to explain fully how their combination works, one is left wondering what the exact relationship among the different arguments is, if they all have equal force, and how they should be balanced in case of conflict among themselves. This phenomenon is, however, relatively rare and it certainly occurs far less often than in instances of juxtaposition of arguments. The general impression, then, is that the worry of being served a bad soup should fade away in the case of well-reasoned combinations of arguments in which the role of the various justifications is explained and in which the potential conflict among justifications is resolved by balancing them against each other. In

[27] See eg Pietro Trimarchi, *Rischio e responsabilità oggettiva* (Giuffrè 1961); Guido Calabresi, *The Costs of Accidents: A Legal and Economic Analysis* (YUP 1970).

[28] See eg Stapleton (n 20) 179–200; Tony Honoré, 'Responsibility and Luck: The Moral Basis of Strict Liability' (1988) 104 LQR 530; George Fletcher, 'Fairness and Utility in Tort Theory' (1972) 85 Harv L Rev 537; Stephen Perry, 'Responsibility for Outcomes, Risk, and the Law of Torts' in Gerald Postema (ed), *Philosophy and the Law of Torts* (CUP 2001) 72 (relying on the idea of 'unilateral risk imposition', which resonates with Fletcher's imposition of a nonreciprocal risk of harm).

[29] See eg Murphy (n 18) 659 (combining the deep-pockets argument with risk–profit); Giovanni B Ferri, 'Garanzia, rischio e responsabilità oggettiva' (2005) 10–12(1) Riv Dir Comm 867, 870 (combining risk–profit with the theory of *rischio di impresa*).

these cases, the soup may not suit our personal taste, but its ingredients are nevertheless properly combined and produce a satisfactory result.

4.3 Justifying Strict Liability: Arguments, Values, and Goals

The analysis of the reasoning conducted in Part 3 has revealed that the significance of each argument varies *within* and *across* legal systems. Following my characterization of arguments as key, secondary, or make-weight, we have seen that legal actors from the same jurisdiction understand each argument in different ways and often attribute to it a different justificatory weight. Also, by exploring the various instances of reasoning and by paying attention to the contexts of strict liability in which arguments are invoked, the analysis has provided an overview of the role and significance of each argument in each of the four laws, and it has compared and contrasted the treatment that each argument receives across them. In doing so, the discussion in Part 3 has reduced each legal system's substantive reasoning in strict liability to its constituent parts (the arguments) in order to provide a fresh analysis. What follows seeks instead to offer an overall picture of each legal system's reasoning by pulling together its constituent parts and by paying attention to the values and goals to which legal actors are committed. This will help us to appreciate and contrast the distinct commitments which shape the role and significance of legal arguments across the four laws and to enhance our understanding of each system's tort culture.

A good starting point for our discussion is French law. As seen throughout Part 3, the value of social solidarity permeates French reasoning and requires that the victims of accidents should be protected by the law and receive adequate compensation for their losses. Driven by a sentiment of compassion for victims in a spirit of solidarity, the French approach to strict liability looks at least prima facie single-minded in seeing victim protection as the ultimate goal and justification of strict liability.[30] In order to guarantee compensation for as many victims as possible, French reasoning relies heavily on risk-based justifications and on loss spreading (while the deep-pockets argument is today marginal and widely seen as old-fashioned).[31] As to the former, since the end of the nineteenth century the idea that the party who creates a risk of harm or gains from that risk should be liable for the losses inflicted on innocent victims has attracted widespread support in France, and even today it is heavily relied upon to justify a wide variety of strict liabilities (with the exception of parental liability).[32] Probably because they spring from authoritative 'sources' such as Saleilles and Josserand, risk-based

---

[30] See subsection 3.6.2.
[31] See subsections 3.2.2 (risk) and 3.5.2 (loss spreading).
[32] See text to nn 7–14 in subsection 3.2.2.

302   JUSTIFYING STRICT LIABILITY

justifications are perceived as prestigious and look intuitively fair (*juste, équitable*) to many French legal actors.[33] As a result, risk creation and the gain-based theories of risk provide considerable *theoretical* support to the imposition of strict liability. Moreover, even though these justifications may, in principle, be used to promote norms of individual justice and responsibility, it is instead clear that, from the time of their eminent proponents, risk-based arguments are indissolubly bonded to victim protection and still today they are typically deployed to achieve this goal.

As to loss spreading, the development of insurance has acted in France as a true 'game-changer', for it has profoundly affected both how accidents are considered and how the law responds to their occurrence. In particular, the existence of insurance fuelled the transformation of French tort law from a system of individual responsibility into a socialized system for the allocation of losses,[34] and as the analysis in Part 3 has shown, the *practical* relevance of insurance has spilled over into French reasoning, so as to make loss spreading—particularly in the form of insurance spreading—a pervasive justification for strict liability.[35] Similarly, the idea that the burdens initially imposed for the common good on a particular individual should be proportionally spread across society provides a powerful justification for the imposition of strict liability on public authorities;[36] practically, this proportional sharing is realized through spreading via taxation, which is the key channel for loss redistribution in the public context.[37] Therefore, besides being *theoretically* very attractive, loss spreading is also *practically* essential, because the availability of spreading mechanisms is what renders socially and economically acceptable the widespread reliance on strict liability in France.[38] Compared to risk-based arguments, then, loss spreading is more attuned to a system geared towards the socialization of losses and more truly reflective of the French commitment to social solidarity. Indeed, unlike risk-based arguments, loss spreading ensures that losses are socialized, meaning that the wider community will bear them and that no one will be excessively burdened by the consequences of accidents. In other words, the spreading of losses protects the interests of *both* claimants and defendants. This is very important, as it leads us to qualify the previous statement that the French approach to strict liability is single-minded because focused exclusively on the victims' interests. While it is certainly true that French legal actors rely on loss spreading as a means to protect victims, the heavy and systematic reliance placed on the loss-spreading justifications suggests that there is a *covert* balancing going on in the minds of French lawyers between the interests of defendants and the interests of claimants, and that the combined effect of strict liability and loss

---

[33] See eg text to and following n 34 in subsection 3.2.2.
[34] See eg text to and following nn 6–9 in subsection 3.5.2.
[35] See subsection 3.5.2.
[36] See text to nn 40–46 in subsection 3.5.2.
[37] See text to and following n 47 in subsection 3.5.2.
[38] See text to n 33 and text to, preceding and following nn 38–39 in subsection 3.5.2.

spreading is deemed to reconcile them appropriately and in obedience to the value of solidarity for all.[39]

The French approach is therefore profoundly instrumental, meaning that strict liability (and one might suspect tort liability more generally) is seen as a tool for the realization of social objectives which are broader than the relationship between the particular claimant and the particular defendant. Largely emancipated from a vision of tort law as a system of individual justice, French legal actors think that it is only by fulfilling the value of social solidarity that tort law can achieve morally satisfactory results. In this sense, focusing too narrowly on the claimant–defendant nexus and too much on norms of individual responsibility would likely result in a retrenchment of tort liability (especially strict) and to a reduction in the protection granted to the victims of accidents. All this would represent a morally repugnant outcome in the view of most French legal actors.

The French instrumentalism is, however, selective because strict liability is used as a tool for the achievement of certain specific goals, namely the compensation and spreading of losses. Consistently with this, the reasoning on strict liability in France is driven by a triad of arguments which serve these aims, namely victim protection, loss spreading, and risk, each with its own justificatory role and significance. As highlighted in our discussion in Part 3, the emphasis of French legal actors on these arguments goes hand in hand with their antipathy towards law and economics.[40] Here, then, French law steers clear of a type of instrumentalism that is common both in Italy and (especially) in the United States. Legal economists focus on incentives and their main concern is to assess and choose liability rules based on their effects on social welfare. This way of approaching the consequences of accidents is perceived in France as at odds with the value of social solidarity and, therefore, as immoral and to be rejected. This hostility towards the economic analysis of law has important repercussions in terms of legal reasoning. Indeed, law and economics places great emphasis on the avoidance of accidents as a key consideration to promote social welfare, and it therefore provides the ideal intellectual milieu for the flourishing of accident avoidance as a justification for strict liability. The absence of this type of analysis in France explains, at least in part, why only few scholars take accident avoidance seriously with the vast majority of them either ignoring or marginalizing it.[41] Similarly, while law and economics gives serious consideration to the administrative costs entailed by different liability rules, only very rarely have French scholars taken these into account,[42] showing once again that the cost–benefit analysis embedded in law and economics is alien to the way in which French lawyers conceive of tort law.

---

[39] See eg text to and following n 39 in subsection 3.5.2.
[40] See text to and following n 169 in subsection 3.3.5, text to n 52 in subsection 3.5.2, and text to and following nn 61–62 in subsection 3.7.5.
[41] See text to and following nn 167–169 in subsection 3.3.5.
[42] See text to nn 52–57 in subsection 3.7.5.

304   JUSTIFYING STRICT LIABILITY

In conclusion, in an environment where notions of individual responsibility have long gone and in which the economic analysis of law is seen as repulsive because of its supposedly 'cold' calculations, there is little left to counterbalance the value of social solidarity and the desire to protect the victims of accidents. Compensation is perceived as a moral and social imperative, and it is therefore not surprising that French law is by far the legal system among the four studied where the rules of strict liability are more numerous and more rigorous. To feed and support the French 'compensation ideology', legal actors from this jurisdiction rely heavily on risk-based arguments and, perhaps more importantly, on loss spreading. The result of combining strict liability with spreading mechanisms is that the costs of accidents are not left concentrated on any one person, whether the victim, the defendant, or a third party. This emphasis on loss spreading shows that, while the French reasoning may appear single-minded in its commitment to protect victims, the interests of defendants and more generally of society are also taken into account. In sum, more than by a compensation ideology, the French approach to strict liability appears to be driven by an ideology of compensation and distribution.

Compared to France, the legal reasoning seeking to justify strict liability in Italy, England, and the United States is more varied. In each of these legal systems, a wider range of commitments inspire it and reflect distinct values and goals which variously affect the role and significance of legal arguments.

In Italian law, the reasoning on strict liability is shaped by the coexistence of two distinct approaches which are committed to *very* different values and goals. First, in keeping with the French approach, Italian tort law finds an important source of inspiration in the value of social solidarity which, formally adopted by the Italian Constitution, has played a key role in shifting the focus of tort law from the defendant's conduct to the victim's need for adequate compensation.[43] Secondly, law and economics has also gained attention in Italy as a credible intellectual movement and it now exerts considerable influence on the debate regarding the functions and goals of Italian tort law by focusing on accidents from the standpoint of their costs.[44] Common to these two intellectual movements is the belief that tort law pursues broader societal goals and that, therefore, there is much more going on in this area of the law than the doing of justice between the particular claimant and the particular defendant on the basis of some norm of individual responsibility. In this respect, then, Italian law displays a markedly instrumental character, in keeping with the French approach, even though it encompasses a wider range of policy considerations and concerns.

It is against this backdrop that we can appreciate in full the Italian reasoning on strict liability and how the various justifications for this type of liability are treated

---

[43]   See eg text to nn 111–116 in subsection 3.5.4, and text to and following nn 27–28 in subsection 3.6.3.
[44]   See eg text to and following nn 52–53 in subsection 3.3.3, and text to nn 117–123 in section 3.5.4.

CONCLUDING REFLECTIONS   305

in the Italian context. First, given the importance of the constitutional principle of social solidarity, it is not surprising that victim protection has become an essential goal of tort law, perhaps the most important one, and that it features very conspicuously in the reasoning seeking to justify all sorts of strict liabilities in Italian law.[45] However, even if the compensation of victims is an essential goal of strict liability, Italian scholars see the latter as in need of more theoretical support than a simple reference to victim protection itself. Therefore, other arguments are relied upon to give effect to the value of social solidarity, namely the various permutations of risk, loss spreading, and (though rarely) the deep-pockets justification. Particularly significant are, in this respect, abnormality of risk which is codified in article 2050 Cod civ as an element of liability and which is also a key justification for this important and ever-expanding context of strict liability;[46] and the gain-based theories of risk, which feature in a wide variety of strict liabilities, even though it is only in the context of liability for animals that they dominate the scene (in the form of risk–benefit).[47] While these risk-based arguments may, in principle, stem from a commitment to norms of individual justice and responsibility, it appears that in Italy they are often used as part of a strategy to achieve wider societal goals, most notably the compensation of victims.[48] In this respect, then, there is some resemblance to the French approach, although the analysis has shown that in Italy risk creation is widely rejected and more emphasis is arguably placed on abnormality of risk.[49] Very importantly, however, a commitment to social solidarity and victim protection should also be sustained by widespread reliance on loss spreading, as evidenced by the French experience. While loss spreading is occasionally mentioned, for example by reference to *rischio di impresa* in the context of employers' vicarious liability[50] or in relation to the liability of public bodies,[51] the argument has failed to thrive both because of several criticisms made to it and because of the scarce attention paid to it by scholars working in the field of law and economics.[52] As a result, while Italian law holds social solidarity and the protection of victims in high regard, it shuns any systematic reliance on the loss-spreading justifications, in striking contrast with the French approach.

A second approach shaping Italian reasoning on strict liability is law and economics, which exercises considerable influence on Italian legal scholars and, through them, on Italian courts.[53] In this respect, there is again a profound

---

[45] See subsection 3.6.3.

[46] Text to nn 91–96 in subsection 3.2.3.

[47] See text to nn 104–113 in subsection 3.2.3.

[48] See text to and following nn 98–100 in subsection 3.2.3 (abnormality of risk). See also Guido Alpa, *La responsabilità civile: principi* (2nd edn, UTET 2018) 467; Griffey (n 21) 91 (both referring to risk–benefit).

[49] See text to nn 68–70 (risk creation) and to nn 91–103 (abnormality of risk) in subsection 3.2.3.

[50] See text to nn 124–128 in subsection 3.5.4.

[51] See text to n 145 and to n 146 in subsection 3.5.4.

[52] See text to nn 133–142 in subsection 3.5.4.

[53] See text to and following nn 52–53 in subsection 3.3.3, and text to nn 117–123 in subsection 3.5.4.

difference with French law, which frowns upon law and economics as a persuasive framework of legal analysis. By focusing on the effects that tort rules have on the behaviour of potential defendants and potential claimants, law and economics seeks to promote social welfare and, for this purpose, it attributes a pivotal role to accident avoidance. While French legal actors typically disregard economic analysis and give little consideration to accident avoidance, these feature prominently in the Italian reasoning justifying strict liability, in essence every time this liability is seen as consistent with the goal of avoiding accidents efficiently.[54] It is also important to underline that a reduction in administrative costs is taken into account in Italian reasoning[55] and that, although spreading considerations too could form part of an approach inspired by economic analysis, most Italian scholars working in the field ignore or marginalize them, largely because they are seen to be in potential conflict with the aim of efficient accident avoidance.[56] In addition to this, the type of cost-benefit balancing typical of law and economics leads Italian scholars to criticize any single-minded emphasis on victim protection as well as any excessive reliance on strict liability whenever its imposition is at odds with the objectives of economic analysis.[57] Therefore, it is very clear that law and economics has a chilling effect on the type of values and reasoning which are instead so jealously cherished in France.

Given all this, the Italian approach to strict liability differs strikingly from the French one. Certainly, social solidarity and the compensation of victims are highly regarded in both legal systems, and risk-based arguments are often used in support as well. However, Italian reasoning shuns any systematic engagement with loss spreading and only occasionally invokes it. Moreover, while Italian legal actors recognize the importance of compensating the victims of accidents, they avoid any single-minded approach, and other key goals (and therefore arguments) enter the picture, most notably the avoidance of accidents. In this respect, the emergence of law and economics has proved to be highly influential in Italian law, introducing a habit for cost–benefit analyses which contrast with the unilateral, pro-victim reasoning dominating the scene in France. As a result, the Italian approach is often characterized by an overt balancing of considerations which, weighed up against each other, may or may not support the imposition of strict liability in different contexts. It is therefore not surprising that Italian law does not rely on strict liability as much as French law does, whether in terms of frequency, breadth, or rigour of the strict liabilities adopted.[58] All this is a reflection of the fact that commitments to different values and goals coexist in the Italian reasoning on strict liability, with some legal actors appealing to the value of social solidarity and the need to protect

[54] See subsection 3.3.3.
[55] See subsection 3.7.3.
[56] See text to nn 139–142 in subsection 3.5.4.
[57] See text to nn 33–40 in subsection 3.6.3.
[58] See section 2.5.

victims, and others invoking economic analysis and the goal of avoiding accidents efficiently. It is around these poles that the argumentation on strict liability revolves and its justifications are articulated in Italian law.

Looking at the broader picture, it is clear that, in keeping with the French approach, the Italian reasoning on strict liability is overtly instrumental, but with significant differences. While French legal actors focus almost exclusively on compensating and distributing losses, Italian reasoning recognizes the importance of these goals while at the same time adding another layer of instrumental thinking, that relating to economic analysis. In a way, therefore, it may be said that while both tort systems and cultures show a taste for instrumentalism, the Italian approach is more varied as it encompasses a wider range of policy concerns and considerations. But as in France, instrumental thinking exhausts the reasoning on strict liability, as it leaves no room for consideration of norms of individual justice and responsibility. These may be given some relevance in relation to liability for fault, but they have never provided appealing justifications for strict liability.[59] In keeping with the French experience, the type of philosophical analysis that would be necessary to ground strict liability in norms of individual responsibility has never taken hold; relatedly, the view that the reasons for imposing liability in tort may be confined to considerations pertaining to the claimant–defendant nexus is frowned upon because seen as limitative of tort law's potential as a tool of social engineering. In sum, strict liability (and probably fault liability as well) is fundamentally seen as an instrument of socio-economic policy which, depending on the particular commitment to which legal actors subscribe, may be bent in one way and then another to fulfil a variety of values and goals.

The English approach to strict liability presents some tenuous similarities with the Italian and French approach, but it is fundamentally different in several key respects. The value of social solidarity is really not part of English tort law, the economic analysis of law has never taken hold, and the view that tort law is better seen as a system of individual responsibility is widespread. In sum, the set of values and goals that inspire the English system contrasts strikingly with the French and the Italian approaches, and, while the types of arguments used to justify strict liability are the same as those encountered in the other two systems, their meaning and significance are generally very different. All this is reflected in the traditionally cautious approach of English law towards the imposition of strict liability.[60]

First, the commitment to social solidarity which pushes Italian and especially French law to rely on strict liability is much less present in England. To be sure, as seen in Part 3, English legal actors show on occasion a desire to ensure that the victims of accidents receive adequate compensation for the losses suffered.[61]

---

[59] See subsection 3.8.4.
[60] See subsection 2.2.
[61] See subsection 3.6.5.

308   JUSTIFYING STRICT LIABILITY

However, this type of commitment is not frequent in most contexts of liability, with an important exception being the law of vicarious liability: here several scholars and even more judges explain or support strict liability on a variety of grounds which include victim protection, loss spreading, and the deep-pockets justification.[62] Moreover, numerous leading scholars (and some courts) put forward burden–benefit proportionality as an attractive justification for the strict liability of public bodies.[63] On the one hand, therefore, a conspicuous number of English legal actors seem attracted by the very sort of ideas which in France and in Italy are associated with the value of social solidarity, even though this value is clearly not recognized as such in English law itself. On the other hand, however, victim protection, loss spreading, and the deep-pockets argument are met with broad and explicit scepticism, especially by legal scholars who perceive these ideas as threatening the values of individual responsibility and as fundamentally at odds with the bilateral and backward-looking structure of English tort law.[64] This resistance to the adoption of an instrumental, pro-victim attitude marks a profound difference between England and France, and, to a lesser extent, between England and Italy.

Secondly, as seen above, a key argument for strict liability in Italian law is accident avoidance, especially—though not exclusively—within the framework of analysis provided by law and economics. Here again, English law adopts a very different approach, with the argument receiving a mixed treatment. On the one hand, many legal actors credit accident avoidance as a plausible goal and justification of strict liability (and tort liability more generally) in a wide variety of contexts.[65] On the other hand, many others doubt whether any meaningful avoidance of accidents can be accomplished through tort law in general, let alone by a type of liability which is independent of any assessment of the defendant's conduct, as is strict liability.[66] Moreover, as already emphasized in Part 3, law and economics has failed to attract meaningful support in England; on the contrary, it is regularly frowned upon for the same reasons which militate against victim protection or loss spreading: these are all forward-looking, instrumental ideas which embody societal goals far removed from the doing of individual justice and are therefore in conflict with an interpersonal understanding of tort law.[67] As a result, while law and economics in Italy (and in the United States) is a well-regarded theoretical basis where (especially) accident avoidance may be cultivated as a justification for strict liability, in England it is seen as an approach that would undesirably distort the essence of tort law.

---

[62] See text to nn 62–67 in subsection 3.4.5, to nn 165–172 in subsection 3.5.5, and n 66 in subsection 3.6.5.

[63] See text to nn 179–184 in subsection 3.5.5.

[64] See text to nn 71–78 in subsection 3.4.5, to nn 194–210 in subsection 3.5.5, and to and following nn 77–87 in subsection 3.6.5.

[65] See text to nn 104–120 in subsection 3.3.4.

[66] See text to and following nn 131–134 in subsection 3.3.4.

[67] See eg text to and preceding nn 141–142 in subsection 3.3.4.

CONCLUDING REFLECTIONS 309

Clearly, then, a common thread in our discussion of the English approach is the effect that notions of individual justice and responsibility have on a variety of justifications for strict liability. In particular, English tort law is often presented as based on such notions and this narrative can work as a brake both to strict liability and to all those arguments which embody goals or concerns going beyond the relationship between defendant and claimant and which contravene norms of individual responsibility. These arguments are accident avoidance, the deep-pockets justification, loss spreading, administrative cost reduction, and victim protection. This does not mean, though, that an approach that values norms of individual responsibility and the claimant–defendant nexus cannot try to justify the imposition of strict liability, or that individual responsibility cannot coexist with broader concerns in a reasoning justifying strict liability. To be sure, a vision of tort law as an ethical system of responsibility can easily accommodate liability for fault, while it may be more problematic, at least prima facie, to recognize a role to strict liability. However, as seen in Part 3 of book,[68] several English legal scholars put forward sophisticated theories of strict liability suggesting that, as a matter of moral and legal justice, individuals ought to take responsibility for the outcomes they bring about in the world, including the harm they cause to others, even if without fault. Moreover, this type of reasoning usually includes a variety of additional arguments. In some instances, space is given to societal goals such the avoidance of accidents, the spreading of losses, or the protection of victims,[69] this showing that, at least for the purpose of justifying strict liability, norms of individual responsibility may sometimes coexist with forward-looking considerations. More often, though, individual responsibility is coupled with justifications of a different nature, namely the various permutations of risk, perhaps because these are generally seen as more in line with a focus on the claimant–defendant nexus than with some broader societal concern. Here, arguments such as abnormality of risk or risk–profit are provided with a moral connotation which brings to the fore norms of individual justice and responsibility, especially—though not only—in relation to vicarious liability.[70] As we saw when discussing France and Italy, risk-based arguments can certainly be used as part of a pro-victim strategy to fulfil the value of solidarity and guarantee compensation; however, this is not the only way in which such arguments can be deployed, and English reasoning provides an example of this pattern by linking risk to individual responsibility. While this phenomenon does not mean that English reasoning is particularly keen on risk-based arguments, as these too attract several criticisms,[71] it shows that the same argument (in this case, risk) may proceed from

---

[68] See subsection 3.8.3.

[69] See text to nn 68–69, to nn 84–92, and to nn 93–97 in subsection 3.8.3.

[70] See eg text to and following nn 82–87 in subsection 3.6.5, and text to nn 64–67, to nn 75–82, and to nn 108–110 in subsection 3.8.3.

[71] See text to nn 185–189 (risk creation), text to and preceding nn 210–220 (abnormality of risk), n 228 and n 235 (risk–profit and risk–benefit) in subsection 3.2.5.

310   JUSTIFYING STRICT LIABILITY

different commitments, including the promotion of norms of individual responsibility, and be therefore used for disparate purposes across legal systems.

To conclude, a variety of distinct values and goals are involved in the English approach to strict liability. First, several instances of reasoning show a desire to ensure compensation to the victims of accidents, this commitment finding expression in arguments such as victim protection, loss spreading, and (occasionally) risk. Secondly, the avoidance of accidents attracts the attention of several legal actors as an appealing justification and goal of strict liability, even though the most formidable framework to support it—law and economics—is rejected in the English context. These two sides of English reasoning show a degree of instrumentalism in English tort culture, and a certain awareness that legal rules, in our case strict liability, may be helpfully deployed to achieve a plurality of societal goals. But there is also a third, important side of English tort reasoning which is quite different in nature from the other two, as it focuses on notions of individual responsibility and justice. On the one hand, this type of reasoning hinders the flourishing of justifications that are divorced from the claimant–defendant nexus and that tend to use tort liability as a tool of social policy. On the other hand, it provides its own set of justificatory strategies, showing a line of argumentation and a commitment to values that are basically absent from both the French and the Italian discourses on strict liability. In sum, the English reasoning on strict liability features a remarkable tension—as well as an interesting interplay—between different arguments and commitments, and strict liability itself constitutes a battlefield for the clash between distinct and contrasting approaches to tort law.

Even more complex is the picture of reasoning in strict liability characterizing the United States. Reasoning in that legal system reflects a variety of commitments to distinct values and goals which connote in different ways the arguments used to justify strict liability. These commitments largely correspond to what we have seen in the other three legal systems—victims' needs, law and economics, and norms of individual responsibility—but this time they all coexist under the same roof, giving rise to a particularly heterogeneous reasoning.

First, while the term 'social solidarity' does not have any currency in the United States, ideas resonating with it played a historically important role in the development of strict liability, especially in the middle part of the twentieth century. In the pursuit of social justice, which really meant meeting the needs of victims, US scholars and courts often relied on the arguments most congenial to that purpose, namely victim protection, loss spreading and, to a lesser extent, the deep-pockets justification, particularly where firms or public bodies were involved as potential defendants.[72] As in France, the emergence of a robust insurance market changed the terms of the discussion regarding the basis of tort liability, and the view became

---

[72] See text to nn 41–43 in subsection 3.4.4, to nn 57–62 in subsection 3.5.3, and to nn 42–44 in subsection 3.6.4.

widespread that the availability of this and other spreading mechanisms rendered any fault requirement superfluous or even an obstacle to justice. While this pro-victim and pro-spreading commitment has driven many courts and legal scholars operating in the second half of the twentieth century, the force of this intellectual movement has diminished with the advent of law and economics and of theories of interpersonal justice and individual responsibility.

Legal economists soon abandoned any particular emphasis on the protection of victims and shifted the focus of legal analysis on the social costs of accidents and on how to minimize them. Largely neglected by the pro-victim approach, the avoidance of accidents becomes of paramount importance in law and economics, because reducing the number or the severity of accidents is the first step to min-imize their social costs.[73] However, in keeping with the Italian approach, it must be noted that accident avoidance is not monopolized by law and economics in the United States because this argument is highly regarded by many legal actors who do not subscribe to the assumptions and goals set by the economic analysis.[74] Besides accident avoidance, many scholars working in the field of law and eco-nomics recognize that once accidents have occurred it becomes a matter of al-locating the attendant costs in a way which is the least detrimental to society. As a result, distributing losses appropriately is key and loss spreading as well as the availability of a deep pocket are significant both in assessing the 'efficiency' of li-ability rules and in justifying a choice among them.[75] Clearly though, the meaning that loss spreading takes on in US law and economics is not the meaning that it has for French legal actors: the latter see it as a gateway to victim protection, whereas the former see it as constituting one of the methods for minimizing the social costs of accidents. Finally, law and economics pays attention to the costs involved in the administration of liability rules, for they too are part of the overall costs of acci-dents.[76] As seen in Part 3, all these considerations are taken into account in eco-nomic analysis, and most scholars working in the field believe that strict liability can score better than fault, although views differ as to the exact circumstances in which this holds true. Contrary to the pro-victim and pro-spreading movement, law and economics has not experienced any decline in importance; quite the op-posite, it appears to be exercising an ever-growing influence on US legal thought. As a result, it is inevitable that the debate on strict liability is heavily influenced by the law and economics literature.

A common feature of the pro-victim/spreading movement and of law and eco-nomics is their instrumental nature, that is their seeing tort law as a tool to achieve societal goals, whether the protection of victims, the spreading of losses, or the

---

[73] See text to nn 3–26 in subsection 3.3.2.
[74] See eg text to n 41 in subsection 3.3.2.
[75] See text to nn 46–48 in subsection 3.4.4, and to nn 64–68 in subsection 3.5.3.
[76] See generally subsection 3.7.2.

312 JUSTIFYING STRICT LIABILITY

minimization of the costs of accidents. It was seen that approaches and arguments of this type are heavily criticized in England, and exactly the same happens in the United States. As seen in Part 3, one criticism common to all instrumental approaches, and therefore to arguments such as accident avoidance, the deep-pockets justification, loss spreading, and victim protection, is that they side-line the relationship between defendant and claimant and the doing of individual justice.[77] In other words, they are at odds with the bilateral structure of tort law and with its underlying principles, if these are understood as relating to norms of individual responsibility. Approaches that see tort law as a system based on these norms are influential in the United States and they have their own ways of justifying strict liability, the fundamental point being their effort to reconcile this type of liability with their own understanding of tort law. Significantly, each approach elaborates its own conception of responsibility and, therefore, its own distinct structure of reasoning in order to justify strict liability (or tort liability more generally). In some instances, it is individual responsibility itself as shaped by moral concepts such as autonomy, choice, duty, or wrong(doing) which does the justificatory work. In other cases, the reconciliation between strict liability and norms of individual responsibility is pursued by including in the relevant reasoning risk-based justifications such as nonreciprocity of risk or risk–benefit/profit, for these are sometimes seen as consonant with norms of moral and legal responsibility.[78] Finally, in very few cases are norms of individual responsibility seen as compatible with broader societal goals such as the spreading of losses, therefore providing an expanded justificatory basis to strict liability in US tort law.[79]

Overall, a variety of distinct commitments are at play in the United States to justify strict liability. Embedded in US legal culture, they reflect values and goals which express different visions about the functions and roles of strict liability (and of tort law more generally). To understand the US reasoning, then, it is very important to distinguish among these various commitments, for each provides a different connotation, meaning and significance to the specific arguments invoked. A commitment which seeks to meet the needs of victims will favour arguments such as loss spreading, the deep-pockets justification, and, of course, victim protection itself. A commitment which instead seeks to minimize the costs of accidents will focus on accident avoidance, while also paying attention to administrative costs as well as to loss spreading and even to the deep-pockets argument (though in a very different way as compared to the previous commitment). Finally, a commitment which seeks to promote norms of individual responsibility and interpersonal

---

[77] See text to n 48 in subsection 3.3.2, to n 49 in subsection 3.4.4, to n 55 and n 87 in subsection 3.5.3, and to n 57 in subsection 3.6.4.

[78] See eg text to and following nn 21–29 in subsection 3.8.2; Gregory C Keating, 'Strict Liability Wrongs' in John Oberdiek (ed), *Philosophical Foundations of the Law of Torts* (OUP 2014) 292, 306–08; Perry (n 28) 114–15 (referring to 'unilateral risk imposition').

[79] See text to and following nn 14–20 in subsection 3.8.2.

justice is likely to reject all or most of these instrumental arguments and to rely instead on justifications which accord with those very norms, including risk in its various permutations. In sum, the emergence and coexistence of distinct and contrasting commitments generates many lines of argumentation which render the US reasoning on strict liability extremely rich and heterogeneous.

4.4 Further Critical and Comparative Thoughts

This study has allowed us to appreciate the chameleonic nature of 'strict liability'. From the perspective of its justifications, there is not one understanding of strict liability across legal systems, nor even has each of the four systems its own, unitary understanding of strict liability. Rather, within each legal system and in the four systems taken together there is a plethora of different understandings of strict liability. These depend on, and vary according to, a number of interrelated factors, including the functions or purposes attributed to strict liability, the type of arguments relied upon and their significance, the patterns of reasoning chosen, and the broader values and goals which inspire the views of individual legal actors.

First, legal actors can select their preferred justifications from a rich menu, depending on their normative or interpretive views and, ultimately, on the broader values and goals that shape their vision of strict liability (and of tort law more generally). For example, there is a profound difference between the views of (say) Viney, whose works are imbued with an ethos of solidarity and therefore rely heavily on victim protection and loss spreading, the views of Trimarchi, who is primarily concerned with providing incentives to potential defendants and claimants and hence relies heavily on accident avoidance, and the views of Epstein, whose theory of strict liability seeks to define the reciprocal autonomy and freedom of individuals and, hence, focuses on norms of individual responsibility. These approaches select largely different justifications for strict liability and attribute to it very different functions. For this very reason, they reflect profoundly different understandings of strict liability.

Secondly, legal actors can choose from a number of patterns of reasoning and decide to deploy their preferred justifications as stand-alone arguments or to put them next to other arguments by way of combination or juxtaposition. The many variations which exist in this respect and which we have seen throughout Part 3 as well as in section 4.2 above translate too into varying ways of understanding strict liability. For instance, and most dramatically, the same justifications may be put forward by way of juxtaposition in one reasoning, and by way of combination in another, giving rise to profoundly different justificatory bases of strict liability. To give an example, a legal actor may suggest that an attractive reason for imposing strict liability on (say) manufacturers lies in their ability to spread losses via insurance or price adjustments, and then may add that a further reason lies in their

314 JUSTIFYING STRICT LIABILITY

ability to take precautions so as to reduce the risk of accidents caused by their products. In this example of reasoning, loss spreading and accident avoidance are juxtaposed. A different legal actor may use these two arguments as well but deploy them in a different way: for example, they may suggest that manufacturers should be liable because they can reduce accidents and spread their costs in a way that minimizes the overall sum of the costs of accidents. In this second example, loss spreading and accident avoidance are combined to accomplish a further objective, namely the promotion of social welfare. Despite featuring the same arguments, these two examples of reasoning reveal a different understanding of strict liability, as they are structured in their own way and attribute (at least partly) different purposes to strict liability.

Thirdly, and quite apart from the chosen patterns of argumentation, the same justification may be accorded varying weight in different instances of reasoning. For example, in seeking to justify (say) strict vicarious liability, a legal actor may deploy and rank in this order arguments such as victim protection, loss spreading, and accident avoidance; others may rely on the same justifications but give priority to accident avoidance and see the other two as carrying only secondary weight. Here again, different ways of understanding strict liability are at play, as the primary functions of strict liability are different, with implications of potentially great import in terms of the requirements or conditions for its imposition.

Fourthly, and perhaps more fundamentally, the way in which strict liability is understood and justified depends on the broader values and goals that inspire the thinking of legal actors. As shown throughout Part 3 and as re-emphasized in section 4.3, courts, scholars, and legislators can proceed from a variety of distinct commitments and their embrace of certain values or goals instead of others determines their choice of arguments as well as the justificatory weight and connotation attributed to these. For instance, those who highly regard the value of solidarity will usually rely on arguments such as victim protection, loss spreading, or the deep-pockets justification; those who are concerned with the promotion of social welfare are likely to focus on accident avoidance, administrative cost reduction, and loss spreading; again, those who value principles of moral agency are going to justify strict liability on the basis of some conception of individual responsibility and, perhaps, of risk-based arguments. This does not mean, of course, that these types of reasoning may not refer to further justifications: for instance, a 'solidarity approach' may also mention accident avoidance, but in all likelihood it will accord to it only secondary importance; similarly, a 'social welfare approach' may well consider victim protection as a respectable goal, though a less important one than the avoidance of accidents; and a 'responsibility approach' may well feature justifications such as accident avoidance or loss spreading along with norms of individual responsibility, even if it is the latter which will take priority in the relevant reasoning. In addition to this, there is a deep interconnectedness between the arguments for strict liability and the broader values and goals informing the views of legal actors. In particular, arguments can acquire distinct connotations and express different visions of strict liability, depending on the commitment from which individual legal actors proceed in putting forward their views. To give one example, loss spreading in the hands of Viney is a very different justification from loss spreading in the hands of Calabresi, in much the same way as risk–profit in the hands of Saleilles is different from risk–profit in the hands of Stapleton. This is so because the values and goals that shape the thinking of these legal scholars about strict liability (and tort law more generally) differ substantially from one another. Put another way, instances of reasoning which include the same justifications will be different if they are based on different ways of understanding the functions of strict liability and the values or goals that this form of liability should fulfil. As emphasized in section 4.3, commitments to distinct values and goals can and do coexist within a single legal system and they shape the legal reasoning in strict liability in various ways, generating complex interactions and clashes between the chosen values and goals and between the arguments themselves.

This brief discussion shows, I hope, that there are many ways of understanding strict liability within and across jurisdictions. Against this backdrop of complexity, though, a tendency has emerged to justify strict liability on the basis of arguments which focus on societal goals more than on the doing of individual justice between claimant and defendant. This may explain, at least in part, why US law and (especially) English law are more cautious than French law and Italian law when it comes to the adoption of rules of strict liability. Indeed, the English and (to a lesser extent) US emphasis on tort law as an ethical system of individual responsibility is likely to water down the attractiveness of strict liability, and the many legal scholars who entertain this vision of tort law often look with circumspection at strict liability and at justifications such as accident avoidance, loss spreading, the deep-pockets argument, administrative cost reduction, or victim protection. By contrast, the more instrumental understandings of tort law which characterize (in partly different ways) the French and the Italian legal systems go hand in hand with those arguments and it is therefore perfectly consistent with the mind-set of French and Italian legal actors to rely more heavily on strict liability for the achievement of societal goals which are broader than the doing of individual justice. Relatedly, a contrast that has emerged between England and the United States, on the one hand, and France and Italy, on the other hand, concerns the significance of individual responsibility as a justification for the imposition of strict liability. As we have seen, many legal scholars from the two common law systems engage in sophisticated moral analysis, and they put forward justifications of strict liability that focus on the moral and legal responsibility of a person for the loss they inflict on others. By contrast, this way of seeing strict liability does not find any meaningful support in the two civil law systems: here, broader societal concerns loom large as justifications for strict liability and consideration of norms of individual responsibility is largely confined to fault-based liability.

316   JUSTIFYING STRICT LIABILITY

Though important, this point of contrast between common law and civil law systems does not mean that the legal reasoning in strict liability traces the distinction between the common law and the civil law tradition. On the contrary, there are profound differences within the same legal tradition. In particular, as made clear throughout the book, the French reasoning on strict liability ignores law and economics, which in France is often seen as a synonym for 'immoral' thinking; by contrast, from the 1960s onwards law and economics has attracted considerable support in Italy, where especially legal scholars bring to bear the insights of economic analysis on the reasons for imposing (or not imposing) strict liability. Moreover, attachment to the value of social solidarity is strikingly more pronounced in France than in Italy despite its formal constitutional recognition there, and it translates into a considerably heavier reliance on strict liability in French law. Contrasts of a similar nature can be seen in the common law tradition as well: US legal actors are the 'masters' of law and economics, and this type of analysis pervades the discussions on strict liability, whereas English legal actors regard this approach with distrust and frame their reasoning on strict liability in very different ways; moreover, US tort law has experienced a pro-victim movement in the middle part of the twentieth century which has profoundly influenced the debate on strict liability and which has never occurred, at least with comparable force, in England. All this shows that the differences in the historical development of common law systems as opposed to civil law systems do not correspond to a substantive difference in the tort cultures of the four systems along the line civil law *vs* common law and that, at least in some respects, there may be more similarities across that line than on the two sides of it. This shows, once again, that the way in which strict liability (and perhaps tort liability more generally) is justified depends on the values, goals, and even ideologies that prevail at different times in different jurisdictions.

Bibliography

Abbagnano N, 'Il giudizio di responsabilità nella morale e nel diritto' (1957) 1 Rivista di filosofia 30

Abraham KS, *The Liability Century. Insurance and Tort Law from the Progressive Era to 9/11* (HUP 2008)

——*The Forms and Functions of Tort Law* (5th edn, Foundation Press 2017)

——and Rabin RL, 'Automated Vehicles and Manufacturer Liability for Accidents: A New Legal Regime for New Era' (2019) 105 Va L Rev 127

Abravanel-Jolly S, 'Art. 1382 à 1386—Fasc. 280-10: RÉGIMES DIVERS. —Circulation routière. —Indemnisation des victimes d'accidents de la circulation. —Droit à indemnisation' JCl Civil Code (updated 28.11.2018)

Addison CG, *Wrongs and their Remedies: Being a Treatise on the Law of Torts* (Stevens and Sons 1860)

Alessi R, *La responsabilità della pubblica amministrazione* (Giuffrè 1955)

Alibrandi A, 'Note sulla responsabilità civile del proprietario del veicolo coinvolto in sinistro stradale' (1991) 7–8 Archivio giuridico della circolazione e dei sinistri stradali 545

Allen CK, *Legal Duties, and Other Essays in Jurisprudence* (Clarendon Press 1931)

Alpa G, 'Prodotti difettosi, danno ingiusto, responsabilità del fabbricante' (1971) I GM 297

——'Costruzione di autoveicoli, clausole di esonero e responsabilità dell'impresa per una diversa lettura dell'articolo 2054, ultimo comma, codice civile' (1975) 4(1A) GI 1975 751

——*Responsabilità dell'impresa e tutela del consumatore* (Giuffrè 1975)

——'Attività pericolosa e responsabilità dell'ENEL. Verso la erosione dei privilegi della Pubblica Amministrazione?' (1982) 4(1) GC 919

——'Il révirement della Corte di cassazione sulla responsabilità per la lesione di interessi legittimi' (1999) 4–5 RCP 907

——*La responsabilità civile: principi* (2nd edn, UTET 2018)

——and Bessone M, *La responsabilità civile* (Giuffrè 2001)

Ambrosoli M, 'I diritto reali e la responsabilità extracontrattuale' in A Gambaro and U Morello (eds), *Trattato dei diritto reali. Volume I—Proprietà e possesso* (Giuffrè 2008) 1033

Amirthalingam K, 'Animal Liability: Equine, Canine and Asinine' (2003) 119 LQR 563

Anderloni L, Tanda A, and Vandone D, *Vulnerabilità e benessere delle famiglie italiane*, available at http://www.forumaniaconsumatori.it/images/pdf/rapporto_vulnerabilit_unimi_2016.pdf at 23

Anderson JG, 'The Rylands v. Fletcher Doctrine in America: Abnormally Dangerous, Ultrahazardous, or Absolute Nuisance?' (1978) Ariz St LJ 99

Anelli F and Granelli C, *Manuale di diritto privato Torrente Schlesinger* (24th edn, Giuffrè 2019)

Arrowsmith S, *Civil Liability and Public Authorities* (Earlsgate Press 1992)

Atiyah P, *Vicarious Liability in the Law of Torts* (Butterworths 1967)

——*Accidents, Compensation and the Law* (3rd edn, Weidenfeld & Nicholson 1980)

——*Essays on Contract* (Clarendon Press 1986)

——'Personal Injuries in the Twenty-First Century: Thinking the Unthinkable' in P Birks (ed), *Wrongs and Remedies in the Twenty-First Century* (Clarendon Press 1996) 1

318 BIBLIOGRAPHY

Avanzini G, 'Nuovi sviluppi nella responsabilità delle amministrazioni per danni derivanti da attività pericolose e da cose in custodia' (2010) 1 Diritto amministrativo 261

Bacache-Gibeili M, *Les obligations, La responsabilité civile extracontractuelle* (3rd edn, Economica 2016)

Bach E, 'Réflexions sur le problème du fondement de la responsabilité civile en droit francais' RTD civ 1977.221

Baffi E, 'Responsabilità "aggravata". Un'analisi giuseconomica' (2011) 4 DR 345

——'La responsabilità del proprietario per danni da rovina di edificio come forma di responsabilità vicaria: analisi giuseconomica' (2017) 6 DR 657

——and Nardi D, 'Colpa e livelli di attività: il contributo della Law and Economics' (2014) 1 RCDP 137

——and Nardi D, 'La responsabilità da custodia della P.A.: prospettive di analisi economica del diritto' (2016) 4 DR 337

——and Nardi D, 'L'analisi economica del diritto e la giurisprudenza' (2016) 10 DR 1012

——and Nardi D, 'Analisi economica del diritto e danno cagionato da cose in custodia' (2018) 3 DR 327

Bagshaw R, 'Rylands confined' (2004) 120 LQR 388

——'The Development of Traffic Liability in England and Wales' in W Ernst (ed), *The Development of Traffic Liability* (CUP 2010) 12

Bandes S, 'Reinventing *Bivens*: The Self-Executing Constitution' (1995) 68 S Cal L Rev 289

Barassi L, 'Contributo alla teoria della responsabilità per fatto non proprio in ispecial modo a mezzo di animali' (1897) Rivista italiana per le scienze giuridiche 325, 174, 379

——'Contributo alla teoria della responsabilità per fatto non proprio in ispecial modo a mezzo di animali' (1898) Rivista italiana per le scienze giuridiche 56

——*La teoria generale delle obbligazioni*, vol 2 (Giuffrè 1946)

Baty T, *Vicarious Liability* (Clarendon Press 1916)

Beever A, *A Theory of Tort Liability* (Hart Publishing 2016)

Bell J, 'Governmental Liability in Tort' (1995) 6 NJCL 85

——'Administrative Law' in J Bell and others, *Principles of French Law* (2nd edn, OUP 2008) 168

——'The Basis of Vicarious Liability' (2013) 72 CLJ 17

——'The Reform of Delict in the Civil Code and Liability in Administrative Law' in J-S Borghetti and S Whittaker (eds), *French Civil Liability in Comparative Perspective* (Hart Publishing 2019) 425

Bénabent A, *Droit des obligations* (19th edn, LGDJ 2021)

Benedetti AP, 'Condotta del danneggiato e responsabilità da cose in custodia: spunti di riflessione' (2011) 3 DR 234

——'La responsabilità dei genitori per il trasporto in motorino di un passeggero da parte del figlio minorenne' (2012) 3 DR 267

——'La caduta di un alunno durante una gita scolastica: chi risponde?' (2012) 7 DR 755

Berlia G, 'Essai sur les fondements de la responsabilité en droit public français' RDP 1951.685

Bessone M, 'Prodotti dannosi e responsabilità dell'impresa' (1971) 1 RTDPC 97

——'Progresso tecnologico, prodotti dannosi e controlli sull'impresa' (1972) 2 Pol dir 203

——'Profili della responsabilità del produttore nell'esperienza italiana' in G Alpa and M Bessone (eds), *Danno da prodotti e responsabilità dell'impresa—Diritto italiano ed esperienze straniere* (Giuffrè 1980) 9

Bianca CM, *Diritto civile. V—La responsabilità* (3rd edn, Giuffrè 2021)

BIBLIOGRAPHY 319

Bin M, 'L'assicurazione della responsabilità civile da prodotti' in G Alpa, M Bin, and P Cendon (eds), *Trattato di diritto commerciale e diritto pubblico dell'economia. La responsabilità del produttore* (CEDAM 1989) 273

Birks P, 'The Concept of a Civil Wrong' in DG Owen (ed), *Philosophical Foundations of Tort Law* (OUP 1995) 31

Bitetto A, 'Danni provocati da animali selvatici: chi ne risponde e perché?' (2003) 3 DR 275

——'Responsabilità da prodotto difettoso: strict liability o negligence rule?' (2006) 3 DR 259

——'"Nuisance" e danni non patrimoniali' (2018) 4 DR 478

Bohlen FH, 'The Rule in Rylands v Fletcher: Part III' (1911) 59 U Pa L Rev 423

Bonvicini E, *La responsabilità civile*, vol I (Giuffrè 1971)

Borghetti J-S, *La Responsabilité du Fait des Produits: Etude de Droit Comparé* (LGDJ 2004)

——'La responsabilité du fait des choses, un régime qui a fait son temps' RTD civ 2010.1

——'The Development of Product Liability in France' in S Whittaker (ed), *The Development of Product Liability* (CUP 2010) 87

——'The Culture of Tort Law in France' (2012) 3 JETL 158

——'La responsabilité du fait des choses et/ou du fait des activités dangereuses. Synthèse comparative' in *Le droit français de la responsabilité civile confronté aux projets européens d'harmonisation* (IRJS Éditions 2012) 279

——'La responsabilité de l'entreprise du fait des activités dangereuses' in N Ferrier and A Pélissier (eds), *L'entreprise face aux évolutions de la responsabilité civile* (Economica 2012) 59

——'L'accident fait générateur de responsabilité' RCA 7–8 July 2015, dossier 3, 12

——'L'avant-projet de réforme de la responsabilité civile. Vue d'ensemble de l'avant-projet' D 2016.1386

——'Legal Methodology and the Role of Professors in France—*Professorenrecht* is not a French word!' in J Basedow, H Fleischer, and R Zimmermann (eds), *Legislators, Judges, and Professors* (Mohr Siebeck 2016) 209

——'Liability for False Information in French Law: The Limits of Civil Law' in H Koziol (ed), *Tatsachenmitteilungen und Werturteile: Freiheit und Verantwortung* (Jan Sramek Verlag 2018) 133

——'Extra-Strict Liability for Traffic Accidents in France' (2018) 53 Wake Forest L Rev 265

——and Whittaker S, 'Principles of Liability or a Law of Torts?' in J-S Borghetti and S Whittaker (eds), *French Civil Liability in Comparative Perspective* (Hart Publishing 2019) 455

Borgo J, 'Causal Paradigms' (1979) 8 J Legal Stud 419

Branca G, 'Sulla responsabilità oggettiva per danni causati da animali' (1950) RTDPC 255

——'Responsabilità dell'usufruttuario per rovina di edificio' (1958) 1 Foro It 1311

Breda R, 'La responsabilità—riformata?—della struttura sanitaria' in N Todeschini (ed), *La Responsabilità Medica* (UTET 2019) 930

Bridgeman C and Goldberg JCP, 'Do Promises Distinguish Contract from Tort?' (2012) 45 Suff U L Rev 873

Brodie D, 'Enterprise Liability: Justifying Vicarious Liability' (2007) 27 OJLS 493

——*Enterprise Liability and the Common Law* (CUP 2010)

——'Employers' Liability and Allocation of Risk' (2018) 47 ILJ 431

Brown LN and Bell JS, *French Administrative Law* (5th edn, OUP 1998)

Brun P, *La responsabilité civile extracontractuelle* (5th edn, LexisNexis 2018)

Burrows A, *Understanding the Law of Obligations: Essays on Contract, Tort and Restitution* (Hart Publishing 1998)

320   BIBLIOGRAPHY

Busnelli FD, *La lesione del credito da parte di terzi* (Giuffrè 1964)
——'Nuove frontiere della responsabilità civile' (1976) 1–2 Jus 41
——and Patti S, *Danno e responsabilità civile* (3rd edn, Giappichelli 2013)
Cadiet L, 'Sur les faits et les méfaits de l'idéologie de la réparation' in *Le juge entre deux millénaires—Mélange offerts à Pierre Drai* (Dalloz 2000) 495
Calabresi G, 'Fault, Accidents and the Wonderful World of Blum and Kalven' (1965) 75 Yale LJ 216
——and Bass KC III, 'Right Approach, Wrong Implications: A Critique of McKean on Products Liability' (1970) 38 U Chi L Rev 74
——*The Costs of Accidents: A Legal and Economic Analysis* (YUP 1970)
——'Optimal Deterrence and Accidents' (1974) 84 Yale LJ 656
——and Hirschoff JT, 'Toward a Test for Strict Liability in Torts' (1971) 81 Yale LJ 1055
——and Klevorick AK, 'Four Tests for Liability in Torts' (1985) 14 J Legal Stud 585
——'L'allievo Carlo Castronovo e le parole del diritto, da Yale a Milano. Spunti e ricordi' in *Scritto in onore di Carlo Castronovo* (Jovene 2018) 1
——'Professor Fleming James Jr (1904–1981)' in J Goudkamp and D Nolan (eds), *Scholars of Tort Law* (Hart Publishing 2019) 259
——and Al Mureden E, '*Driverless* car e responsabilità civile' (2020) 1 Rivista di diritto bancario 7
Calais-Auloy J, 'Le risque de développement: une exonération contestable' in *Mélanges Michel Cabrillac* (Dalloz/Litec 1999) 81
Cammeo F, *Corso di diritto amministrativo*, vol IIII (La Litotipo 1914)
Campeis G and De Pauli A, 'La responsabilità per vizi di costruzione dei veicoli' (1990) Riv giur circolaz e trasp 140
Candian AD, *Responsabilità civile e assicurazione* (EGEA 1993)
Cane P, 'Justice and Justifications for Tort Liability' (1982) 2 OJLS 30
——'Corrective Justice and Correlativity in Private Law' (1996) 16 OJLS 471
——*The Anatomy of Tort Law* (Hart Publishing 1997)
——'Fault and Strict Liability for Harm in Tort Law' in W Swadling and G Jones (eds) *The Search for Principle: Essays in Honour of Lord Goff of Chieveley* (OUP 1999) 171
——'Vicarious Liability for Sexual Abuse' (2000) 116 LQR 21
——'Responsibility and Fault: A Relational and Functional Approach to Responsibility' in P Cane and J Gardner (eds), *Relating to Responsibility: Essays in Honour of Tony Honoré on his 80th Birthday* (Hart Publishing 2001) 81
——'Tort Law as Regulation' (2002) 31 CLWR 305
——*Responsibility in Law and Morality* (Hart Publishing 2002)
——'Rights in Private Law' in D Nolan and A Robertson (eds), *Rights and Private Law* (Hart Publishing 2012) 35
——and Goudkamp J, *Atiyah's Accidents, Compensation and the Law* (9th edn, CUP 2018)
Cantu C, 'Distinguishing the Concept of Strict Liability for Ultra-Hazardous Activities from Strict Products Liability under Section 402A of the Restatement (Second) of Torts: Two Parallel Lines of Reasoning That Should Never Meet' (2001) 35 Akron L Rev 31
——'Distinguishing the Concept of Strict Liability in Tort from Strict Products Liability: Medusa Unveiled' (2003) 33 U Mem L Rev 823
Cappelletti M, 'Comparative Reflections on Punishment in Tort Law' in J-S Borghetti and S Whittaker (eds), *French Civil Liability in Comparative Perspective* (Hart Publishing 2019) 329
Caranta R, 'La pubblica amministrazione nell'età della responsabilità' (1999) I Foro It 3201
Carassale U, *Assicurazione Danni e Responsabilità civile: guida alla lettura della giurisprudenza* (Giuffrè 2005)

Carbone E, 'La responsabilità aquiliana del genitore tra rischio tipico e colpe fittizie' (2008) 1(2) Riv Dir Civ 1

Carbonnier J, *Droit civil. Les biens, les obligations* (2nd edn, PUF 2017)

Cardani V, 'Il danno cagionato da animali' in P Cendon (ed), *Responsabilità civile*, vol III (2nd edn, UTET 2020) 3869

Caringella F, *Manuale di diritto amministrativo. I. La responsabilità della pubblica amministrazione* (Dike 2012)

Carnelutti F, 'La responsabilità civile per gli accidenti d'automobile' (1908) I Riv Dir Comm 401

Carnevali U, *La responsabilità del produttore* (Giuffrè 1974)

Carval S, *La responsabilité civile dans sa fonction de peine privée* (LGDJ 1995)

Castronovo C, *Problema e sistema nel danno da prodotti* (Giuffrè 1979)

——'Danno da prodotti (dir. it. e stran.)' Enc Giur (Treccani 1995) X, 1

——'Responsabilità civile per la pubblica amministrazione' (1998) 3 Ius 647

——*Responsabilità civile* (Giuffrè 2018)

Chapus R, *Responsabilité publique et responsabilité privée: les influences réciproques des jurisprudences administrative et judiciaire* (LGDJ 1954)

——*Droit administratif général*, vol 1 (15th edn, Montchrestien 2001)

Charbonnier L, 'Une notion-clé pour l'indemnisation des victimes d'accidents de la circulation: l' "implication" du véhicule (loi du 5 juillet 1985)' in Rapport de la Cour de cassation 1986, 96

Chiarella ML, 'Minore danneggiante e responsabilità vicaria' (2009) 10 DR 973

Ciliberti O, 'L'elemento soggettivo nella responsabilità civile della pubblica amministrazione conseguente a provvedimenti illegittimi' in E Follieri (ed), *La responsabilità civile della pubblica amministrazione* (Giuffrè 2004) 253

Citron DK, 'Reservoirs of Danger: Evolution of Public and Private Law at the Dawn of the Information Age' (2006) 80 S Cal L Rev 241

Clarke MA, *Policies and Perceptions of Insurance Law in the Twenty-First Century* (OUP 2005)

Coggiola N, 'The Development of Product Liability in Italy' in S Whittaker (ed), *The Development of Product Liability* (CUP 2010) 192

——'The Influence of Foreign Legal Models on the Development of Italian Civil Liability Rules from the 1865 Civil Code to the Present Day' (2019) 5 Italian Law J 441

Cogliolo P, 'La responsabilità riflessa' in *Scritti varii di diritto privato*, vol 1 (4th edn, UTET 1914) 215

Coleman JL, 'Justice and Reciprocity in Tort Theory' (1975) 14 W Ontario L Rev 105

——'Moral Theories of Torts: Their Scope and Limits: Part 1' (1982) Law & Phil 371

——'The Structure of Tort Law' (1988) 97 Yale LJ 1233

——*Risks and Wrongs* (CUP 1992)

——*The Practice of Principle: In Defence of a Pragmatist Approach to Legal Theory* (OUP 2001)

——'Facts, Fictions, and the Grounds of Law' in JK Campbell, M O'Rourke, and D Shier (eds), *Law and Social Justice* (MIT Press 2005) 327

Comandé G and Nocco L, 'The Liability of Public Authorities in Italy' in K Oliphant (ed), *The Liability of Public Authorities in Comparative Perspective* (Intersentia 2016) 251

Comporti GD, 'Responsabilità della pubblica amministrazione' in *Dizionario di diritto pubblico*, vol V (Giuffrè 2006) 5125

——'Il cittadino viandante tra insidie e trabocchetti: viaggio alla ricerca di una tutela risarcitoria praticabile' (2009) 3 Diritto Amministrativo 663

Comporti M, *Esposizione al pericolo e responsabilità civile* (Morano editore 1965)

322 BIBLIOGRAPHY

——*Fatti Illeciti: le responsabilità oggettive—Artt. 2049-2053. Il Codice Civile—Commentario* (Giuffrè 2009)

Cooter R and Ulen T, *Law & Economics* (6th edn, Pearson 2012)

Cooter R and others, *Il mercato delle regole—Analisi economica del diritto civile—I. Fondamenti* (Il Mulino 2006)

——*Il mercato delle regole—Analisi economica del diritto civile—II. Applicazioni* (Il Mulino 2006)

Cornford T, *Towards a Public Law of Tort* (Taylor and Francis 2008)

Corradino M, *La responsabilità della Pubblica Amministrazione* (Giappichelli 2011)

Corsaro L, 'Funzione e ragioni della responsabilità del genitore per il fatto illecito del figlio minore' (1988) IV GI 225

Corso G, 'La responsabilità della pubblica amministrazione da attività lecita' (2009) 2 Diritto amministrativo 203

Cortese F, 'The Liability of Public Administration—A Special Regime between Formal Requirements and Substantial Goals' in G della Cananea and R Caranta (eds), *Tort Liability of Public Authorities in European Laws* (OUP 2020) 61

Cotterrell R, 'Comparative Law and Legal Culture' in M Reimann and R Zimmermann (eds), *The Oxford Handbook of Comparative Law* (2nd edn, OUP 2019) 710

Courtieu G, 'Art. 1382 à 1386—Fasc. 265-10: RÉGIMES DIVERS. —Troubles de voisinage' JCl Civil Code (updated 27.11.2017)

Coviello N, 'La responsabilità senza colpa' (1897) Riv It Sc Giur 188

Covucci D, 'Attività pericolosa e responsabilità oggettiva del produttore di sigarette' (2010) 6 NGCC 667

Craig P, *Administrative Law* (9th edn, Sweet & Maxwell 2021)

Crismani A, *Le indennità nel diritto amministrativo* (Giappichelli 2012)

Croley SP and Hanson JD, 'What Liability Crisis? An Alternative Explanation for Recent Events in Products Liability' (1991) 8 Yale J Reg 1

Cross G, 'Does Only the Careless Polluter Pay? A Fresh Examination of the Nature of Private Nuisance' (1995) 111 LQR 445

Crovetto M, 'La responsabilità oggettiva dei genitori' in P Cendon (ed), *Responsabilità civile*, vol III (2nd edn, UTET 2020) 3706

Davis KC, 'Administrative Officers' Tort Liability' (1956–1957) 55 Mich L Rev 201

——*Administrative Law. Cases—Text—Problems* (West Publishing 1973)

——and Pierce RJ, *Administrative Law Treatise* (3rd edn, Little, Brown and Company 1994)

Davola A and Pardolesi R, 'In viaggio col robot: verso nuovi orizzonti della r.c. auto ("driver-less")?' (2017) 5 DR 616

De Cupis A, *Il danno: teoria generale della responsabilità civile*, vols I and II (3rd edn, Giuffrè 1979)

de Gouttes R, 'À propos des métamorphoses du droit de la responsabilité civile: à la recherche d'une remise en ordre dans le désordre actuel des normes' Gaz Pal 16.2.2012 n.47

de Latournerie M-A, 'The Law of France' in J Bell and AW Bradley (eds), *Governmental Liability: A Comparative Study* (United Kingdom National Committee of Comparative Law 1991) 200

De Menech C, 'Il progressivo (ed irriflessivo) dilagare della responsabilità per fatto dei dipendenti' in C Granelli (ed), *I nuovi orientamenti della Cassazione civile* (Giuffrè 2017) 456

de Naurois L, 'Juriste et moraliste en présence des obligations inter-personnelles de justice' Nouvelle revue théologique 1963.598

de Ruggiero R, *Istituzioni di diritto civile*, vol III (6th edn, Principato 1930)

Deakin S and Adams Z, *Markesinis and Deakin's Tort Law* (8th edn, OUP 2019)

Deards E and Twigg-Flesner C, 'The Consumer Protection Act: Proof at last that it is protecting consumers?' (2001) 10 Nottingham LJ 1

Debard T, 'L'égalité des citoyens devant les charges publiques: fondement incertain de la responsabilité administrative' D chron 1987.157

Degl'Innocenti F, *Rischio di impresa e responsabilità civile—La tutela dell'ambiente tra prevenzione e riparazione dei danni* (Firenze University Press 2013)

Deguergue M, *Jurisprudence et doctrine dans l'élaboration du droit de la responsabilité administrative* (LGDJ 1994)

Dejean de la Bâtie N, *Aubry et Rau, Droit civil français, t. VI-2, Responsabilité délictuelle* (8th edn, Litec 1989)

Delvolvé P, *Le principe d'égalité devant les charges publiques* (LGDJ 1969)

Demogue R, *Traité des obligations en général—Tome V—Sources des obligations* (Rousseau 1925)

Denning ATD, *What Next in the Law* (Butterworths 1982)

Department of Trade and Industry, *Implementation of European Community Directive on Product Liability: An Explanatory and Consultative Note* (1985)

Desnoyer C, 'La jurisprudence relative à l'articulation des articles 1386 et 1384, alinéa 1er du Code civil. L'instrumentalisation de la règle *Specialia generalibus derogant*' RTD civ 2012.461

Diana AG, *Le immissioni. Tipologie, azioni e tutele* (Giuffrè 2013)

Dicey AV, *Lectures Introductory to the Study of the Law of the Constitution* (Macmillan 1885)

Di Rosa J, (2017) 6(1) Foro It 1986

Dobbs DB, Hayden PT, and Bublick EM, *Hornbook on Torts* (2nd edn, West Academic Publishing 2016)

——*Torts and Compensation—Personal Accountability and Social Responsibility for Injury* (8th edn, West Academic Publishing 2017)

Dominici A, 'La responsabilità oggettiva in materia di appalti: il Consiglio di Stato si allinea alle pronunce del giudice comunitario' (2013) 1 Rivista amministrativa degli appalti 41

Duguit L, *L'état, le droit objectif et la loi positive* (Fontemoing 1901)

——*Traité de Droit Constitutionnel*, vol 3 (3rd edn, Fontemoing 1930)

Duni G, *Lo Stato e la responsabilità patrimoniale* (Giuffrè 1968)

Durry G, RTD civ 1976.786

Dyson M and Steel S, 'Risk and English Tort Law' in M Dyson (ed), *Regulating Risk through Private Law* (Intersentia 2018) 23

Edelman J, 'Equitable Torts' (2002) 10 Torts Law J 64

Eekelaar JM, 'Nuisance and Strict Liability' (1973) 8 Ir Jur 191

Ehrenzweig AA, *Negligence without Fault: Trends Toward an Enterprise Liability for Insurable Loss* (University of California Press 1951) (reprinted in (1966) 54 Cal L Rev 1422)

Eisenmann C, 'Sur le degré d'originalité du régime de la responsabilité extra-contractuelle des personnes publiques' JCP 1949.I.751

Elefante F, *La responsabilità della pubblica amministrazione da attività provvedimentale* (CEDAM 2002)

Epstein RA, 'A Theory of Strict Liability' (1973) 2 J Legal Stud 151

——'Defenses and Subsequent Pleas in a System of Strict Liability' (1974) 3 J Legal Stud 165

——'Intentional Harms' (1975) 4 J Legal Stud 391

——'Products Liability: The Search for the Middle Ground' (1978) 56 NCL Rev 643

324 BIBLIOGRAPHY

——'Nuisance Law: Corrective Justice and Its Utilitarian Constraints' (1979) 8 J Legal Stud 49

——'Causation and Corrective Justice: A Reply to Two Critics' (1979) 8 J Legal Stud 477

——*Modern Products Liability Law* (Quorum Books 1980)

——'Products Liability as an Insurance Market' (1985) 14 J Legal Stud 645

——'Causation in Context: An Afterword' (1987) 63 Chi-Kent L Rev 653

——'Toward a General Theory of Tort Law: Strict Liability in Context' (2010) 3 JTL, article 6

Errera R, 'The Scope and Meaning of No-Fault Liability in French Administrative Law' (1986) 39 CLP 157

Esmein P, 'Prendre l'argent là où il est' Gaz Pal 1958.2.46

Ewald F, *L'État providence* (Bernard Grasset 1986)

——'La véritable nature du risque de développement et sa garantie' Risques, 1993, no 14, 9

Ewald W, 'The Jurisprudential Approach to Comparative Law: A Field Guide to Rats' (1998) 46 AJCL 701

Fabre-Magnan M, *Droit des obligations. 2—Responsabilité civile et quasi-contrats* (4th edn, PUF 2019)

Facci G, 'L'illecito del figlio minore, la prova liberatoria dei genitori e la responsabilità oggettiva' (2005) 2 LRC 162

——'La responsabilità dei genitori in caso di incidente stradale del figlio minore: per colpa od oggettiva?' (2006) 2 Fam Dir 138

Fairgrieve D, *State Liability in Tort: A Comparative Law Study* (OUP 2003)

——and Lichere F, 'The Liability of Public Authorities in France' in K Oliphant (ed), *The Liability of Public Authorities in Comparative Perspective* (Intersentia 2016) 155

——and Daniel Squires, *The Negligence Liability of Public Authorities* (2nd edn, OUP 2019)

Fanelli L, 'Fondo stradale dissestato per lavori ed esercizio di attività pericolosa: caratteri e limiti' (2001) 10 DR 925

Farolfi A, 'Il danno cagionato da cose in custodia' in Paolo Cendon (ed), *Responsabilità civile*, vol III (2nd edn, UTET 2020) 3849

Feezer LW, 'Capacity to Bear Loss as a Factor in the Decision of Certain Types of Tort Cases' (1930) 78 U Pa L Rev 805

——'Capacity to Bear Loss as a Factor in the Decision of Certain Types of Tort Cases' (1931) 79 U Pa L Rev 742

Feldman ER, 'Strict Tort Liability for Police Misconduct' (2019) 53 Colum JL & Soc Probs 89

Feliziani C, 'L'elemento soggettivo della responsabilità amministrativa. Dialogo a-sincrono tra Corte di giustizia e giudici nazionali' (2018) 6 federalismi.it 1

Ferrari V, 'Una ipotesi di responsabilità civile in funzione di garanzia' (2011) 1(1) Foro It 203

Ferri GB, 'Garanzia, rischio e responsabilità oggettiva' (2005) 10–12(1) Riv Dir Comm 867

Fleming J, *The Law of Torts* (9th edn, LBC Information Services 1998)

Fletcher G, 'Fairness and Utility in Tort Theory' (1972) 85 Harv L Rev 537

Flour J, Aubert JL, and Savaux E, *Droit civil. Les obligations. 2. Le fait juridique* (14th edn, Dalloz 2011)

Foddai MA, *Sulle tracce della responsabilità. Idee e norme dell'agire responsabile* (Giappichelli 2005)

Forchielli P, *Responsabilità civile* (CEDAM 1969)

Fracchia F, 'L'elemento soggettivo nella responsabilità dell'amministrazione' in *Responsabilità della pubblica amministrazione per lesioni di interessi legittimi. Atti del 54° Convegno di Studi di Scienza dell'Amministrazione, Varenna—Villa Monastero, 18-20 settembre 2008* (Giuffrè 2009) 211

Franklin RB, 'Pouring New Wine into an Old Bottle: A Recommendation for Determining Liability of an Employer under Respondeat Superior' (1994) 39 SD LR 570

Franzoni M, 'La responsabilità del produttore di beni di consumo' (1993) 1 Diritto ed economia delle assicurazioni 3

——*L'illecito. Trattato della responsabilità civile* (2nd edn, Giuffrè 2010)

——*Il danno risarcibile. Trattato della responsabilità civile* (2nd edn, Giuffrè 2010)

Friedman LM, *A History of American Law* (4th edn, OUP 2019)

Fusaro A, 'Attività pericolose e dintorni. Nuove applicazioni dell'art. 2050 c.c.' (2013) (6) Riv Dir Civ 1337

Gardner J, 'The Purity and Priority of Private Law' (1996) 46 U Toronto LJ 459

——'Obligations and Outcomes in the Law of Torts' in P Cane and J Gardner (eds), *Relating to Responsibility* (Hart Publishing 2001) 111

——'What is Tort Law For? Part 1. The Place of Corrective Justice' (2011) 30(1) Law and Phil 1

——'Torts and Other Wrongs' (2012) 39 Fla St U L Rev 43

——'Some Rule-of-Law Anxieties about Strict Liability in Private Law' in LM Austin and D Klimchuk (eds), *Private Law and the Rule of Law* (OUP 2014) 207

Garraffa P, 'La responsabilità del gestore di un impianto di calcio "saponato"' (2018) 7–8 NGCC 1052

Gaudemet Y, *Droit Administratif* (23rd edn, LGDJ 2020)

Geis G and Binder A, 'Sins of Their Children: Parental Responsibility for Juvenile Delinquency' (1991) 5 Notre Dame JL Ethics & Pub Pol'y 303

Geistfeld M, 'Should Enterprise Liability Replace the Rule of Strict Liability for Abnormally Dangerous Activities?' (1997) 45 UCLA L Rev 611

——'Negligence, Compensation, and the Coherence of Tort Law' (2003) 91 Geo LJ 585

——'Hidden in Plain Sight: The Normative Source of Modern Tort Law' (2016) 91 NYU L Rev 1517

Gentile L, 'Parental Civil Liability for the Torts of Minors' (2007) 16 JCLI 125

Geri V, *La R.C. da cose in custodia, animali e rovina di edificio* (Giuffrè 1974)

Ghestin J, JCP 1991.II.169 n.21673

Ghidini G, 'Prevenzione e risarcimento nella responsabilità del produttore' (1975) Rivista delle società 530

Giannini MS, 'Intervento' in *Atti del convegno nazionale sull'ammissibilità del danno patrimoniale derivante da lesione di interessi legittimi* (Giuffrè 1965) 511

Giliker P, *Vicarious Liability in Tort: A Comparative Perspective* (CUP 2010)

——'Vicarious Liability, Non-Delegable Duties and Teachers: Can You Outsource Liability for Lessons?' (2015) 31 PN 259

——'A Revolution in Vicarious Liability: Lister, The Catholic Child Welfare Society Case and Beyond' in S Worthington, G Virgo, and A Robertson (eds), *Revolution and Evolution in Private Law* (Hart Publishing 2018) 121

——'Comparative Law and Legal Culture: Placing Vicarious Liability in Comparative Perspective' (2018) 6 Ch J Comp L 265

Gilli J-P, 'La "responsabilité d'équité" de la puissance publique' D chron 1971.125

Giracca MP, 'Responsabilità civile e pubblica amministrazione: quale spazio per l'art. 2049 c.c.?' (2001) 1 Foro It 3293

Gohin O, 'La Responsabilite de l'État en tant que Legislateur' (1998) RIDC 595

Goldberg JCP, 'Twentieth-Century Tort Theory' (2002) 91 Geo LJ 513

——and others, *Tort Law: Responsibilities and Redress* (5th edn, Wolters Kluwer 2021)

——and Zipursky BC, 'Tort Law and Moral Luck' (2007) 92 Cornell L Rev 1123

——and Zipursky BC, *The Oxford Introductions to U.S. Law: Torts* (OUP 2010)

——and Zipursky BC, 'Torts as Wrongs' (2010) 88 Tex L Rev 917

——and Zipursky BC, 'Civil Recourse Revisited' (2011) 39 Fla St U L Rev 341

326   BIBLIOGRAPHY

——and Zipursky BC, 'Rights and Responsibility in the Law of Torts' in D Nolan and A Robertson (eds), *Rights and Private Law* (Hart Publishing 2012) 251

——and Zipursky BC, 'Civil Recourse Defended: A Reply to Posner, Calabresi, Rustad, Chamallas, and Robinette' (2013) 88 Ind LJ 569

——and Zipursky BC, 'The Strict Liability in Fault and the Fault in Strict Liability' (2016) 85 Fordham L Rev 743

——and Zipursky BC, *Recognizing Wrongs* (HUP 2020)

Goldman B, *La détermination du gardien responsable du fait des choses inanimées* (Sirey 1947)

Goldman BR, 'Can the King do no Wrong? A New Look at the Discretionary Function Exception to the Federal Tort Claims Act' (1992) 26 Ga L Rev 837

Gollier C, 'Le risque de développement est-il assurable?' Risques, 1993, no 14, 49

Goudkamp J, *Tort Law Defences* (Hart Publishing 2013)

——and Plunkett J, 'Vicarious Liability in Australia: On the Move?' (2017) 17 OUCLJ 162

——and Nolan D, *Winfield & Jolowicz on Tort* (20th edn, Sweet and Maxwell 2020)

Gout O, 'Le droit français positif et prospectif de la responsabilité du fait d'autrui' in *Le droit français de la responsabilité civile confronté aux projets européens d'harmonisation* (IRJS Éditions 2012) 291

Graham PK, 'Parental Responsibility Laws: Let the Punishment Fit the Crime' (2000) 33 Loy LA L Rev 1719

Grare C, *Recherches sur la cohérence de la responsabilité délictuelle. L'influence des fondements de la responsabilité sur la reparation* (Dalloz 2005)

Gratton L, 'Le dommage déduit de la faute' RTD civ 2013.275

Gray A, *Vicarious Liability: Critique and Reform* (Hart Publishing 2018)

Graziadei M, 'The Functionalist Heritage' in P Legrand and R Munday (eds), *Comparative Legal Studies: Traditions and Transitions* (CUP 2003) 100

——'Liability for Fault in Italian Law: The Development of Legal Doctrine from 1865 to the End of the Twentieth Century' in N Jansen (ed), *The Development and Making of Legal Doctrine* (CUP 2010) 126

Green L, 'The Duty Problem in Negligence Cases' (1928) 28 Colum L Rev 1014

——'The Duty Problem in Negligence Cases' (1929) 29 Colum L Rev 255

Green MD and Cardi J, 'The Liability of Public Authorities in the United States' in K Oliphant (ed), *The Liability of Public Authorities in Comparative Perspective* (Intersentia 2016) 537

Gregory CO, 'Trespass to Negligence to Absolute Liability' (1951) 37 Va L Rev 359

Griffey M, *La responsabilità civile derivante da circolazione dei veicoli e dei natanti* (Giuffrè 1995)

Griffiths (Lord), De Val P, and Dormer RJ, 'Developments in English Product Liability Law: A Comparison with the American System' (1988) 62 Tul LR 353

Guégan-Lécuyer A, 'Vers un nouveau fait générateur de responsabilité civile: les activités dangereuses (Commentaire de l'article 1362 de l'Avant-projet Catala)' in *Etudes offertes à Geneviève Viney* (LGDJ 2008) 499

Häcker B, '*Fait d'autrui* in Comparative Perspective' in J-S Borghetti and S Whittaker (eds), *French Civil Liability in Comparative Perspective* (Hart Publishing 2019) 143

Halpérin J-L, *Histoire du droit privé français depuis 1804* (PUF 2012)

Hamson CJ, 'Escaping Borstal Boys and the Immunity of Office' (1969) 27 CLJ 273

Hanks JL, 'Franchisor Liability for the Torts of Its Franchisees: The Case for Substituting Liability as a Guarantor for the Current Vicarious Liability' (1999) 24 Okla City U L Rev 1

Harper FV and James Jr F, *The Law of Torts*, vol 2 (Little, Brown and Company 1956)

——and James Jr F, Gray OS, *The Law of Torts*, vol 5 (2nd edn, Little, Brown and Company 1986)

BIBLIOGRAPHY   327

Hassel D, 'A Missed Opportunity: The Federal Tort Claims Act and Civil Rights Actions' (1996) 49 Okla L Rev 455

Hauriou M, 'Les actions en indemnité contre l'État pour préjudices causés dans l'administration publique' RDP 1896.51

——S 1897.3.33

Henderson JA Jr, 'Coping with the Time Dimension in Products Liability' (1981) 69 Cal L Rev 919

——'Judicial Reliance on Public Policy: An Empirical Analysis of Products Liability Decisions' (1991) 59 Geo Wash L Rev 1570

——Kysar DA, and Pearson RN, *The Tort Process* (9th edn, Wolters Kluwer 2017)

Hennette-Vauchez S, 'Responsabilité sans faute' in Répertoire de la responsabilité de la puissance publique (2017)

Hilliard F, *The Law of Torts or Private Wrongs* (Little, Brown and Company 1859)

Holmes OW, *The Common Law* (Little, Brown and Company 1923)

Honoré T, 'Responsibility and Luck: The Moral Basis of Strict Liability' (1988) 104 LQR 530

——'The Morality of Tort Law—Questions and Answers' in DG Owen (ed), *Philosophical Foundations of Tort Law* (OUP 1995) 73

——'Medical Non-disclosure: Causation and Risk: Chappel v Hart' (1999) 7 Torts LJ 1

Horwitz MJ, *The Transformation of American Law 1870–1960: The Crisis of Legal Orthodoxy* (OUP 1992)

Howarth D, 'The House of Lords and the Animals Act: Closing the Stable Door' (Case Comment) (2003) 62 CLJ 548

Huet J, 'Responsabilité du fait des produits défectueux. Objectifs, portée et mise en œuvre de la directive 85/374' JCl E, fasc 2020 (updated 15.2.2017)

Husa J, 'Farewell to Functionalism or Methodological Tolerance?' (2003) 67 RabelsZ 419

Infantini GG, 'La responsabilità civile della pubblica amministrazione per danni causati nell'esercizio di attività pericolose e da cose in custodia' in E Follieri (ed), *La responsabilità civile della pubblica amministrazione* (Giuffrè 2004) 297

Insurance Information Institute, *2021 Insurance Fact Book*, available at https://www.iii.org/sites/default/files/docs/pdf/insurance_factbook_2021.pdf

Iudica G and Scarso AP, 'Tort Liability and Insurance: Italy' in G Wagner (ed), *Tort Law and Liability Insurance* (Springer 2005) 119

James Jr F, 'Accident Liability: Some Wartime Developments' (1946) 55 Yale LJ 365

——'Accident Liability Reconsidered: The Impact of Liability Insurance' (1948) 57 Yale LJ 549

——'Products Liability II' (1955) 34 Tex L Rev 192

——'Tort Liability of Governmental Units and Their Officers' (1955) 22 U Chi L Rev 610

Jault A, *La notion de peine privée* (LGDJ 2005)

Jèze G, *Éléments du droit public et administratif* (V Giard & E Brière 1910)

Jolowicz JA, 'The Right to Indemnity between Master and Servant' (1956) 14 CLJ 101

——'Liability for Accidents' (1968) 26 CLJ 50

——'The Protection of the Consumer and Purchaser of Goods under English Law' (1969) 32 MLR 1

Jones MA (ed), *Clerk & Lindsell On Torts* (23rd edn, Sweet & Maxwell Ltd 2020)

Josserand L, *De la responsabilité du fait des choses inanimées* (Arthur Rousseau 1897)

——D 1925.1.97

——'Les collisions entre véhicules et la responsabilité civile' D chron 1928.33

——'Les collisions entre véhicules et entre présomptions de responsabilité' D chron 1935.41

——*Cours de droit civil positif français* (3rd edn, Sirey 1938)

328 BIBLIOGRAPHY

——*De l'esprit des droits et de leur relativité: théorie dite de l'abus des droits* (2nd edn, Dalloz 1939)

Jourdain P, 'La reconnaissance d'une responsabilité du fait d'autrui en dehors des cas particuliers énoncés dans l'article 1384' RTD civ 1991.541

——D 1997.265

——D 1997.496

——'Commentaire de la loi no 98-389 du 19 mai 1998 sur la responsabilité du fait des produits défectueux' JCP E 1998.1204

——RTD civ 1995.890

——'La responsabilité du fait d'autrui à la recherche de ses fondements' in *Mélanges Lapoyade Deschamps* (PU Bordeaux 2003) 67

——'La responsabilité des père et mère: une responsabilité principale et directe, indépendante de celle du mineur' D 2003.4.231

——RTD civ 2003.305

——*Les principes de la responsabilité civile* (10th edn, Dalloz 2021)

Julien J, 'Les régimes de responsabilité du fait d'une chose' in P le Tourneau (ed), *Droit de la responsabilité et des contrats. Régimes d'indemnisation* (12th edn, Dalloz 2021) 951

Kaplow L and Shavell S, 'Property Rules Versus Liability Rules: An Economic Analysis' (1996) 109 Harv L Rev 713

——*Fairness v Welfare* (HUP 2002)

Keating GC, 'The Idea of Fairness in the Law of Enterprise Liability' (1997) 95 Mich L Rev 1266

——'Distributive and Corrective Justice in the Tort Law of Accidents' (2000) 74 S Cal L Rev 193

——'The Theory of Enterprise Liability and Common Law Strict Liability' (2001) 54 Vand L Rev 1285

——'Nuisance as a Strict Liability Wrong' (2012) 4(3) JTL, article 2

——'Strict Liability Wrongs' in J Oberdiek (ed), *Philosophical Foundations of the Law of Torts* (OUP 2014) 292

——'Products Liability as Enterprise Liability' (2017) 10(1) JTL 41

——'Is There Really No Liability Without Fault?: A Critique of Goldberg & Zipursky' (2017) 85 Fordham L Rev Res Gestae 24

Keeton RE, 'Conditional Fault in the Law of Torts' (1959) 72 Harv L Rev 401

——*Venturing to Do Justice: Reforming Private Law* (HUP 1969)

——and O'Connell J, *Basic Protection for Traffic Victim* (Little, Brown and Company 1965)

——Sargentich LD, and Keating GC, *Tort and Accident Law—Cases and Materials* (4th edn, Thomson West 2004)

King Jr JH, 'A Goals-Oriented Approach to Strict Tort Liability for abnormally Dangerous Activities' (1996) 48 Baylor L Rev 341

Knetsch J, 'The Role of Liability without Fault' in J-S Borghetti and S Whittaker (eds), *French Civil Liability in Comparative Perspective* (Hart Publishing 2019) 123

Kornhauser LA, 'An Economic Analysis of the Choice between Enterprise and Personal Liability for Accidents' (1982) 70 Cal LR 1345

Koziol H, 'Comparative Conclusions' in H Koziol (ed), *Basic Questions of Tort Law from a Comparative Perspective* (Jan Sramek Verlag KG 2015) 683

——'Schadenersatzrecht and the Law of Torts: Different terms and different ways of thinking' (2014) 5(3) JETL 257

Kratzke WP, 'Some Recommendations concerning Tort Liability of Government and Its Employees for Torts and Constitutional Torts' (1996) 9 Admin LJ Am U 1105

Kutz C, 'Responsibility' in JL Coleman, KE Himma, and SJ Shapiro (eds), *The Oxford Handbook of Jurisprudence and Philosophy of Law* (OUP 2004) 548

La Battaglia L, 'Danno da prodotto farmaceutico difettoso e prova liberatoria' (2002) 10 DR 986

La Torre A, *L'assicurazione nella storia delle idee. La risposta giuridica al bisogno di sicurezza economica: ieri e oggi* (Giuffrè 2000)

Laghezza P, 'La responsabilità della P.A. per omessa manutenzione delle strade' (2002) 12 DR 1201

——'Responsabilità per rovina di edificio e uso anomalo del bene' (2010) 10 DR 994

——'Quale causalità per l'art. 2051 c.c.? —Il commento' (2014) 3 DR 258

Lambert-Faivre Y, 'L'évolution de la responsabilité civile d'une dette de responsabilité à une créance d'indemnisation' RTD civ 1987.1

——'L'éthique de la responsabilité' RTD civ 1998.1

Landes WM and Posner RA, 'The Positive Economic Theory of Tort Law' (1980) 15 Ga L Rev 851

——'A Positive Economic Analysis of Products Liability' (1985) 14 J Legal Stud 535

——*The Economic Structure of Tort Law* (HUP 1987)

Larroumet C, D 1980.IR.414

——D 1982.449

Law Commission, *Civil Liability for Animals* (Law Com No 13, 1967)

——*Civil Liability for Dangerous Things and Activities* (Law Com No 32, 1970)

——*Liability for Defective Products* (Law Com No 82, 1977)

le Tourneau P, 'La verdeur de la faute dans la responsabilité civile (ou la relativité de son déclin)' RTD civ 1988.505

Leduc F, 'L'état actuel du principe général de responsabilité délictuelle du fait des choses' in F Leduc (ed), *La responsabilité du fait des choses, Réflexions autour d'un centenaire* (Economica 1997) 35

Lee M, 'What is Private Nuisance' (2003) 119 LQR 298

Leidi L, 'La rovina e i difetti di edificio' in P Cendon (ed), *Responsabilità civile*, vol III (2nd edn, UTET 2020) 3880

Leotta G, 'Sulla responsabilità del datore di lavoro ex art. 2049 cod. civ' (2001) 2 Rivista giuridica del lavoro e della previdenza sociale 399

Lewis R, 'The Relationship between Tort Law and Insurance in England and Wales' in G Wagner (ed), *Tort Law and Liability Insurance* (Springer 2005) 47

Lobban M, 'Tort' in W Cornish and others (eds), *The Oxford History of the Laws of England, Volume XII—1820-1914: Private Law* (OUP 2010) 877

Logue K, 'The Deterrence Case for Comprehensive Automaker Enterprise Liability' (2019) 1 J L & Mob 1

Long M and others, *Les grands arrêts de la jurisprudence administrative* (22nd edn, Dalloz 2019)

Lunney M, 'Professor Sir John Salmond (1862–1924): An Englishman Abroad' in J Goudkamp and D Nolan (eds), *Scholars of Tort Law* (Hart Publishing 2019) 103

Maitre G, *La responsabilité civile à l'épreuve de l'analyse économique du droit* (LGDJ 2005)

Majello U, 'Responsabilità dei genitori per il fatto illeciti del figlio minore e valutazione del comportamento del danneggiato ai fini della determinazione del contenuto della prova liberatoria' (1960) Dir giur 43

Malaurie P, Aynès L, and Stoffel-Munck P, *Droit des obligations* (11th edn, LGDJ 2020)

Marini G, 'Gli anni settanta della responsabilità civile. Uno studio sulla relazione pubblico/privato (parte I)' (2008) 1 RCDP 23

——'Gli anni settanta della responsabilità civile. Uno studio sulla relazione pubblico/privato (parte II)' (2008) 2 RCDP 229

Markesinis B, 'Plaintiff's Tort Law or Defendant's Tort Law? Is the House of Lords Moving towards a Synthesis?' (2001) 9 Torts LJ 168

330 BIBLIOGRAPHY

Marteau-Petit M, 'La dualité des critères de mise en œuvre de la responsabilité du fait d'autrui' RRJ 2002.1.255

Mascia K, 'Responsabilità per i danni cagionati dagli animali' (2020) 4 DR 538

Mattei U, *Tutela inibitoria e tutela risarcitoria: contributo alla teoria dei diritti sui beni* (Giuffrè 1987)

——'The Comparative Jurisprudence of Schlesinger and Sacco: A Study in Legal Influence' in A Riles (ed), *Rethinking the Masters of Comparative Law* (Hart Publishing 2001) 238

——*I Diritti Reali—2—La Proprietà. Trattato di Diritto Civile* (UTET 2015)

Mazeaud H, 'La faute dans la garde' RTD civ 1925.793

——Mazeaud L, and Tunc A, *Traité théorique et pratique de la responsabilité civile délictuelle et contractuelle* (6th edn, Montchrestien 1965)

Mazzola MA, *Responsabilità civile da atti leciti dannosi* (Giuffrè 2007)

Mazzon R, 'Il fenomeno della responsabilità oggettiva nella disciplina prevista dall'art. 2054 c.c. e concernenti la circolazione dei veicoli' in P Cendon (ed), *Responsabilità civile*, vol III (2nd edn, UTET 2020) 4006

McBride NJ, 'Rights and the Basis of Tort Law' in D Nolan and A Robertson (eds), *Rights and Private Law* (Hart Publishing 2012) 331

——*The Humanity of Private Law. Part I: Explanation* (Hart Publishing 2019)

——and Bagshaw R, *Tort Law* (6th edn, Pearson Education 2018)

McKendrick E, 'Vicarious Liability and Independent Contractors: A Re-Examination' (1990) 53 MLR 770

Mead SM, '42 U.S.C. § 1983 Municipal Liability: The Monell Sketch Becomes a Distorted Picture' (1987) 65 NCL Rev 517

Merkin R, 'Tort, Insurance and Ideology: Further Thoughts' (2012) 75 MLR 301

——and Dziobon S, 'Tort Law and Compulsory Insurance' in TT Arvind and J Steele (eds), *Tort Law and the Legislature: Common Law, Statute and the Dynamics of Legal Change* (Hart Publishing 2013) 303

Messineo F, *Manuale di diritto civile e commerciale*, vol V (9th edn, Giuffrè 1957)

Michaels R, 'The Functional Method of Comparative Law' in M Reimann and R Zimmermann (eds), *The Oxford Handbook of Comparative Law* (2nd edn, OUP 2019) 345

Mignon M, 'La socialisation du risque' D chron 1947.37

Millet F, *La notion de risque et ses fonctions en droit privé* (PUF 2001)

Minervini G, 'Orientamenti in tema di responsabilità senza colpa' (1952) GC 626

Mitchell JDB, 'Administrative Law and Parliamentary Control' (1967) 38 The Political Quarterly 360

Mitchell P, 'Professor John G Fleming (1919–1997): "A Sense of Fluidity" ' in J Goudkamp and D Nolan (eds), *Scholars of Tort Law* (Hart Publishing 2019) 289

Molfessis N, 'La jurisprudence relative à la responsabilité des commettants du fait de leurs préposés ou l'irrésistible enlisement de la Cour de cassation' in *Ruptures, movements et continuité du droit, Autour de Michelle Gobert* (Economica 2004) 495

Monateri PG, 'Responsabilità civile' Dig Disc Priv (UTET 1998) XVII, 1

——*La Responsabilità Civile. Trattato di Diritto Civile* (UTET 1998)

——'Il Tort da illegittimo esercizio della funzione pubblica' (1999) 10 DR 978

——*Illecito e responsabilità civile—Tomo II. Trattato di diritto privato* (UTET 2002)

——'Responsabilità del produttore di sigarette per danni da fumo attivo' (2005) 12 DR 1210

——Arnone GMD, and Calcagno N, *Il dolo, la colpa e i risarcimenti aggravati dalla condotta* (Giappichelli 2014)

Monti S, 'Responsabilità dei genitori: alcune riflessioni' (2014) 11 DR 1054

Moreau J, 'Rapport sur les choses dangereuses en droit administratif français' in *Travaux de l'Association Henri-Capitant: Les choses dangereuses: journées néerlandaises* (Dalloz 1971) 256

Morgan J, 'Tort, Insurance and Incoherence' (2004) 67 MLR 384

——'Vicarious Liability for Independent Contractors' (2016) 31 PN 235

Morgan P, 'Recasting Vicarious Liability' (2012) 71 CLJ 615

Morris C, 'Hazardous Enterprises and Risk Bearing Capacity' (1952) 61 Yale LJ 1172

Motzo G and Duni G, 'Rapport sur les choses dangereuses en droit public italien' in *Travaux de l'Association Henri-Capitant: Les choses dangereuses: journées néerlandaises* (Dalloz 1971) 291

Murgo C, 'La responsabilità dei genitori per fatto illecito dei figli minori: una conferma che invita alla riflessione' (2016) 2 RCP 541

Murphy J, 'The Merits of Rylands v Fletcher' (2004) 24 OJLS 643

——'Juridical Foundations of Common Law Non-delegable Duties' in JW Neyers, E Chamberlain, and SGA Pitel (eds), *Emerging Issues in Tort Law* (Hart Publishing 2007) 369

Natoli U, Busnelli FD, and Galoppini A, 'Responsabilità, assicurazione e solidarietà sociale nel risarcimento dei danni' (1970) Annuario di diritto comparato 45

Neely R, *The Product Liability Mess. How Business Can Be Rescued from the Politics of State Courts* (Free Press 1988)

Newark FH, 'The Boundaries of Nuisance' (1949) 65 LQR 480

Newdick C, 'The Future of Negligence in Product Liability' (1987) 103 LQR 288

Nicholas B, *An Introduction to Roman Law* (rev edn, OUP 2008)

Nolan D, 'The Distinctiveness of *Rylands v Fletcher*' (2005) 121 LQR 421

——'Causation and the Goals of Tort Law' in A Robertson and HW Tang (eds), *The Goals of Private Law* (Hart Publishing 2009) 165

——Review of 'Douglas Brodie, *Enterprise Liability and the Common Law* (CUP 2010)' (2012) 41(3) ILJ 370

——'Strict Product Liability for Design Defects' (2018) 134 LQR 176

Nolan VE and Ursin E, 'The Revitalization of Hazardous Activity Strict Liability' (1987) 65 NCL Rev 257

——*Understanding Enterprise Liability: Rethinking Tort Reform for the Twenty-first Century* (Temple University Press 1995)

——'Dean Leon Green and Enterprise (No-Fault) Liability: Origins, Strategies, and Prospects' (2001) 47 Wayne L Rev 91

North P, *Civil Liability for Animals* (OUP 2012)

Occhipinti A, 'La colpevolezza' in P Cendon (ed), *Responsabilità civile*, vol I (2nd edn, UTET 2020) 255

——'The Liability of Public Authorities in England and Wales' in K Oliphant (ed), *The Liability of Public Authorities in Comparative Perspective* (Intersentia 2016) 127

Ollier P-D, *La responsabilité civile des père et mère* (LGDJ 1961)

Orlando VE, 'Saggio di una nuova teorica sul fondamento giuridico della responsabilità civile' (1893) Arch dir pubbl 241

Oudot P, 'La piège communautaire de la responsabilité du fait des produits défectueux' Dr et patrim, January 2003, 40

——'L'application et le fondement de la loi du 19 mai 2008 instituant la responsabilité du fait des produits défectueux: les leçons du temps' Gaz Pal 15.11.2008, 6

Overstake J-F, 'La responsabilité du fabricant de produits dangereux' RTD civ 1972.485

Owen DG, 'Rethinking the Policies of Strict Products Liability' (1980) 33 Vand L Rev 681

332 BIBLIOGRAPHY

——'Moral Foundations of Products Liability Law: Toward First Principles' (1993) 68 Notre Dame L Rev 427

——*Products Liability Law* (3rd edn, West Academic Publishing 2015)

Paillet M and Breen E, 'FAUTE DE SERVICE. —Notion' JCl Admin, Fasc 818, 2008 (updated in 2011)

Pacchioni G, *Elementi di diritto civile* (2nd edn, UTET 1921)

Palmieri A, 'Difetto e condizioni di impiego del prodotto: ritorno alla responsabilità per colpa?' (2007) 1 Foro It 2415

——and Pardolesi R, 'La Cassazione riconosce la risarcibilità degli interessi legittimi. Il commento' (1999) 10 DR 980

Pardolesi P, *Profili comparatistici di analisi economica del diritto* (Cacucci 2015)

——'Riflessioni sulla responsabilità da prodotto difettoso in chiave di analisi economica del diritto' (2017) 2 Riv Dir Priv 87

——and Dimattia M, 'Responsabilità dei genitori per l'illecito dei minori: un esercizio di precomprensione?' (2010) 2 DR 168

Pardolesi R, 'Azione reale e azione di danni nell'art. 844 c.c. —Logica economica e logica giuridica nella composizione del conflitto tra usi incompatibili delle proprietà vicine' (1977) 1 Foro It 1144

——and Ponzanelli G (eds), 'La responsabilità per danno da prodotti difettosi' (1989) (3) Le nuove leggi civili commentate 497

——and Tassone B, 'Guido Calabresi on torts: Italian courts and the cheapest cost avoider' (2008) 4 Erasmus Law Rev 7

Parziale A, 'Il "caso dell'amaca", danno alla persona e costi assicurativi' (2013) 6 DR 688

Patti S, *Famiglia e responsabilità civile* (Giuffrè 1984)

——'Responsabilità dei genitori: una sentenza in linea con l'evoluzione europea' (2001) 4 Familia 1174

Pearson Commission, *Report of the Royal Commission on Civil Liability and Compensation for Personal Injury*, Cmnd 7054-I (1978)

Peck CJ, 'Laird v. Nelms: A Call for Review and Revision of the Federal Tort Claims Act' (1973) 48 Wash L Rev 391

Peel E and Goudkamp J, *Winfield & Jolowicz on Tort* (19th edn, Sweet & Maxwell 2014)

Perry SR, 'The Impossibility of General Strict Liability' (1988) 1 Can JL Juris 147

——'The Moral Foundations of Tort Law' (1992) 77 Iowa L Rev 449

——'Responsibility for Outcomes, Risk, and the Law of Torts' in G Postema (ed), *Philosophy and the Law of Torts* (CUP 2001) 72

——'Torts, Rights, and Risk' in J Oberdiek (ed), *Philosophical Foundations of the Law of Torts* (OUP 2014) 38

Peterson BA and Van Der Weide ME, 'Susceptible to Faulty Analysis: United States v. Gaubert and the Resurrection of Federal Sovereign Immunity' (1997) 72 Notre Dame L Rev 447

Petruso R, 'Immissioni' Dig Disc Priv (UTET 2012 agg) 546

Philipp D, 'De la responsabilité à la solidarité des personnes publiques' RDP 1999.593

Piazza A, *Responsabilità civile ed efficienza amministrativa* (Giuffrè 2001)

Pierce RJ and Hickman KE, *Administrative Law Treatise*, vol 3 (6th edn, Wolters Kluwer 2019)

Pizzetti FG, 'Responsabilità civile del datore di lavoro, occasionalità necessaria e stato soggettivo del danneggiato' (1994) 4 DR 430

Planiol M, 'Études sur la responsabilité civile' RCLJ 1905.277

——'Études sur la responsabilité civile' RCLJ 1909.282

Plunkett J, 'Taking Stock of Vicarious Liability' (2016) 132 LQR 556

Poletti D, 'Le regole di (de)limitazione del danno risarcibile' in N Lipari and P Rescigno (eds), *Diritto civile, Volume IV, Attuazione e tutela dei diritti. Tomo III, La responsabilità e il danno* (Giuffrè 2009) 291

Pollock F, 'Duty of Insuring Safety: The Rule in Rylands v Fletcher' (1886) 2 LQR 52

——*The Law of Torts: A Treatise on the Principles of Obligations Arising from Civil Wrongs in the Common Law* (1st edn, Stevens 1887)

Ponzanelli G, 'Nuove figure di danno alla persona e tecniche assicurative' (1989) RCP 409

——'Il produttore è responsabile del danno cagionato da difetti del suo prodotto' in R Pardolesi and G Ponzanelli (eds), *La responsabilità per danno da prodotti difettosi* (1989) 3 Le nuove leggi civili commentate 506

——*La responsabilità civile. Profili di diritto comparato* (Il Mulino 1992)

——'Dal biscotto alla "mountain bike": la responsabilità da prodotto difettoso in Italia' (1994) 1 Foro It 252

——'Causa probabile del danno e responsabilità del produttore' (2004) 5 DR 527

Posner RA, 'Book Review (reviewing Guido Calabresi, The Costs of Accidents: A Legal and Economic Analysis (1970))' (1970) 37 U Chi L Rev 636

——'A Theory of Negligence' (1972) 1 J Legal Stud 29

——'Strict Liability: A Comment' (1973) 2 J Legal Stud 205

——'Epstein's Tort Theory: A Critique' (1979) 8 J Legal Stud 457

——'Utilitarianism, Economics, and Legal Theory' (1979) 8 J Legal Stud 103

——'The Ethical and Political Basis of the Efficiency Norm in Common Law Adjudication' (1980) 8 Hofstra L Rev 487

——'The Concept of Corrective Justice in Recent Theories of Tort Law' (1981) 10 J Legal Stud 187

——*Economic Analysis of Law* (9th edn, Wolters Kluwer 2014)

Priest GL, 'The Invention of Enterprise Liability: A Critical History of the Intellectual Foundations of Modern Tort Law' (1985) 14 J Legal Stud 461

——'Understanding the Liability Crisis' in W Olson (ed), *New Directions in Liability Law* (Academy of Political Science 1988) 196

——*The Rise of Law and Economics* (Routledge 2020)

Procida Mirabelli di Lauro A, *La responsabilità civile: strutture e funzioni* (Giappichelli 2004)

Prosser WL, *Handbook of the Law of Torts* (2nd edn, West Publishing Co 1955)

——'The Assault upon the Citadel (Strict Liability to the Consumer)' (1960) 69 Yale LJ 1099

——*Handbook of the Law of Torts* (3rd edn, West Publishing Co 1964)

——'The Fall of the Citadel' (1966) 50 Minn L Rev 791

Pugliese G, 'Responsabilità per rovina di edificio in usufrutto' (1957) Temi 471

Puill B, 'Vers une réforme de la responsabilité des parents' D chron 1988.185

Quadri E, 'Indennizzo e assicurazione' in M Comporti and G Scalfi (eds), *Responsabilità civile e assicurazione obbligatoria* (Giuffrè 1988) 97

Rabin R, 'Some Thoughts on the Ideology of Enterprise Liability' (1996) 55 Md L Rev 1190

Radé C, 'Le renouveau de la responsabilité du fait d'autrui (apologie de l'arrêt Bertrand)' D chron 1997.279

——'Art. 1382 à 1386—Fasc. 143: DROIT À RÉPARATION. —Responsabilité du fait d'autrui. —Domaine: responsabilité des commettants' JCl Civil Code (updated 16.5.2016)

Rémy P, 'Critique du système français de responsabilité civile' Revue juridique de l'USEK 1997.5.49

Rétif S, 'Un critère unique de la garde de la chose: la faculté de prévenir le préjudice qu'elle peut causer?' RCA November 2004, 7

334 BIBLIOGRAPHY

Reynolds Jr OM, 'Strict Liability under the Federal Tort Claims Act: Does "Wrongful" Cover a Few Sins, No Sins, or Non-Sins?' (1974) Am U L Rev 813

Ripert G, D 1930.1.57

——*La règle morale dans les obligations civiles* (4th edn, LGDJ 1949)

Rochfeld J, 'La responsabilité' in J Rochfeld (ed), *Les grandes notions du droit privé* (2nd edn, PUF 2013) 481

Rodière R, *La responsabilité civile* (Rousseau 1952)

Rodotà S, *Il Problema della Responsabilità Civile* (Giuffrè 1964)

——'Modelli e funzioni della responsabilità civile' (1984) RCDP 595

Rogers WVH, 'England' in BA Koch and H Koziol (eds), *Unification of Tort Law: Strict Liability* (Kluwer Law International 2002) 101

Romano A, *Giurisdizione amministrativa e limiti della giurisdizione ordinaria* (Giuffrè 1975)

Roppo E, 'Sul danno causato da automobile difettose. Tutela dei danneggiati, regime di responsabilità e incidenza dell'assicurazione obbligatoria' (1978) 12(IV) GI 130

Rosenberg D, 'The Judicial Posner on Negligence versus Strict Liability: Indiana Harbor Belt Railroad Co. v. American Cyanamid Co.' (2007) 120 Harv L Rev 1210

Rossi Carleo L, 'La responsabilità dei genitori ex art. 2048 c.c.' (1979) II Riv Dir Civ 126

Rudden B, 'Torticles' (1991-1992) 6 Tul Civ LF 105

Russo C, *De l'assurance de responsabilité à l'assurance directe: contribution à l'étude d'une mutation de la couverture des risques* (Dalloz 2001)

Sacco R, 'Legal Formants: A Dynamic Approach to Comparative Law' (1991) 39 AJCL 1

Sainctelette C, *De la responsabilité et de la garantie: accidents de transport et de travail* (Bruylant-Christophe 1884)

Saleilles R, 'Rapport' Revue bourguignonne de l'enseignement supérieur 1894.647

——D 1897.1.433

——*Les accidents de travail et la responsabilité civile* (Arthur Rousseau 1897)

——'Le risque professionnel dans le code civil' La réforme sociale 1898.633

Salmond JW, *The Law of Torts: A Treatise on the English Law of Liability for Civil Injuries* (1st edn, Stevens and Haynes 1907)

——*The Law of Torts: A Treatise on the English Law of Liability for Civil Injuries* (2nd edn, Stevens and Haynes 1910)

Salvi C, *Le immissioni industriali. Rapporti di vicinato e tutela dell'ambiente* (Giuffrè 1979)

——'Responsabilità extracontrattuale (dir. vig.)' Enc Dir XXXIX (Giuffrè 1988) 1186

——*La responsabilità civile* (3rd edn, Giuffrè 2019)

Samuel G, 'Can legal reasoning be demystified?' (2009) 29(2) LS 181

Sangermano F, 'La responsabilità dei padroni e dei committenti. La fattispecie del danno cagionato dal preposto al preponente' (2012) 4(2) RCP 1105

Santoro E, 'Il risarcimento del danno da aggiudicazione illegittima prescinde dall'accertamento della colpa? Riflessioni alla luce della giurisprudenza europea e del codice del processo amministrativo' (2011) 2 Foro amministrativo T.A.R. 679

Satta F, 'Responsabilità della pubblica amministrazione' Enc Dir XXXIX (Giuffrè 1998)1369

——'La sentenza n. 500 del 1999: dagli interessi legittimi ai diritti fondamentali' (1999) 5 Giurisprudenza Costituzionale 3233

Savatier R, *Traité de la responsabilité civile*, vol 1 (2nd edn, LGDJ 1951)

——*Les métamorphoses économiques et sociales du droit privé d'aujourd'hui* (2nd edn, Dalloz 1959)

——'Personnalité et dépersonnalisation de la responsabilité civile' in *Mélanges de droit, d'histoire et d'économie offerts à Marcel Laborde-Lacoste par ses collègues, ses élèves et ses amis* (Éditions Bière 1963) 321

Scalfi G, 'Responsabilità per vizi e per difetti dell'autoveicolo' (1974) RCP 323

Scarpelli U, 'Riflessioni sulla responsabilità politica. Responsabilità, libertà, visione dell'uomo' in R Orecchia (ed), *La responsabilità politica. Diritto e tempo* (Giuffrè 1982) 41

Schamps G, *La mise en danger: un concept fondateur d'un principe général de responsabilité* (Bruylant/LGDJ 1998)

Schuck PH, 'Suing Our Servants: The Court, Congress, and the Liability of Public Officials for Damages' (1980) 1980 Sup Ct Rev 281

——*Suing Government: Citizen Remedies for Official Wrongs* (YUP 1983)

——'Municipal Liability under Section 1983: Some Lessons from Tort Law and Organizational Theory' (1989) 77 Geo LJ 1753

Schwartz GT, 'Foreword: Understanding Products Liability' (1979) 67 Cal L Rev 435

——'The Vitality of Negligence and the Ethics of Strict Liability' (1981) 15 Ga L Rev 963

——'Reality in the Economic Analysis of Tort Law: Does Tort Law Really Deter?' (1994) 42 UCLA L Rev 377

——'The Hidden and Fundamental Issue of Employer Vicarious Liability' (1996) 69 S Cal L Rev 1739

——'Mixed Theories of Tort Law: Affirming Both Deterrence and Corrective Justice' (1997) 75 Texas L Rev 1801

Schwartz VE, Kelly K, and Partlett DF, *Prosser, Wade, and Schwartz's Torts—Cases and Materials* (13th edn, Foundation Press 2015)

Scoca FG, *Diritto amministrativo* (6th edn, Giappichelli 2019)

Scognamiglio R, 'Illecito (diritto vigente)' Noviss Dig It (UTET 1962) VIII, 164

——'Responsabilità per fatto altrui' Noviss Dig It (UTET 1968) XV, 691

——'Responsabilità civile' Noviss Dig It (UTET 1968) XV, 628

Scotti E, 'Appunti per una lettura della responsabilità dell'amministrazione tra realtà e uguaglianza' (2009) 3 Diritto amministrativo 521

Sella M, *La responsabilità civile nei nuovi orientamenti giurisprudenziali* (Giuffrè 2007)

Serra MP, 'La natura oggettiva della responsabilità per danni da cose in custodia: le ragioni di una scelta' (2009) 7 DR 751

Sharp C, 'Normal Abnormality? Liability for Straying Horses under the Animals Act 1971: Mirvahedy v. Henley [2003] UKHL 16' (2003) JPIL 172

Shavell S, 'Strict Liability versus Negligence' (1980) 9 J Legal Stud 1

——*Economic Analysis of Accident Law* (HUP 1987)

——'The Mistaken Restriction of Strict Liability to Uncommon Activities' (2018) 10 Journal of Legal Analysis 1

Shugerman JH, 'The Floodgates of Strict Liability: Bursting Reservoirs and the Adoption of Fletcher v. Rylands in the Gilded Age' (2000) 110 Yale LJ 333

——'A Watershed Moment: Reversals of Tort Theory in the Nineteenth Century' (2008) 2(1) JTL, article 2

Sica S, *Circolazione stradale e responsabilità: l'esperienza francese e italiana* (ESI 1990)

Siems M, *Comparative Law* (CUP 2018)

Sirena P, 'The New Design of the French Law of Contract and Obligations: An Italian View' in J Cartwright and S Whittaker (eds), *The Code Napoléon Rewritten* (Hart Publishing 2017) 339

Slavny A, 'Nonreciprocity and the Moral Basis of Liability to Compensate' (2014) 34 OJLS 417

Smith B, 'Cumulative Reasons and Legal Method' (1949) 27 Tex L Rev 454

Smith YB, 'Frolic and Detour' (1923) 23 Colum L Rev 444

——'Frolic and Detour' (1923) 23 Colum L Rev 716

336 BIBLIOGRAPHY

Spencer JR, 'Motor-cars and the Rule in *Rylands v Fletcher*: A Chapter of Accidents in the History of Law and Motoring' (1983) CLJ 65

Stanton KM, *Breach of Statutory Duty in Tort* (Sweet & Maxwell 1986)

——'The Legacy of Rylands v Fletcher' in NJ Mullany and AM Linden (eds), *Tort Tomorrow, a Tribute to John Fleming* (LBC Information Services 1998) 84

Stapleton J, 'Products Liability Reform—Real or Illusory?' (1986) 6 OJLS 392

——*Product Liability* (Butterworths 1994)

——'Tort, Insurance and Ideology' (1995) 58 MLR 820

——'Bugs in Anglo-American Products Liability' in D Fairgrieve (ed), *Product Liability in Comparative Perspective* (CUP 2005) 295

Starck B, *Essai d'une théorie générale de la responsabilité civile considérée en sa double fonction de garantie et de peine privée* (L Rodstein 1947)

——'Domaine et fondement de la responsabilité sans faute' RTD civ 1958.475

——Roland H, and Boyer L, *Obligations*, t. 1, *Responsabilité délictuelle* (5th edn, LITEC 1996)

Steele J, 'Private Law and the Environment: Nuisance in Context' (1995) 15 LS 236

——*Risks and Legal Theory* (Hart Publishing 2004)

——*Tort Law, Text, Cases, and Materials* (4th edn, OUP 2017)

——and Merkin R, 'Insurance Between Neighbours: Stannard v Gore and Common Law Liability for Fire' (2013) 25 JEL 305

Stevens R, 'A Servant of Two Masters' (2006) 122 LQR 201

——*Torts and Rights* (OUP 2007)

Stoppa A, 'Responsabilità del produttore' Dig disc priv (UTET 1998) XVII, 119

Street H, *Governmental Liability* (CUP 1953)

Sykes AO, 'Strict Liability versus Negligence in Indiana Harbor' (2007) 74 U Chi L Rev 1911

Taccini S, 'Il sistema della responsabilità civile dei genitori: tra profili di protezione e di garanzia' (2008) 1 DR 5

Teissier G, *La responsabilité de la puissance publique* (Chez Paul Dupont 1906, reprinted Editions La Mémoire du Droit 2009)

Terranova CG, 'Responsabilità da circolazione di veicoli' Dig disc priv (UTET 1998) XVII, 89

Terré F, *Pour une réforme du droit des contrats* (Dalloz 2009)

——*Pour une réforme du droit de la responsabilité* (Dalloz 2011)

——*Pour une réforme du régime général des obligations* (Dalloz 2013)

——Simler P, Lequette Y, and Chénedé F, *Droits civil, Les obligations* (12th edn, Dalloz 2018)

Testu FX and Moitry J-H, 'La responsabilité du fait des produits défectueux, Commentaire de la loi 98-389 du 19 mai 1998' Dalloz affaires (16 July 1998) Suppl to No 125, 5

Tofaris S, 'Rylands v Fletcher Restricted Further' (2013) 72 CLJ 11

——'Vicarious Liability and Non-Delegable Duty for Child Abuse in Foster Care: A Step too Far?' (2016) 79 MLR 884

Tomkins N, 'Civil Health and Safety Law after the Enterprise and Regulatory Reform Act 2013' [2013] JPIL 203

Torchia L, 'La responsabilità' in Sabino Cassese (ed), *Trattato di Diritto Amministrativo. Diritto amministrativo generale*, vol II (2nd edn, Giuffrè 2003) 1649

Traynor R, 'The Ways and Meanings of Defective Products and Strict Liability' (1965) 32 Tenn L Rev 363

Trimarchi P, *Rischio e responsabilità oggettiva* (Giuffrè 1961)

——'Transfers, Uncertainty and The Cost of Disruption' (2003) 23 International Review of Law and Economics 49

——*La Responsabilità Civile: Atti Illeciti, Rischio, Danno* (Giuffrè 2017)

BIBLIOGRAPHY 337

Tunc A, 'Foreword' in G Viney, *Le déclin de la responsabilité individuelle* (LGDJ 1965)
——'L'enfant et la balle' JCP 1966.I.1983
——*La sécurité routière: esquisse d'une loi sur les accidents de la circulation* (Dalloz 1966)
——'Rapport sur les choses dangereuses et la responsabilité civile en droit français' in Travaux de l'Association Henri-Capitant: Les choses dangereuses: journées néerlandaises (Economica 1967) 50
——'Les causes d'exonération de la responsabilité de plein droit de l'art. 1384, al. 1er du Code civil' D chron 1975.83
——'Responsabilité civile et dissuasion des comportements antisociaux' in *Aspects nouveaux de la pensée juridique: recueil d'études en hommage à Marc Ancel*, vol 1 (Pedone 1975) 407
——*La responsabilité civile* (2nd edn, Economica 1989)
——'L'insertion de la loi Badinter dans le droit commun de la responsabilité civile' in *Mélanges Roger O. Dalcq—Responsabilité et assurances* (Larcier 1994) 557
Ursin E, 'Judicial Creativity and Tort Law' (1981) 49 Geo Wash L Rev 229
Valaguzza S, 'Percorsi verso una "responsabilità oggettiva" della pubblica amministrazione' (2009) 1 Diritto processuale amministrativo 50
Valcke C, 'Comparative Law as Comparative Jurisprudence—The Comparability of Legal Systems' (2004) 52 AJCL 713
Vedel G and Delvolvé P, *Droit administratif*, vol 1 (12th edn, PUF 1992)
Venezian G, 'Danno e risarcimento fuori dei contratti' in *Opere giuridiche, vol. 1—Studi sulle obbligazioni* (Athenaeum 1919)
Ventrella W, 'Danno cagionato da animali: fondamento della responsabilità e individuazione dei soggetti responsabili' (1978) 4(1) GC 741
Vincent F, 'Responsabilité sans faute' JCl Admin, Fasc 824, 2015
Vincenti E, 'La dottrina in dialogo con la giurisprudenza: il pensiero di Pietro Trimarchi in taluni orientamenti della Cassazione civile' (2018) 4 RCP 1396
Viney G, *Le déclin de la responsabilité individuelle* (LGDJ 1965)
——'De la responsabilité personnelle à la répartition des risques' Arch phil dr 1977.5
——'L'indemnisation des victimes de dommages causés par le "fait d'une chose" après l'arrêt de la Cour de cassation' D chron 1982.201
——JCP 1997.II n.22848
——JCP 2000.I.241
——JCP 2002.I.124
——'La mise en place du système français de responsabilité des producteurs pour le défaut de sécurité de leurs produits' in *Mélanges offerts à Jean-Luc Aubert—Propos sur les obligations et quelque autres thèmes fondamentaux du droit* (Dalloz 2005) 329
——'Les trentes ans de la loi Badinter: bilan et perspectives. Propos introductifs' in *Les trentes ans de la loi Badinter—Bilan et perspectives*, RCA September 2015, dossier 12, 7
——*Introduction à la responsabilité. Traité de droit civil* (4th edn, LGDJ 2019)
——and Guégan-Lécuyer A, 'The Development of Traffic Liability in France' in W Ernst (ed), *The Development of Traffic Liability* (CUP 2010) 50
——Jourdain P, and Carval S, *Les conditions de la responsabilité. Traité de droit civil* (4th edn, LGDJ 2013)
——Jourdain P, and Carval S, *Les régimes spéciaux et l'assurance de responsabilité. Traité de droit civil* (4th edn, LGDJ 2017)
Visintini G, 'Immissioni e tutela dell'ambiente' (1976) RTDPC 689
——*Trattato breve della responsabilità civile—Fatti illeciti. Inadempimento. Danno risarcibile* (3rd edn, Cedam 2005)

338 BIBLIOGRAPHY

——*Fatti Illeciti* (Pacini Giuridica 2019)

Volpe G, 'Esercizio di attività pericolose, rischio d'impresa e controllo delle tecnologie' (1974) 4–5 GM 381

Wade HWR and Forsyth CF, *Administrative Law* (11th edn, OUP 2014)

Waline J, 'L'évolution de la responsabilité extracontractuelle des personnes publiques' EDCE 1994.459

Waline M, 'Cinquante ans de jurisprudence administrative' D chron 1950.21

Weinrib EJ, 'The Insurance Justification and Private Law' (1985) 14 J Legal Stud 681

——'Right and Advantage in Private Law' (1989) 10 Cardozo L Rev 1283

——'The Special Morality of Tort Law' (1989) 34 McGill LJ 403

——*The Idea of Private Law* (OUP 2013)

Weir T, *An Introduction to Tort Law* (2nd edn, OUP 2006)

Wester-Ouisse V, Taylor S, and Fairgrieve D, 'Risk and French Private Law' in M Dyson (ed), *Regulating Risk Through Private Law* (Intersentia 2018) 55

White GE, *Tort Law in America: An Intellectual History* (OUP 2003)

Whittaker S, 'The EEC Directive on Product Liability' (1985) 5 YEL 233

——'Privity of Contract and the Tort of Negligence: Future Directions' (1996) 16 OJLS 191

——*Liability for Products* (OUP 2005)

——'The Law of Obligations' in J Bell and others, *Principles of French Law* (2nd edn, OUP 2008) 294

——'The Development of Product Liability in England' in S Whittaker (ed), *The Development of Product Liability* (CUP 2010) 51

——'Contract Law and other Legal Categories' in H Beale (ed), *Chitty on Contracts*, vol 1 (34th edn, Sweet & Maxwell 2021) ch 3

Williams G, 'The Aims of the Law of Tort' (1951) 4 CLP 137

——'Liability for Independent Contractors' (1956) 14 CLJ 180

——'Vicarious Liability and the Master's Indemnity' (1957) 20 MLR 220

——'Vicarious Liability and the Master's Indemnity' (1957) 20 MLR 437

——'The Effect of Penal Legislation in the Law of Tort' (1960) 23 MLR 233

Winfield PH, *Province of the Law of Tort* (The University Press 1931)

Witt JF, *Torts: Cases, Principles, and Institutions* (2nd edn, CALI eLangdell Press 2016)

Witting C, 'Breach of the Non-Delegable Duty: Defending Limited Strict Liability in Tort' (2006) 29 UNSWLJ 33

——*Street on Torts* (16th edn, OUP 2021)

——'Modelling Organisational Vicarious Liability' (2019) 39(4) LS 1

Zito A, *Il danno da illegittimo esercizio della funzione amministrativa. Riflessioni sulla tutela dell'interesse legittimo* (Editoriale Scientifica 2003)

——'Il problema della colpa nella tutela risarcitoria degli interessi legittimi: spunti ricostruttivi' in *Studi in memoria di Franco Ledda* (Giappichelli 2004) 1381

Zweigert K and Kötz H, *An Introduction to Comparative Law* (Tony Weir tr, 3rd edn, OUP 1998)

Index

For the benefit of digital users, indexed terms that span two pages (e.g., 52–53) may, on occasion, appear on only one of those pages.

Abbagnano, Nicola 282, 285n.138
abnormality of risk
  and accident avoidance 89–90, 98–100,
    109, 282
  and administrative cost reduction 98–100
  comparisons among English, French, Italian,
    and US law 88–90, 98–100, 109–
    11, 116–17
  and contexts of liability 294
  criticisms 88n.95, 109–11, 273, 274–76
  definition 73
  English law 107–11, 116–17, 140, 235–36,
    238–39, 271–72, 273, 274–77, 309–10
  French law 78, 79–81, 116–17, 288–89
  and individual responsibility 108–9, 238–39,
    271–72, 273, 276–77, 282
  Italian law 88–90, 116–17, 227–29, 282, 304–5
  and 'law and economics', 89–90, 98–100
  and loss spreading 79–81, 98–100, 288–89
  and patterns of reasoning 295–96, 299–300
  US law 98–100, 116–17, 231–33
  and victim protection 79–81, 98–100, 109,
    227–29, 231–33, 235–36, 282
Abraham, Kenneth 124–25nn.30–31,
  242n.5, 243n.8
accident avoidance 119–53
  activity modification 119–20, 122, 130, 138–
    40, 143, 147–48
  background safety 119, 120, 122, 130–31,
    143, 147–48
  bilateral accidents 122–23, 130–31,
    132, 134–35
  cheapest cost avoider 131, 132, 134–36, 141–
    42, 200–2, 243–44n.11, 281–82
  comparisons among English, French, Italian,
    and US law 120, 129–30, 132–35,
    136–38, 143–44, 145, 147–48, 149,
    150, 151–53
  and contexts of liability 293–94
  criticisms 128–29, 137, 144, 309–10
  definition 119–20
  and individual responsibility 131, 132, 140,
    144, 151–53, 267–69, 271–72, 274–76,
    277, 281–82, 290–91, 310

  in 'law and economics', 67–69, 120–23, 129–
    35, 143–44, 299–300, 303, 305–7, 308,
    311, 312–13
  outside 'law and economics', 127–28, 135–36,
    152–53, 311
  market (or general) deterrence 121–22, 144,
    200–2, 204, 242n.5
  and patterns of reasoning 295–300
  rischio di impresa 85–87, 129–30, 132–34
  situational safety 119, 122, 130–31, 148
  unilateral accidents 122–23, 130–31,
    132, 134–35
actionability *per se* 6–7, 15n.11, 35n.179, 262–63
actual insurance coverage
  comparisons among English, French, Italian,
    and US law 185–86, 195–96, 205, 217–20
  criticisms 175–76, 185–86, 193–94, 195–
    96, 205
  definition 173
  English law 205, 213–14
  French law 176, 178
  Italian law 195–97
  US law 185–86, 193–94
  see also insurability; insurance spreading; loss
    spreading
administrative cost reduction 241–58
  definition 241–42
  comparisons among English, French, Italian,
    and US law 242, 246, 247–50, 252–53,
    254–55, 256–58
  and contexts of liability 293–94
  criticisms 245, 252–53, 255–57, 303, 309–10
  in 'law and economics', 98–100, 187–88, 242–
    48, 256–57, 297–98, 305–6, 311, 312–13
  outside 'law and economics', 242–46, 248–51,
    252–54, 256–57, 297–98
  and patterns of reasoning 296–97, 299–300
  uncertainty on the administrative costs of
    different liability regimes 243–45, 247–
    48, 256–57
  volume of litigation 179n.30, 196–97, 243–45,
    248–51, 252–54
administrative liability *see* public authorities,
  liability of

340 INDEX

agency 259–60, 264–65, 272–73, 274–76, 282–
    83, 284–85, 287, 288–90, 314–15
allocation of resources *see* resource allocation
allocative efficiency *see* resource allocation
Alpa, Guido 87n.84, 92n.118, 199nn.125–26,
    200–2, 221, 229n.40, 283n.128, 283n.131,
    305n.48
animals, liability for
  justifications
    English law 107–8, 107n.191, 109, 111–12,
      138–40, 152–53, 206–7, 216, 250–51,
      257–58, 271–72, 277–79
    French law 81–82, 115–16, 146n.145, 148,
      152–53, 223, 287
    Italian law 86n.77, 88n.93, 89n.96, 90–93,
      115–16, 130nn.55–56, 132–34, 135n.95,
      151–52, 196–97, 202n.140, 304–5
    US law 96–98, 100–2, 122–26, 151–
      52, 263–64
  substantive law
    English law 17–18
    French law 40
    Italian law 53–54
    US law 29–30
arguments *see* justifications for strict liability
assurance oblige see actual insurance coverage
Atiyah, Patrick 142, 144, 168–69, 207–9
autonomy 71n.7, 242n.5, 259–60, 263–64, 276,
    286, 290–91, 311–12, 313
Aynès, Laurent 145–46, 147n.153, 147n.156,
    157n.9, 176n.15

Bacache-Gibeili, Mireille 145n.143, 289–90
Baffi, Enrico 89n.102, 131n.64, 133n.77,
    133n.79, 202n.142, 247–48
Bagshaw, Roderick 106–7, 114n.237, 139n.113,
    141n.125, 168–69, 206–7, 215n.205,
    297n.13
Baty, Thomas 167
Bell, John 106n.189, 114n.236, 169n.75, 181–
    82n.40, 210–12, 237–38, 272–73, 277
Bessone, Mario 137n.102, 201n.133, 227n.32,
    228n.35, 283n.128, 283n.131
Bianca, CM 93n.122, 226–27
Borghetti, Jean-Sébastien 76n.23, 79nn.39–40,
    80n.43, 80n.46, 83nn.63–64, 155n.2,
    156n.6, 157n.10, 176n.9, 177n.20,
    178n.27, 179, 179n.34, 222, 223–24n.18,
    224–25n.23, 225, 229n.37, 254n.57
Bramwell, Baron 143–44, 210n.177, 214–16
Brodie, Douglas 104–5, 112n.224, 112n.229,
    114n.236, 139–40n.114, 297–98n.14
Brun, Philippe 78n.33, 83n.63, 145n.143,
    146n.145, 288–89

burden–benefit proportionality *see*
    proportionality of burdens and benefits

Calabresi, Guido 68n.4, 100–1n.158, 121–22,
    123n.25, 124nn.27–28, 126–27, 129–30,
    131, 133nn.75–76, 134–35, 143–44,
    155, 159n.23, 163–65, 173, 185–86,
    187–88, 193–94, 198–99, 200–2, 204, 209,
    233n.59, 242n.4, 243–44n.11, 248, 268–
    69, 281–82, 300n.27, 314–15
Cane, Peter 103n.174, 103–4n.176, 105n.186,
    107n.192, 107n.194, 109–11, 111n.221,
    112n.226, 112n.229, 140, 142n.133, 144,
    168–69, 213–14, 215n.204, 215n.206, 221,
    238–39, 238nn.78–79, 250n.35, 252–53,
    260n.4, 272n.68, 274–79, 299n.20
Carbonnier, Jean 81–82, 83n.64, 149–50
Castronovo, Carlo 86n.80, 88n.95, 93n.122,
    129n.53, 131, 132, 134–35, 200–2,
    248n.25, 281–82, 283n.131, 285n.138
causation 67–69
  and individual responsibility 261
  theories of pure 67–69
    criticisms 68n.3
Chapus, René 76n.18, 81n.52, 82nn.57–58,
    83n.64, 182n.41, 182n.45
choice 132, 259–60, 263–65, 267–68, 281–82,
    284–85, 290–91, 311–12
Citron, Danielle 124n.28, 268–69
civil recourse, theory of 266–69
Coleman, Jules 98n.141, 164n.49, 233n.57,
    261n.11, 264–65, 267–69
Comandé, Giovanni 137n.103, 204n.148
commitment(s) in legal reasoning 1–2, 109, 120,
    301–13, 314–15
  accident avoidance 135, 305–6, 307, 308,
    310, 311
  individual responsibility 213–14, 233–34,
    309–10, 311–13
  loss spreading 156–57, 301–4, 306–7, 310–11
  minimization of the costs of accidents 120,
    123–26, 151–52, 197–98, 233–34, 304,
    305–6, 307, 310, 311, 312–13
  social solidarity 156–57, 197–98, 255, 288–89,
    301–5, 306–8, 310–11
  victim protection 156–57, 222–23, 225,
    233–35, 239, 255, 301–5, 306–8, 310–
    11, 312–13
compensation ideology 222–23, 239–40, 304, *see
    also* victim protection
compensation *see* victim protection
Comporti, Marco 84n.67, 85nn.69–70, 86n.80,
    88–89, 93n.122, 135–36, 159n.21,
    226n.27, 227n.32

INDEX 341

compulsory insurance 148, 158–59, 160–
    62, 176, 177n.18, 181, 195–96n.97,
    196–97, 205, 206, 210n.176, 214n.201,
    228n.35, 248–50
context-dependence of justifications 69, 293–95
Cooter, Robert 89n.101, 122–23, 130n.60,
    133n.75, 202n.142, 233n.59, 247–48
corrective justice 140, 208n.166, 210n.176,
    213–14, 213n.194, 216, 217–18, 219–20,
    237–39, 245, 260–61, 262–66, 267–70,
    271, 278n.105, 279
cost internalization *see* internalization of costs
Craig, Paul 210–12
creation of risk *see* risk creation
cultures of tort 1–2, 10–11, 301–16

dangerous activities/things, liability for
    justifications
        English law 103n.175, 107–11, 116–17,
            138–40, 152–53, 206–7, 235–36, 251n.41,
            252–53, 271–72, 277–79, see also *Rylands
            v Fletcher*
        French law 78n.35, 79–81, 116–17,
            147n.154
        Italian law 86n.77, 86n.81, 87n.84, 88–91,
            92–93nn.116–19, 93n.122, 116–17, 130–
            31, 132–35, 151–52, 160, 197n.109, 200,
            200n.127, 228nn.35–36, 229n.39, 248n.25
        US law 93–94, 94–95n.129, 96–102,
            116–17, 122–26, 151–52, 162–63, 170–
            71, 185–86, 188–90, 191–93, 231–33,
            233n.55, 242–43, 261, 262–68, 270–
            71, 274
    substantive law
        English law 14–16, 17–18, 20–21, 61, see
            also *Rylands v Fletcher*
        French law 39–40, 44n.240, 47–49, 61
        Italian law 51–53
        US law 27–30, 31, 62–63
dangerousness *see* dangerous activities/things,
    liability for
deeds of things *see* things in one's keeping,
    liability for
deep-pockets justification 155–71
    and accident avoidance 163
    comparisons among English, French, Italian,
        and US law 158, 159, 162, 163, 164–65,
        166, 168, 169–71
    and contexts of liability 294
    criticisms 157–58, 160, 161–62, 164–65, 168–
        70, 301–2, 311–12
    crypto-justification 166
    definition 155
    in 'law and economics', 155, 159, 163–65, 168

and loss spreading 155, 156–58, 160, 161–62,
    164–65, 169–70, 214–16
moral basis 155
and patterns of reasoning 296–97, 298–
    99, 300–1
social solidarity 156–58, 288–89, 314–15
and victim protection 156–58, 159, 163, 168,
    191–92, 221, 224–25, 227–29, 231–33,
    235–36, 310–11, 312–13
Delvolvé, Pierre 82n.59, 83n.64, 181–82n.40,
    182n.44, 183n.49, 224–25n.23
deterrence 127–28, 137, 140, 141–42, 145,
    163, 168n.69, 213–14, 248n.25, 253–
    54, 289–90
    market (or general) deterrence 121–22, 144,
        200–2, 204, 242n.5
    specific deterrence 122n.9, 200–2
    see also accident avoidance
Dimattia Marina 161n.30, 197n.106,
    228n.35, 248–50
distinction between key, secondary, and make-
    weight justifications 70–71, *see also*
    justifications for strict liability
distribution of losses *see* loss spreading
distributive justice, issues of 130–31, 151–52,
    160, 161–62, 163–65, 171, 198, 200–3,
    208n.166, 210n.176, 217–20, 271–72n.65
Duni, Giovanni 85n.69, 203n.145
duty 259–61, 264–65, 267–68, 270, 284–85,
    289–91, 311–12
Dyson, Matthew 73n.2, 105n.184, 105n.187,
    107n.194, 108–9, 112n.228, 139n.113

égalité devant les charges publiques see equality
    before public burdens
employers' vicarious liability *see* vicarious
    liability of employers (or defendants akin
    to employers), justifications for
enterprise liability 94–96, 127–29, 268–69, 273
    reasons for not considering it a justification of
        strict liability 67–69
enterprise spreading
    comparisons among English, French,
        Italian, and US law 184, 185, 206, 217–
        18, 219–20
    and contexts of liability 293–94
    definition 174
    English law 206–9, 219–20
    French law 184, 216–17
    Italian law 197–98, 199–200
    and proportionality of burdens and
        benefits 174–75
    US law 185, 186, 217–18, 230
    see also loss spreading

342 INDEX

Epstein, Richard 68n.3, 101n.161, 102n.171, 193–94, 233n.58, 242–43nn.6–7, 261, 263, 267–69, 313

equality before public burdens 47–49, 74–76, 78, 81n.53, 83n.63, 181–82, 183n.49, 210–12, 216–18

and social solidarity 181–82, 183, 216–17

and taxation spreading 183

see also proportionality of burdens and benefits

Esmein, Paul 156

Fairgrieve, Duncan 78n.35, 81n.53, 183n.47

fairness, reasons for not considering it a justification of strict liability 67–69

'family purpose' doctrine in the United States 31–32, 37, 62–63, 232n.52

first-party insurance 173

Fleming, John 108–9, 112n.229, 139–40n.114, 167n.65, 206n.158, 208n.167, 229n.40, 279n.110

Fletcher, George 73nn.3–4, 80n.48, 96–98, 106–7, 115–16, 193n.87, 263–64, 268–69, 300n.28

Forchielli, Paolo 158–59, 199n.125

Forsyth, Christopher 211n.181

Franzoni, Massimo 91nn.109–10, 91n.112, 92–93nn.118–19, 132n.74, 159n.22, 161nn.35–36, 162n.38, 199n.125, 200n.129, 228n.35, 284n.136

Friendly, Henry Jacob 269–70, 280n.114

Gardner, John 140, 272–73

Geistfeld, Mark 94–95n.129, 96n.136, 97n.138, 98–99n.147, 124n.28, 263–64, 267–68

Ghestin, Jacques 83–84n.65, 178n.26, 178n.27, 184n.50

Giliker, Paula 105n.184, 106n.189, 141n.125, 168n.68, 169–70, 215n.207, 235–36n.66, 236n.68, 238n.79, 239n.86, 278n.105

Gilli, Jean-Paul 82n.60, 182n.44, 224–25n.23

goals

as justifications for strict liability 69–70, 295–316

and means in the reasoning on strict liability 69–70, 298–99, 300–1

and values in strict liability 301–16

Goldberg, John 97n.138, 98n.141, 98–99n.147, 101n.162, 221n.1, 245n.15, 266–69

Goudkamp, James 105n.186, 105–6nn.188–89, 107n.194, 109–11, 112n.226, 112nn.228–29, 138n.104, 141n.126, 142n.133, 144n.139, 169n.74, 213n.194, 215n.205, 238n.85, 250n.36, 251n.41, 251n.43, 252–53, 279, 299n.20

Grare, Clothilde 82–83n.61, 83–84n.65, 179n.34

Gray, Anthony 110n.218, 141n.126, 169n.75, 215n.204

Gray, Oscar 94–95n.129, 125n.31, 128n.47, 190n.75, 232n.50, 233n.55, 296–97n.11

Griffey, Mario 91n.111, 92–93n.119, 227n.32, 282n.123, 299n.21, 305n.48

Häcker, Birke 215n.206

Hamson, Charles 211n.181

harm-based strict liability 262–63, 267–68

Harper, Fowler 94–95n.129, 98–100, 125n.31, 128n.47, 190n.75, 231n.48, 232n.50, 233n.55, 296–97n.11

Henderson, James 100n.156, 102n.166, 242–43n.6, 245n.14

Hirschoff, Jon 121n.3, 124n.28, 185n.54, 187n.65

Holmes, Oliver Wendell 246n.20

Honoré, Tony 108–9, 112n.225, 112n.229, 140, 205, 206, 209–10, 210n.180, 213n.194, 238–39, 271–79, 280n.114, 300n.28

individual responsibility 259–92

and accident avoidance 132, 140, 274–76, 277, 281–82

comparisons among English, French, Italian, and US law 271, 276–77, 279, 280, 281, 282, 285, 286, 289, 290–92

and contexts of liability 293–94

contrast between civil law and common law 290–92

and corrective justice 260–61, 262–66, 267–70, 271, 278n.105, 279

criticisms 270–71, 282–86, 287–89

definition 259–60

and fault 267–68, 277–79, 282–86, 287, 289–90

and patterns of reasoning 295–97, 299–300

and proportionality of burdens and benefits 262–63, 272, 273n.72, 277

and risk 108–9, 111–12, 114, 262–64, 265–66, 271–72, 273–77, 279, 280, 282, 288–89, 291–92, 299–300, 309–10, 311–12

and victim protection 274–76, 277

instrumentalism 144, 271, 284–85, 289–90, 303, 304, 307–8, 310, 311–13, 315

insurability

comparisons among English, French, Italian, and US law 186, 194–95, 196–98, 206, 209, 217–18, 219–20

criticisms 175–76, 193–94, 200–2, 205, 213–16

definition 173

English law 206–9, 219–20

French law 176–78, 184

Italian law 161–62, 196–98
US law 186, 217–18
see also actual insurance coverage; insurance
 spreading; loss spreading
insurance market 179, 194–95, 200–2, 214–16,
 218–19, 310–11
insurance spreading 174
 and contexts of liability 293–94
 criticisms 193–94, 200–2, 213–16, 214n.196
 definition 173
 English law 206, 214n.196, 214n.201
 French law 175, 176–81, 184, 216–17, 302–3
 and individual responsibility 272
 Italian law 195–97, 199–200
 US law 185
 see also actual insurance coverage; insurability;
  loss spreading
internalization of costs 121–22, 143–44, 191–92,
 199–200, 214–16
 reasons for not considering it a justification of
  strict liability 67–69
interpersonal justice 115–16, 128–29, 144, 150,
 152–53, 164–65, 185–86, 193–94, 216–17,
 218–19, 230, 233–34, 239–40, 245, 246,
 252–53, 256–58, 260–61, 271, 285, 289,
 308, 310–11, 312–13

James, Fleming Jr 94–95n.129, 98–100,
 102n.172, 125n.31, 128n.47, 186–88,
 188–89n.70, 190n.75, 201n.134, 230n.44,
 231n.46, 231n.48, 232n.50, 233n.55,
 296–97n.11
Jolowicz, John Anthony 141n.123, 142, 169–70,
 206–7, 210n.177, 212–13, 234–35n.61,
 235–36n.66, 236n.70, 250–52
Josserand, Louis 74–76, 77, 78, 80n.46, 83n.63,
 83n.64, 84–85, 96, 106, 115, 156n.6, 176,
 181n.39, 224–25, 288–89, 299n.21, 301–2
Jourdain, Patrice 78, 79n.37, 81–82, 82–83n.61,
 83–84, 87n.88, 146nn.145–46, 146n.149,
 147n.153, 147n.156, 148–49, 148n.159,
 157–58, 176–78, 176nn.15–16, 178n.26,
 179n.34, 181n.39, 224n.19, 224–25n.23,
 253–54, 297n.13, 297–98n.14
justifications for strict liability
 combinations
  definition 69
  problems of clarity relating to 299–301
  usage of 298–99
 context-dependence 69, 293–95
 juxtapositions
  definition 69
  problems of clarity relating to 297–98
  usage of 296–97
 key, definition of 70–71

make-weight, definition of 70–71
nature, interpretive and normative 71
secondary, definition of 70–71
stand-alone
 definition 69
 usage of 295–96
see also commitment(s) in legal reasoning;
 means; morality; goals; patterns of
 reasoning in strict liability; significance
 of justifications for strict liability; strict
 liability; values in strict liability

Kaplow, Louis 68n.4, 123n.25, 127n.39, 163–65,
 187–88, 193–94, 230n.41, 242n.4, 244n.12
Keating, Gregory 94–96, 98n.141, 101n.161,
 101n.164, 102n.166, 102n.171, 124–
 25n.30, 127–29, 188–90, 245–46, 260n.2,
 262–63, 267–69, 277n.99, 312n.78
Keeton, Robert 93–94, 193–94, 233n.58, 262n.17
key justification *see* justifications for strict
 liability
King, Joseph Jr 100–1n.158, 124n.28, 127n.43,
 241n.1, 242n.5, 244n.12, 245–46n.19,
 296–97n.11, 297–98n.14
Klevorick, Alvin 121n.3, 243–44n.11

Lambert-Faivre, Yvonne 77n.31, 175n.6,
 177n.18, 288n.151
Landes, William 68n.4, 122n.10, 122n.12,
 122n.14, 164–65, 244n.12
liability insurance 78–79, 83–84, 145–46, 148,
 157–58, 161–62, 173–74, 175–79, 180–81,
 184, 186, 194–97, 200–2, 206–9, 288–89
liberal egalitarianism 263–64, 267–68
licensing-based liability 266–67
loss insurance *see* first-party insurance
loss spreading 173–220
 comparisons among English, French, Italian,
  and US law 185–86, 187–91, 194–95,
  196–98, 202–6, 209, 216–20
 and contexts of liability 293–94
 criticisms 175–76, 193–94, 200–2, 205, 213–
  16, 217–18, 219–20, 304–5, 308, 311–12
 definition 173–75
 and individual responsibility 262–63, 268–69,
  272, 276–77
 in 'law and economics', 187–88, 197–99, 200–
  3, 204, 209, 217–19, 305–6, 311
 and patterns of reasoning 295–97, 299–300
 and resource allocation 193
 and *rischio di impresa* 198–200, 204, 218–19
 and social solidarity 175–76, 178–79, 181,
  183–85, 187–88, 190–91, 197–98, 199,
  200, 204, 216–17, 218–19, 226, 301–
  3, 304–5

344 INDEX

loss spreading (*cont.*)
and victim protection 175–76, 186–87, 197–98, 199, 212–13, 216–20, 221, 224–25, 226, 227–29, 230–33, 234–36, 239–40, 301–3, 304–5, 310–11, 312–13
see also actual insurance coverage; enterprise spreading; insurability; insurance spreading; proportionality of burdens and benefits; taxation spreading

Majello, Ugo 158–59
make-weight justification *see* justifications for strict liability
Malaurie, Philippe 145–46, 147n.153, 147n.156, 157n.9, 176n.15
Marini, Giovanni 176n.13, 198n.111, 200–2
Mattei, Ugo 91n.110, 159n.22, 247–48
McBride, Nicholas 106–7, 114n.237, 139n.113, 141n.125, 168–69, 206–7, 213–14, 215n.205, 278–79nn.105–6, 297n.13
means
and goals in the reasoning on strict liability 69–70, 298–99, 300–1
as justifications for strict liability 69–70, 109, 126–28, 129, 132, 151–52, 159, 163–64, 168, 170–71, 178–80, 184n.51, 186, 187–88, 192, 193, 198, 212–13, 221, 224–25, 227–29, 231–33, 235–36, 245–46, 295–316
see also justifications for strict liability
Merkin, Rob 103–4n.176, 205n.150, 207n.159, 214n.201
Messineo, Francesco 91n.112, 92–93n.119, 158–59, 297n.12
minimization of the costs of accidents 67–70, 98–100, 117, 120–22, 126–27, 132–34, 164–65, 168, 187–88, 192, 194–95, 198–99, 216, 217–18, 233–34, 245–46, 247–48, 252–53, 255, 299, 311–14, *see also* social welfare
Monateri, Pier Giuseppe 87n.83, 89n.101, 91n.109, 93n.122, 130–31, 132–34, 196–97n.104, 199n.125, 228n.35, 229n.40, 247–48, 284n.135, 296–97n.11
morality
and individual responsibility 115–16, 117, 259–61, 265–66, 269–70, 272–76, 277–79, 282–85, 287, 289–90, 315
and social solidarity 178, 183, 216–17, 287–88, 289–90
Morgan, Jonathan 139–40n.114, 168n.69, 169n.74, 213–14, 215n.205, 238n.78, 278–79n.106
Morgan, Phillip 106n.189, 114n.237
Morris, Clarence 246n.20

Motzo, Giovanni 85n.69
Murphy, John 103n.175, 108n.199, 111n.221, 112n.225, 112n.229, 138n.105, 141n.125, 166–67, 169n.75, 207nn.159–60, 298n.18, 300n.29

Nardi, Dario 131n.64, 133n.77, 202n.142, 247–48
Neely, Richard 165
negligence *per se* 27n.111
Nocco, Luca 137n.103, 204n.148
Nolan, Donal 107n.192, 108n.196, 109–11, 141n.126, 144n.142, 213–14, 215n.205, 237n.77, 250n.36, 251n.43, 278–79n.106
Nolan, Virginia 94–95n.129, 97n.138, 101–2n.165, 124n.28, 186n.58, 194n.91, 230n.43, 232n.52
non-delegable duty in English law, breach of
justifications 103–4, 108–11, 139–40n.114, 167, 235–36n.66, 276
substantive law 20–21
nonreciprocal risk *see* nonreciprocity of risk
nonreciprocity of risk 114–15
comparisons among English, French, Italian, and US law 115–16
and contexts of liability 294
criticisms 96–98, 106–7
definition 73
English law 103, 106–7
French law 74
and individual responsibility 263–64
Italian law 84
and liberal egalitarianism 263–64
and patterns of reasoning 299–300
US law 93, 94–98
norms of individual responsibility *see* individual responsibility
nuisance, liability for 63
justifications
English law 107–8, 111–12, 138–40, 143–44, 152–53, 210–12, 214–16
French law 75n.13, 80n.46, 82–83, 83n.64, 181–82n.40
Italian law 132–34, 228n.35
US law 96–98, 100–2, 261n.10, 262–63, 266–67
substantive law
English law 14–15, 17–18, 24–26, 61–62
French law 44–45
Italian law 55
US law 32–33

O'Connell, Jeffrey 233n.58
Ollier, Pierre-Dominique 146n.149, 156–57

outcome responsibility
and abnormality of risk 108–9, 238–39, 271–72, 276–77
and accident avoidance 140
avoidability-based conception of 265–66
criticisms 274–76
and loss spreading 272–73, 276–77
and risk–profit 238–39, 273–74, 276–77
and unilateral imposition of risk 265–66
Owen, David 164n.50, 194n.90, 233n.58, 268n.55

Pardolesi, Paolo 132–34, 161n.30, 197n.106, 228n.35, 229n.40, 248–50
Pardolesi, Roberto 133n.75, 133n.80, 202n.139, 247–48
patterns of reasoning in strict liability 69–70, 71, 295–301, *see also* justifications for strict liability; means; goals
Patti, Salvatore 137n.101, 159n.20, 161n.29, 161n.31, 196–97nn.104–5, 197n.107, 229, 249n.30
Perry, Stephen 68n.3, 73n.1, 95n.133, 98n.141, 100–1n.158, 140n.119, 261n.11, 264–66, 267–69, 300n.28, 312n.78
Planiol, Marcel 76nn.20–21, 82–83n.61, 83n.64, 287–88n.148
Ponzanelli, Giulio 200–2, 228n.35, 248n.25, 285n.140
Posner, Richard 68n.4, 98–100, 98n.141, 122, 123n.25, 124nn.27–28, 127n.39, 129–30, 144, 164–65, 173n.1, 193–94, 233n.59, 242n.4, 244n.12, 261n.11
prevention of accidents *see* accident avoidance
products, liability for
justifications
English law 103–4, 105–7, 111–12, 138–40, 141–42, 143–44, 166–67, 168n.71, 206–7, 209–10, 214–16, 236, 237–39, 250–51, 251n.43, 271–72, 274, 278n.105
French law 77–78, 79–81, 82–83, 83n.64, 145–46, 147, 157–58, 178–79, 184, 224n.19
Italian law 86n.77, 86n.79, 87n.84, 90–91, 92n.116, 92–93n.119, 130–31, 132–34, 137, 160, 196–98, 199, 200, 227–29, 247–48
US law 93–94, 96–98, 100–2, 122–26, 127–28, 186–87, 187n.62, 188–90, 191–92, 193–94, 231–33, 233n.55, 233n.58, 242–43, 244n.12, 262–63, 264–65, 266–68
substantive law
English law 21–24, 26
French law 43–44, 45
Italian law 56

US law 33–34, 37
proportionality of burdens and benefits
comparisons among English, French, Italian, and US law 188–90, 203–4, 209–12, 217–18
and contexts of liability 293–94
definition 174–75
English law 209–12, 219–20
French law, as equality before public burdens 74–76, 79–81, 175, 181–82, 183–84, 216–17
and individual responsibility 262–63, 268–69, 272, 277
Italian law 203–4, 218–19
and social solidarity 181–84
US law 188–91, 192, 217–18
see also loss spreading
Prosser, William 102n.167, 102n.171, 124–25n.30, 163n.42, 165n.55, 243n.7
protection of victims *see* victim protection
public authorities, liability of
justifications
English law 209–12, 216, 219–20, 237–38, 307–8
French law 74–76, 78, 79–82, 83n.64, 116–17, 175, 181–84, 216–17, 222–23, 224n.21, 288–89, 302–3
Italian law 85n.69, 90n.107, 91n.109, 93n.122, 132–34, 136n.100, 137, 159, 203–4, 218–19, 227–29, 304–5
US law 98–99n.147, 123–26, 188–91, 217–18, 231–33, 234, 243n.8, 310–11
substantive law
English law 24–26
French law 46–49
Italian law 57–60
US law 34–37
punishment 259–60, 277, 289–90n.159

Rabin, Robert 125n.34, 194n.89
Radé, Cristophe 145–46, 147–48
reasons *see* justifications for strict liability
reciprocity of risk *see* nonreciprocity of risk
relational justice *see* interpersonal justice
resource allocation 85n.69, 107n.191, 121–22, 139n.113, 193, 200–2, 207n.164, 231n.48, 248n.25, 269n.59
see also minimization of the costs of accidents; social welfare; wealth maximisation
respondeat superior see vicarious liability of employers (or defendants akin to employers), justifications for
responsibility *see* individual responsibility
Rétif, Samuel 148n.159, 149–50
richesse oblige see deep-pockets justification

346 INDEX

right-based strict liability 262–63
rischio di impresa 132–34, 134n.82, 134n.89,
    198–200, 204, 218–19, 227n.34,
    300n.29, 304–5
risk 73–117
    see also abnormality of risk; nonreciprocity of
        risk; risk–benefit; risk creation; risk–profit
risk-based justifications of strict liability,
        meaning of 73–74
    see also abnormality of risk; nonreciprocity
        of risk; risk–benefit; risk creation;
        risk–profit
risk–benefit
    comparisons among English, French, Italian,
        and US law 90–93, 100–3, 111–12,
        114, 117
    and contexts of liability 294
    criticisms 76, 86–87, 91–93, 100–2, 112–13,
        114, 309–10
    definition 73–74
    English law 103–6, 111–13, 114, 238–
        39, 309–10
    French law 74–76, 81–82, 83–84, 180, 288–89
    Italian law 90–93, 196–97, 304–5
    and patterns of reasoning 295–96, 299–300
    US law 93, 96, 100–3, 231–33, 262–63, 268–
        69, 311–12
risk creation
    comparisons among English, French, Italian,
        and US law 84–85, 87–88, 96, 106, 115
    and contexts of liability 294
    criticisms 76, 84–85, 86–87, 94–96, 105–
        6, 309–10
    definition 73
    English law 103–6, 112–13, 309–10
    French law 74–76, 77–79, 81–82, 180, 288–
        89, 301–2
    Italian law 84–88, 304–5
    and patterns of reasoning 295–96, 297–98
    US law 93–98
risk–profit
    comparisons among English, French, Italian,
        and US law 90–93, 100–3, 111–12,
        114, 117
    and contexts of liability 294
    criticisms 76, 86–87, 91–93, 100–2, 112–
        13, 309–10
    definition 73–74
    English law 105–6, 111–13, 114, 166–67, 238–
        39, 273–77, 279, 309–10
    French law 74–76, 81–84, 180, 288–89
    Italian law 90–93, 135–36, 282
    and patterns of reasoning 295–96, 297–98,
        299–301, 314–15

US law 93, 96–98, 100–3, 231–33, 311–12
Rodière, René 156–57, 224n.22
Rodotà, Stefano 195n.95, 198n.112, 198nn.114–
    16, 226nn.27–28, 284–85
Roppo, Enzo 91n.113, 92–93n.119, 135–36,
    228n.35, 297n.13
ruinous buildings, liability for
    justifications
        French law 223
        Italian law 88n.93, 90–91, 132–34, 159,
            170–71, 202n.140, 227n.32, 247–48,
            249n.31
    substantive law
        French law 40
        Italian law 54
Russo, Chantal 148n.158, 179n.34
Rylands v Fletcher
    justifications 103–4, 107–8, 109–12, 116–
        17, 138–40, 141–42, 143–44, 152–53,
        162–63, 167n.59, 206–7, 210n.179,
        211n.181, 214–16, 235–36, 265n.34, 266–
        67n.46, 277–79
    substantive law 14–16, 17–18, 24–26
    see also dangerous activities/things,
        liability for

Saleilles, Raymond 74–76, 77, 78, 84–85,
    96, 106, 115, 156n.6, 224–25, 288–89,
    299n.21, 301–2, 314–15
Salmond, John 138–40, 237n.77, 277–79
Salvi, Cesare 85, 86n.80, 87n.84, 92–93nn.118–
    19, 136n.100, 195n.96, 199n.125, 228n.35,
    283n.125, 283n.127, 284n.137, 285
Savatier, René 81–82, 176, 177n.23, 180–81,
    287–88n.148
Scarpelli, Uberto 285n.138
Schamps, Geneviève 80n.46, 299n.24
Schuck, Peter 94–95n.129, 125–26nn.35–36,
    190n.77, 232n.53, 243n.8
Schwartz, Gary 98–99n.147, 125n.31, 127–28,
    128n.50, 163, 194n.90, 243n.8, 245–
    46n.19, 268–69
secondary justification *see* justifications for strict
    liability
Sella, Mauro 87n.83, 132–34, 199n.125
Shavell, Steven 68n.4, 98–100, 122–23,
    123n.25, 127n.39, 129–30, 163–65, 187–
    88, 193–94, 230n.41, 241n.2, 242n.4,
    244nn.12–13
Shugerman, Jed 95n.132, 101–2n.165, 162–63,
    269–70n.60
Sica, Salvatore 88–89
significance of justifications for strict
    liability 70–71, 314, *see also* distinction

INDEX 347

between key, secondary, and make-
weight justifications
Slavny, Adam 107n.192, 112n.226, 140
Smith, Young B 94–95n.129, 100–1n.158,
165n.55
social solidarity 173, 216, 314–15, 316
English law 307–8
French law 74–76, 83–84, 89–90, 116–17,
156, 175–76, 178–79, 181, 183–85,
190–91, 216–17, 222, 255–56, 288–89,
301–4, 313
Italian law 89n.98, 90n.107, 195, 197–98,
199–200, 203–4, 203n.145, 218–19, 226,
227–29, 284–86, 304–5, 306–7
and 'law and economics', 150, 152–53, 184,
197–98, 199, 200, 255, 303–4
morality of 287–88, 289–90, 303
and risk 74–76, 83–84, 89–90, 90n.107, 288–
89, 291–92, 301–5, 309–10
US law 187–88, 310–11
and victim protection 74–76, 83–84, 89–90,
175–76, 178–79, 181, 198, 222, 226,
227–29, 255–56, 288–89, 301–5, 306–7,
309–11, 313
see also commitment(s) in legal reasoning;
deep-pockets justification; equality
before public burdens; loss spreading;
socialization of losses; victim protection
socialization of losses 83–84, 156–58, 160, 175–
76, 212–13, 216–17, 288–89, 302–3, *see
also* social solidarity
social welfare 67–69, 89–90, 126–27, 130,
132–34, 136–37, 151–52, 164n.47, 166,
198–99, 227–29, 243–45, 247–50, 299,
303, 305–6, 313–15
see also minimization of the costs of
accidents; resource allocation; wealth
maximization
Spencer, John 111n.221, 250–51, 251n.43,
278n.102
spreading of losses *see* loss spreading
Stanton, Keith 109–11
Stapleton, Jane 105n.188, 110n.218, 112nn.225–
26, 112n.229, 114n.235, 140, 141–42,
168n.71, 213–16, 237–39, 261n.11,
273–77, 278–79n.106, 279, 299n.20,
300n.28, 314–15
Starck, Boris 76n.21, 76n.23, 77n.32, 181n.39,
223n.16, 223–24n.18, 289–90n.159
statutory duty in English law, breach of
justifications for strict liability 111–12, 140,
152–53, 206–7, 209, 236, 237, 250–
51, 257–58
substantive law 15–16, 20–21, 24–26

Steel, Sandy 73n.2, 105n.184, 105n.187,
107n.194, 108–9, 112n.228, 139n.113
Steele, Jenny 73n.1, 103–4n.176, 104–5,
107n.194, 114n.236, 139–40n.114, 167,
169–70, 207–9, 207n.159, 213n.192,
234–35n.61, 235–36n.66, 236nn.68–69,
250–51, 251n.43
Stevens, Robert 105n.185, 106n.189, 107n.191,
111n.221, 112n.228, 114n.237, 142–43,
168–69, 215nn.204–5, 278–79nn.105–
6, 297–98
Stoffel-Munck, Philippe 145–46, 147n.153,
147n.156, 157n.9, 176n.15
Street, Harry 211n.181
strict liability
choice of justifications 313
context-dependence of
justifications 69, 293–95
patterns of reasoning 295–301, 313–14
significance of justifications 70–71, 314
substantive law
comparisons among English, French,
Italian, and US law 61–63
English law 13–26
French law 37–49
Italian law 49–60
US law 26–37
values and goals 301–13, 314–15

taxation spreading
comparisons among English, French, Italian,
and US law 190–91, 203–4, 212
and contexts of liability 293–94
criticisms 203–4, 212
definition 174
English law 212
French law 181–82, 183, 216–17
Italian law 203–4, 218–19
US law 190–91, 217–18
see also loss spreading
things in one's keeping, liability for
justifications
French law 74–76, 77, 79–82, 115–16,
145–46, 147n.153, 148–50, 152–53, 176,
177n.18, 180–81, 223, 224–25
Italian law 86n.77, 88n.93, 90–91, 92–
93n.119, 93n.122, 115–16, 130nn.55–56,
131n.64, 132–35, 136n.100, 160n.24,
196–97, 200, 202n.140, 228nn.35–36,
229, 247–48
substantive law
French law 39–40, 49, 61
Italian law 52–53, 57–58, 60
third-party insurance *see* liability insurance

348 INDEX

Tomkins, Nigel 140n.115, 207n.161, 209
traffic accidents, liability for
 justifications
  English law 205, 210n.176, 234–35n.61,
   235–36, 250–51, 251n.43
  French law 75n.13, 77–78, 78n.33, 79–
   81, 79n.37, 100–2, 116–17, 145–46,
   147n.153, 148n.159, 178–79, 180–81,
   222–23, 224n.19, 224–25n.23, 253–54,
   255n.60, 257–58
  Italian law 85, 87n.84, 88–89, 90–91,
   92nn.116–17, 92–93n.119, 100–2,
   130n.56, 158–59, 160–61, 196–97,
   202n.140, 226–27, 227n.32, 228n.35
  US law 123–26, 230, 231–33, see also
   'family purpose' doctrine in the
   United States
 substantive law
  English law 19–20, 26, 61–62
  French law 44–45, 49, 61
  Italian law 52, 60, 62
  US law 31–32, 37, 62–63
  see also 'family purpose' doctrine in the
   United States
Traynor, Roger 123–26, 186–87, 231–32n.49
Trimarchi, Pietro 68n.3, 84n.67, 85–88, 90n.104,
 93n.122, 94–96, 129–31, 132–34,
 134n.82, 135n.94, 143–44, 148n.157, 160,
 195n.95, 196n.101, 198–202, 200n.129,
 204, 218–19, 229, 247–48, 284–85,
 300n.27, 313
troubles du voisinage see nuisance
Tunc, Andrè 80nn.47–48, 83n.63, 145n.143, 147–
 48, 156n.6, 173n.2, 176, 177n.18, 179n.31,
 179n.34, 181–82n.40, 224–25n.23, 253–
 54, 286–87, 288n.150, 296–97n.11

Ulen, Thomas 122–23, 233n.59, 247–48
unilateral imposition of risk 265–66, 267–68,
 300n.28, 312n.78, see also outcome
 responsibility
Ursin, Edmund 94–95n.129, 97n.138, 101–
 2n.165, 124n.28, 186n.58, 194n.91,
 230n.43, 232n.52

values in strict liability 301–16
Vedel, Georges 82n.59, 83n.64, 182n.44
Venezian, Giacomo 68n.3, 283n.130
vicarious liability of employers (or defendants
 akin to employers), justifications for
 English law 103–6, 111–14, 138–40, 141–43,
  152–53, 166, 167–70, 205, 207–9, 210–13,
  214–16, 219–20, 234–36, 237–40, 272n.69,
  275n.89, 275n.92, 280, 307–8, 309–10

French law 79–81, 82–84, 145–46, 147,
 147n.153, 148n.159, 156–58, 176–78,
 179n.34, 184n.51, 223, 224–25
Italian law 86–87, 90–91, 92n.116, 92–
 93nn.118–19, 93n.122, 130nn.55–56,
 131n.64, 132–34, 134n.82, 135n.95, 158–
 59, 160, 195–96n.97, 196–98, 199–200,
 204, 218–19, 226–27, 228n.35, 304–5
US law 94–95n.129, 100–2, 102n.172, 122–26,
 162–63, 165n.55, 186, 188–92, 231–33,
 233n.55, 262–63, 264–65, 265n.41, 266–
 68, 269–70
vicarious liability of parents, justifications for
 English law 278n.105
 French law 79n.37, 82–83, 90–91, 145–46,
  147n.156, 156–58, 176–78, 179n.34, 222–
  23, 224–25, 253–54, 301–2
 Italian law 90–91, 93n.122, 135, 136n.98,
  137n.101, 158–59, 160–62, 196–97, 227–
  29, 248–50
 US law 123–26, 231–33
vicarious liability for organising and controlling
 the way of life of another (French
 law) 178
vicarious liability for traffic accidents see traffic
 accidents, liability for
vicarious liability, substantive law of
 English law 18–20, 24–26
 French law 40–43
 Italian law 50, 54–55, 57–58, 60
 US law 31–32, 34–37
victim protection 221–40
 comparisons among English, French, Italian,
  and US law 222–23, 226, 227–30, 231–
  35, 236, 237, 239–40
 and contexts of liability 293–94
 criticisms 222, 229, 233–34, 237–38
 definition 221
 and the deep-pockets justification 156–58,
  159, 163, 168, 191–92, 221, 224–25,
  227–29, 231–33, 235–36, 310–
  11, 312–13
 and individual responsibility 274–76, 277
 and loss spreading 175–76, 186–87, 197–98,
  199, 212–13, 216–20, 221, 224–25, 226,
  227–29, 230–33, 234–36, 239–40, 301–3,
  304–5, 310–11, 312–13
 and patterns of reasoning 295–99, 300–1
 and risk 83–84, 224–25, 227–29, 231–33,
  235–36, 301–5, 306–7, 310
 and social solidarity 74–76, 83–84, 89–90,
  175–76, 178–79, 181, 198, 222, 226,
  227–29, 255–56, 288–89, 301–5, 306–7,
  309–11, 313

INDEX 349

Viney, Geneviève 78–79, 79n.39, 80n.48, 82–83, 83n.64, 145–46, 147nn.152–53, 147n.156, 148n.159, 156n.6, 157–58, 176–78, 178n.27, 179n.30, 179n.32, 184n.51, 223, 224n.19, 224–25n.23, 253–54, 255n.60, 288n.154, 313, 314–15
Visintini, Giovanna 87n.82, 91n.109, 133n.80, 159n.21, 228n.35

Wade, Henry 211n.181
wealth equalization 164–65
wealth maximization 165n.53, 245n.16, *see also* minimization of the costs of accidents; social welfare; resource allocation

Weinrib, Ernest 95n.133, 128n.48, 164n.49, 185n.55, 193–94, 233n.57, 245n.16, 261n.11, 268–69
Whittaker, Simon 237n.76
Williams, Glanville 142n.133, 167, 199n.124, 207–9
Witting, Christian 112n.229, 139–40n.114, 276, 277, 296–97n.11
wrong 259–61, 262–63, 264–65, 266–68, 270, 277, 290–91, 311–12
wrongdoing *see* wrong
wrongful *see* wrong
wrongs-based liability 266–68

Zipursky, Benjamin 97n.138, 98n.141, 98–99n.147, 101n.162, 245n.15, 266–69